Unsettled States, Disputed Lands

THE WILDER HOUSE SERIES
IN POLITICS, HISTORY,
AND CULTURE

The Wilder House Series is published in association with the
Wilder House Board of Editors and the University of Chicago.

David Laitin, *Editor*
George Steinmetz, *Assistant Editor*

EDITORIAL BOARD

*Unsettled States, Disputed Lands: Britain and Ireland,
France and Algeria, Israel and the West Bank—Gaza*
by Ian S. Lustick

UNSETTLED STATES
DISPUTED LANDS

Britain and Ireland, France and Algeria,
Israel and the West Bank-Gaza

IAN S. LUSTICK

Cornell University Press

ITHACA AND LONDON

First published 1993 by Cornell University Press.

Library of Congress Cataloging-in-Publication Data
Lustick, Ian, 1949—
  Unsettled states, disputed lands : Britain and Ireland, France and Algeria, Israel and the West Bank-Gaza / Ian S. Lustick
    p.   cm. — (The Wilder House series in politics, history, and culture)
  Includes bibliographical references (p.   ) and index.
  ISBN 0-8014-2840-8 (cloth : alk. paper). — ISBN 0-8014-8088-4 (pbk. : alk. paper)
    1. Acquisition of territory. 2. Sovereignty. 3. Ireland. 4. West Bank. 5. Algeria. I. Title. II. Series.
JX4088.L87   1993
341.4'2—dc20   93-4449

Printed in the United States of America

⊗ The paper in this book meets the minimum requirements
of the American National Standard for Information Sciences—
Permanence of Paper for Printed Library Materials, ANSI Z39.48–1984.

For Terri, Hilary, and Alexander

Contents

Contents

List of Figures

Preface

This book studies the incorporation of additional territories into existing states and the equally problematic process of how states relinquish control over territories. The theory I develop views state expansion and contraction as closely related but asymmetric political achievements. Though the initial impetus for the analysis was the relationship of Israel and the West Bank and Gaza Strip, and though I developed my theory by comparing the changing relationships of Britain to Ireland (1834–1922) and France to Algeria (1936–62), this book has a larger purpose—to explain patterns of similarity and difference in the expansion and contraction of any state by treating states as institutions subject, in their own way, to the laws governing all institutions.

I began this project as an analyst in the Bureau of Intelligence and Research of the Department of State in 1979–80. Among other things, I was charged with evaluating scenarios for the eventual disposition of the West Bank and Gaza Strip, occupied by Israel since the June 1967 war but inhabited, despite intensive Israeli settlement efforts, by overwhelming majorities of Palestinian Arabs. It was clear enough that the goal of Israeli government policy at the time was to incorporate the territories into the Jewish state by policies of de facto annexation. But how likely were these policies to succeed, and on what factors would this success depend? What theory of state expansion and contraction, I wondered, when applied to the forces pushing toward incorporation or separation of these territories, could sort the impossible from the possible, the possible from the probable, the probable from the inevitable?

Inside the State Department there was not much I could do about my need for such a theory except sharpen my appreciation of its absence. But when I left the Department in the summer of 1980, I returned to academia with concrete questions about Israel and the territories and the knowledge that if I could not produce a theory of state expansion and contraction I would not be able to answer them. To inform my choice of factors likely to be decisive I studied the debate in Israel over whether policies designed to ensure the incorporation of the occupied territories were succeeding. I then sought historical cases of expansion and contraction with enough structural similarities, but enough substantive differences, to test the theory that began to emerge—a theory that might not only account for the trajectory of the Israel–West Bank/Gaza relationship but also identify the conditions for Israeli absorption of or withdrawal from these areas.

While I immersed myself in the long and intricate histories of these relationships, the world outside my study was being dramatically reshaped. In eastern Europe, central Asia, south Asia, and Africa the abstract problems my detailed inquiries were designed to address—of the presumptively permanent but actually contingent nature of state boundaries, of the relationship between the internal complexion of states and their external shape, and of the mysterious links between gradual processes of political metamorphosis and sudden transformations—took on an obviousness not present when I began the study, as well as an aspect that was as often horrifying as it was inspiring. With these developments in mind I try, at both the beginning and end of this book, to explain why I think that the theory I advance, although developed and tested in three specific settings, has robust implications for explaining patterns of order and disorder associated with any large-scale discontinuity in the size and shape of states that does not primarily and directly result from war.

In the decade and a half it has taken to bring this project to completion I have accumulated more debts to colleagues, friends, students, institutions, and relatives than I could possibly list here. I hope those who aided, abetted, or just tolerated the various obsessions associated with this work will accept my thanks and forgive me if by accident they are not named.

Foremost among the institutions whose generous support permitted me to make this book what I wanted it to be are Dartmouth College, the National Endowment for the Humanities, and the United States Institute of Peace. With its steadfast commitment to research by Dartmouth faculty and its various fellowship and support programs, including funds provided through the John Sloan Dickey Endowment for International Understanding and the Nelson A. Rockefeller Center for the Social Sciences, Dartmouth College gave me the freedom and resources to sustain a long-term, intrinsically speculative research program. My colleagues at Dartmouth, especially in the Government Department, were a constant source of encouragement and reassurance. I especially thank the staff of the Goverment Department—Kathy Donald, Eunice Lemkul, Suzanne Markloff, and Earl Raymond—for their steady, capable, and good-humored assistance. Just as important to me was the ingenuity of Dartmouth's superb reference librarian, Robert Jaccaud, and the dedication and skill of its interlibrary loan specialists, Patricia Carter and Marianne Hraibi. A special thanks is also due to a dozen students who worked assiduously as research assistants in the accumulation, sorting, and filing of information, and to the many more, at Dartmouth and at the University of Pennsylvania, whose hard work in courses spun from this project made crucial contributions to my thinking and learning.

The bulk of this book was written under the terms of substantial grants from the United States Institute of Peace and, especially, from the Interpretive Research Program of the National Endowment for the Humanities. Without the confidence in me expressed by these grantors and the generosity of their support I could not have completed this project and would probably not even have been able to try. In addition I am delighted to acknowledge the support received for the final stages of manuscript preparation from the staff of the Political Science Department at the University of Pennsylvania and from the resources of the Richard L. Simon Term Chair in the Social Sciences, which I currently hold.

For assistance of various kinds in connection with visits to Britain, Ireland, France, Algeria, Israel, and the West Bank and Gaza Strip, I thank the International Relations Department at the London School of Economics, the Political Science Department at University College, Dublin, the United States Embassy in Algiers, the United States Embassy in Tel-Aviv, and the U.S. Consulate-General in Jerusalem, the Maison des Sciences de l'Homme in Paris, and the Centre de Recherche et d'Etudes sur les Sociétés Méditerranéennes and the Dépôt des Archives d'Outre-mer in Aix-en-Provence. I also express my thanks for the hospitality I was shown by the Political Science Department of Tel-Aviv University, the Sociology and Anthropology Department of the Hebrew University in Jerusalem, the staff of the International Center for Peace in the Middle East, the Eretz Yisrael Academy, Rafi and Shoshana Menachem, David and Laura DeNola, Avner and Noga Bar-Ilan, Yoram and Penina Peri, and Assem Tahhan.

Next to the financial assistance I have acknowledged and the support of my family, the contribution to my work for which I am most grateful has been the commentary provided by colleagues, in many disciplines, on preliminary drafts (sometimes several different drafts) of various portions of this work. First among these is Yoram Peri, my Israeli consultant on this project, as supported by the National Endowment for the Humanities.

His unmatched knowledge of Israeli political life, and his intense, good-humored curiosity about it, were constant sources of enlightenment and encouragement. Just as steadfast in his readiness to respond to my appeals for comment and advice was David Laitin, whose intellectual instincts I have relied on so heavily to guide me through difficult choices. For the rest I can only express my appreciation by listing their names: Avner Bar-Ilan, Paul Bew, Thomas Callaghy, Jack Censer, Martha Crenshaw, Laurence Davies, Irene Gendzier, Adrian Guelke, Ernst Haas, Peter A. Hall, Lawrence Kritzman, Gene Lyons, the late Bernard McLane, Bruce Marshall, Roger Masters, James Mayall, Nelson Kasfir, Baruch Kimmerling, Andrea Leskes, Benjamin Neuberger, Eric Nordlinger, Brendan O'Leary, Margaret Pearson, Donald Pease, Dani Rubinstein, Anne Sa'adah, René Seve, Gershon Shafir, Kenneth Sharpe, Immanuel Sivan, Sammy Smooha, Charles Townshend, the late John Whyte, and Frank Wright. Since I disagree on some matters of consequence with each of these people, and on many matters with some of them, I stress that I list them here to thank them for the benefit of their critical thinking, not to associate them in any way with my argument or conclusions.

I also owe a great deal to the editorial staff of Cornell University Press, especially Roger Haydon, Kay Scheuer, and Joanne Hindman for their professionalism, their good judgment, and their sympathetic understanding of the objectives of this study, and to Kathryn Gohl, for an excellent job of copy-editing.

An earlier version of Chapter 3 appeared in *Politics and Society*, 18, 1 (1990), and I am grateful to Sage Publications, Inc. for permission to use material from that article in this book.

I am beholden, above all, to my wife Terri. Without her love and her confidence in me and in this project I could not have carried it to completion.

                                                                    IAN S. LUSTICK

Philadelphia, Pennsylvania

Unsettled States, Disputed Lands

PART I

The Changing Shape
of States

In the world as we know it in the 1990s, no fact about states is more obvious than the impermanence of their boundaries. United Germany represents, above all, a tremendous expansion in the territory ruled by the state formerly known as the Federal Republic of Germany. Meanwhile, states ruled from Belgrade and Prague have shrunk drastically in size: the only certainty about the borders of the states replacing Yugoslavia is that they will be changing. In 1988 the Soviet state had boundaries encircling fifteen socialist republics. In 1991 the state with Moscow as its capital exercised its claims to authority within the Russian Federated Republic only. Questions about its ability to uphold those claims over all the autonomous republics and regions within its designated borders suggest that the shape of the Russian state itself may undergo significant change. Meanwhile, other successor states of the Soviet Union, including Armenia, Azerbaijan, Moldova, Georgia, and Ukraine, struggle to expand or maintain their boundaries.

But eastern and central Europe and central Asia are not the only areas of the world where fluctuation in the shape of states is evident. The industrial democracies of western Europe are making fundamental decisions that will determine their future as separate territorial states or integral components of a "United States of Europe." The Anglo-Irish agreement of 1985 officially marks British rule of Northern Ireland as contingent on political trends within Ireland. Basque separatists continue violent challenges to the integrity of the Spanish state.

In Africa the separation of Eritrea from Ethiopia has substantially reduced the territory ruled by that state. With separatist pressures on the rise in other regions, the shape of the state ruled from Addis Ababa will remain problematic for a long time. Whether or not part of Chad is ever attached to Libya, it is an open question what borders the Chadian state will have by the end of the century. Morocco, it appears, has successfully expanded its boundaries to include the western Sahara.

In the Middle East, the Jordanian state formally and substantially revised its boundaries in 1988 by excluding the West Bank from its domain. On the other hand, the merger of the two Yemeni states into one seems relatively successful. Lebanon survives on paper, but in its eastern and southern provinces the Syrian and Israeli states appear the actual rulers. Having failed to expand its borders to include Kuwait, Iraq now fights, along with Turkey, to prevent chunks of territory from emerging as a Kurdish state.

In South Asia, central governments in India and Pakistan strain to contain ethnic and religious movements threatening to splinter the subcontinent into at least as many states as were produced by the end of the Soviet Union. Tibet is increasingly restive, returning the question of Chinese rule over that country to the international agenda. Sri Lanka continues to be torn by vicious fighting between Tamils and Sinhalese, suggesting the inability of the Sri Lankan state to maintain the whole island within its domain.

Cyprus, the Koreas, Indonesia, Liberia, Sudan, Somalia, Zaire, and Canada are only some of the other states whose territorial shape is under pressure or may change as the result of hostile action, cooperative agreements, or both, within the next decade.

From a historical perspective the spatial malleability of states is neither surprising nor extraordinary. Even states that today appear endowed with relatively stable borders are in fact products of wars and other processes of territorial aggrandizement, contraction, or consolidation. Closely examined, the territorial shape of any state reveals itself as contingent on as well as constitutive of political, technological, economic, cultural, and social processes.

Despite the complexity of these processes, change in the size and shape of individual states has often been presented as (and sometimes is) a straightforward function of armed conflict—of the application of force majeure to extend or defend boundaries. Certainly the United States owes its continental size to the forcible seizure of Mexican territories and the victory of the North ("the Union") in the Civil War. War was also decisive in the mid–nineteenth-century expansion of the German state in central Europe, its reduction in size after World Wars I and II, the enlargement and reduction of the Japanese state's boundaries in the 1930s and 1940s, and the expansion of the Vietnamese state in the 1970s. Similarly today, in the Balkans, on the Horn of Africa, in Ngorno-Karabakh, and on the

Iraq-Kuwait border, states and would-be state-makers do battle with one another over territories to be or not to be included within their domains.

But the intricate histories of British, French, and Italian state formation show that coercion is usually only a partial explanation, and sometimes no explanation at all, for the changing size and shape of states. Ongoing negotiations over the possible secession of Quebec from Canada, the essentially nonviolent detachment of the non-Russian republics from Russia and of Slovakia from Czechoslovakia, and the reunification of Germany clearly demonstrate that peaceful separation of territories from existing states is possible, that conquest of territories does not necessarily mean their political integration, and that acquisition of a territory in war does not necessarily mean its permanent separation from rival claimants. With respect to territorial expansion and contraction as a *political* problem, it is precisely those cases where force majeure was not decisive in the determination of outcomes, or where it is not expected to be decisive, which are of the greatest interest.

These simple considerations have profound but usually unnoticed implications for the study of states. Most working definitions of the state treat its shape as exogenous to its operation, suppressing the fact of territorial variability by treating borders as historically or externally imposed constants. But since boundaries of states change, the territorial composition of any particular state is a variable.[1] Since variation in the shape of states is politically consequential, definitions that treat the territorial compass of a state as fixed make it difficult to pose crucial research questions because, in addition to clarifying meaning, definitions also place limits on research. By making certain things "true by definition," every definition automatically prevents questions about those things from being asked.

For the last twenty years, students of the state have typically begun their work with Max Weber's classic definition—"a human community that (successfully) claims the *monopoly of the legitimate use of physical force* within a given territory."[2] Dozens of scholars have tinkered with Weber's formulation to suggest, for example, that an organization might qualify as a state whether or not it seeks to legitimize its use of violence, whether or not its authority is deemed legitimate, or whether or not it possesses or seeks to hold a monopoly on coercive authority. With these adjustments researchers have been able to ask many questions of great interest. But since almost all variants of Weber's conception abide, implicitly or explicitly, by his stipulation of the exogenously determined or a priori "givenness" of the territorial shape of the state, they exclude or discourage questions about the construction and maintenance of boundaries of "established" states or about the implications of change in those boundaries.[3]

I should emphasize that most analysts neither assert nor believe that the borders of a state cannot change. Rich literatures trace the expansion and interaction of various "conquering cores," patterns of European state development that include treatment of changing boundaries as both dependent and independent variables, and the artificial imposition of colonial state boundaries as the historical basis for the shape and size of contemporary third world states.[4] But the existence of these boundaries is usually treated as foundational—as accomplished historical fact, as an externality, or as a function of "international relations," and thus as "background knowledge" for the application and evaluation of propositions about state attributes and behavior. Even analysts such as J. P. Nettl and James N. Rosenau, who emphasize the multiple respects in which "the state" should be treated as "variable," imagine states to exist within territorial borders that, once arrived at, are constants.[5]

Indeed a rather sharp line has divided study of state formation or development from studies of state behavior. The metaphor of state "building" has perhaps contributed to this dichotomization, implying that, once "built," a state is "finished" and can then be observed in operation as an intact, completed entity. In general, questions about the territorial composition of states are seen to pertain to their "formation" or "development" rather than to their operation once they have "taken shape." Thus the "boundaries of the state" have been a major focus of contemporary scholarship, but the boundaries in question are those that separate "the state" from "the society" within which it is embedded, from which it extracts resources, or over which it rules. Meanwhile the territorial boundaries of the state, which circumscribe the lands and peoples within its domain, which determine what are "internal" and what are "external" affairs, or which present the state with that "society" to which it must relate, are seldom present the state with that "society" to which it must relate, are seldom considered as politically constituted, or as having the same constitutive effects, as the boundaries between the state and society.[6]

The main benefit of ignoring the constituted and constitutive aspect of territorial boundaries is to simplify analysis of state operations within those boundaries. There have been other benefits as well. Much of the reason for renewed interest in statist analyses came from the frustration of societally based explanations for economic and political distress in Africa and elsewhere in the third world. Since in Africa, especially, both analysts and protagonists endorsed the boundaries of postcolonial states as sacrosanct, the failure of European-based theories of the state to integrate boundary change into their models was not a problem. Quite the opposite—it helped suppress separatist forces by keeping questions of ethnic or cultural self-determination *within* the boundaries of the new states off political and scholarly agendas.[7]

But when these pressures and proposals do appear on public agendas, and when change in the territorial composition of the state is either the effect to be explained, the mechanism for explaining that effect, or the prime motive or fear of ruling elites, then it is self-defeating for scholars to pretend the immutability of territorial boundaries and ignore their problematically institutionalized nature. If we wish, in other words, to explain the suddenness with which change in the shape of states can occur; why expansion is so common and contraction is so rare; why some large-scale morphological transformations can be accomplished with almost no violence while disputes about relatively small territorial adjustments can produce some of the bitterest, most violent, and most prolonged struggles of our time; and why changes in the shape of states are so often associated with changes in the character of the regimes that rule them and the identity of governing elites; then we need a theory of state expansion and contraction that obviously cannot be based on a definition of the state which treats its territorial composition as a given.

In this light Israel's disputatious and uncertain relationship with the Arab-inhabited territories it occupied in 1967—especially the West Bank and Gaza Strip—can be seen to pose just the mix of substantive and conceptual problems which need to be addressed by any theory of state expansion and contraction.[8] The purpose of this book is to develop such a theory. Chapter 1 shows that the most puzzling questions asked about the Israel–West Bank/Gaza Strip relationship cannot be answered without a conceptually coherent approach to territorial state-building and state contraction. In Chapter 2 a theoretical framework with the potential for producing answers to these questions is adapted from the "punctuated equilibrium" approach to the evolution of states advanced by Stephen Krasner, Theda Skocpol, and others. I present a model suggesting those answers in Parts II and III, testing and refining it in an extended comparison of two historical cases—Britain's relationship to Ireland from the 1830s to 1922, and France's relationship to Algeria from the 1930s to 1962.

For both contemporaries and historians, the relationship of Britain to Ireland and France to Algeria posed most of the same questions now confronted by both protagonists in, and observers of, the Israeli-Palestinian case. Accordingly, in Part IV hypotheses about conditions for state expansion and contraction that emerge from and survive the extended British-French comparison are used to address the questions originally posed about the Israeli-Palestinian case and about general processes of change in the size and shape of states. The enterprise explains differences and similarities in the outcome of the British-Irish and French-Algerian relationships, specifies the conditions for Israel either to absorb or to relinquish the West

Bank and Gaza Strip, and suggests plausible interpretations for other salient cases, such as the sudden but uncertain emergence of the Russian Federated Republic out of the Soviet Union. More broadly, by integrating analysis of the psychological constructedness of states as arenas for political competition with analysis of how the rules for conducting that competition are exploited and changed, the model and the conceptual framework surrounding it illustrate how research on institutions can be stripped of its bias toward growth and sensitized to both continuous and discontinuous aspects of contraction as well as expansion.

CHAPTER ONE

Israel and the West Bank and Gaza Strip: Disengagement or Incorporation?

Since 1967, Israel has been faced with an agonizing dilemma. The West Bank and Gaza Strip are inhabited by more than 1.8 million Palestinian Arabs and 250,000 Jews.[1] Many Israelis see these territories as integral, even sacred parts of their country. But their problematic status has accounted for the most significant political division in the country's history—pitting those Israelis who favor permanent incorporation against those who favor relinquishing most or all of the West Bank and Gaza Strip in return for a peace agreement with the Arab world and resolution of the Palestinian problem.

The outlines of the debate over what *should* be done with the territories can briefly be sketched. Among the key claims of the annexationists is that Israel needs the territories for security, to prevent terrorism and give the Israeli army maneuvering room in time of war. Anti-annexationists respond by saying that the occupation breeds terrorism and that ending it can reduce the likelihood of war. Anti-annexationists also contend that modern weaponry reduces the importance of territorial expanse and increases the value of demilitarization agreements. Annexationists argue that roads, powerlines, waterworks, and economic ties bind the West Bank and Gaza so tightly to Israel that withdrawal would subject the Israeli economy and the Israelis who have settled in the territories to intolerable dislocations. Those who favor territorial compromise point to the continuing cost of the occupation, the millions of hours spent in policing operations, and the enhanced opportunities for trade and investment that would be associated with a peace agreement. Anti-annexationists also argue that demographically Israel will cease to be Jewish if it absorbs the large Arab population of the territories, adding them to the 750,000 Arabs already living within Israel. They point out that there are already more Arab children in the area between the Jordan River and the Mediterranean Sea than Jewish children, and argue that with such a large and hostile Arab population Israel will be forced to become substantially less democratic in order to remain "Jewish." Annexationists, however, contend that demographic trends can be misleading. They point to the influx of Russian immigrants and the potential of a similar wave from the United States. Furthermore, they argue, regardless of whether Israel relinquishes the territories it will have to deal with a large internal and discontented Arab population. On the ideological level, annexationists argue that withdrawal from the heartland of biblical Israel and the abandonment or dismantling of settlements would be a betrayal of the Zionist principles upon which the state was founded. Anti-annexationists stress that equally important Zionist goals—creating a Jewish working class and a model society and achieving peace with the Arabs—are betrayed by the employment of tens of thousands of semilegal Arab laborers from the territories and the prolonged occupation's corrosive effects on the country's moral spirit.

As confounding as the polemics over what *should* be done with the territories have been, by the early 1980s an equally complex but theoretically more interesting debate emerged over what the Israeli political system *could* do with them. Arguments over whether Israel's absorption of the territories had already, would soon, or could eventually become permanent required participants in this debate to argue as if they had powerful theories—about the political dynamics of state expansion and contraction and about constraints on the institutionalization of territorial states. Because each side of the struggle to ensure or prevent Israel's permanent incorporation of the West Bank and Gaza Strip has treated the size and shape of the state of Israel as contingent on the outcome of this struggle, their efforts, and their evaluations of success and failure, can be understood as expressive of hypotheses about how territorial states expand and contract. The theory of state expansion and contraction advanced and tested in this book is built on the logics embedded in these hypotheses.

Precisely because no theory capable of conditioning or integrating insights standing behind rival claims does exist, protagonists and observers on both sides of the issue have repeatedly been forced to reverse categorical assessments of the possibility of Israel's disengagement from the territories. One result of this inquiry should therefore be the introduction of considerably more coherence into the argument over de facto annexation's reversibility than has ever been present. More generally, it should make guidelines available for judging, in other settings, the plausibility of policy options entailing the political separation or combination of territories.

De Facto Annexation of the West Bank and Gaza Strip

One needs a certain amount of historical background to the current relationship between Israel and the Palestinian territories to understand the terms of the debate, the theoretical questions it raises, and how those questions relate to broader issues in the study of state-building and state contraction. In the history of the Arab-Israeli conflict only one kind of proposed solution has ever received substantial support from mainstream elements on both sides—partition. Firm and explicit Zionist support for the division of the Land of Israel came in 1947 with acceptance of the terms of the United Nations partition resolution. Israel's commitment to the principle was reaffirmed by its interpretation of the 1949 armistice agreements and by its acceptance, in 1970, of United Nations Security Council Resolution 242. Even while successive right-wing governments, from 1977 to 1984, and from the spring of 1990 to the summer of 1992, rejected the division of the "Land of Israel west of the Jordan," 40 percent to 70 percent of Israeli Jews have continued to express support for a territorial compromise.[2]

Following the 1967 war, the future of the West Bank and Gaza Strip came to form the central focus of the Arab-Israeli conflict. Before 1967 support for partition among Palestinian Arabs as a solution to the Arab-Israeli conflict was limited to the Communist party, which followed Soviet policy by accepting the idea of an Israeli state in part of Palestine alongside an independent Palestinian Arab state. After the June war of 1967, groups of notables and intellectuals within the West Bank and Gaza Strip became convinced that a Palestinian state in these areas, including East Jerusalem as its capital, could be a viable solution to the Palestinian problem. Although rejected at first by the Palestine Liberation Organization, this "separate-state solution" soon became the actual, if not always the public and explicit position, of Fatah and the mainstream of the PLO. The governments of Saudi Arabia, Jordan, Egypt, Kuwait, Morocco, and even Syria, Algeria, and Iraq have all, since the early 1970s, moved toward this same position—that peace with Israel is possible, but only with return of the territories captured in 1967 to Arab rule.

Thus the policy preferences of many Israelis, Arab positions since at least the early 1970s, and the stance of the major powers as reflected in UN Security Council Resolution 242, all shared a common denominator in the formula of "territory for peace." In 1977, however, the Likud, led by Menachem Begin, came to power in Israel. For the first time in Israel's history the Revisionist wing of the Zionist movement controlled the government. Since it was founded in 1925 the Revisionist movement has advocated a Jewish state in the "whole Land of Israel." Indeed, the Revisionism, its youth movement, Betar, its military arm, the Irgun (New Military Organization), and the Herut (Freedom) party to which it gave birth in 1948 have each regarded the East Bank of the Jordan (Trans-jordan), in addition to "Western" Palestine, as a rightful part of the area over which Jews should exercise political sovereignty.

Herut had little electoral success in the 1950s and 1960s. Without formally renouncing Israel's right to more territory, the dominant Labor party was nevertheless rather easily able to dismiss Herut's emphasis on "liberating the whole Land of Israel" as unrealistic and dangerous bombast. Begin himself was denounced as a demagogue. Until 1967 Herut was effectively excluded from the mainstream of Israeli politics.

The emotional upheaval produced by Israel's victory in 1967 reinforced strong sentiments of attachment to the areas occupied as a result of the fighting, particularly the West Bank, containing the core areas of the ancient kingdoms of Judah and Israel, including, in particular, the site of the First and Second Temples in the Old City of Jerusalem. Five days before the outbreak of the war, a "national emergency government" had been formed which brought Begin into the cabinet for the first time. Within weeks after the end of the fighting this government moved quickly to incorporate East Jerusalem and a number of surrounding villages into the Israeli municipality of Jerusalem. Although some Labor party ministers tried to resist the temptation, the government as a whole soon responded positively to pressures for the establishment of settlements in various strategically and emotionally important locations within the captured (or "liberated") territories.

In the 1970s, Labor party vacillation concerning the proper future of the West Bank and Gaza Strip added to the party's growing image among Israelis as incapable of continued leadership. In the 1970s the Labor party lost credibility and popular support among the new generation of Israelis, particularly among voters whose families came from Islamic countries. Taking advantage of decades of accumulated social and economic resentment, and of a new militance on matters of territory and security, the Herut-led Likud bloc achieved a decisive victory over Labor in the 1977 elections. The Likud was quickly able to form a governing coalition with religious parties increasingly controlled by advocates of Jewish sovereignty over the "whole Land of Israel" and increasingly wary of the secularist tone of the Labor party.

During the seven years of its first two terms in office the Likud plunged into a rapid, wide-ranging, and expensive effort to annex the territories without formally changing their legal status. By the end of this period approximately half of all West Bank and Gaza land had been transferred to Israeli government or Jewish control through expropriations, requisitions, legal redefinitions of public and private land, zoning regulations, and purchasing programs. While the government virtually prevented investment by Arab inhabitants of the West Bank and Gaza in industry or agriculture, it spent billions of dollars on Jewish settlements and the infrastructure to support them, concentrating on those areas, heavily populated by Arabs, that had previously been avoided by Labor government–supported settlement efforts. In 1982, for example, the Ministry of Housing and Construction spent 44 percent of its entire budget to support settlement projects in the West Bank (excluding expanded East Jerusalem).[3] When Likud took office in 1977, 5,023 Jewish settlers were living in the West Bank (excluding expanded East Jerusalem). By the time elections were held in 1984, however, that number had climbed to nearly 44,000. Housing contracts and other commitments made before the elections raised this number to 53,000 by the end of 1985.[4] Settlement activity decelerated somewhat between 1986 and 1990, during which the Likud shared power in uneasy coalitions with the Labor party, but exploded again under the auspices of the third Likud-led government from 1990 to 1992 (see Fig. 1).

The Debate over Irreversibility

By the mid-1980s the West Bank and Gaza Strip contained more than 140 Jewish settlements, including half a dozen towns, large-scale military dispositions, billions of dollars of infrastructural investments, and more than 140,000 Jewish settlers, about two-thirds of whom lived in neighborhoods built within the seventy-five square kilometers of expanded East Jerusalem. These developments led many Israelis to the conclusion that the Likud was succeeding, or even had succeeded, in eliminating options for Israeli withdrawal from the West Bank and Gaza, making their permanent absorption into Israel only a matter of time. Included among those who came to view the annexation process as irreversible (or virtually so) were both delighted advocates of the policy and despairing opponents.

On the other side of the "empirical" argument over the relative likelihood of incorporation or disengagement were those who maintained that the links between Israel and the territories could still be severed. They included advocates of permanent incorporation who still doubted that the absorption process had been completed, joined by those who opposed annexation and believed the struggle against processes of incorporation should continue. For some Israelis, including settlers made uneasy by Israel's evacuation of the Sinai settlements in April 1982, and for dovishly inclined politicians, whose platforms required the possibility of a territorial

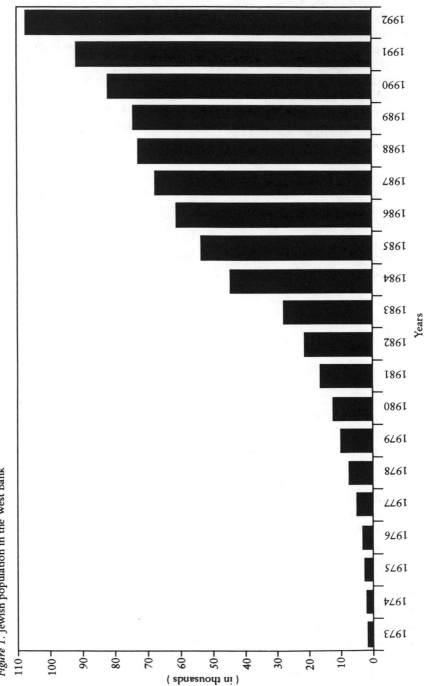

Figure 1. Jewish population in the West Bank

compromise with the Arabs, conclusions of irreversibility seemed premature. These participants in the debate, both annexationists and anti-annexationists, argued that however difficult it might be to disengage Israel from the territories, and although the crisis surrounding such a decision might even lead the country into civil war, disengagement could still not be considered impossible.

The protagonists in this debate over whether Israel could (not "should") disengage from the territories seldom argued over the "facts" of the matter. But the disagreements were vivid. The best known and most influential advocate of the irreversibility thesis was Meron Benvenisti, an urban planner by profession, a former deputy mayor of Jerusalem, and a well-known political activist on the dovish-liberal left. In a widely publicized speech in Washington, D.C., in October 1982, Benvenisti described Israel's ability to reverse the "de facto annexation" of the territories as "five minutes to midnight." Within three more years, he predicted, there would be one hundred thousand Jewish settlers in the West Bank (excluding expanded East Jerusalem). "If this occurs, it will become impossible for any Israeli government to relinquish control." "Time is running out," he wrote in late 1982. "The data show us clearly that the processes of integration known as 'annexation' (although this is no more than a legal expression for a much deeper process) are advancing very quickly to a point of no return."[5]

Benvenisti's warnings about a swiftly approaching "point of no return" pleased dovish/Labor party circles in Israel and even many Arabs because they gave urgency to struggles against annexation. The question before the country, said former Foreign Minister Abba Eban in 1982, was whether the desire of half the Israeli nation "to have permanent control over the West Bank and Gaza can be effective against all the dynamics of objective fact that work in a different direction."[6] Peace Now, the largest nonpartisan organization in Israel dedicated to achieving a territorial compromise, issued a fifteen-page pamphlet in 1983 comparing the settlements to the "baobob tree" in the children's book *The Little Prince*. In this fable, seeds of the baobob tree produce roots that spread with unstoppable force until they destroy the entire planet in whose soil they are planted. According to the analysis in this pamphlet, the settlement of a hundred thousand Jews on the West Bank would turn the "Greater Israel" idea of the annexationist right into a "self-fulfilling prophecy"—described as a "terrifying prospect" liable to be achieved "in another five—or even three—years." "Peace Now," the pamphlet was subtitled, "*before it's too late.*" In 1983 Palestinian notables such as Elias Freij of Bethlehem and Rashad a-Shawa in Gaza, as well as King Hussein of Jordan and President Husni Mubarak of Egypt, warned that the "point of no return," after which

Israel's de facto annexation of the territories would be irreversible, was only months or even weeks away.[7]

But by 1983 and 1984 Benvenisti had completed a number of studies documenting just how pervasive was the Israeli presence in the territories and how routinized the dynamic of its expansion had become. No longer did he argue that it was "five minutes to midnight." Instead, he declared, midnight had arrived. Like it or not, he maintained, the "critical point" had been passed. For all intents and purposes, Israeli separation from the territories had become impossible.[8]

According to the settlers themselves, their presence was meant to have just the effect Benvenisti was describing, to "reduce the ability of a government—any government—to play 'tricks' with the political future of Judea, Samaria, and the Gaza District."[9] It was hardly surprising, therefore, that annexationist politicians, settlement planners, and many settlers themselves were delighted with Benvenisti's findings. Yuval Neeman, head of the extreme right-wing Tehiya (Renaissance) party, predicted that by stepping up its settlement efforts, "in two years, a situation will be reached where there will no longer be a physical possibility of tearing off any part of Eretz Yisrael."[10] Eliyahu Ben-Elissar, appointed by Begin (during his first government) as chairman of a semisecret committee to plan and coordinate policies toward the territories, proudly cited Benvenisti's findings.

> The policies of the government were indeed designed to guarantee Israeli rule over Judea, Samaria, and the Gaza District for an unlimited period. I am delighted that Benvenisti arrived at the conclusion, by means of scientific research, that the facts on the ground prove the success of the government in fulfilling its mission. Certainly this finding is contrary to his political position, but the fact that he came to his conclusions through purely scientific research can only make me happy.[11]

By the middle of 1984, declared *Nekuda*, the leading journal among settlers in the territories, the point of no return had been passed. It claimed that "by the end of this summer there will be, with the help of God, nearly 50,000 Jews living in Judea, Samaria, and the Gaza district . . . enough, in terms of creating settlements and political facts, to guarantee the hold of the Jewish people on the heart of the Land of Israel for generations to come."[12]

Not all Israelis who accepted the irreversibility thesis were as pleased as annexationist politicians, settlement planners, and Gush Emunim settlers. The rush by middle-class Israelis to buy government-subsidized land and homes in the West Bank intensified in 1983 and was deeply disturbing to many Israelis opposed to the annexation of the territories. Dovish journalists, with reputations for being better informed than virtually anyone else on the situation in the West Bank and Gaza Strip, were torn between sensations of despair and desperate hopes that somehow territorial compromise might still be possible. At the beginning of 1982, Dani Rubinstein, who subsequently won Israel's top journalism prize for his reporting on West Bank affairs, cited a lecture by Benvenisti which helped him formulate his own judgment more clearly, "the gist of which is that there is no chance that Israel will be able to give up as much as one meter in the West Bank and in Gaza, even if it wishes to do so."[13] Yehuda Litani, West Bank correspondent for *Haaretz,* commented in January 1983 that seven weeks was not an exaggerated estimate for the amount of time left before negotiating initiatives toward a territorial compromise might be irrelevant.[14] In early February Amos Elon wrote that settlement of the Nablus area was "ruling out (perhaps forever) the possibility of repartitioning Palestine/ Eretz Yisrael."[15] Later that same month Elon wrote that "for all practical purposes [Judea, Samaria, and Gaza] have already been annexed to the State of Israel, perhaps irrevocably."[16]

On the other hand, despite dovish despair and the informed judgments of most journalists and observers, plenty of annexationists still worried that perhaps the point of no return had not yet been passed. In February 1984, Yuval Neeman, head of the government's Interministerial Committee on Settlement, complained that cuts in the settlement budget were very dangerous, precisely because an irreversible situation had not yet been created: "Settlement is the key. Every one million dollars that settlement lacks [today] could boomerang on us later."[17]

Indeed the economic crisis in Israel that began in 1984, combined with instances of corruption and mismanagement in the implementation of settlement policies and Labor party participation in the first national unity government, contributed to something of a slowdown in the rate of settlement expansion. Benvenisti, however, no longer even bothered to qualify his declarations of irreversibility. In his institute's report on West Bank developments for 1986, he argued that since 1983, in fact, "a 'West Bank entity' had no longer existed except in theory." Scathingly he attacked Israeli doves who still maintained that a solution based on the separation of Israel from the territories was possible, characterizing the "liberal psyche" as "too fragile for . . . cruel facts" and as desperately seeking to ignore "the phantoms whispering that the future has already arrived, that we have passed the point of no return, that we have crossed the red line." By January 1987, when these words were written, he maintained that what had emerged was a new, larger state: "The distinction between Israel's sovereign territory and the area in which it rules by military government has long since lost its meaning, as it acts as sovereign, for all intents and purposes, in the whole of the area west of the Jordan river, changing the law as it wishes, and creating permanent facts."[18]

According to Benvenisti, the Palestinian problem had been transformed from a foreign policy question to a protracted "communal war" *within* a binational society.[19] The corollary of this analysis, that the cumulative array of social, economic, and political forces driving Israel toward a situation of permanent incorporation of the West Bank and Gaza Strip had become unstoppable, was that Israelis with progressive values as well as U.S. policymakers were wasting their time unless they virtually reversed the focus of their activities. If Israeli progressives and U.S. policymakers were sincere in their commitment to justice for Arabs, then they must shift their efforts, he argued, toward improving the conditions of life for West Bank and Gaza Arabs within the "dual society" and "*herrenvolk* democracy" into which Israel had been transformed by the annexation process. By continuing a fruitless struggle to reverse a completed process of de facto annexation, Israeli doves and U.S. diplomats were only aggravating the problem by preserving false hopes, justifying the exclusion of Palestinian Arabs from access to political rights, and postponing the mobilization of Palestinian sentiment behind demands for Israeli citizenship.[20]

With the continuation of rapid settlement expansion in the West Bank, anti-annexationist reaction to Benvenisti's warnings of irreversibility began to change. By 1984 both Palestinians and Israeli doves had become increasingly sensitive to the depressing effect which the apparent success of the de facto annexation process was having on the morale of the anti-annexationist camp.[21] "Never in politics is never," said Elias Freij in April 1984, a year after he had endorsed Benvenisti's conclusion that the "midnight" of annexation was only weeks or months away.[22] By 1984 Eban shifted from use of Benvenisti's argument and data to mobilize anti-annexationist forces and encourage international involvement to scornful rejection of their importance and of Benvenisti himself as a defeatist and Likud ally. Eban labeled Benvenisti's analysis of the impact of settlement "nonsensical." "So the Arabs aren't a hundred percent [of the West Bank and Gaza Strip population], they're only 98 percent. So what? There's nothing that can change the predominantly non-Jewish character of those territories. . . . If the logic of the partitionist position is destroyed by 7,000 families—of whom some thousands have, incidentally, retained their solid foothold on the Israeli side—that's absurd." According to Eban, it was not Benvenisti's dovish critics, but Benvenisti himself and those who hailed his findings as sealing the fate of the Land of Israel, who suffered from a psychologically based distortion of reality, including "an almost fetishistic attachment to roads." "Benvenisti goes on to say, 'Look at the infrastructure.' He stands before these great road systems and asks how people are going to move out now that so many great roads have been built. I wish he'd go see the roads in Algeria and in Kenya. The world is full of road systems, built from Roman times onward, and the architects of those systems have long since vanished."[23]

Two years and twenty thousand settlers later, Eban still dismissed the argument that settler political pressure had robbed future Israeli governments of disengagement options. Indeed, he now appeared to reject the principle that settlement of the territories, however substantial and long-lived, could rule out Israeli disengagement from them. The idea that the "spectacular marginality" of fifty thousand "puny illicit squatters" could prevent territorial compromise in this way was "preposterous" and "an insult . . . on Israel's statehood." Such "seditious nonsense," he continued, "deserves therapeutic treatment, with all possible patience and concern."[24] Some doves began to argue that Benvenisti, Likud politicians, government officials, Gush Emunim settlers, and the "expert" journalists were wrong about de facto annexation having passed the point of no return. The opposite was the case. It was Israeli withdrawal from the West Bank and Gaza that was inevitable, not the permanent incorporation of those areas. "Nothing will help the settlers," wrote Boaz Evron. "The basic reason is that the tide of history has simply begun flowing against them. The fundamental facts of policy and demography that cannot be overcome have begun to make themselves felt."[25] The absorption of the territories into Israel neither had been nor was being achieved. Of all the possible scenarios it was, said Eban, the "only intrinsic impossibility, because it goes against the laws of political gravity."[26]

The debate seesawed, responding year to year and even month to month to changes in the identity of key ministers, the size of budgets, and the demand for West Bank housing as well as to fluctuations in the vigor of Palestinian, American, and other international opposition to de facto annexation. The switch of so many anti-annexationists, from warning of or perceiving irreversibility to denouncing the very possibility of a point of no return, was neatly mirrored in the fears aroused among Gush Emunim settlers that their euphoria over the putative passage of the point of no return, in 1983 and early 1984, had been premature. In the midst of the painful aftermath of the Lebanon War, with Israeli troops still struggling to maintain order among warring Muslim, Christian, and Druse factions, and the economic disaster of triple-digit inflation, the 1984 elections brought down the Likud government. However, the electorate was so evenly divided between annexationists and anti-annexationists that the Labor party and its allies were not able to establish a government of their own.[27] The result was an awkward arrangement, known as a "national unity government." Beginning in September 1984, Shimon Peres served as prime minister, until the "rotation" in October 1986, at which time Likud leader Yitzhak Shamir took his place—each presiding over a cabinet evenly divided between the two large parties and their respective allies.[28]

During Peres's premiership he made energetic efforts to negotiate with Jordan over the future of the territories and implemented austerity measures, including a freeze on the construction of new settlements. Combined with several highly publicized scandals in which would-be suburban settlers lost considerable amounts of money, and the embarrassing discovery of a Jewish terrorist underground comprised of Gush Emunim activists, these policies encouraged anti-annexationists even as they weakened the confidence of the annexationist camp. *Nekuda* editorials, which in the spring and summer of 1984 had been trumpeting the effective consummation of the de facto annexation process, now began to warn that Israeli disengagement from at least parts of the West Bank and Gaza Strip was still a dangerous possibility. In November 1984, *Nekuda* described the threat of a renewed effort by newly reelected President Ronald Reagan to implement the September 1982 "Reagan plan" for granting West Bank Arabs "autonomy" within the framework of Jordanian rule. Current speculation about the plan, the editors pointed out, would be enough to cause many potential settlers to reconsider their decisions if now were the time they had intended to move. To avert this threat, the editors called upon Gush Emunim and its supporters to "persuade potential settlers that, *precisely because it appeared to be so unpropitious a time*, that now is the time to settle. *The great and growing Jewish presence in Judea, Samaria, and Gaza is the surest guarantee that the Reagan plan—and all other similar plans that may appear—will not be brought to fruition*."[29]

For the next two years *Nekuda* editorials and articles emphasized the deleterious effects of cutbacks in expenditures, the failure of government and World Zionist Organization agencies to meet the targets specified in the "100,000 plan," the gradual return of Arab farmers and home-builders to lands transferred to Israeli control, and the lack of vigor with which parties supposedly committed to the integrity of the "whole Land of Israel" were defending the interests of the settlement movement.[30] In June 1985 one *Nekuda* editorial typical of the period criticized the previous government "for having done too little to close options."[31] In August *Nekuda* warned the Herut party, "the central political body committed, absolutely, to the integrity of the whole Land of Israel," that while it was absorbed in destructive internal rivalries, "the Labor party is preparing to surrender the heart of the Land of Israel and is freezing the growth of settlements there."[32]

During this period, however, Benvenisti's view did not change. From 1983 until 1988, support for his view of the impossibility of separating the West Bank from Israel came not only from confident Israeli annexationists and their pessimistic opponents, but from sober, middle-of-the-road Israeli academics and politicians, respected non-Israeli observers, U.S. diplomats, and even some Palestinians. In June 1983 a political solution based on unification of Israel and the territories was described as an "inevitability" in a report prepared by nine well-known Israeli academics and political figures.[33] Between 1983 and 1988 Benvenisti's views were quoted dozens of times by American journalists based in Israel. Many outside observers and U.S. diplomats responded to images of irreversibility by opposing, de-emphasizing, or abandoning efforts to achieve negotiations toward a land-for-peace settlement. "The burden of proof is now awesome," wrote Larry Fabian of the Carnegie Endowment in the spring of 1983, "for anyone wishing to conclude that Israel can or will turn back the clock on the West Bank." Despite his sympathy for the Labor party's traditional policy of "land for peace" and his appreciation of why its leadership had to act "as if it genuinely believes that the passage of so much time on the West Bank has mattered so little," Fabian remarked that "Labor's solutions for the West Bank and Palestinians simply strain credibility."[34] In August 1983 a State Department official explained the U.S. veto of a United Nations Security Council resolution condemning West Bank and Gaza settlements by labeling the debate over the legality of Israeli settlements "sterile." It was no longer "practical," he said, "or even appropriate to call for the dismantling of the existing settlements."[35]

Even some Palestinians began to interpret the de facto annexation process as demanding a fundamental reorientation of Palestinian political strategy. In October 1985, Sari Nusseibeh, a leading Palestinian intellectual and scion of a well-known family, suggested that Palestinians consider the option of demanding annexation and full rights as Israeli citizens as the "best solution under present circumstances." He predicted that "if Palestinians were to become Israeli citizens, they could win between twelve and sixteen Knesset seats and exert influence to attain their interests by means of the state."[36] In February 1987 he described as "already evident" the Palestinians' " 'instinctive' shift from outright rejection of Israel to exploitation of its social, economic and legal resources."[37] In 1987 Hana Siniora, editor of the East Jerusalem newspaper *Al-Fajr* and a prominent supporter of the Arafatist mainstream within the PLO, announced his intention to run as a candidate in upcoming Jerusalem municipal elections. This move represented a sharp break with the Palestinian consensus since 1967, which was to boycott Jerusalem municipal elections in order not to give legitimacy to Israeli claims of annexation.[38] On the eve of the *intifada* Moshe Amirav, a former Likud activist dismissed from the party because of his contacts with PLO supporters, reported on his conversations with "a new group of Palestinian figures." They had reached the conclusion, he said, "that in the present circumstances it is no longer possible to divide the land between two peoples. Therefore they would rather become part of the State of Israel and conduct a national struggle from within through political means."[39]

A Conflict of "Inexorable Logics"

A striking feature of the de facto annexation debate is that what many who argued the irreversibility point deemed "illusion" or "fantasy" (that Israel could ever disengage from the West Bank and Gaza) was often interpreted as obvious and even inevitable by those who argued disengagement options were still open. On the other hand, what the latter held to be utterly impossible, namely, a stable but unannounced incorporation of the West Bank and Gaza into Israel, "irreversibilists" labeled as either palpable reality or inevitable.[40] "Who here has the Messianic fantasy," asked one journalist writing about West Bank settlements, "Sarid [a prominent secular anti-annexationist] or Levinger [a firebrand Gush Emunim rabbi]?"[41] In 1985 Jonathan Frankel, a historian at the Hebrew University in Jerusalem, expressed the frustration of observers confronted with two utterly persuasive but contradictory answers to one of the most important questions facing the country: "Is this situation permanent?" He responded that "one form of inexorable logic says that close to 1.5 million people cannot be permanently deprived of political rights by a parliamentary democracy in the twentieth century and that autonomy, some form of independence, must result eventually. But is it no less logical to argue that 50,000–100,000 colonists, backed by a population ever more accustomed to rule over others, will never voluntarily permit such liberation?"[42]

Subsequent events seemed, temporarily at least, to deprive this conundrum of some of its vexing symmetry. The Palestinian uprising, which began in December 1987, led many doves who had despaired of ever separating Israel from the West Bank and Gaza Strip to declare that the process toward separation had now itself become irreversible and the establishment of a Palestinian state in those territories inevitable. For example, in 1982 Dani Rubinstein had declared that because of massive settlement and other related activities, there was "no chance that Israel will be able to give up as much as one meter in the West Bank and in Gaza." In July 1988, after only seven months of *intifada*, Rubinstein described the significance of the settlements in different, but no less categorical terms.

What future can there be for a few thousand, or even several score thousand Israelis, awash in a sea of more than 1.5 million Palestinian Arabs who want only to rid themselves of Israeli governance? How many more millions can we invest in this movement which, under the circumstances, hasn't a prayer of attracting Jewish settlers—and all the dreams of "Judaizing" the West Bank and Gaza are (and always have been) but vain illusions?[43]

In the United States, much attention was given to an August 1989 Rand Corporation study titled *The West Bank of Israel: Point of No Return?* Reflecting the impact of the *intifada* on perceptions of the de facto annexation process, the "point of no return" at issue in this study was not the putative irreversibility of Israeli absorption of the territory, but what the author judged the irreversible emergence of an independent Palestinian state in the West Bank and Gaza Strip.[44] Likewise, in September 1989 an Israeli journal linked to the Ratz party devoted an entire issue to the practical aspects of accommodating what it announced was the "inevitable" emergence of a Palestinian state in the West Bank and Gaza Strip. "It may be far away," wrote the editors of *Politika*, "and for some Israelis a Palestinian state is a nightmare ... but it is an unavoidable solution. A public willing to open its eyes must begin to get used to it."[45]

Even Meron Benvenisti reformulated his position. In a symposium held on January 30, 1990, at the Van Leer Institute in Jerusalem, Benvenisti no longer argued that the annexation process was "irreversible" or that it had passed some sort of "critical point" or "turning point." Rather, he said, "it is possible to partition the land, to create a Palestinian state ... but a partition solution is not a necessary or inevitable scenario ... it can happen, but it is not true that it *must* happen."[46] Thus did the problem, as defined by Benvenisti, also shift from whether permanent incorporation had been made inevitable to whether its opposite, territorial withdrawal and creation of a Palestinian state, had become inevitable.[47]

On the other side of the political fence, most of those annexationists who had argued that the process had become irreversible also appeared to modify or abandon their claims, though without giving up their belief that permanent incorporation of the West Bank and Gaza into Israel could or would be achieved. In the spring of 1990 even Gush Emunim's most optimistic, confident leaders changed the substance and tone of their analysis. Rabbi Yoel Ben-Nun was the leader of the camp within the settler movement that had stressed the decisiveness of what had already been accomplished and the importance of avoiding expressions of nervousness, threats of violence, or other strident challenges to government authority.[48] In the spring of 1990, however, even Ben-Nun warned of the imminent danger of decisions leading toward territorial compromise. The announcement of such decisions by a government dependent in the Parliament on non-Zionists (Israeli Arabs and ultraorthodox Jews) would, he declared, cross "our red line," leading, "God forbid," toward "transformation of the war of the people of Israel and its state against the Palestinians, to another sort of war, worse than all others, a civil war."[49]

Thus virtually every participant in this debate over the "irreversibility" of de facto annexation changed position on the issue in the face of fluctuating rates of settlement activity and changing political, economic, and demographic trends. These fluctuations continued. By mid-1991 a combination of high levels of immigration and accelerated construction of new settlements in the territories led many protagonists and observers to warn of, or celebrate, the soon-to-be inevitable incorporation of the territories—judgments they suddenly very much doubted due to the victory of anti-annexationist parties in the June 1992 elections.

Between "Secession" and "Decolonization"

In the modern world, empires are expected to break apart. In accordance with that expectation political scientists and historians studying relationships between established states and territories under the rule of those states have been limited by an implicit distinction between relationships seen as natural and permanent and those seen as artificial and temporary. Separation of an outlying territory from an established state is usually considered "secession" if the link between the state and the outlying territory is or was presumed permanent and "decolonization" if the link is or was presumed temporary.

Thus Ronald Reagan's depiction of the Soviet Union an "evil empire" was understood as a rhetorical challenge to both the legitimacy and permanence of Moscow's rule over its territories and peoples. As things turned out, the characterization was potent analytically as well as polemically. The size and shape of the Soviet state was far more susceptible to large-scale change than Reagan or any of his advisers had imagined. Nevertheless, when independent republics proliferated in the wake of a Soviet state unwilling or unable to enforce its claims to sovereignty, the achievement of independence by these new states was almost always termed "secession," not "decolonization." This "ordinary language" description reflected preexisting assumptions that the Soviet Union was a coherent and, for all intents and purposes, permanent entity; it also reflected desires to distinguish the end of the Soviet "empire" in eastern Europe from the end of the Soviet state's control over the territory of the USSR.

The surprise and terminological confusion occasioned by the breakup of the Soviet Union were partially due to the underdevelopment of theory about change in the size and shape of states, conceptual limits which forced category errors on observers of Soviet and post-Soviet society. If all relationships between central states and peripheral territories are to be divided into those presumed permanent and those presumed temporary, and if pressures to sever those relationships can only be understood as secessionism or decolonization, then how can problematic relationships be analyzed—relationships for which neither sort of presumption exists? If the Soviet Union were an empire, then why would the independence of Ukraine or Uzbekistan be understood as "secession?" But if the separation of those territories from the state ruled from Moscow were deemed "decolonization," then with what justification would separatist efforts by any of the Russian Federated Republic's 131 nationalities or 31 autonomous republics and regions not also be understandable as decolonizing struggles?

This problem is not only taxonomic. Secession and decolonization are categories often used by politicians to label what they do to prevent or achieve changes in the shape of a state. In the modern era, if an outlying territory is accepted within the core of a state as a commonsensically integral, permanent part of the national domain, efforts by inhabitants of the periphery to achieve independence are understood as "secession." To the extent that this categorization is accepted, both the inhabitants of the core state and the international community of sovereign states tend to accept the prerogatives of state authorities to treat struggles for separation as treasonous. The population of the core state is expected to support efforts to "crush the rebellion," to prevent the amputation of the national patrimony, without measuring the costs and benefits of doing so. Any outside intervention on behalf of the "secessionist" population's putative right to "national self-determination" is deemed thoroughly illegitimate. To the extent that the government's struggle against attempts to achieve territorial disengagement is accepted as necessary to prevent "secession," drawing resources from the population to support this struggle is not difficult. The struggle may entail heavy sacrifices; it may succeed or fail; but since the objective is defined in such intimate relationship to well-established collective identities, it will not divide the political community in a regime-threatening manner.

Consequently, few movements seeking political independence for a peripheral territory will define the struggle to achieve autonomy from a central state as "secession," since that implies the right of the dominant core to retain control of the territory in question at any cost. The struggle over the fate of the territory is much more likely cast as a question of "decolonization." Aside from the negative connotations associated with imperial political formulas and the positive connotations presently associated with "anticolonialist" struggles, portraying a relationship between two territories as colonial or imperial implies that the population of the superordinate region ought to decide on its policies in an instrumentalist fashion—by measuring the costs and benefits entailed in keeping the territory against those associated with disengagement from it. For the government of a central state, categorization of a territorial problem as one of "decolonization" implies that eventually a change in the political status of the territory will occur, that disengagement will not unacceptably insult the national honor or cultural identity of the core population, and that the pace of the decolonization process and the mix of costs and benefits associated with alternative paths to separation are legitimate issues for public debate—issues over which "reasonable persons" may differ without being accused of treason. Such debates may be bitter; the costs of eventual disengagement may be light or heavy; but because the categorization of the territorial issue as an instrumental one is widely accepted, typical political processes of bargaining, compromise, and trial-and-error decision making can proceed without serious threat to the integrity of the political order.

But what about cases, such as post-1983 Israel or post-Soviet Russia, when the shape of the central state is itself problematic, that is, when territorial questions arise whose very categorization as either "secession" or "decolonization" is at issue? One would expect such questions to pose particularly intractable and dangerous challenges to democratic institutions, highlighting both the opportunities and constraints that democratic leaders confront when tasks of political education loom as large as requirements for resource mobilization or interest group satisfaction. Comparably challenging methodological and conceptual questions are raised for scholars studying such problems, since decisions about how to pose the questions must be made without prejudging their categorization as one of either "secession" or "decolonization." Accordingly, the structure of the analysis must be capable of comprehending processes of change in the intellectual premises of political life as well as reactions to and strategic manipulations of the interests, resources, and constraints that crystallize in relationship to those premises.

Consideration of the debate over the course and prospects for Israeli absorption of the West Bank and Gaza Strip brings into sharp focus the limitations of "decolonization" or "secession" as constructs for guiding analysis when the presumptions associated with these terms are themselves the subject of dispute. These presumptions, attached to opposing images of these territories as "integral parts of the state" or as colonial-style possessions, have powerful effects on the assessments, strategies, and actions of those who accept them as definitions of the problems they address.

As strong as these effects may be, however, the presence of annexationists and anti-annexationists on both sides of the argument over the permanence of Israeli rule of the territories, and the way both annexationists and anti-annexationists have changed, and even rechanged, their minds about the "reversibility" of annexation suggest how little confidence they have in the knowledge of the processes they deem so crucial.

As time passes, without stabilizing the relationship between Israel and the territories by eliminating fears, hopes, or expectations of either absorption or disengagement, the hard outlines of the fundamental theoretical/analytical problem emerge with increasing clarity. Amid the welter of events, the changing judgments of observers, and the shifting hopes and fears of various opposing groups of Israelis and Palestinians, what survivable picture can be drawn of the relationship between Israel and the territories? What framework of analysis can be constructed to accumulate insights—not only those produced from analysis of the dynamics of this particular relationship, but also insights that can be distilled by mobilizing the potential for comparability of other, structurally similar, episodes?

In Chapter 2 a conceptual framework for solving this problem is described, based on images of Israel as engaged in what is best understood as a problematical effort at state expansion or state contraction. I argue that by posing the problem as one of the conditions under which preexisting states expand and contract, theories useful for solving the problem can be developed and even tested by studying two other substantially similar but strategically different cases—the relationship between Great Britain and Ireland from the early nineteenth to the early twentieth centuries, and the relationship between France and Algeria from the late 1930s to the 1960s. Subsequent chapters analyze these cases. The results of this comparative analysis are used in the concluding chapters of the book to identify conditions under which Israel could stabilize its relationship to the territories (through disengagement *or* incorporation); to establish particular scenarios as considerably more plausible than others; and to suggest regularities in the experience of any state whose territorial constructedness loses its invisibility.

CHAPTER TWO

Thresholds of State-Building
and State Contraction

The heroic model of Israel's socialist-Zionist founders is based on the movement's success in building a state in as much of the Jewish people's ancient homeland as possible. This state-building project was understood as dialectically related to rebuilding the Jewish nation—a relationship expressed in the popular Zionist slogan "to build and to be built by." Although willing to accept partition in order to consolidate Jewish sovereignty in part of the Land of Israel, David Ben-Gurion and other mainstream Labor Zionist leaders always maintained the superiority of Jewish rights to the whole land—rights that could be exercised whenever circumstances might make it prudent to do so.[1] Combined with the "pioneering" ethos of state- and nation-building, this ideological position made it difficult for most of the Israeli political class to resist the attraction of resuming state-building tasks in those portions of the Land of Israel brought under the jurisdiction of the Jewish state in 1967.

Revisionism, Labor Zionism's historic rival for leadership of the Zionist movement, was founded primarily on its rejection of any sort of territorial compromise. Although Herut's participation in Israeli elections signaled Revisionism's acceptance of democratic competition as a route to power, Begin and his followers never formally accepted the legitimacy of the state's borders. The party's platform emphasized the imperative of Jewish rule over both the western and eastern sections of the Land of Israel.[2]

For Herut, opportunities for state expansion that appeared as a result of the Six Day War were more than an irresistible temptation. The victory and the emotional climate that followed were seen as a glorious affirmation of national destiny and national spirit. The territories that were "liberated," according to Herut, should never have been considered anything but core elements of the state. But Herut lacked the ability to express its ideological commitments by establishing settlements in the newly won territories. For all its militance and maximalism, the Revisionist Zionist movement had traditionally emphasized formal/legal declarations, treaties, and international guarantees, albeit backed up by military force, as the key elements in state creation. Revisionists had always disparaged "close settlement on the land" as a state-building technique. Herut's own settlement movement was extremely weak. In the context of the Zionist movement it was therefore ironic, but historically and politically correct, for Herut-dominated governments to characterize their "fait accomplis" policies of settlement and de facto (as opposed to de jure) annexation as "building the Jewish state in Judea, Samaria, and Gaza."

Theoretical Implications of the Debate over "Irreversibility"

Considered analytically rather than in historical, ideological, or polemical terms, attempts to incorporate the territories into Israel (or facilitate Israeli disengagement from them) are interesting for the theories of state-building and state contraction they imply. Protagonists in the debate over irreversibility surveyed in Chapter 1 tried in particular ways to achieve or prevent permanent incorporation of the West Bank and Gaza into Israel. They evaluated the success of their efforts and those of their opponents according to certain yardsticks and used their assessments as a basis for self-criticism and for designing more effective means of struggle. By so doing they displayed implicit commitments to theories of how states are built out of culturally heterogeneous, even hostile territories, and how existing states can build themselves into other territories, or, it may better be said, how existing states build such territories into themselves.

Thus the state-building theory implied by Likud government policies emphasized settlement, elaboration of administrative, economic, and social institutions among the settler population, land transfers, and control of (rather than elimination or assimilation of) indigenous inhabitants. If the ambitious plans developed under the auspices of the first and second Likud governments are viewed as hypotheses growing out of that theory, the energetic efforts of Likud governments to implement their plans and the anti-annexationist camp's struggle to thwart them can all appropriately be viewed as tests of these hypotheses. It follows that the confusion of the debate over the conditions under which Israel's ties to the territories could be said to be unbreakable reflected a lack of coherence to the theory itself, including disagreement on how the dependent variable (establishment of one set of borders or another as "permanent") could be specified.

This chapter elicits from this rich but confused debate a framework for the analysis of change in the shape of a state. The framework is then used throughout the book to compare cases of state expansion and contraction, testing the plausibility of hypotheses about the political dynamics of state re-formation. To this end, the various and changing conclusions of participants in the Israeli debate over de facto annexation are not as important as the reasoning used to support these judgments and reject others. Contained in these claims are choices as to what data are deemed relevant to the question and what measurements of those data will permit confident judgments about state-building or state contraction.

Two instructive areas of tension appear in the debate over the putative irreversibility of de facto annexation. In the first, discontinuous, nonlinear images of territorial incorporation, or disengagement, are set against linear images of continuous processes. In the second, a substantive distinction appears between two kinds of factors considered decisive in the struggle over the disposition of the territories. One perspective emphasizes leadership abilities, changing constellations of political interests, electoral clout, and the governing coalitions these factors make more or less likely. Another view stresses changing perceptions of the territories in the minds of Israelis—changes attendant on a growing Israeli presence in the territories and increases in and routinization of transactions across the Green Line.

As I argue below, these oppositions are less contradictory than they may appear if the process of state expansion and contraction is properly conceptualized. The initial plausibility of my analytic framework is based on its ability to glean insights available within each of these perspectives and clarify the relationships among them.

State Shaping as a Discontinuous Effect

Phrases such as "irreversible" or "point of no return," "five minutes to midnight" or "critical point," and focus on the attainment or prevention of particular settlement goals (e.g., the "hundred thousand" plan for settlers in the West Bank outside of expanded East Jerusalem), suggest a theory of state expansion in which incremental changes could produce relatively sudden and categorical changes in the character of the political relationship between core and periphery. More specifically, this theory of the state-building process holds that the continuous accretion of small changes in the status quo (land transferred to Israeli control, public works projects completed, change in the number and location of settlements and settlers, or gradual elaboration of Israeli administrative and legal procedures) will at some relatively discrete point trigger a discontinuous change in the character of the relationship between the central state and the peripheral territory.

For my purposes, whether it was argued that a point of no return had been or might be passed in the Israeli-Palestinian case or where it might be located is less interesting than the very imputation of the existence of a "point of no return." By using concepts and images portraying the process of state-building as marked by a sharp discontinuity, Benvenisti and those who echoed his views were proposing a theory envisioning a radical separation between a breakable relationship linking the central state and outlying territory, on one side of a "point of no return," and an unbreakable relationship on the other. To the extent that a truly "irreversible" situation was said to exist on the "other side of midnight," the theory stipulated that beyond this "critical point" only state expansion or (presumably) destruction was possible, not state contraction. But if a somewhat looser meaning is attached to "irreversible," and in Benvenisti's writings there is ample justification for doing so, the passage of the "critical point" can be understood to mean substituting territorial disengagement as "secession" for territorial disengagement as "decolonization."

State Shaping as a Continuous Process

Decolonization is the process of ending a colonial relationship. The picture conveyed by the word "colonial" contains a metropole controlling a possession, separate from the metropole itself, and exploiting that control to its own advantage. Accordingly, decolonization is almost always viewed as resulting from metropolitan calculations, usually belated, that, because of unrest in the colony, changing international circumstances, or shifting interests or economic conditions, the military, political, and/or economic costs of controlling the possession outweigh the perceived benefits.

In the Israeli debate over de facto annexation, many of Benvenisti's most articulate critics employed a thoroughly "colonial" model of the continuing occupation. In contrast to a single point of qualitative change, brought about by quantitative increases in various measures of the process of de facto annexation, those invoking a colonial model of the relationship portrayed the cost of breaking the ties between Israel and the territories as tracing a continuously rising cost curve. Writing in 1985, Milton Viorst admitted that "disentangling the structure created by seventeen years of occupation will be difficult."[3] The question, however, was not whether transfer of a territory to the rule of a core state, "once done, can be undone. The potential for change obviously exists. The question is, at what price?"[4]

Abba Eban described Israel's rule of the territories in similarly linear, continuous terms. "The longer it goes on, the more adhesive it will become, and the less easy it will be to disentangle ourselves from it."[5] The implication, however, was that the task of disentangling the relationship would not rise to a point after which the possibility, and not the cost, of doing so would become the dominant question. "Aside from death and the passage of time," said Knesset member Yossi Sarid in 1984, "nothing is irreversible. Certainly not with such thoroughly political matters."[6] For Viorst, Eban, and Sarid, whatever drastic or qualitative change in the relationship was deemed possible was not envisioned as something that could occur as a function of settlement, road construction, land acquisition, and other techniques of de facto annexation. These investments would make it increasingly difficult, increasingly costly, to disengage. But even if the slope of the cost curve could become rather steep, the result would only be a higher price for disengagement, for "decolonization."[7]

Political Mechanisms of State-Building and State Contraction

The second area of tension in the de facto annexation debate pertained to the mechanisms envisioned as consolidating Israeli rule of the territories or capable of ending it, whether gradually or abruptly. One mechanism deemed crucial in promoting or reversing processes of incorporation was the changing level of political support within Israel for politicians favoring disengagement.

Benvenisti's most prominent explanation as to why he believed the "critical point" had been passed by 1984 was that the Likud's settlement effort had gathered sufficient momentum to reach its goal of a hundred thousand settlers. The Likud, he said, had "estimated correctly that the decision about the future of the territories would result from domestic political struggles within the state of Israel." Translation of settlement into statebuilding on the political level would be accomplished at the ballot box by a powerful prosettler constituency. According to Benvenisti, "Knowing that the percentage of the floating vote in Israel is small, the Likud estimates that 100,000 people, representing four or five marginal seats in the Knesset, would be an effective barrier to any political alternative espousing the principle of territorial compromise. The suburban settlers need not hold with Likud ideology; they simply wish to protect their investment and the higher quality of life they will have attained."[8]

The rejection of this argument by Sarid and other Israeli doves nevertheless revealed their acceptance of electoral and coalition-building factors in measuring the difficulty of withdrawal and setting the conditions under which it could be accomplished. After Benvenisti made his prediction of irreversibility in 1984, Sarid asked how he or the Likud could imagine that the settlers could prevent the opening of negotiations over the future of the West Bank? Their votes, according to Sarid, could elect not three, but no more than one deputy to Israel's 120 member Parliament. "Further, since these votes will be divided up among the Likud, Tehiya, Tzomet, the National Religious Party, Orot, and who knows who else, it is clear that this population lacks any political importance." Even if the number of settlers would increase, and even if the electoral power of the annexationist bloc might at some point become well established, that did not mean, according to this view, that the sentiments supporting such a political alignment could not shift or that effective leadership by anti-annexationist politicians could not bring a government power capable of implementing policies that would bring about disengagement.[9]

Again, what is instructive about such an analysis is not the conclusion—that the settlers were not as weighty a factor as Benvenisti thought—but the acceptance of shifting prospects for hawkish versus dovish governments as the appropriate measure for judging the tightness of bonds between Israel and the territories.

Associated with the explosive increase in settlement activity, however, was a change in the nature of the domestic political forces which both supporters and opponents of de facto annexation imagined as decisive. Increasingly both sides argued that the crucial obstacle to disengagement would not be the constraints on government policy produced by the pressure of new constituencies within normally operating Israeli political institutions (e.g., marginal increases in the size of the annexationist bloc within the Knesset), but rather the fear that efforts to achieve a territorial compromise would trigger challenges to those institutions, including armed clashes among Jews. In particular, both Gush Emunim settlers and Israeli doves, and both those who believed it would be possible to overcome such challenges to legally constituted authorities and those who did not, traced scenarios in which settlers, right-wing ideologues, frustrated or hawkish generals, and religious fundamentalists would take up arms against the government and precipitate civil war rather than tolerate Israeli "abandonment" of key portions of the national patrimony.

Among those who believed such a crisis would certainly erupt in connection with attempts to reach a territorial compromise was Yehosafat Harkabi. His fundamental argument against settlements and in favor of moving sooner rather than later toward negotiated compromise was his concern that the scope of the inevitable crisis would increase with the size and density of Israeli settlement of the territories. As time went on, interests in the continuation of Israeli rule of the territories would proliferate and attitudes toward the Arabs would harden. Harkabi stated, "This development will intensify the internal crisis in Israel when it becomes clear that Israel must nonetheless make concessions for the sake of an agreement, even if such conditions are imposed." He argued that skillful leadership could prepare Israeli society for the stresses it would experience and help it overcome whatever violent challenges would erupt. But he was bitter about the scale of the damage that Israel would suffer, predicting the Jewish state would eventually pay an unnecessarily "exorbitant" and "very painful" price for withdrawal.[10]

Some doves took a more sanguine view, identifying the particular combination of policies and coalitions that might be able to overcome such extralegal challenges.[11] Others, however, doubted whether Israeli democracy could survive a clash with those ready to resist withdrawal at all costs, or whether any government, faced with such a risk, would ever take it.[12] This latter judgment was accepted with satisfaction by Gush Emunim settlers and other hardline advocates of annexation. Indeed this same "hypothesis," that threats of institutional collapse would translate de facto annexation into political constraints against state contraction, was endorsed by the Council of Jewish Settlements in Judea, Samaria, and Gaza. This was readily apparent when it issued its October 1985 warning that negotiations toward a territorial compromise would mark any Israeli government that engaged in them as illegitimate and justify "Gaullist"-style resistance to a "Pétainist" regime.[13]

Psychological Mechanisms of State-Building and State Contraction

Apart from the political obstacle to withdrawal which the settlers and their supporters might constitute as a voting bloc, or as the instigators of civil strife, many participants in the debate over de facto annexation stressed the overriding importance of psychological factors. The settlements were not crucial, they argued, because of the direct impact they would have on the calculations of politicians or the probability of one sort of coalition government or another. Rather their presence and the networks of relationships linking them to inhabitants of Israel proper were understood to contribute to a transformation in the way Israelis viewed the natural shape of their country. As a result of the success of the West Bank settlement effort, said one deputy minister in the second Likud government, "the political controversy will be completely different. Every Jew who settles . . . strengthens our ownership of the areas, and increases our sense of belonging to those areas, and their belonging to us."[14]

The basis of this argument is a substantially different kind of (hypothesized) barrier to reversing the process of de facto annexation than the shifting calculations of politicians responding to either electoral pressures or threats of regime disruption. The crucial variable here is the inclination, or even ability, of Israelis to view the West Bank and Gaza Strip as territories separate from Israel itself, and therefore potentially (at least) disposable. According to the official "Master Plan for the Development of Samaria and Judea to the Year 2010," the primary objective of the massive settlement effort it proposed was to transform the image of the territories in the psyche of Israelis.[15] For the authors of this 134 page study, the objective of permanent incorporation of "Judea and Samaria" into the state of Israel was not the issue.[16] What was problematic was how that objective could be achieved. Of primary importance to the planners was the transfer of large numbers of Jews from Israel proper, across the 1949–67 Green Line border, into "Judea and Samaria." But they judged that the commitment of Israeli Jews to the "pioneering Zionism" exhibited by Gush Emunim settlers, who lived in trailers, on windy hilltops, far from metropolitan comforts, was not sufficient to achieve this goal. Instead the planners suggested the kind of massive program of roadbuilding, housing construction, infrastructural development, and industrial and residential subsidies which the Likud government undertook. According to the plan, offers of higher standards of living than were available within the Green Line, and employment opportunities and transportation networks arranged so as to minimize contacts between new Jewish residents and Arab inhabitants, would pull half a million Jews into the West Bank (excluding East Jerusalem) by the year 2010.[17]

In the study itself there is no attempt to identify a particular point after which political outcomes other than the permanent incorporation of the West Bank into the State of Israel would be ruled out. The planners neither anticipated that a Jewish majority would be created in the West Bank nor considered a Jewish majority necessary to build the area into the state of Israel.[18] To be sure, a hundred thousand settlers in this area was established as an "interim" target for 1986, but neither this target nor any other numerical objective was characterized by the planners as a sufficient condition for the permanent incorporation of the West Bank. In the planners' view the critical variable was not the relative size but the physical distribution of the Jewish and Arab populations. The plan put highest priority on the establishing Jewish concentrations in salient, highly visible locations, such as along the central mountain ridge where the main north-south highway connects a series of sizable Arab towns and cities. Such reassur-

ingly continuous belts of Jewish settlement would create a "mental barrier," linking compact blocs of Jewish towns and villages with one another
and to Israeli metropolitan areas by a network of highways bypassing
Arab population centers.[19]

By preempting available land around urban areas, by physically blocking
the "ribbon development" of Arab towns and villages, and by organizing
economic opportunities for Arabs near but not inside of already existing
Arab municipalities, the Israeli government hoped to prevent West Bank
Arabs from leaving their widely scattered towns and villages for urban
areas or from developing larger, more imposing metropolitan centers. By
avoiding Jewish settlement within Arab cities and towns, by keeping Arabs
divided, "out of sight" in their rural villages, and more or less separate
from Jewish communities and Jewish-used transportation links, Israelis
could come more quickly to feel at home in the area and to sense no
difference between one side of the Green Line and the other. Under such
circumstances the "psychological" integration of the West Bank into Israel,
along with its physical integration, could be ensured.[20]

What was required, in other words, was a presumption among Israeli
Jews that Israel's relationship to the West Bank had ceased to be problematic. To achieve this objective it would not be necessary to legitimize
Israeli control of the area in the minds of local Arabs. However, a degree
of Arab acquiescence was seen as important for conditions in the territories
to be blended into the Israeli routine, so that Israeli Jews would evaluate
opportunities to visit, work, or move to the West Bank and Gaza according
to the same criteria they would use to plan travel, work, or residence in
other parts of "Israel." Compared to the enormous expenditures proposed
as necessary for roads, housing subsidies, land development, and other
infrastructural investments for settlers, the planners believed that the necessary level of Arab quiescence was obtainable relatively cheaply, by small
but steady increases in Arab standards of living and employment
prospects.[21]

Again, for the planners, the ultimate significance of the projects they
advocated was the contribution they were likely to make to the cultivation
of a habit of thinking among Jewish Israelis that the West Bank and Gaza
were part of their state. State expansion was thus seen as a psychological
process taking place (mostly and decisively) within the dominant (Jewish)
population of the core state (Israel). By depriving the old Green Line of
all practical meaning, and by habituating Israelis to a country in which
territories acquired in 1967 were no less accessible or attractive, no more
dangerous or alien, than territories acquired in 1948, Israelis would lose
not only the inclination but the ability to distinguish "Israel" from the
"occupied territories." No formal declaration of "annexation" would be

necessary. The decisive fact would be that political programs suggesting that Israel's interests could be served by making territorial concessions in the West Bank or Gaza Strip would become more than unpopular; they would appear silly or even nonsensical. By thus removing the disposition of the territories from the national political agenda, the stable and permanent expansion of the state would be accomplished.

The emphasis in this plan on the psychological aspects of the process of expanding the territorial ambit of the state of Israel was consistent with conclusions drawn by many settler activists after Gush Emunim's failure to stop Israel's withdrawal from Yamit.[22] An important strain in the thinking of Gush activists, reinforced by the Yamit evacuation and Israel's return of Sinai to Egyptian control, was that incorporation of the territories into Israel would occur only if settlement were part of a broad process of acculturation—an educational, cultural, and psychological process that would bring Israeli Jews to see the State of Israel as naturally and necessarily coextensive with the whole Land of Israel.

"Settlements are not enough!" was a slogan that emerged from a Gush Emunim symposium convened immediately after the evacuation of Yamit.[23] Nekuda editorials and the comments and essays of numerous Gush activists stressed the decisive importance of sustained educational and cultural activities to reshape basic Israeli attitudes toward the shape of the Land of Israel and the significance of Jewish rule over it. What was necessary was to erase the Green Line from the public imagination. Toward this end, the first thing Rabbi Yisrael Ariel recommended was "to burn the old maps, and put before the youth the map of the Land of Israel as written in the Bible.... Every child must see before him all of the Land of Israel, from the river of Egypt to the Euphrates."[24] The public must be educated not only to know but to feel—to feel, wrote one prominent Gush leader, that "if those who raise a hand against a soldier must receive one month in prison, two months, or half a year, whoever uproots settlements deserves life imprisonment."[25]

While the spectacular success of the "suburban" settlement campaign began by the Likud in 1983 encouraged many settlers again to deemphasize the educational dimension of their project, still, in January 1984, a Nekuda editorial noted that settlement was only one component of the state-expanding process.

> The central goal of settlement—aside from the basic establishment of settlements—is to bring about the complete organization—psychological and concrete—with the State of Israel. Integration can be achieved in several ways, the first of them, of course, would be the extension, and rapidly, of Israeli law on the territories of Judea, Samaria, and Gaza. But that is not enough.

In order that the public will have a psychological sense that indeed Judea, Samaria, and Gaza are integral parts of the state, these areas must cease to be problematic.[26]

In the long run, argued Yoel Ben-Nun, that would require a veritable cultural revolution. Settlement of the territories was the practical basis for the eventual success of the necessary "kulturkampf," but was not itself the sign of success. Only if Israeli Jews could be brought to accept the redemptive mission of the state of Israel, and the central role of Jewish sovereignty over the whole Land of Israel in accomplishing that mission, could Israel's rule of the territories be stabilized. According to Ben-Nun,

> There is no longer the possibility of evading the decisive stage of the process of redemption. Beyond establishing the infrastructure of the ingathering of the exiles, the blossoming of the desolated land and the construction of a strong state, what is now demanded is a clear concept of the state and its relationship to the people and the land, to Judaism, to diaspora Jews, and also to the Arab minority. Thus has the long delayed *kulturkampf* erupted.[27]

Opponents as well as supporters of de facto annexation shared the view that new cognitive habits, determining what was considered possible or impossible, natural or unnatural, problematic or inevitable, would ultimately be decisive in the struggle over the disposition of the occupied territories. Thus in the early and mid-1980s dovish groups such as Yesh Gvul (There Is a Limit) and Peace Now organized events during which their members used green paint to mark the location of the Green Line. Yochanan Peres, a Tel Aviv University sociologist prominent in the ranks of Ratz, expressed his concern in 1984 that seventeen years after the beginning of the occupation, it was "Greater Israel," and not Israel of the 1949 armistice lines, which seemed to young voters to be the natural shape of their country:

> They grew up in an occupying state. For them the State of Israel is a State of Israel that includes Judea and Samaria. Any change in that situation is a change in what they have felt they belonged to for as long as they can remember. Just as someone who grew up in Israel before the founding of the state would not consider it possible to give Ramle and Jaffa back to the Palestinians, so those whose world-view includes Judea and Samaria as part of Israel cannot grasp any other reality.[28]

In 1985, however, the dovish journal *Koteret Rashit* published a lead article about the outlook of high-school graduates born in the year of the Six Day War who were about to enter the army. The author was happy to report that the student he interviewed as representative still considered the fate of the territories an issue to argue about. "At least," commented the author, "from that perspective we have achieved something: there are still arguments going on."[29]

A Framework for Theory Building

Each approach to measuring the success of de facto annexation policies offers insights into different aspects of state expansion and contraction. To integrate them within one framework, discontinuous and continuous processes of institutionalization must be linked to the forms that politics takes at different stages of institutionalization: rule-governed competition within an institutionalized setting; competition over the parameters of the institution itself; and competition over the establishment or elimination of presumptive beliefs which can protect institutions from, or expose them to, fundamental challenges.

As a theoretical baseline, a general notion of institutions is required within which the problem of accounting for the variable boundaries of states can be situated and solved. An institution is a framework for social action which elicits from those who act within it expectations of regularity, continuity, and propriety. Such a framework is institutionalized to the extent that those expectations are reliably reproduced. Institutionalization is a process by which change in the rules of political competition becomes increasingly disruptive and decreasingly likely to be part of the strategic calculus of competitors within the institutional arena.

States are special institutions. They are the institutions which enforce property rights and provide sufficient order to permit persons within their purview to build and maintain other institutions.[30] In the building of states, as in the building of any institution, the process by which positively valued and stable expectations are produced or destroyed includes both continuous and discontinuous elements and both political and psychological aspects. These facets of institutionalization and de-institutionalization processes can be located in relation to one another if the continuous aspects of institution-building, including gradually increasing propensities to expect norms, rules, and boundaries to be adhered to and symbols to be honored, are understood to surround two distinct thresholds. These thresholds mark discontinuities in the process of institutionalization, dividing it into three stages. Movement from one stage to another entails a shift in the order of magnitude of political conflict that would surround efforts to change a particular institution along a salient dimension (see Fig. 2).

The morphological variability of all states indicates the need for a dynamic conception of the size and shape of the state. The long time periods through which such shifts manifest themselves, and the suddenness or "lumpiness" of those transformations, suggest the need to temper awareness of fluidity with expectations that change in the contours of states will not respond smoothly to marginal changes in patterns of popular loyalty, economic interest, elite ideology, or even military strength. What, then, endows the nominal border of a state with long-term political significance? Study of the dynamics of state expansion and contraction requires a fairly precise answer to this question—one that combines the notion of ultimate fluidity with the expectation of sluggishness and discontinuity in patterns of border change.

According to one formulation offered by Max Weber, the sociological meaning of a state is the observer-determined probability that individual action is grounded in the expectation that an authoritative framework for political competition exists. "If there is no such probability the State does not exist any more."[31] This fundamentally psychological character of stateness is also captured in Joseph Strayer's dictum that "A state exists chiefly in the hearts and minds of its people; if they do not believe it is there, no logical exercise will bring it to life."[32] From a political perspective these formulations suggest that borders of states describe boundaries between political arenas within which it is believed that available power resources will be mobilized according to different sets of norms and legal arrangements. Accordingly, from the internal perspective of any state, stable borders are reflections of presumptive beliefs which remove potentially intractable questions of the composition of the political community from the political arena. The usefulness of these formulations is that they remind us of the constructedness of states and the contingency of their compass, while also suggesting the potential for stability in their size and shape which can attend deeply embedded, widely shared, and uncontested beliefs.

Considering state boundaries as institutionalized features of states also suggests why internal political struggles over the proper and permanent territorial definition of the state are typically so intense when they do erupt. What is likely at stake is not only the instrumental value of the territorial adjustment to the state as a whole. Territorial expansion or contraction can be expected to trigger shifts in the distribution of power within a state by changing the resources available to different groups and, ultimately, by changing prevailing norms and legal arrangements to correspond with the interests of newly dominant groups. Substantial change in the shape and size of a state thus has long-term implications for the relative power position of different groups within it. Accordingly, unless the border of the state is accepted as an immutable given, we can expect that different groups within the state will align their own perceptions of the proper border in light of the implications different borders, or different principles of inclusion and exclusion, may have for their chances to achieve and/or maintain political power.[33]

My two-threshold model of institutionalization, applied to the expansion and contraction of states, is designed to facilitate cross-cultural and diachronic comparison of reciprocal relations between change in the institutional context of political competition and the competition itself. A concrete illustration of the need for such an approach was inadvertently but conveniently presented by Andrew Mack. In 1975 he argued that small nations can win wars against large states because (in colonial or neocolonial situations) the definition of the stakes of the game is "asymmetric": absolutist and total within the small nation, but instrumentalist and partial within the large state. He thus sought, for example, to explain the success of the Vietnamese against the United States, and the failure of the Palestinians against the Israelis. In the former case the political will of the large state could be affected by the high cost of the continued war, while in Israel rising costs were deemed incapable of affecting the state's willingness to commit resources to the struggle. Mack ignored the possibility that shifts within Israel or among Palestinians could transform the struggle against Israel's existence into one focused on establishing a separate state in the territories occupied by Israel in 1967 (an outcome substantial numbers of Israelis might be prepared to consider acceptable). The fact is that within Mack's static and strictly dichotomous typology of territorial relationships, the possibility that the problem might "move" from one category to another cannot be entertained. Thus Mack is encouraged if not required to ignore crucial and empirically open questions about whether the definition of the problem, among both Palestinians and Israelis, might change, how such changes might come about, and what they might imply.

The absence of any way to interpret changes in the perceptions or objectives of the protagonists as factors that might help transform the character of the struggle between them is also reflected in Mack's characterization of the French-Algerian conflict. Focusing only on the Algerian War of the 1950s and early 1960s instead of the much longer relationship between France and Algeria, he notices French rationality in responding to the rising political costs of holding Algeria, while ignoring the more decisive question of how France came to define the Algerian problem as one of decolonization instead of separatism or secession. Mack thus ignores the crucial failure of earlier French attempts to foster non-instrumentalist conceptions of France's relationship to Algeria. By labeling the Algerian problem "throughout" as "asymmetric," he exposes the inability of his model to entertain change in the categorization of particular relationships.[34]

Mack's view of Algeria's status—independent and separate from "France"—as a given of the relationship between them, reflects as much the biases of studies of the state cited in Chapter 1 as it does the bias of hindsight in this particular case. Yet it is relatively easy, at least for institutionalist theories of the state, to accommodate variability in its size and shape. In large measure only habit has led theorists such as Stephen Krasner and Theda Skocpol to take the territorial composition of a state as a given— as a structural feature of political life which sets, once and for all, certain limits on the population, the resources, and the myths that could become politically significant. The fact is that their approaches to the study of states as institutions emphasize the need to treat the norms and expectations from which states are constituted as ultimately subordinate to the outcome of political processes. There is no good reason why geographical boundaries should not be treated in just this way—as a problematically institutionalized dimension of the state, affecting but also subject to both continuous and discontinuous processes of political competition.

For example, Krasner views the "symbols embodied in the state and representing basic political and ethical sentiments [permeating] the polity," as "a fundamental institutional constraint that channels the behavior of individuals even to the point of endangering or sacrificing their lives."[35] The debate in Israel over the territories illustrates that borders, that is the territorial dimension of the state, constitute just such an institutional constraint—one that is neither permanent nor given but which shapes political outcomes in fundamental ways. In general, analysis of how struggles over the inclusion or exclusion of substantial territories are linked to institutional consequences (both intended and unintended) for future competition within the new boundaries is perfectly consistent with the "Tocquevillian" approach to the study of the state advocated by both Krasner and Skocpol.[36] This approach gives "crises" in the life of states particular importance. During such episodes of rapid and fundamental change in state institutions, according to Krasner, politics "becomes a struggle over the basic rules of the game rather than allocation within a given set of rules."[37] Such crises may be seen as responses to pressures accumulating slowly over time by institutions which cannot "respond in any rapid and fluid way to alterations in the domestic or international environment."[38] Such dramatic kinds of change have systematic and long-term consequences for the organization of political competition. These consequences include institutional shifts that create new political realities unanticipated by the protagonists during crisis itself. Since, again in Krasner's words, "the interests and political resources of actors are a function of existing institutions," institution-transforming episodes are "watersheds" separating periods during which different sets of institutional arrangements and institutional constraints "seem to be part of the basic nature of things."[39]

My point here is that borders are institutional constraints, subject to change in time of crisis, which advantage certain groups and rival elites within the state at the expense of others. Substantial changes in the territorial shape of a state represent institution-transforming episodes. Struggles over the size and shape of the state must accordingly be understood as struggles over the "rules of the game." Boundaries specify who and what are potential participants or objects of the political game and who and what are not. Different borders have different demographic implications and different political myths associated with them. The territorial shape of a state thus helps determine what interests are legitimate, what resources are mobilizable, what questions are open for debate, what ideological formulas will be relevant, what cleavages could become significant, and what political allies might be available.

A Two-Threshold Model of State Expansion and Contraction

The process of territorial state-building, or the expansion of an existing state to include additional territory, can be portrayed as a process of change in the kind of political conflict within the core state which would attend efforts to *disengage* from the new territory. More precisely, the scale of the internal political dislocation which the political class within the core state expects to be associated with efforts to disengage from an outlying territory measures the extent to which that territory has been built, or integrated, into the central state. State contraction involves reducing the scale of the internal political dislocation which would be associated with disengagement, while state expansion involves increasing it. The "regime" and "ideological hegemony" thresholds divide political conflicts pertaining to the territorial shape of the state into three types or stages, linked to one another in Guttman-scale fashion. These stages correspond to struggles over incumbency; over incumbency and regime integrity; and over incumbency, regime integrity, and ideological hegemony (see Fig. 2).

Conflict at the incumbency stage may be thought of as normal political competition conducted as an iterated game according to established and expectedly stable rules. Such "incumbent-level" conflict over a government policy designed to achieve disengagement from a closely held territory might be intense. Indeed the political future of incumbents and their rivals may be at stake in any effort to move toward disengagement. But if competition is limited to political bargaining, threats to bolt from the ruling

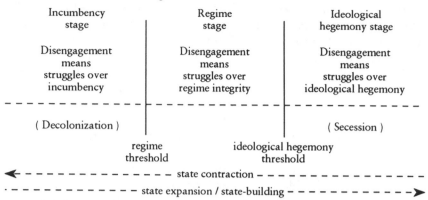

Figure 2. Territorial state-building and state contraction

coalition, electoral campaigns, and so forth, it is easily contained within the political institutions of a developed polity. In such conflicts the rules of the allocative game are not the issue. Neither the integrity of the regime nor the underlying balance of power enshrined by state institutions is threatened. The scale and content of struggles over separation of the territory from the state would challenge neither the structure of state institutions nor the underlying beliefs and identities of the state's population. Precisely for this reason such conflict can be interpreted to mean that integration of the peripheral territory into the state-building core is in its early stage.

The territory can be considered much more closely integrated into the core state if proposals for disengagement from the territory raise in the minds of competitors for political power not only the danger of losing coalition partners, partisan advantages, or career opportunities, but also the real possibility of violent opposition and the mounting of extralegal challenges to the authority of state institutions. Conflict at the regime stage, in other words, portends or includes "illegal" competition over the rules themselves in a game treated at least in part as an "end of the world" contestation. Following Antonio Gramsci, I analyze these struggles (in Part III of this volume) as "wars of maneuver." By struggling not just over the fate of the no-longer-so-peripheral territory but over the right of the state to determine it, the protagonists bear witness to the territory's drastically different status. Clearly, state-building has proceeded much further if conflict over disengagement is conducted about the "rules of the game," that is, about state institutions, and not within them. At this "regime" stage of political struggle over the inclusion or exclusion of the territory, the issue is not only "Should the state, for its own interests or the interests of those it is deemed to represent, disengage from the territory?" It is also

"Should the future of the territory as a part of the state be legitimately entertained as a question of interests, costs, and benefits, by government officials or by participants in the wider struggle for power in and over the state?"

The concept of "threshold" suggests a racheting effect that might be the consequence of incremental state-building efforts—an effect that may be reversible, but not by purely incremental "state-contracting" efforts. There are three reasons why an asymmetrically discontinuous notion, such as threshold, is needed to label the transformation of a territorial question from a cost-benefit, allocative policy problem (at the incumbency stage) to a struggle (at the regime stage) that puts the legal structure of the state in doubt. First, not merely a quantitative, but a qualitative change in the character of political competition is indicated. Second, the political dynamics of such critical junctures and the crises or periods of rapid change associated with them deserve analysis in their own right. Third, reversing the process, by returning to incumbency struggles even after the regime has been put at risk by the territorial issue, can be expected to be peculiarly difficult, but not impossible.

The need to think in terms of *two* thresholds dividing the process of territorial state-building into three kinds of political situations is apparent if the idea of the shape of the state as one of its key institutional features is kept clearly in mind. The fundamental characteristic of institutions is that they establish certain parameters of political competition as not only difficult to change, but as "givens" that permit decision-making, bargaining, and other forms of political activity to proceed "normally." By effectively ruling out many of the most basic questions that could otherwise be raised in any political context, well-developed institutions permit political actors to focus on particular issues, calculate the consequences of different outcomes, and make appropriate trade-offs. The establishment of a belief as commonsensically, necessarily true privileges it—by protecting it from reevaluation in the face of events or pressures that might otherwise affect it, and by diverting political responses to strains associated with the state of affairs it describes. This agenda-shaping effect of deep-seated, unquestioned beliefs represents a qualitatively different kind of protection against de-institutionalization than the incumbency or regime-level concerns of political actors.

The way embedded beliefs shape outcomes by excluding certain questions from appearing before the public as relevant, or even meaningful, is what Gramsci emphasized in his study of how hegemonic beliefs, that is, maximally institutionalized norms, set limits to the rational pursuit of self-interest. Conflict surrounding transitions across the ideological hegemony threshold concerns the establishment or disestablishment of presumptive expectations about rules for political competition, that is, about the character of the background knowledge used by those who play by or enforce iterated games. Again following Gramsci, these struggles are analyzed (in Part II of this study) as "wars of position." When maximally institutionalized, the territorial expanse of the state—its border—is the boundary of the institution (the state), which people within it expect/presume to be a permanent, proper, and unquestioned features of their public life. A particular territory incorporated into a core state is fully "institutionalized" only when its status as an integral part of the state, not as a problematically occupied asset, becomes part of the natural order of things for the overwhelming majority of the population whose political behavior is relevant to outcomes in the state. Operationally, the territorial expanse, or shape, of a state has been institutionalized on a hegemonic basis when its boundaries are not treated by competing political elites within it as if those boundaries might be subject to change. If typical political discussions imply that such change might be advisable or possible, and certainly if debate rages over whether a particular area and its population are or are not to be considered integral parts of the state, the state-building process with respect to that boundary and territory is plainly incomplete.[40]

In other words, surrounding the second threshold (ideological hegemony) is a second kind of discontinuous change in the process of territorial state-building or state contraction. The ideological hegemony threshold divides political struggles over the authority of the state to determine the fate of the territory (regime stage), from a political context within which no serious contender for political power finds it advisable to refer to the area as if its permanent incorporation as a part of the state had not been decided. At this ideologically hegemonic stage of state-building, its least reversible stage, advocacy of "disengagement" would be expected to produce not vigorous intrainstitutional competition, or polarized and possibly violent political struggle, but a discourse marked by all but universal rejection of the idea as impossible, unimaginable, absolutely unacceptable, and certainly irrelevant. Real movement toward "disengagement" or "state contraction" (now more appropriately labeled "secession") would, at this stage, require raising fundamental questions about the community's sense of itself and its rightful political domain. The political unpalatability of raising such necessarily iconoclastic questions and the difficulty of waging a successful political struggle within or against state institutions by doing so are what, ultimately, defend the integrity of the new and larger state. The absence of struggle about the shape of the state is, accordingly, what indicates its successful institutionalization.[41]

In sum, we may think of two different thresholds that must be crossed by a state if an outlying territory is to be incorporated on as permanent a basis as possible. The first—the "regime threshold"—is the point at which a government interested in relinquishing the area finds itself more worried about civic upheavals, violent disorders, and challenges to the legitimate authority of governmental institutions than with possible defections from the governing coalition or party. The second—the ideological hegemony threshold—signals a deeper kind of institutionalization, though it still does not represent an intrinsically irreversible state of affairs. This stage begins when the absorption of the territory ceases to be problematic for the overwhelming majority of citizens of the central state, that is when hegemonic beliefs prevent the question of the future of the territory from occupying a place on the national political agenda. The presence of such beliefs is revealed when, in public, ambitious politicians systematically avoid questioning, even by implication, the permanence of the integration of the territory.

Much of the confusion attending the debate over Meron Benvenisti's "irreversibility thesis" was due to a failure to disaggregate the process of territorial expansion. Benvenisti was clearly correct in his sense that in the early 1980s some drastic change was occurring in the status of the relationship between Israel and the West Bank. He was wrong, however, insofar as he suggested either that this transformation was irreversible or that it could be identified as occurring at one singular point. Many of his severest critics, such as Abba Eban, were right in their basic point—that in politics virtually nothing is truly irreversible. They were also correct in their overall view that as the state-building, territorial incorporation process proceeded, the costs (to the center) of eventual disengagement would continue to rise. They were wrong, however, to suggest that disengagement was inevitable, and to deny the distinctive contribution that routine processes and habits, such as those emphasized in the Tzaban plan (see note 15, above) and in Benvenisti's analysis of "suburban" settlers, could make to the possible success of de facto annexation. They were also mistaken to have focused so strongly on the notion of continuously rising, but always payable, costs for withdrawal as to ignore or belittle changes in the order of magnitude of those costs.

The framework of state-building and state contraction presented in this chapter has been designed to highlight the reality of discontinuities in the rising cost curve associated with state-building in a target territory, while disaggregating notions of "irreversibility" or "point of no return" into two different kinds of thresholds. State-building, or expansion, is thus conceived of as a process of accumulating more kinds of disruption in the center that would be associated with disengagement. Threats to the regime of the core state emerge, accompanying and even overshadowing incumbency concerns. Subsequently the larger conception of the state may become part of the common sense of political life, a hegemonic level of institutionalization attained as politicians who might otherwise have reason to oppose permanent incorporation of the target territory adopt vocabularies and rhetorical strategies which imply presumptions of its inclusion within the state. State contraction, accordingly, is conceived as a process of moving "backward" through these thresholds, first by legitimizing public discussion of disengagement as a credible or sensible option, and then by eliminating from public debate and private calculation the threat of challenges to the legal order should a coalition favoring disengagement be in a position legally to implement its preferences.

Justification and Design of a Structured, Focused Comparison

As suggested in the conclusion to Chapter 1 and my discussion of Mack's argument, another way to analyze qualitative changes in the relationship between a core and a periphery is to consider the differences between those struggles to break the relationship which are understood within the core as "decolonization" versus those struggles for which the categorization itself is the focus of contention versus those understood as "secessionist." These three kinds of political competition correspond, respectively, to the stages previously labeled "incumbency," "regime," and "ideological hegemony." They may be used to sort the arguments made within the Israeli debate over the reversibility of de facto annexation. But crucial questions about what is required and/or sufficient to move a relationship across one or both thresholds, in either the state-building or state contracting direction, cannot be answered by the framework itself or by the Israeli case. What is required is a collection of propositions made plausible by the historical experience of states involved in comparable episodes of expansion and contraction. The episodes I have chosen involve the relationships between Great Britain and Ireland from 1834 to 1922 and between France and Algeria, from 1936 to 1962. These are the best-known historical cases of democratic states faced with major territorial problems located "between" secession and decolonization. Each is treated as displaying the results of a series of struggles to institutionalize (and de-institutionalize) state boundaries—struggles susceptible to classification and comparative diachronic analysis according to the framework outlined above.

By plotting and comparing shifts in the relationship between the core states and the outlying territories, according to the categories and expectations contained in the two-threshold framework, I develop a series of propositions to explain those patterns—propositions that, in the final chapters of the book, help guide analysis of the Israeli-Palestinian case and separate probable from improbable outcomes.

Despite very substantial cultural, geographical, and historical differences, the British-Irish and French-Algerian cases display the similar effects of similarly structured political legacies. The incompleteness with which Ireland and Algeria were integrated into late nineteenth-century Britain and mid-twentieth-century France meant that these core states would eventually be subjected to severe strain.[42] Indeed, prior to British withdrawal from three-quarters of Ireland in 1922 and French withdrawal from all of Algeria in 1962, the Irish and Algerian questions afflicted both Britain and France with chronic, deeply divisive political controversies over the disposition of territories that legally, historically, and ideologically had been treated as integral parts of the central state. The severity of these problems was manifest in regime threatening crises, climaxing in Britain from 1912 to 1914 and in France from 1957 to 1961.

It is remarkable that despite the intriguing similarities between these two most salient of all territorial issues in British and French political history, and despite the truly enormous amount of scholarship produced concerning them, no systematic comparison of the two cases has ever been written.[43] One reason is that any objective effort to study the changing dynamics of these episodes requires what is developed here for the first time—a framework of analysis focusing as much on the categorization process (Are these episodes to be considered examples of "decolonization" or "secession?") as on the implications of each category.

The basis of the comparison presented in bulk of this book, and its suitability for elaborating and testing a model of state-building and state contraction relevant to the Israeli-Palestinian case, is the opportunity to compare the conditions under which the relationships between Britain and Ireland, and France and Algeria, moved across the thresholds of state-building and state contraction—into and out of circumstances requiring core-state disengagement to be studied as either secession or decolonization. By comparing patterns associated with these movements I develop an explanation of why these two democratic states failed to absorb these territories and how, instead, they managed to disengage from all or most of them. The propositions developed and corroborated in this effort, pertaining to general processes of state expansion and contraction, are then available as a basis for offering plausible interpretations of the Israeli-Palestinian case.

These operations entail learning from the mix of similarities and differences in the three cases.[44] There are several basic similarities. In each case a parliamentary democracy faced (faces) chronic and extraordinarily stressful decisions as to the ultimate disposition of outlying territories containing hostile indigenous majorities. In each case the outlying territory(ies) was (are) too close to the "metropole," too extensively settled by nationals of that country, too tightly bound by legal, economic, ideological, and/or security-related ties, for decisions to be taken concerning their separation from Britain, France, or Israel without unprecedented risks of mutiny or civil conflict. In each of these cases settler communities (Protestants in Ireland, Europeans in Algeria, and Jewish settlers in the West Bank and Gaza Strip) contributed, or have contributed, to strong commitments by large proportions of the British, French, and Israeli populations to establishing these areas as permanent parts of the national domain.

At the same time substantial portions of the political communities in Britain, France, and Israel came or have come to believe that withdrawal was (is) necessary to avoid catastrophe. In all three cases as well, nationalist sentiment, in Ireland, Algeria, and among the Palestinians, developed to challenge continued rule by the metropolitan country. Prolonged debate among Israelis over whether the PLO should be treated as a gang of terrorists or recognized as a representative *interlocuteur valable* is evocative in tone, content, and polemical elaboration of similar debates in Britain and France over how to combat, whether to recognize, and when to negotiate with the IRA and the FLN. In each case terrorism played (is playing) a key role. Finally, in each case changing pressures and attitudes in the international arena shaped (are shaping) core state policies and the outcomes of repeated struggles within the core state over continued rule of the outlying territory(ies).

Among the most important differences between the two European cases are the much more rapid pace of change in the French-Algerian case, the implementation of a complete French withdrawal from Algeria (1962) but only a partial British withdrawal from Ireland (1922), and the demise of the French Fourth Republic in the face of severe strains engendered by the Algerian debacle, compared to the survival of the British regime despite comparable threats from Ulster Protestants, Unionist politicians, and a mutinous military in the years preceding the outbreak of World War I.

Among the differences between the Israeli-Palestinian versus the British-Irish and French-Algerian cases are some which suggest that disengagement might be less feasible in the Israeli case and stable incorporation more likely. Other differences suggest the contrary. Unlike the Palestinians, neither the Irish nor the Algerians entertained irredentist ambitions with respect to the core territory of the ruling state. Despite the historical importance of Britain's security concerns—that Ireland had been used as a staging area by such continental enemies as Catholic Spain, Napoleonic France, and Wilhelmian Germany—and despite the French army's insistence that neither France nor the West could survive without French Algeria, there is strong reason to consider that neither Algeria nor Ireland constituted security problems for France and Britain as delicate or as complex as the security implications for Israel of relinquishing the West Bank and Gaza.

On the other hand, the permanence of Israel's hold over the Palestinian areas is not nearly as widely supported within the Israeli political arena as was the integrity of the "Union" in Britain or the principle of *Algérie Française* within the Third and Fourth Republics (1871–1958). Leading Israeli politicians have, ever since 1967, publicly condemned the idea of permanent incorporation of the West Bank and Gaza on ideological, demographic, pragmatic, and even security grounds. Nor, in contrast to Britain and France, has Israel declared these areas (apart from East Jerusalem) to be legally integral and inseparable parts of the state. Moreover, Israel faces and seems likely to continue to face a greater array of international pressures toward disengagement than those which impinged on either Britain or France. These differences suggest that Israel's disengagement from the West Bank and Gaza might be considered less difficult to orchestrate, and more likely to take place, than were British and French withdrawals from southern Ireland and Algeria.

Nor do the obvious geographical differences imply anything determinative about the likelihood of integration or disengagement. While Algeria and Ireland are separated from France and Britain by the Mediterranean and Irish seas, no substantial geographical features divide the West Bank and Gaza Strip from Israel proper. For generations, however, what was striking for British and French politicians about the geographical location of Ireland and Algeria was not that those territories were separated from the mainland by sea water, but that they were so close as to make integration seem necessary, natural, and inevitable. Aside from the obvious constructedness of most claims about geographical "imperatives," there are certain respects in which the small distances involved in the Israeli case may serve as a factor facilitating disengagement. One reason both Ulster Protestants and French Algerians fought with such tenacity to prevent British and French disengagement was that they knew relocation to the "mainland" would entail destruction of their way of life, loss of their jobs, and resettlement in a very different kind of environment. Most West Bank and Gaza settlers, however, although prepared to struggle hard to prevent disengagement, might draw back from certain kinds of confrontation, knowing that relocation would involve a trip of less than an hour to homes, jobs, and neighborhoods only marginally less agreeable, and in some cases more so, than those left behind.

In the final analysis, political change in Britain and France resulted in the reversal of seemingly "irreversible" policies and the surrender of sovereignty over what were widely supposed to have been permanently incorporated territories. In addition to helping construct plausible arguments about the circumstances under which adjustments in Israel's relationship to the West Bank and Gaza might take place, the British and French cases can also help identify elements in the Israeli-Palestinian case which *cannot* be considered decisive in determining the ultimate disposition of the occupied territories. For example, neither enormous infrastructural investments nor a settler community equaling 13 percent of the total Algerian population were sufficient to ensure permanent French rule over Algeria.

For comparative purposes, one unfortunate similarity between the British-Irish and French-Algerian cases is that neither witnessed the successful construction of a hegemonic conception of the state which included Ireland or Algeria.[45] Nevertheless, drawing on these cases to understand the factors that contributed to the failure of hegemonic projects describing Ireland as "British" and Algeria as "French" does *not* require reaching the conclusion that such efforts cannot, or will not, succeed in the Israeli case. Explanation of the failure of hegemonic construction in the British and French cases will help identify those factors likely to determine the success or failure of efforts to promote images of the "whole Land of Israel" as a hegemonic conception of the Israeli state which would include the West Bank and Gaza Strip.

The comparison is organized according to the framework outlined in this chapter, moving from political competition surrounding the ideological hegemony threshold to political competition surrounding the regime threshold. Thus the focus of Part II is on the psychological and cultural aspects of state-building and contraction. Chapters 3 and 4 trace the problematic construction, defense, and ultimate failure of hegemonic projects in Britain (Chap. 3) and France (Chap. 4) which portrayed Ireland and Algeria, respectively, as integral parts of the British and French states. In Chapter 5 the wars of position attending these struggles are analyzed by drawing on Gramsci's seminal discussion of the determinants of such conflicts. This analysis yields propositions which explain patterns displayed in Chapter 3 concerning Britain and Ireland, and in Chapter 4 concerning France and Algeria.

Part III (Chaps. 6, 7, and 8) focuses on the political mechanisms of state expansion and contraction evident in struggles surrounding transitions across the regime threshold, that is those in which threats to seize, challenge, or overthrow regime authority become salient. Chapters 6 and 7 plot changes in the level of institutionalization of British rule over Ireland and French rule of Algeria, focusing on the shifting balance between incumbent and regime-level concerns attached to the possibility of disengagement. Chapter 8 then compares the wars of maneuver fought in these two cases, identifies four "rescaling mechanisms" as strategies for "de-institutionalizing" state control of the territory across the regime threshold, and advances explanations for how and when this was accomplished in Britain and France.

Part IV applies what is learned about both wars of position and wars of maneuver to evaluate alternative trajectories for the relationship between Israel and the territories and provide guidelines for the analysis of other cases of state expansion, contraction, and collapse.

P A R T II

Wars of Position and the
Fate of Hegemonic Projects

Before departing for armistice negotiations in 1949, the Israeli delegation received instructions concerning boundary questions from Prime Minister David Ben-Gurion.

> As for the setting of borders—it's an open-ended matter. In the Bible as well as in our history, there are all kinds of definitions of the country's borders ... No border is absolute. If it's a desert—it could just as well be the other side. If it's a sea, it could also be across the sea. The world has always been this way. Only the terms have changed. If they should find a way of reaching other stars, well then, perhaps the whole earth will no longer suffice.[1]

Ben-Gurion was of course correct—borders can be anywhere. Over the long term the size and shape of a state is fluid. But beliefs about where borders "really" are can be established so firmly that the idea they could change seems absurd. The three chapters of Part II focus on struggles to create, defend, or destroy such ideologically hegemonic beliefs within Britain and France about the inclusion of Ireland and Algeria within the compass of the British and French states.

I use the term "ideological hegemony" to specify the concept of "hegemony" (egemonia) developed by Antonio Gramsci. Gramsci and his interpreters have used the notion to explain the successful containment or dissipation of tensions—tensions that would be expected to strain the political order if the belief, or belief system, of the ruling strata were not shared unquestioningly by broader strata. From this perspective, the widespread diffusion and the deeply embedded nature of a particular conception of reality, implying a restricted set of intellectually or politically conceivable alternatives, is seen to shape outcomes in powerful and systematic ways. The shaping of outcomes is accomplished through the effective exclusion of alternatives falling outside the range of choice implied by hegemonic beliefs.

By labeling the uncontested acceptance of a state's borders an "ideologically hegemonic" belief, I make no claims to be applying Gramsci's concept in the one and only way he meant it to be used; I claim only to be developing the concept in a way consistent with Gramsci's overall intention to elucidate the impact on political outcomes associated with the transformation of particular beliefs into uncontested, and virtually uncontestable, "commonsense" apprehensions.[2] When and if these ideological constructions enjoy the kind of immunity from public scrutiny or evaluation that distinguish hegemonic beliefs, they enhance the power position of those best able to mobilize political resources from within the geographical, social, economic, and cultural limits they specify.

Studying the dynamics of change in the shape of a state therefore must include consideration of the breakdown of ideological hegemony and its reconstruction. When breakdown occurs, the actual question of whether a particular territory should be included within the state can be placed on the "national" political agenda—stimulating direct and public examination of the idea. Reconstruction occurs when the border of a state is not only removed from the political agenda but treated, again, within the state's dominant political arena, as a commonsensical "given."[3]

However, to analyze boundaries of states as ideological constructions with the potential to achieve the psychological status of collective presumptions, we must be able to tell if and when particular beliefs enjoy the kind of immunity from public scrutiny or evaluation that distinguishes them as hegemonic, to determine, in other words, when they are present and when they are absent. This is no simple matter. The problem is similar to that confronting any inquiry into hegemonic effects. It is virtually impossible to show that any particular conception is not only believed to be proper and/or permanent by the overwhelming majority of the politically active population, but presumed to be so. If a belief is accepted as a "given," alternatives to it are not entertained. Since it is logically impossible to prove a negative, to demonstrate directly that certain conceptions of reality have been excluded from consideration within a political arena, how can concepts designed to help explain political outcomes by focusing on what is not discussed, not fought about, or not seriously considered be operationalized?

Faced with such difficulties, one might be tempted to reject such categorical notions in favor of more continuous images of beliefs and of political questions concerning which there may be relatively more or less discussion, more or less agreement, more or less certainty. But this analytical response has severe drawbacks of its own. If key variables change in discontinuous fashion, if changes in the qualitative character of political struggle are more important to explain than changes in the amount of political struggle, or if dramatic changes in the character of political behavior precede or lag behind quantitative changes in the pressures to which such change is attributed, then concepts must be fashioned to capture those "discontinuous" effects, and methodologies must be developed to operationalize them.

The identification of instances of breakdown or reconstruction in the hegemonic status of an ideological belief entails demonstrating that a certain class of political outcomes was politically "unthinkable" at one point in time and "thinkable" at another. This is not a matter of showing that something not "on the agenda" subsequently was, since there can be many explanations for why particular beliefs and their alternatives are not discussed. A hegemonic explanation is but one of them. Labeling a belief as hegemonic, or its problematization as a "breakdown of ideological hegemony," therefore requires more than pointing out that critical discussion of the belief or alternatives to it are (or were) absent. Since no tools exist for penetrating the consciousness of individuals, the best analytic opportunity for observing the presence of a hegemonic belief is examining the terms according to which it is defended against challenges. Although this means that the best established hegemonic beliefs, those that never are challenged, cannot be confidently identified, this method is the only way to conduct hegemonic analysis without either presuming knowledge of intrapsychic phenomena or labeling many beliefs hegemonic which are not, but are simply "not on the agenda."

It follows that "unthinkable" cannot be taken in a literal epistemological sense to mean "impossible of imaginative conception," or in the cognitive psychological sense to mean assuredly "incapable of being thought of" or "not thought of" by specific individuals or groups.[4] Rather, the operational definition of "unthinkable" used in this study connotes the systematic exclusion from political discourse, within the dominant political arena of the state, of argument and appeal which imply that beliefs held by the speaker/author or audience include the possibility that a specifiable set of outcomes might and/or should occur. Once presumably rational and ambitious politicians (or commentators) present arguments and appeals which, albeit designed to encourage opposition to a particular set of outcomes, yet imply by their rhetorical strategy that such outcomes might be considered or preferred by significant elements within the dominant political arena, then the hegemony of an ideological belief excluding that outcome can be said to have broken down. A question foreclosed by what had been treated as common sense becomes a choice. What was given becomes problematic. What was context becomes content. Conversely, the success of a hegemonic project is indicated by the transformation of a choice into a commonsensical given. What was problematic becomes given. What was content becomes context.

Employing this operationalization of hegemony, I devote Chapter 3 to establishing the presence of an ideologically hegemonic belief in Britain about Ireland's inclusion in the United Kingdom. I document the successful defense of that belief in the 1830s and 1840s, and demonstrate its absence in the 1880s. Chapter 4 is devoted to establishing the variable outcome of three post–World War II attempts in France to establish as hegemonic belief that Algeria was an integral part of the French state. Chapter 5 then compares patterns in the timing, success, and failure of the hegemonic projects traced in Chapters 3 and 4 in order to test explanations about when wars of position erupt and how they are conducted, which is to say, explanations about the conditions under which that threshold may be crossed and how, around those junctures, it displays its "threshold effects." The hypotheses advanced to explain these patterns, refined by consideration of the British and French cases, are then in the last part of the book used to judge the potential for establishing or disestablishing hegemonic beliefs about various pictures of the shape of the Israeli state and to suggest the consequences of hegemonic failure and the challenges of hegemonic construction for any state whose territorial composition may be open to question.

CHAPTER THREE

Becoming Problematic: Breakdown of a Hegemonic Conception of Ireland

Defending Ideological Hegemony: The Defeat of Repeal

An unsuccessful challenge to the ideological hegemony of the shape of the British state took place in the United Kingdom from 1834 to 1844. Under the leadership of Daniel O'Connell, whose thirty-year struggle for Catholic emancipation had earned him the title of "Liberator," the Irish Catholic masses demanded "Repeal of the Union." At first their demand for an Irish legislature was primarily a tactic to convince the British to take specific Irish grievances seriously—land reform, tithes, Catholic education. When the British government failed to respond, the demand for a redefinition of the political community itself became the main impetus for Catholic mobilization. O'Connell, the Catholic hierarchy, Irish "Repealer" members of Parliament, and hundreds of thousands of Irish Catholic members of the Repeal Association petitioned and loudly demonstrated (in Ireland) for an end to the United Kingdom (as established by the Act of Union in 1801) and for a separate, autonomous legislature for Ireland.

When O'Connell raised the demand for Repeal, the political future of Ireland was not an issue on the agenda of the British state. When he tried to put it on that agenda, he met an absolutely solid wall of opposition. British opposition was not grounded in a calculation of political cost and benefit, but in a fundamental incapacity and unwillingness publicly to imagine such a drastic change in the territorial composition of the state. The reestablishment of any sort of legislative independence for Ireland contradicted what had come to be a "given" of British political life—the political unity of the British Isles. Virtually no one in Britain, and certainly no important political figure, advocated Repeal or anything like it to solve the various administrative, economic, social, and religious problems with which Ireland chronically burdened the United Kingdom.

Indeed the struggle for Repeal is better understood not as a struggle over whether such a program would be passed and implemented, but as a challenge to the ideologically hegemonic position of the concept of Ireland as immutably integrated within the British state. My analysis of the defense of ideological hegemony against Irish Catholic attempts to put Repeal of the Union on the British political agenda is conducted by noting the judgments of Continental observers, surveying the treatment accorded the topic by the contemporary British press, and especially by evaluating the rhetorical appeals of British politicians. In their response to the Repeal movement, politicians successfully defended the British public's *presumption* of the "givenness" of the incorporation of Ireland within the British state by appeals based solely on assumptions that the audience shared with them about the universally acknowledged, unchangeable, and absolutely valued shape of the British state. The breakdown of ideological hegemony is then apparent in the very different appeals made by opponents of Irish home rule in 1886—appeals characterizing, both implicitly and explicitly, the relationship of Ireland to the British state as fundamentally contingent.[1]

In 1835 Alexis de Tocqueville and his companion Gustave de Beaumont traveled to Ireland. Both were horrified by the misery of the Catholic peasants and their oppression by the Protestant Ascendancy. To ameliorate conditions in Ireland and relieve the great strain on the British state associated with the festering problem of Ireland they advocated drastic social, economic, and political reforms, including overthrow of Protestant Ascendancy. Indeed Beaumont thought that from the Irish point of view, the obvious remedy was to "separate, and form a distinct state, having its own nationality and proper government." But, wrote Beaumont, this could and would never come about: "We may regard it as certain that Ireland will never form a state separate from England." He took it as "nearly certain" that "the re-establishment of the Irish legislature . . . will never take place."[2] He based his predictions on his understanding of historical destiny and the laws of geopolitics.

> It is sufficient to consider the geographical position of Ireland and England, to see that the latter will never renounce her sovereignty over the former. Ireland is a vital member of the British empire—a gangrened member, but one without which the empire could not exist. In truth, if any convulsion of the globe sank Ireland in the bottom of the seas, England might be strengthened by the loss; but whilst this country, holding the place of an arm to the

body, keeps its present position in the ocean, England must assert supremacy over it.[3]

Beaumont saw Ireland and England, who "must adhere together," as "monstrous twins, which, condemned by nature to form only one body and the same flesh, have, nevertheless, contrary tastes, and which incessantly afflicted with the desire of parting, are forced to move together, to live and die externally united, but internally discordant."[4] For both Beaumont and Tocqueville, "it seemed axiomatic that, for its own survival, no English government could contemplate dissolving the Act of Union."[5]

Count Emilio Cavour visited England in 1843 and wrote an essay on the Irish problem. His reaction to the Repeal agitation was similar. He too was moved by the depth and urgency of Ireland's problems. But he too judged that their amelioration should and could be sought only through reform within the bounds of the "British constitution." Thus Cavour based his analysis and his recommendations, just as Tocqueville and Beaumont had, on the immutability of the Union of Great Britain and Ireland. Aside from the reasons which he thought made it necessary and right for Britain to rule Ireland, Cavour also declared that, in any event, British opposition to the idea of autonomy for Ireland was so wide and deep that any Irish efforts to raise that banner in British politics were "doomed to be and to continue barren."[6]

> The Repeal of the Union is rightly regarded in Britain, by all parties, as a question of life or death; all, with equal energy, have declared against the separation of the two kingdoms. Though divided in opinion as to the best means of governing that country, and restoring it to tranquillity, the British people are unanimous as to the necessity of maintaining, by all possible means, the incorporation of Ireland with Great Britain. Let it be remembered that the gentlest, the most humane, the most liberal, the most sincere member of the Whig party—Lord Spencer—when he was minister, declared without hesitation that, rather than consent to the Repeal of the Union, he would advise parliament to maintain a war of extermination.[7]

Some might think, continues Cavour, that just as Catholic emancipation was granted after a long and arduous struggle, and after the threat of civil war had made it seem prudent in British eyes, so too might Repeal some day be achieved. Cavour rejects the analogy. Again he stresses the "universal agreement . . . which regards the disruption of the bond that unites the British islands as a hateful and criminal enterprise." Parliament, he believed, would forever supply ample resources to British governments "to maintain in Ireland the existing legal order."[8]

The judgments of Continental observers as to the intrinsic necessity and immutability of the Union of Ireland and Great Britain, though proven inaccurate by subsequent events, reflected contemporary British beliefs. British editorial opinion toward Repeal during the height of O'Connell's 1843 activities indicates both the unanimity of British opposition to the idea and the prominence accorded by opponents of Repeal to declarations of the proposal's impossibility or even absurdity. After virtually ignoring the Repeal agitation in Ireland, in which hundreds of thousands of Irish Catholics were mobilized in orderly attendance at various "monster" meetings, the *Times*, in May 1843, simply insisted that "Repeal is madness and no English ministry will grant it." The leading Whig journal, the *Edinburgh Review*, viewed Repeal as an "impossible proposition." The two leading conservative periodicals, *Blackwood's* and *Quarterly Review*, "agreed that Britain's interests would not tolerate an independent and potentially hostile Ireland. The laws of nature—'moral,' 'political,' and 'physical'—clearly demonstrated that 'the greatest body shall overbalance and control the lesser.' Ireland could not more have separate status within the British system 'than the moon could abandon the earth and set up for herself as an independent planet.' "[9]

The *Illustrated London News*, whose sympathies with Ireland and commitment to alleviating social and economic distress in Ireland were indisputable, also rejected Repeal out of hand. Its judgment, like that of the conservative press, was that the integrity of the Union was an unquestionable and absolute necessity—Ireland and Britain "must hold firm and binding companionship to the 'crack of doom'."[10] The Union was, in any case, permanent, and agitation for its abolition nothing but a "mad folly," a "wicked delusion," and "a morbid but wild ambition."[11] As did the other observers and journals surveyed above, the *Illustrated London News* emphasized the unanimity of British opposition to any notion of Irish separation: "As for the plain question of repeal of the Union, it is nonsense to entertain it, except for purposes of riot, disaffection, and bloodshed. Those English who would do anything else for Ireland are against it to a man ... would halt indignantly at the sound of the trumpet of repeal, and 'wage war with the worlds' before they would dismember the empire, unsettle the constitution, and insult the throne."[12]

Even in the pages of the *Westminster Review*, reflective of advanced radical opinion, deep sympathy for the historical wrongs committed in Ireland, and the critical need for comprehensive reforms, opposition to O'Connell's demand for Repeal of the Union was expressed in terms indicating the hegemonic status of the belief in the permanence of the Union. Repeal was deemed "a simple impossibility."[13] The *Review* allowed that dismemberment of the empire, through some violent separation, could not be entirely ruled out. But the *Review* treated this theoretical possibility facetiously. It was only even theoretically possible because of the "genius of disorganization" characterizing "our present rulers."[14] As did the mainstream conservative and liberal journals, the *Review* refused to consider any form of separation as a solution to Irish problems worthy of evaluation on its own terms. Repeal would, the *Review* argued, lead automatically to separation, and separation ran directly counter to common sense, "to the natural course of things progressively advancing towards completeness."[15] Ireland was described as the "western division of Great Britain." Its separation, whether possible or not, was described as contradicting the most fundamental commitments of British radicals to "the cause of peace and civilisation."[16]

Thus, across the whole spectrum represented within the British political class, and among the intellectuals and journalists who shaped its view of national life, the formation of the United Kingdom in 1801 constituted a basic and final solution to the question of Ireland's political fate. To be taken seriously, those who would advance new departures in policy toward Ireland would either have to frame their proposals in a manner convincingly consistent with the integrity of the legislative union of Great Britain and Ireland or be prepared to overthrow some of the most fundamental expectations and values of the British governing strata.

Such was the meaning of the Union in Britain. In Ireland, on the other hand, Repeal of the Act of Union, signifying at least the reestablishment of an Irish legislature in Dublin, was discussed by some almost as soon as the act went into effect on January 1, 1801.[17] In the 1830s and 1840s Daniel O'Connell organized an unprecedentedly massive and disciplined popular movement in support of "Full and Prompt Justice for Ireland, or Repeal." By 1841, abandoning direct efforts to achieve reforms via the United Parliament, the movement adjusted its objectives and its name (it became the Loyal National Repeal Association) in a straightforward struggle for Repeal of the Union. But support for Repeal was forthcoming only in Ireland. Although O'Connell had succeeded in mobilizing substantial British support for Catholic emancipation, and although he tried hard to distinguish between "Repeal of the Union" and "separation" of Ireland from Great Britain,[18] he failed to attract even minimal support for the idea in Britain.

The massive agitation for Repeal was, of course, a topic of considerable discussion and some concern in Britain. Although it heightened the awareness of the need for basic social and economic reforms, the primary issue it raised was not whether or in what form to maintain the political relationship of Britain to Ireland, but how to enforce the law in Ireland in the face of widespread and potentially violent disturbances. Repeal, in other words, never touched British politicians or the British people as a question to be responded to on its own terms. Even those sympathetic to the problems of Ireland and Irish Catholics were unable or unwilling to permit consideration of any measure that entailed reducing the intimacy of Ireland's incorporation into the British state.

In the first half of the nineteenth century, then, the United Kingdom was a state whose borders included Ireland, not because all within those borders, or even a majority of each region within those borders, had transferred their loyalty to the state, but because, in the dominant political arena, those borders were nonproblematic. "The Union," as Patrick O'Farrell has written, "was a true union to the extent that it bred an attitude of English mind which refused to accept that Ireland might be anything more than a distinctive region within the realm."[19]

Thus had the Act of Union "with the solemnity of fundamental law" and the "finality of a vast constitutional rearrangement... fenced in the range of the politically possible."[20] In this sense the conception of the United Kingdom of Great Britain and Ireland had achieved a position of ideological hegemony in Great Britain. Independent of any particular interests at stake, or any particular technical difficulties associated with the implementation of this or that version of Repeal, the deeply embedded and widely shared belief that the United Kingdom of Great Britain and Ireland was the proper and permanent conception of the "British" or "English" state kept the issue of Ireland's political future off the British political agenda, thereby blocking Irish efforts to move toward autonomy or independence.

Nowhere were the implications of ideological hegemony more apparent than in Parliament. Just as Repeal never emerged on the political agenda of British politics, so neither did a motion for Repeal of the Act of Union ever appear as a formal item on the official agenda of the Imperial Parliament. But just as the agitation for Repeal attracted widespread attention in Britain, so did Parliament engage in lengthy debates on the issue—debates not about Repeal of the Union per se, but about a variety of related procedural and substantive issues. The political meaning of ideological hegemony as a barrier to Irish autonomy, and of its breakdown as a stage in the evolution of the Irish question in British politics, can be usefully explored by comparing parliamentary action and debate in 1834 and 1843–44 relevant to the Repeal agitation to parliamentary action and debate in 1886 relevant to home rule. It is particularly instructive to compare the different assumptions about Ireland's place in the United Kingdom implicit in the arguments of those MPs who opposed Repeal, with those implicit in the arguments of MPs who, forty to fifty years later, opposed home rule.

When, on April 23, 1834, Daniel O'Connell rose to address the House of Commons on the subject of Repeal, he acknowledged the overwhelming opposition of the Commons to the sentiments he would be expressing. "No man," he said, "ever yet rose to address a more unwilling audience."[21] This was perhaps the primary reason why neither he, nor any Irish MP elected as a "Repealer," ever offered a formal motion to that effect. What O'Connell did move was not Repeal, but the appointment of a select committee "to inquire and report on the means by which the dissolution of the Parliament of Ireland was effected; on the effects of that measure upon Ireland; and on the probable consequences of continuing the legislative Union between both countries."[22]

After a week of debate the House voted 523 to 38 to defeat the motion. Only one British MP (whose political career thereupon ended) voted affirmatively. But an amended version of O'Connell's motion was passed, one which completely reversed the intent of the original. Instead of appointing a committee of inquiry into the state of the Union, the motion that was adopted called for an address to be presented to the queen "to record in the most solemn manner our fixed determination to maintain, unimpaired and undisturbed, the Legislative Union between Great Britain and Ireland."[23] This "address to the throne" was then forwarded to the House of Lords. The upper house expressed its unanimous and enthusiastic endorsement of the message and transmitted it to the queen.

Parliament did not again give sustained attention to Irish demands for Repeal until 1843. By then Parliament, having failed to grant land, tithe, and other reforms that O'Connell had hoped to gain by agitating for Repeal, could no longer ignore that agitation. At weekly rallies, hundreds of thousands of Irishmen, disciplined, sober, and generous in their contributions, assembled to hear fiery speeches against continuation of the Union. Nor could the House of Commons ignore the small but vigorous group of "Repealers" included in Ireland's parliamentary delegation. Although in 1843 and 1844, as in 1834, Parliament did not consider Repeal in its own right, as a separate and formal item on its agenda, nevertheless rejection of Repeal was the overriding theme in long debates over the Arms (Ireland) Bill (1843), the dismissal of Irish magistrates for attending Repeal rallies (1843), a proposal to move the House of Commons into a Committee of the Whole to consider the "State of Ireland" (1844), and the imprisonment and trial of O'Connell on charges of "attempting to undermine the Constitution and to alienate the loyalty of Her Majesty's forces in Ireland" (1844).[24]

At stake in all of these debates was not what degree of autonomy would be granted to Ireland nor whether this or that procedural motion, or resolution of the sense of the Parliament, would be passed, but whether the question of change in Ireland's political status would be recognized as discussable in *British* politics. In other words would, or would not, the ideologically hegemonic conception of Ireland as a permanent part of the United Kingdom be broken? The desire to preserve ideological hegemony, to prevent the legitimization of public consideration of the question, was reflected in the substance of the argumentation against it.

Thomas Spring-Rice, an Irish Protestant serving as secretary to the treasury, made what was subsequently referred to as the most effective response to O'Connell's motion for a select investigating committee. It was certainly the longest—more than one hundred *Hansard* columns. He treated the House to a point-by-point rebuttal of O'Connell's interpretation of Irish history, of the means by which the Act of Union was passed in 1800, and of the economic consequences of Union for Ireland. Significantly he did not think it necessary or advisable to evaluate Repeal as a means of coping with Irish problems. But he did feel it necessary to justify not so much the length of his speech, but the appropriateness and wisdom of any attempt at reasoned discussion of the issue.

After explaining his intention to address O'Connell's proposal, to rebut his charges in a systematic fashion, and to propose a solemn address to the queen categorically affirming Parliament's commitment to the Union, Spring-Rice urged his audience to guard against the assumption that the ideologically hegemonic conception of the United Kingdom inclusive of Ireland did not itself need protection:

> Let not honorable Gentlemen think, that the course proposed exceeds the necessity of the case; let them not think, because so far as their opinions are concerned, that the discussion of this question here is futile, and its agitation in Ireland is fruitless; let them not think, because they do not apprehend that any impression can be raised in reasonable minds, that the Repeal of the Union can ever be carried; let them not think that, therefore, the course I propose is inexpedient. I assert that, if any single individual proposes to this House the dismemberment of the British empire, and proposes thus to deprive the State of its force and its dignity, it behoves the Legislature, as a matter of duty and of necessity, to express its most decided opinion, recorded in the most authoritative manner, on so unjustifiable and so fatal a proposal.[25]

In the midst of his speech Spring-Rice apologized. In spite of his own elaborate justification for opposing Repeal via systematic argument, he confessed that he was "truly ashamed" to have had occasion to discuss "these absurd consequences" or even "to argue the question."[26]

In Spring-Rice's speech, as in virtually all others made by British and Irish Protestant parliamentarians on the subject of Repeal, the same themes predominated: unanimity, impossibility, and catastrophe—the unanimity of British opposition to the idea, the impossibility of autonomy of any sort for Ireland, and the utterly catastrophic implications that any move toward Irish separation would have for everything that British citizens, or even civilized human beings, held dear.

These are precisely the arguments one would expect to characterize any effort to protect a belief whose hegemonic position is being challenged. For theoretically, each, if accepted, would require that any alternative contradicting the belief in question be deemed outside the range of sensible political debate. Each appeals to "common sense." Each is a basis for labeling alternatives as "nonsense." In a democracy the one insurmountable barrier to any political program must be assumed to be unanimous or virtually unanimous opposition to its acceptance. Whether opposition to a proposal is considered strong or weak, if its passage is considered impossible of achievement, it is illogical to devote resources to that end. Finally, unless implementation of the proposal in question is itself considered an ultimate value, then belief that its consequences would interrupt absolute and ultimate values would render its consideration as a policy option nonsensical. If all three are held to be true of the proposal—unanimity of opposition, impossibility of achievement, and absolute inconsistency with ultimate values—the hegemonic position of the principle it challenges is that much more secure.

A comprehensive review of the thousands of columns of debate pertaining to Repeal would be prohibitively long, but illustration of the centrality of these themes in the speeches of opponents of Repeal is possible. Of greatest interest in this context are those cabinet ministers, Irish civil servants, leading politicians, and Irish Protestant representatives whose speeches set the tone of the deliberations and whose contributions triggered approving comment by their parliamentary colleagues.

The single most important participant in the Repeal debates of 1834, 1843, and 1844 was Sir Robert Peel. Chief secretary for Ireland from 1812 to 1818, Peel had a reputation as a proponent for toughness in Ireland which had earned him the sobriquet "Orange Peel." Eventually, however, he supported Catholic emancipation; indeed as home secretary and leader of the House of Commons in 1829 he introduced the Emancipation Bill. In November 1834, seven months after the first Repeal debate, he became prime minister and chancellor of the exchequer. Founder of the Conservative party, he assumed the premiership again in 1841 and was still in office for the Repeal debates of 1843 and 1844.

Peel made one speech during the 1834 Repeal debate. Although he praised the efforts of Spring-Rice and others to refute attacks made on the Union by Irish advocates of Repeal, he himself wondered "(if any there be) who entertain an honest doubt upon this subject." For himself Peel considered the integrity of the United Kingdom to be one of those "truths which lie too deep for argument; truths, to the establishment of which, the evidence of the senses, or the feelings of the heart, have contributed more than the slow process of reasoning; which are graven in deeper characters than any that reasoning can either impress or efface."[27]

Consistent with this view of the question of Repeal as beyond the pale of reasonable discussion, Peel apologized for the responses he did offer to specific charges made by Repeal proponents. His purpose in speaking was not to convince the House or the country of the necessity of rejecting Repeal, but to protect the presumption of the Union's permanence. He thus devoted most of his efforts to portraying opposition to Repeal as virtually unanimous, the breakup or "dismemberment" of the British Empire[28] as an unutterable catastrophe, and Repeal as, in any case, impossible. "Look at the map," he said, "Look at the geographical position of the British Islands, their relative position to the Peninsula, to France, to that great empire which is rising in the West on the opposite shores of the Atlantic.... Do not you feel convinced, by the evidence of the sense, that there exists an obstacle to Repeal, more powerful than any that mere argument can suggest? *Opposuit natura.* There is a physical necessity that forbids Repeal."[29] Attempts to tinker with the fundamental political relationship between Ireland and Britain he likened to efforts to change the course of planets and their satellites—a task "far beyond the grasp of your limited faculties—far beyond any intelligence, save that of the Almighty and Omniscient Power which divided the light from the darkness, and ordained the laws that regulate in magnificent harmony the movements of countless worlds."[30]

Peel also ridiculed the cry for Repeal of the Union, likening it to a cry that might just as sensibly be raised to "Restore the Heptarchy!"[31] Describing in great and graphic detail the ancient Gaelic ritual of crowning kings by bathing them in the blood of a cow, Peel pretended to be offering the Irish proponents of Repeal "this valuable record... to be reserved for future use if occasion should require it."[32] In the long debate over the Coercion or "Arms" Bill for Ireland in 1843, the only explicit reference to Repeal he thought it necessary to make was that opposition to the measure was "the unanimous opinion of every member of this House, from England and Scotland, and of a great number of Members from Ireland... [who consider Repeal] to be equivalent to a dismemberment of the empire and a separation of Ireland from the sister country."[33]

In 1834 much was made of the overwhelming approval given to Spring-Rice's address to the throne affirming the inviolability of the Union. Moving approval of the address forwarded to the House of Lords from the House of Commons, Prime Minister Earl Grey emphasized that the measure "had been carried by a majority [523 to 38] almost unparalleled in the annals of Parliament."[34] He entertained, he said, "no doubt whatever of receiving the decided, and the unanimous support of their Lordships," and hence did not think it "necessary [to] go into a very large field of argument and detail on this most important subject."[35] The House of Lords thereupon endorsed the address and passed it on to the queen with not one word or vote against it.

Lord Brougham, a Scotsman and one of Britain's leading jurists, made essentially the same points about unanimity in an 1843 speech to the House of Lords, hailing the duke of Wellington's declaration on behalf of the government to maintain the Union inviolate. Demonstrations of unanimity would help demoralize proponents of Repeal.

> Let their Lordships recollect the majority by which the address referred to by the noble Duke was passed in 1834; and let those who cherished the hope that they might receive some support in this country for their abominable projects in Ireland, also recollect what took place at that period, and then let them feel their hearts sink within them. Of all the Members for England, Wales, and Scotland ... but one single British Member had ceased to support that project; and that Gentleman had ceased to adorn the House of Commons. It was his belief that now there would not be found one single British voice raised in support of this mischievous project.[36]

Indeed, Brougham interpreted the inclination of most members of the upper house to abstain from comment on Repeal to the assumption they all shared of their own unanimity. He felt "quite confident that his noble Friends who sat near him remained silent on the present occasion simply because they considered, as every one must, that there could not exist the possibility of any doubt or hesitation in agreeing heartily to the observations of the noble Duke opposite."[37]

In 1844 the government did come under strong criticism from Whig and Radical members of Parliament who favored a more vigorous program of reforms in Ireland. They used the turmoil in Ireland surrounding the arrest and trial of O'Connell on sedition charges to raise their complaints. John Russell, for example, who led the opposition to Peel's government, moved that the House of Commons resolve itself into a committee of the whole to consider the "state of Ireland." After nine full days of debate the motion was defeated. What is interesting, however, is the virtually unanimous presumption in favor of the Union reflected even in the arguments of those such as Russell who were prepared to struggle so vigorously against the government's Irish policies. Introducing his motion, Russell made this presumption explicit.

I am about to ask the House to consider what have been our relations with Ireland since the period of the Union. I will take it for granted, as I very fairly may, until some one in this House shall make a motion for the Repeal of the Union, that we all desire and are resolved to maintain that Union; that we all wish to preserve its principal conditions; that we wish to have an Imperial Parliament of the United Kingdom, containing representatives, in both Houses, of Ireland as well as of Great Britain.[38]

The unanimity theme blended naturally with the claim of Repeal's impossibility. Thus Emerson Tennet, a Protestant member of Parliament from Belfast, seconded Spring-Rice's motion in 1834 with the argument that demonstrations of unanimity would prove the "utter emptiness and delusion" of Repeal.[39] In light of the fact that the "reflecting portion" of Britain and Ireland was "so fully satisfied of [the Union's] advantages, as it exists, and of the ruin which must inevitably ensue from its repeal," he declared "accomplishment of that measure as utterly and absolutely impracticable."[40] Tennet asserted the impossibility of Repeal's implementation, however, on grounds other than the unanimity of informed opinion against it. As Peel had stressed the laws of geopolitics, so did Tennet. Ireland's location rendered irrelevant the question of whether the Union be for "good or bad."

Had [Ireland], instead of having risen from the waters within 60 miles of the coast of Britain...been situated far off in the bosom of the Atlantic, and remote from the contending States of Europe...she might have been quietly abandoned to her own resources, and her own unaided and distinct independence. But situated as she was, innumerable causes have conspired not only to make a close political connexion between her and England but to render a union of interest between the two countries, a community of fortune, and identity of object, and a co-operation in action, indispensable to the power, prosperity, and security of the British empire.[41]

The theme of the "impossibility" of Repeal, or political autonomy for Ireland, was most prominent in the stigmatization of the idea as an evident and ridiculous absurdity. In 1843 D. R. Ross, a Protestant from Belfast, told the House of Commons that the forty years of union between Ireland and Britain had created an unchangeable reality. It thus seemed to him "absurd to talk of a Repeal of the Union. The Union had now existed for upwards of forty years, and had so blended itself with the condition, the feelings, and the prosperity of the two countries, that to dissolve it would be ruinous—if it were possible. To attempt a division between the Saxon and Celtic families would be an attempt equally absurd, because equally impossible. They had been so mixed together, that the two races were now in reality one nation."[42]

Thomas Bateson, an MP from Londonderry, was one of the few Irish Protestants to oppose the 1843 Irish Coercion Bill. But though he sympathized with the evils that produced the agitation in Ireland, Repeal itself he too considered absurd—as absurd as "restoring the Heptarchy." He then sought to "turn" that virtually unanimous presumption "to an account different from that to which it is applied" by arguing that separate coercionist legislation for Ireland would be as absurd as passing separate legislation for Essex, Northumbria, or Sussex.[43] The key point for this analysis is the assumption implicit in his argument that his audience deemed the separation of Ireland from Britain an absurdity akin to the idea of treating the former Heptarchic kingdoms as separable units.

The absurdity of Repeal was just as prominent in the debates of the House of Lords in 1843. Lord Brougham, who took the lead in these debates, called Repeal a "wild project" and a "detestable, if not grossly absurd scheme." He found it "almost impossible to conceive how such a fancy came into existence."[44] John Campbell, lord chancellor of Ireland in 1841 and a leader of the upper house, who criticized the government for firing magistrates who attended Repeal rallies, was nevertheless categorical in his view that "the very notion that Ireland should have a separate Legislature independent of the Imperial Legislature was most absurd."[45]

In view of these perceptions of the intrinsic impossibility and absurdity of Repeal it cannot be surprising that participants in these debates seldom if ever tried to predict how implementation of different interpretations of Repeal might affect various Irish and/or British interests. But, as reflected in the speeches of Spring-Rice and Peel, opponents of Repeal sought to characterize the potential damage that Repeal of the Union could wreak. Instructively, they did so in cataclysmic terms—terms implying the irrationality of wasting time considering the exact meaning of this or that version of Irish autonomy, or calculations showing that even the limited benefits associated with Irish autonomy would be outweighed by the disadvantages attending the implementation of such a scheme.

Earl Grey, prime minister during the 1834 Repeal debate, told the House of Lords that the Union was "a thing, perhaps, which at the time should not have been done; but which, having been done, they would by undoing hazard the undoing of the country."[46] Indeed, the most common epithet used to telegraph the utter unacceptability of movement toward political devolution in Ireland was "dismemberment of the empire." To appreciate the meaning of this phrase to contemporaries as equivalent to the "undoing of the country," we must keep in mind that before the 1860s the term "British Empire" referred clearly and unmistakably not to the "British

Isles" and Britain's worldwide network of colonies, but to the United Kingdom of Great Britain and Ireland *only*. In India Great Britain had an empire (the British Empire *in* India), and other territories in Africa, Asia, and America might have had dominion or colonial status vis-à-vis the United Kingdom, but it was the United Kingdom only, or the "Three Kingdoms of England, Scotland, and Ireland," which was referred to as the British Empire. Over and over again speakers referred to the "dismemberment of the empire," meaning the separation of one part of the United Kingdom (Ireland) from the rest, to signal their categorization of the question of Repeal as one which no loyal subject could be prepared to contemplate. Legally as well as emotionally, the legislative separation of Ireland from Britain would be a "dismemberment." For only with the implementation of the Act of Union between Britain and Ireland on January 1, 1801, had the Parliament in London officially declared itself the "Imperial Parliament."[47]

The point is that in the first half of the nineteenth century, "dismemberment of the empire" did not mean, and was not intended to mean, the loss of important appendages of the metropolitan political community. Rather, as a description of the consequences of Repeal, the phrase was understood by members of Parliament, and the wider public attuned to the debate, to mean what one outspoken Irish Protestant member of Parliament called it in 1834—"national dismemberment."[48]

With the failure of the Repeal movement to generate any significant support in Britain, in the final analysis, the government found it easy to bring an end to the agitation. By banning the Clontarf "monster meeting" in October 1843, and subsequently arresting and trying O'Connell (even though he had canceled the banned meeting), the government took effective political advantage of the gap between what was, strictly speaking, legal and what in fact it was able to treat as intolerable. In this very specific way the demise of the Repeal movement can be traced to the successful defense of an ideologically hegemonic belief in the integrity of the "United Kingdom."[49]

The 1886 Defeat of Home Rule

Freed from prison, O'Connell ran unsuccessfully for Parliament and died in 1847. The Repeal movement had in any case split between O'Connell's followers and young nationalists who resented O'Connell's nonconfrontationist tactics and who were unwilling to consider the struggle for autonomy as a possible means to achieve fairness for Irish Catholics within an integrated United Kingdom. This split, and the famine that ravaged

Ireland from 1845 until 1849, spelled a temporary end to significant agitation for Irish political autonomy. Such agitation was slowly renewed, first under the rubric of Isaac Butt's Home Government Association, and then, in the late 1870s and 1880s, by the Home Rule party under the leadership of Charles Stewart Parnell.

In 1886 a new Liberal party government, the third under William Gladstone's leadership, sponsored a Home Rule Bill for Ireland. It was defeated in the House of Commons, leading to new elections. In these elections the Conservative party won a resounding victory. The Tories, allied with Whigs and Radicals who deserted Gladstonian Liberalism over the issue of political autonomy for Ireland, dominated British politics for seventeen of the next twenty years.

The outcomes of the struggles for Irish self-government which took place in the 1830s and 1840s, and then forty to fifty years later, were the same. Each was conspicuously unsuccessful. But the terms of the struggles and the real stakes involved had shifted dramatically. In the 1880s opponents were no longer trying to prevent a question about Ireland's political future from being placed on the British political agenda. It was on the agenda. Opponents might try to remove it, but first they had to defeat it—to actually prevent the political system from accepting a serious, and seriously debated, proposal to bring an end to the legislative union between Great Britain and Ireland.

This shift was indicated by a dramatic change in the character of the arguments used by parliamentary opponents of the 1886 Home Rule Bill in contrast to those which dominated Parliamentary opposition to Repeal forty to fifty years earlier. In the interim the ideologically hegemonic position of the concept of Ireland as a permanent and necessary part of the British state had broken down. As a consequence it no longer made sense to defend that position by declaring the overwhelming "unanimity" of opposition to any form of Irish autonomy, the "absurdity" or "impossibility" of any such scheme, or its evident, absolute, and utterly "catastrophic" consequences. In 1886 the arguments employed by those who defended the integrity of the United Kingdom (expressed in the form of the legislative union) reflected a new set of assumptions. In the mid-1880s at least, political autonomy for Ireland was a question which, however regretfully from the point of view of many who opposed it, was open to legitimate public debate—a question that would be decided, in some sense or other, on the basis of reasoned consideration of the merits and demerits of specific proposals.

Indeed the specificity of the proposal for home rule—an elaborate bill, drafted and presented by William Gladstone, prime minister, chancellor of the exchequer, and the politician with the largest personal following in

Great Britain—signaled more clearly than anything else the transformation that had occurred in the meaning of Irish autonomy as an issue in British politics. In the 1830s and 1840s the formal context for much of the Repeal debate was provided by motions to conduct parliamentary inquiries into the "state of Ireland," motions advanced in lieu of specific proposals for Repeal. As noted earlier these motions for inquiries were opposed and refused as implicit suggestions that the political relationship between Ireland and Britain could be legitimately questioned. During the 1886 debate over home rule, however, it was a leading opponent of the bill who spoke in explicit support of an official inquiry into the state of British-Irish relations. The marquess of Hartington, the Whig leader who split with Gladstone on home rule to found the Liberal Unionist party, indicated that however deep his opposition to home rule, he and his supporters would see nothing wrong if "a Committee of the House of Commons or a Royal Commission might undertake an inquiry."[50]

Thus the 1886 debate was not over whether to admit a question existed by launching an investigation, but whether to pass, amend, or reject a bill for changing Ireland's status which did indeed lay before the House. The debate on this bill was longer than the debate on the first and second readings of any other legislation in the history of the United Kingdom. When the final vote came on June 8, 1886, more members of the House of Commons (656) participated than had ever participated in a single division.[51]

In the tradition of those who led opposition to Repeal, leading opponents of home rule identified Irish autonomy as a singularly momentous subject. But unlike their predecessors in 1834 and 1843, they did not fashion their appeals by considering how best to declare an opinion presumed to be shared by all British politicians. Nor did they apologize for the arguments they did make. Instead, the Unionist position in 1886 was based on an image of the decision process as a choice between conceivable and analyzable alternatives—reflecting judgments that many Britons had come to doubt the wisdom of the Union inaugurated in 1801, and that the commitment of many others to the preservation of that Union was no longer absolute.

Joseph Chamberlain, the Radical mayor of Birmingham, deserted Gladstone on home rule. He went on to become spokesman for Britain's new imperialism as secretary of state for the colonies (1895–1903) in a future Unionist government. Charles Stewart Parnell, the Irish nationalist leader, called him "the man who killed the Home Rule bill."[52] Chamberlain was convinced that his hopes for a consolidated British worldwide empire required England to retain "the Imperial Parliament in its present form and authority."[53] But despite his vigorous opposition, Chamberlain was unwilling to reject home rule "in principle." He declared, "I really think much as I dislike this bill, if I could have honestly convinced myself that it was to be accepted as a final settlement—I do not mean absolutely a final settlement, but practically a final settlement for our time—I believe I should have voted for the Bill, bad as I think it to be."[54]

In this way even Chamberlain, and others whose references to the "integrity of the empire" echoed phrases of those who had opposed Repeal, did not claim that the "unity" of that empire was such an obvious and vital necessity, and the "disintegrative" implications of home rule so direct and automatic, that reasonable men could not differ on the matter. The home rule debate was, declared Chamberlain, a "great Constitutional discussion...a great controversy." A choice had to be made between two alternatives—alternatives he was willing to describe to the House in fair terms, indeed in terms that implied the choice would not be an easy one.

> On the one hand, we have the Government honestly and sincerely believing that these proposals will bring about a final and friendly settlement of the difficulties which have existed for centuries between Ireland and Great Britain, and which have acted so injuriously to the interests of both countries alike. That is a settlement which may well evoke passionate enthusiasm, and to accomplish which effectually would be the crowning glory of an illustrious career. On the other hand, those who oppose this measure believe with equal honesty and with equal conviction that they form an irretrievable and fatal step, which will lead to animosities more dangerous than any with which we have hitherto had to deal, which will destroy the influence of the United Kingdom...and which will postpone indefinitely measures of domestic reform and progress if the complications which we anticipate should unfortunately result from this legislation. I do not say now which of these alternative hopes and fears have the better foundation.[55]

The point is not, of course, that Chamberlain's own preferences were not clear or that his opposition was not genuine. Indeed he often declared that England ought be as prepared as the American North was in the 1860s to wage bloody war in Ireland to maintain the Union.[56] The point is that the issue of political, specifically legislative, autonomy for Ireland was treated as a discussable problem to be addressed and solved by the British political process. Anticipating new elections after what he believed would be the defeat of the bill, Chamberlain said he was "glad that this great issue, having been raised, is to be submitted to the only tribunal whose decision we can all accept, and which is competent to pronounce it."[57]

But a common willingness to submit to the democratic will was not the only basis of agreement between supporters of home rule and Unionists. In the Repeal debate O'Connell and his supporters repeatedly argued that the unity of the British Empire—meaning, at that time, the United Kingdom—would be placed on a firmer foundation by repealing the Union and cultivating a sentimental and material basis, under a common Crown, for a united political future. Such arguments were not only treated as false but as absurd and dishonest to boot. In 1886 supporters of the Union heard similar arguments from Gladstone: as Canadian loyalty to the British Empire (meaning, in the late nineteenth century, the worldwide network of British dominions and possessions) had been enhanced by prudent grants of political autonomy, so would home rule bind Ireland tighter to the British Empire than would any other policy. Opponents of autonomy for Ireland in 1886 may well have believed these arguments to be as absurd or as dishonest as those advanced by O'Connell, but most no longer felt it proper or productive to say so.

Sir Michael Hicks-Beach, twice chief secretary of Ireland and chancellor of the exchequer in Conservative governments, as well as Leader of the House of Commons from 1886 to 1887, concluded his sharp attack on the Home Rule Bill by characterizing the issue as a choice of efficient means to a achieve a *commonly* valued end—the unity of the British Empire.

> We are the trustees and inheritors of the Parliamentary privileges of a free and historic Kingdom—a Kingdom which is the centre of a great but loosely united Empire. Many Members on both sides of the House are looking for means to unite and weld together that Empire more firmly than at present. Let us beware how we admit the canker of disintegration into its very heart. There may be dangers in the rejection of this Bill. There may be difficulties in store for us in this House or in Ireland. But these dangers and difficulties will vanish before a bold determination to confront the responsibility from which we cannot escape, and to maintain the union of our Government and our Parliament before the nations of the world.[58]

For George Goschen, a Liberal Unionist who served as chancellor of the exchequer in Salisbury's second administration (1887–92), as well as Chamberlain and Hicks-Beach, the question was not whether in principle some sort of enhanced Irish control over "Irish" affairs was unacceptable, but whether commonly held objectives would be served by the provisions for Irish autonomy contained in the Home Rule Bill.[59] It was a matter, Goschen stated, properly the subject of careful analysis. As he explained, "It has been assumed—what we all wish in our hearts might be true— that if you grant Home Rule to Ireland the grant will be followed by smiling plenty in every part of the country—that the Land Question, that the poverty of Ireland, and that all those causes of misery which reach so deep down into her social system, will vanish with Home Rule. But is that so?"[60]

Lord Hartington as well accepted the notion that the political future of Ireland was fundamentally both problematic and appropriately viewed in instrumentalist, cost-benefit terms. Nicholas Mansergh described Hartington's address as "the most effective denunciation of the Home Rule Bill in the House." "There is no attempt," says Mansergh of Hartington's speech, "to minimize the consequences of rejection, merely a balanced but authoritative statement of the case against change."[61] At long last, said Hartington, the British people had come face to face with "the enormous question of the future legislative relations between Great Britain and Ireland."[62] After setting out the practical and specific difficulties he thought would attend implementation of the bill in a manner consistent with the effective supremacy of the Imperial Parliament and protection of Protestant rights in Ireland, Hartington expressed his confidence in the judgment of the British people in making an admittedly difficult choice. "I believe, at all events," he said, "that now if ever—now that the people of this country have been brought face to face with the alternative of the disruption of the Empire on the one hand, or all the evils and calamities which I admit will follow on the rejection of this unfortunate scheme, I believe that now, at all events, the people of this country will require that their Representatives shall ... unite as one man for the maintenance of this great Empire."[63]

But perhaps no opponent of home rule spoke more clearly than did Major E. J. Saunderson, an Irish Protestant MP and leader of the Irish Unionist party, of the need to approach this "great question" by carefully measuring the interests it would serve and the costs it would entail against those associated with alternative policies toward Ireland. For Saunderson, home rule was a question that "ought to be dealt with on its merits. Is it likely to succeed? That is the question which the House of Commons ought to ask themselves. Is it likely to be a final settlement, or a successful settlement; and is the House of Commons asked by this Bill to pay too dearly for the operation?"[64] In opposing the bill Saunderson said it was "our duty to show that there is a less expensive and more satisfactory way of accomplishing the objects the Prime Minister has in view."[65] In this context he told the House that home rule would cost the Treasury at least fifty million pounds sterling.[66]

Opponents of home rule such as Lord Randolph Churchill, first chancellor of the exchequer and leader of the House of Commons in the subsequent Tory government, often called it "Repeal" in an attempt to stigmatize the proposal, but they could not argue effectively against it with the same tone of outraged and categorical denunciation which pervaded attacks on Repeal when it was proposed forty years earlier.[67] The kind of evaluative discourse in which they were constrained to engage entailed discussion of exactly what was likely to occur *if* home rule were implemented. Thus they not only conceded the measure's conceivability, but by criticizing relatively minor and technical points, they gave implicit support to the definition of autonomy for Ireland as an open question, to be approached by serious politicians with an eye to its practical utility as a response to widely recognized problems.

The detailed, explicit elaboration of scenarios depicting the aftermath of home rule was a necessary part of this "conditional" analysis (if home rule, then . . .). In this context much was made of very specific fiscal, procedural, legal, commercial, and other problems that would attend its implementation. For example, amid his more fundamental objections to the Bill, Joseph Chamberlain criticized as "unsatisfactory" the clauses that would permit invitations to be extended to Irish representatives to participate in taxation debates at Westminster. How, he queried, would such debates be identified?[68] The marquess of Hartington criticized the bill for not specifying clearly enough the status of the paramilitary police force known as the Royal Irish Constabulary.[69] George Goschen supported his more general objections to home rule by predicting the ruin of the Ulster linen industry if the bill were passed. He also predicted that heavy new taxes would have to be levied on Irish peasants because of the effect on revenues available to the Irish Parliament of previously enacted land reforms.[70] Churchill offered extended comment on what he saw as flaws in the procedures outlined in the bill for choosing peers in the projected Irish upper house.[71]

During the Repeal debates many MPs referred to the awful consequences for Britain, and even for mankind, of ending the legislative union. They employed "if—then" argumentation also. But such apocalyptic rhetoric played a different role and served a fundamentally different purpose than did the careful measurement of causes and effects, and costs and benefits, that opponents of home rule used as one element in their campaign to defeat it. In the 1830s and 1840s when some opponents of Repeal spoke of the government's willingness to fight a civil war in Ireland rather than accept dissolution of the United Kingdom, no members of Parliament, neither supporters nor opponents of Repeal, questioned the credibility or sense of these declarations. They were neither meant as nor heard to be policy prescriptions for a contingency that could well arise, but as rhetorically powerful signals of what the speaker viewed as virtually inconceivable catastrophe.

In 1886 the prospect of widespread political violence in reaction to Irish autonomy was a prominent feature of opposition argument. In the 1830s and 1840s such predictions of violence and civil war that were made were based on the anticipation of outraged British opinion which would commit the country to the reconquest of Ireland. In 1886 the source of violence was identified as the Protestants in Ireland, who, it was said, would take up arms to resist the authority of the Irish Parliament. In further contrast to the Repeal debates, almost every mention of the possibility of violent resistance was preceded and followed by discussion of exactly how probable such developments ought be considered and how much weight, if any, ought properly be attached by legislators to the anticipation of violence. Altogether arguments pertaining to protection of the rights of Irish Protestants and their resistance to home rule figured in importance second only to the "constitutional" question of whether the "supremacy of the Imperial Parliament" and the unity of the wider empire could be preserved if home rule were granted to Ireland.

In further contrast to the vague warnings of Catholic oppression and revenge against Protestants that issued from some opponents of Repeal, the predictions of home rule opponents as to what Protestants would suffer at the hands of the Catholic majority if home rule were passed were usually highly specific and based on careful scrutiny of protective arrangements that could (or could not) be devised. These warnings, both of the consequences of home rule for Irish Protestants ("the loyalist minority") and of the resistance they were likely to offer its implementation, were advanced most vividly by the parliamentary representatives of the Irish Protestants themselves.

In the 1830s and 1840s Irish Protestant MPs had been anxious to avoid creating doubts in anyone's mind that they considered Repeal something that could ever conceivably be implemented. In general, therefore, they did not present themselves as advocates for the particular interests of their constituents. Had they argued as if specific interests were at stake, they would have implied that some sort of Repeal bill had a chance of passage. Representatives of Irish Protestants tended to defend the ideological hegemony of Ireland's place in the United Kingdom in terms that were virtually identical to those used by the leading British politicians.

In 1886, however, Irish Protestant MPs were unabashed in representing their "interest group." Abjuring the florid and occasionally violent rhetoric of Ulster Unionist rallies, they nonetheless warned the House of Commons not to enforce home rule against the wishes of the Protestant minority. Implementation of the measure would be resisted. If, in the end, it were enforced, the stage would be set for the pillage and persecution of Protestant loyalists by Roman Catholics.[72]

Most clearly reflective of the breakdown of the ideological hegemony of the concept of Ireland as a part of the United Kingdom was the willingness of some Irish Protestant MPs to advocate the "exclusion" of Ulster, or the predominantly Protestant areas of Ulster, from the jurisdiction of the Irish Parliament which would be established with the passage of home rule.[73] Thus began the idea that eventually took on so much importance in the post–World War I Irish settlement. What is important at this point to notice is that its appearance in 1886 reflects a decisive change, as compared with the Repeal debates, in the thinking of even the most determined opponents of Irish political autonomy. Proposals to exclude some or all of Ulster from home rule were designed to make the best of an undesired contingency. Such proposals meant that those advancing them no longer thought that they, or their audience, could presume the defeat of any effort to separate Ireland from the jurisdiction of the Parliament of the United Kingdom.

Conclusion

In the final analysis what is striking about the Repeal and home rule controversies is not that two substantively similar proposals for solving the Irish problem both failed to gain the approval of the British state, but that such different meanings attended those failures. The failure of Repeal reflected Britain's unwillingness and/or inability to entertain autonomy for Ireland as a debatable question, meaning that for several more decades practical efforts to alleviate the distress associated with Ireland's relationship to Britain would have to take the integrity of the United Kingdom as a given. The failure of home rule in 1886, on the other hand, could be and was rightfully interpreted by those who had supported it as a sign that wider alliances, more effective mobilization of resources, and the imposition of higher costs for refusing to grant Irish autonomy could achieve a favorable decision in the future.

After the vote against home rule and the crushing defeat of his Liberal party in the 1886 election, Gladstone said he would "not venture to forecast the future," but was sure that a decisive victory had been won on the road to self-government for Ireland. He had no doubt, he said, "that a measure of self-government for Ireland, not less extensive than the proposal of 1886, will be carried. Whether the path will be circuitous; whether the journey will be divided into stages, and how many these will be; or how much jolting will attend the passage; it is not for me to say."[74]

Those who had successfully opposed home rule agreed with Gladstone, to the extent of understanding their victory in 1886 as but one indecisive battle in what would be a long and bitter campaign—a campaign to block passage and implementation of proposals for Irish political autonomy and then, once again, remove that form of the Irish question from the British political agenda. Consider Prime Minister Salisbury's trenchant remarks, on the limited significance of home rule's defeat, to a crowd of Conservative party supporters in 1887. Under the Unionist banner Salisbury had led the Tory party to its victory over the Liberals in 1886. But with the breakdown of ideological hegemony over what constituted the boundaries of the political community, he considered that a serious threat to the integrity of the United Kingdom remained. There was, he said, one great condition necessary to insure that Britain's hold over Ireland would be consolidated on a permanent basis. "It is necessary that the generations, as they grow up, should believe that the consolidation is inevitable."[75]

Salisbury thus viewed the very fact that the fate of Ireland was a "momentous issue before the country" as a serious problem. Whether the Irish question would once again be removed from the political agenda, and the consolidation of British rule in Ireland thereby assured, would require an act of will on the part of Englishmen and their adherence to beliefs that would drive debate over proposals for home rule from the realm of legitimate political discourse. What was required, in other words, was reestablishment of the ideological hegemony of the concept of Ireland as part of the United Kingdom. Salisbury instructed his followers accordingly. Certain lines of argumentation, used against those who favored Irish autonomy, would have to be abandoned.

> We have for many years—almost for a whole generation—pursued the wrong path. . . . We have pursued conduct, and we have held language which has led them [Irish nationalists] to believe that, if they only pressed earnestly enough, the necessary consolidation would not take place. That has been a lamentable and a most disastrous injury, not only to the Empire at large, but to Ireland itself. . . . The issue depends on you—on you the constituencies of England. If you resolve that the inevitable and beneficent process shall be carried through it will be carried through, and no evil will result.[76]

A hegemonic belief is one that enjoys a presumption of truth. This means it is protected against inferences challenging its validity that would normally be drawn from changing conditions—inferences that, absent the presumption of truth, would lead to reevaluation, amendment, and/or abandonment of the belief. But as Gladstone and Salisbury both understood, to presume something true does not make it true or permanently believed to be true. This principle is demonstrated by the eventual separation of most of Ireland from Britain and, before that, by the loss of presumptiveness attached to British beliefs about Ireland's inclusion within the United Kingdom. However, to offer plausible explanations for how beliefs achieve and lose presumptive status, explanations which could guide analysis of the Israeli-Palestinian case, requires more data. The French-Algerian case, treated in the following chapter, offers three attempts to establish presumptive beliefs about Algeria's inclusion within the French state. Analysis of these three failures of hegemonic construction, combined with consideration of why a hegemonic belief about Ireland, successfully defended in the 1830s and 1840s, lost that status by the 1880s, is the basis for Chapter Five's general explanation for hegemonic construction and deconstruction.

CHAPTER FOUR

Where and What Is France?
Three Failures of
Hegemonic Construction

In the British-Irish struggle over Repeal of the Union, I examined the successful defense of an ideologically hegemonic conception—that Ireland was an integral part of the territory ruled by the British state. I showed that this conception, defended successfully in the 1830s and 1840s, had broken down by the mid-1880s. In contrast, the French-Algerian case, from 1945 to 1958, presents a series of unsuccessful attempts to construct a hegemonic conception of Algeria, or of "overseas France," as an integral part of the territory ruled by the French state. The two cases are similar in the importance attached in each to questions pertaining to what was considered "commonsensical" about the definition of the political community. Another key similarity is the emergence of Ireland and Algeria as issues, within British and French politics, whose resolution was perceived to entail threats to regime stability as well as to the careers of leading politicians and parties.

As early as 1848, Algeria was officially declared an integral part of France. In 1871 Algeria was divided into metropolitan-style departments, shifting primary administrative control of the territory from the Ministry of Colonial Affairs to the Ministry of the Interior. The hundreds of thousands of European settlers in Algeria at that time were to be treated as French citizens residing in the three "departments" of Algeria. In principle, French citizenship and voting rights were open to indigenous Algerians, but the requirement that Muslims renounce Islam to become eligible made attainment of citizenship virtually impossible. It was in this context that the European settlers, a 10 percent 20 percent minority, emerged as the real rulers of Algeria and its Muslim majority.

Before World War II Algeria's status had not been a regular source of contention in French politics. Although debates over policies toward Algeria and relations between its European and Muslim inhabitants were not uncommon, the question of whether Algeria was or would remain a part of France almost never presented itself. This exclusion was achieved, however, not because of a hegemonic or even widely agreed upon perception of Algeria as equivalent to Normandy or Anjou, but because strain associated with Algeria's anomalous relationship to continental France was too small to attract attention or trigger controversy.[1]

The post–World War II period was the first time in France's 115-year rule of Algeria that serious efforts were made to address its anomalous status—to devise formulas, at first for the empire in general and later for Algeria in particular, which would endow the legal fiction of Algeria's integration into France with a sufficiently convincing basis in French perceptions of their political community so as to remove questions about the territory's future from the French political agenda. To understand what impelled French elites toward more formally institutionalized relations with "overseas France" as well as the obstacles they faced in this effort, French colonialism's earlier failure to build a hegemonic conception of *la plus grande France* and the political consequences of France's defeat in World War II must be examined.

French Images of Their Empire

From the mid-1880s through the first decades of the twentieth century, France was subject to the same economic, social, and political forces which pushed most major European powers into bursts of imperial expansion. At the outbreak of World War I, France governed an overseas empire second only in size to Britain's.

The development of a particularly French imperialist doctrine in this period and the images of the empire fostered within the metropole were shaped by France's defeat in the Franco-Prussian War in 1871. French overseas expansion coincided with both the circumscription of the nation's ambitions in Europe and the establishment of a new regime—the Third Republic. Among the republican political elite were those who believed that blue-water colonialism was the only activist option available to France in the face of German power in Europe. Conscious of France's precarious hold on its great power status, Third Republic imperialists such as Eugène Étienne, Jules Ferry, Théophile Delcassé, and Gabriel Hanotaux evoked a republican myth of empire to generate renewed French enthusiasm for the idea of their country's career as that of bringing reason, progress, and universalist ideals to all peoples.[2]

Before World War I, however, French supporters of empire were less successful than British and German imperialists in convincing their countrymen that their empire was both a vital interest and a key element in the fulfillment of the national vocation. In the 1880s French parliamentarians castigated Foreign Minister Jules Ferry for his policies of colonial expansion. He was dubbed "Ferry le Tonkinois" and accused of deserting his national duty by "forgetting the blue line of the Vosges."[3] Despite the activities of numerous societies formed to increase metropolitan appreciation of French possessions, public opinion was at best indifferent and at worst hostile to imperial affairs.[4]

World War I gave French imperialists a new opportunity. During the late nineteenth century, France's longstanding demographic predominance in Western Europe disappeared. By 1918 the massive casualties suffered in the trenches produced a manpower shortage which threatened France's ability to withstand an imminent German offensive. In this crisis the arguments of those advocating la plus grande France, the France which, including its colonies, could muster a population of one hundred million, were as convincing as they were convenient. Under this slogan the Clemenceau government mobilized nearly 300,000 North African Muslims to fight in Europe. Algeria alone had provided 173,000 soldiers and 119,000 workers to metropolitan France, equaling more than 6 percent of the total Muslim population.[5] To effect this mobilization, colonial recruits were promised equal political rights. After the war few of these promises were kept, but the colonial contribution to victory left a powerful impression. Alongside metropolitan troops, representatives of the native units, in their colorful uniforms, marched in parades commemorating the sacrifices of French soldiers, blending vivid images of Senegalese and North African soldiers into the honored figure of the *ancien combattant* in the French popular imagination. Praise of their heroism in battle portrayed the native troops as loyal to a France that properly included them.[6]

In the 1920s popular interest in the romance and exoticism of France's possessions was expressed in many spheres, including anthropology, geography, and a colonialist literature exemplified by authors such as Louis Bertrand, whose stories glorifying the development of a new and vigorous French race in North Africa made him one of France's most influential writers of the interwar period.[7] In primary and secondary schools during the interwar period, students were taught that France's overseas possessions were of crucial importance for her welfare and security and that her rule over them was a great "civilizing" influence on their native inhabitants.

The empire as a whole was portrayed as "an integral part of the national territory."[8]

The period from 1930 to 1935 marked the "apotheosis" of the idea of "greater France" in the consciousness of the metropolitan population.[9] World depression and the tariff wars accompanying it encouraged France and the other major powers to emphasize the economic development and political unity of their empires as secure markets and fields for future investment. In 1933 the French Empire absorbed 33 percent of French exports and furnished 23 percent of continental France's imports, compared to twenty years earlier, when only 13 percent of France's trade was conducted with the empire.[10] In 1935 plans for great infrastructural investment in the empire, including a trans-Saharan railway, were enthusiastically discussed as the key to France's economic future. Still, consistent with French memories of World War I and perceptions of a newly menacing Germany, "it was the role of the empire in defense and security of the national soil, in safeguarding these supreme imperatives, with which the primordial necessity of the empire was most frequently and most strongly underlined."[11]

Complementing this view of the empire as vital to France was the widespread belief in the positive contribution of French colonizing activity to the well-being and political liberation of native peoples—what is usually referred to as France's *mission civilisatrice*. Saint-Simonian commitments to the spread of progress through technology combined with Christian religious motifs and republican values to create assumptions among most of the French that "once having been exposed to the advantages of the French culture, no native would wish to continue his own cultural tradition."[12]

The French were encouraged to view France's rule of Algeria as emblematic of its global imperial mission. In May 1930 seventy thousand metropolitan Frenchmen, the president of the republic, and a fleet of fifty warships visited Algeria to mark the centenary of its conquest by France. When France arrived there in 1830, said the National Metropolitan Committee for the Algerian Centenary, it found "a rude country and a bellicose population." Gradually, thanks to "the French Peace," it had been pacified, "persuaded both by our superiority and our arms."[13] The conquest of Algeria in 1830 was characterized as marking the real end of the Middle Ages, with North Africa recovered for civilization and for republican values.[14]

The Algerian centenary was followed by a comprehensive French celebration of colonialism in general, and the French Empire in particular—the massive Colonial Exhibition held in Vincennes from May through November of 1931. The French government used this extravaganza to endorse an expansive view of France as a world power, by not only entertaining ordinary French citizens with the exoticism of their far-flung empire, but by promoting an international political culture fully supportive of colonialism as a vehicle for spreading "progress" and transforming industrial nation-states into world powers. At the center of the exhibition were archaeological displays, produce, crafts, performers, and military units from every part of the "great human collectivity of France."[15] At the formal opening of the exhibition, the Minister of Colonies Paul Reynaud declared its purpose to be the encouragement of the concept of "greater France"—"France of 100 million Frenchmen on five continents"—of which the hexagon was to be understood as comprising only one-twenty-third of what another speaker described as "one indissoluble whole."[16]

The dominance of colonial ideas in the international political culture of the early 1930s was reflected by pavilions representing all the major imperialist powers, including the United States. Each was ceremoniously opened by representatives of the sponsoring metropolitan government, whose speeches offered words of praise for France's own imperial mission. In the five and a half months of the exhibition it was visited by more than thirty-two million people, helping change the empire "from a vague entity to a familiar reality" for many ordinary Frenchmen.[17]

But despite feelings of attachment to French colonies by many, and the development of strong loyalties by some, metropolitan opinion remained ambivalent. Even during this pre–World War II peak of enthusiasm for what was now increasingly referred to as *France d'outre-mer* or la plus grande France, the French cannot be said to have constructed a natural view of their country as extending with roughly equivalent levels of empathic concern to areas on five continents. In polls reported in August 1939, evidence showed that French perceptions had changed, but not to the point of having established la plus grande France as a hegemonic conception. Forty-four percent of respondents indicated that they were "prepared to fight rather than cede even the smallest part of colonial possessions." Forty percent said they were not prepared to fight, with 16 percent not responding. Fifty-three percent said they would "see ceding a part of the colonial empire as painful as ceding a part of France." But 43 percent said they would not view such a cession as comparable to losing a part of the hexagon.[18]

Additional evidence for the failure of greater France partisans to establish their perspective as the definitive conception of the French political community is the incoherence of colonial policy. In 1939 Robert Montagne, an official in the Colonial Ministry and an ardent supporter of the "greater France" idea, noted how embarrassing it had been to have admitted to the British, at an international conference on colonial affairs, that "we

lacked any common institutional structure for our three Maghreb provinces." Montagne detailed the demise of four kinds of administrative reforms, from 1923 to 1938, each designed to help French possessions in
the Mediterranean basin take their rightful place in a unified empire.[19]

Failure to devise and implement systematic policies did not mean that
any part of the French elite considered abandoning the empire. Beset by
increasingly deep divisions between right and left, Third Republic politicians from all parties embraced a Republican/imperial ethos as an important source of regime legitimacy. According to D. Bruce Marshall, "In the
face of mounting tension the preservation of the colonial status quo tended
to become a primary goal of national policy admitting of no inquiry except
where circumstances made it absolutely unavoidable. . . . The future of the
French colonies had become an integral part of the French political mythology and was intimately related to the self-image that French leaders
had evolved."[20]

In the interwar years some questions were raised about French rule of
its overseas possessions. There were reports of outrages against natives by
colonial governments. Leftist intellectuals responded sympathetically to
scattered insurrections. Memory of the horrors of the Great War challenged
beliefs in the obvious superiority of European culture. But the general
response to criticism, insofar as it was acknowledged as valid, was agreement that a new and better relationship between continental and overseas
France was needed, one more authentically reflective of French values and
aspirations.[21] In explaining this response Marshall cites what he might
have termed "hegemonic" aspects of the metropolitan "conviction that
the republic was multinational and indissoluble": "if basic [colonial] structures and doctrines were left unaltered . . . it was because none of the critics
ever was able to conceive of the fundamental issue of France's relationship
to the colonies in any other terms than those derived from a century or
more of a tradition that excluded political separation as a legitimate goal
of national policy."[22]

From Empire to Overseas France: The Impact of World War II

By the end of the 1930s two beliefs regarding empire appear to have
been treated within metropolitan France as unquestioned assumptions.
The first, as noted by Marshall, was that the ties between France and that
substantial part of the world influenced by French rule and French culture
were indissoluble. The second was that France's civilizing mission toward
humanity, expressed in great part by France's impact on the territories
and peoples brought under its rule, was a necessary part of France's great-

ness as nation. After 1940 these beliefs were resources for, but also limits on, efforts by French men and women seeking to reconstitute a political order within which continental and overseas France could be linked in a stable, legitimizable, manner.

The undiscussed and undiscussible status of these beliefs is suggested by the terms of debate between Vichy and the Free French during World War II. With the Germans in Paris, the meaning of the attachment between overseas and continental France became a key issue between those who favored signing the armistice with Germany and who went on to participate in the collaborationist Vichy government, and those who rallied to de Gaulle and the Free French movement. Vichyists tended to see the empire as subordinate to metropolitan France. If the fate of metropolitan France was defeat, occupation, and subservience to Germany, then that was also the proper fate of the empire, entailing, of course, rule by the Vichy government. Accordingly, the proposed Vichy constitution completely integrated the empire into the political domain of metropolitan France, while consigning it to an irrevocably subordinate status.[23]

Despite the depth of his disagreement with Vichy, de Gaulle also embraced the concept of the empire as just as truly "France" as the metropolitan territory. Consistent with his interests, and those of the Free French, de Gaulle argued that German occupation of Paris and control of the European hexagon did not constitute defeat of "France," that overseas France remained, and that only traitors would agree to Germany's terms for an armistice while so much of the country's territory remained available to continue the fight. What is significant is that both arguments, and the long-term planning of both Vichy and the Free French during the war, implicitly accepted the same conception of a panoply of overseas territories that were properly, vitally, and immutably French.[24]

For the French public as well as French political elites, the overall effect of World War II was to increase the perceived importance of the empire. The humiliation of military defeat, the rigors and brutality of occupation, and the servitude of millions of French citizens in German factories were an even more shattering assault on the nation's self-confidence and its future than had been the carnage of World War I.[25] Again colonial troops had been active in the fighting on the side of the Allies. Nor had any French colony used the war as an opportunity to sever its connection to France.[26] Indeed the headquarters of de Gaulle's provisional government were in Algiers, so that, as one postwar observer remarked, "the Mediterranean emerged not as a frontier, but as a bridge, which linked the Metropole with its African territories."[27] The effective military and diplomatic use which the Free French made of colonial territories appeared to support more substantially than anyone might have imagined the argument made before the war that "If France is not in Algiers, Dakar, and Hanoi, it is questionable whether she will remain in Paris."[28]

Specifically, World War II gave an even stronger boost than had World War I to the sense that the French had of the empire's importance to their country's future as a great power. In his broadcasts from London in 1942 and 1943 de Gaulle called on "Moslem France, from Nigeria to Casablanca," to rally to his side and spoke glowingly of the "union of all Frenchmen, regardless of race or creed." "The Moslems of French Africa," he declared, "will be ready to do their duty towards their great motherland, the France of yesterday and forever."[29] National Council of the Resistance declarations about the future rights of all inhabitants of the empire assumed, they did not assert, France's continued sovereignty.[30] Although resistance movements within the continental hexagon gave little systematic consideration to the future of overseas France, this was a matter of great importance for Free French circles in Algiers, where the provisional government entered into direct competition with Vichy for the loyalty of North African Muslims.[31]

In an often-quoted phrase de Gaulle warned that were France to lose its empire after the war, the country "might count for nothing more in the world than Greece does in Europe."[32] This reference to the wholly unacceptable possibility that France, without France d'outre-mer, would occupy a place in the world no different in its fundamental character from that of any other country reflected a widespread concern within the French elite in the final years of the war and in the immediate postwar period.[33] The demographic specter that had haunted French leaders during and after World War I had become even more frightening. Between 1900 and 1939 British, Italian, and German population growth rates were, respectively, twelve, eleven, and seven times higher than the meager 3 percent rate recorded by France.[34] For Marius Moutet, Socialist minister of colonies in the 1930s and minister of overseas France after World War II, France was at a crossroads. The successful incorporation of the overseas portions of France would determine "whether France would be a great power or not—a nation of 110 million or only 40 million."[35]

The search for an appropriate political formula for the postwar relationship between continental and overseas France began in earnest at the Brazzaville Conference, convened by the Free French in February 1944. The conference was charged with developing "a constitutional regime, both republican and democratic, consistent with the notion of Empire."[36] Jacques Chaban-Delmas, administrator in chief of the colonies in the Free French government, declared that "The Empire, which is to say continental France and overseas France, are not associated but united, with France as a single and indivisible organism as formed by a Fourth Republic, based on respect and recognition of the three Republics from which it grew."[37]

Belief in the absolute necessity of French rule over much more than the hexagon if France's status as a great power was to be preserved helps explain why the Brazzaville Conference categorically rejected "even the distant establishment of 'self-government' " in any part of what was henceforth known offically as "overseas France."[38] During the conference, continued rule of all French possessions was treated as an obvious necessity. British predilections for devolution of authority were understood as the result of the limitations of Anglo-Saxon (as opposed to French/Latin) culture.[39]

In 1945 the affairs of "overseas France" did not matter much to the people of newly liberated France. But elite perceptions of links between France's great power status and the future of its former empire did correspond to much wider streams of opinion. A survey of French public opinion in 1946 showed the French divided over whether the colonies should be governed "for the profit of France, or above all for the profit of the indigenous population." The crucial element in the survey, however, was the assumption implicit in the poll itself that the colonies would continue to be ruled by France.[40] Native demands for political change that were seen to challenge this assumption exposed French sensitivities. According to Philippe Devillars, "National feelings, whipped up by the war, were becoming extremely irritable as soon as it appeared that France's future as a great power was at stake. Public opinion, while ready to accept any transformation—even a radical one—in the colonial system, was on the other hand, absolutely unwilling to permit the slightest attempt at secession."[41]

These sentiments help explain the popular support the government received for its savage attacks on Muslims in eastern Algeria. On May 8, 1945, VE-day, Muslim veterans in the Algerian town of Sétif staged a victory march demanding political reforms. Some nationalist banners were raised, triggering violent attacks by Europeans. These led to a wave of outrages against European homes and farms and resulted in the death of at least one hundred Europeans. Both the colon population and the military struck back with extraordinary ferocity. The government's own best estimate was that at least fifteen thousand Muslims were killed by air force attacks on villages, naval bombardment, and repressive measures taken by army units and vigilantes.

In the months that followed both provisional government officials and observers treated the Sétif affair as an object lesson in France's need to be categorical and internally united in its stand against nationalist agitation and foreign encroachments in any of the colonies. "The whole world," declared Interior Minister Adrien Tixier, "must understand that victorious France has the firmness of will and the necessary means to resist any blow to the sovereignty of France in Algeria."[42] Discussion of the matter in the Provisional Consultative Assembly drew extended comments from Communists, native deputies, and colon representatives as well as provisional government officials. While disagreeing vehemently over what precipitated the violence, all agreed that the events signaled a threat to French sovereignty, that such threats could not be tolerated, and that any measures required to subdue "separatist" agitation would be justified.[43]

However, French elites were broadly aware that something more than repression would be necessary if the reconstruction of continental and overseas France into a global entity with great power status were to succeed. Important themes in French political culture, mentioned earlier in connection with the development of French imperial ideology, reinforced realistic calculations with traditional sentiments. Provisional government spokesmen also emphasized the need to implement the Ordinance of March 7, 1944 (a set of decrees designed to grant Algerian Muslims the political rights contained in the stillborn Blum-Violette project of 1936). Such reforms were seen as crucial if ties of loyalty between Algerian Muslims and France were to be strengthened. But this was only one element in the array of political, administrative, social, and economic reforms it promised for Algeria.

For many French people, yearning to believe in a future for their country which could overshadow the consequences of June 1940, and inspired by the sacrifices and heroism of the maquisards, the idea of France's "civilizing mission" toward the rest of the world took on unprecedented significance in the postwar period. Overseas France appeared in this context, and against a background of the emergence of the two superpowers, as the final field within which the French genius for cultivating humane values could show itself, and within which France could reestablish itself as the most vibrant force in the world on behalf of "liberty, equality, and fraternity."

If these aspirations were to be realized the French Empire could not be allowed to go the way of others, such as the British or the Americans. "Decolonization" would have to mean not a devolution of French authority and influence, but a process of emancipation which would bring the peoples under French rule into a fuller sense of freedom and accomplishment *within* the French republic—one and indivisible. Achieving decolonization by incorporating the colonies into a new French superstate could thus be seen as a bold, even desperate attempt to regain France's lost grandeur and world role through institutions modeled, at least officially, on Jacobin values. These were the concerns and aspirations that dominated French thinking about the empire in the years immediately following the liberation and that produced discussions of the distinctly French form of "federalism" that could tie overseas France to the hexagon.

On March 24, 1945, the provisional government's minister of colonies, Paul Giacobbi, introduced the term "French Union" to describe the federal-type relationship he envisioned as developing between France and French-ruled Indochina. The term was quickly adopted as an image for relations between France and all its overseas departments and territories. Giacobbi's idea, wrote Robert Delavignette, a colonial governor and director of the École Coloniale, was an authentic expression of the message of Brazza-ville.[44] The provisional government's grant of citizenship in the French Union to all inhabitants was equivalent to the Emperor Caracalla's grant of Roman citizenship to all peoples of the Roman Empire.[45] The French Union would be "a world organism which includes within it the imperial overseas territories and that which is in metropolitan Europe.... *The old notion of the metropole and the colonies is outmoded. A new notion is developing and flourishing, that of a common entity that is superior to all its elements.* Brazzaville does not supplant Paris; Brazzaville is not equal to Paris; but Brazzaville and Paris are part of one new organic unity, a united new world organism."[46]

From this perspective, noted Delavignette, it was entirely fitting that soldiers from France's empire were the first to enter Paris on August 24, 1944.[47] Clearly the "colonies" could no longer properly be referred to as such, as if they were the "property" of the metropole.[48] Nor could overseas France any longer be "decomposed" into a series of small administrative problems. Such a renunciation of the challenge facing France would ignore the profound change that had taken place in the colonial problem and would betray France's eternal "vocation"—its transformation into a worldwide multiracial community, pooling its resources to enhance the quality of life "for all of us." Accordingly, "sovereignty" would no longer be a rationale for expansion, but a framework for human development. Whether the French would indeed open their political community to the variety of peoples inhabiting overseas France would test the nation's special genius for responding to the essential "indivisibility of humanity."[49]

The boldness, not to say extravagance, of these ideas assuredly went far beyond what the great mass of French people experienced as the empathic reality of their political life. But the myth of Brazzaville and evocative, idealistic descriptions of France's global mission were characteristic of the period—a discourse common to both native and colon representatives and to metropolitan politicians of every persuasion: conservative, Gaullist, radical, socialist, Catholic, and communist.[50]

Postwar Constructions of the "Indivisible Republic"

Aside from satisfying their need to believe in France's continuing status as a great power and expressing their genuine enthusiasm for her special vocation, French elites had two very practical reasons to espouse grand images of the French Union's future. One pertained to France's participation in the international community; the other to the process of reconstituting a legitimate political order within the country.

During the war the principle of self-determination for colonized peoples was enshrined in the Atlantic Charter and later in the founding documents of the United Nations. In the postwar era the doctrine of independence for former colonies was advanced vigorously by native nationalists and both superpowers. If France, needful of continued economic and political support, was to maintain its sovereignty over former colonies, it required a justification that could be defended in terms of this new international political culture—a framework of thinking which treated European rule of non-Europeans as oppressive and decolonization as obviously necessary and inevitable. In Washington, D.C., on July 10, 1944, de Gaulle demonstrated his understanding of this requirement by evoking the "myth of Brazzaville," describing France's policy as "elevating its territories as fast as possible; for each to administer in its own interests and represent itself within a federal system."[51] Three months later he explained that he had meant "not a French federation... but a French system where each part will have its role," illustrating that however wise it might be to describe the as-yet-unnamed "French Union" in generous terms, de Gaulle's first commitment was to preserve French sovereignty over all imperial possessions.[52]

In an extended effort to spell out the logic that lay behind French responses to new international political norms of anticolonialism and "self-determination," Jean de la Roche and Jean Gottmann stressed how completely the world would be transformed in the aftermath of the war. Small territorial nations would be passé. Imaginative leaps and political inventions comparable to the contribution of the French Revolution in its day were required. France, based on her long history of "federating" various tribes into a larger "Gaul" and combining a heterogeneous mix of provinces and ethnic groups into the united hexagon, would employ the "French federation" to achieve "a profound union of peoples of French culture living on the national soil—able to be a great force for the establishment and maintenance of world peace... and for putting a final end to the 'colonial cycle.' "[53] This "enlargement of the national consciousness" in which "the idea of the Nation extends beyond the limits of France in Europe and extends throughout all the French territories" would serve as a model for "all of humanity, white, black, or yellow, on the march toward a new destiny."[54]

From this perspective, renewal of the mandate system requiring individual colonies to be guided toward independence was a backward step. By "imposing an evolution toward (separate) self-government as the definition of success," it contradicted the need for more comprehensive forms of political loyalty and organization.[55] British, Soviet, and U.S. professions of support for such old-fashioned self-determination schemes were seen by France as camouflage for those powers' own neo-imperialist designs on French possessions.[56]

In addition to the demands of a new international political culture, establishment of an authentically French, legitimized relationship to overseas France was response to political imperatives within the metropole. The Third Republic had been thoroughly discredited. No one questioned that France would be republican, that it would be governed from Paris, that French would be the official language, or that it would honor the tricolor and sing the "Marseillaise." Little else, however, was taken for granted. There was, in effect, a scarcity of hegemonic beliefs.

Writing and ratifying a constitution for the Fourth Republic which most French people could deem legitimate and which might have a chance of producing expectations of stability was a long and tortuous process. A premium was placed on any elements in French political culture which could plausibly be seen as expressions of what the French people might consider the common sense of their collective life. In addition to international considerations, this need for ingrained beliefs, to which appeal could be made in struggles over the design of the new regime, encouraged emphasis on the two aspects of France's relationship to its overseas holdings that appear to have been hegemonic before World War II—the indissolubility of ties linking France d'outre-mer to the metropole, and the vital role overseas France played as a field for the expression of France's special vocation.

In this context, what Marshall called the "colonial myth" was of great value—a set of beliefs that by the 1930s had come to provide "a common universe of discourse to virtually all segments of the political elite, both metropolitan and colonial."[57] These beliefs were a resource for as well as a constraint on efforts to rebuild a legitimate political order. But after the "tidal wave of the war"[58] and amid a tempest of conflicting interests and ideologies, they did not provide a clear design for a stable regime linking continental and overseas France.

From 1945 to 1958 three attempts to translate myth into common sense were made. These took the form of three overlapping but distinct formulas for naming and legitimizing the postwar regime as a set of institutions reflecting the indissolubility and importance of ties between continental and overseas France. More precisely these attempts may be understood as ways of shaping continental and overseas France as a single political community which could be acceptable as hegemonic constructions. Each was advanced by different political groups within the reemerging political system as part of their proposals for the constitution of the Fourth Republic. Each formula experienced a degree of success before being effectively replaced as a candidate for hegemonic status by a successor that, in important respects, was less ambitious. This series of failures at the hegemonic level contributed to the weakness of the Fourth Republic at the regime level and the explosive emergence of the Algerian problem in French politics.

The French Union of Free Consent

The first hegemonic project held out the image of France as the French Union—a global political community "of free consent." It addressed native elites as full partners in designing the new France that would emerge from the war and in exercising political power within it. Through Union with its former colonies, France would articulate its global political vocation. The indissolubility of la plus grande France would be guaranteed by the empathic generosity of the French in welcoming tens of millions of former subjects as equal citizens and by the enthusiasm with which the formerly colonized peoples would freely maintain their loyalty to France and French culture.

Consistent with this image of France was de Gaulle's unopposed decision in the summer of 1945 to permit native peoples from overseas France to elect delegates to the Constituent Assembly in Paris.[59] In July 1945 a two-part article in *Le Monde,* titled "The Colonies and the Constitution," urged the French people to make sure that the language of the new constitution would recognize France's nature as a world power and not "reduce her to the status of a European nation." This would entail abandoning a system of legal relationships "which united metropolitan France and the French overseas territories as a sovereign is united to its vassals," and building instead "a French community with opportunities for each people within it to find its just place." This would also require change in the terms of public discourse about formerly "colonial" affairs. According to *Le Monde,* "We say: 'France and *its* empire,' 'France and *its* colonies,' 'France and *its* overseas possessions.' This terminology reflects an outdated 'colonialism' ... distinguishing citizens from subjects."[60]

Many participants in post-war debates within the Provisional Consultative Assembly and the first Constituent Assembly made similar points.

One was Jacques Soustelle, a left-leaning Gaullist who served as commissioner of information in the Free French government and minister of colonies in 1945. Soustelle's reputation as an anthropologist enhanced the importance of his views on the future of the empire. France, he argued, was a great Eurafrican power. The French Union would make it a global state. It was therefore quite literally improper to speak of a debate over "colonial affairs." These were essentially "provincial" matters. Soustelle insisted that "This is not a 'colonial debate.' Nor is it a discussion of arranging relations between a metropole and its colonies, as if it were a matter of external relations. It is an attempt to resolve the internal problem of the new France, which is the French Union."[61] He went on to explain how the "antimony between colonizer and colonized" would be overcome by recognizing African vernaculars as having the same status as Provençal or Basque and by making the French Union "a true political democracy."

As noted, Soustelle was a Gaullist, but this formula, as a candidate for hegemonic definition of the French political community—of the French Union as France, and of France as a global republican community—was advanced primarily by Socialists, Communists, and native deputies to the first Constituent Assembly, with some support as well from liberal Catholic elements within the Resistance organizations. Rejecting, along with all other French people, any diminution in French sovereignty, the Communists "demanded a constitutional new deal for the colonial natives, by which the latter would receive citizenship and political rights."[62] Maurice Thorez, leader of the PCF (Le Parti Communiste Français), looked forward to the creation of a "free, confident, and fraternal union of the colonial peoples and the people of France."[63]

After the election of delegates to the Constituent Assembly in October 1945, a constitutional committee was chosen. Among its more difficult tasks was to design legal formulas for governing the relationship between continental France and the former French Empire. This committee's basis of discussion was a constitutional project for the "French Union," produced by the Socialist party, which commanded the largest bloc of delegates in the Assembly. The committee's chairman, Marius Moutet, representing the Socialist party, characterized the objective of the Socialist proposal as the creation of a transitional arrangement "to put an end to the colonial regime, juridically, to the system of dependency of colonies on the metropole, and to substitute an organization both supple and articulated."[64]

According to the terms of the committee's proposals, which were mainly the work of left-wing and native members of the SFIO, native inhabitants of overseas territories were guaranteed all the rights in the Declaration of the Rights of Man, universal suffrage was to be implemented, and a council of the French Union would be established, with representatives from territorial assemblies to be established throughout overseas France. The text declared that the French Union would be a "free union of consent," implying the right of secession, although the "absolute right" of all peoples and collectivities "to independence and to expression of their civilization, culture, and language" was to be exercised only "within the limits of the cohesion of the French Union."[65] The Socialist project also affirmed "the principle of national sovereignty" as the highest source of authority and the intrinsic unity of the French republic "one and indivisible." In this way, although not without a certain "audacious ambiguity," the Socialists sought to translate the twin hegemonic conceptions of mission and indissolubility into a legitimizing basis for combining continental and overseas France into a single political community.[66]

The high watermark for this particular hegemonic project was reached in the spring of 1946 when a draft constitution for the Fourth Republic was approved by the Constituent Assembly and presented to the French people for ratification. Article 41 of this draft constitution declared "France, with its overseas territories, on the one hand, and with the associated states, on the other, a union of free consent." Articles 44 and 45 established the fundamental political equality of all inhabitants of metropolitan and overseas France. Indeed, before dissolving itself, the Constituent Assembly put into effect one of the draft's provisions by enacting the Loi Lamine-Gueye, a sweeping grant of French citizenship to all inhabitants of overseas France, regardless of cultural, religious, or previous legal status.[67]

In a referendum on May 5, 1946, the French people rejected the draft constitution presented to them by the first Constituent Assembly. The debate preceding the referendum paid relatively little attention to the question of overseas France. But the returns from the colonies signaled trouble for the concept of a French Union of "free consent." Europeans living in overseas France, especially in North Africa, voted overwhelmingly against the draft. Their representatives to the second Constituent Assembly, elected in June 1946, sought to convince that body of the impossibility of ensuring French sovereignty over overseas possessions, or of remaining true to France's civilizing mission, if the French Union's provisions permitted political equality for natives and even theoretical opportunities for territories to opt out of the Union altogether.

By August 1946 left-wing and native proposals for a French Union of "free consent"—proposals that matched or exceeded in generosity those contained in the draft constitution produced by the first Constituent Assembly—attracted so much attention that they "threatened to dominate the entire constitutional debate."[68] Deputies representing Europeans in the overseas territories relentlessly attacked what they called the "shameful syndicate of separatists" that had produced the proposals.[69] While endorsing the principle of a federalist French Union, Edouard Herriot labeled the proposals a form of "acephalous and anarchic federalism [that]...we shouldn't be afraid to treat as treason." Troubles with the Viet Minh in Indochina, Algerian proposals for an Algerian republic that could still, supposedly, remain within the French Union, and the specter of "alien interference in the affairs of continental France"—of France becoming "a colony of her former colonies"—stiffened centrist and right-wing opposition to a French Union based on political equality and "free consent."[70] These deputies found it increasingly difficult to believe that French sovereignty could be preserved by relying on the loyalty and free choice of the inhabitants of overseas France. On August 29 the Assembly removed these provisions from the draft constitution.

Doubts about whether a union of free consent could guarantee the sovereignty of France in its overseas territories echoed the severe criticisms de Gaulle had leveled at the first Constituent Assembly draft. Shortly following its defeat he had proposed a hierarchically organized French Union, governed by the president of the republic, who would appoint premiers and viceroys for its various parts, including the metropole. The president himself would conduct the foreign and security affairs of the French Union as a whole. In reaction to the reappearance of the looser union of "free consent" during the deliberations of the second Constituent Assembly, de Gaulle issued a blunt and categorical rejection of the Assembly's entire constitutional project. He concentrated his attack specifically on the weakness of the president and the slackness of the ties linking the metropole to overseas France.[71] Georges Bidault, leader of the MRP (Mouvement Républicaine Populaire) and president of the provisional government, declared his agreement with de Gaulle and those nationalists, conservatives, and rightward-leaning Socialists who warned of "secessionist anarchy" if free consent were to be established as the basis for the French Union. Unless this principle were abandoned, Bidault warned, he would resign the presidency.[72]

Native deputies, on the other hand, had come to Paris committed to preserve and even strengthen the foundations for a multinational French political community. But the fears and distrust expressed by so many metropolitan deputies and political leaders undermined their faith in France's real willingness to leave colonialism behind. Felix Tchicaya, from French Equatorial Africa, warned against attempts to use "federalist" terminology to conceal continued subordination of overseas possessions by metropolitan France. He stated, "Do not lead the peoples overseas to believe in a vast mystification, in the existence of principles for internal usage which, outside the metropolitan hexagon, will be nothing but advertising slogans whose authors laugh among themselves."[73]

Thus, during the deliberations of the second Constituent Assembly, both opponents and proponents of the French Union of "free consent" explicitly questioned each other's motives. This public skepticism signaled the inadequacy of "the myth of a unity of desires" and "the ideal of a large, multinational community of French peoples" as credible candidates for an ideologically hegemonic conception of France.[74]

The French Union of Tutelary Subordination

With Bidault's assent, new language outlining the terms of the French Union was provided to the Constituent Assembly and incorporated into the draft constitution. It was approved (narrowly) by the French people in an October referendum, thereby becoming the constitution of the Fourth Republic.

As inelegant and as ambiguous as they may be, the portions of the Constitution dealing with the French Union should be understood as the second substantive effort to advance a hegemonic basis for French authority over the former empire—what may be termed the French Union as a form of "tutelary subordination." As with the Union of free consent, the Union of tutelary subordination relied upon and sought to protect hegemonic beliefs about the indissoluble ties between continental and overseas France and the special French vocation to humanity expressed in that relationship.

However, in contrast to the French Union described in the April draft, the pertinent articles in the constitution of the Fourth Republic described a hierarchical structure designed to maintain metropolitan predominance at every crucial point. Complex, interlocking, and scattered throughout the text, the French Union provisions nonetheless clearly reflected Bidault's "rejection of the pluralistic conception of the union."[75] Where the April draft had referred to "France" as "a Union of free consent," with "overseas territories" and "associated states" as component parts of that same union that was "France," the new constitution described the French Union as formed "on the one hand by the French Republic which includes Metropolitan France, the Overseas Departments and Territories, and on the other hand by Associated Territories and States." By mentioning "Metropolitan France" as distinct from both overseas departments and territories, the constitution established the basis for the superordinate status of the metropolitan government. In the absence of any reference to the "free consent" of its component parts, the constitution stated that this government would rule not only the "French republic," but the French Union as a whole, including, in addition to overseas territories and departments, both "Associated Territories and States." The hierarchical relationship between the "metropolitan" portion of the "French republic" and the overseas portion was institutionalized by concentrating all legislative power in the National Assembly in Paris and by establishing a two-college system that gave preponderant representation to European residents of overseas France as opposed to natives. The Assembly of the French Union was granted consultative and advisory powers only. Even so it was to be composed "half of members representing Metropolitan France and half of members representing the Overseas Departments and Territories and the Associated States."

The hierarchical, tutelary ethos of the constitution, in contrast to the pluralist, egalitarian thrust of the April draft, was expressed by the last paragraph of the constitution's preamble, declaring France as "Faithful to her traditional mission...to lead the peoples under her tutelage to the liberty of administering themselves and of managing democratically their own affairs." Absent any provisions for secession from the Union, or for control by inhabitants of specific overseas territories of their status within it, these principles of "self-administration" were clearly to be realized only within a French Union over which metropolitan France could exercise unchallengeable sovereignty.

In the traditions of French colonialism, in the repertoire of French political mythology, and in wartime thinking about French ties to former colonies, it was as easy to find raw material for fashioning this alternative political formula as it had been to construct images of a pluralist union of free consent as the authentic expression of France's eternal mission. Although the official message of the French civilizing mission was "Liberty, Equality, Fraternity," associated beliefs in French intellectual prowess and the superiority of French culture and language reflected a profound sense that France was endowed with a unique gift for raising the cultural and spiritual level of the rest of humanity. Victorious generals and colonial administrators such as Thomas-Robert Bugeaud, Joseph Galliéni, and Hubert Lyautey were honored as imperial "proconsuls." Such iconography enlivened colonialist doctrines portraying France as heir to the Roman tradition of civilized world leadership, dedicated to raising the level of brave but benighted peoples through the patient and confident extension of imperial law. Associated with this self-image was a traditional commitment to centralized control of imperial affairs, dedicated, in principle at least, to the transformation and assimilation of colonized areas—their "evolution" toward additional provinces of France. Because the vast majority of the French were convinced of their culture's superiority and attractiveness, insistence that subject peoples remain under the sovereignty of France could be combined with genuine commitments to political self-determination. Thus native preferences for independence over continued rule by France were often interpreted as prima facie evidence of the need for more guidance and more exposure to France.

During World War II the "tutelary subordination" formula for the French Union was foreshadowed in the thinking of both Vichyite and Free French circles. Under the slogan "Order and Progress" the Vichy publicist René Maunier argued for an organic conception of the empire, with assigned roles for its component parts. Each part of the empire, he stressed, should be tied to the metropole as Algeria had been, so that the territory of each colony would be "united as a *national* territory and, this being the case, that *the French State [would be] the French Empire.*" The indissolubility of the Empire would be accomplished by formally proclaiming it so in a constitution that would establish the legal basis for governing different parts of the imperial state by different laws, according to the various "levels of advancement" attained by local peoples. Through subordination to the metropole the "national unity of the whole empire" would be assured in "authentic Roman style, without abstract and inapplicable notions of assimilation."[76]

Within Free French circles similar ideas existed, sometimes in awkward proximity to the Jacobin, universalist egalitarianism that lay behind the Union of free consent. On Bastille Day 1945, the National Council of the Resistance published suggestions for a new constitution that promised "full citizenship rights" for all inhabitants of overseas France—this while allocating four times as many seats in the Parliament to representatives of 40 million metropolitan French as to 70 million inhabitants of overseas France.[77] At the very beginning of the Brazzaville Conference's report on its proceedings and recommendations, two paragraphs set forth the actual frame of reference of the conferees and the assumptions they were suggesting as appropriate for the Free French on the subject of imperial affairs. Although "little by little" colonial peoples were to be "elevated toward participation in the conduct of public affairs . . . the purposes of the civilizing work accomplished by France in the colonies dispel any idea of autonomy, and any possibility of evolution outside the French imperial bloc. Even the eventual establishment of self-government, in the distant future, is to be avoided."[78]

Contrary to the myth cultivated soon after the Brazzaville Conference, examination of the published summary of the discussions that took place there shows that the participants had uppermost in their minds the need to strengthen metropolitan France's rule over its colonies. This consolidation was to be achieved by giving powers and responsibilities previously vested in Parisian ministries to "local" (mainly European) civil servants. To be sure, some enhancement in the status of native peoples was to be allowed. But the most important rationale for a degree of "decentralization" was increased administrative efficiency. In this context "federalism" and federalist institutions were discussed, but the conclusions reached were that the federal mode of organization, as conventionally imagined, was inappropriate and that it was inconsistent with France's "Roman sense"— its particular "spirit of civilization."[79] Education in French was to displace all schooling in vernacular languages. The idea of an imperial or federal citizenship seemed premature to the conferees, liable to result in the subordination of metropolitan affairs to native concerns in a "federal Parliament," or to open up avenues for the empire, apart from continental France, to establish itself as a separate and equal unit. The conclusion was that if, eventually, some sort of federalist formula might be implemented, it would have to be molded in a distinctly French fashion, featuring the "subjugation" in legislative matters that was traditional in French colonialism—"a subjugation tempered by humane sensibility, beneficence, and competence."[80]

The image of the French state as a well-ordered array of territories governed for the benefit of all its peoples by a republic anchored firmly in the European hexagon was little more successful as a candidate for hegemonic status than its pluralist predecessor. Support for the constitution as a whole was anything but enthusiastic. Only 35.8 percent of the electorate voted in its favor; 31.6 percent were opposed, and 32.6 percent abstained. In overseas France the constitution was supported by only 20 percent, with 29 percent opposed and more than 50 percent abstaining.[81] Prior to the referendum, Gaullists and Radicals as well as political parties representing conservatives and peasants urged the French people to reject the draft. While some of these groups gave scant attention to its French Union provisions, others feared French sovereignty in overseas France was still not well enough protected. Ferhat Abbas's party declared its profound dissatisfaction with the draft, calling it a rejection of the principle of a "free federation of free peoples," and urged abstention. The Communists, leftist Resistance militants, and the Socialists expressed disappointment at the abandonment of principles enshrined in the first draft. Offering lukewarm and often apologetic support, they promised to struggle vigorously to refashion the constitution as "an instrument of liberation." Of the parties that supported the Constitution, the MRP, whose leader, Georges Bidault, had framed its French Union provisions, was the "least unenthusiastic." But even MRP propaganda, though it claimed the Constitution would "guarantee the French Union's future," admitted the draft contained "substantial problems," describing it only as a necessary compromise and as "eminently perfectible."[82]

To be sure, some limited success was registered in establishing the centralized Union as a fact of French political life. Although world maps produced in the late 1940s and early 1950s by major French publishing houses and the National Geographic Society distinguished between "La France Metropolitaine" and "Les Territoires d'Outre-mer," they also displayed a transcontinental French Union, in one solid color, common to both the metropole and overseas France.[83] This latter notion was consistent with the official shape of the French state as outlined in the constitution. Public inclination to accept official doctrines was also reflected in the absence of any significant metropolitan criticism of costly and repressive government policies in Indochina and Madagascar. France's long and bitter war in Indochina began in December 1946, when hostilities between the Viet Minh and French forces commenced over the terms of Vietnam's incorporation into the French Union. In Madagascar, four months later, a nationalist rebellion was crushed at a cost of thirty thousand dead Malagachies. A Communist party proposal to create a commission of inquiry into the events in Madagascar was defeated in the National Assembly by a vote of 415 to 199. Instead the Assembly passed (375 to 41, with the Communists abstaining) a resolution expressing full confidence in the government's policy. Raoul Girardet characterized the early response of Fourth Republic parliamentarians to anticolonial movements as a kind of "imperial optimism"—"a wall of massive assurance, a faith shared by almost everyone: assurance of cohesion, faith in the solidity of the community of peoples assembled under the domination or protection of the French flag."[84]

In principle, all those living under French rule had rights to be citizens of the French Union, and all "subjects of the Overseas Territories" were accorded "the same rights of citizenship as French nationals of the Mother country."[85] In practice, persons within each category (subject, citizen with French civil status, citizen without French civil status, etc.) in each overseas jurisdiction awaited the National Assembly's passage of implementing legislation to specify how the rights attached to their status could be exercised. The French Union's failure as a hegemonic project serving as a source of legitimacy for the Fourth Republic became apparent as soon as the government sought such legislation for Algeria—the putative cornerstone of the entire postimperial edifice.

What success the Fourth Republic's version of the French Union had as a hegemonic project should have been evident in the 1947 debate over passage of the Organic Statute for Algeria. Success would have been reflected by the absence of dispute over the proper status of Algeria in relation to France and the French Union. Success would also have been indicated by a pattern of argumentation used by both proponents and opponents of the law which implicitly accepted the French Union "of tutelary sub-ordination" as a given. However, in the debate over the 1947 statute, no constitutionally implicit, "natural," and obvious view of Algeria prevailed. Nor was the metropolitan-dominated image of the French Union treated presumptively.

Despite official protestations of Algeria's status as "thoroughly assim-ilated departments of France," there was serious and spirited debate over exactly how the statute itself should describe Algeria. Among the com-peting formulations were the following: "a collective territory of the French Republic composed of Overseas departments"; "French departments con-stituting a collective territory of the French Republic"; "a special collec-tivity composed of Overseas departments"; "an Overseas territory"; and "a prolongation of the metropole composed of French departments."[86] Some native deputies supported an amendment that would have designated Algeria as "a Republic" which in the future would enjoy the status of an "Associated State," "within the bosom of the French Union." Along with the Communists, they demanded that Algeria, in its present circumstances, be referred to as a "colony," so that demands for "liberation" could be formulated precisely. If these ideas did not find favor with the majority of Assembly deputies, they were nonetheless treated by government spokes-men as representing a point of view no less conceivable among the French than any other.[87]

The draft statute presented to the National Assembly by the Socialist-led government also stood in sharp contrast to the hierarchical concept of the French Union that had finally been endorsed by the second Constituent Assembly. Disagreement within the committee that drafted the proposed legislation had been intense, belying any effort to portray France's rela-tionship to Algeria as "obviously" or "commonsensically" describable. Despite vigorous opposition from the right and center, the Socialists found it necessary to accept amendments proposed by Communists and Muslim members of the committee in order to preserve a majority. These amend-ments liberalized provisions in the government draft regarding Muslim political rights and the amount of autonomy Algeria would enjoy. Mod-ification in the Socialists' position could not be concealed. In February 1947 the party had taken a firmly assimilationist view, asserting that "Algeria constitutes a collective territory of metropolitan France." Ac-cording to the Socialist rapporteur for the committee, by summer his party's position had shifted: "Having studied the problem thoroughly, we now have a detailed understanding of it. Seeing the problem from a dif-ferent angle, we have changed our view. Today we think we are right."[88]

Far from exhibiting presumptive beliefs about the French Union of "tutelary subordination," participants in the parliamentary debate over the proposed statute seldom drew on this image. Communists and native deputies did stress the importance of the French Union as an institution. But their appeals were to images of the Union of free consent that had been rejected by the second Constituent Assembly. Their commitment to revive that notion was apparent in their attempt (both in the committee that formulated the proposed legislation and on the floor of the Assembly) to characterize Algeria as "the pillar of the French Union," while recategorizing it as a territorial entity apart from France.[89] They advocated granting the country substantial autonomy as an "associated state" and extending maximum political rights to Muslims. During the debate Leopold Senghor, for example, argued that the meaning of the French Union was not so much "French sovereignty," but "the preeminence of the French Republic," within which a very large measure of autonomy or "self-government" for Algeria, as for other parts of the Union, was the goal.[90]

The French Union was also mentioned by some right-wing critics. They pointed out that the draft statute ignored the consultative role of the (yet to be constituted) Assembly of the French Union in adjusting the categorization of any territory within the Union. But the brunt of the criticism leveled by the colons and the right wing at the draft statute had nothing to do with the French Union. It was that the statute threatened the survival of the colon community and the integrity of what they characterized as Algeria's historic incorporation into metropolitan France itself—"a French province of the same type as Burgundy, Flanders, Brittany, le Comtat Venaissin or Savoy, which after all were attached to France after Algeria."[91] De Gaulle himself implicitly criticized the legislation as equivocal. Algeria, he emphasized, was subject to "the sovereignty of France. This signifies, first of all, that we must not allow any question to be raised in any form, neither at home, nor abroad, about whether Algeria is our domain." In his declaration on the subject, de Gaulle avoided any mention of the French Union.[92]

Conservatives and MRP deputies as well as Gaullists were particularly bothered by the draft statute's placement of Algeria within the category "overseas departments." They argued that the absence of any explicit mention of Algeria in the constitution implied and required its consideration as simply "three French departments." Since article 73 of the constitution explicitly declared that "the legislative form of government for the Overseas Departments is the same as that of the Metropolitan departments," they insisted that transfer of legislative and taxing powers to an Algerian Assembly was unconstitutional. "The government project," declared General Adolphe Aumeran, "tends very much to transform the

Algerian departments, which today are just that, from French departments to an overseas territory."[93] According to the constitution, recategorization of parts of the French Union could take place. But, argued one MRP deputy, since Algeria was comprised of French departments it was not eligible for recategorization, with or without consultation of the Assembly of the French Union.[94] René Capitant, a prominent Gaullist, even accused the government of moving, purposefully and effectively, if not explicitly, toward sovereign independence for Algeria.[95]

The outcome of a full-scale parliamentary debate in the summer of 1947 over the Organic Statute for Algeria was a complex and awkward compromise. Approved in August 1947 by a vote of 320 to 88, with 186 abstentions, the statute's first article described Algeria as "constituting a group of departments endowed with a civil personality, with financial autonomy and with a special organization."[96] Drawn from both the assimilationist and associationist traditions of French colonialist policy, this mix of phrases reflected the government's failure to sustain the hegemonic project incorporated into the regime established by the Fourth Republic Constitution. The formulation was far too awkward and complex to be considered a "natural" or commonsensical categorization under the rubric of the French Union of "tutelary subordination," (or, for that matter, of the French Union of "free consent"). Blatant rigging of the 1948 and 1951 elections to the Algerian Assembly, which deprived Algerian nationalists of most of their representation, only confirmed native beliefs that the reforms described in the statute would not be implemented.[97] In light of the pivotal position within the French Union Algeria was said to occupy, and the historic intimacy of ties between continental France and Algeria, failure to maintain the credibility of the regime's hegemonic project with respect to Algeria betokened the Union's demise, within the metropole, as a formula to legitimize French political domination in the former empire or to bolster the Fourth Republic's authority.

From 1948 until 1954 Algeria was largely ignored by metropolitan politicians and intellectuals, reflecting a general loss of interest in the affairs of overseas France.[98] Partisans of the French Union found themselves fighting the same battles as earlier generations of French colonialists had fought, against the chronic indifference of a French public mostly ignorant about overseas France. As early as 1948 they began warning that for the French Union as conceived in the constitution to survive, a substantial reinvigoration of national commitment and reinforcement of the authority of the French executive would be needed.[99] At the end of 1949, according to Roger Quilliot, "the system was everywhere confronted with the violent hostility of overseas elites, and also faced with the hostility of some governments of the fourth republic, . . . public opinion was totally indifferent, attaching hardly more importance to the war in Indochina as to a death in the place Pigalle."[100]

Increasingly, those who expressed sympathetic concern about the Union's future, or who defended French authority in its former colonies against international criticism, characterized the Union's institutional framework as "federalist," as ready to accommodate nationalist desires for political autonomy, and as necessarily evolving toward looser forms of association based on the principle of "independence within interdependence."[101] In this way the "tutelary subordination" conception of the French Union, within which the "tensile strength of imperial ties"[102] binding overseas France to the metropole was to have been preserved, was gradually abandoned. This process is neatly traceable in the gradual change of subject heading used by the conservative, semi-official *L'Année Politique*. In its chronological annex, events were divided into topic areas, one of which, in 1947, was "The French Union." By 1950 this heading had been changed to "The French Union and Protectorates." Shifts in 1952 to "French Union Overseas and Protectorates" and in 1956 to "French Union Overseas and Interdependent Countries" reflected gradual acknowledgment of the fundamental cleavage between the European and overseas segments of the Union and the declining salience of claims to French sovereignty over the Union as a whole. Though the French Union was not formally abolished until the inauguration of the Fifth Republic, by the mid-1950s its obituary could be written.[103]

In 1954 France left Indochina. In 1955 it granted "home rule" to Tunisia. In 1956 it recognized the sovereign independence of both Tunisia and Morocco and promulgated a *loi cadre* which effectively, if not explicitly, revoked the constitution's insistence on French sovereignty throughout the French Union. Universal suffrage within single electoral colleges was established throughout French Equatorial Africa, French West Africa, and Madagascar. The autonomy achieved by administrative districts within these territories set in motion a rapid process of political evolution, resulting in the emergence of fifteen independent states by the end of 1960.[104]

The demise of the French Union spelled the end of the idea of a global French state. Cartiérisme, an approach to former French colonies that dictated maintaining ties to them only as long as they turned a profit for metropolitan France, had carried the day. "The argument," Alfred Grosser observed, "was very matter of fact, 'If it will cost us more than it will bring in, why bother?' " But Grosser also noticed that "in a paradoxical fashion, one found among the partisans of a French retreat many of the intransigent defenders of a fully French Algeria.... What would have been scandalous applied to Algeria was reasonable applied to Senegal."[105]

In fact, traditional beliefs about the indissolubility of France's ties to its overseas possessions and its special Jacobin vocation remained salient aspects of French Republican political culture. But by the mid-1950s increasing proportion of the French people had come to believe that the only place these ideas could be given permanent expression was in Algeria, where the presence of over one million European citizens of the republic seemed naturally to distinguish it from any other part of overseas France. In this context the Fourth Republic produced its final candidate for a hegemonic formula describing the metropole's ties to France d'outre-mer: the idea of *Algérie française*—French Algeria.

Algérie, c'est la France

On September 30, 1955, the French government withdrew its delegation from the United Nations in protest against the General Assembly's decision to put the "question of Algeria" on its agenda. In his speech to the agenda committee the French representative had quoted article 2, paragraph 7, of the UN charter, insisting that Algerian affairs were "essentially within the domestic jurisdiction of France." Instructively, he did not mention the French Union, or Algeria's status within it, though such references had been prominent in Foreign Minister Robert Schuman's 1952 speech to the General Assembly protesting UN consideration of unrest in Tunisia and Morocco. At that time France had described both Tunisia and Morocco as lying within the "domestic jurisdiction" of France by virtue of their membership in the French Union.[106] In 1955, by classifying Algeria as part of metropolitan France itself and labeling that as "domestic," the French government signaled the change that had occurred in the conception of France it was promoting. As recorded in the minutes of the meeting, held on September 22, 1955, the French ambassador to the UN proceeded to argue that "Algeria had been united to France by the ordinance of 1834 and had since formed an integral part of metropolitan France, on an equal footing with the Île de France, Brittany, or Auvergne.... Some French provinces, whose French character no one dreamed of disputing, such as Savoy or the county of Nice, had been French for a shorter period than Algeria."[107]

As with each version of the French Union, so too this Algeria-centered hegemonic project required a highly selective construction of evidence and precedent.[108] Indeed the evidence is very strong that from the late nineteenth century through the 1950s, when citizens in European France imagined or heard reference to "la France," what they naturally and unselfconsciously called to mind were images of the hexagon, along with Corsica. In the French popular imagination, and within the perspective of the French political class, Algeria was a "colony," a part of "overseas France," not a portion of the metropole itself.

Traditional, matter-of-fact perceptions of Algeria as a colony are evident in the location and treatment accorded Algeria by French schoolbooks before World War II—in sections dealing, not with metropolitan France, but with the French Empire; in maps that mark Algeria as distinct from metropolitan France, submerged by its color code within the empire as a whole, and by its location within typologies of France's "possessions."[109] Both before and after World War II, maps labeled "France" produced by private as well as government publishers (and by mapmakers in countries friendly to France) depicted the hexagon only, often accompanied by an inset of Corsica, but almost never including the Algerian departments. Instead, Algeria was included within the colonial category by all major French world and colonial atlases.[110] In French art and literature an "exotic" Algeria was naturally and invariably evoked as a part of the "colonial" milieu. Just as Algerian veterans were counted among the colonial units marching in commemorative parades after World War I, so too was a large Algerian pavilion featured as a part of the great Colonial Exhibition of 1931.

The working perception of French political elites in the interwar period— that Algeria was *not* part of metropolitan France—are also reflected in the substance of interwar proposals to streamline policies toward overseas France by shifting responsibility for Algeria from the Interior Ministry to a larger Ministry for Overseas France, or some other similar framework. On the cover of a college textbook published in 1942 under Vichy auspices, Algeria was depicted as one of eleven different "colonies" linked to a hexagonal emblem by arrows radiating from "France."[111] Algerian affairs were also discussed within the colonial, not interior affairs section of L'Année Politique for the years 1945 and 1946 (before the formal establishment of the French Union). Despite the Fourth Republic's claims of the "metropolitan" status of Algeria, that area's separateness from the metropole was vividly and practically if not explicitly recognized when Algerian representatives to the Assembly of the French Union were included within the 50 percent drawn from France d'outre-mer and not from the 50 percent drawn from metropolitan France.

The claim that Algeria was neither a colony nor a part (however important) of France d'outre-mer relied heavily on the area's distinctive administrative history and formal juridical status as three departments of France, on the existence of a large number of European settlers (12 percent of Algeria's population in 1900 and far more in absolute terms than lived in the rest of overseas France), and on the results of viniculture, which helped transform the landscape and economy of Algeria into what many experienced as a trans-Mediterranean "prolongation of metropolitan France." It was true that during the 1930s Algeria was the only major part of the French Empire included automatically within French tariff boundaries.[112] In 1945 Robert Delavignette, whose pre- and post–World War II position as head of the School for Colonial Affairs constrained him to be as precise as possible in his formulations, footnoted his analysis of the challenges facing France in its former empire with the reminder that he was "not speaking here of Algeria."[113] In that same year the commission established by the Ministry of Colonies to study the question of colonial representation in the political institutions of the Fourth Republic delivered its report. Its proposal (never discussed by the first Constituent Assembly) was that approximately one-sixth of National Assembly deputies be drawn from the colonies, but not from Algeria, which was envisioned as part of metropolitan France.[114] Indeed, even after the establishment of the French Union (which, as noted, counted Algeria within overseas France and not the metropole), France had successfully insisted, in negotiations with its Western allies, that for purposes of both the Marshall Plan and the North Atlantic Treaty Organization, Algeria be considered an integral part of metropolitan France.[115] Public opinion surveys suggested that the population of the metropole saw Algeria as much more solidly tied to the hexagon than was the rest of overseas France. In 1954, polls showed that even the 35 percent of the French public who anticipated the eventual separation of French colonies from the metropole, did not include Algeria in that expectation.[116]

The potential for constructing a myth of France which included Algeria but not the rest of the prewar empire was obvious in the immediate postwar years. A leader of the Algerian Muslim delegation to the first Constituent Assembly introduced a bill in February 1946 for the complete enfranchisement of Algerian Muslims and creation of a binational parliament in Paris with a hundred Algerian deputies.[117] Partly as a result of fears raised by the Sétif disturbances of May 1945, parliamentarians representing Algeria's European population provided the Provisional Consultative Assembly and both Constituent Assemblies with a chorus of claims that Algeria enjoyed a special, even uniquely intimate relationship to continental France. "The two banks of the Mediterranean," said Charles Serre, colon deputy from Oran, "are the soil of the same fatherland."[118] None of this rhetoric evoking the principle of Algérie française was ever directly challenged by metropolitan politicians, foreshadowing this conception's potential as a candidate for hegemonic status. For metropolitan politicians with scant knowledge of overseas France, Algeria presented itself as the most convenient way to pledge their allegiance to the fundamental principle of permanent French sovereignty over all former dependencies. Thus did

Algeria feature far more regularly than any other single part of France d'outre-mer in postwar declarations by metropolitan personalities on behalf of the "undiscussability" of France's continued sovereignty over its prewar possessions. If, in the 1940s, few were willing to make a qualitative distinction between Algeria and other parts of overseas France, still the real intensity of commitment expressed by metropolitan politicians toward French Algeria, as opposed to French West Africa, French Equatorial Africa, French Indochina, or French Madagascar, was unmistakable. Even if all French territories were the "children of France," Algeria was "the most beautiful daughter," "the oldest daughter," "a region of France," or "nothing but a prolongation of France."[119]

Eight to ten years later, with the failure of both the French Union of free consent and the French Union of tutelary subordination as candidates for ideologically hegemonic notions of France, these sentiments, and the rhetoric surrounding them, were exploited to promote the more limited hegemonic project of Algérie française. In the 1870s and 1880s Algeria had been portrayed as the "New France," settled by heroic pioneers from Alsace and Lorraine. Their courage and determination were interpreted as the nation's historic riposte to the loss of those provinces to Germany in 1870. In the 1950s the concept was revived under a new name. Visions of French energy independence, linked to projected Saharan oil reserves, and of a vast frontier for economic expansion, helped transfer to Algérie française the concerns about France's great power status which had led to the migration of Alsatians and Lorrainers seventy years before, and which had fueled interest after World War II in the French Union. Without Algeria, warned Guy Mollet in December 1955, "France, would become a small power, in the second or third rank, deprived of its world role."[120] As constructed by the mythmakers of Algérie française, Algeria presented the only reliable, satisfying, and appropriate vehicle for expressing the civilizing mission of "eternal France." Algeria would be for France what North Africa had been for France's greatest ancestor, Rome—her richest and most important province.

The immediate impetus for the emergence of this Algeria-centered hegemonic project was a scattered outbreak of violence in the Aurès Mountains on the night of October 31–November 1, 1954, that signaled the beginning of the Algerian Revolution. The Mendès-France government's official reaction shows how disposed (or constrained), by the mid-1950s, even liberal elements within the French political class were to distinguish categorically between Algeria and the rest of overseas France. François Mitterrand was minister of the interior and therefore responsible for Algerian affairs. His immediate comment on the outbreak of the rebellion was to distinguish between "Tunisian and Moroccan nationalists," on the one hand, and "the rebels in Algeria," on the other. With the latter "the only negotiation is war. Algeria is France." With Algeria part of the metropole, he declared "secession [of Algeria] is inconceivable."[121]

Mitterrand's words were a faithful reflection of Pierre Mendès—France's own position, which the premier proclaimed in no uncertain terms before the National Assembly on November 12.

> One does not compromise when it comes to defending the internal peace of the nation, the unity and the integrity of the Republic. The Algerian departments are part of the French Republic. They have been French for a long time, and they are irrevocably French.... Between them and metropolitan France there can be no conceivable secession.
>
> This must be clear once and for all, in Algeria and in metropolitan France as much as in the outside world. (Applause from left, centre, right and extreme right.) Never will France—any French government or parliament, whatever may be their particularistic tendencies—yield on this fundamental principle.
>
> Mesdames, Messieurs, several deputies have made comparisons between French policy in Algeria and Tunisia. I declare that no parallel is more erroneous, that no comparison is falser, or more dangerous. Ici, c'est la France![122]

In the final months of his premiership Mendès-France appointed Jacques Soustelle as governor-general of Algeria. In spring 1946 Soustelle had been an enthusiastic supporter of the French Union of free consent. In 1954 Soustelle still clung to hopes that the French Union could be reinvigorated along federalist lines. However, during his year as governor-general of Algeria he came into intimate contact with the large French population of Algeria. Influenced by their passionate commitment and convinced that only France could rescue the Muslim majority from impoverishment and National Liberation Front (FLN) tyranny, Soustelle abandoned the French Union and emerged as the leading apostle of the complete integration of Algeria, and only Algeria, into France. The dramatic shift in Soustelle's thinking corresponded exactly to the displacement of conceptions of a global French state under the rubric of the French Union by a vision of France, in the hexagon and in Algeria, divided by the Mediterranean "as Paris was divided by the Seine." If "Tunisian solutions" (i.e., various degrees of autonomy or independence) might be implemented for restless parts of the Union, a more profound and intimate integration of its Algerian departments could be France's only response to troubles there. Soustelle argued,

> France is at home here, or better still, Algeria and all its inhabitants form an integral part of France, one and indivisible.

That is the alpha and omega. All must know, here and elsewhere, that France will no sooner leave Algeria than she will leave Provençe or Brittany. Whatever may happen, Algeria's destiny is French.

Yes, gentlemen, the destiny of Algeria is French! That is the significance of the choice that France has made—the choice whose name is integration.

We must pursue this objective unswervingly and unreservedly.[123]

Soustelle's term as governor-general ended in January 1956, at which time he issued a report containing the definitive exposition of the hegemonic project with which he had become so closely identified—establishment of Algeria as a commonsensical part of France's self-conception. "Integration" would mean strict "equality of rights and duties among both the French-born and the Moslem citizens in Algeria." This notion would require sweeping administrative reforms, the unification of public services between Algeria and metropolitan France, the application of identical labor codes and pension plans, the abolition of the governor-general's office and the Algerian Assembly in favor of a Ministry of Algeria, and a much larger Algerian delegation to the National Assembly (to be chosen by a single electoral college).[124] He stressed how important it was not to evince even a theoretical willingness to negotiate with rebel leaders. To do so, he argued, would be to suggest the possibility that France's commitment to maintain its sovereignty over Algeria might not be permanent.[125] This had been, in fact, the policy of Prime Minister Edgar Faure's government, which defined "complete integration" as meaning that "without discrimination all inhabitants [of Algeria] would enjoy and be subject to the rights and duties, the opportunities and obligations, which pertain to the status of French citizens."[126]

During the election campaign which ended in December 1955 the Socialist leader Guy Mollet implied his willingness to consider reforms in Algeria. But soon after assuming the premiership, Mollet visited Algiers and was confronted with a massive and violent display of European opposition to his appointment of the liberal-minded General Georges Catroux as resident minister for Algeria. The depth of these sentiments, expressed by working-class people with whom Mollet closely identified, and the echoes they produced in metropolitan France convinced Mollet to shift his government's policy from a willingness to experiment toward an uncompromising commitment to the maintenance of Algérie française. The Catroux nomination was withdrawn. In his stead Mollet picked Robert Lacoste, whose firm attitudes toward Algeria mirrored those of Soustelle. Giving full-throated endorsement to Mollet's request for special powers to prosecute the war in Algeria, Soustelle urged the premier to define the question of Algeria in terms that would identify it with French concerns

about the basic integrity of the country: "Tell France that this is not a
police operation nor is it a colonial war.... Algeria is not far away... it
is French soil, so close to us, so close to our heart, to our will, that it is
a province of the continent. Tell the country that the moment has come
to choose between an effort that will bring salvation, and an incurable
decline. I am convinced that it will refuse decline. (Lively applause except
on the extreme left)."[127]

France's behavior at the UN, from 1955 through 1957, was consistent
with the Algeria-centered hegemonic project for the definition of France
which Soustelle articulated and Mollet embraced. When, in 1957, France
agreed to address UN meetings on the subject, Foreign Minister Christian
Pineau described as "indisputable" the principle that the "question of
Algeria was... a French domestic matter."[128] France, Pineau explained,
would make its views known to members of the committee. But that did
not mean "we ask them to make their views known to us."[129] The French
government's position was that the UN Charter's prohibition against interference in affairs that were "essentially within [a member state's] domestic jurisdiction" applied unambiguously to Algeria.

Pineau cited the NATO treaty, which included the Algerian departments
within French territory, to support the view that the frontiers of Algeria
"were the frontiers of France." And he cited the opinions of selected
international jurists to the effect that "Algeria was a group of French
departments and formed part of the metropolitan territory." With similar
arguments emphasizing the financial sacrifices France had made on behalf
of its Algerian departments and the more than one million European French
living there, both Pineau and Soustelle insisted that images of the rebellion
in Algeria as an anticolonialist struggle for national self-determination were
inadmissible. "The existing situation in Algeria," said Pineau, "was nothing more nor less than a rebellion aiming at the dismemberment of the
territory of France."[130] In support of the government's propaganda campaign the French embassy in the United States published a brochure,
"France Overseas," whose first sentence began, "Algeria has never been
a colony." On the cover of the brochure was a world map portraying
Algeria—distinguished from "overseas territories," "trust territories," and
"overseas departments"—in the same black ink as the continental
hexagon.[131]

The success of this third postwar "hegemonic project," compared to its
predecessors, was indicated by the explicit acceptance expressed by the
Western democracies of French claims that Algeria formed an integral part
of France.[132] Within France itself its relative success is evidenced by the
consistency with which every governing coalition, between 1954 and the
end of the Fourth Republic in May 1958, whether led by liberal-leaning

Radicals, conservative-leaning Radicals, or Socialists, maintained a high-profile commitment to one or another version of French Algeria. Although by 1956 the Communist party and elements within other parties favored the effective separation of Algeria from France, the strong commitments of the Europeans of Algeria, Gaullists, Conservatives, Poujadists, the MRP, as well as many Socialists and Radicals to the principle of Algérie française made it impossible for any government to form that was not willing to commit itself to permanent French rule over Algeria. Indeed, as I. R. Campell and others have observed, by the mid-1950s the question of Algeria had become determinative not simply of which political coalitions could be governing coalitions, but also of whether the regime defined by the constitution of the Fourth Republic could survive.

In 1959 Charles de Gaulle, president of France within the new Fifth Republic, publicly included Algeria among those overseas dependencies which would be given a choice of three options: integration into France, association with France, or independence from France. According to Albertini, "No other than de Gaulle himself had thus given up the traditional premise, hitherto considered indisputable, that Algeria was an indivisible part of the national territory."[133] Albertini's claim that Algeria's status as an "indivisible part of the national territory" had been "hitherto considered indisputable" and was a "traditional premise" of French political life is tantamount to asserting that, under the Fourth Republic, the ideological hegemony of Algérie française had indeed been established.

Acceptance of this view put forward by Albertini, Tony Smith, and other observers would entail a judgment that Algeria's status as an "integral part of France" had, at least for a period of time in the mid-1950s, passed the ideological hegemony threshold.[134] Indeed several Fourth Republic governments did their best to act as if Algeria was an unquestionable part of the national territory. As early as March 1955 the National Assembly approved a government request for authority to declare "a state of emergency" in any department of France (including those of Algeria). The special powers accruing to the government in affected departments, and the attendant restrictions on civil rights and civil liberties, were justified as necessary to defend "the territorial integrity of the Republic," in view of the "threat to the national collectivity" posed by the rebellion in Algeria.[135] Although the government acknowledged that the legislation would infringe on democracy in designated departments, it successfully opposed an amendment that would have limited the legislature's grant of authorization to the Algerian departments.[136] Whereas only professional soldiers had been sent to fight in Indochina, hundreds of thousands of conscripts were dispatched to Algeria. French officials described the struggle in Algeria not as a war, but as a "pacification" campaign to defeat "terrorism" and restore order. In accordance with this terminology, captured FLN fighters were treated as criminals, not prisoners of war.[137]

During the first year and a half of the insurrection, most of the press exercised a substantial amount of self-censorship. But by 1956 the government felt it could no longer rely on the instincts or prudence of many editors and publishers. Reflecting its commitment to constructing a hegemonically established conception of Algeria as France, the Faure government "responded to press criticism of the war or of pacification techniques by seizing the offending papers."[138] This seizure was part of a widening campaign of prosecution and censorship against publication of "seditious," "treasonous" or "defeatist" material. In Algeria itself virtually all leftist and progressivist newspapers from mainland France were banned. Certain issues of "moderate" newspapers, such as *Le Monde, France-Soir, La Croix,* and even the *Saturday Evening Post,* were also seized in Algeria. Seizures on the mainland of "leftist" newspapers, including *France-Observateur* and *L'Express,* "rose from nine in 1955 to 17 in 1956; 34 in 1957 and 23 in the last five months of the Republic in 1958."[139]

Far from exhibiting consensus over the definition of Algeria as France, however, the very need to control through censorship the range of public debate suggests the failure of this hegemonic project, the failure to institutionalize France's incorporation of Algeria past the ideological hegemony threshold. This failure is also apparent in the habits of government ministries and in the ordinary language which even its partisans used to advance the idea of Algérie française. The official view of the last several Fourth Republic governments was that Algeria was France, even, it was often said, an "integral part" or a "prolongation" of the metropole. Until the summer of 1958, however, stamps issued for use in Algeria bore an *Algérie postes* or *Algérie, RF* inscription which distinguished them from stamps issued for use on the mainland (including Corsica). Routine maps produced by the Ministry of Public Works displayed France as a continental hexagon, with Corsica included as an "insert," and no depiction of or reference to Algeria. Enunciation of the official view of Algeria's status, in books, articles, and public forums, almost invariably included references to metropolitan France's policies *toward* Algeria, to the strength of ties *between* the metropole and Algeria, or *between* France and Algeria.

Thus no deputy objected to what was in fact the perfectly natural wording of the government's request for emergency powers in 1955. The bill, as proposed and passed, gave the government power to declare a state of emergency "in any part of the metropolitan territory, of Algeria or the overseas departments." Had Algeria genuinely been understood as an integral part of the metropole, or even of "France," it would not have been necessary or appropriate to include "Algeria" in such a list of the "French territories" to which the law would apply. As minister for Algeria, Robert Lacoste offered the government's primary defense before the National Assembly of its September 1957 *loi cadre* for Algeria—a proposal for the reorganization of Algerian departments and the abolition of the Algerian Assembly. While explicitly declaring Algeria "an integral part of the French Republic," he implicitly acknowledged the separateness of Algeria from France by endorsing the legislation as capable of maintaining "indissoluble bonds *between* France and Algeria."[140]

After beginning his February 1957 speech at the United Nations by explicitly endorsing the view that "Algeria was a group of French departments and formed part of the metropolitan territory," Foreign Minister Christian Pineau went on to explain how his government's policy of pacification was designed to bring the French and Moslem communities of Algeria closer together "and to increase their common trust *in metropolitan France*." In the latter portion of his address Pineau discussed the merits and demerits of various solutions to the problem of relations "*between* France and Algeria."[141] He reminded his audience that Algeria was "a poor country" which needed France because it "could not live without *external* assistance." Jacques Soustelle spoke on behalf of the French government to the same session of the United Nations. In his remarks about subsidies for Algeria drawn from the budget "of metropolitan France" he evinced the same disjunction between an official commitment to Algeria as an extension of metropolitan France and his own working conception of Algeria as a separate entity.[142] Similar language was used in the propaganda in favor of Algérie française distributed by the French government.[143]

By their very syntax these claims, and the everyday pattern of French political discourse they illustrate, prove that the cognitive integration of Algeria into France had not been accomplished. What is implied, instead, is a commonsensical, presumptive image of Algeria as a separate entity with a relationship *to* France. For only if the speakers or authors themselves did not share, or did not believe their audiences shared, commonsensical images of Algeria as a part *of* France would such language have been uttered or written so regularly, unselfconsciously, and without objection, comment, or correction.

To appreciate this point about the commonsensical image the French had of their country in the mid-1950s, one need only consider how "nonsensical" it would have been for these speakers to have discussed problems relating to other "regions of France," such as Burgundy, by referring to relations "between" France and Burgundy, or to the policies "of metropolitan France toward Burgundy." Far from supporting images of a united country, such language, had it ever been uttered, could only have been understood by French audiences to imply some sort of radical reinterpretation of the meaning of France that excluded Burgundy as an integral part of it.

In October 1955 the leftist *Les Temps Modernes* published a lead editorial titled "L'Algérie n'est pas la France."[144] By mid-1956 respectable members of the French political class were beginning to offer arguments which explicitly treated Algeria as an asset or a liability to France rather than as a part of it, and abandonment of Algeria as at least an option deserving of serious consideration. The single most important of these contributions to the French debate over Algeria was made by Raymond Aron, a respected, "nonpolitical" staff writer for the conservative newspaper *Le Figaro,* in a booklet titled *La tragédie algérienne.* His purpose, he declared at the beginning of his essay, was "without illusions...to analyze the particulars of this diabolical problem, which obstructs the future of France."[145] Explicitly questioning the claim that "indissoluble ties" bound Algeria to the French mainland, he contended that Algerian independence could no longer be excluded as a possibility. Aron portrayed the insurrection as part of an irresistible tide of decolonization, France's transition from a world power to a European power as inevitable, and the cost of ruling Algeria as far higher than any benefit accruing to France. If nothing else, he said, "it seems necessary for me to break the taboos"— taboos responsible for freezing French attitudes toward Algeria.[146] Aron's booklet was immediately attacked by *Le Figaro,* but proponents of Algérie française found it impossible to avoid responding directly to Aron's explicit attempt to change the terms of legitimate debate about Algeria.

Soon after Aron's essay appeared, Soustelle published his rejoinder— *Le drame algérien et la décadence française: Response à Raymond Aron.* The main thrust of Soustelle's attack reflected his commitment to the hegemonic project of Algérie française—the establishment of tight links between unquestioned French beliefs about their country and the maintenance of Algeria as part of it. Aron, argued Soustelle, made a fundamental error by referring to the Muslims of Algeria as "our friends" and not "our brothers."[147] He categorically rejected Aron's argument from analogy, which classified Algeria with Indochina, Tunisia, and Morocco, instead of as part of France. According to Soustelle, "We must say once, and say twenty times, 'The Algerian problem is not a classic problem of decolonization.' Trying to stretch Algeria on the Procrustean bed of a rhetorical theme: colonialism—independence, one mutilates it or kills it."[148] Soustelle labeled as signs of decadence Aron's willing embrace of a despairing view of France's future, his refusal to apply the lessons of the Resistance to the challenge posed by the struggle in Algeria, and his "defeatist" attempt to portray "abandonment" as "heroism." Aron thereby betrayed the ideals of universalism, freedom, and greatness, without which France could not be France. These direct appeals to elements of French political culture which remained hegemonic reflected the grounds of argumentation Soustelle preferred.

But for all his attention to the fundamental flaws in Aron's terminology, categorizations, and system of values, Soustelle could not afford to ignore the substantive claims Aron had made about Algeria's contingent relationship to France. Although he rejected Aron's application of cost-benefit thinking to Algeria as no more appropriate than questioning whether "Corsica, la Lozere, les Causses, or the mountains of Cevennes" were turning a profit, he apparently found it necessary to do his own cost-benefit analysis. On the benefit side he described Algeria's essential role as a market for French manufactured goods, a field for investment, and a source of oil.[149] As for costs, he calculated it would take four trillion francs to "repatriate" the Europeans of Algeria in the event of an FLN victory— much more, he averred, than the cost of continuing the pacification campaign to a successful conclusion.[150]

The direction of change within French political discourse in general is indicated by the questions asked by French pollsters about Algeria and in the responses they received. These trace a definite trend toward classifying Algeria as separate and separable from France. The French Institute of Public Opinion conducted many different surveys of French opinion about Algeria beginning in August 1955. In the questions the pollsters asked one can see their implicit judgment of the boundaries of acceptable debate. In August 1955 the only question focusing specifically on Algeria asked respondents no more than their degree of "interest in news about Algeria." Beginning in October 1955 respondents were offered choices about the possible future status of Algeria, but the range was limited to favoring "the status quo of Algeria as departments of France" or supporting "less tight bonds." In April 1956 the range was widened and the possibility of separation made explicit in a poll that posed two, and only two, extreme alternatives—"to repress the rebels using all necessary military means" or "to negotiate with the rebels to accord independence to Algeria." In that same month a survey, repeated several times over the next year and a half, asked respondents if they thought "Algeria will be French within five (ten) years." In July 1957 two new questions appeared asking whether respondents favored independence for Algeria and negotiations with the rebels. By 1959 respondents were being presented with "secession" of Algeria as one "option" for French policy, in a list of other options that included "Frenchification" and "association."[151]

In his analysis of the data generated by these polls Charles-Robert Ageron argues that Lacoste was clearly wrong in September 1957 when he

claimed that "French opinion was entirely hostile to Algerian independence."[152] The data Ageron presents demonstrate that the proportion of
French who doubted France could or should maintain Algeria as "departments of France" decreased steadily beginning early in 1956, and that
diehard Algérie française sentiment did not exceed 25 percent by the end
of the Fourth Republic.[153]

Conclusion

Between 1945 and 1958 three substantial attempts to establish a hegemonic conception of France larger than the hexagon (plus Corsica) failed.
Yet the level of institutionalization achieved by the third of these projects,
focused on Algeria and not on the former empire as a whole, differed
qualitatively from its predecessors.

Abandonment of the Union of free consent during the second Constituent Assembly was linked to the replacement of one governing coalition,
among Socialists, Communists, and overseas native deputies, with another—between the MRP and Socialists. Socialists abandoned the idea of
the Union of free consent in favor of the Union of tutelary subordination.
This shift was precipitated by politicians calculating that within the second
Constituent Assembly and in the emerging Fourth Republic the Union of
free consent could not form part of the platform of a winning coalition.
Thus the amount of "disruption" its abandonment triggered within the
French political community could be measured only in terms of the change
in the opportunities of different parties or individuals to participate in
governing coalitions. Failure to include even an evocation of the Union of
free consent within the constitution of the Fourth Republic, and the domination of "incumbent level" rather than "regime level" concerns in determining political stands on the issue, makes it clear that the hegemonic
project associated with the Union of free consent fell considerably short
of passing the regime threshold.

Although vaguely incorporated within the terms of the Fourth Republic
Constitution, the global Union of tutelary subordination was only marginally more successful as a hegemonic project for the definition of the
French political community. Its failure is indicated by the absence of any
sense of threat to the integrity of the Fourth Republic regime attendant
upon policies which actually, if not formally, abandoned the French
Union's constitutive meaning. Between 1947 and 1957, whatever difficulties various Socialist-, MRP-, and Radical-led governments may have
experienced in connection with policies toward Indochina, Tunisia, Morocco, French West Africa, or French Equatorial Africa, decisions about

these policies were not shaped by concerns that the regime itself could collapse as a result of a failure to abide by the official terms of the French Union.

But Algeria was different—marked out from the rest of the French Union by successive Fourth Republic legislatures, by the presence of more than a million European settlers, by the reactions of Mendès-France and Mitterrand to the outbreak of the revolt, by Soustelle's energetic campaign in favor of *intégration* and Algérie française, by the behavior of French diplomats, and by large-scale military operations and economic investments intended to maintain Algeria as a "prolongation of France." The zenith of this hegemonic project was reached in 1955 and 1956, during which time the terms of French political discourse strongly discouraged, if they did not forbid, discussion of Algeria in terms which questioned its future as part of France.

Proof that this project had at least passed the regime threshold in the state-building direction is the crisis of 1958, when the Fourth Republic regime collapsed amid accusations that the succession of fragile governments it was producing endangered France's ability to maintain sovereignty over Algeria. As analyzed in Chapter 7, what had come to preoccupy Fourth Republic politicians by late 1957 was not the ways the Algerian question might affect their careers or their parties, but the possibility that it could trigger civil war or otherwise endanger the regime itself. Such concerns remained decisive in government calculations about Algerian policy until June 1961, two and a half years after the establishment of the Fifth Republic, thus locating the Algerian problem of late 1957 to mid-1961 as near, but to the right, of the regime threshold.[154]

Of course France did subsequently separate from Algeria. A necessary condition for the disengagement policies which led to that outcome was the inability of partisans of Algérie française to establish their commitments as hegemonic beliefs. But though necessary, this was not a sufficient condition. The policies that led to separation of Algeria from France were sustainable only within the framework of a new regime in which, eventually, the consequences of moving toward resolution of Algeria's status could be measured by the careers of politicians and not of republics.

CHAPTER FIVE

Patterns of Hegemonic Change: Britain and Ireland, France and Algeria

Chapters 3 and 4 have shown how the British and French states failed to sustain the integration of Ireland and Algeria. In Britain a hegemonic conception of Ireland's incorporation within the United Kingdom, successfully defended in the 1830s and 1840s, no longer prevailed in the 1880s. In France, three successive attempts to establish hegemonic presumptions regarding Algeria's status, either as part of a French Union, or as part of France itself, failed. In both cases, in Britain by 1885 and in France by 1957, the boundaries of the state and of the political community emerged on the national agenda as bitterly divisive but open questions. In this chapter I examine explanations for why and how this happened.

Gramscian Explanations for Outcomes of Wars of Position

Ideologically hegemonic conceptions provide stabilizing distortions and rationalizations of complex realities, inconsistent desires, and arbitrary distributions of valued resources. They are presumptions which exclude outcomes, options, or questions from public consideration; thus they advantage those elites well positioned to profit from prevailing cleavage patterns and issue definitions. That hegemonic beliefs do not shift fluidly with changing realities and marginal interests is what makes them important. That they require some correspondence to "objective" realities and interests is what limits their life and the conditions under which they can be established and maintained. Though no detailed theory of hegemonic change can be crucially tested by comparing the Irish problem's reemergence in late nineteenth-century Britain with the failure of three post–World War II efforts to achieve hegemonic status for enlarged notions of France, the cases can establish the plausibility of some key hypotheses. This effort can be understood in Gramscian terms as a probe into the dynamics of "wars of position."

Antonio Gramsci distinguished between "wars of position" and "wars of movement," both of which terms refer to political struggles within a territorial state. A "war of position" entails political competition over which ideas and values will be accepted by leading strata of a state as the "concrete fantasy" that will achieve hegemonic status. Though such struggles are subtle, nonviolent, and conducted as much in the press and in educational and religious institutions as in the political arena, their outcome is of far-reaching importance. For whatever particular interpretation of reality is contained in the set of conceptions enshrined as hegemonic will decisively advantage certain groups by privileging their particular preferences and attitudes as unassailable assumptions of community life. By linking particular conceptions and preferences to commonsensically established myths, symbols, and categories, hegemonic ideas camouflage particular distributions of power. "Wars of movement," on the other hand, refer to the direct clash of interests that surround acute crises, when governments or regimes can change hands as a result of illegal or semi-legal actions by political groups.[1]

Gramsci lays great stress on the investigation of wars of position and the "organic crises" that surround them. He advocates diachronic comparisons of societies at different stages of struggle to discover the conditions under which different ideologies attain or lose hegemonic status.[2] In *The Modern Prince* Gramsci attempted to generalize about the patterns such struggles display and the factors that determine the outcome of competition among hegemonic projects. The result of his effort, though limited, is suggestive. The origin of organic crises, he maintained, lies in drastic changes which bring to light "incurable contradictions." These shocks undermine the self-confidence of state elites and ruling groups and weaken the ability of prevailing conceptions to limit entry of new kinds of questions into the public domain. Among the likely precipitants of such crises (which, Gramsci notes, may last for decades) are failure in some crucial enterprise, such as defeat in war, or a large-scale increase in the political mobilization of lower strata.[3]

These contradictions, or shocks, in effect create gross discrepancies between prevailing conceptions and "stubborn realities." Although the central tenet of Gramscian thinking is the susceptibility of people to accept contingent or even false and counterproductive beliefs as commonsensically valid, Gramsci also emphasized the difficulty of sustaining beliefs which too explicitly, directly, and systematically are contradicted by immediate perceptions. This may be thought of as a hypothesis about the impossibility of "absolute distortion" in achieving and maintaining hegemonic status for particular beliefs. Implicit here is the notion that only by arranging at least a modicum of satisfaction for the groups from whom consent is required and reaching a minimum correspondence between objective conditions and ideological pictures, can hegemonic conceptions fulfill their primary function: the containment and political neutralization of latent tensions which, if unleashed, would threaten the power of those whose interests the conceptions serve.[4]

In this regard, Gramsci suggests that counterhegemonic ideas, offering a more comforting and "parsimonious" mystification of both "stubborn reality" and elements of irreducible self-interest, will be a necessary component in the overthrow of an existing hegemonic conception or an important factor in the failure of some other contender for that status.[5] The point is that no politician, confronted with beliefs honored or advanced as hegemonic, is likely to treat them as problematic unless another available schema can articulate those beliefs as *an interpretation* of reality and the imperatives of national life, rather than as the direct and unavoidable expression of immutable facts and ultimate values. It is thus reasonable to expect that change in the status of hegemonic beliefs, and the outcome of struggles to establish beliefs as hegemonic, will be linked to the availability and mobilization of new ways of thinking, and not simply to the accumulation of evidence.

Political and ideological entrepreneurship is the transmission belt which carries ideas with hegemonic potential forward into the political arena. It is practiced by bold leaders, intellectuals, and the organizations they build or control. Of course most people who challenge basic assumptions of their community's political life fail. Whether because of their own shortcomings, the solidity of prevailing beliefs, or the ineffectiveness of their ideas, their likely fate is dismissal as either cranks or criminals. Still, the inventors and promoters of hegemonic projects are people who understand the decisive importance of "reclothing political questions in cultural forms."[6] By shaping the cognitions and values of elites and masses, these entrepreneurs seek to (re)define, for their own purposes, the allowable boundaries and the appropriate stakes of political competition.[7]

In sum, what Gramsci seems to think necessary for the establishment or breakdown of hegemonic constructions is a combination of three elements. To overthrow an established ideologically hegemonic conception or explain its breakdown Gramsci posits the presence of all three of the following:

> a severe contradiction between the conception advanced as hegemonic and the stubborn realities it purports to describe;

an appropriately fashioned alternative interpretation of political reality capable of reorganizing competition to the advantage of particular groups;

dedicated political-ideological entrepreneurs who can operate successfully where fundamental assumptions of political life have been thrown open to question, and who see better opportunities in competition over basic "rules of the game" than in competition for marginal advantage according to existing rules.

Obversely, establishing a belief as hegemonic, or successfully defending its status as such, requires *at least* one of the following: substantial correspondence between the claims of the belief and the political realities it purports to describe; the absence of a widely accepted basis for an alternative interpretation; *or* the absence of political entrepreneurs capable of profiting from its overthrow or breakdown.

This chapter treats these inferences from Gramsci as explanations for the success or failure of hegemonic projects. The breakdown and failure of British and French hegemonic projects pertaining to Ireland and Algeria, as traced in Chapters 3 and 4, are interpreted in this chapter as functions of the ways grossly discrepant beliefs, new ways of thinking, and entrepreneurial leadership interacted with each other. Testing the plausibility of these Gramscian explanations for patterns of change in British and French beliefs about the shape of their states requires analyzing the impact of Irish and Algerian national mobilization on the integrity of official British and French claims regarding the status of Ireland and Algeria; the role of historicist, imperialist, and social Darwinist ideas in Britain, and of cultural relativism, Cartiérist rationalism, and desperate yearnings for national vindication in post—World War II France; and the leadership strategies of British and French politicians who sought to exploit the circumstances of wars of position over Ireland and Algeria to further their own interests.

Ireland Erupts, 1867–1885

The Irish question faded into obscurity after the failed 1848 "rising." From the mid-1880s until World War I, however, the political disposition of Ireland was the single most important issue in British politics. Breakdown of the ideologically hegemonic status of British beliefs about Ireland's place in the United Kingdom was the permissive cause of this transformation. But how is this breakdown of hegemony to be explained?

From the point of view of practical politics, consideration of the national dimension of the Irish question began with Herbert Gladstone's sudden disclosure on December 15, 1885, that his father favored home rule for Ireland. This event was followed by William Gladstone's proposal of his first Home Rule Bill in the House of Commons in 1886. Gladstone's move marked the end of all taboos discouraging British politicians from treating the national-political future of Ireland as if it might not already have been permanently settled. Three moments of Irish nationalist mobilization laid the groundwork for Gladstone's bill. Cumulatively they presented the British political elite with Irish realities that were grossly discrepant with official presumptions of Ireland's unproblematic and undisturbable integration into the Union. These were, first, the abortive rising of March 1867 and the subsequent terrorism of Irish nationalist groups associated with it; second, the Irish National Land League's mass mobilization of Irish peasants from 1879 to 1882, known as the Land War; and third, the transformation, between 1877 and 1885, of a timid and largely ineffective Irish parliamentary presence into a bold and disciplined nationalist delegation to the British Parliament.

The poorly coordinated Fenian rising of February–March 1867, sponsored by the U.S.-based Irish Republican (Revolutionary) Brotherhood, was easily crushed. Subsequent actions in Ireland and Britain by frustrated Fenians included the killing of a British policeman in Manchester and the dynamiting of the wall of Clerkenwell Prison in London, which killed 12 civilians and injured 120. This violence, in combination with the rising itself, attracted more British press attention to Irish affairs than in any period since the end of the great famine. Figure 3 illustrates the changing percentage of space allocated by the *Times* to matters pertaining to Ireland.[8]

Fenian rebellion in Ireland and terrorism in Britain led John Stuart Mill to consider the Irish question anew. For a generation there had been no public discussion of the once and future question "What is to be done with Ireland?" In his 1868 pamphlet "England and Ireland," Mill warned that with respect to Ireland the "upper and middle classes [were] basking in a fools paradise." "Fenianism," he continued, "has burst, like a clap of thunder in a clear sky, unlooked for and unintelligible."[9] Much as they condemned Fenian terrorism, conservative commentators shared this view of its stimulative effect. While quoting old anti-Repeal polemics to argue that any contemporary separatist proposal was "nonsense," the *London Quarterly Review* admitted that in the immediate aftermath of the Clerkenwell bombing, Ireland had become "the problem of problems to the English statesmen."[10]

Gladstone construed "these painful and horrible manifestations" as perhaps designed by Providence "to invite this nation to greater search of its own heart and spirit and conscience with reference to the condition of

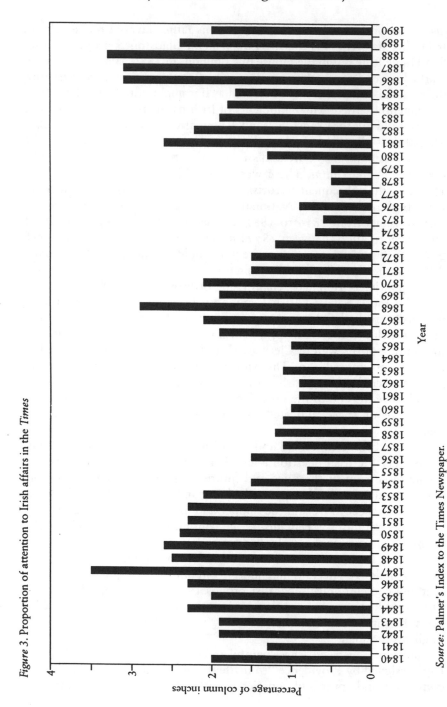

Figure 3. Proportion of attention to Irish affairs in the *Times*

Source: Palmer's Index to the Times Newspaper.

Ireland and the legislation affecting that country."[11] Indeed Ireland dominated the election of 1868, bringing William Gladstone his first premiership and eliciting from him a pledge that would shape his entire career.
"My mission," he declared, "is to pacify Ireland." Addressing Parliament
in 1869 concerning his bill to disestablish the Irish (Anglican) church,
Gladstone offered a compelling analysis of Fenian terrorism's role in providing the shock necessary to remove the "privileged" status of popular
beliefs about Ireland and the institutions of British rule there.

> The influence of Fenianism was this—that when the habeas corpus Act was
> suspended, when all the consequent proceedings occurred, when the tran-
> quillity of the great city of Manchester was disturbed, when the metropolis
> itself was shocked and horrified by an inhuman outrage, when a sense of
> insecurity went abroad far and wide . . . when the inhabitants of the different
> towns of the country were swearing themselves in as special constables for
> the maintenance of life and property—then it was when *these phenomena
> came home to the popular mind, and produced that attitude of attention and
> preparedness on the part of the whole population of this country* which
> qualified them to embrace, in a manner foreign to their habits in other times,
> the vast importance of the Irish controversy.[12]

Twelve years separate the Fenian rising from the outbreak of the Land
War in 1879, and another three years separate the end of the Land War
in 1882 from the sweeping victory of Parnell's Home Rule party in 1885.
Historically, however, Fenianism, the Land War, and Parnell's hold on
the balance of power in the House of Commons are best understood as
components of an unprecedentedly sustained mobilization of Irish nationalism that intruded with increasing disruptiveness into the consciousness,
and the calculations, of the British political class.

With most of the Irish Republican Brotherhood's main operatives in
prison, IRB-sponsored violence subsided after 1869. Once released, however, many veterans of the rising found in the severely depressed agricultural conditions of 1877–79 a ready-made opportunity to resume the
national struggle in a broader-based, more effective manner. Taking advantage of peasant fears of another catastrophic famine, the sympathy of
Catholic priests for the suffering of their parishioners, and long traditions
in Ireland of organized agrarian violence, Michael Davitt and other former
Fenians initiated the Irish National Land League in October 1879. Closely
if not officially tied to the Clan na Gael and other Fenian groups in the
United States, and enjoying financial support from Irish Americans, the
Land League developed quickly. Its founders hoped that, in what was
called a "New Departure" from straight-out insurrectionism, a large-scale

movement for tenant rights and land ownership would develop into the mobilizational basis for a disciplined national revolution.[13]

Low grain prices, a series of bad harvests, and the return of starvation to some sections of Ireland made it increasingly difficult for landlords (virtually all Protestant) to collect rents from their Catholic tenants. Eviction rates rose to unprecedented levels, producing much bitterness. The Land League called for an end to evictions and for substantial reduction in rents as a prelude to subsequent demands for peasant proprietorship. Its declaration of a rent strike was accompanied by waves of violence against landlords, estate agents, and farmers who agreed to occupy the houses and lands seized from tenants who had not paid their rent. Juries refused to convict the perpetrators. In some parts of Ireland it was reported that courts set up by the Land League exercised more authority than those of the state. From late 1879 through 1882 much of Ireland was effectively ungovernable.[14] London responded with both a severe Coercion Act, under which the law was suspended in wide areas of Ireland and the leadership of the Land League imprisoned, and substantial land reform—the Land Act of 1881.

The Land War, it has been said, "is to Irish history rather as the revolution of 1789 is to French history."[15] It combined, within a quasi-legal framework, mass demonstrations, support for evicted tenants, legal protection, ostracism, and violence. Its intrusion upon the consciousness of the British political class is evident by the steep rise it triggered in the *Time's* coverage of Irish affairs (see Fig. 3). The apparently wild nature of the Irish, as conveyed in hundreds of stories under the heading "agrarian outrage," and the explicit threat to property rights expressed by tenants' refusal to pay rents may not have generated sympathy in Britain, but they did gain attention. Most fundamentally the Land War registered the fact of an Irish discontent so deep and pervasive that blame for the disturbances could no longer be attributed simply to the outside agitation of U.S.-based Fenians.[16]

In 1880 Disraeli dissolved Parliament, hoping to exploit British backlash against Irish unrest. In the general election of that year, Disraeli demanded rigorous coercion in Ireland. Gladstone countered with a call for reforms to reconcile the Irish to union with Great Britain. The sweeping victory gained by Gladstone was his second. Both were built, in large measure, upon his public commitment to solve the Irish problem by prudent reforms. These victories were followed by at least five general elections between 1885 and 1922 whose outcome was largely determined by struggles over what to do with Ireland.[17]

For British politicians as well as the British public, the galling intrusion of Ireland into "their" affairs was identified with the rise to power of one man—Charles Stewart Parnell, "the uncrowned king of Ireland." He appeared at Westminster at the head of an Irish nationalist party large enough to disrupt the regular conduct of parliamentary business and trigger fundamental realignments within and between the dominant British parties. Parnell's tactics and the discipline of his party made it impossible for British politicians to escape the "incurable contradictions" entailed in treating Ireland as both colony and home territory.[18]

Corresponding to an odd tradition in Irish nationalist history, Parnell was a Protestant landlord. As a young man he was inspired to enter politics by the Fenian rising of 1867. In 1875 he was elected to Parliament. For twenty-five years Irish members of Parliament, whether returned as members of the Independent Irish party, or Isaac Butt's Home Rule party, and for whatever reasons of corruption, timidity, sloth, or circumstances, had failed to generate parliamentary interest in the problems of Ireland. Butt's 1874 motion for home rule was defeated by a vote of 458 to 61.

In 1877, against this background, Parnell and a few close associates gained control of the Home Rule party. They replaced Butt's loyalism and insistence on "respect for the traditions of the House." Parnell organized repeated filibusters, forcing the attention of members to Irish matters while obstructing parliamentary business in all other areas.[19] Obstruction, and the militant nationalism which it conveyed, brought wide support to Parnell in Ireland and among Irish Americans. It also gained the grudging respect of the IRB, which had until Parnell's appearance opposed all forms of "constitutionalist" agitation. In fact the creation of the Land League in 1879 was the direct result of meetings between Davitt, Parnell, and Clan na Gael members of the IRB in which it was decided that Parnell's strategy of pursuing both land reform and home rule, while leaving open the question of eventual independence, would be joined by the league's mass mobilization of peasants as described earlier.

Imprisoned in Kilmainham Jail by Gladstone in 1881 for refusing to halt the Land War, Parnell achieved martyr status in Catholic Ireland. By calling off the land agitation in return for Gladstone's 1881 land reforms, Parnell was able to gain his release from prison while retaining both the loyalty of Irish peasants and his nationalist credentials. For Parnell, as for Davitt and the IRB, however, it was not land for Irish peasants that was of central importance, but an end to British rule of Ireland. In February 1881 the enactment of cloture rules had brought a halt to Parnellite obstructionism as a means of forcing British politicians to confront Irish demands for political autonomy. Accordingly, the most important consequence of what Gladstone's opponents called his "Kilmainham Treaty" with Parnell helped establish Parnell and the Home Rule party as major players in the formation and demise of British governments. This was crucial in translating Fenian violence and peasant discontent into a nationalist struggle by constitutionalist means. To give him the balance of power in the House of Commons he desired, Parnell ordered his supporters in Britain to vote Conservative in the elections of 1885. Conservative gains in Britain plus his own party's sweep of all Irish seats apart from Ulster insured that neither a Liberal nor a Conservative government could be formed without his support. As a result, no British politician could any longer deny that Ireland's political future had been placed squarely on the national agenda.[20]

Between 1867 and 1885 the Irish created extraordinarily large discrepancies between Irish realities and the official, and previously hegemonic, view of Ireland as no different in the naturalness of its incorporation into the British polity than Scotland or Northumbria. But as Gramsci's analysis anticipates, the mobilization of Catholic Irish discontent, in all its forms, cannot itself be credited with breaking the hegemonic idea of Ireland as an integral part of the United Kingdom. As we shall see, new ways of thinking about cultural differentiation and the natural scope of modern states, as well as the entrepreneurship of both Liberal and Tory politicians, played crucial roles.

Upheaval in Algeria, 1954–1957

The Algerian Revolution, from 1954 to 1962, was the first violent and sustained mobilization of Algerian Muslims against French rule since the Moqrani Rebellion of 1870–71. By its end upward of seven hundred thousand Algerian Muslims had been killed. Millions more were either confined to *regroupement* camps or forced to take refuge in overcrowded cities. Nomadic groups were wiped out, agricultural resources destroyed, and the entire fabric of traditional society "pulverized" by implementation of the French army's new doctrine of counterinsurgency—*la guerre révolutionnaire.*"[21] One final blow to the integrity of the economic and administrative infrastructure of Algeria was the flight, in 1962, of almost one million European inhabitants—skilled workers, artisans, merchants, technicians, and civil servants, many of whom did their best to destroy as much public and private property as possible before their departure. In metropolitan France the political and economic disruption attendant on the revolution was far more severe than that associated with change in any of France's former colonial relationships, including *la sale guerre* in Indochina from 1946 to 1954.

The origins of the revolt lay in the nationalist organizations that began forming during the interwar period among Algerian workers in metropolitan France. The charismatic leader of this movement, Messali Hadj, formerly a member of the Communist party, blended Marxist terminology with Islamic and nationalist appeals. Rejected by mainstream reformist intellectuals in the 1930s, and by the militant Ben-Badis movement of Islamic clerics as well, Messali nevertheless nurtured ideas of complete Algerian independence from France. This, while other Algerian elites were still advocating inclusion of Algerian Muslims within the French republic, federal solutions, or equal participation of an Algerian republic within the French Union.

During the repression that followed the Stif disturbances of May 1945, Messali was deported and his organization, the Parti Progressiste Algérien (PPA), was banned. As noted in Chapter 4, the French reaction to Sétif caused the deaths of many thousands of Algerians. Thousands more, including veterans and professionals, were imprisoned. Among the latter was Ferhat Abbas, an Algerian *évolué*—a pharmacist, married to a French woman. His father was a member of the French Legion of Honor. The son began his political career in the 1930s as president of the Muslim Students Association in Paris, fully committed to achieving equality for Algerian Muslims as French citizens. In 1936 he declared, in support of his vision of an Algeria fully assimilated to France, that Algeria had never been and never could be a nation.

But if at the outset of World War II Abbas's nationalist credentials were not strong, the war, and Sétif, changed him. In the early 1940s, Abbas and the *évolués* who supported him were frustrated by the futility of appeals to the Free French for guarantees of political equality for Algerian Muslims. Attracted by the slogans of self-determination advanced by the Allies in the Atlantic Charter, Abbas issued what he called the Manifesto of the Algerian People in February 1943. In this document he condemned France for treating Algerians as French when recruits were needed for the battlefield, but as colonial subjects when they returned home. Joining with Messali's PPA, Abbas' supporters formed a broad nationalist grouping in March 1944 known as the *Amis du Manifeste et de la Liberté* (AML, or Friends of the Manifesto). The group called for an autonomous Algerian republic federated to the French republic. Along with the PPA, the AML was banned in the wake of Sétif, and Abbas himself imprisoned.

Following an amnesty in 1946, Abbas broke with Messali. In the elections to the second Constituent Assembly in June 1946 Abbas's Democratic Union for the Algerian Manifesto (UDMA) won 75 percent of the vote in the second (Muslim) college, electing eleven of thirteen deputies. In the general elections of November 1946, and in subsequent municipal elections, the UDMA enjoyed continued success. Messali's Movement for the Triumph of Democratic Liberties (MTLD) also participated in these elections, winning between 30 percent and 33 percent of the vote. But attached to the MTLD was a clandestine unit known as the Special Organization (OS), dedicated to violent revolution. In 1950 the OS was destroyed by the French authorities. Survivors were frustrated by Messali's authoritarian leadership style and convinced that more thorough preparation would be necessary before a successful insurrection could be launched.

Meanwhile, thwarted by the dual electoral college system from achieving effective power within the Algerian Assembly, and deprived of significant representation in the National Assembly in Paris by the machinations of French administrators in Algeria, elements within Abbas' UDMA turned toward nonconstitutionalist paths to establish an autonomous Algeria. After the fraudulent Algerian elections of 1951, the UDMA, the MTLD, militant Muslim clerics, and the Algerian Communist party joined in the Common Front for the Defense and Respect of Liberty. Shortly thereafter, veterans of the OS established another clandestine organization—the Comité Révolutionnaire d'Unité et d'Action (CRUA). Encouraged by the example of the newly independent countries comprising the Arab League, and the success of the Viet Minh against the French army in Indochina, the CRUA began systematically organizing a violent overthrow of French rule. After the rebellion was initiated, during the night and morning of October 31/November 1, 1954, the CRUA reconstituted itself as the executive committee of the National Liberation Front (the FLN—Front de Liberation Nationale).

Those who launched the revolution late in 1954 had reason to be optimistic about their prospects for success. The experience of famine, during and after World War II, was fresh in the minds of Algerian peasants, as was the slaughter in Sétif and the savage bombardment of other villages by the French navy and air force. The crushing poverty of the Algerian masses was intensified by a population explosion that threatened to double the size of the Muslim population every ten years. Peasant hostility to European settlers was intense, bred by memories of massive land expropriations and the exploitative, often racist, labor arrangements enforced by Europeans in their vineyards and on their farms. Among the educated portions of the population, frustration also ran high. Broken promises by French governments to improve living conditions and implement political reforms contained in the statute of 1947, and the insult to the évolués constituted by flagrant manipulation of two successive elections, had all but destroyed the ability of the Muslim elite to imagine itself satisfied within a French-ruled Algeria. In this context the hope of the founding "chiefs" of the revolution was that the initiation of hostilities would trigger a popular uprising throughout the country.

The scattering of attacks against targets in different parts of Algeria resulted in only moderate damage and fewer than a dozen fatalities. The French authorities estimated that the rebel force consisted of no more than eight hundred poorly armed men.[22] Indeed the violence of November 1 attracted little more than passing references in the French and international press. Except for parts of the Aurès region, the response of the Algerian population was also scanty. Moreover, by the spring of 1955, effective police work had resulted in the death or imprisonment of much of the FLN leadership.

However, the French army's enforcement of "collective responsibility" in its search and destroy operations soon swelled rebel ranks. The revolution drew support from frustrated intellectuals, land-hungry peasants, a small urban middle class jealous of European prerogatives, and Muslim leaders anxious to maintain the Islamic complexion of the country. Despite severe internal rivalries, by the late 1950s the leadership of the revolution had displaced virtually all other native claimants to authority over Algerian Muslim society. Abbas signaled his own growing disillusionment with France by insisting that Algeria was either Arab or Algerian, but not French.[23] Still, by the early summer of 1955, the leaders of the revolution were desperately searching for a way to meet the challenge of the rapidly growing French army in Algeria.

As suggested in Chapter 4, enactment of the vague and convoluted statute on Algeria marked the failure of the tutelary subordination model of the French Union as a formula with hegemonic potential. In addition the French Union, apart from Algeria, was disintegrating. After eight years of war in Indochina, the defeat at Dien Bien Phu, and more than ninety thousand French soldiers killed in action, few French could take seriously the Union as described in the Fourth Republic's constitution, let alone imagine it as inevitable and permanent. To be sure, images of a French-governed "Eurafrica," including slogans of France as stretching "from Flanders to the Congo," were occasionally advanced by politicians and commentators on the affairs of the French Union. By 1955 these claims rang hollow. They fell victim to the increasing assertiveness among nationalist parties and elites in French Equatorial Africa and French West Africa and to effective, partially violent, nationalist mobilization in Tunisia and Morocco. In March 1956 the national sovereignty of these "protectorates" was formally recognized. In that same month, a new loi cadre put all of French black Africa on a rapid road to independence.

In contrast to much of the rest of the French Union, Algeria was perceived as quiet from 1945 to the end of 1954. Although pollsters found that the political problems most on the mind of metropolitan French in the late summer and early autumn were "international questions and issues pertaining to Overseas France" (especially Indochina, Tunisia, and Morocco), little if any concern was expressed about the situation in Algeria. Writing after "the outbreak of the troubles," the editors of *Sondages* attributed this lack of concern to the fact that "at the time of the survey, in August and September of 1954, Algeria seemed calm."[24] The more or less casual inference of most French in this period was that Algeria, at least, was loyal to France.[25]

The Mendès-France government's immediate response to the outbreak of violence in Algeria had been to treat French sovereignty there as categorically different from previous claims to French sovereignty over most of the rest of the French Union. Algeria was France, the *fellagha* were "outlaws," and the FLN was a criminal, terrorist organization. On one level this simple and politically useful response helped Mendès-France bolster his threatened premiership against accusations of treason—accusations made in reaction to his conclusion of the Indochina War and his policy of concessions in Tunisia. But Mendès-France could make this calculation only because metropolitan beliefs (including his own) about Algeria's status *were* different from beliefs, by that time largely discarded, about France's attachment to Indochina, the Ivory Coast, or Tunisia.

The formula adopted by the Mendès-France government in reaction to the events of November 1, 1954, was embraced, in one fashion or another, by every subsequent government of the Fourth Republic. Treating the violence as an attack on a portion of France itself, Parliament declared a state of emergency. Reinforcements for the 50,000 French troops stationed in Algeria in November 1954 were quickly dispatched. Within six months the number of French troops in Algeria had doubled. In another six months the number had again doubled. By the end of 1956 there were over 400,000 French soldiers in Algeria.

The revolution was in a precarious state by spring 1955. Despite some increasing support in the Algerian countryside and among educated Muslims, it had yet to make much of an impact in France. The French public's relative lack of concern with unrest in Algeria mirrored official attempts to treat the area as if its status as integrally part of France were hegemonically established. Under these circumstances the FLN decided, in June 1955, to launch a terrorist campaign against French civilians and Muslim opponents. Its purpose was to provoke French responses that would undercut Soustelle's campaign for socioeconomic reforms and irretrievably polarize the situation.

In August the FLN organized a brutal attack in the Constantanois region which left more than a hundred civilians dead. The Philippeville Massacre triggered a massive campaign of repression and the virtual abandonment of Soustelle's reformist program. In response a majority of Muslim delegates to the Algerian Assembly rejected Soustelle's integration formula. In

January 1956 the Muslim caucus within the Algerian Assembly formally endorsed the principle of an Algerian nation, setting the stage for dissolution of the Assembly three months later. In this rapidly polarizing situation Abbas rallied to the FLN, fled Algeria, and announced from Cairo the dissolution of the UDMA, urging his supporters to join the revolution.

In December 1955 still only 25 percent of the French public considered "the disturbances in Algeria" as France's most important problem.[26] Yet from the perspective of the metropole, the Constantanois atrocities and the repression that followed had brought an end to what many had been calling *drôle de révolution* (the phony revolution). Soon a debate took shape in France whose terms reflected not a presumption of Algeria's permanent status as part of France, but the belief that Algeria's fate was problematic and would be determined by a combination of war in Algeria and politics in the hexagon. In November 1955 a group of French intellectuals published the first of many petitions opposing French policy in Algeria.[27] Despite censorship and other restrictions, press coverage of Algeria skyrocketed. According to one study of *Le Monde,* France's "newspaper of record" for the political class, the proportion of front-page news pertaining to Algeria rose from 3.45 percent in the last two months of 1954, to only 4.1 percent in 1955, but to 15.5 percent in 1956.[28] In April 1956, fully 63% of those surveyed by IFOP (Institut Français d'opinion publique) rated Algeria as France's most important problem.[29]

It was in this context of increasing French attentiveness to the Algerian conflict and the breakdown of taboos protecting French policy in Algeria from serious scrutiny that Algérie française as a hegemonic project began to take shape. This ideological program was advanced by those whose personal, political, or material stake in keeping Algeria French was greatest and was developed in response to their realization that the idea of Algeria as France was a casual attitude for most French people—not a deeply ingrained, presumptive belief. This meant that mobilization of metropolitan political support for crushing the rebellion could not be based on simple appeals to French patriotism in the face of an assault on the national territory. The definition of Algeria as part of the national territory first had to be established as a given of French political life.

Thus the problem to be analyzed in the French-Algerian case is not why an ideologically hegemonic conception lost that status (which was the problem posed by the British-Irish case between the 1850s and 1880s). The problem at hand in the French-Algerian case (1955–58) is why a relatively promising hegemonic project failed.

The partisans of Algérie française included most of the officer corps, rank and file soldiers in the professional army, one million French of European extraction living in Algeria, and important elements within the

Catholic hierarchy, among the Gaullists, and within every political party to the right of the Communists. Algérie française not only was advanced as the official view of successive governments, it also expressed Algeria's actual legal status. Supported by massive economic and coercive resources and accepted at face value (until 1957) by the industrial democracies, Algérie française also enjoyed the initial disposition of most French people to view Algeria as permanently French. The question is why such a powerful, well-endowed coalition failed to translate this construction of the France-Algeria relationship into a presumptive, hegemonic belief.

By 1958 the ruthless determination of the French military and the construction of electrified barriers along the entire length of Algeria's eastern and western borders had forced the FLN to abandon hopes of a military victory. But the objective of French governments and the French military was more ambitious. They sought to erase the image of Algeria as possibly separate from France. The problem was that the effort required to achieve this objective was so large and disruptive, *within the metropole,* that one of its consequences was to overwhelm initial dispositions inside France to perceive Algeria as quiet, loyal, and unproblematically French. Certainly there can be no question about how grossly discrepant from official images of Algeria as a "natural," permanent, and productive part of France was the revolutionary mobilization of Algerian nationalist sentiment against French rule and the size of the effort required to contain it.

For one thing, the war played havoc with the French economy. Despite the significant drain of the Indochina War, the French economy had made a remarkable recovery after World War II. In August 1955, shortly before the rapid escalation of French military operations in Algeria, Prime Minister Faure celebrated the country's economic achievements. Industrial production, he pointed out, was 76 percent above that of 1938 and 11 percent above that of 1954. National income was increasing at a rate of $2 billion annually. France's foreign currency reserves were well in excess of $1 billion. Faure predicted the French standard of living would double within ten years.[30] Instead, the enormous cost of the Algerian War plunged France into an economic crisis.

From 1949 to 1953, metropolitan France had contributed $714 million in development assistance to Algeria and had spent another $190 million per year in military, technical, and administrative tasks. The total annual expenditure for Algeria of approximately $332 million equaled a sum, in that period, corresponding to virtually the entire amount transferred to France from the United States under the Marshall Plan.[31] With the onset of serious fighting, however, Algeria's cost to France went even higher. In 1956 alone, French military and development expenditures in Algeria totaled approximately $830 million, in addition to an estimated $312 million in revenues lost as a result of workers conscripted for military service in Algeria. In 1957 the direct costs of Algerian military operations alone were estimated to have risen to $1.1 billion.[32]

As a result of these economic subsidies for Algeria and military operations, the government announced in April 1956 a projected budget deficit of $1.67 billion out of a total budget of $11.3 billion, representing a 33 percent increase over the previous year's deficit.[33] To finance the "pacification" campaign in Algeria, the government called for $600 million in new taxes and across-the-board cuts in salaries and other expenditures.[34] In order to protect long-promised increases in pensions and other social programs, foreign currency reserves were rapidly drawn down.[35] In June 1957 the government projected a budget deficit 27 percent higher than that of the previous year. "The Treasury," announced the government, "can no longer meet the commitments of the state."[36]

High levels of social spending, acceleration of demand associated with the Algerian fighting, contraction of the labor force following mobilization of the reserves, and a 20 percent devaluation of the franc brought inflation. Despite a government-ordered price freeze, the wholesale price index in France rose 5 percent in 1956 and 14 percent in 1957.[37] Meanwhile, Germane Tillion, who had served as Soustelle's top adviser on socioeconomic reform in Algeria, published a book arguing that Algeria could remain French only if its Muslim population enjoyed at least a "minimally acceptable" standard of living. This, she insisted, would require an annual investment in infrastructure, agriculture, industry, services, and housing of $1 billion per year for four to five years.[38]

Expert observers were agreed that even without the investment of the staggering sums called for by Tillion, no solution to France's economic distress was possible without a quick end to the fighting. But in keeping with their effort to discourage debate over Algeria from being framed in cost-benefit terms, successive governments were usually careful to avoid linking the country's economic problems to the cost of the Algerian military operations. The public made the connection anyway. Polls conducted by IFOP began posing questions in these terms in July 1956. Fifty-one percent indicated their disapproval of new taxes to finance the war in Algeria while 48 percent said they would refuse to pay supplementary taxes to finance escalation of the conflict.[39]

The rapid escalation of the pacification campaign also had noneconomic effects on French society which could not be ignored. In April 1956 the government put 200,000 reservists on alert and began sending conscripts to Algeria. By October 1957 72 percent of the 408,000 French troops in Algeria were draftees.[40] Conscripts were paid thirty dollars per month, and resistance to the draft, including riots and mutinies by draftees boarding troop trains and ships bound for Algeria was widely publicized. In May 1956, twenty two members of an infantry platoon were killed in an FLN ambush and their bodies horribly mutilated. The victims, Parisians, were among the first reservists to die in the war. The incident led to a severe crackdown in Algiers, including five thousand arrests, but the furor surrounding the reservists' deaths "brought home to France for the first time, and more sharply than anything else could, the cruel realities of the Algerian war."[41]

Reports of French atrocities in Algeria began circulating in metropolitan France in 1955 and 1956. By 1957 enough was known in metropolitan France to produce a full-scale debate over the techniques used by the army in its "pacification" campaign, including what appeared to be the systematic use of torture. Some, such as Pierre Vidal-Naquet, have argued that the widespread use of torture was a natural concomitant of a struggle officially defined not as colonial, but as a defense of France itself. Thus defined, the struggle justified and elicited "the use of the whole machinery of the state, and the full forces of the nation. There could be only one result. The willingness to use any means, even torture."[42]

However, Mollet's government refused to justify torture on the basis of *raison d'état,* denying that torture had ever been officially authorized. Military men and journalists who reported on its use were branded as "defeatist" and prosecuted for seeking to "demoralize the army." Newspapers and journals whose coverage of the issue was too explicit were seized.[43]

But the flow of conscripts returning from Algeria with grisly eye-witness accounts and a number of celebrated cases of Europeans subjected to torture made it impossible for the government to ignore the issue. Good French patriots in the Socialist party and the MRP, whose political identities were forged during the struggle against the Nazis, and whose comrades suffered and died at the hands of Gestapo torturers, were traumatized by images of men in French uniforms beating prisoners, inflicting electric shock treatments on genitalia, insertion of pressurized gas or liquid into body cavities, and participating in semi-drownings. Liberal Catholic intellectuals were particularly sensitive. Although not usually linked to demands for French withdrawal from Algeria, petitions, exposés, declarations of outrage, and demonstrations against the "means used to implement pacification" proliferated.

In spring 1957 the government created a commission to investigate alleged abuses, but then refused to publish its mildly critical report. At the end of the year *Le Monde* published it anyway. But after the paratroopers' brutal dissection of the FLN network in the casbah of Algiers—the Battle of Algiers during January–March 1957—and the increasingly explicit justifications for torture by theoreticians of *la guerre révolutionnaire,* few French people were left with many illusions about what continued prosecution of the war entailed. Although humanitarian objections to the use of torture were not, as some antiwar activists had hoped, the grounds upon which the war could be brought to an end, *la question,* as Henri Alleg called it, did force the intrusion of clear and painful questions about continuing the war into the consciousness of the French public.[44] The salience of this issue, which conflicted so directly with hegemonic ideas of the French as guardians of humane values and civilized standards of behavior, made it doubly difficult for those seeking to raise the idea of Algérie française to that status as well.

Re-cognizing Ireland: The Availability of Counterhegemonic Interpretations

In both the British-Irish and French-Algerian cases the sustained mobilization of peasant masses was guided by nationalist elites. In Britain and France these upheavals created enormous discrepancies between palpable realities and officially hegemonic conceptions. But according to the theory adumbrated at the beginning of this chapter, the discrepancies themselves cannot explain the breakdown of the Union's ideological hegemony in Britain and were insufficient to ensure the failure of the Algérie française hegemonic project in France. No matter how large the intrusion of events on the public consciousness, and no matter how difficult it may be to account for these events within prevailing hegemonic conceptions, effective challenges to those conceptions also require, or are likely to require, counterhegemonic interpretations. Such formulas are combinations of suggested presumptions and inferences in light of which disturbances can be explained as the unfortunate result of a *contingently* held set of beliefs and the *particular* character of the institutions they support. By definition, however, beliefs which exclude contemplation of alternatives cannot *themselves* generate or support alternative interpretations. Still, consistent with the great range of ideas available within any political culture, counterhegemonic interpretations can be expected to emerge from new combinations of images, theories, and values, contained within or filtered through the cultural repertoire of the dominant community. In the latter part of the nineteenth century British images of Ireland as naturally distinct from Britain were encouraged by the growing importance of historicism, social Darwinism, and the new imperialism within British—especially English—political culture.

Historicism

From the end of the Great Famine until the mid-1870s, John Stuart Mill was one of the most influential Englishmen debating Irish affairs. Mill's particular interest was the organization of land use in Ireland and the evils of "landlordism." In his seminal work *Principles of Political Economy* (1848) and in a series of newspaper editorials, Mill made a strong theoretical case for fixity of tenure, if not peasant proprietorship, to enhance the productivity of Irish agriculture. Irish agricultural problems and the larger Irish political problem, he contended in the late 1840s, could be solved by measures that would "facilitate 'the introduction of English capital and farming' over the greater part of Ireland."[45]

Twenty years later, in the aftermath of the Fenian rising, Mill published a pamphlet, titled "England and Ireland," advocating a radically different approach to reconciling Ireland to English rule. In the pamphlet Mill characterized the attempt to solve an *Irish* problem by applying *English* agricultural techniques and modes of land use as itself the problem. The general question Mill posed in 1868 was no longer how to extend the rationality of English ways of doing things to Ireland, but how to discover "what laws and institutions are necessary for a state of society and civilization like that of Ireland."[46] The root of Britain's historical difficulty in Ireland, and the only way to avoid future rebellions that could lead to separation, would be to recognize just how qualitatively different Ireland and Irish culture were from England and "English" ways of thinking, feeling, and behaving. Regarding England, Mill wrote, "there is no other civilized nation which is so far apart from Ireland in the character of its history, or so unlike it in the whole constitution of its social economy; and none, therefore, which if it applies to Ireland the modes of thinking and maxims of government which have grown up within itself, is so certain to go wrong."[47]

Despite the radical shift in Mill's thinking about Ireland, his desire to achieve the permanent and stable integration of Ireland into the United Kingdom had not changed. What had changed was a fundamental way Mill thought about relationships between culture, history, economics, and government. In 1868 Mill's emphasis was on designing policies to correspond to the peculiar combination of historical and cultural attributes of specific countries—in this case Ireland. This was in sharp contrast to his approach, twenty years earlier, based on the application of abstractly derived general laws, or a model of English organization held as the exemplar of economic rationality. In this substitution of historical and cultural determinism for cross-cultural general laws of rationality Mill, was reflecting what was later recognized as a sea change in modes of thinking that occurred in Britain between 1860 and 1875.[48]

Expressed in Henry Sumner Maine's Oxford lectures on the history of institutions (1875), and analyzed in A. V. Dicey's lectures on the history of British thinking about the origins of law (1898), this intellectual transformation entailed the displacement of universalistic, abstract approaches to human behavior by historicist paradigms. Maine rejected the Benthamite approach to law of those whom he called the "Analytical Jurists," whose enchantment with Hobbesian abstractions led them to approach politics and law as if they were branches of mathematics. While describing the historical determinants of legal norms in Ireland and India, Maine took the analytical jurists to task for ignoring the decisive role played by "the entire history of each community":

> It is its history, the entire mass of its historical antecedents, which in each community determines how the Sovereign shall exercise or forbear from exercising his irresistible coercive power. All that constitutes this—the whole enormous aggregation of opinions, sentiments, beliefs, superstitions, and prejudices, of ideas of all kinds, hereditary and acquired, some produced by institutions and some by the constitution of human nature—is rejected by the Analytical Jurists.[49]

Dicey portrayed Bentham's systematic utilitarianism and the Manchester school of laissez-faire liberalism as most fully expressive of an age dominated by what Dicey called "Benthamism" or "individualism"—a "sentiment" which, he argued, came to an end between 1865 and 1870. The subsequent enactment of "collectivist" types of legislation replaced laissez-faire policies at home and abroad with energetic state regulation in social and economic spheres, which was accompanied by imperialist expansion. The new weltanschauung upon which these policies were based, Dicey argued, incorporated a presumption of differentness from culture to culture; a sentiment, if not a doctrine, emphasizing distinctive histories as the sources of that differentness; and the primacy of passion and instinct, as opposed to reason, in the shaping of institutions.[50]

This new "historicist" way of thinking was an important factor in the breakdown of the ideological hegemony of Ireland as an integral part of the United Kingdom. It provided a conceptual framework for debating Ireland's future which treated "Ireland" as inescapably different from "England." The wide variety of specific political positions encompassed within this framework is illustrated by the intriguing case of Matthew Arnold—a dedicated opponent of Irish home rule. In 1867 he published his Oxford lectures under the title *The Study of Celtic Literature*. As Seamus Deane has argued, by emphasizing the "Celtic idea" and making it respectable in British intellectual circles, Arnold helped establish "a differentiating fact between Ireland and England."[51] In sharp contrast to the philistinism he found so prevalent among the English bourgeoisie, Arnold extolled the virtues of "the dreamy, imaginative Celt...at home in wild landscapes far from the metropolitan centres."[52] Arnold's opposition to home rule was therefore not based on Britain's obligation to bring civilization to Ireland. Quite the opposite. Arnold hoped that maintaining British rule of Ireland would lead England to absorb some of the Celtic spirit, a share of the "imaginative intensity" with which the "genius of the Celtic race produces...a domestication of poetry into daily life."[53] Only thus, said Arnold, might England be saved from "a defective type of civilization" propagated by an increasingly "vulgarised middle class." Ireland's specific function within the Union was "to be teaching England and the English middle class how to live."[54]

Much more typical of British historicism was an unrestrained glorification of England and all things English. In his famous Crystal Palace speech in 1872, Disraeli captured this mood and foreshadowed the crucial role of invigorated, extravagant English nationalism in the imperialist ideology which dominated British views of their country and the world for the next forty years. Seeking to enlist newly enfranchised workers on the side of the Tories, Disraeli told them they were, above all, "English to the core. I mean that the people of England, and especially the working classes of England, are proud of belonging to a great country, and wish to maintain its greatness—that they are proud of belonging to an Imperial country, and are resolved to maintain, if they can, their empire—that they believe, on the whole, that the greatness and the empire of England are to be attributed to the ancient institutions of the land."[55] Disraeli's was a myth of an English nation that stood splendidly apart from the "cosmopolitan" states of the Continent. England, in this view, was providentially gifted with skills of entrepreneurship and governance; a nation fundamentally different from the Dutch or the Venetians, who had abandoned their empires; a nation "more calculated to create Empires than to give them up."[56]

It was this idea that lay behind the goal of uniting all lands of Anglo-Saxon colonization into a "Greater Britain," a vision first put forward by Charles Dilke in 1867: "Nature seems to intend the English for a race of officers, to direct and guide the cheap labor of the Eastern peoples." Dilke included among these "Eastern peoples" the Chinese, whom he instructively labeled the "Irish of Asia."[57] In his 1883 book *The Expansion of England*, John Seeley gave Dilke's celebration of Anglo-Saxonism its most systematic and influential expression. Having spread abroad the genius of its nation and the authority of its state, he argued, England was in the 1880s situated at a great decision point. Would it abandon the global array of territories its energy and emigrants had stamped with an English complexion, thereby acquiescing in the status of a middling European power? Or would England embark on a great consolidative enterprise to weld all of "Greater Britain" into a "political union" that would surpass the Russian superstate, if not the American?[58]

In Seeley's embrace of an English-led Greater Britain the deep imprint of the "historicist reaction" is apparent. Thus Seeley excluded India from Greater Britain. Ruled by the English nation, India was culturally and "racially" too alien to be a genuine part of an Anglo-Saxon Greater Britain. But for Seeley, history in most of the rest of the empire contained a clear imperative. Having traced "how England has been entirely engaged for the last three centuries in this expansion into Greater Britain," Seeley observed that "if once we grant that historic truth is attainable, and attainable it is, then there can be no further dispute about its supreme importance. . . . It is by this consideration that I merge history in politics. I tell you that when you study English history you study not the past of England only, but her future."[59]

The perceived distinctiveness of England, as opposed to the empire England had acquired and the problematique associated with it (Could England hold what she had gained?), implied that successful British rule of Ireland was *contingent* upon laws and policies that took account of the fact that Ireland was Irish, not English. For members of the British elite such as William Gladstone, disposed to take a solicitous attitude toward "others," this meant openness to generous measures of land reform and self-government and a tendency to think of Scotland and even Canada, rather than Northumbria, as appropriate models for Ireland's future relationship to England. But to members of the British elite disposed to view "others" in terms of their location in a hierarchy ranging from highly civilized to barbaric, or, in social Darwinist terms, from strong to weak, historicism meant an invigorated assertion of "English" imperatives and power over an Ireland seen more readily as akin to India than Scotland.[60]

Thus Clive Dewey identifies Gladstone's enthusiasm for Irish land reform between 1870 and 1882 with the broad shift of intellectual climate described here—the eclipse of "classical political economy and analytic jurisprudence" in favor of a "historicist reaction." According to Dewey, historicism encouraged supposedly intrinsic differences between Celtic Ireland and Anglo-Saxon Britain to assume decisive significance. Dewey shows that scholarship in the 1860s, drawing on a Celtic revival in Ireland and reflecting the influence and prestige of German sociology, described a rich history of Celtic institutions and customary law. This work shaped the findings of British commissions of inquiry on Irish land questions. It also provided Gladstone and his lieutenants with the imprimatur, and the intellectual equipment, to overcome objections by classical political economists and convince a Parliament still largely comprised of landed aristocrats to accept state interference in the disposition of private property.[61] Utilitarian axioms of political economy, according to Gladstone, now seeing Irish society "in evolutionary perspective," were as relevant to the Irish as to "the inhabitants of Saturn and Jupiter." Arguing that intellectual trends in mid-nineteenth-century Britain had gradually changed the premises of acceptable "scientific" argumentation, Dewey comments that "Gladstone's relegation of political economy to outer space rapidly attained public notoriety. Twenty years earlier, it would have encountered polite incredulity."[62]

Once British elites saw Ireland and the Irish as intrinsically different from Britain and things English, it was considerably easier for politicians to treat discontent in Ireland—even its violent manifestations—as political rather than criminal.[63] This view encouraged accommodative change in the terms of Union between the two countries to be understood as a natural constitutional process rather than betrayal of an eternal principle. Ireland, argued Gladstone in his 1868 campaign, could be pacified if it were governed by "Irish ideas," not subject to the enforcement of laws that came, as he later put it, "in a foreign aspect, and a foreign garb." Thus in 1834 a British prime minister (Peel) could, as noted in Chapter 3, dismiss Irish Repeal agitation as absurd by citing ancient Celtic rituals for baptizing kings with cow's blood, while forty years later another British prime minister (Gladstone) could draw explicitly on the hoary traditions of Celtic life as guidance for the design of legislation.[64] The same intellectual fashion enabled Gladstone first publicly to entertain, but reject, home rule; then privately to accept it; and then, finally, publicly to embrace it as a vehicle for expressing distinctly Irish political identities. After his defeat in 1886 Gladstone wrote, "We may fairly say of the policy which aims at giving Ireland an Irish Government . . . it is a policy which, instead of innovating, restores; which builds upon the ancient foundations of Irish history and tradition; which, by making power local, makes it congenial, where hitherto it has been unfamiliar, almost alien; and strong, where hitherto it has been weak."[65]

Social Darwinism

But the darker side of historicist thinking proved more robust than the liberal impulses that could be associated with it. In the context of a late nineteenth-century jingoist tide that affected all sectors of English opinion, it was not Gladstonian generosity but a disposition toward viewing others as unequal and undeserving which carried the day.[66] "The real bane of Ireland," wrote Edward Dicey in 1885, "is the possession of parliamentary institutions, which the character of her people, the stage of her civilisation, the conditions of her national existence, render her unfit to employ with advantage to herself or others."[67] The proportion of the British intelligentsia who shared these views was so great that on the key question of Irish home rule it was reliably observed that "never in the history of England was there such a consensus of intellect arrayed against statesmen as is now arrayed against Mr. Gladstone."[68]

The historicist paradigm, an obsession with Darwinism, and an international culture of *macht-politik* produced a "science" of racialism embraced by the elites of almost every Great Power.[69] In Britain such theories endowed traditional stereotypes of Irishmen as irrational, lazy, dirty, violent, stupid, drunk, and collectively retrograde with a pseudoscientific cachet, and contrasted England's continued and effective rule of Ireland with the specter of "a Balkanised Britain [which] must sink, Darwin-like, to decay and decline."[70] The marquess of Salisbury, the new leader of the Conservative/Unionist party, call the Irish "Hottentots," a slur which played well in this environment. So did Salisbury's calls, on behalf of England and the empire, for "twenty years of coercion" (instead of home rule) and the emigration of one million Irish to Canada. Gladstonian protests against such misanthropic appeals only added to the stigma increasingly attached to his brand of Liberalism as too sentimental, and too prepared to accommodate the desires of the non-English, to be trusted with the interests and the destiny of the British Empire.[71]

In the end, however, the important point is not that social Darwinism strengthened resistance to accommodating Irish demands for self-government, but that by the 1870s and 1880s both opponents and advocates of home rule were thinking about politics in terms that encouraged viewing Ireland as fundamentally distinct from England, and liable, under specifiable circumstances, to be separated from the British state.

The New Imperialism

One of the best established facts about political culture in late Victorian England is the general and intense upsurge of excitement about almost everything associated with the British Empire. In 1885, Gordon of Khartoum was a martyred saint; at the turn of the century Rudyard Kipling was a virtual poet laureate. The public's interest in imperial affairs was regularly stimulated by gala celebrations and exhibitions, its attention riveted on the overseas exploits of British military forces by a penny press that relished action and exoticism. As the nineteenth century drew to a close, British competitive instincts were reinforced, by fears that African markets and fields of investment would be lost without bold expansion, and by evocations of Britain caught in a bitter struggle for power with the leading states of Europe and America.[72] No less important, British, especially English, vanity was flattered by the "white man's burden" image and the visions of Dilke, Seeley, W. E. Forster, and Cecil Rhodes of an ever-expanding domain of Anglo-Saxon culture and English political power.[73]

The triumphalist imperial sentiments promoted by these men are often cited to explain the defeat of Gladstone's first Home Rule Bill and the subsequent political ascendance of a Unionist party committed to the military, political, and economic consolidation of a widening empire.[74] The general argument is powerful. But an important point about the effects of the new imperialism is missed if the question is posed as most historians of the period have posed it: why was home rule defeated? The question I pose here is not why Irish home rule was defeated, but how and why it emerged at all as a serious issue on the agenda of British politics.

In this context the new imperialism had a larger significance. Its emphasis on Englishness, and its substitution of a global empire or a "Greater Britain" for the United Kingdom as the main institutional expression of English political authority, had unintended consequences for the terms of British political discourse applicable to Ireland. The new imperialism, latching itself onto Ireland as a test case for England's determination to resist pressures toward "dismemberment of the empire," effectively "demoted" non-British, and certainly non-English, Ireland from the status of an integral part of the "United Kingdom of Great Britain and Ireland" to that of one territory in a panoply of imperial dependencies scattered around the world.[75]

Some in the ideological vanguard of "Unionism," such as Edward Dicey, made this recategorization explicit. Maintaining the empire meant protecting "British authority over a vast outlying territory."[76] The empire, according to Dicey, was "everywhere the English race rules; English laws prevail; English ideas are dominant; English speech holds the upper hand."[77] The legitimizing basis for English rule of so many colonies, he contended, could not admit the principle of "consent of the governed"— not in India or in Ireland. He continued, "If the consent of the governed is a *sine qua non* of all just government, then we have no right to hold

Gibraltar, or Malta, or Shanghai, or Singapore. Nor can we lay down any theory by which, though we are not at liberty to hold India against the wish of the Hindoos, we are at liberty to hold Ireland against the wish of the Irish."[78] In 1885 Dicey applied the logic of his position by recommending that Ireland be governed "as a crown colony till her people have become fit to enjoy political liberty without abusing it."[79]

But if the kind of policy Dicey inferred from Ireland's demotion to "colonial" status was what appealed to most of the English, it was not the only kind of inference British politicians could credibly draw. For some Gladstonians, such as John Morley, enlightened aspects of British administration in India suggested the efficacy of generous reforms in Ireland. Gladstone's own approach relied heavily on the success of the 1867 British North America Act, which maintained Canada within the empire as a "dominion." He remarked in Parliament in mid-1886 that "as it has been perfectly easy to reconcile the rights of Canada with the supremacy of the Imperial Parliament, it will not be less easy in practice to reconcile the rights and the autonomy of Ireland with the same supremacy."[80]

Indeed Gladstone's argument for Irish home rule never departed from the pro-imperialist spirit of the time. He first entertained, then advanced, measures of self-government for Ireland as fully consistent with Britain's proven tradition of devolving power to its colonies in order to increase their loyalty and bind them more securely to England.[81] Blending this vision of the empire with his generally optimistic view of human nature and the historicist emphasis he had come to place on the importance of indigenous institutions, Gladstone developed a coherent rationale for home rule based on precisely the values his Conservative/new imperialist opponents claimed they cherished. Quoting Edmund Burke he argued that home rule was certainly not a narrowly "Liberal" policy for preserving the empire's integrity, but "eminently Conservative."

> For it is especially founded on regard for history and tradition. It aims in the main at restoring, not altering, the Empire. In this vast mass are straightway discovered a multitude of subaltern integers; municipalities, counties, colonies, and nations. Does a true conservative policy recommend that the dividing lines, which hedge about these secondary organisations, should be eyed with an eager jealousy, and effaced upon any favorable occasion?...It is surely most desirable that every subaltern structure in an enormous political fabric, having joints and fastenings, tie-beams and rafters of its own, should contribute, by the knotted strength thus inhering in each part, to increase the aggregate of cohesive force, which guarantees the permanence and solidity of the whole.[82]

By joining in the disposition to classify Ireland as a colony, and in the prevailing concern to prevent "dismemberment of the empire," Gladstone ignored evidence that for most Irish Catholics, the substantive purpose of home rule, was as a first stage to eventual independence. Thus he was able to characterize legislative home rule for Ireland as the best way to preserve British sovereignty there and so protect "the unity of the empire." Inaugurating the government that produced the home rule Bill, Gladstone described the first condition of an acceptable Home Rule plan as "Union of the empire and due supremacy of Parliament."[83] Invitations to participate in his cabinet informed each prospective minister that Gladstone intended to seek establishment of a legislature in Dublin "calculated to support and consolidate the unity of the empire on the continued basis of imperial authority and mutual attachment."[84]

Unionists could and did attack Gladstone as sophistic and disingenuous, but they could not so easily dismiss Joseph Chamberlain or Cecil Rhodes. Chamberlain compared Parnell to Arabi, leader of the Egyptian nationalist revolt crushed by the British in 1882. Both, he said, "threatened the empire."[85] Though opposed to the particulars of the Home Rule Bill, Chamberlain described the Irish problem as one susceptible of solution only within a large-scale "Imperial Federation," and drew on the Canadian government's relationship to its provincial legislatures as a model for England and Ireland.[86] The expansiveness of Rhodes's imperial views were unsurpassed by any Unionist. But Rhodes *supported* home rule as consistent with his Round Table organization's program for a centrally governed federation of English settled territories. Indeed he contributed ten thousand pounds to Parnell's party.[87]

The fact is that as evocative as it may have been for portraying home rule as "imperial dismemberment," new imperialist rhetoric had blurred, if not virtually destroyed, public images of the empire as that which, according to the Act of Union of 1801, it still legally described—the United Kingdom of Great Britain and Ireland. Beginning with Disraeli, Tories had effectively redefined "empire" to connote English possessions around the world. Unable to argue against devolution as a useful consolidative technique in portions of the empire, the Unionists had unwittingly provided a theoretical and rhetorical basis for Irish home rule to be presented as a service to, rather than a betrayal of, imperial unity.[88] Thus their schema for interpreting England's place in the world contributed to the breakdown of the ideologically hegemonic status of Ireland as an integral part of the United Kingdom, even though the appeals this schema made possible also played a key role in preventing timely realization of the program (Irish autonomy) whose place on the political agenda it had helped prepare.

Relativism, Realism, and Political Entrepreneurship in the Failure of Algérie Française as a Hegemonic Project

In the previous section I analyzed the role that historicist, social Darwinist, and imperialist modes of thought played in reshaping British categories applied to Ireland. Emerging in the 1850s and 1860s, these ideas had their most potent impact on British-Irish relations in the 1880s and 1890s. The partisan exploitation of a re-cognized Ireland by Gladstone, Salisbury, and other leading British politicians is treated later in this chapter. In the French case the time span is much smaller. Accordingly, the impact of changing modes of thought on France's relationship to its non-European territories is more difficult to analyze without simultaneously considering the use made of those ideas by key political actors.

An ambitious politician's decision to challenge popular, let alone hegemonic, beliefs is always risky. That is why neither the existence of opportune circumstances nor the availability of ideological alternatives is sufficient to explain the breakdown of hegemonic beliefs or likely to provide a full explanation for the failure of candidates for that status. Politicians themselves play a crucial role, for no belief loses or gains hegemonic status unless strategically placed political actors calculate that substantially advancing their fortunes requires it.

The evidence suggests that in postwar, France new ways to interpret the metropole's relations to overseas France were available, but that their impact on French political thinking, especially with regard to Algeria, was limited. Their most important role was indirect, helping to problematize Algeria's status by invigorating a discourse that made Algeria the crucial test of the Fourth Republic's claim to legitimate authority. The direct influence of postwar intellectual trends on French views of decolonization in general, and France's relationship to Algeria in particular, is clearly apparent only after 1958. At that point de Gaulle, after establishing the Fifth Republic, advanced yet another formula for understanding France's "natural" and "inevitable" relationship with Algeria and the balance of France's remaining overseas territories—the idea of the "community." Although as an institution the community hardly mattered at all, as a formula permitting the metropole to reconstitute itself as "France" it was important. It replaced sovereignty with cultural and economic association as the expression of the indissolubility of French ties to its former empire and France's global, civilizing mission. This approach, including the grant to each French possession of the right to choose independence, entailed official acceptance of the contingent character of French rule over non-European territories and implicitly acknowledged the integrity of autochthonous cultures.

In promoting this view after 1959, de Gaulle was able to draw on converging trends in cultural and economic domains which, together with a radically changed international attitude toward colonialism, had been used before 1958 by some critics of the French Union and by opponents of Algérie française. In the cultural sphere, new relativistic ideas challenged the traditional French understanding of the transcendent role played by their own culture and language as the appropriate standard (and goal) for all peoples.[89] These ideas had been carried into the political domain by left-wing intellectuals, led by Jean-Paul Sartre and Maurice Merleau-Ponty writing in *Les Temps Modernes.* Their stinging indictments of French colonialist abuses reflected a radical change in international political culture. In the 1930s, European colonialism was hailed throughout the West as a progressive, liberating, and civilizing force. This notion was replaced after World War II by a stringently anticolonialist international political culture which viewed colonialism as exploitative, national self-determination as progressive, and decolonization as inevitable.

In French literary and philosophical circles this massive reorientation toward understanding relations between colonizer and colonized was expressed by the Negritude movement—whose most important exponents gained prominence in the 1950s; by "native" commentators on colonialism, such as Albert Memmi and Franz Fanon; and by the structuralist anthropology of Claude Levi-Strauss and Michel Leiris, which honored the quality of "primitive" thought and the essentially incommensurable achievements of separate cultures. Also important were notions of a new "universal civilization" advanced by André Malraux and Paul Ricoeur, within which "dialogue between cultures" would replace the diffusion of one. The sympathy if not outright support for third world nationalist movements, as expressed with increasing vigor in the pages of *Esprit* and *Témoignage Chrétien,* reflected changing attitudes within the Vatican, and among some French Catholics, toward acceptance of cultural diversity and an understanding of colonialism as an obstacle to, rather than an instrument of, Catholic objectives in the third world.[90]

However, the cultural relativism implicit in this literature and scholarly work, and in the evolution of the Catholic church's thinking, was generally too abstract or too new to transform political attitudes toward the entire *ensemble* of France d'outre-mer. Indeed, the French public as a whole, and French politicians in particular, rejected the dissolution of ties between France and its former colonies which might well have seemed inevitable if the premises of cultural relativism were accepted. Most French intellectuals continued to understand Western culture and ideas, whether specifically French, or Marxist, to be the solvent for all "indigenous" cultures and identities, the standard for their evaluation, and the medium for their most fitting expression.[91] As discussed in Chapter 4, the theory behind both versions of the French Union, as well as Algérie française, was that where France had planted her flag, decolonization would mean not independence from France, but participation in the French republic itself. The demand for colonial liberation appeared as "the rejection of the gift of a superior culture."[92] "The English," said Maurice Duverger in 1955, "would be shocked that a foreigner could have the idea of becoming British; the French are shocked when a foreigner does not have the idea of becoming French."[93]

These intellectual trends did have some political impact. With the stagnation of the French Union and metropolitan distraction from the affairs of French West Africa and French Equatorial Africa, these new ways of thinking probably encouraged promulgation of the 1956 loi cadre, permitting the introduction of sweeping reforms and the granting of opportunities for virtual self-government to restive sub-Saharan colonies. This process was also influenced by a "new realism" in the economic sphere associated with the men who supervised France's successful economic revival in the early 1950s.[94] Pierre Mendès-France, an economist by training, stressed the principles of efficiency and rationality as the basis of France's future. He advocated a well-run economy as the engine for continuing expansion and for maintaining France's rank and influence as a world power. Applying such thinking to overseas France, Mendès-France supported a reorganized French Union, emphasizing economic cooperation and political autonomy, to preserve the French presence overseas while treating nationalists in the developing world with respect. As noted in Chapter 4, some, such as Raymond Cartiér, went much further in advocating the "rationalization" of France's relations with its former colonies, suggesting that the economic interest of metropolitan France be the only criterion for maintaining links with them.[95]

As prime minister, Mendès-France pursued a policy of retrenchment overseas and reconstruction at home. He cut French losses in Indochina and struck deals with nationalists in Tunisia and Morocco, permitting rapid French disengagement from those territories. But as premier, Mendès-French found it politically impossible to apply the same ideas to Algeria. Cartiér likewise refused to apply his profit-and-loss logic to Algeria. Other journalists, especially those representing the French business community, did explain just how costly and burdensome Algeria was likely to become. But in contrast to the conclusions they were willing to draw about other portions of overseas France, they generally refused even to consider "disengagement" from Algeria as an option, at least until 1959.[96]

Indeed before 1958, ambitious politicians generally avoided using principles of cultural relativism or economic realism when discussing Algeria.

Instead of providing the basis for a reevaluation of French policy in Algeria, the main contribution of these ideas to the problematization of Algeria's status, and thus to the failure of Algérie française as a hegemonic project, was to help serve as a foil for de Gaulle's special kind of appeal—an appeal he used to destroy the Fourth Republic before discarding its attempt to include Algeria within France. From 1946 to 1958, de Gaulle strengthened his political reputation by opposing any concession made by Fourth Republic governments to nationalist demands in any of France's former colonies, by appearing as the champion of French Algeria, and by seeming to foreswear the "relativist" and "realist" ideas of those who opposed continuing the war—ideas which included categories, expectations, and beliefs on which his future policies of disengagement from Algeria would be based.

The key element in the psychological, intellectual, and cultural landscape of France which gave de Gaulle the opportunity to pursue his war of position so successfully was the collective embarrassment of the French people. Of all the major protagonists in World War II, France was the most thoroughly humiliated. At least that is how most French felt afterward. A country that viewed itself as the cultural if not the political leader of Europe, with an army that significantly outnumbered Nazi Germany's, had surrendered after offering only minimal resistance. Pétain's German-supported regime enjoyed, in its first years at least, overwhelming popular support. "It would not be wrong," commented Stanley Hoffmann in 1961, "to describe French policy in the last two decades as a battle against humiliation."[97] This search for renewed self-esteem gave France's external relations, especially its struggle to resist decolonization, their central importance in postwar French politics.

Hoffmann's emphasis on the French quest for self-esteem corresponds to the arguments that virtually all those who have studied the relationship between French political culture and decolonization have made. Raoul Girardet describes decolonization as "a profound shock to the national sensibility,"[98] an insult to France's "collective amour propre" which was experienced across the political spectrum.[99] This "resistance to abandonment" he traces to an overpowering sense of national humiliation: "The background to the movement to resist colonial abandonment was the effort to erase the memory of the 1940 defeat, which remained tragically present in the French consciousness. Neither the liberation of its territory, nor finding itself, in the end, among the victors, sufficed to eradicate a dominant mood of humiliation and anguish."[100] After June 1940, Dien Bien Phu, the loss of Tunisia and Morocco, and the Suez disaster, France was, Girardet quotes Bidault as saying in 1957, "tired of humiliations."[101] Yet it was the problem of Algeria which Girardet says intensified feelings of "wounded pride" to an extreme degree, and posed itself, agonizingly, as the decisive test for France. He asserts that "the struggle for Algérie française nourished the singularly tenacious conviction that, on this issue, hung the future, the very destiny, of the national community. At stake was whether the French nation would survive as a great power, or sink into irremediable decay."[102]

The popularity of Jean Dutourd's *The Taxis of the Marne* is cited by Hoffmann, Girardet, and other students of postwar France as evidence of the tremendous psychological and political trauma which was June 1940's legacy to the Fourth Republic. Written just as the Algerian conflict was beginning to assume the dimensions of a full-scale revolt, Dutourd's novelized account of his experiences during World War II savagely attacked the generation of Frenchmen whose cravenness, he maintains, led to France's defeat. It epitomized the sense of humiliation born by the French over their country's collapse in 1940—a sentiment sharpened by defeat in Indochina and the embarrassing debacle at Suez in 1956.

For Dutourd, writing in the 1950s, the defeat suffered by France in World War II was a present reality. In Indochina, as in Africa, France was being "beaten everywhere." The humiliating abandonment of France's mission, of its very raison d'être, was bound to continue as long as her destiny was consigned to men as unworthy of France as they were representative of their unmanly generation. Yet the "gnats" running France since the war, wrote Dutourd, "make the insects of the Third Republic look like giants." Dutourd insisted that only a France which occupied the center stage in world affairs was a country he cared to live in. Further, he stated, "I don't give a damn for what the world will be tomorrow if this future has not got French civilization as its foundation...I have every right to want no future for the world if it cannot be created through France....I am not resigned to ending my days in the prisons of the puritans of America or the atheists of Russia...not only can I not conceive the world without France, I cannot conceive that the world might be led by any other nation."[103]

Dutourd's expression of shame, outrage, and desperate self-assertion reflected the deep sense of insecurity among the French about the validity of their nation's claims to greatness. These sentiments discouraged any politician from presenting himself as ready to compromise, no matter how sensibly, by trading principles for profit or safety—especially if those principles included defending the integrity and sovereignty of France itself.[104]

One crucial attempt to discuss Algeria in terms that were not consistent with this psychological and cultural stance was, as noted in Chapter 4, Raymond Aron's treatment of what he called "the Algerian tragedy." This was a hard-hitting, "realist" analysis of France's incapacity to sustain its rule over Algeria at a bearable cost. Employing his characteristically de-tached, "rational" style of analysis, Aron marshaled evidence that was difficult to ignore. The staggering costs of the war, even larger estimates of what it would require to raise Algerian living standards to "minimally acceptable levels," and the global tidal wave of anticolonialism were widely appreciated. Originally composed as a memorandum to the Mollet gov-ernment in early 1956, Aron's argument was expanded and published as a book after Mollet solidified his alliance with the partisans of Algérie française.

But not one important political group before 1958 adopted Aron's po-sition as the basis of its appeal for an end to the war. Critics of government policy in Algeria instead argued that the French conscience could not abide the repressive measures necessary to win the war or that the European settlers had created an intrinsically oppressive and exploitative system. The appeal of these critiques was limited, however, to students and intellectuals. From the outbreak of the rebellion on November 1, 1954, until end of the Fourth Republic in June 1958, the critiques of Algerian policies which affected the composition and tenure of governments were mainly, if not solely, those from the right, offered by parties and politicians who ques-tioned the sincerity of official commitments to Algérie française and the willingness or ability of the authorities to prosecute the war with sufficient vigor.

From 1955 on, Fourth Republic governments were closely monitored by representatives of the one million European French living in Algeria and by an army seeking the victory it had so long been denied. The army and the settlers were supported by right-wing political parties in the me-tropole, such as the Indépendants and Poujadists, and by important ele-ments within the SFIO, the Radical party, the Gaullist movement, and the MRP. Their common response to any suggestion that improved French-Algerian relations could be achieved by loosening ties between the two countries was to excoriate such ideas as "retreat," "surrender," "betrayal," or "abandonment." Their message was clear and, to most French, painfully reminiscent of choices they had confronted fifteen years earlier. Now, having lost most of the French Empire already, the government was taking a stand in Algeria. If the will to defend France had been lacking in 1940, it would not be lacking in Algeria. If Indochina was far away, a part of the French Union perhaps, but certainly not of France, Algeria was nearby, heavily settled by French people, and legally a part of the country. To apply relativist or realist logics to Algeria seemed, in this context, to reflect spinelessness, not empathy, and cowardice, not rationality. From 1955 through 1957, whatever shades of difference can be found in the Algerian policies of Fourth Republic premiers—Mendès-France, Faure, Mollet,

Maurice Bourgès-Maunoury, and Félix Gaillard—each adopted the rhetoric of *résistance à l'abandon* in Algeria.

The widespread disposition to accept construction of the situation in these terms did not guarantee that Algeria would remain French, but it did discourage Guy Mollet, and the Socialist party leadership to whom Aron had addressed himself, from approaching the Algerian problem as Aron had suggested. To have done so, Mollet, or any other French leader, would have had to promote a very different kind of discourse, defining Algeria, for example, as a French territory rather than as a part of France. The French could then have been encouraged to treat the disposition of Algeria as a discrete problem whose solution lay in a pragmatic adjustment of relations. To be sure, a year and a half after the fall of his cabinet, Mendès-France did adopt such a stance, but by that time his political base in the Radical party was shattered and his increasingly vigorous opposition to the war practically ruled him out as a candidate for the premiership. As we see in Chapter 7, no French politician except de Gaulle (*after* his return to power) was both willing and able to assume the burdens of political education associated with turning Aron's arguments into a formula for political success.

If the ease with which Algeria could be portrayed as a last line of defense for French greatness, a "new Verdun," deterred some politicians from following their inclinations toward compromise on Algeria, it opened valuable opportunities to others. Political entrepreneurs operating mainly against, and not within, the Fourth Republic were particularly well positioned to advance their fortunes by casting doubt on the regime's ability to keep Algeria as part of France. Thus the two political actors who capitalized most spectacularly on the construction of Algeria as a test of national virtue—Pierre Poujade and Charles de Gaulle—were those whose appeals rested on critiques of the regime itself, not on the policies of any particular government. Ironically, however, exploitation of these opportunities, by reinforcing inclinations to view Algeria's status in problematic terms, contributed directly to the failure of Algérie française as a hegemonic project.

The Poujadist movement began in 1953 as a reaction by small farmers and shopkeepers against the effects of French economic modernization. Led by Pierre Poujade, a stationer with real organizational and rhetorical talent from a small town in the Auvergne, the movement embraced what Stanley Hoffmann identified as "the two issues which 'le Système' had been unable to resolve." These were "the plight of the shopkeepers" (who were threatened by new products and by national and international marketing networks) and "the humiliation of France."[105] Poujade cast the clerks, technocrats, tax collectors, and party politicians of the Fourth Republic as responsible for the decline in France's international standing and the panic felt by so many of his small-town, self-employed constituents. Portraying his movement as a continuation of the French Revolution, he declared that only a reconstituted "estates general" could reestablish the "Republic of good sense," and halt the damage done by those who had betrayed the *fraternité française*."[106]

The French political class at first dismissed Poujade as an ignorant, anti-Semitic demagogue. But it was shocked by his success in the elections of January 1956. Poujade's movement received 2.6 million votes (nearly 10 percent), giving it fifty two deputies in the Assembly. Support was particularly strong among the *pieds noirs*. Poujade claimed a hundred thousand adherents in Algeria at the end of 1955. Many of the organizers of the violent demonstration against Mollet in February 1956, and of the settler uprising in spring 1958 which helped bring an end to the Fourth Republic, were Poujadists.[107]

With the return of inflation the economic fortunes of retailers improved dramatically, and Poujadist strength began to decline. But from January 1956 to May 1958, Poujade's sizable parliamentary delegation helped prevent any government from moving toward compromise on Algeria, while his extremist rhetoric contributed to a high level of national tension over the issue. Poujade could not, however, present himself as a candidate for national leadership capable of resolving the problem. De Gaulle could, and did.

One of de Gaulle's most visible supporters was Jacques Soustelle. Before agreeing to serve in the government Soustelle had asked for and received the general's blessing. In Soustelle's public argument with Aron, conducted after Soustelle's term as governor-general of Algeria was over, he attacked Aron's "so-called realism" as a symptom of a national malaise, which was France's most basic problem. The struggle over Algeria was a struggle to overcome this malaise, to resist the tendencies toward decadence and rationalized surrender that had led to the humiliations of World War II and the postwar period. Soustelle noted that Sartre, and many intellectuals on the left, increasingly treated Algeria as another case of "decolonization," and praised third world revolutions as the most positive force on the world scene. Along with other leading partisans of French Algeria, such as the former prime minister Georges Bidault, Soustelle castigated the timidity of "salon intellectuals" and condemned the relativistic thinking that, he maintained, led them to betray traditional French commitments to the "Rights of Man" in favor of terrorist movements and authoritarian regimes in Asia and Africa.

In Soustelle's construction, and from a Gaullist perspective, the Algerian problem threw into bold relief the very aspects of France intrinsic to its greatness, which both World War II and Dien Bien Phu had called into question, and for which de Gaulle stood as the paragon. By this account nothing less than the legitimacy of French claims to glory and greatness was at stake. Evoking the Cassandra type warnings de Gaulle issued before his retreat from public view in 1955, Soustelle's polemics helped establish as salient, and even decisive, the principles de Gaulle had sought to in-carnate—steadfast commitment to the grandeur of France and courageous refusal to surrender French sovereignty in the face of military threat. Sous-telle used these ideals to frame his attack on Aron, pitting them against Aron's "realism" and "overvaluation" of materialist forces.[108]

After coming to power in May 1958, de Gaulle, with his unassailable credentials of steadfastness and *grandeur*, acted, as Tony Smith put it, as France's "master therapist"[109] to reinterpret decolonization. De Gaulle declared that decolonization was a French decision—an expression of the greatness of France, rather than proof of its decadence. He proclaimed it the culmination of France's work in Africa—a process of state creation rather than imperial contraction. The credibility de Gaulle brought to this construction of events and these decisions allowed the domestic political strains associated with relinquishing France's non-European territories, including Algeria, to be contained within the institutions of the Fifth Republic.

But de Gaulle reinterpreted French decolonization *after* he came to power. Before May 1958 he did nothing to discourage interpretations of decolonization as evidence of awful failure. Before May 1958 it was not his reinterpretive virtuosity which counted, but his special position in French politics as a historical figure, a political entrepreneur, and the leader of a movement (the Gaullist movement) that had never accepted the Fourth Republic as worthy of France.

A "realist" political discourse which enlisted, as Aron sought to do, the logic of the balance sheet to calculate the most profitable direction for French policy toward Algeria was then to play directly into de Gaulle's distinctive political strength. His image, created during the war, was of a leader who responded to principles, not trade-offs, who would fight for France, and for French honor, regardless of what might seem the "rational" course. As Dutourd described the situation, "On the one side there was refinement, elegance, conformity, and realism. This was Vichy, toward which rushed everything France contained in the way of eminent minds, accomplished politicians, and ambitious soldiers. On the other side there was the absurd, the apparently useless gesture, the conventional attitude of the elementary-school textbooks on civic behavior. This was De Gaulle."[110]

With frustration over the Algerian debacle increasingly melding in

French minds with frustration over what de Gaulle called "the absurd ballet" of weak coalition governments, it was reassuring for the French public to remember the central theme of postwar Gaullism—the Fourth Republic's incapacity to preserve the grandeur of France. Drawing on a deeply embedded tradition in French political culture, of "eternal France" manifested by an absolutist "millennarian" state, de Gaulle presented himself as the link between France's past and future greatness—a claim to legitimacy distinct not only from the Fourth Republic, but from the post-Revolution republican tradition itself.[111] By focusing attention on issues of pride, and linking disappointments to faults in the regime rather than to the decadence of "France" or the French people as a whole, de Gaulle could use his unassailable credentials as guardian of France's honor to overcome doubts about his authoritarian tendencies or his specific attitudes toward Algeria.[112] By casting the regime as the problem in 1958, and not the misconceptions of the French about themselves, their place in the world, and the wisdom of preserving French Algeria, de Gaulle offered the kind of comforting and "parsimonious" mystification of a painful, "stubborn reality" which Gramsci suggested would be necessary to achieve victory in a war of position.

De Gaulle's critiques of institutionalized immobility in the Fourth Republic implied nothing, however, about what policy might actually succeed in Algeria. As it happened, de Gaulle used the carefully redesigned institutions of the Fifth Republic, which concentrated substantially more power in the hands of the president, to sustain policies of disengagement from Algeria which were the reverse of what most French had expected from him. But this course became clear only late in 1959. Before May 1958 the specifics of his thinking about Algeria hardly mattered. In private his interlocutors were told contradictory things about his opinions. In his rare public comments he avoided referring to Algeria as part of France itself, while emphasizing the unassailability of French sovereignty and speaking of a "sincere integration" that clearly distinguished Algeria from Indochina, Tunisia, or Morocco. What mattered, in the Algerian context, was that de Gaulle's mythic stature and his regime-centered analysis reassured the deeply troubled Frenchmen masses. In their interpretation of reality the Algerian debacle could be understood as contingent on political decisions de Gaulle could make; it was not a reflection of deep flaws in themselves, in France, or in their conception of France's role in the world.

De Gaulle's studied availability as one who could save France by transforming the regime, instead of forcing the French to discard cherished beliefs about themselves and their nation, corresponded perfectly to his postwar political strategy for "winning completely" by playing the political game only when he could determine the rules. In 1946 de Gaulle resigned the premiership rather than exercise either of two other available options. Had he chosen to lead his own political party within the rough and tumble of Fourth Republic parliamentary life, he almost certainly could have returned to power. But he would have forfeited the opportunity, at some later date, to use his "unsullied" reputation to replace the regime. On the other hand, had he sought to seize power in 1946, that is, had he sought to initiate a "war of movement" against the regime, the blatant contradiction of "republican" norms involved would have split the people. Afterward it would have been impossible for him to present himself as the voice of a united France, thereby robbing whatever institutions he might have created of the legitimacy he saw as his most valuable asset.

And so de Gaulle chose a war of position. He boycotted all public ceremonies sponsored by the Fourth Republic.[113] In 1955 he expressed "total disinterest" in the outcome of general elections. He refused, he said, to participate in what he contemptuously referred to as "that which may be called, for convenience sake, 'the conduct of public affairs.' "[114] Abandoning his loyalists in Parliament in favor of uncompromising (but legal) opposition to the regime, he displayed a haughty self-confidence in his prediction of its eventual demise. His consistency on this point, even as his critics described the "death-agony of Gaullism,"[115] later proved valuable by demonstrating once again the apparent prescience that was an intrinsic element of his charismatic appeal.[116]

In the posture he adopted, of the man who had saved and would again save France from the humiliations associated with governments unworthy of her destiny, in all his public utterances, and in private interviews, he encouraged the development of a particular political discourse. The myths and predicaments underlying this discourse, however, required appropriately structured, "catastrophic" circumstances to become the basis for a successful Gaullist challenge to the regime. Thus did de Gaulle trust in the development of a kind of political crisis he believed would come, but could not publicly hope for. In Algeria he found it—a problem eminently constructible as "the dreaded yet necessary *secousse.*"[117]

De Gaulle's shrewd judgment of events in 1958, his deft timing, and the terms upon which he agreed to return to power were key elements in his reemergence as France's savior and the architect of the Fifth Republic. These moves, and the developments his careful formulations were designed to promote and forestall, were elements in the war of movement which de Gaulle waged from early 1958, when the death knell of the Fourth Republic began to sound in his ears, to the middle of 1961, when he stabilized the authority of the Fifth Republic by thwarting an attempted military coup. These maneuvers are analyzed in Chapter 7. What is crucial here is that his opportunity to undertake this war of movement was due to a prior victory in a quite different kind of struggle—a war of position—in which the framing of issues, rather than the seizure of power, was the center of contention.

Political Entrepreneurship and the Problematization of Ireland's Status within the United Kingdom

In Britain there was one first-rank politician—Gladstone—who made systematic efforts, both as prime minister and as opposition leader, to advance the cause of Ireland's political autonomy. In France, however, no powerful politician campaigned explicitly and systematically for separating Algeria from France. In both France and Britain those who clearly benefited most from the salience of the controversies over the fate of Algeria and Ireland were political entrepreneurs opposed to disengagement from these territories. I have just shown how Poujade, but especially de Gaulle, used a posture of opposing abandonment of Algeria to spectacular political advantage. I now show how Conservative and Unionist leaders in Britain, such as Salisbury, Chamberlain, and Randolph Churchill, embraced the controversy over Ireland as politically advantageous. By actively elaborating upon it they advanced their careers. However, as with comparable activities in France with respect to Algeria, British Unionists thereby strengthened the cause of Irish separatism by reinforcing in the consciousness of British citizens an image of Ireland as a territory only problematically linked to their state.

The Impact of Suffrage Extension

Between 1867 and 1885 Parliament enacted a series of electoral reforms which extended suffrage to male workers, introduced the secret ballot, eliminated most "rotten boroughs," and reapportioned or "redistributed" parliamentary districts, thereby substantially increasing the electoral weight of expanding metropolitan areas at the expense of agricultural "counties" in southern England. The fundamental impetus for this legislation was the transformation in the British economic landscape that industrialization produced. Both the Liberal and Conservative parties emerged from the middle of the nineteenth century as representatives of opposing tendencies within a relatively homogeneous landed and titled oligarchy. But economic power was shifting from the "field of corn" to the "field of coal." The mills and factories of Manchester and Birmingham, the trading houses of London and Liverpool, the coal mines of Cardiff and Newcastle, and the shipyards of Glasgow and Belfast were producing enormous new wealth. Associated with industrialization was urbanization, and the transformation of most British citizens from villagers to towns-people or city dwellers. By the late 1860s leaders of both parties recognized that whichever could more effectively broaden its appeal to reflect new British economic and social realities would enjoy a decisive advantage.

For the Conservatives the future seemed bleak. The cumulative effects of economic change and the extension of the franchise would throw power into the hands of those best able to rally support among the working classes. The danger was evident in Gladstone's crushing defeat of the Tories in 1868, the first election held after the Reform Act of 1867. The predic-ament that mass democracy posed for conservative, tradition-oriented par-ties would eventually be the same in every European industrial democracy as it was in Britian at this time. In Britain, as in France and Germany, the expansion of political participation set the stage for a war of position over the contours of the national agenda. The stakes were roughly the same in each country. If class-oriented issues were dominant, mass participation would benefit liberal, radical, or socialist parties. But if other issues could be made to loom largest, issues which aristocratically based, conservative parties were relatively better equipped to address—national prestige, in-ternational power, or cultural superiority—the right wing would benefit.

Disraeli's response to this predicament in Britain was "Tory democracy," a combination of social reform and jingoist imperialism which fired the imagination of the urban proletariat and, in the spirit of the times, appealed directly to ethnic and racialist pride in "English" superiority. Abandoning his 1852 view of the "wretched" colonies as "a millstone around our neck,"[118] Disraeli instead portrayed the empire as a glorious and essential part of England's domain, but as beset internationally by economic and military threats. Attacking the Liberals as the party of "Little England," Disraeli sought to cast doubt on Gladstone's ability to stand up for the Empire and its interests. Set forth most memorably in the Crystal Palace speech of 1872, this doctrine was the basis for Disraeli's 1874 campaign. That election brought the Tories to power, substituting a 109-seat parlia-mentary advantage over the Liberals for the 100-seat margin gained by the Liberals in 1868.

But in key respects Disraeli's appeal was ahead of its time. General Charles Gordon had not yet died in Khartoum. Disraeli's spirited foreign policy lacked immediacy for Britons who still knew little about interna-tional affairs, and were still attracted by the "sensible" Victorian reformism and studied fair-mindedness of Gladstone. The latter had great success using Disraeli's policies of "realpolitik" to embarrass him with florid ac-counts of Balkan Christians massacred by Disraeli's Muslim/Turkish allies.

To rescue his faltering ministry Disraeli picked the Irish question. Catholic Irish attacks on the economic and political status quo, construed as threats to national greatness and the integrity of the empire, were far more familiar, and so more menacing and convenient, than developments in far-off colonies. The revulsion of most Britons toward Irish lawlessness and terrorism and the results of by-elections in which anti-Irish sentiment among English workers contributed to Tory victories were both factors in Disraeli's decision.[119] In 1880, at the height of the Irish Land War, Disraeli dissolved Parliament, intending to fight the election on a platform of coercion in Ireland and die-hard opposition to home rule. In the sympathy for Irish home rule which he ascribed to the Liberals, Disraeli accused them of plotting to extend their policy of colonial "decomposition" to the "disintegration of the United Kingdom."[120] His failure to win reelection on this issue showed his timing was wrong. The subsequent success with which the Conservative party used the Irish question and anti-Irish sentiment to overthrow Liberal ascendancy shows, however, that Disraeli's instincts were correct.

Gladstone's 1880 Midlothian speeches roused the moral fervor of the country against what he portrayed as an unscrupulous "Beaconsfieldism" whose lack of respect for principles of justice and equity were responsible for economic distress in Britain, unrest in Ireland, and waste and outrage abroad. The theme of his campaign, which ended in a sweeping Liberal victory, was economic justice. Depicting it as a struggle of the "masses," which he and his party claimed to represent, against the "classes," he succeeded in shaping the agenda of national politics in a way that suited his needs and those of his party, replacing the Disraelian emphasis on prestige abroad and coercion in Ireland, with democratic appeals against privilege and concentrated wealth.

> We have great forces arrayed against us... we cannot reckon upon what is called the landed interest, we cannot reckon upon the clergy of the established church... we cannot reckon on the wealth of the country, nor upon the rank of the country, nor upon the influence which rank and wealth usually bring. In the main these powers are against us, for wherever there is a close corporation, wherever there is a spirit of organized monopoly, wherever there is a narrow and sectional interest... we, the liberal party, have no friendship and no tolerance to expect.[121]

The defeat shocked the Conservative party. With Disraeli's retirement, a leadership struggle ensued. Apart from the clash of personalities, the substance of the struggle revolved around the precise balance to be struck between social reform and jingoism in the "cry" of the party.

"Playing the Orange Card"
The Struggle for Leadership in the Conservative Party

The two main contenders for leadership of the Conservative party were Lord Randolph Churchill, the young and dynamic parliamentarian, and the marquess of Salisbury, Disraeli's first secretary of state for India and his second foreign minister.[122] In 1883 Gladstone made a stinging attack on Salisbury and the right wing of the Conservative party. His rhetoric suggested the potency of the appeal to democracy and economic justice which the Liberal party, comprised of Radicals, Gladstonian Liberals, and progressive Whigs, could make. He inveighed, "Lord Salisbury constitutes himself the spokesman of a class—of the class to which he himself belongs, who *toil not neither do they spin;* whose fortunes—as in his case—have originated by grants made in times gone by for the services which courtiers rendered kings, and have since grown and increased, while they have slept, by levying an increased share on all that other men have done by toil and labour to add to the general wealth and prosperity of the country."[123]

As a potential leader of the Conservatives, Randolph Churchill was less vulnerable to such attacks than Salisbury. Churchill's passionate oratory and virile demeanor made him popular among urban workers. Among party leaders, Churchill advocated emphasizing the social reform component of "Tory democracy" as a direct response to Gladstone's challenge. He believed the continued expansion of the electorate was inevitable, and he was anxious to find a formula for establishing the Conservatives as the ruling, not the opposition party. "Parliamentary reform," he wrote in 1883, "is the gage of battle, and the Party which carries it will have power for a quarter of a century."[124] His Primrose League, named after Disraeli's favorite flower, was a network of Tory activists as committed as he was to displacing Liberal party predominance by a full-blooded Tory democracy. In the League's platform, priority was given to ambitious schemes for improving the living conditions of urban workers.

Salisbury's aristocratic manner and distaste for the laboring masses, which made him an unlikely party leader should such a strategy have been adopted, argued against fighting the Liberals on their own ground. Despite a large increase in the size of the British electorate (the Franchise Act of 1884 raised the number of eligible voters in the United Kingdom from three million to five million), Salisbury insisted that the future of the Tory party could not be built on competition with the Liberals over social reform. Standing for "resistance to disintegration" at home and abroad, Salisbury wanted a Conservative party whose appeal would center on themes of English traditionalism, imperial power, and pride of place. The classes, he pointed out to Churchill, could not and would not fight in direct defense of the rights of property. Instead Salisbury advocated a more indirect strategy, one consistent with the natural disposition of the upper strata and the credulity of the lower. The key to electoral success would be for the "classes" to ignore economic issues and to select instead "some other matter on which they can appeal to prejudice."[125]

Salisbury not only understood this strategy as the best opportunity available to the Conservative party, but also viewed it as the most effective way to advance his own candidacy as party leader. By the time of Gladstone's public "conversion" to home rule, in late 1885, Salisbury had also come to see in Irish home rule that "other matter" which would enable politics to be shifted from interest to prejudice. It was in May 1886, as Gladstone's Home Rule Bill was being debated in the House of Commons, that Salisbury made his famous "manacles and Manitoba" speech. He compared the Irish to the "Hottentots"—a people too primitive to be granted self-government. He offered "government that does not flinch" as an alternative; resolute enforcement of coercion "for twenty years" and subsidies for the emigration of one million Irish to Canada. He also "sounded the tocsin of empire," asking whether rejection of the Home Rule Bill would be "only a halt in the gradual process of disintegration and decay, or whether it shall be the first step in a new and bolder Imperial policy."[126] Ireland was, says Peter Marsh, "a point where [Salisbury's] desires, the interests of his party, and the prejudices of his country came together powerfully. He used the Irish question to consolidate his primacy over the party, to stiffen its reflexes, to forge an alliance with the Unionist defectors from the Liberal Party, to get rid of Churchill, and hence to establish himself in office for almost fourteen years until he chose to lay the burden down."[127]

Making the Irish question work in this way required a particular construction of it. The home rule movement had to be cast as a mortal threat to the integrity of the "Union" (i.e., the United Kingdom of Great Britain and Ireland) and to the British Empire as a whole; as a betrayal of Protestant kith and kin in Ulster; and as an insult to the presumed superiority of the English over the Irish. Disraeli had tried and failed to do this in 1880. But five years later, with Parnell's ascendancy over a large Irish delegation at Westminster, the Irish party's increasingly militant nationalist rhetoric, Gladstone's apparent sympathy for home rule, and Ulster Protestants frightened about prospects for their continued predominance, there was considerably more to work with in conjuring English prejudice and patriotism than Disraeli had had at his disposal.

Extravagant imperialist themes, ethnocentric applications of historicist thinking, and social Darwinist nostrums were readily available to Salisbury. Systematically, in a manner epitomized by Salisbury's "manacles and

Manitoba" speech, Conservative politicians and publicists used them to construe Irish national demands as an insulting challenge to English pride and power—a challenge which, if not confronted with tough-minded determination, meant "imperial dismemberment" and national decline.[128] This "entrepreneurial" strategy, seeking to exploit the intrusion of Irish demands into British consciousness without satisfying them, entailed focusing public attention directly upon the eruption of Irish discontent and the nationalist demands it had spawned. It did not discourage—it *required* public perceptions of Ireland's political status as problematic. Remaining taboos that treated Ireland as if its permanent status as a part of the United Kingdom could be *presumed,* and not debated, had to be discarded. To construe Irish nationalists as a threat, to legitimize misanthropic appeals to British workers fearful of competition from masses of Irish Catholic immigrants, and to saddle the Liberal party with a reputation for being soft on the Irish and careless about imperial requirements, the separation of Ireland from Great Britain, however floridly opposed, had to be portrayed and debated as a real possibility.

Beginning in 1885 with Salisbury's formation of a short-lived minority government, he served as prime minister for thirteen and a half of the next seventeen years. "Defense of the Union with Ireland was the keystone" of his political strategy. It was fashioned as part of the war of position in which Salisbury saw himself engaged—a struggle to construct alignments of party and cleavage that would work to his advantage. With this strategy, Salisbury "placed his impress upon the Conservative Ministry, the Unionist alliance, and the politics of the ensuing generation."[129]

Thus did Irish demands for political autonomy become a political resource for Tory entrepreneurs able to mobilize Protestant loyalism in Ireland and antipapist sentiment among British workers on behalf of what would henceforth be called the Unionist party. Ultimately Salisbury used the Irish issue to better effect than his chief rival within the Conservative party, Randolph Churchill. But it was Churchill, again following in Disraeli's footsteps, who sought most spectacularly to exploit the specific opportunity that Irish nationalism created—to play, as he put it, "the Orange Card."[130]

Gladstone's Political Entrepreneurship and the
"Ripening" of the Irish Question

On December 15, 1885, Herbert Gladstone told several British newspaper editors that his father favored home rule for Ireland. The report was published on December 17, while the elder Gladstone was resting in

Hawarden, Scotland, after his November election victory. There has been much debate about whether the statement was an indiscretion on the son's part or a trial balloon. Most evidence suggests the former. The incident is nonetheless known as the Hawarden Kite. It figures prominently in all efforts to explain the timing of Irish home rule's appearance on the agenda of British politics. Four months after the kite, Gladstone came forward with the first Home Rule Bill (discussed in Chap. 3), marking the beginning of a thirty-year period during which the national demands of the Irish shaped and disrupted British political life more powerfully and consistently than any other single issue, domestic or foreign.

Focus on these particular events—the Hawarden Kite and introduction of the Gladstone's first Home Rule Bill—reflects a traditional emphasis in the pertinent historical literature. In the work of unabashed admirers of Gladstone, his personal crusade to bring justice to Ireland is seen as the decisive factor in the late nineteenth-century resurrection of the Irish question.[131] Gladstone is depicted as he wished himself to be understood—as a farseeing statesman, convinced by his unusual powers of analysis that only sweeping political concessions to Irish demands for autonomy could prevent social revolution in Ireland, stabilize the relationship between the two islands, and prevent a terrible struggle within Britain over Irish independence. In Gladstone's view, as in that of his admirers, the eruption of such a struggle was liable to severely damage, if not destroy, British democracy. For the good of the country and for the sake of justice, so the account goes, Gladstone jeopardized his political career and brought an end, in the process, to nearly four decades of Whig and Liberal party dominance. A contemporary description of Gladstone's bearing immediately preceding the 1886 vote to reject home rule captures the spirit of this conception. "The Grand Old Man might have been an early Christian martyr marching to his doom . . . the sight was most sublime—the look of fixed, almost agonized resolve of a great leader to sacrifice his proud position at the head of a great and powerful party to satisfy the claims of justice and to bestow the blessings of peace and prosperity upon a sorely vexed country."[132]

Lord Salisbury exaggerated when he said that Gladstone, and Gladstone alone, had "turned Home Rule from a chimera into a burning issue."[133] But Gladstone's willingness, especially after 1885, to stake out a position on Irish home rule far in advance of that of his country, and his party, is undeniable. Considering the veto which he knew the House of Lords would exercise against his first Home Rule Bill, had it passed the House of Commons, Gladstone's commitment to home rule as a vehicle for political education of the British public is also clear. In this regard, current scholarship agrees with the older, hagiographical literature on Gladstone and

Ireland. Gladstone's alliance with Parnell's Home Rule party in his third ministry, and the formal proposal of a Home Rule Bill in the House of Commons, meant that "maintenance of the union had ceased to be a basic assumption of British politics and had become an open issue between the parties."[134]

Without denying Gladstone's crucial role, and against the background of Irish events and intellectual trends described above, more recent work has sought to contextualize and demystify Gladstone's policies toward Ireland. In their often contradictory analyses, contemporary scholars share a broad interest in the implications for political competition of dramatic changes in late nineteenth-century Britain's economy, international position, and electoral system. All agree that these transformations pushed both the Conservative and Liberal parties toward painful realignments and that leading British politicians began to see the problematization of Ireland's status as posing unusual, albeit risky opportunities to advance or protect their own political fortunes. In other words, these transformations were the setting within which pressures created by events in Ireland, and the newly available interpretations of those events described above, could be translated into opportunities with unusually large payoffs for ambitious and imaginative elites—including Gladstone.

Indeed Gladstone was the first major British politician to appreciate the pressing nature of Irish demands as well as the political opportunities they presented. It is instructive to consider how Gladstone's public presentation of his view of the Irish question evolved from his anti-Repeal vote in 1843 to his sponsorship of home rule forty-three years later, and why his publicly stated views lagged so far behind his private assessments of what, eventually, would be necessary to solve the Irish problem.

The political mobilization of Irish Catholics occurred amid the struggle to synchronize change in party programs and appeals with the aforementioned shifts in the composition of the electorate. But because many reform bills distinguished between England and Ireland, and because Irish Catholic society was overwhelmingly rural in nature, the consequences of franchise extension in Ireland were not strongly felt until 1884, when agricultural laborers were given the vote.[135] The result of the sudden enfranchisement of virtually all Irish Catholic males, and Parnell's success in translating that voting strength into a disciplined, nationalist political party, was that every Parliament between 1885 and 1916 included at least eighty Irish nationalists, who often held the balance of power between the Unionists and the Liberals.

As noted earlier, following the Fenian rising Gladstone began to turn his party's attention to satisfying Irish social and economic grievances. In the 1868 campaign he promised to destroy the Protestant ascendancy in

Ireland, referring to it as a "tall tree of noxious growth . . . lifting its head to Heaven and poisoning the atmosphere of the land so far as its shadow can extend. It is still there, gentlemen, but now at last the day has come when as we hope, the axe has been laid to the root. . . . There lacks, gentlemen, but one stroke more—the stroke of these Elections."[136]

This kind of talk represented a dramatic change in Gladstone's public approach, though not necessarily in his private convictions. As early as 1845, only two years after joining in the overwhelming majority that blocked Irish efforts to promote Repeal of the Union, Gladstone wrote to his wife about the eventual need to make right the depredations inflicted on Ireland. "Ireland, Ireland!" he declared, "that cloud in the west, that coming storm, the minister of God's retribution upon cruel and inveterate and but half-atoned injustice! Ireland forces upon us those great social and great religious questions—God grant that we may have courage to look them in the face, and to work through them."[137]

A key feature of rule in Ireland by the Protestant "Ascendancy" was the established Episcopal Church of Ireland and the tithes it exacted from Ireland's Catholic majority. Although in 1865 Gladstone had voted against a radical member's bill to consider the status of the Irish church, in 1868 he addressed the issue head on.[138] Aware of the bitter resentment expressed by Catholics over the establishment of a minority sect's church in their country, considering the Conservatives vulnerable in their identification with so "manifestly exploitative" an institution, and able to link the disestablishmentarianism of his nonconformist followers in Scotland and Wales to Irish Catholic demands, Gladstone included reform of the Irish church as part of a comprehensive package of reforms for Ireland outlined in December 1867.[139] In March 1868 he declared in favor of disestablishing the Church of Ireland, making it the primary issue of the campaign.[140] The 1868 campaign ended in a Liberal victory and a 20 percent increase in the party's parliamentary majority, an increase due entirely to the success of the Liberal party among Catholics in Ireland. In 1868 twenty-five Liberals were elected in Ireland, compared to five in 1865.

Gladstone's government quickly passed legislation disestablishing the Irish church. Efforts to respond to Irish grievances in other areas, notably the Land Act of 1870, were less successful but reflected the same attempt to extend to Ireland, and to Irish voters, the practical, reformist liberalism Gladstone advocated in Britain.[141] Gladstone did not yet see, or at least did not depict, the Irish problem as that of a "nationalist" movement demanding political autonomy, if not independence. In his 1880 campaign against Disraeli, Gladstone emphasized the need to reestablish law and order in Ireland; at the same time he promoted a number of economic measures, especially land reform. Once in office he implemented a forceful

Coercion Act, but also provided Irish tenant farmers with substantial loans and legal protection against abuse by landlords.

Gladstone retrospectively explained his unwillingness to advocate home rule until 1886 by judgments that the issue had not sufficiently "ripened" in the public mind, that explicit initiatives toward that end were likely to trigger dangerously deep divisions in the country, and that, until 1885, the Irish people had not "unequivocally" (that is, via elections) endorsed national autonomy. Less generous interpretations of Gladstone's record on Ireland contend that Gladstone knew and cared little about Irish affairs and that, until the 1880s, held conventional views toward the Union and Ireland's permanent place within it. According to these accounts, Gladstone embraced home rule in 1886 out of error or self-interest: because he construed it as a great and terrible issue whose threat to the nation could only be met by his special talents, and with which he could rationalize his reluctance to retire from politics (Jenkins); because his own brand of liberal imperialism required its extension to Ireland as to England's other colonies (Dunne); because of an "eccentric historicism," and because he was panicked into an unreasoning fear of Irish social revolution by the exaggerated reports of key advisers (Loughlin); because by 1886 an alliance with Parnell was the only way could he form a government (Kee, Marsh); because he could thereby purge the Liberal party of Radicals and Whigs who opposed his leadership (Cooke and Vincent); or, somewhat contrarily, because he saw home rule as a great unifying theme for a Liberal party divided and confused by "faddism" (Hamer).[142]

Despite their differences, these scholars clearly establish how crucial were Gladstone's partisan political calculations in linking structural changes in British society and in the electoral system to a redefinition of the Irish question in British politics. However, in their urge to debunk accounts of Gladstone's foresight and courage by proving his self-interested behavior in 1885 and 1886, these authors often ignore the importance of the changing terms with which Gladstone dismissed or criticized home rule proposals in the 1870s and early 1880s. For what was at stake was not whether home rule would be legislated into reality, but whether consideration of fundamental changes in the constitutional shape of the United Kingdom would be admitted as discussable in British politics and, theoretically at least, open to modification by parliamentary action.

Looking back to his first ministry (1868–74) from the vantage point of 1886, Gladstone identified, in the shift he had made in the rhetoric with which he had opposed home rule, what he considered his most significant contribution to the gradual achievement of national autonomy for Ireland. Protesting against the idea that "it is the duty of every Minister to make known... every idea which has formed itself in his mind,"[143] Gladstone characterized himself as having believed in the possible advisability of home rule even while his colleagues were rejecting the idea in principle as either monstrous or absurd. Convinced of the dangers associated with the premature consideration of the idea in Parliament, he claimed to have decided to wait and hope that home rule would not be necessary. Still, he contended, he had at no time regarded "domestic government for Ireland... as necessarily replete with danger, or as a question which ought to be blocked out by the assertion of some high constitutional doctrine with which it could not be reconciled."[144]

Home rule for Ireland, he claimed, was one of those things in politics which "cannot properly become the subject of action until they have been seen as well as foreseen."[145] Listing a number of conditions under which he had considered that "the question of a statutory Parliament for Ireland could be warrantably entertained," he summed up their significance with the concept of "ripeness."[146] What was required before an issue such as Ireland's status had "ripened" to the point of action were more subtle forms of political education. As evidence that this was what he had been about for some time, Gladstone quoted his well-known 1871 speech which firmly rejected Isaac Butt's proposals for home rule, or home government, in Ireland. Gladstone pointed out that despite the fact that, at that time, he advocated and still hoped for implementation of reforms for Ireland which could cement the union between it and Great Britain, he did not condemn political autonomy as fundamentally inconsistent with reason or with the honor, sovereignty, or vital interests of the British state. By criticizing the proposal on its merits "instead of denouncing the idea of Home Rule as one in its essence destructive of the unity of the Empire," Gladstone described himself as having opened the door to "a recognition of the question in a different state of things.... Thus, at the very first inception of the question, I threw aside the main doctrine on which opposition to Irish autonomy is founded. This was the first step, and I think a considerable step, towards placing the controversy on its true basis."[147]

Historians sympathetic to Gladstone implicitly accept his own portrayal of the delicate and sustained contribution he made to the breakdown of an ideologically hegemonic conception of Ireland's relationship to Britain. More skeptical historians stress how late it was before Gladstone actually advocated home rule, and how unsympathetic were his motives in doing so. But even those most hostile to the image of Gladstone as a farsighted statesman agree that by the early 1880s he had come to favor some sort of political devolution for Ireland, at least as a way to deflect Irish demands for a national legislature (which was the operational meaning of home rule).[148] He began advocating the establishment of county councils and wider forms of municipal government in Ireland. He responded favorably to Joseph Chamberlain's proposal in 1882 for a "Central Board" that would meet in Dublin to handle purely Irish affairs. In his contribution to the debate over extending the franchise to Irish agricultural workers in 1884, Gladstone's growing sympathy with Irish demands for home rule was evident. He argued that the measure deserved support precisely because it provided an opportunity for the Irish masses to declare themselves in support of it.[149] In all these ways, without actually proposing home rule, Gladstone sought to establish it as a matter of practical politics, an idea to be evaluated, amended, criticized, and improved, but an idea that itself did not run counter to fundamental principles of British political life or the assumptions that governed political competition.[150]

Gladstone's expectations were met by Parnell's sweeping success in the 1885 elections. From then on, however, Gladstone was unable to guide Ireland's entry onto the British political agenda with quite the precision he desired. Parnell's descriptions of what home rule would and could mean left little doubt that he saw it as a first stage toward as much independence as Ireland could achieve. Asked repeatedly whether he considered home rule a final settlement of Irish demands, or whether total separation from Britain would eventually be demanded, Parnell declared in 1885 that "No man has a right to fix the boundary to the march of a nation. No man has a right to say to his country: thus far shalt thou go and no further. We have never attempted to fix the *ne plus ultra* to the progress of Ireland's nationhood and we never shall."[151]

Despite Parnell's tacit endorsement of maximal nationalist demands, he was obviously ready to play the game of British parliamentary politics. During the 1885 election campaign he ordered his supporters in Britain to vote Conservative so as to demonstrate to the Liberals their need for his support. By that time politicians from all streams of British political life—including Tories, Radicals, and Whigs—had begun seeking parliamentary alliances with Irish Home Rulers. Although this competition for Irish nationalist political support accelerated the breakdown of the ideological hegemony of the concept of a British Ireland, it also presented Gladstone with a set of circumstances toward which he had always maintained a deep aversion—a situation in which leading British parties would seek to outbid each other for Irish nationalist support. Whether motivated by idealism, concern for the stability of British constitutional life, or by calculations of expediency, Gladstone urged his Conservative rivals to consider home rule for Ireland to be in the same category as the Great Reform Act of 1832, the repeal of the Corn Laws in 1846, and the partial enfranchisement of English workers in 1867. These were all adaptations by the state to dangerous pressures—measures advocated by Whigs or Liberals, but implemented in the end by Conservatives. When the Conservatives formed a minority government (with Parnell's tacit support) in November 1885, Gladstone engaged in intensive efforts to convince Salisbury and other Whig and Tory politicians to implement home rule on the basis of national consensus.

But by the time of the Hawarden Kite it was clear this effort would fail. If Gladstone interpreted the precedents of 1832, 1846, and 1867 as statesmanlike acts of Conservative leaders anxious to protect the political system from polarized conflict, Salisbury remembered that Conservative support for those reforms had each time been immediately followed by long periods of Whig or Liberal rule.[152] Now that the idea of Irish home rule was conceivable and discussable, and therefore capable of frightening British voters, Radical, Whig, and Tory politicians all saw much greater political opportunities in rousing imperial, Protestant, and misanthropic sentiment against it (and against the Catholic Irish in general), than in supporting measures by which Irish nationalist aspirations might prudently be satisfied.

Along with the views of Salisbury, Churchill, and Gladstone, the responses of Radical and Whig leaders (Joseph Chamberlain and Lord Hartington) to the Irish question contributed to the breakdown of the ideological hegemony of a British-ruled Ireland. By portraying the Parnellites as "potential allies rather than revolutionary separatists," Joseph Chamberlain indicated early in 1885 that he was prepared to recognize the Irish as "a separate nation" and ready to meet "in the fullest possible way, the legitimate aspirations of the Irish people towards entire independence in the management of their local affairs."[153] But in successive drafts of what he called his "Central Board," "National Board," or "National Council" scheme for Ireland, Chamberlain reduced the scope of the proposal, finding in Parnell a much more useful enemy than friend.[154] The direction of change in Chamberlain's thinking, and his dramatic break with Gladstone in March 1886, stemmed directly from his view of Ireland as part of an English dominated "imperial federation," his belief that Radical support of the Irish was weak, and his discovery that an "aggressive unionism" was a much livelier electoral appeal than accommodating the "local patriotism" of Irish Catholics. Citing strong anti-Irish feelings among "artisans and non-conformists" and "English and Scotch workmen," he foresaw a Whig-Tory coalition whose appeal to prejudice would "carry all before them."[155] Loyal to the "consolidationist" imperialism that had served him, and would serve him, so well, he led the Radicals out of the Liberal party. Together with their traditional "class" enemies, the Whigs, the Radicals formed the Liberal Unionist party. In permanent coalition with the Tories, Chamberlain rose to power on a platform of coercion in Ireland and vigorous new imperialist policies abroad.

Hartington's break with Gladstone occurred immediately after the Hawarden Kite. Despite his support for moderate local government reforms in Ireland he (and most of the Whigs), remained resolutely opposed to home rule. Like Salisbury, Hartington saw home rule as a threat to the empire as a whole. He also believed he could not maintain the confidence of his supporters if he took anything less than a strong position against it. He was therefore deaf to Gladstone's pleas to remain loyal to the Liberal party. Nor was he impressed by Gladstone's attempt to find common ground with him on the Irish issue by stressing that change in Ireland's status was now, as much for Hartington as it was for Gladstone, an instrumental question—not one of fundamental principle.[156] Hartingtonian Whigs had become increasingly uncomfortable with radically tinged Gladstonian liberalism. In opposition to home rule and loyalty to the "Union," many Whigs found the firm basis they needed to forge an alliance with the Tories.[157]

Even Randolph Churchill and Lord Salisbury, whose use of home rule as a foil for their militantly anti-Irish appeals has already been discussed, flirted with Parnell in 1885. Churchill's opposition to Gladstone's renewal of coercion, Salisbury's appointment of the liberally minded Carnarvon as Irish secretary in 1885, and the Conservative government's promulgation of the Ashbourne Land Purchase Act for Ireland served as a basis for exploratory contacts between Parnell and the Conservative party. For Parnell the possibility of an alliance with the Conservatives was meant to strengthen his hand in bargaining with Gladstone. For the Conservatives, these maneuvers were mainly designed to embarrass the Liberals and increase the price they would be compelled to pay for Parnell's support. After the Hawarden Kite in December, the Conservative government swiftly reversed its field and endorsed coercion in Ireland. This change forced Gladstone, with neither Whig nor Radical support, into an open declaration of his home rule views and a full-fledged alliance with Parnell. Despite some claims to the contrary, there was little more than tactical maneuvering in Tory overtures to the Irish nationalists. But even as tactics, these overtures contributed to the legitimization of Irish nationalist politicians as players in the British parliamentary game, and to the appearance of their demands on the agenda of British politics.

In 1885 and 1886 Gladstone had tried to persuade both his allies and his opponents that conditions were ripe for passing home rule legislation. He was clearly wrong in this assesment. Instead of implementing home rule as a historic solution to the Irish question, his bill accomplished just what he said he feared most—a polarization of political opinion on the Irish issue that inflamed passions to dangerous levels and made the Liberal party politically dependent on Irish nationalist support. On the other hand, the transformation of home rule from an idea "dismissed in England as a bogey or no more than a distant possibility ... to the centre of debate"[158] he saw as a major accomplishment. In this respect Gladstone's judgment after his bill's defeat, and after the Unionist landslide of 1886, was more sound than his assessment or his tactics a year earlier. He concluded, "I do not venture to forecast the future, beyond the expression of an undoubting belief that a measure of self-government for Ireland, not less extensive than the proposal of 1886, will be carried."[159] The Irish, he continued, needed only to persevere to eventually achieve the satisfaction of their just demands—demands which had finally been accepted as a legitimate matter of dispute, susceptible to reasonable measures which the institutions of the British state could adopt.[160]

If Ireland had therefore benefited from Gladstone's exertions on behalf of home rule, the Liberal party's career at the same time was dealt a shattering blow. And if Britain was now to be subjected to the kind of long, wrenching, and polarized struggle Gladstone had emphasized he wanted to avoid, Gladstone himself did not go unrewarded. With another "great controversy" raging across the country, and his main rivals for party leadership now departed from Liberal ranks, the Grand Old Man yet again postponed his retirement, positioning himself to gain the premiership one more time in 1892.

Regardless of whether they supported or opposed autonomy for Ireland, and regardless of whatever other motives may have been involved, politicians such as Salisbury, Randolph Churchill, Gladstone, Joseph Chamberlain, and Hartington all contributed to the breakdown of the hegemonic idea of Ireland as an integral part of the United Kingdom. They did so by treating change in the terms of the Union between Britain and Ireland as a *possibility* and by seeking to exploit that possibility for their own purposes. Each drew on historicist, social Darwinist, and/or new imperialist ideas to interpret Ireland's changing status. Each sought to use the emerging problematization of Ireland's status to create or consolidate winning coalitions or to break those of their opponents. They tried, in other words, by the exercise of political entrepreneurship, to guide processes of issue definition and party realignment in profitable directions. The construction of an Irish national question, legitimately and vigorously debated within British politics, and the consequent breakdown of a previously hegemonic view of Ireland as a part of the Union were encouraged by their efforts.

Conclusion

In Part II I have explained how the political classes in two metropolitan states came to view the status of two territories ruled by them as problematic. Wars of position among Liberals, Unionists, and Irish nationalists, and among Gaullists, Poujadists, and mainstream Fourth Republic politicians, account for the emergence of Ireland and Algeria as issues on the agendas of Great Britain and France. Despite the metropolitan focus, however, processes leading to this recategorization were seen to have begun in the nationalist mobilization of the Irish and the Algerians.

In the British-Irish case, the problematization of Ireland's status required the overthrow of an existing hegemonic conception. It was necessary, in terms of the model presented in Chapter 2, to move the Irish problem back through the ideological hegemony threshold. The expectation associated with this metaphor was that such backward movement through a threshold could be accomplished only when forces pushing in that direction were overwhelming. In accordance with this expectation, and in the context of the three-factor theory of hegemonic stability discussed in this chapter, it is not surprising that severe discrepancies between Ireland's officially equal status within the United Kingdom and the reality of Catholic subordination, along with the intrusion of Irish discontent into British consciousness associated with that discrepancy, were not sufficient to bring an end to the ideologically hegemonic status of Ireland's integration within the United Kingdom.

Figure 3 shows that Irish events and Irish discontent, including the Repeal agitation, the consequences of the Great Famine, and the 1848 rising, intruded more thoroughly and for a longer period of time into the consciousness of the British political class in the 1840s than in the 1860s, 1870s, or 1880s. But breakdown of ideological hegemony occurred in the latter part of the century, rather than earlier, because of two factors absent in the 1830s and 1840s: popular perspectives on culture, history, and politics which encouraged the analysis of Ireland as contingently linked to Britain; and electoral, economic, and international circumstances within which reinterpretation of Irish discontent, and struggle over Ireland's status, could be profitably exploited by ambitious political entrepreneurs. In the absence of these factors, the "gross discrepancies" between the official status of Ireland (an integral part of the United Kingdom) and Irish realities (millions of its inhabitants could starve, die of disease, or emigrate without producing a sense of national catastrophe in Britain) were insufficient to displace hegemonic British beliefs about Ireland's future.

In the French-Algerian case, as demonstrated in Chapter 4, Algeria's status as a part of France was never established as hegemonic. The absence of struggles over Algeria's status before the mid-1950s was explained by the lack of significant strain on that relationship. The relative rapidity with which the Algerian revolt triggered debates in France over the future of Algeria is thus partially explained by the absence of a hegemonic conception of Algeria as an integral part of the French state, whether defined as metropolitan France (including Algeria) or as the French Union. Had one of the three attempts to hegemonize larger conceptions of France succeeded, it could have acted as the same kind of cognitive and political barrier against entry of the Algerian question onto the French agenda that presumptions of Ireland's permanent incorporation into the United Kingdom formed against introduction of the Irish question into British political life in the 1840s.

It is unclear whether the Algerian revolt and the massive discrepancies between the reality of war in Algeria and the official status of Algerian territory as a collection of French departments were themselves sufficient to place the issue of Algeria onto the metropolitan political agenda. What is apparent is that the revolt triggered the first serious effort to develop a hegemonic project focused specifically on Algeria's status—Algérie française. Explaining the failure of that project required analysis of intellectual trends as well as political entrepreneurship. As in the British-Irish case, these factors played a role more complex than anticipated in the model I have inferred from Gramsci. Neo-realist economic ideas, relativistic trends in philosophy and anthropology, as well as an international political culture favoring decolonization were available for interpreting and legitimizing Algerian Muslim demands for political autonomy from France. Sartre, Aron, and eventually Mendès-France drew on these ideas to fashion critiques of French policy. However, before 1959, and in the context of the central motifs of postwar French political culture (shame, fear of humiliation, fear of loss of great power status), the importance of these alternative visions was not that they convinced the French to abandon beliefs that Algeria was or could be made part of France, or that politicians gained support by using them. The visions' most important contribution to the construction of Algeria's future as an explicit issue in French politics was the opportunity they provided antiregime political entrepreneurs (especially de Gaulle) to depict a politically unwinnable war as a decisive test of the Fourth Republic's legitimacy and of the *vertu* of its leaders.

In the British-Irish case, Gladstone did draw on historicist and imperialist ideas to legitimize discussion of Irish home rule and recast Ireland's political links to Great Britain as contingent on British generosity toward Irish Catholics and toleration of Irish nationalist sentiments. Gladstone's electoral victories in 1868 and 1880 (especially the former) and his 1886 success in purging the Liberal party of Whig and Radical rivals for his leadership are in line with Gramsci's expectation that political entrepreneurs can use counterhegemonic conceptions to advance their own careers. But as in the French-Algerian case, "new ways of thinking" in the British-Irish case played their most important role as a vehicle for raising nationalist demands for autonomy onto the agenda of metropolitan politics.

Chamberlain, Churchill, Hartington, and Salisbury used historicist, imperialist, and social Darwinist ideas to construct Irish home rule as an insulting, dangerous threat to England and to the British Empire. Their efforts, while substantially advancing their own careers, blocked home rule legislation in the House of Commons in 1886 and the House of Lords in 1893.[161] Anchored in its opposition to Irish home rule, the Unionist coalition they brought into existence among English aristocrats, Ulster Protestants, working class Tories, and Radical imperialists ended the Liberal party's career as Britain's governing party. The matrix of ideas promoted by the founders of this coalition helped establish the political dominance of the Unionist party from 1886 to 1906. But just as Gaullist and Poujadist dramatizations of the real threat of Algerian separation helped prevent efforts to make Algeria appear to the French as a natural, inevitable, and permanent part of France, so did Unionist use of the Irish question as a political resource help remove presumptions of inevitability and naturalness from the image of Ireland as an integral, permanent part of the United Kingdom.

In both cases the long-term consequence of hegemonic projects based on global images (of the "British Empire" and the "French Union") was to make it difficult if not impossible for less ambitious hegemonic projects to succeed. We cannot know for sure whether the ideologically hegemonic status of Ireland's incorporation into the United Kingdom could have survived the forces that transformed both Britain and Ireland in the late nineteenth and early twentieth centuries. Nor can we know for certain that Soustelle's dream of establishing Algeria in French minds as equivalent to a collection of hexagonal departments was doomed to failure. What is fairly obvious, however, is that neither the Anglo-Saxon Empire espoused by Dilke and Seeley nor the imperial federation of Chamberlain and Rhodes had a better chance of acceptance as the commonsensically correct description of the British political community than a United Kingdom limited to the "British Isles." Likewise, it is clear from the dismal failure of both versions of the French Union discussed in Chapter 4 that widening the French public's commonsensical view of France to include Algeria was considerably more promising than promoting a France that would equally include Dahomey, Indochina, and Madagascar.

In the British political lexicon of 1800, "the Empire" was constitutionally established as the United Kingdom of Great Britain and Ireland. Accordingly, as noted in Chapter 3, the Parliament at Westminster was officially renamed the "Imperial Parliament." But in the latter third of the nineteenth century public sentiments and patriotic enthusiasm were distracted from this "United Kingdom," as "the Empire," to a smaller unit—England—and to a much larger one—the "British Empire," upon which it was said "the sun never sets." In addition to providing Gladstonian advocates of Irish autonomy with arguments for enhancing imperial unity via Irish home rule, celebrations of *English* superiority and efforts to institutionalize various versions of an English-ruled "Greater Britain" diverted public attention from the affairs of the United Kingdom. In effect, Unionists sought to draw the hegemonic mantle which had come to cover Ireland's incorporation into the United Kingdom over a much larger array of territories. Thus despite its name (Unionism), the movement in opposition to Irish home rule was largely founded on images of the British political community which contradicted the constitutional definition of the "Union" (between Great Britain and Ireland). Moreover, by exploiting and reinforcing anti-Irish sentiments among British workers, the Tories effectively abandoned efforts to appeal for political support among Irish Catholics. This contributed to a cleavage pattern which deprived the majority of the Irish of the integrative effects that would have accompanied vigorous Liberal-Tory competition for their electoral support.

In light of the Catholic church's conservative inclinations, and the eventual success of the Conservative party in solving the Irish land problem, British Conservatives would likely have enjoyed considerable advantages in competition for Irish Catholic votes. But such competition would have presupposed a genuine commitment to the integration of Ireland into the United Kingdom, on terms that respected Irish as well as English national sentiments. It would also have entailed the subordination of blue-water imperial affairs to those of the United Kingdom. Since both of these commitments would have run counter to the ideas that excited the country and dominated the thinking of party activists, a strategy based on rallying Irish Catholics to the Conservative banner did not present itself as an attractive formula for ambitious Tory political entrepreneurs. Instead, by building its political base on opposition to Irish Catholics, the Tory party helped construct an electoral system that pitted an imperialist-Unionist England (with Protestant Ulster) against a Liberal and (Irish Nationalist) Celtic periphery. In this way, and despite the election victories it enjoyed as a result, Unionism helped intensify the strains that led eventually to the breakup of the United Kingdom.[162]

As seen in Chapter 4, Algeria's close relationship to France, and the general, if casual, inclination of most French people after World War II to see that relationship as permanent, encouraged advocates of the French Union to use Algeria as an exemplar for supposedly similar ties between the hexagon and each part of overseas France. But just as Ireland's demotion from an integral part of the mother country to one of a panoply of English possessions undermined the hegemonic status of conceptions of Ireland as a permanent part of the British state, so too did the submergence of Algeria within the vast expanse of the French Union prevent a timely and focused evocation of Algeria as a true prolongation of the metropole.

Whatever real prospects existed in the postwar period for a larger redefinition of France depended on the full integration of Algerian Muslims into French political and economic life. For this to have occurred, Algérie française would have had to be advanced as the first, not the third, candidate for hegemonic status. In retrospect it is apparent that had the Fourth Republic's constitution enshrined incorporation of Algeria, and only Algeria, into France, its terms would have corresponded much more closely to what postwar France was actually capable of being than what was described in the drafts produced by either constituent assembly. In support of that objective, the legal, diplomatic, demographic, and geographical factors that lent credence to Algérie française in the 1950s would have had more time to establish themselves as natural. The political, military, and economic resources wasted on the hopelessly ambitious institutions of the French Union, a major war in Indochina, repression in Madagascar, Tunisia, and Morocco, and minimally satisfactory reforms elsewhere in French Africa could instead have been devoted to raising Muslim living standards in Algeria, establishing political equality among all French Algerians, and cultivating positive images of Algerian Muslims as culturally distinct but loyal French.

The motives of both British and French political entrepreneurs who helped frame the Irish and Algerian issues were mixed. Gladstone, Salisbury, and de Gaulle, at various times, each saw ways to improve their own political prospects by persuading constituents to view links to the peripheral territory as (dangerously) problematic, or by reinforcing and exploiting beliefs that they were. One major difference between the two cases is that British politicians anticipated that the outcomes they hoped for or feared would emerge within a stable institutional context. Although Gladstone often argued that too prolonged and explicit a struggle over Irish autonomy might threaten the stability of the British regime, it is difficult to say how genuinely he feared such an outcome. The argument seems mainly to have been advanced as a way to encourage support for his preferred solution to the problem (a Liberal/Tory–sponsored Home Rule Bill). On the other hand, in strong contrast to the French case, no leading British politician (including Parnell) ever considered the problematization of Ireland politically useful *because* it would help destroy the regime.[163] In the French case, however, no leading politician even pretended to seek the problematization of Algeria's status and advance solutions entailing partial or complete disengagement out of concern for the stability of the Fourth Republic.

There was one specific reason why no French head of government, or candidate for the premiership, ever made as active an effort as did Gladstone to problematize the territorial issue and seek satisfaction of indigenous political aspirations. Although the French National Assembly was even more delicately divided along party lines than the British Parliament, it did not include a "Parnellite" Algerian party, able to trade decisive numbers of votes for recognition if not satisfaction of its demands. This lack was largely due to the relatively complete success enjoyed by Europeans in Algeria, who prevented virtually all efforts to extend political rights to Algerian Muslims, in comparison with the gradual failure of Irish Protestants, between 1800 and 1884, to prevent the gradual extension of political rights to Irish Catholics.

The presence of an Irish nationalist party in the British Parliament was a key element in transforming the Irish question from a revolutionary threat to a hotly contested, prolonged, but primarily legal and parliamentary political issue (at least until 1912). The absence of a comparable party in the French National Assembly deprived Mendès-France or Mollet of coalitions excluding the *pieds noirs* and their supporters. This in turn drove Muslim évolués into the arms of the FLN, made revolt in Algeria virtually inevitable, and helped turn the struggle over Algerian policy from a factor determining the composition of governments to a threat to the stability of the regime.

An even more fundamental factor accounting for these differences in the consequences of hegemonic failure regarding British Ireland and French Algeria is that the British constitutional monarchy, established in 1688, was much more fully institutionalized than the Fourth Republic. In this context it was possible for one element in the ideological basis of the British regime's legitimacy (the hegemonic status of legislative integration between Great Britain and Ireland) to be removed without presenting a clear and immediate danger that the authority of the regime would be questioned. Unlike Britain, France has had a long history of weakly institutionalized regimes susceptible to internal destabilization and collapse. As indicated in Chapter 4, the Fourth Republic relied heavily on myths about the indissolubility of ties to non-European territories over which France had been sovereign and on the special vocation of France to transmit the civilizing influence of French culture to non-European peoples. Its founders treated these myths as resources for the construction of a "greater France," as candidates for hegemonic status which could endow the new regime with legitimacy and authority. It was therefore much more difficult for French politicians in the 1950s than for British politicians in the 1870s and 1880s to imagine, or help their publics to imagine, that the fate of a territory officially portrayed as a part of the state could be treated as an open question without undermining the ability of the regime to keep other dangerous issues off the agenda.[164]

PART III

State Contraction and the Regime Threshold in Britain and France

In the spring of 1988, several months after the outbreak of the intifada, a Zionist conference was convened to discuss the prospects for Israeli democracy. At the opening session Yaron Ezrahi, a Hebrew University political scientist, described the country as evenly divided between those who thought it "mortally dangerous to the State of Israel" to trade territories for peace and those who thought it mortally dangerous not to do so. The pertinent question, he said, "is how can we as a democratic state survive the kind of decision we have to take in the near future?"[1]

What he was describing as at stake in the struggle over the shape of the state was no longer the nature of Israeli political discourse, not the psychological "erasure" of the Green Line, not the possible success of annexationist efforts to instantiate presumptive beliefs that could prevent territorial issues from arising, but the stability of the regime—the legal order whose rules would otherwise be expected to govern competition over government policy. His concern, in other words, was not with a war of position, but a war of maneuver, not with prospects for state-building associated with establishing a new hegemonic conception of the state, but with prospects for securing the integrity of the regime against the forces liable to be unleashed by state contraction.

Part III of this volume follows Part II in a sequence that corresponds to the sequence of struggles over Israeli rule of the West Bank and Gaza carried on within Israel during the last decade. As in Part II, I analyzed the dynamics of wars of position to explain Britain's and France's failure of hegemonic state-building regarding Ireland and Algeria, so in Part III I focus on the dynamics of wars of maneuver to explain the variable success of state contraction in these cases. While struggles surrounding movement toward and across the ideological hegemony threshold were at the center of concern in Part II, struggles surrounding movement toward and across the regime threshold are of central concern in Part III. In Part IV the results of both these analyses are applied to the oscillation of the West Bank–Gaza problem between these two thresholds.

This volume's theoretical framework guides us to imagine wars of position and wars of maneuver as two kinds of contestation linked within a single, reversible, but asymmetric process of institutionalization. Part II explained the breakdown or absence of hegemonic beliefs that otherwise would have insulated British sovereignty in Ireland and French sovereignty in Algeria from effective political challenges. In Britain the very occurrence of conflict over Ireland's status was the result of the breakdown of a previously established hegemonic belief in Ireland as an integral part of the British state. In France, conflict over Algeria's relationship to the metropolitan hexagon was the result of the failure to establish as hegemonic prevailing beliefs about, and official claims of, Algeria's status as an integral part of France. The continuation of British rule of Ireland and French rule of Algeria was thereafter directly exposed to the cut and thrust of political competition and the vicissitudes of international circumstances and domestic interests. What was explained in Part II—the problematic status of Ireland and Algeria in British and French politics—is the point of departure for Part III.

From the mid-1880s in Britain and from at least 1957 in France, the struggles in those countries over whether and at what pace to disengage from Ireland and Algeria were qualitatively different than they were in the periods discussed in Part II (1834–86 and 1945–57 respectively). Subsequently, agreements on the terms of political separation between Britain and Ireland, and France and Algeria were reached—in 1921 in the British-Irish case and in 1962 in the French-Algerian case. However, in both cases, reaching these agreements entailed yet another qualitative shift in the stakes of political conflict. In Britain, between 1912 and 1916, and in France, from late 1957 to mid-1961, the problem of what to do with the outlying territory was transformed from questions whose resolution was perceived by governing elites to threaten the legal/parliamentary order, to questions whose resolution would threaten no more than the political careers of particular leaders, parties, and/or governments. According to the model presented in Chapter 2, this transformation occurs when a state crosses the regime threshold in the state-contraction direction.

Before proceeding, let me recapitulate the main elements of the model and the status of the argument thus far in terms of those elements.

The intimacy of a connection between an outlying territory and a central state is measured by the character of disruption in the central state which severing that connection would entail or is perceived to entail. Three qualitatively different sorts of disruptions are contemplated. To locate a problem to the right of the ideological hegemony threshold (see Fig. A-1, in the Appendix) is to indicate that disengagement from the territory in question would entail all three. Political separation from the territory, in other words, would require abandonment of settled presumptions about the boundaries of the political community, destabilization of central decision-making institutions, as well as challenges to the reputations and careers of governing politicians and their parties. Locating the problem of the disposition of an outlying territory to the left of the ideological hegemony threshold means that moving toward disengagement from the territory entails destabilization of central institutions and threats to political incumbents, but not the overthrow of fundamental presumptions about political life. Locating the problem to the left of the regime threshold means that moving toward disengagement would still present challenges to the political standing of governing elites, but would no longer entail fears that the regime—the formal/legal institutions of parliamentary life—would be disrupted.

Part II compared change in the location of the question of Ireland's status in British politics (from a point to the right of the ideological hegemony threshold to a point to the left of it) to the failure of three attempts to change the location of different definitions of Algeria's relationship to France (from various points to the left of the ideological hegemony threshold to some point to the right of it). Part III compares change in the location of both the Irish and Algerian problems from points to the right of the regime threshold to points to the left of it. In Part II, political struggles surrounding movement or attempted movement through the ideological hegemony threshold were analyzed as wars of position. The focus of Part III is on struggles surrounding movement through the regime threshold that are more appropriately labeled, again in Gramscian terms, as wars of maneuver.

Corresponding to the organizational scheme of Part II, Part III is divided into three chapters. Chapter 6 shows that between 1886 and 1921 a qualitative change took place in the character of the disruption which government officials in Britain believed would accompany movement toward political disengagement from Ireland. During this period, specifically between 1914 and 1916, the location of the Irish problem in British politics is shown to have crossed the regime threshold in the state-contraction direction. Chapter 7 shows that in 1961 a similar change took place in the character of the disruption which government officials in France believed would accompany movement toward political disengagement from

Algeria. Chapter 8 compares the wars of maneuver which accompanied these two processes of problem transformation in an attempt to explain similarities and differences in the contraction of the British and French states.

CHAPTER SIX

The Irish Question in
British Politics, 1886–1922

Incumbent-Level Factors, 1886–1911

In 1887 the *Times* published a series of letters, ostensibly written by Charles Stewart Parnell, suggesting links between him and agrarian "terrorism" in Ireland. Not until February 1889 were the letters proven to be forgeries. The *Times*'s involvement in the attempt to smear Parnell, the widespread popularity Parnell enjoyed after his vindication, continued strife over land questions in Ireland, and Gladstone's introduction of a second Home Rule Bill in 1893 insured that Irish affairs remained prominent in British politics during this period. But from 1894 to 1911, the Irish question in all its forms moved from the center of British politics. Home rule remained an important plank of the Liberal party platform, and opposition to home rule remained the keystone of the Unionist alliance between the Tories and the Liberal Unionists. But the crisis that surrounded defeat of Gladstone's first Home Rule Bill had faded. The question of Ireland's political status reappeared, and in a much sharper form, but not until 1912.

A variety of factors account for the changing prominence of the Irish question in the twenty-five years between 1887 and 1912. The Plan of Campaign launched in the late 1880s by the Irish Land League never generated the momentum of the 1880–81 period. Lacking Parnell's wholehearted support, it was starved for funds. It was also confronted by unprecedented rigorous coercion—a policy implemented by a Conservative government resolved to rule Ireland effectively, with or without the consent of the ruled. Arthur J. Balfour, Salisbury's nephew, served as chief secretary for Ireland from 1886 to 1892 and remained the guiding hand in Unionist policy toward Ireland. Although his coercion policy earned him the nickname "Bloody Balfour," his efforts to "kill home rule with kindness" had a longer-lasting effect in dampening Irish unrest.

The capstone of Balfour's Constructive Unionism was the Wyndham Land Act of 1903, promulgated soon after Balfour succeeded Salisbury as prime minister. This legislation provided low interest loans to two hundred thousand Irish tenants to finance purchase of their farms. By buying out the landlords, the Unionists transformed agrarian relations in the Irish countryside, creating a great mass of peasant proprietors. The Irish peasants' land hunger, which Irish nationalists had seen as the "locomotive" for their political campaign, was thereby largely satisfied.[1]

However, the heaviest blow to the Irish nationalist movement in this period was not the result of Unionist policy but of personal scandal. Parnell's affair with a married woman, Katherine O'Shea, had been generously ignored by his political enemies for several years.[2] In 1889, however, public discussion of the adulterous affair brought an end to Catholic church support for Parnell in Ireland as well as a demand from Gladstone, pressured by the nonconformist wing of the Liberal party, that Parnell resign as leader of the Irish party. Parnell refused, precipitating a rancorous split in the Home Rule party between Parnellites and anti-Parnellites. Depressed and exhausted, Parnell died in October 1891 at the age of forty five. His passing, and the internecine feuding that followed, incapacitated the Irish home rule movement. It took ten years before John Redmond could restore some of the discipline, unity, and direction Parnell had given it.

The relatively meager attention given home rule between 1894 and 1911 was also due to the electoral calculations and intraparty competition of Liberal party leaders. In the mid-1890s jingoist sentiments were at their peak. By the end of the century the pro-Boer sympathies of Irish nationalists were apparent to all. After the Liberal party's second successive defeat, in 1900, even home rule enthusiasts such as Herbert Gladstone and John Morley thought it would be best to "stand and wait," to let the question "sleep awhile."[3] The fact is that the elder Gladstone's retirement in 1894 left the party in the hands of men who lacked the crusading impulse of the "Grand Old Man." Nor was Irish support in Parliament any longer a crucial commodity. The margins of Unionist victories were so large in 1895 and 1900 that whether allied to the Irish party or not the Liberals could not form a government.

Despite the willingness of Gladstonian Liberals to compromise their commitment to home rule, a deep split emerged within the Liberal party in the early years of the twentieth century. The Liberal imperialist Lord Rosebery, who served briefly as prime minister when Gladstone retired, insisted on outright "repudiation" of home rule. Necessary unity was achieved in 1905 by a compromise that home rule would be pursued, but only "step by step," and a public stance suggesting that no full-scale home rule measure was contemplated. In 1906 the Liberals finally returned to power following a campaign dominated by their opposition to tariff reform. This time the scale of the Liberal victory made it easy to keep home rule on the back burner. It was so large that Irish support was unnecessary for the formation of a government.

The decisiveness of these incumbent-level considerations in lowering the profile of the Irish question is apparent by the Liberal party's return to the home rule banner in 1910. Both the January and December elections in 1910 produced such narrow margins between the dominant parties that Liberal governments could only be formed in coalition with the Irish nationalists. This result gave the Irish the leverage necessary to the revive Liberal commitments to home rule.[4] In April 1912 the Liberal prime minister, Herbert Asquith, introduced the third Home Rule Bill.

In sum, between 1894 and 1910, Unionist political predominance and the prudence of Liberal leaders in the face of English opposition to home rule were the primary obstacles to movement toward Irish political autonomy.[5] But if electoral considerations, growing out of normal political competition within the institutions of the British state, were the operative barrier to changing the terms of the Union, a very different sort of obstacle to British disengagement from Ireland was also evident during this period. Any government seeking to pass and implement home rule legislation could do so only after substantial change had taken place in the parliamentary role of the House of Lords, and only by withstanding violent challenges to the authoritativeness of parliamentary decisions. The role of these regime-level constraints became increasingly clear following the passage in the Commons of Gladstone's second Home Rule Bill in 1893, and especially following manifestations of potentially violent resistance to home rule in Ulster in 1886 and 1892–93.

Regime-Level Factors, 1886–1911

In September 1893 the House of Lords rejected Gladstone's second Home Rule Bill after only four days of discussion (compared to six months of consideration in the House of Commons). No one was surprised. The Lords was a predominantly Tory and Unionist body. But few anticipated the size of the margin by which home rule was defeated. More peers participated in the vote than in any other division in the history of the upper chamber. There were 419 votes against the bill and only 41 in favor of it. Every bishop joined in the majority along with most Liberal members. Clearly, as long as the House of Lords maintained its veto over legislation passed by the House of Commons, home rule for Ireland would be a practical impossibility.

Although his cabinet rejected Gladstone's request to dissolve Parliament and call a general election on the constitutional issue of the House of Lords's veto, his advice was put into effect seventeen years later. After the Lords rejected the People's Budget of 1909, two elections were held on the question in 1910. Narrow Liberal victories in each and the failure of a constitutional conference to resolve the question led to passage of the Parliament Act in 1911, which removed the Lords's veto over any legislation passed three times within the same Parliament by the House of Commons. In that year, deprived of the protection of the House of Lords, Ulster Protestants organized to resist the implementation of the third Home Rule Bill by force of arms. Enjoying the active support of the Unionist party, Ulster Protestants plunged the country into the regime crisis of 1912–14. Their defiance pushed the United Kingdom to the brink of civil war, undermined the army's capacity to enforce parliamentary decisions, and deterred the government from proceeding with home rule.

Though not the decisive factor blocking Irish political autonomy until the crisis of 1912–14, the regime-challenging character of Ulster "loyalist" opposition had been evident as early as 1886. In the early months of that year, Irish Protestants responded to the debate over the first Home Rule Bill with a stunned realization that self-government for Ireland was no longer beyond the bounds of the possible. Their fury and their distrust of both the Liberal and Unionist parties were expressed by mass demonstrations and announcements in the Ulster press of preparations to resist implementation of home rule. Agitation for such measures was centered in the lodges of the anti-Catholic Orange Order.

The Orange Order emerged in 1795 amid fights in Ulster between Protestant and Catholic peasants over land. It drew strength from a general sense of unease among Protestants which accompanied the relaxation of the anti-Catholic penal laws.[6] Orange Order activities emphasized celebrating Protestant ascendancy over Irish Catholics in ways calculated to wound Catholic sensibilities as deeply as possible. Although usually able to find some among the landed gentry to lead them, Orangemen were largely disdained by "respectable" people as vulgar bigots. From the 1840s through the 1870s the order virtually disappeared. Its reappearance in the 1880s was in reaction to the Land War and Gladstone's Home Rule Bill.

The strength of the order was concentrated in Ulster. Since the Cromwellian settlement of the mid-1600s, the nine counties of Ulster have contained the overwhelming majority of Irish Protestants—nearly six hundred thousand in 1911. Concentrated further in the six northeastern counties, Protestants were 57.8 percent of the inhabitants of Londonderry, Antrim, Down, Armagh, Tyrone, and Fermanagh, and 75 percent of the citizens of the city of Belfast. In February 1886, Lord Randolph Churchill traveled to Belfast to play what he called the "Orange card." His rhetoric there was designed to inflame anti-Catholic, antinationalist sentiments, to stiffen Protestant resolve to resist home rule by any means, and to exploit aroused passions for his own purposes and those of the Unionist party. After portraying Gladstone as akin to "Macbeth before the murder of Duncan," hesitating before "plunging the knife into the heart of the British Empire," Churchill promised English help for Ulster resistance to home rule.[7] "I do not hesitate to say and to tell you, and tell you most truly," he said, "that in that dark hour there will not be wanting to you those of position and influence in England who are willing to cast in their lot with you—what ever it may be, and who will share your fortune."[8] Two months later Churchill, serving as leader of the Unionist party, contributed a slogan for Ulster resistance which would echo for decades to come. "Ulster," he wrote in April 1886, "at the proper moment will resort to the supreme arbitrament of force: *Ulster will fight; Ulster will be right;* Ulster will emerge from the struggle victorious."[9]

Churchill's visit to Belfast had been arranged by the Ulster loyalist Anti-Repeal Union, founded in January to resist Gladstonian home rule. In the months before the vote on home rule, the Anti-Repeal Union and the Orange Order issued warnings that Ulstermen would respond to passage of the bill by armed resistance. One of the Anti-Repeal Union's leaders, who was also an important figure in the Orange Order, called for "an appeal to Germany, if the one to England fell on deaf ears."[10] Early in April one hundred Orange activists met to discuss arming their lodges. A minor sensation was created in Britain by a flurry of Ulster newspaper advertisements calling for arms and drill instructors, unrepudiated claims that Field Marshal Lord Wolseley, commander of British forces in Ireland, and Lord Charles Beresford, a naval hero and an MP then serving as fourth lord of the admiralty, were ready to support an Ulster revolt, publication of a list of fifty-one prominent Orangemen purportedly involved in the organization of a rebel army, and British press reports of training maneuvers and arms purchases.[11]

The intent of those who threatened resistance was to refuse to pay taxes to a Dublin Parliament established by home rule legislation and to prevent by violence any attempt to establish its authority in Ulster, but their expectation was that "when the moment of coercion comes the people of England and Scotland would not permit the Queen's troops to be sent against them."[12] Indeed many Unionists in both Ulster and Britain believed the British army to be "so 'honeycombed' with Orangemen that it would not march on Ulster."[13] How serious this regime-challenging mobilization was in 1886 may be doubted, but there is good reason to think that even at this early date real fears had been raised in the mind of the British public that implementation of home rule would indeed likely trigger armed resistance in Ulster.

In any event, the defeat of the Home Rule Bill on June 8 brought an end to these threats of violence, and to speculation in the British press over whether the navy would obey orders to bombard Belfast.[14] But the character of the forces at work was signaled by the government's failure to gain indictments against participants in illegal military drills,[15] and by the outbreak of Protestant riots in Belfast in the days surrounding the House of Commons vote. Despite the deployment of army units to keep order, fighting in Belfast and other Ulster locales continued through the summer, leaving 32 dead, 442 arrested, and 377 police injured.[16]

After six years of Unionist government, Gladstone's Liberals gained a narrow victory over the Unionist party in the general election of July 1892. The scant six-seat margin between the two large parties again gave the Irish nationalists the key to forming a Liberal government. The imperatives of coalition formation, combined with the strength of Gladstone's personal commitment to Irish self-government, made proposal of a second Home Rule Bill a virtual certainty. With more time to prepare, and faced with the real possibility that the House of Commons would pass a Home Rule Bill, Protestant Ulster responded with an amplified version of the 1886 agitation. One month before the election, twelve thousand delegates, including four thousand tenant farmers, attended an Ulster Unionist Convention in Belfast. On the walls of the pavilion specially constructed to house the gathering was painted in giant letters the slogan: "If necessary we must shed blood to maintain the strength and salvation of the country."[17] The resolution adopted by this assembly expressed Protestant Ulster's determination that under no circumstances would home rule be accepted. This meeting, and the subsequent establishment of the Ulster Defence Union in 1893, inaugurated a process that would reach its climax in 1914. The Ulster Defence Union was, remarked Charles Townshend, a "quasi-constitutional mass organization with the capacity, if not yet the intention, to act as an alternative government."[18]

In 1892–93 practical discussions among Irish unionists about resistance to home rule again centered on passive acts of disobedience, especially refusal to pay taxes to a Dublin-based Parliament. But evidence of widespread discussion of armed resistance against the authority of an all-Ireland legislature or the British government was readily available. In the House of Lords, the marquess of Londonderry declared that Irish loyalists "would be justified in shedding blood to resist the disloyal Catholic yoke."[19] Colonel E. J. Saunderson, an Orangeman who led the Ulster Protestant delegation in the House of Commons, warned the government that the army would follow orders to impose home rule on Ireland only if home rule were passed by a majority of *British* MPs, deeming decisions reached with the support of Irish nationalist MPs illegitimate.[20] Lord Wolseley, commander of the British army in Ireland, told his superiors in England that "Ulster Protestants would 'fight *a outrance*' if they were placed under a Dublin parliament."[21]

Even more significant than the escalation of Ulster Protestant rhetoric was the substantially greater encouragement for extraconstitutional resistance to home rule expressed by Unionist party leaders in 1892 and 1893 as compared to 1886. Joseph Chamberlain advised the Ulster Unionist Convention "to have a large subscription list opened and show that you are determined to resist. No Government will ever dare to coerce you."[22] Addressing the Conservative Primrose League in London in 1892, Salisbury compared Ulster's defense against home rule as comparable to its legendary defiance of Catholic King James II in 1689, in support of Protestant King William. Salisbury noted that "James II had stepped outside the limits of the spirit of the constitution, and they knew how the people of Ulster had met him. If a similar abuse of power on the part of a parliament or a king should ever again occur, he did not believe 'the people of Ulster have lost their sturdy love of freedom nor their detestation of arbitrary power'."[23] After reviewing a march of a hundred thousand Ulster loyalists in April 1893, Arthur Balfour predicted that, should home rule pass, "Ulster can at all events fight: the last refuge of brave men struggling for their freedom cannot be denied them."[24]

The predominant Liberal and Irish nationalist response to Unionist threats of armed resistance was to dismiss such talk as typically frivolous Orange "bluster."[25] Gladstone assured Parliament and the British public that Ulster's discomfiture would be alleviated by the equitable reality of home rule, once legislated and implemented. He described the Protestants of Ulster as "intelligent and reasonable men." These clumsy attempts at "spin control," meant to lessen the impact of Ulster's threats on the prospects for home rule legislation, suggest that the menace of extraconstitutional resistance *was* considered politically relevant.[26] On the other hand, threats to the legal order were not the factors which actually determined the fate of either the first or second Home Rule Bill. Certainly they induced no cabinet ministers, in either 1886 or 1893, to abandon or substantially amend their support for home rule. In this context, John Morley's comment that in 1893 there was "no fear of an organized rising" is significant. Morley was Gladstone's chief secretary for Ireland in 1886 and in 1893.

He was also a member of Asquith's cabinet during passage of the third Home Rule Bill. His judgment about the cabinet's perceptions in 1893 must be taken as convincing when contrasted with his own dramatic change on home rule, triggered by what both he and the rest of the cabinet understood as the real threat of civil war posed by Ulster and its British Unionist allies in 1912–14.[27]

The Regime Crisis of 1912–1914:
Ulster, Home Rule, and the Threat of Civil War

The Organization of Rebellion in Ulster

The primary organizing framework for Ulster's nascent rebellion of 1912–14 was the Ulster Unionist Council. The UUC brought together Ulster members of Parliament with representatives of the Orange Order and various local Unionist associations. In 1908 the UUC joined with the Irish Unionist Alliance, representing antinationalist opinion in the south of Ireland, and later with the London-based Union Defence League. The vigorous political activities of these groups helped discourage the Liberal party from presenting home rule for Ireland as an important part of its platform in the elections of 1910.[28] But these organizations also provided the machinery for escalating struggle against home rule from attacks on candidates and parties to attacks on the regime itself. In January 1913 the UUC founded the Ulster Volunteer Force, a private army whose purpose was to deter and, if necessary, prevent implementation of home rule. In March 1914, officers of the British army in Ireland, faced with well-organized armed opposition by Ulster Protestants, and encouraged by Conservative party leaders, successfully demanded that the Asquith government renounce its intention (and virtually its right) to impose home rule on Ulster. As we shall see, by this time the struggle over home rule had produced a constitutional crisis more serious than any to befall a British government since the seventeenth century.

The trigger for escalating the home rule struggle from ballots to bullets, from conflict within the rules of the game to conflict over the authority of the rules themselves, was passage of the Parliament Act in 1911. The Lords approved the legislation in August 1911, after receiving a royal threat to pack the House of Lords with Liberal peers if they refused. The Lords thereby deprived themselves of a veto over any bill passed in three successive "circuits" by the House of Commons in the same Parliament. Unionists, as well as Liberals and Irish nationalists, knew that ending the Lords's veto rendered probable the eventual passage of home rule for

Ireland. In fact, deep disagreement over home rule had prevented a "set-tlement by consent" of the constitutional role of the House of Lords at an all-party conference called for this purpose by the king in 1910.

The effect of the loss of the Lords' veto was quickly apparent in the changed role of extraconstitutional resistance to home rule for Ireland. In 1886 and in 1892–93, warnings of civil war served as colorful, if fore-boding, accompaniment to primarily legal and *parliamentary* struggles. In contrast, from 1911 to 1914 the organization of violent resistance to home rule was the decisive political instrument of Unionists in both Britain and Ireland. In 1834, 1843, 1886, 1893, and 1905, legal attempts to gain or grant varying degrees of political autonomy to Ireland were thwarted as an outcome of legal competition within the institutions of the British state. Unionist success in blocking the third Home Rule Bill, however, was due to the unwillingness, and even the proven inability, of those institutions to enforce the result of legal competition within them by overcoming *illegal* threats to parliamentary authority.

The unchallenged leader of Irish Unionism and the rebellious loyalists of Ulster during this period was Edward Carson. Carson was a hard-working Dublin lawyer who served as Crown prosecutor against the Na-tional League's Plan of Campaign during the late 1880s and was appointed Ireland's solicitor general by Balfour in 1892. From 1900–1906 he served as England's solicitor general, representing the University of Dublin in the House of Commons. Carson's baleful expression and rigorous prosecution of Irish nationalists contributed to a well-earned reputation for ruthless effectiveness. In 1910 he was elected leader of the Ulster Unionist party and quickly emerged as the undisputed "king" of Protestant Ulster.[29]

Carson's chief lieutenant was a former army officer named James Craig, a self-made millionaire from Belfast, and a dominant figure in the Orange Order and the Ulster Unionist Council. Under Craig's direction, prepa-rations for a mass demonstration at his estate were begun in the weeks before the Parliament Bill became law. One month after the bill received the royal assent, fifty thousand Ulstermen gathered at Craigavon, near Belfast. With thousands of Orangemen and Ulster Unionist club members marching in military-style review, Carson outlined what became known as the "Ulster programme." Besides defying any Dublin-based Parliament, Ulster loyalists were told to build the military, economic, and administra-tive capacity to govern the "Protestant province of Ulster." This was a public signal to both Irish and British Unionists that the struggle against home rule had entered a new phase.

The chief secretary of Ireland since the 1906 Liberal landslide, Augustine Birrell, believed as early as August 1911 that civil war would erupt if the government sought to implement the Irish Home Rule Bill then being drafted.[30] Undoubtedly his judgment was based on the work of the Dublin Castle investigators who reported to him. But even they were unaware of how extensive and how early were the preparations to resist home rule by force of arms. It is in part the secrecy of these activities which today suggests the seriousness of their intent. Their deliberate and clandestine nature contrasts sharply with the flamboyant posture of resistance adopted in 1886 and 1892–93. In 1911 Protestant activists explicitly discussed and rejected a proposal to import openly a thousand weapons as a publicity stunt to impress British opinion. Instead Craig assured Colonel Frederick Crawford, mastermind for most of the gun-running operations into Ulster during 1911–14, of his "unequivocal commitment to effective—secret and continuing importation."[31]

Still, Edward Carson wondered whether Ulster Unionists would follow where he was prepared to lead them. Late in July 1911 Carson had written to Craig of his concerns: "What I am very anxious about is to satisfy myself that the people over there really mean to resist. I am not for a mere game of bluff, and unless men are prepared to make great sacrifices which they clearly understand, the talk of resistance is of no use."[32] Indeed it appears that one of the main purposes of the Craigavon demonstration in September 1911 was to convince militant activists—such as Crawford and Ulster's political leaders, especially Edward Carson—that those who were planning for armed resistance were to be trusted. The Craigavon meeting dramatically revealed the depth of Protestant Ulster's commitment to extraconstitutional means of struggle and set the stage for Carson's call to stop home rule by any means necessary.

As early as November 1910, the Ulster Unionist Council established a secret committee "to oversee aproaches to arms dealers, and to select weapons for an Ulster army."[33] By April 1911, Belfast loyalists were beginning to drill. At least two thousand weapons were delivered in the next few months.[34] These efforts were given added impetus in April 1912, with Asquith's formal introduction of the third Home Rule Bill.[35] Two months later James Craig's brother, Charles Craig, told the House of Commons that Ulster Protestants knew the difference between Catholic emancipation and home rule. When Catholics had been emancipated by Parliament in 1829, there was nothing to be done to nullify the decision. But, he said, "if this Bill is passed into law and Home Rule is set up, we can fight against the results of this Bill. . . . We have said in Ulster and elsewhere that we will resist and never allow ourselves to come under the influence of a Parliament in Dublin. We have said in pursuing that determination that we are prepared to use any means, the most extreme means, we have at our disposal."[36]

On September 28, 1912, a huge convocation was held in Belfast, presided over by Edward Carson, for the signing of a text titled "Ulster's Solemn League and Covenant." Proclaiming their loyalty to King George V and their refusal to recognize the authority of a Home Rule Parliament, the signatories pledged themselves "throughout this time of threatened calamity to stand by one another in defending for ourselves and our children our cherished position of equal citizenship in the United Kingdom and in using all means which may be found necessary to defeat the present conspiracy to set up a Home Rule Parliament in Ireland."[37]

Was such a pledge seditious? A week earlier Carson had told an Irish audience that he did "not care twopence whether it is treason or not."[38] Within several days nearly a quarter of a million Ulstermen had signed the document. An equal number of Ulster women signed a declaration of support for the men in their fight against home rule.[39] By the end of 1912, according to A. T. Q. Stewart's authoritative account, "the whole province seemed in a fever of military preparation."[40]

At the beginning of 1913, the roster of the Ulster Volunteer Force listed a hundred thousand men, all signatories of the covenant. Within this rubric, Orange lodges and Unionist clubs throughout the province were enlisted to form regiments, battalions, companies, and sections in proportion to their local strength and in conformance with district boundaries determined by the UUC's military committee. In July 1913, Sir George Richardson, a retired, highly decorated lieutenant general in the British army, moved to Belfast to become commander in chief of the Ulster Volunteers. He had been nominated for the post by Field Marshal Earl Roberts, a "national idol," a hero of innumerable colonial campaigns, and still on the army's active list.[41] Assisted by the British League for the Support of Ulster and the Union, formed in March 1913 by 100 peers and 120 members of Parliament, the UVF recruited sympathetic reserve officers from England to establish logistical, transport, intelligence, administration, medical, and communications units.[42] By the end of 1913, according to Stewart, "the Ulster Volunteer Force had virtually created a state within a state," complete with its own postal service, nursing corps, motorized transport, food supplies, armories, and mobilization plans.[43]

Carson acknowledged that these activities went well beyond what could be considered legal, even under a liberal interpretation of the law. "The Volunteers are illegal," he said in a speech in County Down, "and the Government know they are illegal, and the Government dare not interfere with them. Don't be afraid of illegalities."[44] The crystallization of a substantial rebel army, with the public support and involvement of well-known British military figures, gave credibility to Carson's claims, in July 1912, that "the Government know perfectly well that they could not tomorrow rely upon the army to shoot down the people of Ulster.... The army are with us."[45] To another Ulster audience in late September 1913, Carson declared that "we have pledges and promises from some of the greatest generals in the army that, when the time comes and if it is necessary, they will come over to help us keep the old flag flying and to defy those who dare invade our liberties."[46] On September 24, 1913, climaxing a tour during which Carson and Richardson inspected twenty-two thousand men on parade in six different counties, the Ulster Unionist Council "formally organised itself into a 'Provisional Government.' "[47]

The preparations for rebellion had a dynamic of their own. After months of regular training with wooden rifles, the UVF battalion commanders and the recruits themselves increasingly pressed their demands for weapons— demands that far outstripped the available supply. The pressures arising from this discrepancy, and a December 1913 government ban on importing arms and ammunition into Ireland, led to a secret decision in January 1914 by Carson, Craig, and Richardson to escalate the UVF's gun-running efforts.[48]

The planning department of the UVF general staff had already estimated that to threaten England effectively with civil war, and thereby either deter implementation of home rule or stop its enforcement if attempted, "a big fight" would be necessary requiring 30,000 rifles and 2.5 million rounds of ammunition.[49] Sufficient funds were provided to smuggle 20,000 rifles from Europe into Ulster along with 2 million rounds of ammunition. The project was begun under the utmost secrecy and came to fruition on the night of April 24–25, 1914, with the clandestine delivery of 24,600 rifles and approximately 3 million cartridges.[50] In an extraordinarily well-orchestrated operation, the guns and ammunition were distributed overnight throughout the province and concealed in tiny arms caches, making it impossible for the authorities quickly to disarm the Volunteers. As a result the UVF became more than a political threat; it "could no longer be seen as anything but a formidable military force."[51]

The training and organization of the UVF, and weapons acquisition on this scale, were consistent with the outline of a plan for a "coup" in Ulster drafted early in 1914 and labeled the No. 1 Scheme. It emphasized organizing a "special flying column of 5,000 men" in Belfast and assigning particular tasks and targets to specific units. The plan included taking control of key roads, cutting all railway, telegraph, telephone, and cable lines into the province, seizing arms and ammunition depots, and capturing artillery pieces. Commanders were advised to build, wherever possible, a local force with the capacity to overwhelm army, police, or constabulary units, so as to achieve their objectives with a minimum of bloodshed.[52] Belfast magnates and the Protestant aristocracy of Ulster supported these schemes financially. They also used their resources to create a one-million-pound indemnity fund for families of UVF men who might be killed or wounded in the fighting.[53]

The UVF's readiness to resist the implementation of home rule was a key element in the strategy of Carson and Craig. But they preferred to deter the government decision to proceed with home rule rather than to resist it successfully once the decision to implement it had been made. Constant emphasis during UVF rallies and operations on solemnity, discipline, and silence reflected the leaders' preoccupation with their own ability to control UVF troops and with the need to signal the government that they had the power to remove the threat of violence as well as to put it into effect. This meant creating the specter of civil war, without inciting their followers to unauthorized action and without losing public sympathy by appealing directly for the mutiny of British soldiers—a narrow path to tread. How Carson sought to follow it is illustrated by a speech he delivered in Manchester on December 3, 1913.

> It would be a bad day for the country if the army under any circumstances were to refuse to obey the lawful orders of those who are put in command over them. Of course they must. But it is for that very reason that statesmen and politicians ought to look ahead. It is for that very reason that statesmen and politicians ought to know to what their acts lead. No one will blame the army for shooting upon Ulstermen. But the country will hold the Government that puts forward the army as responsible.[54]

Carson's strategy, in sum, was to make convincing threats of violent and sustained resistance which would intimidate the government into abandoning its home rule policy. He and the rest of the Ulster Provisional Government hoped this strategy would suffice—that the army would be seen as an unreliable means of coercing Ulster and that a frightened, disoriented public and worried financial institutions would induce the government to back down. In one of Carson's scenarios, the government would "learn wisdom when a few days after we move the big banks in London begin putting up their shutters."[55] As late as July 1914, when home rule awaited only the royal assent to become law, Carson was still warning Asquith that without a settlement "there would be demonstrations in Ulster 'with inevitable collisions and bloodshed leading to a general outburst.' "[56] At the same time, the Ulster Provisional Government announced that in the event home rule was implemented, it had been authorized "to take any action it thought necessary to carry out for themselves the power exercised hitherto by the Imperial Government. It further added that it would hold 'the Ulster area' in trust for the constitution of the United Kingdom and with the intent that the Ulster area shall continue an integral portion thereof."[57] On July 12, 1914, at Protestant Ulster's annual celebration of King William's 1690 victory over the Catholic King James II at the Battle of the Boyne, Carson dared the government to exclude the six northeastern counties of Ulster from the application of the bill or face the UVF. "Give us a clean cut," he said, "or come and fight us."[58]

British Tories and Ulster Rebels: A Regime-Threatening Alliance

Protestant Ulster's strategy was effective because it was enthusiastically endorsed by the leadership of the British Conservative party. During 1886–1905, the Tories had acquired the idea that they were the natural rulers of the country. The party's embrace of Ulster Unionism's vehement challenge to parliamentary authority was linked to the shock of the party's defeat in three successive general elections (January 1906, January 1910, and December 1910). Passage of the Parliament Act of 1911 also spurred Conservative disillusionment with prevailing constitutional arrangements. Besides enabling budgets to be passed which Tories considered outright attacks on the propertied classes, this act, with its removal of the veto of the House of Lords, also held out the possibility and even the probability of home rule for Ireland. These events and prospects produced a fierce belief among Tory leaders that the unwritten British Constitution had been illegitimately overturned and was no longer capable of protecting the upper classes against the passions mass democracy could unleash. They now blamed passage of the Parliament Act and plans for a new Home Rule Bill on "a corrupt bargain" between the Liberals and the Irish nationalists—specific evidence of just how unsafe was the British state if its stewardship were left to non-Conservatives.[59]

Beginning with the great Craigavon demonstration in September 1911, British Unionist leaders publicly declared their approval of Ulster rebelliousness. Compared to the kind of encouragement they gave Ulster loyalists in 1886 and 1892–93, the steep rise in Tory support for the Ulster Unionist Council, the Ulster Volunteer Force, and the Ulster Provisional Government, from 1911 through the summer of 1914, parallels the tremendous difference between Ulster's comprehensive military preparations during this latter period and the essentially symbolic militancy of the two earlier episodes. The tone of British Conservative support for Protestant Ulster was reflected in Rudyard Kipling's "Ulster, 1912," published in London's *Morning Post* newspaper in January of that year. The poem depicted Ulster loyalists as betrayed by the England they had so long served and bound over for sacrifice to ancient enemies. Kipling concluded the poem with two stanzas appealing to anti-Catholic sentiment and justifying violent resistance.

> We know the wars prepared
> On every peaceful home,
> We know the hells declared
> For such as serve not Rome—
> The terror, threats, and dread
> In market, hearth, and field—
> We know, when all is said,
> We perish if we yield.
>
> Believe, we dare not boast,
> Believe, we do not fear—
> We stand to pay the cost
> In all that men hold dear.
> What answer from the North?
> One Law, one Land, one
>   Throne.
> If England drive us forth
> We shall not fall alone![60]

Public declarations of unstinting support for Irish Protestant resistance were issued by the Conservative party chief Andrew Bonar Law.[61] Beginning in January 1912, these exhortations to defy Parliament should home rule be legislated became increasingly vitriolic. On January 26, 1912, Law told a London meeting of ten thousand people that "We who represent the Unionist Party in England and Scotland have supported, *and we mean to support to the end,* the loyal minority [in Ireland]."[62] In Balmoral, near Belfast, Law addressed a massive demonstration timed to coincide with the government's official introduction of the Home Rule Bill. Accompanied by seventy British Unionist MPs, and blessed by the Anglican primate of all Ireland and the moderator of the Presbyterian church, Law watched as a hundred thousand men marched in review.[63] Speaking on behalf of the Unionist party, Law labeled the Home Rule Bill "a treacherous conspiracy" and compared Ulster's stance against it to the legendary Protestant defense of Derry against the forces of King James in 1689—90.[64] In the midst of a June 1912 debate on the possible exclusion of Ulster from the terms of the bill, Law told the House of Commons that "If Ulster does resist by force, there are stronger influences than Parliament majorities. ...no Government would dare to use their troops to drive them out... the Government which gave the order to employ troops for that purpose would run a greater risk of being lynched in London than the Loyalists of Ulster would run of being shot in Belfast."[65]

Law's willingness to commit the Conservative party to the extremities promised by Carson and the Ulster Unionist Council was given its most comprehensive expression at a July 1912 rally at Blenheim Palace in England, where he attacked the Liberal government as "a Revolutionary Committee which has seized upon despotic power by fraud." Such a government, he continued, did not deserve, and would not enjoy, the protection of restraints accepted by the Conservative party in opposition during "an ordinary Constitutional struggle." In terms very similar to those employed by Ulster leaders, Law stressed that passage of home rule legislation would not mark the end of the struggle.

> They may, perhaps they will, carry their Home Rule Bill through the House of Commons, but what then? I said the other day in the House of Commons and I repeat here that there are things stronger than Parliamentary majorities.
> ... Before I occupied the position which I now fill in the Party I said that, in my belief, if an attempt were made to deprive these men of their birthright—as part of a corrupt Parliamentary bargain—*they would be justified in resisting such an attempt by all means in their power, including force.* I said it then, and I repeat it now with a full sense of the responsibility which attaches to my position, that, in my opinion, if such an attempt is made, *I can imagine no length of resistance to which Ulster can go in which I should not be prepared to support them, and in which, in my belief, they would not be supported by the overwhelming majority of the British people.*[66]

According to his biographer, "Bonar Law's violent public declarations during these months were not belied by his private remarks.... He saw little hope of averting civil war, or, failing that, a degree of dissention in the country which would strain the constitution to its uttermost."[67] In a talk with Winston Churchill, Law told the then first lord of the admiralty that if a united Unionist party were ready to be turned out of the House of Commons for their support of Ulster, Churchill could not "suppose that the Army would obey orders to exercise force in Ulster!... in that case undoubtedly we should regard it as civil war, and should urge the Officers of the Army not to regard them as a real Government but to ignore their orders."[68]

Bonar Law had strong personal ties to Ireland. Though born in Canada, he was of Ulster Scottish ancestry. But his commitment to resist home rule by "whatever means" necessary was shared by virtually all top-ranking Tory leaders. These included Walter Long and Austen Chamberlain, Bonar Law's two main rivals when he assumed the leadership of the Conservative party in 1910; former Tory Prime Minister Arthur Balfour, F. E. Smith (later Lord Birkenhead), a rising star in Unionist circles who became solicitor general in 1915, then attorney general, and then lord chancellor during 1919–1922; Hugh and Robert Cecil, sons of former Prime Minister Salisbury; and Lord Alfred Milner, former high commissioner of South Africa, a leader of Tory diehards, and guru of the influential Round Table group. Milner's reputation for unswerving dedication to imperial consolidation made him the intellectual and political inspiration for British imperialism following Joseph Chamberlain's incapacitating stroke in 1906.

In his address in Belfast on Boyne Day, July 12, 1912, F. E. Smith told Ulster Unionists that if home rule passed "[you would be] entitled to forget the community which has driven you forth, and to combine in opposition to the community which claims your allegiance as the fruit of a corrupt and abominable bargain." More ominously, he promised that "in that dark hour of your trial, should it unhappily come, you will not lack the active support of thousands in England." The extent to which the Unionist leadership's commitment to oppose home rule was intended to challenge the regime which produced the "corrupt bargain," and not just the incumbent Liberal leadership, was apparent in his peroration.

> The crisis has called into existence one of those supreme issues of conscience amid which the ordinary landmarks of permissible resistance to technical law are submerged. We shall not shrink from the consequences of this view, not though the whole fabric of the Commonwealth be convulsed, and we shall tread with you the path of your destiny knowing that, whether it leads to freedom or to disaster, it is the only road which does not lead to dishonour.[69]

Passage of the third Home Rule Bill on its first circuit, in January 1913, provoked crescendos of Unionist anger in both Ulster and Great Britain. In March 1913, Lord Willoughby De Broke announced formation of the British League for the Support of Ulster and the Union, with the endorsement of a considerable portion of the British aristocracy. At the end of July 1913, Law and Lord Landsdowne, head of the southern Irish Unionists, submitted a lengthy and virtually unprecedented memorandum to the king which warned that "the Constitution was in a state of suspense; that a dissolution [of Parliament] was the only method of averting civil war; that, if Asquith declined to recommend a dissolution, the King had a right to dismiss him and send for someone who would do so."[70] Confronted with Asquith's adamant opposition and warned that the position of the monarchy would be forever changed if he acted in accord with the Unionist suggestion, the king demurred.

From this point, however, until the eruption of World War I a year later, Unionist speeches increasingly dwelled on the support British citizens would give Irish Protestants in their militant resistance to home rule and the uncertain loyalty of the Army to a deceitful, corrupt, and immoral government. In early November 1913, Arthur Balfour was recruited to substitute for Edward Carson at an anti–home rule rally in Aberdeen, Scotland. His theme was that the whole country, and not just Ulster, was faced with one of the greatest calamities to threaten it in "many generations" and that in their struggles, both parliamentary and extraparliamentary, Ulstermen could rely on "the whole force of the Unionist Party." In effect, Balfour argued, passage of the Parliament Act had actually "suspended" the British Constitution, substituting for it an "interim constitution." He placed the entire blame on the Asquith government for the "tragic catastrophe ... of civil war" which he saw looming on the horizon. In a resolution passed by acclamation at the end of the meeting, the three thousand attendees pledged themselves "to aid their loyal fellow-subjects to the uttermost in their resistance" to home rule.[71]

Other Unionist leaders were even less temperate than Balfour in their challenge, throughout 1913, to the legitimacy of the government's authority. The choice, wrote Lord Hugh Cecil in a letter to the *Times,* "will be between no Home Rule and civil war, and that choice neither the Government nor the House of Commons, but the people only, have a right to make."[72] British Conservatives, F. E. Smith told an anti–home rule rally in Ulster in September 1913, "would stand side by side with loyal Ulster ... prepared with them to risk the collapse of the whole body politic to prevent this monstrous crime."[73] Late in November, after secret talks between Asquith and Law failed to produce an agreement to move toward compromise, Law again compared the government's emphasis on "legality" to the claim of King James II in his unsuccessful struggle to defend his crown against the Protestant King William in 1690. In the process Law came close to inciting the British army to mutiny. He claimed that "King James had behind him the letter of the law just as completely as Mr Asquith. ... In order to carry out his despotic intention the King had the largest army which had ever been seen in England. What happened? There was no civil war. There was a revolution, and the King disappeared. Why? Because his own army refused to fight for him."[74]

The most vigorous and extreme efforts to organize British assistance for the nascent Ulster rebellion, and to deprive the government of the army's loyalty in case of a clash of arms, were led by Lord Milner. In December 1913, he wrote to Carson as a British citizen who was "completely in accord with you about Ulster," but who "disbelieve[s] in mere talk." Milner told Carson that "it would be a disaster of the first magnitude" if the Ulster "rebellion" he took to be nearly inevitable were to fail. "But it must fail," he warned, "unless we can *paralyse* the *arm* which might be raised to strike you. How are we to do it? That requires forethought and organisation *over here*."[75] Shortly after this letter was written, Milner was chosen by the Ulster Unionists to replace Carson in the event Carson were arrested.[76]

To "paralyse the arm," that is, to make the army useless as an instrument of coercion against Ulster, Milner enlisted a group of brilliant young admirers who shared his enthusiasm for the empire and his conviction that a sweeping overhaul of British institutions was required to achieve its consolidation. Known as Milner's Kindergarten, these men—such as Leo Amery, F. S. Oliver, Philip Kerr, and Lionel Curtis—edited the prestigious magazine *The Round Table* and enjoyed close ties with high-ranking military officers, cabinet members, and leaders of the English aristocracy. With their help Milner breathed new life into Willoughby De Broke's British League for the Support of Ulster and the Union and Walter Long's Union Defence League. Under the auspices of these organizations, the Ulster Volunteers were provided with military supplies, staff officers, trained commandos, and assistance in evading the efforts by the authorities to prevent importation of arms.[77] But Milner and his disciples had much more substantial plans in mind.

Early in 1914, Milner drew up a British Covenant, modeled on Ulster's Solemn League and Covenant, which declared its signatories justified "in taking any action" to prevent home rule from becoming law or Crown forces from "depriving the people of Ulster of their rights as citizens of the United Kingdom."[78] Using the Union Defence League as an organizing base, Milner launched a public campaign for signatures at the beginning of March 1914. Original signatories included Milner, retired Field Marshal Earl Roberts, A. V. Dicey the well-known constitutionalist, and Rudyard Kipling. Roberts was elected the first president of the British Covenanters, with Milner, Dicey, F. E. Smith, and Kipling serving on its executive committee.[79] By July 1914, when the campaign for signatures was halted, organizers claimed that two million British citizens outside of Ulster had signed the Covenant.[80]

The explicit purpose of the British Covenant was to strengthen the resolve of the Ulster Volunteers by assuring them they enjoyed broad political support in England. Milner also wanted to signal army officers that their inclinations to refuse orders to impose home rule, or to resign their commissions if ordered into Ulster, were understood and approved by leading elements within British society. His propaganda activities within the officer corps were facilitated by his close ties with Major General Sir Henry Wilson, director of military operations, and with Lord Roberts.

Aside from his immense popularity with the public, Roberts was a leader of the National Service League, an organization favoring universal military training, with which Milner was also closely associated.[81]

As early as November 1913, Wilson had told Bonar Law that "if we [the army] were ordered to coerce Ulster there would be wholesale defections."[82] These sentiments Milner sought to encourage. By "winning the officer corps" to the anti–home rule camp, he intended that "Ministers and the people of England would be uncertain of the army in case of a crisis in Ulster."[83] Privately Milner planned to use the British Covenanters as a roster for a "network of local units" throughout the country, just as the Ulster Covenant had been used to register men for units of the Ulster Volunteer Force. To support these various activities, Milner tapped his circle of wealthy friends and sympathizers.[84]

Milner enthusiastically supported a bold legislative maneuver designed to "paralyse the arm" by interfering with Parliament's annual Army Act. Yearly passage of this bill, a routine adopted after the 1688 revolution, was intended to offer the army an annual reminder of its financial dependence on Parliament and its subordination to parliamentary authority. In the first months of 1914, Law, Chamberlain, and Landsdowne, Balfour, Milner, and Lord Selborne explored the possibility of rejecting the annual Army Bill in the House of Lords or attaching a crippling amendment to it in the House of Commons. Their intent was to create a constitutional crisis so severe that the king would be forced to dissolve Parliament, thereby preventing enactment of the Home Rule Bill. In February a committee including Edward Carson and several Conservative party leaders was formed to draft a suitable amendment.[85] On March 18, Milner met with Carson, Sir Henry Wilson, and other Unionist leaders. After an evening's discussion, all agreed that the "Lords must amend the Army Annual Act."[86] The scheme was laid aside, however, after dramatic events in Ireland made it irrelevant.[87]

On March 12, the cabinet formed a committee including Lord Crewe, Ireland's Chief Secretary Augustine Birrell, Minister of War J. E. B. Seely, and Winston Churchill, first lord of the admiralty. The committee's charge was to meet the Ulster and Unionist threat of resistance to home rule. Among the measures taken by the committee was to order troops stationed at the Curragh military base in southern Ireland to protect arms depots in Ulster from seizure by the UVF. Both Bonar Law and Edward Carson responsed to these preparations in the House of Commons. Law declared that British Unionists would assist Ulster "in their resistance . . . to whatever extent our power goes." But his main objective, clearly, was to deter the government from acting. He stated, "I am sure of this, as sure of it as I can be of anything, that if blood is shed in Ulster there will be precisely the same outburst of feeling here [in Britain] as that which took place in the United States when the first shot was fired at Fort Sumner [*sic*]. There will be an outburst of feeling which will shake to its foundation the whole structure of society in this country."[88] Both Law and Carson questioned the army's loyalty to the government: "Soldiers are citizens like the rest us (Hon. Members, 'NO!'). It never has been otherwise in any country at any time. If it is civil war whether it is right or wrong...the Army will be divided and you will have destroyed the force, such as it is, upon which we depend for the defence of this country."[89] So said Law. Carson declared that in view of the government's hostile intentions, his place was not in London but in Belfast. Before leaving for the train station, he challenged Asquith directly, demanding, "Let the Government come and try conclusions with us in Ulster. Ulster is on the best of terms with the Army. It is the only part of Ireland of which that can be said."[90]

The next day the British army in Ireland seemed to make good on Carson's claim by defying orders to secure Ulster for the enforcement of home rule. Amid rumors that the government was arresting scores of Ulster Unionist leaders, and aware of the anti–home rule sentiments of Arthur Paget, commander in chief of the forces in Ireland, fifty-eight officers at the Curragh formally notified the War Office that they preferred to resign rather than lead their men into Ulster. "If it came to civil war," said their spokesman, Brigadier General Hubert Gough, "I would fight for Ulster rather than against her."[91] According to Generals William Pulteney and Charles Fergusson, who also commanded divisions in Ireland, the "great majority" of their officers could not be relied on to enter Ulster. Fergusson reported that the troops themselves "can only be depended on to do their duty up to a certain point—if the situation develops into civil war they will in the end disintegrate."[92] To make sure the government understood the seriousness of the crisis, General Douglas Haig, commander of the Aldershot military base southwest of London and future chief of Britain's expeditionary force in Europe, visited the prime minister personally to tell him that "his own officers strongly supported Gough."[93]

The reaction of army officers to implementing orders that probably would have entailed clashes with Ulster Volunteers frightened the king and the Bank of England as well as the cabinet. The king summoned Arthur Balfour and Lord Roberts, leader of the British League for the Support of Ulster and the Union, for emergency consultations. The cabinet received a solemn and unprecedented communication from the Bank of England—an official warning that any attempt "to force the home rule bill upon Ulster [would] have a very serious effect upon the financial position of Great Britain and upon monetary conditions generally within its borders."[94]

As so many Unionists had been predicting since mid-1913, the army had indeed proven to be a "broken reed" for any Liberal-nationalist government intent on imposing home rule on Ulster. "The Army," declared the *Morning Post* on March 26, "Has Killed Home Rule!" In a humiliating reversal of previous decisions, warships heading for Belfast were recalled. The dispatch of troops to Ulster was halted. Signed guarantees were provided to the officers at the Curragh that the troops under their command would "not be called upon to enforce the present Home Rule Bill on Ulster."[95] Adjutant-General Sir Spencer Ewart, chief of the imperial general staff, Field Marshal Sir John French, and War Minister John Seely all resigned. Asquith quickly assumed the post of war minister in addition to his premiership. Formally, he asserted the government's right to call on the army to enforce any law the Parliament might pass, but the spectacularly successful landing of arms at Larne in late April forced even Asquith to admit that the army could no longer "be used in or against Ulster."[96]

Encouraged by the success of the Curragh "mutiny," General Henry Wilson now informed the Unionist leadership of every move made by the government in dealing with Ulster resistance. Milner's appetite for an extra-constitutional showdown with the Liberal government was also whetted. "My own hope is that the Revolt, having gone so far, will go still further. We shall then be relieved from this horrible nightmare."[97] Milner's activities were intended, as far as possible, "to make the Gov't openly contemptible."[98] He vigorously opposed any inclinations among Unionists to accept compromise proposals for Ulster's exclusion from home rule that might have rescued the government from its difficulties. With his aides, Milner drew up a detailed plan for a convention of Ulster magistrates. Acting in the name of their responsibility to uphold "the King's peace," the convention would provide a pseudoconstitutional basis for the Ulster Provisional Government, supported by the UVF and sympathetic units within the armed forces, to seize complete control of northeastern Ireland.[99]

The openness of British Conservative leaders to these ideas is indicated by the invitation extended to Milner at this time to join the party's "shadow cabinet."[100] Although Carson had tactfully kept Law in the dark about the details of the Larne gun-running, once the weapons had been landed and safely distributed, observes Law's biographer, Law "at once associated himself with Carson and took full responsibility for what had happened."[101] In June Lord Roberts declared that "any attempt to coerce Ulster would result in the utter disintegration of His Majesty's Armed Forces."[102] At the beginning of July, Wilson assured Milner that as long as events were properly presented to the army, "if Carson and his Government were sitting in the City Hall, and we were ordered down to close the hall, we would not go."[103] Late in July, King George V asked all parties in the dispute to a conference at Buckingham Palace to find a way to come back from "the brink of fratricidal strife."[104] On July 17, 1914, just prior to the conference, Asquith asked Law to reconsider the position of his party, drawing attention to the far-reaching amendments to home rule proposed by the government and the clear willingness of many Unionists to accept some sort of Ulster exclusion. Asquith maintained that "it would be a crime if civil war resulted from so small a difference." Law's response was obdurate: "The people of Ulster know that they had a force which would enable them to hold the Province, and with opinion so divided in this country, it was quite impossible that any force could be sent against them which could dislodge them, and that therefore they knew that they could get their own terms, and that it was certain they would rather fight than give way."[105]

Unionist rejection of every government proposal for effecting the exclusion of Protestant Ulster is best explained by the confidence of both British and Irish Unionists that, in the "war of maneuver" that had developed, they had the whip hand. With the UVF armed and brimming with confidence, with the apparent inability of the government to rely on the army to enforce home rule, with the opposition of southern Irish Unionists in mind, and with diehard Conservative leaders such as Milner working for as thorough a humiliation of the Liberal government as possible, every compromise was refused.[106] The Buckingham Palace conference thus ended in deadlock. With the dramatic announcement of war in Europe, however, a basis for agreement was reached. After receiving the royal assent, home rule was placed on the statute books, but with two conditions attached. Enforcement would be delayed until the end of the war with Germany and until enactment of an amending bill which would, in some unspecified fashion, exclude Ulster from its provisions.

Bluster or Bloodshed:
The Perceptions and Concerns of Government Leaders

During one of their secret meetings in late 1913, Asquith asked Bonar Law why the leader of a conservative party, a party fundamentally opposed to disorder and founded on respect for constitutional traditions, was willing to speak with such apparent recklessness in support of Ulster's threats of violent resistance to the authority of the state. Law replied that what he had said at Blenheim and elsewhere was "in substance...simply a repetition" of what had been said in 1886 by Randolph Churchill, Salisbury, Balfour, and Hartington.[107] Law was correct, but after 1911 the scale and explicitness of Unionist readiness to challenge Westminster's constitutional authority reflected a dramatic escalation from 1886 and 1892–93 in the type of struggle conducted by opponents of home rule.

The events of 1911–14 challenged the legitimacy and stability of the British state more fundamentally than any crisis since the overthrow of the Stuart monarchy near the end of the seventeenth century. Most historians agree that only the outbreak of a world war prevented a civil war in Ireland which could well have spread, with disastrous consequences, into the rest of the United Kingdom.[108] In his private papers, Asquith himself referred to "*Luck* ... in external things" as having played a major role in his political success, "above all (at a most critical and fateful moment ...) in the sudden outbreak of the Great War."[109]

But to test the role of the regime threshold and a war of maneuver in my model of state contraction, it is not enough that I retrospectively judge the prewar crisis as regime-threatening. I need to show that unlike previous *or* subsequent episodes of contentiousness regarding Ireland, concerns about "regime-level" disruption figured more prominently than "incumbent-level" calculations in cabinet decisions about how, when, or even if to implement its policy of political disengagement from Ireland.

The fact is that prior to these events, Britain had enjoyed more than two centuries of nonviolent political change. This record of regime stability can be expected to have prejudiced governing elites against taking threats of violent resistance to parliamentary decisions very seriously. An impression that this was the case might easily be formed not only by the sudden completeness with which the domestic crisis was submerged by the world crisis of August 1914, but also by the record of official government pronouncements from 1911 through the middle of 1913. These characterized seditious activities and talk of civil war or violent resistance as bluffs that were best ignored. Such opposition that might in the end materialize could, in this view, be easily swept aside.

Until 1912 the diaries and private correspondence of prominent Liberals, in sharp contrast to those of Unionist party chiefs, reflect little or no interest in the Ulster question or the possibility of extraconstitutional resistance to home rule.[110] In February 1912, after a full-scale debate in which Lloyd George and Winston Churchill found themselves in the minority, the decisive majority of the cabinet dismissed the notion that serious resistance to home rule would be offered in Ulster and rejected arguments that use of the army would be necessary to enforce a parliamentary decision.[111] Even after Bonar Law's appearance in Balmoral on April 9, 1912, most Liberal ministers chuckled at what the colonial secretary, Lewis Harcourt, dismissed as "bombastic threats."[112]

But government spokesmen found it increasingly difficult to maintain this construction of the burgeoning crisis. In a speech in the Commons during debate over the Home Rule Bill in April 1912, Winston Churchill cited the possibility of Ulster resistance as the main obstacle confronted by the government.[113] Privately he mentioned to Lloyd George (chancellor of the exchequer) and Redmond that temporary exclusion of Ulster from the purview of the Home Rule Parliament might be necessary to avoid a violent constitutional crisis. In September 1912, Churchill outlined an ambitious scheme of political devolution throughout the United Kingdom, including the division of England itself into several different "self-governing" districts. The Heptarchy Kite, as Churchill's quickly forgotten elaboration of "Home Rule All Round" was labeled, was interpreted by both Liberals and Unionists as "a signal of distress, and was taken to mean that a section at least of the Government had come to realize that it would be impossible to force the Protestant community of Ulster to submit to the provisions of their Home Rule Bill."[114]

In October 1912, Prime Minister Asquith attacked both Bonar Law and the Ulster Covenanters. Unwilling as yet to admit that extraconstitutional threats would affect the policies of his government, Asquith nevertheless acknowledged the extraordinary dimensions which opposition to home rule had assumed. He declared that "the reckless rodomontade at Blenheim in the early summer as developed and amplified in this Ulster campaign [the signing of the Ulster Covenant], furnishes a complete grammar of anarchy.... If they were to succeed—they will not succeed ... a more deadly blow has never been dealt ... at the very foundations on which democratic government rests."[115]

From the end of 1912 and through the early months of 1913, the cabinet several times discussed the credibility of Unionist threats to resist home rule in Ulster, if only to place the onus of responsibility for the outbreak of violence on the opposition. In his diary entry for December 31, 1912, Charles Hobhouse, a member of Asquith's cabinet, reported his own contribution to one such discussion as including the judgment that the government actually had "no means of coercing Ulster, for the troops were not to be relied on, even if we wished to coerce."[116] But in January 1913, the government decided to go forward with the third and final reading of the Home Rule Bill for its first circuit through the House of Commons–House of Lords loop. The cabinet was in fact divided over whether serious violent resistance would materialize and in the end whether some sort of special treatment would have to be accorded Ulster. The cabinet majority chose to stand fast on the bill's formula of home rule for a united Ireland, to place the burden of initiating acceptable formulas for the temporary exclusion of Ulster on the Unionists themselves, and to minimize (at least in public) their concerns about the menace of extraconstitutional challenges to parliamentary authority. Unionist proposals for permanently excluding all nine Ulster counties were rejected as attempts to wreck any kind of home rule by sabotaging the intricate financing of the bill.[117]

Many Liberal backbenchers, however, were worried about the government's "happy-go-lucky" approach.[118] To avoid what they viewed as the calamitous possibility of civil war in Ireland, many expressed support for some sort of Ulster exclusion. With the strength and determination of the British Unionist/Ulster Protestant alliance becoming increasingly apparent, not only the king but a number of cabinet ministers—including Crewe, Grey, Haldane, and Morley—joined Churchill and Lloyd George in their judgment that some sort of Ulster exclusion would be the only way to avoid civil war. Of Morley, for example, Asquith commented that he "had been one of the two most vehement opponents of Ulster exclusion in February 1912, whereas he had become one of its leading supporters by Nov. 1913." Morley's attitude shifted, apparently, "as his dread of bloodshed increased."[119]

Asquith's approach to the problem also changed. He now realized that the extraconstitutional resistance of which Ulster and the Unionists were capable was the decisive factor in the political equation, and he came to accept the inevitability of some sort of Ulster exclusion. But instead of pursuing a settlement of the dispute "by consent," Asquith adopted a forceful posture. If necessary, he declared publicly in October and November, armed force would be used to coerce Ulster into accepting the will of Parliament. In secret meetings conducted in November and December 1913 with Law, Asquith refused to commit his government to any form of Ulster exclusion acceptable to Law. By pretending that the parliamentary system "was working normally, even if it was not," he sought to place Carson and Law in the politically uncomfortable position of having to initiate violent resistance.[120] Asquith hoped they would instead accept home rule in principle, on the understanding that Protestant Ulster would somehow be excluded.

There was no small measure of bluff in the government's attitude. In the face of the clearly seditious activities of leading Unionists, both in Ulster and in Britain, Asquith refused to arrest anyone on charges of rebellion or incitement to rebellion. In October 1913, he had informed the king that "the Government did not intend to arrest Carson for sedition, because it would 'throw a lighted match into a powder barrel.'" Admitting, in effect, that the government could no longer enforce the law in Ulster, he added that "however conclusive the evidence, no Irish jury would convict, and popular passions in Ulster would be inflamed."[121] In November 1913, Asquith warned Redmond of the "probability of very numerous resignations of commissions of officers in the event of the troops being used to put down an Ulster insurrection."[122]

By 1914 the government was in essence engaged in a game of "chicken" with the Unionists. While both sides saw the activities of Parliament as nearly irrelevant to the outcome of their (extraconstitutional) war of maneuver over home rule, each side wanted to use parliamentary debates during the final circuit of the Home Rule Bill to force the other into appearing responsible for the outbreak of violence.[123] The Unionists wanted the government to commit itself to permanently excluding Ulster without their being required to accept home rule for southern Ireland. The government wanted the Unionists to accept the principle of home rule for all of Ireland, but at least for the south, before it would officially endorse even the temporary exclusion of northeastern Ulster.

While prominent personalities on both sides of the political fence advanced various schemes of devolution, federation, or "Home Rule All Round," the king implored Asquith to extend maximum concessions toward Ulster, "which policy I have always maintained is the only means of averting civil war." In response to these pressures, and before the Curragh episode virtually eliminated the government's coercive options, cabinet policy seemed to waver between conciliation and truculence. On March 9, Asquith proposed a plan in the House of Commons which Lloyd George had been advocating for at least five months. The idea was to give each county in Ulster an option by plebiscite to exclude itself from home rule for six years. Asquith justified his willingness to make this (in Unionist eyes) minor concession by admitting that if the bill were passed unamended, the country would face "the prospect of acute dissension and even of civil strife" in Ulster.[124] The Unionists rejected the proposal. "We do not want a sentence of death," said Carson, "with a stay of execution for six years." Bonar Law insisted that Parliament dissolve and that an election be called on the question of Irish home rule. Evidence of just how conditional was Unionist acceptance of parliamentary authority was contained in Law's unblinking "offer," on the floor of the House of Commons, to abide by the will of the people in regard to Ulster exclusion if the results of a new election supported that policy.[125]

Two days later the cabinet held a detailed discussion of how to prevent the UVF from seizing military stores in Ulster and establishing the authority of a provisional government there. The special cabinet committee to deal with these problems, with Churchill as its moving force, was named at this time. Churchill's speech in Bradford on March 14 reflected the deliberations of the committee. It was similar to Asquith's Parliament address in its explicit recognition of extraconstitutional concerns as decisive, but contrasted sharply with the prime minister's remarks in its unprecedentedly belligerent tone. Churchill denounced Bonar Law as "a public danger seeking to terrorize the Government and to force his way into the Councils of his Sovereign." Carson's shadow government in Belfast was described as "a treasonable conspiracy." There were, Churchill declared, "worse things than bloodshed even on an extended scale." He concluded his speech with the kind of distinctively Churchillian vigor that cabinet members had urged him to employ.

> If Ulster men extend the hand of friendship, it will be clasped by Liberals and by their Nationalist countrymen in all good faith and in all good will; but if there is no wish for peace; if every concession that is made is spurned and exploited; if every effort to meet their views is only to be used as a means of breaking down Home Rule and of barring the way to the rest of Ireland, if Ulster is to become a tool in party calculations; if the civil and Parliamentary systems under which we have dealt so long, and our fathers before us, are to be brought to the rude challenge of force; if the Government and the Parliament of this great country and greater Empire are to be exposed to menace and brutality; if all the loose, wanton, and reckless chatter we have been forced to listen to these many months is in the end to disclose a sinister and revolutionary purpose; then I can only say to you, "Let us go forward together and put these grave matters to the proof."[126]

This speech was cited by Unionists after the Curragh episode as evidence that the government had planned to provoke the Ulster Volunteer Force into attacking the army. The UVF attacks could then have been used to justify a comprehensive crackdown, wholesale arrest of Unionist leaders, and establishment of martial law in Ulster. In the Commons, Unionist leaders charged the government with malicious intent, asserted that it had no right to employ the army to coerce Ulster, and held that officers refusing to comply were doing their national duty. "Nothing can save the army now," Law declared, "except a clear declaration on the part of the Government that officers will not be compelled—(Hon. Members: 'And men!')—and men will not be compelled—to engage in civil war against their will."[127]

On April 3, the Unionists organized what the *Times* described as perhaps the largest demonstration ever held in London. The vast crowd that gathered in Hyde Park heard speeches from virtually the entire Unionist leadership, including Arthur Balfour, Edward Carson, Austen Chamberlain, F. E. Smith, Walter Long, Lord Milner, Robert Cecil, and Lord Roberts. They hailed the stalwart loyalty of Ulster Protestants and their readiness to defend their ties to England by force of arms, while the "Radical" government was condemned for its "plot" against them. Churchill, in particular, was vilified (by Sir Charles Beresford) as "a Lilliput Napoleon, a man with an unbalanced mind, an ego maniac." Robert Cecil declared he could not know "what was in the dark and tortuous mind of Mr. Churchill, but he did know that he contemplated the slaughter of hundreds of thousands of his fellow-men." An official resolution expressing the opinion of those assembled demanded that the government renounce any use of British troops to enforce home rule.[128]

Despite outrage among rank and file Liberals at the army's entry into politics, and demands that the officer corps's challenge to British democracy not go unpunished, cabinet ministers found themselves on the defensive. In private correspondence immediately after the Curragh episode, Asquith expressed "no doubt [that] if we were to order a march upon Ulster, about half the officers in the Army—the Navy is more uncertain—would strike.... that is the permanent situation, and it is not a pleasant one."[129]

Repeatedly official spokesmen were forced to deny that the government had plotted to coerce Ulster. Instead of justifying the actions it had taken as precautionary measures against the seditious activities of the UVF, the government repeatedly apologized for what it described as a series of misunderstandings and administrative errors which had led to the events at the Curragh. The opposition scoffed, and the unmistakable impression was created that, however certainly home rule for Ireland would finally be passed by the House of Commons, it would not be implemented in the north of Ireland.

It was in this atmosphere, in late April, that the UVF was able to conduct the massive gun-running operation described earlier. Police reports said that "any attempt to arrest leaders or to seize the arms of the Ulster Volunteers would without doubt lead to bloodshed and precipitate what would practically amount to war all over Ulster."[130] Convinced of the army's unreliability, the government thus found itself forced to retreat from any attempt to prosecute those responsible for the gun-running. Instead it sought an accommodation with the Unionists.[131] Ten days after the guns and ammunition were unloaded at Larne, Asquith met secretly with Law and Carson. The objective of the government, said Asquith, was to reach a compromise regarding Ireland that the Unionists could accept. Asquith's decisive concession was to promise that although the Home Rule Bill would pass its third and final reading in the House of Commons later in May, it would not receive the royal assent and be placed on the statute books until an Amending Bill, containing special (but unspecified) provisions for Ulster, could also be put into effect.

On May 25, the Home Rule Bill passed its third reading, on its final circuit through the House of Commons–House of Lords loop. But the House of Lords, still under the complete control of Unionist peers, torpedoed the government's Amending Bill, which provided for the six-year exclusion of any Irish county voting to opt out of home rule. The upper chamber changed the bill to require the exclusion, without time limit, of all nine Ulster counties (including predominantly Catholic/nationalist Donegal, Monaghan, and Cavan).

By this time even John Redmond admitted that armed rebellion, or the convincing threat of civil war, would determine the fate of Ireland—not the legislative action of Parliament. Redmond's entire career had been based on his position as leader of the Irish Parliamentary party and on a strategy of political cooperation with British Liberals to achieve home rule legislation. Fundamentally opposed to the creation of nationalist volunteer units modeled after the Ulster Volunteer Force, he yet found it politically impossible to condemn their formation in autumn 1913. In June 1914, Redmond put his party forward as the political voice of the new nationalist paramilitary force—the Irish National Volunteers.[132]

In the kind of regime-threatening politics that had developed in Britain, Redmond's adoption of the Irish Volunteer movement was a crucial counterweight to the Ulster Volunteers. Mesmerized by the military preparations of the Ulster Volunteer Force, public opinion in Britain was "suddenly confronted with the fact that the Irish Volunteers were in existence as a larger force, and were enrolling at the rate of 15,000 men a week.... While the Cabinet were attempting to formulate the terms of their proposed Amending Bill, they too realized for the first time that if Carson's demands were to be granted in deference to threats of armed disorder a much more formidable outburst would occur in the rest of Ireland."[133]

The last effort to avoid a violent confrontation was the Buckingham Palace conference. Personally convened by the king on July 21, the conference began ten days after the first official meeting of the Ulster Provisional Government and just four days after Law told Asquith that without the exclusion of Ulster from home rule, "an independent state would be set up within the United Kingdom and there would be nothing left for us but to support Ulster to the utmost."[134] The Buckingham Palace conference ended in deadlock after just three days of deliberations. Two days later, substantial arms supplies were landed near Dublin for the Irish National Volunteers. On the very eve of World War I there were, as Charles Townshend has said, four armies operating in Ireland—five, if nationalist terminology is used to classify the Royal Irish Constabulary as "an occupying army." One of these, of course, was the British army, but events had demonstrated to the government that its army had become nearly as much a protagonist in the struggle over the fate of Ireland as the Ulster or the National Volunteers.[135]

The regime crisis over Irish home rule, that is, the challenge to the authority of the British state to determine its own geographical shape, produced neither civil war nor political collapse. One might be tempted to say the crisis ended "not with a bang, but a whimper." In truth it ended with a bang and a whimper. The whimper was the Liberal government's abandonment of what had been the party's single most important goal for thirty years—home rule for a united Ireland. This decision was taken not solely or most saliently because of parliamentary barriers (which did not exist) or fears for the political interests of incumbents, but because of concerns over the implications of the measure for the integrity and stability of the regime. The bang was the outbreak of a world war. Construing the German threat to the inhabitants of both Britain and Ireland as more fundamental, even, than imperatives associated with change in the political status of Ireland, Carson, Law, Asquith, and Redmond agreed to shelve both home rule and the question of Ulster exclusion until military victory had been achieved.

Crossing the Regime Threshold: De-escalation of the Controversy

From 1911 to 1914, government concerns about potent threats to the parliamentary regime obscured incumbent-level fears by Liberal ministers that acquiescing to Conservative demands for a new election would lead to a Liberal defeat. Asquith thus had good partisan reasons for not calling a new election. The Liberal party was no more confident than it had been since its crushing defeat in 1895 that an election fought on the home rule issue would lead to victory. British Conservatives, on the other hand, relished the idea of new elections fought explicitly on the principle of Irish home rule, and demanded a new election as soon as the third Home Rule Bill was introduced.

Such incumbent-level concerns were thus never absent. But for several years following the Parliament Act, as the Irish question moved against the right side of the regime threshold, they had been displaced by a regime-threatening war of maneuver. After 1914, however, they were the only kind of British political competition associated with the Irish problem.

This order-of-magnitude change in the character of the concern which impressed itself most disturbingly on leading politicians will be taken to mark the relocation of the Irish question in British politics—a crossing of the regime threshold in the state-contracting direction.[136] To show that this threshold was indeed crossed (in the state-contracting direction) requires demonstrating how quick and radical was the disappearance of these regime threats. Indicators of this shift are the felt concerns of the government ministers most actively involved in attempts to lighten the burden of the Irish question on British political life. As we shall see, important and virtually irreconcilable differences remained among British elites over what to do about Ireland, but these disagreements no longer produced threats of civil war. No longer were policies of disengagement from Ireland (or part of it) framed against scenarios in which armed resistance to constituted authority would disturb the stability of monarchical or parliamentary institutions.

After September 1914, Cabinet policies toward Ireland were fashioned *only* on the basis of calculations about how the government's prospects for achieving wider objectives could be enhanced and how the partisan interests of key players and parties could be served. Ireland's future continued to matter, and matter greatly, to politicians concerned about careers, coalitions, party prospects, and policy outcomes, but such preoccupations, based on expectations that the boundaries of legal political maneuver would be respected by all competitors, are what ordinarily attend political controversy in a well-instututionalized democracy. These "ordinary" considerations, not concerns pertaining to the integrity of the legal order in Britain, were the *only* serious obstacle remaining to dramatic change in the British state's relationship to Ireland. These incumbent-level concerns influenced and doomed three abortive efforts to solve the Irish problem: Lloyd George's negotiating initiative in 1916; the 1917–18 Irish Convention; and the 1920 Government of Ireland Act. They, and not threats to the regime, were also the only salient considerations surrounding British policy during the Anglo-Irish War (1918–21) and the negotiations which ended that war and led to the Irish Free State.

The Negotiations of 1916

The outbreak of World War I elicited an enthusiastic response from Ulster Unionists. At the Battle of the Somme in July 1916, the Ulster Division suffered extremely heavy casualties—fifty-five hundred killed, wounded, and missing in only two days. More suprising than Ulster's response, however, was Redmond's announcement that the Nationalist party would assist the government in recruiting Irishmen to fight against Germany. With home rule at least officially on the statute books, Redmond was anxious to establish a record of Irish loyalty to the British Empire that would help insure generous and speedy implementation of Irish self-government after the war.[137]

Much of the leadership of the National Volunteers, however, repudiated Redmond's endorsement of the British war effort. Radical Irish nationalists were impatient with the never-ending postponements of home rule. In September 1914, the Supreme Council of the IRB made a secret decision to launch an insurrection before the end of the war. On Easter Monday, in April 1916, it set in motion a poorly coordinated revolt, supported by elements of the National Volunteers and James Connoly's small citizen Army. The Easter Rising brought the Republican vanguard within the Irish nationalist movement into public prominence. The leaders of the revolt were under few illusions that their action could lead directly to an independent Ireland. They feared, however, that without the inspiration of a serious attempt at armed struggle, the nationalist movement might pass into oblivion.

The rebellion, centered in Dublin, was crushed by British artillery within two weeks, amid widespread destruction and the general indifference of the city's population. In its aftermath, martial law was imposed under which innocent civilians as well as rebels suffered violent retribution and imprisonment. In the two weeks following the revolt, fifteen of its leaders, including all the members of the Provisional Government of the Republic of Ireland who had not already been killed in the fighting, were executed. The heavy-handed British response transformed Irish opinion. Overnight the dead men became martyred heroes and saints. A wave of disgust with British rule swept the country, radicalizing public sentiment and threatening to deprive Redmond's party of the mass electoral base, and the maneuvering room, it relied on for its strategy of working within the British Parliament.

The cabinet's lack of attentiveness to Irish matters before the Rising and its clumsy reaction to it must be understood in the context of Britain's deadly struggle against the Central Powers and the sustained political intrigue that surrounded debates over how to reverse the war's dismal course. When a crisis in April 1915, over an apparent shortage of artillery shells on the western front, led the Liberal government to accede to a Liberal-Conservative coalition, Lloyd George was given the crucial job of minister of munitions. His success in that position and his popularity as a war leader encouraged him to escalate his attacks on Asquith's conduct of the war. The press said and Asquith feared that Lloyd George was after the premiership. But Lloyd George's hawkish posture, and his support of both industrial and military conscription, had alienated him from many rank and file Liberals and from the emergent Labour party as well. This meant his political future was linked, aside from his personal popularity, to the ties he could cultivate with Tory politicians.[138]

It was to fend off American criticism of British army outrages against the Irish (at a time when the United States's entry into the war was of dominant importance to the British government) and to ruin his rival's chances to forge an alliance with the Unionists that Asquith tapped Lloyd George to respond to the Irish mess.[139] Lloyd George's acceptance of the Irish assignment appears to have been motivated by his interest in persuading Washington to enter the war, his wish to regain the allegiance of Radicals upset by his advocacy of conscription, and his desire to build his own reputation as a statesman who could get things done. His failure was due in part to differences between the Irish sides over the terms of Ulster's exclusion, but even more directly to his underestimation of the pressure Irish Unionist ministers could exert to oppose a settlement and of Asquith's susceptibility to it.[140]

In June and July 1916, while carrying on intensive negotiations with Redmond and Carson, Lloyd George offered both sides what they wanted. To the nationalists he seemed to promise immediate home rule with fiscal autonomy and only a temporary exclusion of some Ulster counties. To Carson he seemed to promise implementation of home rule after the war, limitations on the fiscal autonomy of the home rule government, and the option of permanently excluding six Ulster counties. Despite the gap between permanent versus temporary exclusion of Protestant counties which still remained between Redmond and Carson, many factors were working in favor of Lloyd George's scheme. Redmond was ready to accept extraordinary concessions before Sinn Fein's growing strength made his party an anachronism. Carson was deeply concerned about gaining the United States's entry into the war. In sharp contrast with their position in 1914, many Unionist leaders as well as such conservative newspapers as the *Observer,* the *Daily Telegraph,* the *Times,* and the *Daily Mail,* now supported (or had come to accept as inevitable) a settlement along home rule lines.[141]

Lloyd George rapidly gained agreement from Carson and Redmond to terms somewhat contradictorily described to each, but generally consistent with the immediate creation of a Dublin-based Home Rule Parliament and the exclusion of Protestant Ulster counties, at least until reconsideration of the terms of inclusion could be undertaken after the war.[142] But the southern Irish Unionists in the cabinet—Walter Long and Lord Lansdowne, whose personal fortunes and careers would be most directly affected by a change of regime in the south of Ireland—objected bitterly. One of their English supporters—Lord Selborne, minister of agriculture—resigned forthwith. Confronted by rank and file opposition to any compromise on the permanent exclusion of Ulster from Irish home rule, Bonar Law withdrew his support for an amended version of Lloyd George's scheme. With the coalition government's cabinet "on the brink of breaking up," Asquith indicated that he would not risk ministerial resignations or dissolution of the government to push through an Irish settlement of the sort Lloyd George had proposed. On July 27, 1916, the cabinet met to "bury the agreement," returning Ireland to the old Dublin Castle system of close surveillance and coercion.[143]

Neither the determinants nor the consequences of this episode had anything to do with threats to defy or disrupt the institutions of the British state and can be assessed in conventional terms with respect to the careers and partisan interests of different players. The episode was a terrible blow to Redmond's party, boosting Sinn Fein as the leader of Irish nationalism and setting Ireland on a direct course for violent confrontation with Britain in 1919–21. Referring to Bonar Law's retreat in response to opposition among Unionist party activists and southern Irish Protestant leaders, F. S. L. Lyons has described the failed 1916 negotiations as a "great opportunity for reconciliation ... sacrificed ... to sordid party interest."[144] But it would be incorrect to see only Unionist party interests as responsible for the outcome. It was Asquith who decided not to go forward with the initiative, hazarding die-hard Unionist resignations, but counting on Balfour, F. E. Smith, and other Tory leaders to stick by him. Part of his motivation was fear that collapse of the talks would damage Lloyd George's political reputation. Lloyd George was forced to back down on his promise to Redmond to resign if his commitments were not supported by the cabinet. The *Manchester Guardian* woundingly noted his apparent surrender to "a little aristocratic clique."[145] The experience left Lloyd George "disgusted with Asquith's behavior," but convinced that the Irish problem was not a useful political vehicle with which to advance his prospects for taking Asquith's place as prime minister.[146]

The Irish Convention, July 1917–April 1918

In the summer of 1916, the full dimensions of the disaster on the Somme became apparent. As the slaughter continued without noticeable effect, an irresistible tide of dissatisfaction with Asquith's leadership swept the country. One of the only successes in the British war effort had been Lloyd George's stunning performance at the Munitions Ministry.[147] His reputation grew as the only cabinet member equipped to fight the war with the necessary imagination, vigor, and determination. He was therefore well positioned to demand the job of war minister, left vacant by the death of Lord Kitchener in June 1916.

After receiving the appointment, Lloyd George moved quickly to push Asquith into resigning or granting full control over the war effort to his new war minister. In December 1916, with setbacks in Russia, the defeat of Romania, heavy losses of merchant shipping, and the shortages and price rises that accompanied these losses, Asquith resigned. Most of the Liberal party followed him into opposition. Lloyd George thereupon became prime minister of a coalition government supported by approximately one-third of the Liberal delegation to the House of Commons, the Labor party, and, most importantly, the Conservative party. The strength of this parliamentary bloc, along with establishment of a secretariat within the prime minister's office and creation of a five-member "war cabinet" with full authority over all aspects of the war effort, gave Lloyd George more power than any British leader since Cromwell.

As a Welshman, Lloyd George was sympathetic to Ireland's quest for a measure of autonomy from England. But he rejected Irish claims to nationhood and resented how often Irish demands had forced Welsh grievances to be held in abeyance. To put the new prime minister's attitude toward Ireland in its proper perspective, it is also necessary to understand his ascendancy in December 1916 as approximating his long-cherished vision of a powerful, centralized, efficient state apparatus and the majority-party alignment necessary to establish and maintain it. Since the late 1890s, Lloyd George's career had been shaped by a series of attempts to engineer a centrist, patriotic, social-reforming "national fusionist" party. By joining, under his leadership, the Joseph Chamberlain–style consolidationist and energetic elements of the Unionist party to the "ginger" right wing of the Liberal party, he believed a dynamic welfare state could be created at home and a strong federated empire abroad. With this kind of majority party and the state it would control, the Irish question could finally be prevented from distracting British political debate from what he considered really crucial problems. Within a general scheme of imperial and United Kingdom reorganization, Ireland could then be granted a form of home rule which would prevent separation. This devolution of power to Irish nationalists could be achieved by the dominant centrist party he saw himself as forming out of the wartime coalition. Such a "fusionist" party could then address the Irish problem without having to bow to demands by Irish nationalists or Unionist diehards.[148]

In the meantime he would approach Ireland as a troublesome but substantively unimportant problem posing some short-term risks to British interests which had to be minimized, not eliminated. This attitude and the incumbent-level character of the concerns that dominated policy-making toward Ireland during this period are illustrated in the way Lloyd George handled cross-pressures arising from demands by the British public to extend conscription to Ireland and from the need to avoid U.S. displeasure at the harsh measures that would unquestionably be necessary to enforce the draft on Irish Catholics.[149]

In the wake of the Easter Rising (April 1916), and in line with the judgment of all expert observers, Asquith had decided not to extend conscription to Ireland.[150] But by the beginning of 1917, public outrage that Irish Catholics were substantially being spared the sacrifices required of all other British subjects forced the government to reconsider the issue. It was intimated that home rule for the south of Ireland could be carried through if accompanied by Irish acceptance of conscription. Redmond, however, rejected any linkage between home rule and conscription. To do otherwise would have destroyed what credibility remained to his party, and his leadership of it. Meanwhile, although the United States had officially entered the war on April 6, 1917, the extent of U.S. commitment to victory was much in doubt. The war cabinet was thus very sensitive to U.S. attitudes toward Ireland and the political clout of the Irish-American lobby.[151]

Accordingly Lloyd George was forced to come up with something for Ireland, though his approach had to be particularly delicate. Bonar Law was a member of the war cabinet, and Lord Milner was the prime minister's most important ally within that inner sanctum. Though Milner subsequently proved supportive of initiatives toward Ireland, Lloyd George could not be sure how Milner's genuine antipathy to home rule would affect this crucial personal alliance. More worrisome still was Edward Carson, now first lord of the admiralty. Lloyd George feared that pushing any kind of amending legislation for home rule which might be acceptable to Redmond would trigger Carson's resignation from the cabinet and the breakup of the government. Indeed Carson threatened to resign from the cabinet if the government proceeded with its plan to introduce a complex Amending Bill to the Home Rule Act which would have granted self-government to Ireland, while excluding, via "county option" plebiscites, four (not six) of Ulster's counties.[152]

The government was stymied. Cabinet members even feared a collapse that might stem from the humiliation of abandoning its stated plans to amend and implement the Home Rule Act.[153] In mid-May, however, the prime minister proposed to both sides a scheme that achieved just what he (and his cabinet) needed, and no more. Representatives of Irish from all points of view were to be invited to a convention charged to find an agreement acceptable to all. If "substantial agreement" on a settlement was reached among the Irish delegates themselves, Lloyd George promised that the British government would implement it. Accorded a disproportionate number of seats at the convention, and in receipt of confidential assurances from Lloyd George that Ulster would have a veto over any agreement a majority of the convention might produce, Irish Unionists could not refuse the proposal. Sinn Fein called its own counterassembly in Dublin, but Redmond, heartened by the fact that the convention was based on the image of a unified Ireland, saw it as his last chance. For Lloyd George what was important was that there was no time limit imposed on the discussions, nor any clear definition of what the government would be required to interpret as "substantial agreement." Thus the convention could drag on indefinitely. This tactic would shift attention and blame for lack of a settlement from the government to the "querulous" Irish themselves and eliminate the need for a confrontation with Carson and the diehards.

This is precisely what happened. The convention began in July 1917 and ended inconclusively in April 1918, putting the nettlesome issue back on the government's agenda. In certain respects the problem was unchanged. In the midst of the most dangerous German offensive of the entire conflict (February–August 1918), Irish affairs were still treated as one of many peripheral matters whose significance paled in comparison to the awful struggle on the Contintent. Ireland, in that context, was addressed, as it had been in 1916 and 1917, as an ordinary problem.

As the maximum age of conscription in Britain was raised from forty-two to fifty, the British public demanded with increasing anger that conscription be extended to Ireland.[154] As before, this pressure was matched by overwhelming Irish Catholic resistance to conscription. A general strike against conscription on April 23, 1916, united the Catholic hierarchy with parliamentary nationalists, Sinn Fein, and "physical force" republicans and shut down everything in Ireland except the city of Belfast. Further complicating the government's desire to satisfy British opinion was an abiding concern for the U.S. reaction to coercion in Ireland. Dozens of U.S. divisions were promised for the western front but had not yet arrived.

In two other respects, however, the Irish problem had changed since Lloyd George's consideration of it in 1916 and 1917. First, Redmond's Irish Parliamentary party had been supplanted by Sinn Fein.[155] If home rule was still the slogan most British politicians used to frame proposals for Irish self-government, the old Parnell-Redmond formula—working for maximum political autonomy "within the empire," using constitutional methods, and cooperating with Britain—was thoroughly discredited in Ireland. Irish nationalists now made little or no effort to camouflage their intention to seek complete independence from Britain or their willingness to use both peaceful and violent forms of resistance to achieve it.

The second change in the problem was that Unionist opposition to home rule for the south of Ireland had substantially weakened. The Unionist party as a whole still looked on any sort of special treatment for Ireland, or even the south of Ireland, with disfavor. Nevertheless, proposals made within the government to implement various forms of home rule were no longer perceived to jeopardize the stability of the governing coalition or the political careers of their advocates. Along with general concerns for the political repercussions of Irish policies, straightforward cost-benefit calculations were the cabinet's decisive criteria.

Lloyd George's initial response to the reemergence of the Irish conscription issue in 1918 was to propose the immediate establishment of some sort of home rule as a means of "gilding" the enforcement of conscription. Though rank and file Unionist opposition to home rule did lead to warnings of severe strain within the party, and though Unionists preferred to shelter home rule for Ireland within theoretical offers of similar arrangements to Wales, Scotland, and England, the Unionist leadership in the cabinet did not threaten resignation.[156] The government's decision to legislate conscription, but delay its implementation indefinitely, was based on general agreement both within Dublin Castle and among responsible ministers in London that whatever matter of principle might be involved (regarding the officially equal rights and responsibilities of Irishmen as citizens of the British state), the costs of enforcing conscription in Ireland would far outweigh the concrete benefits that could be obtained.[157] Similar considerations stymied the efforts of a heavily Unionist cabinet subcommittee, including Lord Curzon and Austen Chamberlain and chaired by Walter Long, to frame a Home Rule Bill. Its failure to produce a proposal acceptable to the cabinet in June 1918 was based not on opposition to the idea itself, but on the judgment that support for a Dublin Parliament, whether or not packaged within a broader "federalist" scheme, was unlikely to be forthcoming soon from *any* quarter in Ireland.

The subordinate status of the Irish question, for cabinet ministers reeling from the shock of General Ludendorff's offensive which threatened to destroy both the British and French armies, was reflected in the hurried, impatient, even reckless attitude adopted in these months by Lloyd George. In private conversations the prime minister responded to appeals for conciliation of Ireland by minimizing the importance of the problem and suggesting the use of airplanes, armored cars, and Paris Commune–style summary executions to terrorize Ireland into submission at tolerable cost. On another occasion during this period, Lloyd George "half jokingly" told C. P. Scott "the only way to deal with Ireland is for some one to open a sluice and submerge her." On April 10 the cabinet devoted only two minutes of its deliberations to the massive anticonscriptionist campaign in Ireland, and this only a week prior to legislative approval of Irish conscription. At the June 29 cabinet meeting, when a final decision on the Long Committee's recommendations was to be made, Lloyd George admitted he had not even had time to read the committee's report.[158]

Meanwhile the German offensive had finally shot its bolt. An Allied counterattack, made possible by the engagement of half a dozen U.S. divisions, achieved the long sought "break-out," forcing Germany to sue for peace and making Lloyd George's political position unassailable.

Ireland in general, and the inevitable destruction of the Irish Parliamentary party in particular, figured not at all in Lloyd George's immediate decision to call new elections—elections, in December 1918, in which Sinn Fein candidates committed to absenting themselves from Westminster won 73 of 79 Irish nationalist seats. The stage was thereby set for what Walter Long predicted would be a "fair and square fight between the Irish Government and Sinn Fein as to who is going to govern the country."[159]

The Incumbent-Level Politics of Britain's War in Ireland, 1919–1921

The escalation of Irish nationalist demands, and the government's refusal to recognize Sinn Fein as a legitimate interlocutor, led to two and a half years of violence in Ireland. During this period, however, the character of the concerns determining British policy toward Ireland did not change. Neither the government's refusal to negotiate with Sinn Fein until June 1921, nor its formulation of the Better Government of Ireland (Partition) Act of 1920, nor the stands it took during the final negotiation of the Irish Free State treaty in December 1921 were affected by the kind of regime-level apprehensions that commanded cabinet attention in the years immediately prior to World War I.

Taking full advantage of the public's "Hang the Kaiser!" mood, the Conservative-Unionist party won 338 seats in the election of December 1918. Combined with 136 "Lloyd George Liberals," the coalition enjoyed an enormous margin over the opposition. Its political strength rested more or less equally on the huge mass of Conservative MPs and on the personal popularity of Lloyd George. The Labor party, with 59 seats, became the official "Opposition" in place of the Asquith Liberals, who won only 26 seats. The Irish Parliamentary party was virtually wiped out.

In accordance with Sinn Fein's refusal to accept British institutions as the decisive arena for its nationalist struggle, Sinn Fein's 73 successful candidates refused to take their seats in Westminster. Instead they convened an Assembly of Ireland, or Dail Eireann, in Dublin. On January 21, 1919, at the first meeting of the Dail, 27 of the elected Sinn Fein MPs were present; 34 were in jail. A provisional constitution was read which "ratified" the Irish republic that had been "established" at the beginning of the Rising on Easter Monday 1916.

Eamon de Valera, the senior surviving commander of the Rising, escaped from British custody on February 3, 1919. The Dail unanimously elected him president of the republic. De Valera appointed a cabinet and, officially at least, brought the National Volunteers (more commonly known, by this time, as the Irish Republican Army) under the authority of the Defense Ministry. Through the Dail and the cabinet, a nascent judicial system, and a network of local government institutions, de Valera sought to displace British rule of Ireland and gain recognition, at Versailles and in the capitals of the world, of an independent Irish republic. He also stepped up attacks on Irishmen employed as policemen. By the end of 1919, the IRA had killed twenty-one Irish policemen. Soon a bitter guerilla war was raging between the forces of the Crown and the Irish Republican Army—the latter guided and supported by an underground authority structure comprised of de Valera's cabinet and the shadowy but effective apparatus of the Irish Republican Brotherhood.[160]

The British responded to this mix of civil resistance and armed struggle by proscribing the Dail, Sinn Fein, the Irish Volunteers, and the Gaelic League. The government's objective, Lloyd George declared in October 1920, was to break up "a small body of assassins, a real murder gang." The police and the demoralized Royal Irish Constabulary (RIC) could neither defeat the IRA nor destroy the Sinn Fein underground government, both of which enjoyed the sympathy of most Catholics. Yet reinforcements were not readily available. Postwar demobilization and retrenchment left British military resources stretched to the breaking point. To catch "murder by the throat," a special gendarmerie of ex-British servicemen was recruited. Named after the colors of their makeshift uniforms, the first hundreds of these Black and Tans were sent to Ireland in the spring of 1920, joined later by another, larger batch of Auxiliaries. By the time of the cease-fire which ended "the Troubles" in July 1921, seven thousand of these troops had been sent to Ireland.[161]

The men who joined these units were not typical British soldiers. Many had been so brutalized by their years in the trenches that they had found it impossible to reintegrate into civilian life. Equally contemptuous of regulations, private property, and the legal rights of the Irish as British citizens, they proved impossible to control once exposed to the strain of ambush and insult in Ireland. There remains much debate over how much authorization they were given for their tactics of reprisal and collective punishment. The demolition of houses belonging to Sinn Fein suspects certainly was authorized, but the amount of violence, looting, and arson for which the "forces of the Crown" were responsible became so great that by fall 1920 the British public had become accustomed to discussing "terrorism" in Ireland when referring to the actions of the government, not those of the IRA.[162]

Despite the violence in Ireland, the official end of the war meant that the government would be required to implement the terms of the third

Home Rule Bill. Spurred also by international embarrassment, the cabinet appointed Walter Long, the southern Irish Unionist, to chair a cabinet committee to study available options. The committee recommended establishing two Irish Parliaments, each with narrowly defined powers,—one in Belfast for the six counties of Armagh, Antrim, Down, Londonderry, Tyrone, and Fermanagh, and one in Dublin for the remaining twenty-six counties. A Council of Ireland would also be established as a symbol of Irish aspirations for unity.[163]

Early in 1920 the government accepted the committee's recommendations and introduced a bill "to provide for the better government of Ireland." Debated in desultory fashion, the Better Government for Ireland Act passed its third reading in November 1920. Elections were held in May 1921 for the Parliaments of what were called Southern Ireland and Northern Ireland. As expected, these elections produced a Unionist-dominated Parliament in the North, with Sir James Craig (now Lord Craigavon) as president, and a debacle in the South. All 124 Sinn Fein candidates in the South won uncontested victories, but refused to constitute an assembly under the terms of the legislation.

In 1921, to the extent that Britain continued to govern Catholic Ireland at all, it did so by the direct use of force. The legal status of the twenty-six counties was clouded by the 1920 Better Government Act's requirement that "Southern Ireland" be ruled as a "Crown Colony" in the absence of a duly constituted Parliament. Regardless of how British rule of Ireland was to be named, however, the most important question was whether the government's commitment to brutal techniques of repression could be sustained long enough to destroy the IRA's ability to fight, or whether a rising tide of British revulsion at such techniques, and divisions within the government over their efficacy, would lead to political negotiations with Sinn Fein before the collapse of the IRA.

Graphic newspaper coverage of large-scale property destruction and the cold-blooded killing of civilians by officers of the law shocked the British public. The government's lukewarm condemnations of the most egregious excesses provoked a firestorm of criticism, even from those who shared the government's abhorrence of Sinn Fein. Anglican clergymen, the Trades Union Congress, the Labour party, Asquithian Liberals, "High Tories" such as Lords Robert and Hugh Cecil and Oswald Mosley, most of the press, and virtually the entire intellectual establishment censured the government for its brutality and lawlessness.[164] Both the Oxford and Cambridge Unions passed resolutions condemning government actions in Ireland. The archbishop of York declared he could see no difference between Britain's actions in Ireland and Germany's treatment of Belgium during the war.[165] Herbert Samuel compared British conduct in Ireland with the "tyranny of the Hapsburgs."[166] Even General Gough (formerly of the Curragh), whose sympathies for Ulster Unionists had led him to defy the Asquith government in 1914, compared England's record of "vindictive and insolent savagery" in Ireland *unfavorably* to the outrages "of any nation in the world, not excepting the Turk and the Zulu."[167]

In June 1921, the cabinet abruptly changed course. De Valera was invited to London for talks with Lloyd George. On July 11, a cease-fire was was put into effect. By September, agreement had been reached that formal negotiations could be conducted between the government and Sinn Fein for the purpose of "ascertaining how the association of Ireland with the community of nations known as the British Empire can best be reconciled with Irish national aspirations."[168] After hard bargaining over the terms of Northern Ireland's exclusion and the exact wording of Southern Ireland's relationship to the British Crown, a treaty was signed on December 6, 1921, which recognized Sinn Fein's cabinet and Dail Eireann as the government and Parliament of the Irish Free State. The Northern Ireland Parliament, however, was given the right (promptly exercised) to exclude the six counties under its purview from the authority of the new state. This exclusion was subject only to the findings of a boundary commission that would be charged to make adjustments "in accordance with the wishes of the inhabitants" in districts of mixed Catholic and Protestant habitation.

The treaty was ratified by the Dail Eireann, but important elements within the IRA, and de Valera himself, refused to accept it. In the name of a united Ireland, and abjuring any sort of oath of allegiance to the Crown, they revolted against the Dail. A bloody civil war ensued during which British arms and ammunition supplied to the pro-treaty forces helped defeat de Valera and the anti-treaty irregulars. A total of seventy-seven anti-treaty leaders and fighters were executed. In May 1924, after an estimated five thousand Irishmen on both sides had been killed or wounded, the fighting came to an end.[169] In 1925 the boundary commission disappointed Irish Free State leaders by recommending no changes in their favor. In 1927 de Valera entered the Dail, and as a result of the 1932 Free State elections he was able to form a government. In a series of dramatic unilateral actions de Valera broke virtually all formal ties to the British Crown. His constitution of 1937 proclaimed Eire (Ireland) the new name of the Irish Free State and claimed sovereignty over the entire island.[170] British ministers chafed at the Irish actions, which flouted the terms of the treaty. Some economic sanctions were imposed, but no thought was given to forcible intervention. Through the entire course of World War II, Ireland remained neutral. After eight hundred years of British rule, most of Ireland was independent—in word and in deed.

Perceptions, Motives, and Concerns regarding Ireland, 1919–1922

Historians differ over whether the IRA would soon have been eliminated as a fighting force had the British continued their rigorous policies in Ireland past June 1921.[171] They agree, however, that the crucial factors in the British offer of negotiations and a truce were political, not military. D. G. Boyce, in the most thorough study of the question available, concludes that the government's sudden willingness to agree to a cease-fire and a negotiated settlement with Sinn Fein was not based on a judgment that military victory was impossible. He tells us that "the revolt of the British conscience, not the defeat of the British army,...obliged Lloyd George to seek terms of peace and settlement with Sinn Fein."[172]

It would be difficult to think of a formulation that would point more neatly to the radical change in the determinants of British policy toward disengagement from Ireland. In 1914 it was not the revolt of the British conscience but of portions of the army which, at the Curragh, had deterred the government from proceeding with implementation of home rule. Aside from advising about the resources required to restore order in Ireland, army officers were substantially uninvolved in the political debates of 1920 and 1921. That soldiers or officers might not follow orders in Ireland did not occur to cabinet ministers during 1919–1921. When in July 1919 Edward Carson threatened to call out the Volunteers again, as in 1914, if Ulster's rights were not properly respected, even Unionist newspapers reacted with anger and ridicule rather than sympathy.[173]

Analysis of British policy toward Ireland during this period, which ended with the British government granting much more autonomy to (southern) Ireland had ever been envisioned within the rubric of home rule, reveals the partisan calculations and other incumbent-level concerns which motivated cabinet members and led to the practical withdrawal of British authority from most of Ireland. Indeed, through the entire two and a half years of fighting in Ireland as well as the six months of negotiations with Sinn Fein, the Irish question was *never* perceived by elites or the attentive public in Britain as a matter whose denouement might affect the stability or integrity of the regime. Political elites instead viewed the problem of Ireland as they had since 1916—as an issue liable to disturb the internal harmony of the Conservative party and the "coalition Liberals," threaten the stability of their coalition government, and/or affect the firmness of Lloyd George's grasp on the premiership. Government policies toward Ireland thus changed as a function of struggles for advantage among politicians concerned with a complex range of difficult but ordinary issues. Writing to Bonar Law, who temporarily withdrew from public life because of high blood pressure in the spring and summer of 1921, Lloyd George complained that the "whirling world" of politics was raising his blood pressure as well. Within this world, the Irish question figured on a par with all the other "crises," which seemed to Lloyd George as "chasing each other like shadows of clouds across the landscape. Miners, unemployment, Reparations, Silesia, and always Ireland."[174]

To be sure, in the first year following the armistice, Ireland hardly figured in the concerns of high-echelon British leaders. For most of the period between February and July 1919, Lloyd George and Bonar Law were absent from London—immersed in peace negotiations at Versailles. In the detailed journal kept by Thomas Jones, a confidant of Lloyd George who served in these years as the principal assistant secretary to the cabinet, only two entries mentioning Ireland appear for the entire year of 1919.[175]

Lloyd George's own peculiar political position in the years immediately following the First World War and his schemes to enhance that position are the keys to understanding the pattern of his responses to the Irish question in this crucial period. His charismatic appeal to the average Britisher, his close association with victory in the war, and his international prestige as one of the Big Four encouraged him to treat the affairs of government in a "quasi-presidential" style of "Olympian isolation from the day to day skirmishings of politics."[176] On the other hand, the 1918 election, by eliminating the possibility of a Lloyd George–led Liberal government, made him completely dependent on the loyalty of the Unionist party. However close his ties had been with various members of the Unionist leadership, he had never enjoyed the trust of Conservative backbenchers. This predicament, combining apparent ascendancy with real vulnerability, drove Lloyd George to preserve the image of his personal indispensability and build upon it by reviving his old dream of founding a new, dominant centrist party.[177]

After two shocking coalition defeats in 1919 by-elections, Lloyd George began discussing his plans to transform the coalition into the kind of centrist "fusionist" party he had aspired to lead ever since the 1890s. Liberalism, he argued, was "a dying creed." The coalition had been successful, but it needed a more "positive identity" to build a secure electoral base. "No-one," he told his friend, Lord Riddell, "will take the Coalition brew." From late 1919 through the spring of 1920, he devoted himself to convincing his Liberal supporters—the "Coaly Libs"—to "fuse" with the Unionists into what his advocates proposed be called the United Reform party.[178]

Lloyd George drew support for his project from Liberal MPs within the coalition who saw little political future for themselves in Asquith's declining Liberal party. Nor could they depend on the good graces of the Unionists. Their ties to Lloyd George, however, could provide a wealth of possibilities if his undisputed personal popularity could be harnessed within a specially designed political party. Support for the idea was also linked to the reformism animating many new entrants into political life who railed against the abuses of petty competition that they said had marred British life before 1914 and had interfered with the running of the war. A fusionist center party, they hoped could build a country "fit for heroes" by tapping the spirit of bold enterprise and state-guided collective action which Lloyd George had generated during the war. Winston Churchill viewed a large center party as a bulwark against Labor party–sponsored socialism at home and Bolshevism abroad. Some Unionist leaders, especially Birkenhead and Balfour, agreed, anticipating a broad consensus around Disraeli-style formulas of Conservative social pragmatism. Law and Chamberlain were less enthusiastic; to maintain their alliance with the prime minister they soon swung behind the proposal.[179]

It was in March 1920, just as the first Black and Tans were being sent to Ireland, that Lloyd George and Law agreed to propose a fusionist reorganization of their party organizations. But the strident anti-Red rhetoric and cautious domestic agenda Lloyd George had used to cement his ties with the Unionists struck a sour note with his Liberal backbenchers. If this was what "fusionism" meant, it seemed an abandonment of cherished ideas concerning foreign policy, taxation, social reform, and Ireland. Law also confronted opposition to fusion expressed by Unionist rank and file anxious for a more assertive, independent Conservative party. Exploiting Lloyd George's failure with the Coaly Libs, he canceled plans to make suggestions for amalgamation to the Unionist party.[180] Although Lloyd George, Churchill, Birkenhead, and Chamberlain remained committed to the idea, by April 1920 fusion had been all but dropped in favor of lukewarm resolutions of greater cooperation between Liberals and Unionists.

Had the fusionist project succeeded, Lloyd George would have enjoyed a firm political base for pursuing an Irish settlement. Until it was in place, however, and with all the other issues on his plate at the time, he preferred to postpone Irish initiatives. Once the fusionist effort dissolved, in the spring of 1920, relations between Lloyd George and Law deteriorated and the future of the coalition itself seemed tenuous. Ireland then became one of many domains in which Lloyd George felt it necessary to tailor his position to what the great bulk of the Unionist party would be willing to support. This encouraged continued neglect of Irish affairs and the promotion of confused but generally hard-line "law and order" policies, reflecting the lowest common denominator of the coalition.

But the cabinet could not rely solely on repression to keep the Irish question from occupying more of their time and energy. By the end of 1919, deteriorating conditions in Ireland and the unavailability of military reinforcements had raised real questions in ministerial minds about whether the British government would be able to enforce a policy of strict coercion. In light of Britain's postwar diplomatic alliance with and economic dependence on the United States, U.S. pressure for progress toward a solution was a substantial prod to action, as it had been during the war. Finally, the fact that the Home Rule Bill was on the books and would have to be either enforced or superseded forced the government to at least seem to be seeking a political solution to its Irish difficulties.

This particular combination of pressures and constraints (not his own preference with respect to Irish policy) explains Lloyd George's appointment of the southern Unionist, Walter Long, to chair the cabinet committee charged with drafting new Irish legislation. It also explains Lloyd George's subsequent decision to proceed with the 1920 Better Government for Ireland Bill (despite the certainty of its failure in the south of Ireland) and his ferocious public stance toward Sinn Fein, from mid-1919 to June 1921. The difference between public display and private consideration is exemplified by the contrast between his fervid 1920 and early 1921 speeches in support of the Black and Tans, and his apparent encouragement of a "back-channel" link to the IRA.[181] It is also revealed by Lloyd George's confidential discussions held during the summer and fall of 1920 with Dublin Castle administrators about the possibility of satisfying Sinn Fein demands by offering dominion status[182] to Ireland. Given to understand that even this, especially if Ulster were to be excluded, would not be easily accepted by the nationalists, Lloyd George bided his time.[183]

Lloyd George's retreat from these explorations in December and his full-throated endorsement of repression were also due to political expediency and bargaining tactics rather than his own settled conviction of what could bring stability to the British-Irish relationship. At the end of February 1921, Law and Birkenhead were publicly speaking in traditional Unionist terms about Ireland.[184] Though "secretly convinced" that some form of dominion status would finally have to be granted, and increasingly willing to speculate about "conciliation" based on "loyal membership in the British Commonwealth," Lloyd George was reluctant to offer clear proposals for a truce or a settlement that could provoke his Conservative supporters or give away too much too early to Sinn Fein.[185]

He preferred to let the Irish pot boil until Unionist leaders were themselves prepared to take the first public steps toward disengagement. The strategy worked. By April 1921, the Irish situation had become the "main preoccupation" of the government.[186] Assailed at home for an uncontrolled policy of coercion and reprisal in Ireland, subjected to withering criticism abroad for denying the rights of small nations for which Britain claimed to have fought the Great War, and saddled with the imminent prospect of enforcing Crown colony government on the twenty-six counties of southern Ireland, the cabinet accepted Lloyd George's judgment in May that the time for decision had come.

Still concealing his sympathy for a dominion home rule solution, Lloyd George allowed the cabinet discussion on May 12 to run its course before identifying himself with Balfour's opposition to the dominion-status idea and ranging himself with the Unionists against the Liberals in rejecting a truce.[187] Nonetheless the political environment with respect to Ireland was becoming increasingly malleable. General Crozier, commander of the Auxiliaries in Ireland, had resigned in February 1921 to protest the undisciplined behavior of his own troops. In April he called publicly for a truce. Albeit under somewhat confused pretenses, the Ulster Unionist leader James Craig had met secretly with de Valera in Dublin on May 5. Subsequently, various Unionist opinion leaders, both inside and outside the government, indicated the time had come for conciliation. In the House of Lords, several Unionist peers, including southern Irishmen such as Midleton and Dunraven, supported a resolution calling for negotiations with Sinn Fein.[188] On May 24, General Nevil Macready, commander in chief of British forces in Ireland, submitted an unpredentedly gloomy assessment of the Irish situation. To bring an end to the revolt Macready said he needed cabinet support for an intensified onslaught against the IRA and replacements, by October, for most of his officers and men.[189] On June 12, Macready delivered an even more disturbing assessment to the cabinet's Irish Situation Committee. Accompanied by predictions of "one hundred shootings a week," his proposal to the committee for the formal introduction of martial law included a rigorous system of travel permits, an end to all court proceedings against soldiers or police, an economic blockade, the suppression of newspapers, and the death penalty for Dail members[190] To put Macready's recommendations into effect would have required raising the number of British troops (and constabulary) in Ireland from 40,000 to 100,000.[191]

The members of the heavily Unionist cabinet subcommittee were shaken by the drastic steps Macready and other military men told them would be necessary.[192] Already in May, Birkenhead, Chamberlain, and Churchill had insisted on "an offer of a much larger measure of self-government for the Twenty-six Counties than was contained in the Home Rule Act" as a condition for responding positively to the demands Macready was making.[193] Not coincidentally, according to Dangerfield, Birkenhead and Churchill were also joined in a mid-June attempt to unseat Lloyd George from the premiership. With relations between the Tory party and Lloyd George unsettled by Bonar Law's earlier resignation, Birkenhead, along with Lord Beaverbrook and Robert Cecil, took the lead in seeking to organize a distinctly more "Conservative" government, with himself as prime minister. Its basis would be protectionism, a decisive response to two years of severe labor disputes, and pursuit of a political rather than a military solution in Ireland.[194]

This was the moment for Lloyd George's volte-face on Ireland. It was signaled by his decision to provide the king with a dramatically conciliatory speech to open the Northern Ireland Parliament on June 22. After a cabinet decision on June 24, which supported his new policy, Lloyd George issued a formal invitation to De Valera to come to London, and soon followed it with the declaration of a cease-fire. Lloyd George's timing was significant on two levels. First, his offer to negotiate helped him thwart the Birkenhead-Churchill-Cecil effort to oust him, by stealing the limelight and adopting the very policy toward Ireland they were suggesting. More broadly, it corresponded to (and even lagged behind) a shift of Unionist sentiment toward accepting negotiations with Sinn Fein. His months of delay and his fiery rhetoric had constructed a bulwark protecting him from any move against him from the right.[195] Even Balfour was now supporting negotiations with De Valera,[196] and diehard opponents lacked confidence in the political attractiveness of their position.[197]

The unbending attitude which Lloyd George had for so long displayed in public, and to his cabinent colleagues, must also be seen in light of his memory of 1916. Then he had gone out on a limb for a negotiated settlement, only to have it sawed off behind him by Unionist leaders unwilling to confront die-hard opposition within their party to any sort of British disengagement from Ireland. Having been exposed since the beginning of his career to Unionist dogma on Ireland, and so badly burned by Unionist opposition to Irish self-government, Lloyd George was "somewhat incredulous" in May and June 1921 about the change in Unionist views. He appears to have been genuinely surprised that neither Austen Chamberlain, nor Balfour, nor Birkenhead had the stomach for the kind of "pure coercion" described by Macready.[198] A combination of political prudence and skepticism, then, explain why Lloyd George waited so long to change his public position on Ireland. When the change came it came suddenly, because intellectually he had long been convinced it would be necessary. He reversed course when, and only when, Unionist party leaders gave unambiguous signs of their readiness to support peace overtures and of their ability to deliver their followers for a negotiated settlement.

The labyrinthian and dramatic story of the treaty negotiations in October, November, and December of 1921 has been fully and trenchantly told by Frank Pakenham (Lord Longford) in *Peace by Ordeal*. To account for a settlement based on a strained version of dominion status, Pakenham properly stresses Lloyd George's magnetic personality, his diplomatic virtuosity, and the relative inexperience and confusion of the Sinn Fein delegation. In the end the settlement required nothing more from Ulster than what it had already conceded in the 1920 Act, while eliciting from the new Irish government terms which at least formally expressed loyalty to the British Crown. However, Lloyd George's decisive contribution to the negotiated end of the fighting was not so much his treatment of the Irish but his "manipulation of the political situation at Westminster."[199]

Lloyd George knew his reputation could be reinvigorated by a historic settlement of the age-old Irish question. But his continued desire to construct a great, patriotic-fusionist center party also meant that the terms of the Irish treaty had to include a fig leaf for the continued supremacy of the Crown and empire, however real separation of Ireland from Britain would be in practical terms. Within this matrix of political ambitions and fear, the imperative under which he labored was to implicate the Unionist party leadership as thoroughly as possible in the negotiating process.[200]

Nothing shows so clearly how dominant were Lloyd George's concerns to maintain Unionist support for his Irish policy than the composition of his negotiating team. Except Lloyd George himself and Churchill (the "crypto-Conservative"), every ministerial member on the British side of the table was a Unionist—Austen Chamberlain, Birkenhead, and Worthington-Evans. The latter served as secretary of state for war and had been the cabinet's most resolute supporter of all-out coercion in Ireland. Lloyd George's main concern was with Bonar Law, who had returned to Parliament but not yet to the front rank of power. The chiefs of the Conservative party in 1921—Chamberlain, Birkenhead, Balfour, and Curzon—were stalwart Unionists, but each had also shown his attitude toward Ireland in general and Ulster in particular to be conditioned by a more profound commitment to the interests of England. In this they differed from Carson and Law, whose flexibility regarding an Irish settlement during the war had been largely replaced, after its conclusion, by the sentiments of personal attachment to Ulster which had governed the intensity of their stance before the war.

Bonar Law kept his counsel during the treaty negotiations and backed away, at a November 1921 party convention in Liverpool, from a showdown with the cabinet over its pursuit of an Irish settlement. Carson reacted to the treaty bitterly but ineffectively during the debate over its ratification in 1922.[201] Indeed the immediate impact of the settlement, hailed by the *Daily Telegraph* as "the greatest [event] that has happened in the internal affairs of the country for generations," was a badly needed boost for Lloyd George personally and the coalition in general.[202] But Conservative party activists rejected two suggestions made by the prime minister to hold elections promptly in order to capitalize on the popularity of the Irish settlement.

Public enthusiasm was indeed quickly dispelled, influenced by widespread violence in both northern and southern Ireland and dissatisfaction with Lloyd George's apparent inclination to go to war with Turkey on behalf of Greece. In October 1922, exactly one year after the formal beginning of the Irish negotiations, the Conservative party left the coalition, triggering the collapse of the government, the fall of Lloyd George, and the rise of Bonar Law to the premiership. One element in the Conservative party's decision to desert the coalition was the support Law drew from British diehards and Ulster Unionists anxious to punish Lloyd George.

Conclusion

If the success of the cabinet's Irish policy was not reflected in the government's long-term survival, it was apparent in the extent to which Ireland and its problems faded from the consciousness of leading British politicians. "Nothing in the history of the Irish question," observed C. L. Mowat, "is so surprising as the suddeness and completeness of its end. It simply disappeared as a major factor in British politics."[203] As continued strife in Northern Ireland indicates, the treaty of 1921 was hardly the end of conflicts over the political status of Ireland. But it was a solution to what D. G. Boyce has called "the most pressing objective" of British policy— "[removal of] the Irish Question from British party politics."[204]

The brunt of my argument in this chapter is that this achievement—the disengagement of Britain from most of Ireland and the consequent "removal" of the Irish question from British public life—must be seen as resting upon a prior transformation in the meaning of the Irish problem in Britain, even more than on the rising cost of repression in Ireland and the undeniable talents of David Lloyd George. To be sure, reinforcements were scarce and British losses in Ireland were painful. But the war against the IRA could certainly have been won. The total number of British killed and wounded in Ireland from 1919 through 1921 was smaller than a typical day's casualties on the western front. It may certainly be granted that without Lloyd George's unusual shrewdness, his ruthless exploitation of tactical advantage, and the flexibility of Birkenhead and Chamberlain, the Irish problem would have continued its intrusion upon British political life even longer and in more disruptive ways than it has since 1921. However, what enabled Lloyd George to exercise his skills, and what made relevant the personal and political interests which led key Unionist leaders to shift their ground, was a war of maneuver fought seven to eight years earlier and won, in substantial degree, by the Protestants of Ulster. The result of that crucial episode was a qualitative change in the imperatives governing British political competion over Ireland. This change was a reduction in the *scale* of internal disruption perceived as likely to accompany British attempts to disengage from Ireland.

As modeled in this volume, this change in the context of political decision is treated as the crossing of the regime threshold in the state-contracting direction. The threshold effect is indicated by the contrast between elite concerns about the integrity of the institutions governing the British state—concerns present in 1886 and 1893, and dominant in 1914—versus elite expectations, from 1916 through 1921, that payoffs and repercussions associated with attempts to disengage from Ireland would be calculated solely in terms of partisan advantage within presumptively stable state institutions.

In Chapter 7 another, more complex and extended war of maneuver, but entailing a similar kind of problem transformation—crossing through the regime threshold in the state-contracting direction—is traced in the France-Algeria case. Then in Chapter 8 I seek explanations for differences and similarities in the way these transformations were accomplished.

CHAPTER SEVEN

The Algerian Question in
French Politics, 1955–1962

In 1838 Algeria's conqueror, Marshal Thomas-Robert Bugeaud, fore-shadowed the need for two distinct kinds of analyses of French-Algerian relations when he told the Chamber of Deputies that he saw "no prospect of a government strong enough to get out of Algeria, even if such a step were indicated by the trend of events there." Since France was politically too weak to leave Algeria, the only alternative, Bugeaud continued, was "total domination."[1] But as we have seen in Chapters 4 and 5, France also failed to dominate Algeria by establishing French rule of the country on a hegemonic basis. In this sense, following Bugeaud, France was not only too weak to leave Algeria, but also too weak to stay. In this chapter, Bugeaud's line of analysis is continued, although applied not to France but to the regime of the Fourth Republic. As things turned out, the regime was unable to keep Algeria part of France, but also too weak to separate France from Algeria and survive. In other words, the Fourth Republic was, à la Bugeaud, an obstacle to the production "of a government strong enough to get out of Algeria," even when such a step was indicated "by the trend of events there."[2]

This chapter's point of departure is the emergence of the question of Algeria onto the French political agenda. Its purposes, analogous to Chapter 6's treatment of the Irish question in Britain from 1886 to 1922, are to establish the changing scale of political disruption in France following the failure of the Algérie française hegemonic project and to demonstrate that the pattern of these changes corresponds to the Guttman-scale expectations of my two-threshold model. In Chapter 8 the differences in the outcomes of the Ireland- and Algeria-related wars of maneuver in Britain and France are explained by focusing mainly on differences in resource distribution among the protagonists and strategic choices made by political leaders.

The Changing Location of the Algerian Problem in Postwar French Politics

For some years after its outbreak at the end of 1954, the war in Algeria enjoyed broad support in France. Positions taken by virtually all politicians, excluding the Communists, emphasized reestablishment of law and order and Algeria's permanence in the French Republic. By late 1957 and early 1958, however, widening differences emerged, ranging along a continuum anchored at one end by die-hard Algérie française supporters and at the other by advocates of open-ended negotiations with the FLN prior to arrangement of a cease-fire. As the debate over Algeria polarized between politicans willing seriously to entertain negotiated solutions versus those entirely committed to the forcible imposition of French preferences, the French most strongly committed to sovereignty in Algeria began to fear real movement toward disengagement might be possible. This fear turned latent threats to the regime associated with the Algerian question into explicit challenges. The result was a war of maneuver, lasting from May 1958 to June 1961, that brought the collapse of the Fourth Republic and seriously threatened the stability of the Fifth. By the middle of 1961, however, de Gaulle and the Fifth Republic had won the war of maneuver over Algeria, recasting the Algerian problem as an incumbent-level issue in French politics. Whereas between late 1957 and June 1961 French political elites saw the nature and survival of the regime as at stake in the struggle over Algeria, by mid-1961 neither de Gaulle nor his critics were any longer concerned that policies of disengagement from Algeria could destabilize the Fifth Republic. In that context, negotiations with the FLN were vigorously pursued. The result was establishment of an independent Algeria in July 1962 and the near total evacuation of Algeria's European population.[3]

As in my treatment of the British-Irish case in Chapter 6, I use details of political competition within France to indicate these changes in the location of the Algerian problem in French politics. By documenting transformations in the order of magnitude of disruption contingent on the outcome of political competition over Algeria's disposition, I provide the basis, in Chapter 8, for analyzing and explaining patterns in those transformations. As in the British-Irish case, this discussion of France and the Algerian question also represents a test of the two threshold model's effectiveness as an organizer of insights and information about processes of state expansion and contraction. Additionally, along with Chapter 6, this discussion will help generate and judge hypotheses about the dynamics of the Israeli-Palestinian case.

The Dominance of Incumbent-Level Factors, 1955–1957

Algeria was the single most important and most divisive issue confronting French governments and politicians during the last three and a half years of the Fourth Republic. In the context of an elaborate "game" of politics, however, those who sought to lead or serve in cabinets learned that within the arena established by the constitution of the Fourth Republic, it was necessary to form alliances among parties with deep disagreements over Algeria's future and with strong fissiparous tendencies of their own.[4] Since any government opposed by a majority of National Assembly deputies could be forced to resign, and since the resignation of a government did not automatically entail new elections, politicians were continually reminded of the imperative to operate on the basis of policies reflecting the lowest common denominator among incumbent parliamentarians, party leaders, and other influential politicians. The particular way competition for power was structured thus gave a veto over Algerian policy to those parties and parliamentarians who combined strong views on the subject with political eligibility[5] and enough seats in Parliament to establish and protect the government's majority.

As in Britain with respect to the Irish problem from 1886 to 1911, so in France from 1954 to 1957, the absence of practical possibilities for disengagement temporarily concealed regime-threatening aspects of the Algerian problem. Not until late 1957 were incumbent-level concerns in France over the success or failure of governing coalitions and the fate of individual political careers overshadowed by threats to the regime associated with the question of what to do with Algeria. But until the Galliard and Pflimlin ministries, each of four governments, between Mendès-France in 1954 and Bourgès-Maunoury in 1957, drew back from compromise oriented policies toward Algeria for incumbent-level reasons.

The Mendès-France government (June 1954 to February 1955) was the first to fall on the specific issue of Algeria. Since this government made the most successful attempt to sustain a cabinet by breaking the rules of the political game while remaining loyal to the Fourth Republic regime, its demise is evidence of the difficulties that faced any Fourth Republic government seeking to fashion policies toward Algeria capable of responding to rapidly changing circumstances.

As described in Chapter 4, Mendès responded to the November 1, 1954, outbreak of violence in the Aurès Mountains by declaring that Algeria was absolutely different from Indochina or the other French territories in North Africa. Algeria, the Assembly was assured, was an integral part of France. Within three months a hundred thousand French troops were deployed there. Whatever psychological or ideological factors may have encouraged Mendès to portray the Algerian problem as he did in the months immediately following the outbreak of hostilities, twenty-five years later he cited incumbent-level factors as determinative—his desire to avoid a political crisis liable to overturn his ministry. As he put it, "[I] had to keep in mind the political context. I was involved in the Tunisian negotiation, which was already very difficult to make people swallow. I could not risk an overload, making my position even worse."[6]

But despite its militant posture, the Mendès government was destroyed by the political repercussions of events in Algeria. The attack on Mendès was led by René Mayer, an Algiers-based leader of Mendès's own Radical party, the colon lobby, and leaders of the right-wing political parties. They charged that Mendès's talk of large-scale reforms, including implementation of the 1947 Organic Statute on Algeria, would lead eventually to concessions of the sort he had granted Tunisia and favored in Morocco.[7] In part because of his success at extricating France from Indochina, Mendès was unable to neutralize accusations of "surrenderism" by partisans of French Algeria.

The collapse of the Mendès government was the first in a long series of cabinet crises attributable to an alliance between colons and right-wing deputies committed to maintaining French Algeria. From the fall of Mendès to the final days of the Fourth Republic, politicians designated by the president to form governments were constrained to build coalitions around Algerian policies tough enough or vague enough to satisfy at least a large portion of the colonialist right.[8]

France's next government, formed by Edgar Faure, lasted from February 1955 to the end of the year. It was based on an alliance between his own faction of Radicals and five parties on the right—Gaullists, dissident Gaullists, Indépendants,[9] the Peasant party, and Independent Peasants. As a typical Fourth Republic politician, Faure avoided clear-cut positions and saw in Soustelle's slogan of *intégration* a useful name for a policy of repression that yet suggested the possibility of enhanced political rights and economic reforms for Algerian Muslims. Faure was forced into dangerous clarifications of his government's position, however, when the economic costs of "integrating" Algeria into France became known and as the situation in Morocco rapidly deteriorated.

Seeking to defuse right-wing and colonialist opposition to his policy of political liberalism in Morocco, Faure adopted an uncompromising approach to repression in Algeria. But his policies lost him support on both sides of the spectrum—from Mendèsiste Radicals opposed to his emphasis on repression in Algeria and from Gaullists and Indépendants disposed to seeing reformism in Morocco as evidence of future weakness in Algeria. Declaring that the Assembly was too fragmented to provide a basis for making necessary choices about Algerian policy, Faure dissolved Parliament, forcing a new general election almost immediately.[10] Despite the surprising showing of the Poujadist movement, identified with as rigorous a policy as possible in Algeria, and the gains made by the conservatives, Philip Williams and other observers have interpreted the results of the election, but especially the tone of the campaign debate over Algeria, as amounting "to a mandate—as plain as mandates can ever be—for a liberal attitude to a problem [Algeria] far harder to solve than Britain's in India nine years ago."[11]

After the election and Faure's failure to establish a new government, the president of the republic designated Guy Mollet to form a cabinet. Displaying an initial disposition toward Algeria consistent with his dovish campaign rhetoric, Mollet announced on January 9 that Jacques Soustelle would be replaced as resident-minister in Algeria by the reform-minded General Georges Catroux. With both Mendès-France and Mitterrand in Mollet's cabinet, the Europeans of Algeria and the partisans of Algérie française in mainland France would seem to have had a great deal to be concerned about from the new government. Yet a careful reading of Mollet's investiture speech to the National Assembly on January 31 might have reassured them. "Our goal," he declared, "is to maintain and strengthen the indissoluble union between Algeria and Metropolitan France." Such language did not directly contradict Socialist campaign rhetoric, but the shift in emphasis was clear. Once faced with their political inexpediency, Mollet abandoned the idea of free elections which would lead to negotiations and then a peaceful rearrangement of the French-Algerian relationship. Instead he offered the outlines of his famous "triptych"—cease-fire, elections, and negotiations (in that order). The people of Algeria, he said, "should be consulted as soon as possible, by means of free elections," but "first and foremost" his government was determined "to restore peace, to free the minds of men on both sides from the burden of fear, and for that purpose, to put an end to terrorism and repression." Only after that was accomplished would the "next step" be taken—"to continue organizing the institutions on a democratic basis."[12] In sharp contrast to his message during the campaign, a French military victory over the FLN was, in effect, made a requirement for free elections, and hence for negotiations.

The Europeans of Algeria, however, did not read the speech for the reassuring nuances it contained. On February 6, 1956, Mollet went to Algiers, where he was pelted with tomatoes, cursed, and otherwise humiliated by thousands of pieds noirs convinced his government was preparing a "sellout." During the next few months Mollet led his Socialist party and his government in a dramatic volte-face toward Algeria. Georges Catroux's nomination was withdrawn. His replacement as resident minister was Robert Lacoste, known henceforth for his commitment to rigorous "pacification" and his often-repeated readiness to fight the rebels "to the last quarter of an hour." The Soustelle plan for the thorough integration of Algeria became the government's strategic conception. In March the cabinet requested and received special war powers from the Assembly. In April the Algerian Assembly was dissolved. At the same time, decrees were issued authorizing the recall of two hundred thousand reservists for combat in Algeria. After just seven months of the Mollet government, the number of French soldiers in Algeria doubled, numbering nearly four hundred thousand in August 1956.

It is a serious error to view Mollet's sudden hardline posture toward Algeria as the result of his shocked reaction to the pied noir riots in Algiers, just as it is a mistake to attribute public commitment to Algérie française by subsequent Fourth Republic governments to the uncompromising sentiments of the French electorate.[13] Scrutiny of Mollet's shift to the right in his approach to Algeria, his success in eliciting disciplined support within his own party for "national *molletisme*," the loyalty of subsequent governments to the same basic mix of policies, and the results of public opinion surveys during this period suggest instead how decisive were the constraints which forced Mollet and the Socialists to adapt to the imperatives of *le système*.[14] The fact is that neither the Mollet government nor its successors viewed their policies in Algeria as responsive to the implacability of French public opinion. Lacoste's May 1956 exhortation to French soldiers in Algeria, for example, implied that strong public support for achieving a thoroughgoing victory over the Algerian rebels was only a future possibility, not a present reality. "I think," he said, "that there is *very great hope* that national public opinion, warned of the importance of the Algerian problem, *will increasingly support* our efforts to re-establish peace with justice in the land."[15]

Contrary to the image of overwhelming French support for maximum objectives in the Algerian War, polling data suggest how much range and flexibility existed in French public opinion, even in early 1956, and how significant was the willingness to compromise. During precisely the period of Mollet's escalation of the war (from April 1956 to March 1957), polls asking respondents whether they had "confidence in the present government to settle the Algerian problem" showed virtually no change in the proportions of those responding affirmatively or negatively.[16] In a survey of French opinion conducted in October 1955, a plurality of respondents (47 percent) said they favored maintaining Algeria's political status as French departments versus any arrangments signifying less tight bonds between Algeria and mainland France. But a substantial minority, 26 percent, said they favored less tight bonds, while 27 percent cared or knew too little to offer an opinion. The percentage of respondents favoring less tight bonds remained steady through late 1955 and 1956, rising to 35 percent in March 1957 and 40 percent in September 1957.[17] At this point the percentage of those favoring less tight bonds between France and Algeria surpassed, for the first time, the percentage of respondents favoring maintenance of the official status quo, that is, Algeria's status as departments of France (36 percent).[18] During the same time period, the proportion of respondents identifying as "partisans of Algérie française" dropped from 47 percent in October 1955, and a high of 49 percent in February 1956, to 40 percent in April 1956, and 36 percent in September 1957.[19]

These data do not suggest that by late 1957 more French wanted to leave Algeria than remain there. Nevertheless, those insisting on establishing Algeria as an integral part of their state, and fighting as hard and as long as necessary to "liquidate" the rebels, were becoming a distinct minority. A poll in April 1956 which asked respondents to choose between two extreme choices showed the country was evenly divided. Thirty-nine percent preferred to "repress the rebels using all necessary force," while the same percentage—preferred to negotiate with rebels to accord independence to Algeria.[20] Eighteen months later, in July 1957, virtually the same division of opinion (when the question was posed in such stark terms) was found: 38 percent favored negotiations toward independence while 36 percent favored all-out repression.[21] Other polls asked the French whether they favored negotiations toward a cease-fire, without specifying the contours of the eventual settlement. These polls elicited responses with substantially higher proportions favoring negotiations with the rebels— 53 percent in July 1957, 45 percent in September 1957, and 56 percent in January 1958.[22]

By 1958 a large middle portion of the French appeared willing to settle for a solution that would leave Algeria "French," though not "France." Influenced by the increasing cost of the war, and their reluctance to accept the political and social implications of absorbing eight million Algerian Muslims into the life of the metropole, these French people supported or were willing to accept a progressive evolution of relations leading to an Algeria "federated" or "associated" with France. Polls in July 1956 showed 51 percent of respondents disapproved of new taxes to finance the Algerian

War, while 48 percent said they would refuse to pay supplemental taxes if levied to pay for its escalation.[23] In a July 1957 poll offering three options, only 36 percent favored maintaining Algeria's status as a collection of departments of France. Thirty-four percent favored "a regime of internal autonomy within the French framework," while an additional 18 percent of respondents "favored complete independence for Algeria." In September 1957 only 17 percent of respondents favored "a policy of integration pure and simple." Algerian independence, in this poll, was supported by 23 percent, while 21 percent favored some sort of "progressive autonomy."[24]

However, responding to shifting public sentiments or expressing prevailing conceptions is not what kept Fourth Republic governments in power. They survived only by satisfying the imperatives of *le système*—a game whose main field of play was the National Assembly. Failure of the Algérie française hegemonic project meant that the most important and the most restrictive of these imperatives pertained to Algeria. As structured by the institutions of the Fourth Republic, the systematic effect of partisan competition on the Algerian question was not to attune policy to the fluidity present in public opinion, but to separate it from that fluidity. The determinative influence of coalition politics on the rigidity of French policy toward Algeria lasted until the end of 1957. At that point, as we shall see, incumbent-level factors were superseded by calculations, aspirations, and fears concerning the fate of the regime.

In mid-January 1956 the Republican Front had boldly declared its readiness to form a minority government dependent on alternating majorities, accepting Communist or right-wing support without "making deals" with either extreme. It was intimated that a quick and peaceful "Indochina-style" solution to the Algerian problem would then be attempted. But this plan was abandoned. It would have required complete dependence on Communist support, thereby triggering opposition by both the MRP and those Indépendants inclined to support the government if it adopted a tough line in Algeria. Meanwhile, Mollet was aware of how desperate the Communists were to avoid an open break with the government over Algeria that would doom their efforts to form a Popular Front government. Mollet also calculated that in the long run his government needed non-Communist votes from outside his Socialist-Radical coalition to survive. Conducting secret though shortlived contacts with the FLN to retain the support of Mendèsistes and anti-war students, and promising expensive economic reforms for Algerian Muslims to camouflage the real thrust of his policy, Mollet responded to the demands of Fourth Republic coalition politics by swinging his party and his government behind the program of Algérie française and an escalating war against the FLN.[25]

The political expediency of the Mollet government's approach to Algeria was evident not only in the support it drew from right-wing deputies, fearful that if Mollet's government collapsed negotiations with the Algerian rebels would ensue,[26] but also in the attitude of MRP *syndicalistes,* Radical anticlericalists, and anticolonial Socialists. These groups, who favored conciliation in Algeria, abandoned all but lipservice to serious reforms in Algeria. They supported Mollet because of his social program and in order to prevent the ascendancy of the clericalist right.[27] In March 1956 even the Communists voted with the government, albeit reluctantly, to accord Lacoste special powers in Algeria.[28]

The clearest examples of how the fear of losing his governing coalition deterred Mollet from pursuing initiatives in Algeria that might well have commanded widespread public support are his reaction to the military's seizure of five FLN leaders in October 1956 and the fate of his January 1957 suggestions for an Algerian loi cadre.

In March 1956 Mollet initiated secret contacts with FLN representatives in Cairo. His conditions for a cease-fire, elections, and negotiatiations were never accepted by the other side, and Mollet later denied that he had ever entertained any real hope for the success of this effort.[29] But Morocco, Tunisia, and at least some FLN leaders did take the contacts seriously. A high-level delegation was formed to continue the dialogue in October at a conference in Tunis. To disrupt the diplomatic effort, the French air force (in league with Algerian diehards, and having consulted Max Lejeune, the Socialist minister of state for war) hijacked the plane carrying the delegation.[30] Ahmed Ben Bella and the four other FLN leaders on board were taken into custody. This action forced Mollet to choose between treating the Algerians as the criminals they were, under French law, or continuing his secret dialogue. Though reportedly furious at the army's unilateral action, Mollet did not disavow it. The FLN leaders were duly imprisoned, and contacts with the organization were suspended. "I could not liberate men who were condemned under common law," Mollet later explained, "my government would have fallen overnight."[31]

One other attempt by the Mollet government to take a fresh look at the Algerian problem was made on January 9, 1957, when Mollet indicated the government's desire to promulgate a new loi cadre for Algeria to replace the never implemented and virtually irrelevant 1947 statute. The loi cadre outlined in general terms by Mollet would have created, formally at least, a single electoral college for Muslims and Europeans. The project was primarily motivated by a desire to strengthen France's position at the United Nations, in anticipation of the upcoming General Assembly debate on Algeria. But whatever the reasoning, its fate demonstrates just how decisive were incumbent-level fears of losing a coalition majority in blocking new initiatives toward Algeria, and how narrow were the bounds within which Mollet's government could maneuver on the Algerian question without serious risk to its survival. Faced with strong opposition from Indépendants and representatives of the colon lobby to the very idea of a single electoral college, no matter how qualified and restricted by gerrymandering or administrative rigamarole, Mollet withdrew his initiative.[32]

Mollet also faced problems from the left. In 1956 Mendès-France resigned from the cabinet, protesting the Government's abandonment of campaign promises to begin negotiations with Algerian nationalists. But Mendès's departure from the cabinet did not affect the support his followers were still ready to give the government. In June 1956 Mollet received a vote of confidence from the Assembly on his Algerian policy. Although Mendès and the Communists abstained, a majority of the deputies in every major party to the right of the Socialists (except the Poujadists) supported the government. Mollet's strategy of war in Algeria, expansion of the welfare state at home, and alternating majorities to protect the cabinet from defeat in the National Assembly kept him in power longer than any other Fourth Republic prime minister.

By 1957, however, intensifying opposition on the left to the Algerian War, and confidence on the right that no government could form that was not committed to Algérie française, deprived Mollet of the revolving support he had attracted from Communists, Mendèsiste Radicals, and Indépendants.[33] Expecting his ministry to end in the near future, Mollet sought to bolster his position within the Socialist party by proposing, in mid-May 1957, higher taxes to pay for both the Algerian War and an expanded array of domestic programs.[34] The government was immediately overturned when the bulk of the Indépendant deputies joined the Communists in opposition.

Considering the relative longevity of Mollet's government, and the extent to which both the Bourgès-Maunoury and Gaillard governments emulated (with decreasing success) his political strategy, it is worth laying out its logic with some precision. The *immobilisme* of Mollet's Algerian policy prolonged his government's tenure by serving a variety of contradictory purposes. On the one hand, tentative efforts to establish a dialogue with the FLN and the regular promise of political reform in Algeria salved the consciences of Socialists and Radicals who favored conciliation in Algeria, but who appreciated Mollet's domestic legislation even more and who also enjoyed the fruits of office. It was necessary, on the other hand, to pursue the war with sufficient toughness to encourage Indépendants and Gaullists to tolerate the continuation of the government, despite their exclusion from it.

In order to sustain this delicate equilibrium, proposals for political reform, however attractively packaged, could not offer real political equality to Muslims. While serious efforts to begin negotiations with Algerian nationalists had to be foregone, they could not be ruled out completely. The great accomplishment of the "triptych"—cease-fire, elections, negotiations—was to provide a coherent sounding cover for a policy of nervous paralysis. By never specifying the nature of the elections to be held after a cease-fire, or the parameters of the negotiations to be conducted with those elected, this formula was one that could *not* be accepted by the FLN, that could be interpreted by partisans of Algérie française as fully consistent with their position, but which could also be portrayed, to dovish-leaning deputies anxious for their parties to remain in office, as plausible and even eminently reasonable. The result was a relatively long-lived government, but at the price of political stalemate in Algeria.

Following the collapse of the Mollet government in May 1957, three more governments were installed before power was transferred to General de Gaulle on June 1, 1958—the Bourgès-Maunoury cabinet (June 1957 through September 1957), the Gaillard ministry (November 1957 to April 1958), and the Pflimlin government (May 14–28, 1958). In the long intervals separating resignations from investitures, during which more than a dozen official and unofficial attempts to form cabinets were made, France was without any effective government. The brevity of the Bourgès-Maunoury, Gaillard, and Pflimlin governments and the difficulty of their formation were due primarily to increasing polarization on the Algerian question, which had intensified the constraints operating on the Mollet government and finally destroyed it.[35]

With the Socialists out of office after Mollet's fall, the dimensions of the Procrustean bed upon which any prospective premier was forced to lie became even more uncomfortable. In addition to Mendèsiste Radicals and Mitterrandists within the small UDSR (Union démocratique et socialiste de la résistance), many Socialists were now unwilling to support governments without receiving some assurance that serious political initiatives would be undertaken in Algeria. At the same time, Indépendants and Soutellian Gaullists, concerned about international pressure on France to grant independence to Algeria and the increasing willingness of the French publicly to entertain independence as an option, were now unwilling to tolerate as much official ambiguity as Mollet had required them to accept. Combined with Socialist suspicion of MRP commitments to clericalism, these more rigid demands regarding Algeria foiled efforts by both René Pleven (UDSR) and Pierre Pflimlin (president of the MRP) to form lowest-common-denominator "national union" governments.[36]

Bourgès-Maunoury (a right-wing Radical) succeeded where Pleven and Pflimlin failed. As defense minister in the Mollet government, Bourgès-Maunoury had vigorously prosecuted the Algerian War and enforced severe censorship restrictions on metropolitan newspapers critical of French policy in Algeria. His hawkish credentials were further strengthened by the highly visible role he had played in the British-French invasion of Suez. He was also known to be the personal choice of Guy Mollet. Bourgès-Maunoury was therefore in a position to make his contradictory promises appear more credible than those communicated by Pleven and Pflimlin— promises capable of attracting support from both extremes, at least until their contradictoriness became impossible to conceal (which took about four months). "I once again solemnly declare," he said in his investiture speech, "that the union between Metropolitan France and Algeria is indissoluble. The Government will fight to keep France in Algeria, and she will remain there." When he made it clear that Lacoste would continue in his post as minister in Algeria, and announced that Max Lejeune would head a new Ministry of Saharan Affairs, it was difficult for the right wing to question his commitment to maintaining of French Algeria. But in his investiture speech he also promised to "build a new Algeria" and announced that a federative loi cadre for Algeria would soon be introduced. These promises, commitments, and evocations attracted just enough support from the left and the right for his government to be installed.

Despite his obvious lack of enthusiasm for political reform, Lacoste went along with the premier's insistence on a new loi cadre.[37] According to the first, informal proposals of the government, Algeria was to be divided into administratively autonomous territories with both European and Muslim representation. Although the possibility was mentioned that after conditions in Algeria stabilized, the territorial assemblies could decide to transfer portions of their (limited) powers to a Federative Council in Algiers, responsibility for military and diplomatic affairs, general financial questions, civil and criminal justice, administrative litigation, secondary and higher education, mining, and publicly owned enterprises would remain in the hands of the Paris government.

The narrow scope of this "administrative autonomy" drew protests from the left that only a federal assembly in Algiers "wielding substantial, real powers of legislative import" and an Algerian executive operating outside the purview of a resident minister could attract meaningful Muslim support.[38] Bourgès-Maunoury responded by proposing some enhancement of the powers and responsibilities of the Federative Council and by giving the French Parliament the right to transfer even more authority later. But in consultations with leaders of right-of-center parties (Radical dissidents, Social Republicans [Gaullists], and the Indépendants) and in cabinet debates, opposition to the new loi cadre broke out in full fury, focusing particularly on the idea of a single-electoral college for both Muslims and Europeans, the establishment of any sort of semiautonomous Algiers executive, and the official creation of opportunities for political evolution in the France-Algeria relationship. The loi cadre, it was contended, would be but a way station to the oppression and expulsion of the European population and the secession of Algeria. Faced with resignation threats from Algeria Minister Robert Lacoste, Defense Minister André Morice, and two other dissident radical ministers,[39] the energetic opposition of Soustelle and his supporters (inside and outside the Gaullist parliamentary delegation), and the virulent hostility of Roger Duchet and other Indépendant leaders, Bourgès-Maunoury permitted a shift in the terms of debate over the loi cadre. Discussion now centered on a bill restrictive enough to preserve a governing parliamentary majority, regardless of the legislation's appeal to the Muslims whose demands and aspirations it purported to address. Still, no agreement was forthcoming.

Finally, in a desperate effort to maintain a working majority, and in a signal admission of how intractable the Algerian problem had become for the institutions of the Fourth Republic, Bourgès-Maunoury withdrew the measure from the Assembly and invited the leaders of the parties that had voted for his investiture to extraparliamentary, "round table" discussions at his residence—the Hôtel Matignon. Again, Bourgès-Maunoury's objective was to "thin out" the proposed loi cadre, thereby making it acceptable to enough right-wing party leaders to assure the survival of his government. Europeans were given a veto over adjustments in the distribution of powers between the territorial assemblies and the Algiers Council. Assemblies were no longer to be designated "legislative." Parliament's authority to transfer additional responsibilities to the federative organs in Algeria was deleted. Establishment of the Federative Council was to be postponed for at least eighteen months, by which time, it was anticipated, a new general election would be held.

Despite these changes, which stripped the bill of its potential as a vehicle for political evolution, right-wing opposition was not assuaged. Indépendant representatives, Soustelle, and others pressed for amendments to eliminate any mention of federalism from the loi cadre. Finally Bourgès-Maunoury insisted on an up or down vote on the much diluted legislation, which would also be a vote of confidence in his government. On September 30, 1957, his ministry was overturned on a vote of 279 to 253—the result of substantial defections by Social Republicans (Soustellian Gaullists) and Indépendants.[40]

The five weeks between the end of the Bourgès-Maunoury government and the investiture of Felix Gaillard was the longest period between ministries since the founding of the Fourth Republic. Algeria was now the problem that "blocked all roads," and for the first time considerations about whether or not the regime itself would survive efforts to address the Algerian debacle began to overshadow concerns of specific politicians or parties about their relative standing in, or influence over, the government that would be created.

The Dominance of Regime-Level Factors, November 1957–June 1961

Up against the Regime Threshold: Algeria and the Collapse of the Fourth Republic

On November 5, 1957, a successor government to the ministry of Bourgès—Maunoury finally received a vote of investiture from the National Assembly. The new prime minister was Felix Gaillard, another Radical party member who served as finance minister in the Bourgès-Maunoury government. Gaillard's solution to the the loi cadre problem was to extend the Mollet–Bourgès-Maunoury strategy of contradiction, ambiguity, and *immobilisme* to its logical conclusion. Unable to come up with an image of Algeria's future or a plan for its achievement any more capable of attracting a parliamentary majority than his predecessors, he incorporated virtually all the amendments supported by right-wing deputies into his draft, thereby eliciting their votes for a measure which they, no less than the Muslims, realized was and would remain a dead letter. Whatever little of interest to Muslims was left in the statute was made irrelevant by "the firm understanding that it could not be implemented until three months after the end of all hostilities."[41] On November 29, 1957, the Assembly voted 269 to 200 to adopt the bill.

What is of primary interest about Gaillard's loi cadre is the changed mix of motives behind it. Not only Gaillard and his ministers but many of those on the left who had favored substantial change in the French-Algerian relationship and who were deeply disappointed in the character of the bill as it finally emerged supported the virtually meaningless draft. Indeed though it was opposed by some Mendèsiste Radicals, not a single Socialist or Popular Republican deputy voted against it. For many of these politicians a collapse of the Fourth Republic itself, triggered by the fall of yet another government on the Algerian issue, was more important than their preferences on the issue at hand or their desire to protect a cabinet in which their parties were included.

The argument that maintaining Algeria (or Morocco) for France was a necessary condition for the survival of the Fourth Republic was not new. Faure's retreat from his liberal Moroccan policy in 1955 was linked to fears for the integrity of the regime.[42] In January 1956, amid the uncertain efforts of the Republican Front to form a government in the absence of a coherent parliamentary majority, a wave of gold hoarding swept through the middle class. Observers attributed the phenomenon to fears of regime destabilization in the context of the government's apparent inability to respond effectively to the Algerian dilemma.[43] In April 1956 one Socialist, arguing in favor of considering a solution based on creation of an Algerian state, had first to address the argument that such proposals were irrelevant since the threat of rebellion by the colons rendered any such outcome impossible.[44] A year later military officers and leading French politicians were found implicated in an assassination attempt on Raoul Salan, newly appointed head of French forces in Algeria, who at that time was considered dangerously "soft" by the partisans of French Algeria. The cover-up of this affair was maintained by successive governments, illustrating the fear felt by leading Fourth Republic politicans of an attempt by the army and the "Algiers thugs" to destroy the regime.[45] In June 1957, Mendès-France warned the new Bourgès-Maunoury government that the republic was in danger. The French people, he said, must be made to understand that "the Algerian drama and the crisis of the republican regime are one and the same problem."[46] Indeed what disturbed the French public most about the allegations of torture in Algeria was not so much that it was used against FLN suspects, but that the torturers in Algeria might eventually use their techniques against political opponents on the mainland.[47]

Within Socialist circles, Max Lejeune argued in 1955, and Mollet agreed, that if France lost North Africa, "the regime would disappear."[48] The SFIO was more closely identified with the establishment of the regime and more invested in its continuation than any other party. Accordingly, aside from appealing to the desire of Socialist militants to share in the exercise of power, and to an image of an "emancipated" Algeria, bound to the Republic by ties of mutual advantage and democratic sentiment, Mollet repeatedly used the argument that safeguarding Algérie française was necessary to protect the republic against internal enemies. Throughout his premiership he used the possible disintegration of the regime as a supplementary means of disciplining intraparty criticism of his Algerian policy.[49]

Thus beliefs that the fate of the regime was linked to maintenance of French sovereignty in North Africa had been present for some time. But previous to the Gaillard ministry, the fears associated with these beliefs had played a secondary role, or had been submerged altogether beneath partisan rivalries contained within the institutions of the Fourth Republic and focused on control of them.[50] What was new was the extent to which these "regime-level" considerations were displacing incumbent-type concerns in the calculations of French politicians.[51]

Plainly, Galliard was aware of the situation. His investiture speech emphasized a deepening crisis of the state which required extraordinary measures. He indicated that Bourgès-Maunoury's extraconstitutional "round-table" technique for dealing with the Algerian problem would be applied to all "national problems confronting our political life." Gaillard described the primary goal of his government as the "restoration of the fundamental rules of the functioning of parliamentary democracy," characterizing his coalition as comprised of "all those who respect Republican legality." But his Algerian policy contained the same contradictory elements that had been both the mainstay and the doom of previous governments. Gaillard demanded immediate Assembly approval for two measures—a renewal of the government's "special powers" to prosecute the Algerian War with full vigor, and passage of a loi cadre for Algeria in order to seek "a political solution of the Algerian problem . . . within the framework of indissoluble ties between Metropolitan France and this territory."[52]

Despite Gaillard's talk of pursuing a political solution, it was no easy task to persuade the increasingly antiwar Socialists to participate in his government. The controversy in France over the army's use of terror and torture was reaching its peak. Robert Delavignette, France's veteran colonial administrator, resigned in protest from the Committee for the Safeguard of Rights and Freedoms, set up by the government in May 1957 to ensure the legality of army operations in Algeria. In December 1957, Delavignette warned that the state "was destroying itself. In Algeria we are witnessing the decomposition of the State, and this gangrene is threatening the nation as a whole."[53] Against a background of intensifying controversy over army and police methods in Algeria, Mollet managed to bring the Socialist party into the Gaillard government *only* by declaring that the fate of the regime was immediately at stake. Speaking publicly in December, Mollet noted a dual threat from "Rightist Fascism as well as Stalinist Fascism." He explained the Socialists' decision to participate in the government "because they feared the Republic was on the verge of collapse." In March Mollet's policy of participation in the government was again endorsed by a majority of his party in the belief that "the system was so threatened that a continuing crisis provoked by the refusal of the SFIO to join the government might bring about its collapse."[54]

Another indication that the regime, and no longer merely a government, was at stake was the steep rise in public support for the return to power of France's most famous opponent of the Fourth Republic—Charles de Gaulle. In December 1955, only 1 percent of those polled named de Gaulle as the man they wanted to form the next government. By September 1957, 11 percent preferred de Gaulle, putting him ahead of Mendès-France (9 percent), the Conservative leader Antoine Pinay (8 percent), and the Communist Maurice Thorez (7 percent). Only Mollet's rating (14 percent) surpassed his. But beginning in January 1958, the percentage of respondents preferring de Gaulle exceeded all Fourth Republic politicians by rapidly expanding margins.[55] Another sign of the times was a violent demonstration by seven thousand Paris policemen on March 13, 1958. Detachments of gendarmes only barely prevented the mob from invading the National Assembly. Fascist and antiparliamentary sentiments prevailing in the ranks of the police were evident from the insults they hurled at the deputies. *Le Monde* interpreted the riot as one more bit of evidence that "no one trying to overthrow the regime is treated as a Rebel any more; only those are treated as Rebels who show up the weaknesses of the Government and the regime."[56]

Ironically, the gathering crisis that toppled the Gaillard government in April and the Fourth Republic in May was played out against a background of demonstrable French military success in Algeria. In Algiers Massu's paratroopers had destroyed the FLN infrastructure, even if they did not end its influence over the Muslim population. In the countryside, years of intensive efforts by the "psychological bureau" of the French army were showing results. In part thanks to its maneuvers, a series of exhausting feuds had ravaged the FLN's in-country command structure. An electrified barrier running from the sea into the Sahara Desert along the entire length of the Algerian-Tunisian border, and a less impressive but still effective chain of barricades along the Moroccan frontier, cut off rebels inside Algeria from supplies and reinforcements and tied down three-fourths of the FLN's National Liberation Army in costly efforts to penetrate the barriers from bases in Tunisia and Morocco. From January 1957 to May 1958, the monthly total of French army–recorded "incidents" inside Algeria dropped from four thousand to fifteen hundred.[57]

But these military accomplishments were expensive. As described in Chapter 4, the French economy slipped badly in 1957. In January 1958, Jean Monnet was sent to the United States to arrange a large and desperately needed loan from Washington. Meanwhile the Tunisian leader Habib Bourguiba, concerned that the stalemated war in Algeria might radicalize the revolution there and lead eventually to a pro-Soviet state, began pushing for a diplomatic solution. This squared with an FLN decision to deemphasize the flagging armed struggle in favor of "internationalizing" the conflict. It was in this context that the FLN provoked and welcomed a French retaliation raid that leveled the Tunisian village of Sakiet on February 8, killing seventy civilians. World opinion was outraged. The United States and Britain offered their "good offices" in an effort to find a diplomatic solution to the tangled set of relationships between France and Tunisia and France and Algeria. The offer was made somewhat more compelling (given any French government's need to protect itself against charges of toadying to the Americans) by Eisenhower's suggestion that the newly granted French loan would be reconsidered if France failed to respond to the diplomatic initiative.

For Algérie française supporters in the military, among the settlers, and in the metropole, the tantalizing prospect of military victory enlivened fears that just at the decisive moment a weak government, produced by a rotten regime, would acquiesce in an Anglo-American brokered sellout. These fears were accentuated by a Galliard interview on January 13, 1958, in which he said that "there could be no question of granting Algeria independence . . . at least not in the near future." This qualification, along with his government's acceptance of Anglo-American mediation, infuriated the rightist press. Demands for the end of Gaillard's government, spiced with strong doses of anti-Americanism, echoed across France in a campaign described six months later by Christian Pineau as part of an organized conspiracy against the Fourth Republic.[58]

On April 15, when Felix Gaillard presented the Assembly with the Anglo-American "good offices" proposal, he knew his government was doomed. He urged National Assembly deputies to support him not so much because they agreed with his policies, but because of the dangerous and open-ended political crisis that would result if they did not.[59] But by this time the creation of an untenable parliamentary situation, with the chaos, uncertainty, and antiregime frustration it would entail, was precisely what most Gaullists and many other right-wing politicians wanted. In the two days of Assembly debate preceding the vote of confidence, former Prime Minister Bidault, an ardent partisan of Algérie française, made a violent attack on the government's "internationalization" of the Algerian question, referring to the government's policy in North Africa as "a consent to suicide." Targeting the Socialist Foreign Minister Pineau, Michel Debré declared that the "Social Republicans were under no circumstances ready to accept . . . a government containing any minister whose policy was that of Munich." These attacks were supported as well by Roger Duchet, secretary general of the Indépendants.[60] At the beginning of March the Indépendants had demanded that eighty thousand additional French troops be sent to Algeria, regardless of the cost. Three weeks later Indépendant ministers in the cabinet threatened to resign, and thereby bring down the government, if the concessions to Tunisia proposed by Britain and the United States were accepted. They argued that these proposals (for French recognition of Tunisian sovereignty over French air and naval bases in Tunisia) were designed to pave the way for the same sort of "foreign intervention" in France's Algerian affairs.[61]

The Gaillard government was defeated in the vote of confidence on its North African policy (255 in favor of the government and 321 opposed). At his investiture Gaillard had received overwhelming support from Gaullists, Indépendants, and Peasant party deputies. Five months later, in what was as much a vote on the regime as on the government, almost all the Gaullists, and two-thirds of the Indépendant and Peasant party deputies, voted in opposition.

Little more than a month after the fall of the Gaillard government, European ultras in Algeria, supported by the army and guided by Gaullist activists, seized power in Algiers. Under the specter of a threatened invasion of the mainland by troops from Algeria, and rather than risk the complete destruction of French democracy at the hands of a straight-out military coup ("fascism in a leopard suit"), Fourth Republic politicians in the left and center parties put aside their fears of a Gaullist dictatorship, joined right-wing politicians confident of de Gaulle as the savior of French Algeria, and granted the general the "Republican legality" he wanted in his bid to replace the moribund regime with one of his own design.

Thus may the enormously complex events of May 1958 be summarized. However, the beliefs, objectives, and main lines of activity of the principal actors must be traced if de Gaulle's subsequent policy shifts toward Algeria, and the nature of the challenges faced by the Fifth Republic, are to be appreciated, and if the effects of the regime threshold are to be examined.

After the resignation of the Gaillard government, President René Coty asked Georges Bidault to form a government. Bidault was forced to give up his attempt to form a strong Algérie française government when his own party—the MRP—voted to oppose his effort. Coty then turned to the opposite side of the spectrum. Refused by several other politicians, Coty approached former Prime Minister René Pleven. Despite Pleven's elaborate explanations of a policy essentially no different from those pursued by previous governments, thirty thousand demonstrators in Algiers condemned what they characterized as his attempt to form a "government of abandonment."[62] Leaflets began to appear in the streets of Algiers calling for establishment of a "government of public safety" in Paris as "the last hope of France."[63] To reassure the right, Pleven designated André Morice as his minister of defense, to which the Radicals responded by joining the Socialists in opposing the proposed cabinet. When the Assembly refused permission for an extraconstitutional preinvestiture vote on his Algerian policy, Pleven withdrew.

Coty then asked Pierre Pflimlin, president of the MRP and finance minister in the Gaillard government, to form a cabinet. Associated with a growing trend within the MRP toward negotiations in Algeria, Pflimlin said publicly on May 2 that the only "real solution" in Algeria was a "political solution." To increase military expenditures any further, he warned, "may well immensely aggravate our financial and economic position." To reassure the right, he promised a stepped up military effort in

Algeria, but one justified as preparation for the beginning of negotiations "from a position of strength."[64]

Pflimlin outlined plans for a minority government that would contain no politicians known for their enthusiasm for Algérie française and would formally exclude the Socialists and Indépendants while depending on many of their votes to prevent another crisis. This move meant replacing the hardline Lacoste as resident minister in Algeria. Lacoste reacted by predicting that with Pflimlin in charge Algeria would soon be treated to a "diplomatic Dien Bien Phu," and accusing upper-echelon officers in Algiers of moral cowardice for hesitating to make known the views of the army.[65] On May 9, General Raoul Salan, supreme commander of French forces in Algeria, sent a telegram to President Coty. The telegram, signed in the presence of Generals Jouhaud, Allard, and Massu, strongly implied that the army would revolt should the Pflimlin government be invested. The army, warned Salan, "would unanimously feel the abandonment of this national patrimony to be an outrage. It would be impossible to foretell its despairing reaction."[66]

The Europeans of Algiers dubbed the premier-designate "the abominable Pflimlin," an out-and-out surrenderist, a symbol of *le système* who was all too likely to be made prime minister by the Fourth Republic's "parliament of cowards."[67] A huge Algiers demonstration on May 13, the day of the vote on Pflimlin's investiture, turned into a riot. The riot turned into an assault on the Government General, and the assault resulted in a Committee of Public Safety, formed by the ultras of Algiers and Gaullist representatives, headed by General Massu, and joined soon by Salan and Soustelle. Rallying briefly around slogans of "the Republic in danger" and "Fascism shall not pass!" the Assembly deputies invested Pflimlin's government. But fearing the imminent disintegration of public authority and an army takeover on the mainland, the new government shifted its ground and agreed to de Gaulle's terms. On June 1 he was invested as prime minister. On the following day he was granted six months of dictatorial "emergency powers" and the prerogative of writing a new constitution. Thus the Fourth Republic, threatened with death, committed suicide; in doing so it provided de Gaulle with the "legal" but substantially unencumbered route to power he had desired.

Antiregime Plots against the Fourth Republic

The intricate parliamentary moves described above could obscure but not hide the fact that crucial players in the political game were no longer playing by Fourth Republic rules. The objectives of the protagonists in this struggle were not to overthrow, establish, or maintain governments, but to overthrow, establish, or maintain regimes. Bidault's failure to form a government had convinced Algérie française partisans in France and in Algeria—in the army and out of it—that within the Parliament of the Fourth Republic no majority existed to support a fight to the finish in Algeria. The conclusion was obvious. As Werth has observed, "it was decided not to think any longer in terms of Parliamentary arithmetic." After abandoning his effort to form a government, Bidault signaled his embrace of a war of maneuver by commenting that there soon would be a majority to support his policy and save Algeria, not a majority in a parliament of the Fourth Republic, but a majority "in the Nation . . . and amongst our soldiers."[68]

Compared to the elaborate, disciplined, and sustained efforts of Ulster Protestants and British conservatives from 1911 to 1914, the preparations for revolt by army men, settlers in Algeria, and metropolitan politicians were unimpressive. But the target of these activities in France (the Fourth Republic) was considerably more vulnerable than was the constitutional regime in pre–World War I Britain. Accordingly, the threat these plots posed was genuine and apparent enough to focus virtually all the attention of the French political class, in this period, on the dangers and opportunities likely to surround collapse of the regime.

The various antiregime conspiracies under way in late April and May of 1958 had three things in common.[69] First, they depended on the accumulated fury and frustration of the army. Humiliated by nearly twenty years of defeat and, in their eyes, betrayal, the overwhelming majority of professional officers and many top commanders were now willing to abandon the Fourth Republic or help overthrow it, if that was necessary to prevent surrender to the FLN in Algeria. Second, the various groups of plotters relied on the Europeans of Algeria, and their representatives and sympathizers in mainland France, to provide activists, mass demonstrations, and economic resources. Third, most of the conspirators imagined that in one way or another de Gaulle would play a key role in the revolt. For Gaullist plotters, that role would be to found a new regime and lead the state toward renewal. For most Gaullists, a prime function of that regime was presumed to be maintenance of Algeria as an integral part of France. Some non-Gaullist plotters, however, such as radical army officers and ambitious pieds noirs, viewed de Gaulle as little more than a useful figurehead, a popular and innocuous "Neguib" for the authoritarian "Nasserist" regime they intended to establish.[70]

By 1958, the long French tradition of separation between military and political affairs had become a casualty of the Algerian War.[71] In its place many French officers developed an ideological and emotional posture which made the army, on behalf of the French nation, the arbiter of the French state. But the French officer corps was increasingly isolated from the main currents of postwar French society. Most officers serving in Algeria had spent more than 60 percent of their time, since 1947, outside of metropolitan France.[72] Military officers suffered not only a severe decline in social status but also in income level relative to that of other professions. Many younger officers, especially those who had served in Indochina, adopted "Spartan" attitudes. They deemed technocratic "push-button" generals and "bourgeois" civilians incapable of appreciating the sacrifices made in their name by French soldiers, too soft to withstand the global challenge of communist subversion, and all too ready to abandon the fruits of hard-won victories.[73] According to army theorists of *la guerre révolutionnaire,* only an army and a nation as disciplined, as capable of self-sacrifice, and as ruthless as France's totalitarian enemies could win in Algeria and thus preserve both France and Western civilization.[74]

For much of the French military, Algeria had become nothing less than the definitive test of its claims to effectiveness and glory. But would "the politicians" even give the army a chance to pass that test?[75] The army had been required by the governments of the Fourth Republic to turn Algeria into a veritable military province. The unprecedented array of administrative tasks it assumed included responsibility for education, youth and women's organizations, economic development projects, welfare services, newspaper publishing, policing of cities, elaboration of informational, surveillance, and political networks in the countryside, and the relocation and supply of up to a million refugees. These tasks corresponded to and reinforced the French military's own theory of how to fight a revolutionary war, on all fronts—social, educational, economic, ideological, and military.[76] A key element in this approach was the creation of *certainties* for the Muslim population—especially the certainty that France would never leave Algeria, and that French protection would therefore always be available to those who sided with the army against the FLN.

In addition to this specific imperative (forbidding doubt to be cast on France's future presence in Algeria), the broader implications of the doctrine of "total war," the scale of the resources required for victory, and the increasingly polarized debate in France over whether the whole enterprise was worthwhile focused the attention of many officers on the decisiveness of the political situation at home for the outcome of the struggle in Algeria. Corporate interests were also at stake. High-ranking officers feared the army itself would not survive loss of the Algerian War, or even a continuing stalemate.[77]

The French public was not unaware of discontent in the ranks. In the latter years of the Fourth Republic, "unrest in the army" had become a prominent theme of commentaries and reportage in the French press. But serious, clandestine antiregime activities did not begin until late 1957, during the lengthy hiatus between the Bourgès-Maunoury government's fall and the investiture of Gaillard. They increased rapidly during the last months of the Gaillard government and the weeks of political turmoil that followed the vote of no confidence. Antiregime activities within the military reached a climax during the second week of May, when Pierre Pflimlin appeared on the verge of forming a new government.

Among the military plotters was General René Cogny, commander of French forces in Morocco until March 30, 1958. Cogny was planning a military putsch in Paris and was in contact with CANAC—the Veterans' Action Committee founded in 1957 by nineteen veterans' associations to fight for Algérie française. General Lionel-Max Chassin, air defense co-ordinator for NATO and honorary president of the most militant of the veterans' organizations—the Veterans of Indochina and the French Union[78]—and retired General Paul Cherrier, a former commander of French forces in Algeria, were also planning a coup d'état. They planned an insurrection in Algiers to be followed by the abandonment of the government and the seizure of Paris. General Roger Miquel, commander of the Toulouse military district, agreed to lend his paratroop units to the cause if a coup in Algiers should require military support in mainland France.[79] In January 1958, Miquel had already established a secret communications network among like-minded commanders in Lyons, Dijon, Bordeaux, and Algeria.[80] They were joined later by General Maurice Challe, head of the French air force, and his chief of staff, General André Martin. They agreed to provide air transport for the Algerian-based paratroopers of Operation Resurrection, a plan (formulated in detail in mid-May by General Massu) for the military occupation of continental France.[81]

In Algeria the paratroop colonels most passionately committed to Algérie française and most disgusted with the Fourth Republic were in close touch with ultra-"activists" busily agitating among the pieds noirs. The most important of these colonels were Roger Trinquier, head of the paratroop regiment stationed near Algiers, and Jean Thomazo, commander of the twenty-two thousand strong pied noir militia known as the UT (Territorial Units).[82] Their key contacts among the pieds noirs included Pierre Lagillarde, a former paratrooper, now head of the student federation at Algiers University; Robert Martel, head of the Christian-Fascist French North African Union; local Poujadist leaders such as Jo Ortiz and Bernard Lefèvre; and Jean-Baptiste Biaggi, a Corsican lawyer who had played a key role in orchestrating the Algiers riots against Mollet in February 1956.[83]

In every respect these men were peripheral figures in the political life of

France. Their flamboyant personalities and violent temperaments were appreciated, however, in the pied noir milieu. If they could not develop coherent ideas about ruling France or winning the Algerian War, if their Poujadist loyalties or fascist affiliations made it impossible for them to be considered as leaders of a new French state, they could express the passions of the Algiers mob, its fears of abandonment and its anger toward the series of "lilly-livered" premiers and premier-designates cluttering the Parisian political landscape. This gave them the vital capacity to mobilize scores of thousands of pieds noirs for violent Algiers demonstrations—situations of anarchy that could serve as a pretext for an army-supported Committee of Public Safety to take charge of the city and from that base to challenge the regime.

Seven of these activists, calling themselves the Group of Seven, formed in March under the patronage of the powerful editor of *L'Echo d'Alger,* Alain d'Sérigny. On March 15, at the height of the Anglo-American "good offices" controversy, Sérigny had traveled to the mainland to meet with Gaullist representatives. Convinced a sellout was approaching, he met with Soustelle, Debré, and three others, all of whom eventually served as ministers in Fifth Republic governments. These men were as anxious as Sérigny to bring an end to the staggering regime. With some difficulty, but claiming his assurances were based on a personal conversation with de Gaulle about the future of Algeria, Soustelle convinced Sérigny of de Gaulle's trustworthiness on the Algerian question. Despite his Vichyist resentment toward the general, Sérigny agreed to help set up a Gaullist network in Algiers and pressed Lacoste, among others, to join the anti-regime movement in support of de Gaulle.[84] Editorials in Sérigny's newspaper called for drastic political change in Paris, for an end to "this paradox of monstrous absurdity," and for de Gaulle to break his silence and return to power.[85]

For all the cloak and dagger arrangements of the military conspirators, and the amateurish but explosive efforts of the Algiers activists, "what counted in the end was the flexible Gaullist 'plot.' "[86] In the increasingly combustible atmosphere surrounding Sakiet and the "good offices" crisis, supporters of General de Gaulle saw their long-awaited opportunity: by making France ungovernable under the Fourth Republic, their own champion could return, and on his own terms. Acting in the spirit of what they knew de Gaulle desired rather than on explicit instructions from him, they abandoned all efforts to influence outcomes within the institutions of the Fourth Republic. In the name of Charles de Gaulle and Algérie française they unleashed a public challenge to the regime's legitimacy which de Gaulle's broad-based popularity and his twelve-year refusal to play the game of Fourth Republic politics made possible. Separated from the regime, the army could be rallied to the general, as it had been called upon to do in 1940. In a moment of upheaval, precipitated by an activist insurrection in Algiers, the "princes"[87] of the Fourth Republic would be forced to make way for de Gaulle. With the army and the people behind him, so went the hope and the plan, a new "Gaullist" regime for a revived and renewed France would be inaugurated.

Upon his return from Algeria in 1956, Soustelle had founded the Union for the Safeguarding and Renewal of French Algeria, to mobilize metropolitan support for *intégration*. At that time Soustelle's emphasis on raising Muslim living standards and democratizing relations between the communities in Algeria had attracted relatively wide support. But as the struggle for Algérie française became less focused on the quality of life for Algerian Muslims and more on the enforcement of French sovereignty and the protection of colon interests, the more liberal members of the organization—such as Maurice Violette and Robert Delavignette—resigned. By late 1957 the USRAF was an organization of ten thousand members committed, above all, to saving Algeria for France. For Soustelle, and most USRAF adherents, this meant creating conditions for the collapse of the Fourth Republic and the return of de Gaulle to power.[88] In 1957 Michel Debré (de Gaulle's future prime minister) started a newspaper, *Courrier de la Colère,* dedicated to the glorification of de Gaulle, to convincing the French that the Fourth Republic was dooming France to a "sellout" in Algeria, and to preparing the ground for extraconstitutional resistance against policies of disengagement.[89] "To abandon French sovereignty," Debré wrote in December 1957, "is to commit an illegal action, in other words such an action places all those who take a part in it in the category of outlaws, and all those who oppose those outlaws by whatever means are acting out of legitimate defence."[90]

In November, Soustelle founded the journal *Voici Pourquoi* as a platform for his increasingly bitter attacks on government policy in Algeria. At the end of February he wrote in *Voici Pourquoi* that "traitors" was the only appropriate designation for French who were "evoking the possibility of Algerian independence."[91] Early in 1958, committees of the USRAF and Committees of Public Safety were formed in various cities on the mainland and in Algeria. Through these committees close contacts were maintained with veterans' organizations and with CANAC, the umbrella Veterans' Action Committee, created as a result of USRAF encouragement. Although its claims to speak for the two million veterans belonging to its affiliated organizations were exaggerated, CANAC could quickly mobilize thousands of French for peaceful or violent street demonstrations on behalf of French Algeria and against the Fourth Republic.[92]

As the Anglo-American "good offices" crisis reached its climax in March and April 1958, Soustelle framed the specific question at hand as the government's apparent willingness to participate in negotiations over the future of Algeria. Politicians and newspapers associated with the USRAF denounced the Gaillard government's acceptance of Anglo-American mediation in North Africa as "a new Munich." With increasing audacity, Gaullist politicians redirected their attacks from the Gaillard government to the regime itself. In March, Soustelle told a Social Republican meeting that France and the French Union were suffering a grave crisis, soluble only by the return of de Gaulle. "The regime," he declared, "by its feebleness, its discontinuity, its total absence of prestige, is not up to the challenge."[93] Along with non-Gaullist hardliners associated with the USRAF, such as Bidault, Morice, Duchet, and Sérigny, Soustelle called for the establishment of a "government of public safety"—since the French Revolution the traditional vehicle for a change of regimes.[94] In the French Senate, Debré explicitly evoked the French revolutionary tradition in his call for creation of a government of public safety and the return of a man "with the political authority of a Clemenceau." "You must do what your ancestors did in 1789, in 1830, in 1848," Debré told the senators. "You must rebel!"[95]

Still closeted at Colombey-les-deux-Eglises, de Gaulle intensified his private consultations with supporters anxious to see him enter the fray. The general maintained a public silence, but took care not to discourage those who talked of seizing power or those actively conspiring to achieve that objective.[96] On March 27, de Gaulle granted an interview to the leaders of CANAC anxious to avoid a "new June 1940." In its record of their discussions the delegation noted de Gaulle's opinion that CANAC's vigorous activities had "made a start in . . . reclaiming independence for France and that it must persevere because it is the only way to provoke one day the *psychological shock* permitting the renovation of the nation's institutions."[97] In early May, President Coty secretly contacted de Gaulle to ask whether he would respond positively to an invitation to form a government. De Gaulle answered by demanding authority to inaugurate a new regime as a precondition of his acceptance. This ended the negotiations, but de Gaulle's response, transmitted to his supporters through his inner circle of confidants, encouraged them to act.[98]

The Gaullists' public campaign was complemented by equally energetic clandestine activities. With support now from wealthy colons in Algiers, USRAF members began gathering weapons and distributing leaflets in preparation for overthrowing the regime.[99] Léon Delbecque, a functionary in the Social Republican party, was assigned responsibility for coordinating psychological warfare against the FLN by Minister of Defense Chaban-Delmas. But Chaban-Delmas was himself involved in the Gaullist plot.

Under his protection Delbecque set up an office in Algiers and targeted his psychological warfare activities not against the FLN, but the Fourth Republic.[100]

Serving as the Gaullist "antenna" in Algeria, Delbecque made some twenty-eight trips between Paris and Algiers between December 1957 and early May 1958.[101] Besides maintaining close relations with rebellious officers, he also created, in April, a Vigilance Committee embracing more than a score of "patriotic" groups and organizations in Algiers, and participated as well in the deliberations of the settler-activist Group of Seven. With military assistance, Delbecque orchestrated a large rally at the War Memorial in Algiers on April 26, denouncing Pleven's attempts to form a government. Under instructions from Delbecque, de Gaulle's name was not invoked, but reminiscent of Ulster's Solemn Oath and Covenant, the crowd swore an oath "before their dead," in the name of all the French of Algeria, "to oppose by all means the formation of a government of abandon [requiring] the formation of a government of national safety, for only such a government is capable of restoring the grandeur of the country."[102] In light of the rally's success, Delbecque telegraphed his supporters in France that "I now have Algeria in hand!"[103]

De Gaulle au pouvoir: From Colombey to Paris via Algiers

During the second week of May the preparations by military, pied noir, and Gaullist plotters came to fruition. Gaullist activists in France, joined by Sérigny and Delbecque, contemplated the opportunity presented them by the passions aroused over the FLN's retributive execution of three French soldiers and the conjuction, on May 13, of Pflimlin's investiture and the memorial rally in Algiers. Newspapers, especially on the right, were filled with appeals to de Gaulle to break his public silence and return to the political stage. On May 10, after reportedly advising an Algiers politician to "have a fine demonstration and sack the town hall," Lacoste had departed for the mainland, leaving his office in the massive Government-General building vacant and no one of real political authority in Algeria.[104] Although Salan's loyalties were unclear, his deputies—Allard and Jouhaud—had been won over to de Gaulle by General Petit, himself a member of the general staff in Paris.[105] On May 12, de Gaulle received a letter from the chief of the general staff, General Paul Ely, "informing him of the danger that the army would assume directly a political role by opposing the next government, which could lead to the secession of Algeria from France." Ely's appeal to de Gaulle "to save the unity of the army and the nation" was persuasive evidence for the once and future leader of

France that the regime was on the brink of collapse, that his hour had finally struck.[106] Whether, as some argue, an explicit directive "to go ahead on May 13" was received from Colombey, or not, the signals were clear enough and the decision to do so was made.[107] Despite their original intention to move in August, Soustelle and his associates now gave Delbecque instructions to arrange, in the event of Pflimlin's investiture, disruptions in Algiers severe enough to prompt an army takeover.

On May 13 a general strike shut down all of Algiers. As Salan laid a wreath at the War Memorial, cries of "the army to power" and "Massu to power" were heard from a crowd estimated at nearly a hundred thousand. At the close of the ceremony, Lagaillarde, accompanied by other members of the Group of Seven, gave the signal to change the demonstration into a revolt. Thousands of ultra activists and pied noir youth began a rampage toward the Government-General building (the G-G). With Lagaillarde in the vanguard, and Trinquier's paratroopers opening their ranks to the rioters, hundreds stormed through the gates.[108] Offices were ransacked, dossiers rained down upon the crowd from upper-level windows, and Poujadist flags were raised.

As word of the takeover spread, thirty thousand more pieds noirs flocked to the Forum—an esplanade adjacent to the Government-General building. Generals Massu and Salan also arrived. Massu accepted an invitation by leaders of the assault to serve as president of a Committee of Public Safety, with Delbecque presented as vice-president. Massu read the text of a telegram to the government demanding establishment of a government of public safety in Paris which would alone be "capable of preserving Algeria as an integral part of metropolitan France." A subsequent communiqué announced that "Pflimlin's government of abandonment has just been invested by 273 votes against 124, with the aid of Communist votes, and that Soustelle had been detained by the government but was on his way to Algiers. Also included in this Communiqué No. 1 of the Algiers Committee of Public Safety was an "entreaty" to General de Gaulle "to break his silence and address the country with a view toward formation of a government of public safety, which alone can save Algeria from abandonment."[109]

By May 15, hundreds of Committees of Public Safety had appeared throughout France. While admirals and generals in the metropole had refused suggestions by cabinet ministers to enforce a blockade on Algeria, the various military conspirators set in motion their plans for action in the mainland.[110] General Ely resigned as chief of staff when his deputies, Challe and Martin, were arrested. Speaking to the crowd from the offices of the Algiers CPS in the Government-General building, Salan concluded a congratulatory panegyric to Algérie française and the people of Algiers by exclaiming "Vive la France! Vive l'Algérie française!" and then, prompted by Delbecque, "Vive de Gaulle!"[111]

The next day army operatives pulled thirty thousand Algiers Muslims into the streets to hail the apparently spectacular change that was occurring in the situation. Huge banners carried by the crowd read "De Gaulle au pouvoir." The unprecedented image of the Casbah rallying with the pieds noirs, dubbed by journalists the Miracle of Algiers, gave the revolt considerable credibility. Soustelle's escape from Paris and his arrival in Algiers on May 17 sustained the momentum. The Europeans of Algiers exulted as their former governor-general, the fugitive deputy, the defender of Algérie française, and the champion of General de Gaulle appeared together with Salan on the balcony of the G-G. Behind the scenes, Massu, Salan, and Jouhaud sent representatives to the mainland to meet with General Miquel, rally him and his network of conspirators to de Gaulle, and finalize plans for invading the metropole.[112] On May 21, Salan made his own break with the regime unmistakable. To the crowd on the Forum he declared that "we are now all united, and thus we shall march together up the Champs Élysées, and we shall be covered with flowers."[113]

In his investiture speech, Pflimlin labeled Massu and Salan as "factious generals" who had assumed an "insurrectionary attitude toward the Republic," but tellingly refrained from dismissing them. De Gaulle seized the opportunity afforded him by the ambiguous legal situation in Algeria, the government's indecision, the fears of widening disorder, and the appeals made to him. Likening the emergency to June 1940, when "the nation from its heart placed confidence in me to lead it to safety," he declared his readiness "to assume the powers of the Republic."[114] In a press conference on May 19, de Gaulle expressed understanding for the motives of both the settlers and the army in Algeria, but stated that the situation was leading to an "extremely grave national crisis." De Gaulle also held out hope (in terms heavy with meaning to those officers involved in Operation Resurrection) that the situation might yet lead France, under his guidance, to "a sort of resurrection."[115]

The last straw for the Pflimlin government was a rebellion in Corsica on May 24–25, engineered from Algiers as a warning of what was to come on the mainland if de Gaulle's demands were not acceded to. Greeted by tumultuous crowds, and assisted by 250 Corsican-based paratroopers, Delbecque, Thomazo, Sérigny, and other Algiers ultras replaced local prefects in the main Corsican towns and set up Committees of Public Safety in their stead. The Ajaccio Committee of Public Safety declared Corsica's confidence in Soustelle and Salan and demanded "the formation of a French Government of Public Safety, within the framework of the Republic, under the presidency of Charles de Gaulle."[116] A detachment of gendarmes sent to Corsica was easily disarmed by the paratroopers. One thousand additional loyalist soldiers were stranded on the mainland, the aircraft necessary for their transportation having been commandeered for Operation Resurrection.

Not only was the government unable to enforce its claims to authority in Corsica, but there was real doubt about its ability to do so anywhere in France. Socialist, Mendèsiste, and MRP attempts to organize Republican Defense Committees foundered, in part because they excluded the Communists. But even the Communists failed to rally more than a small proportion of their own supporters to demonstrations and strikes on behalf of the regime. In Pflimlin's cabinet, René Pleven took issue with Minister of Information Albert Gazier, who warned against a "power vacuum," which, he stated, "is what we now have. Let's not play with words. We no longer have any power. The Minister of Algeria cannot cross the Mediterranean. The Minister of National Defense commands no army. The Minister of Interior commands no police."[117]

De Gaulle's role in creating the sense of imminent danger which led Pflimlin's ministers to accept de Gaulle's conditions for forming a new government is well documented. On May 26, Foreign Minister Maurice Schumann received a telephone call from Oliver Guichard, one of de Gaulle's closest confidants, who told Schumann that "the General does not wish to arrive at the Élysée in a paratroop helicopter. He intends to save the Republic by legally assuming control of a Republican government."[118] While negotiations were under way between de Gaulle and Pflimlin, Pinay, Mollet, and other parliamentary leaders, Algiers radio broadcast Gaullist slogans intermixed with coded messages designed to create expectations of an imminent invasion.[119] On May 27, de Gaulle issued a communiqué falsely suggesting that he and the government had reached an agreement for a transfer of power, and he delivered a public warning to Algiers not to launch Operation Resurrection, at least not yet.

> I began yesterday the regular procedure necessary to the establishment of a republican government. In these conditions, any action from whatever side it might come, which places in question the public order, might have serious consequences. Even making allowance for circumstances, I cannot approve such actions. I expect the ground, naval, and air forces now in Algeria to remain exemplary under the orders of their chiefs, General Salan, Admiral Auboyneau, General Jouhaud. To these chiefs, I express my confidence and my intention to establish contact with them immediately.[120]

Pflimlin was in no position to quarrel with de Gaulle's version of his negotiations with Fourth Republic leaders, no matter how false it was.

After General Ely's resignation and the Corsican fiasco, Pflimlin knew exactly how defenseless the metropole was. "I was convinced," said Pflimlin three days after his resignation, "that in the actual circumstances, about which I knew all the facts, civil peace could only be preserved by the legal formation of a government headed by General de Gaulle."[121]

Nevertheless, government negotiators still hesitated to accept de Gaulle's conditions. De Gaulle thereupon advised Salan and Miquel, via secret emissaries, archly phrased telegrams, and telephone calls from his aides, to act so as to "force the hand" of the government and "make necessary" his return to power.[122] Operation Resurrection was accordingly rescheduled for May 30. Fearing both civil war ("Spain, but without the Republican Army," as Mollet put it) and outright military rule, the ministers gave way.[123] De Gaulle's terms were accepted. In his request to the National Assembly that General de Gaulle be asked to form a new government, President René Coty described the country as "on the verge of civil war." "Both sides," he said, "seem to be getting ready for a fratricidal combat."[124]

The initial reaction of Socialists, Radicals, Communists, and Popular Republican deputies to the arrogance of de Gaulle's pronouncement of readiness "to assume the powers of the Republic" and the insurrectionary threats with which he accompanied it was outrage, supplemented by declarations to defend the republic against a military-Gaullist dictatorship. On May 27, the Socialist caucus voted 112 to 3 never to "support the candidacy of General de Gaulle, which ... will remain under all possibilities a defiance of republican legality."[125] But the knowledge was spreading that thousands of paratroopers were poised to land in France, supported by tens of thousands of other soldiers loyal to Algiers and de Gaulle, and that no substantial means of armed resistance was available.[126] On the morning of May 28, Pflimlin presented his cabinet's resignation to President Coty. Messages from President Coty and Vincent Auriol (a former president of the republic and the grand old man of the Socialist party) warning of civil war and placing their trust in de Gaulle set the stage for a stunning reversal of parliamentary sentiment.[127] On May 29 the Socialist parliamentary group approved Vincent Auriol's approach to de Gaulle by a vote of 62 to 29, and two days later the party's caucus of deputies and senators voted 77 to 74 in favor of de Gaulle's investiture.[128] On the same day Coty formally announced his intention to ask General de Gaulle to form "within the framework of republican legality ... a Government of National Safety," a move supported by *Le Monde's* editor in chief, who spoke for much of the French political establishment when he wrote, on May 29, that "Today, right now, whatever reservations one could have about the present, and still more for the future, General de Gaulle would appear the lesser evil, the least poor risk."[129]

In negotiations with leaders of all the major parties except the Communists and the Poujadists, de Gaulle insisted on two decisively important conditions: Parliament be dissolved for six months, during which he would rule with "full powers,"[130] and at the end of that period a referendum would be held to approve a new constitution of his design. De Gaulle's cabinet included himself as both prime minister and minister of defense, with Mollet, Pflimlin, Debré, Pinay, and Lejeune in other posts. The outcome of the June 1 investiture vote was a foregone conclusion. Even Mendès-France, who voted against the new government in protest against extraconstitutional pressures, characterized the Fourth Republic as a "disappearing regime" that was "dying of its own failings" and endorsed de Gaulle's leadership as the best available for France.[131] With only the Communists, a bare majority of Socialists, and some Radicals voting no, de Gaulle was returned to power and the Fourth Republic brought to an end.

Regimes Change, but Not the Algerian Problem

The army-settler-Gaullist takeover in Algeria, the uprising in Corsica, and the credibility of the threatened invasion of the metropole produced within the legislature elected in 1956 a parliamentary majority unlike any other. The basis of this majority, which had voted for a change in regime and placed its confidence in de Gaulle to accomplish the change, was a right-of-center bloc of Indépendants, Social Republicans, Poujadists, dissident Radicals, and others committed above all to keeping Algeria French. Added to it were MRP, Socialist, and Radical deputies who preferred taking a chance on de Gaulle's authoritarian tendencies to the only alternatives they could envision—civil war or a fascist-military dictatorship.

Clearly then, the main representatives of the French political class viewed themselves as acting in the context of a severe regime crisis. Pflimlin's desperate efforts to reassure the Algerian generals of the hard line he intended to take in Algeria (including an appeal to Bidault to serve as minister for Algeria), his last minute inclusion of Morice and Lejeune in his cabinet, and the decision of so many Socialists, Popular Republicans, and Radicals to vote for de Gaulle's investiture suggest not only how clearly the risk of regime collapse was perceived, but that, in the end, most of those in favor of Algerian disengagement thought the risk too great to run.

At this juncture the problem faced by de Gaulle was not how to disengage from Algeria, but how to establish a regime with a better chance of surviving efforts by its governments to do so. In this chapter it remains to be shown that the disposition of Algeria remained a regime-level problem until three years after de Gaulle's return to power. During this time, however, de Gaulle's government, and the Fifth Republic to which it was a prelude, were not exposed to constant and serious threats of overthrow. The sustained regime crisis was instead apparent in much the same way that Thomas Hobbes observed that war and bad weather make themselves felt. As a state of war can be experienced in the absence of actual fighting, so "the nature of foul weather, lieth not in a shower or two of rain." For Hobbes, war and bad weather each describes "a tract of time" containing a chronic inclination toward violence (or inclemency) and the expectation of their continuation.[132] Similarly, the regime-level status of the threats associated with disengagement from Algeria was apparent in the chronic expectation among French political elites, and in de Gaulle's governments, that severe challenges to the constitutional order would accompany efforts to disengage from Algeria.

De Gaulle's perfunctory investiture address on June 1, 1958, contains telling evidence that even as he assumed power he judged the Algerian problem capable of triggering successive threats to the regime he intended to establish. One of the concessions Coty and Pflimlin claimed to have wrung from him was a six-month limit on the period of Parliament's dissolution and the duration of his "full powers" (reduced from the two years de Gaulle had demanded). But in his investiture speech, after again expressing sympathy for the army's tribulations and warning of civil war, de Gaulle voiced concern about threats his own regime would encounter. The genuineness of this concern is indicated by his wording; he risked a breakdown in the delicate transer-of-power process by refusing to commit himself to give up "full powers," or reconvene Parliament, at the end of six months. Full powers would be requested, he said, "for a period of six months, *hoping that at the end of this time*—order having been re-established in the state, hope regained in Algeria, unity restored in the nation—*it will be possible* for the public powers to resume their normal course."[133]

When he issued this caveat, the danger looming largest in de Gaulle's mind was the potential of the military men and ultras of Algeria to do to his regime what they had helped him do to the Fourth Republic. The fate of his enterprise—establishment of a presidential-style regime as his historic contribution to the reconciliation of French grandeur with French democracy—would hinge, he realized, on his ability to end the Algerian War on terms France could be led to accept as consistent with the legitimacy of the Fifth Republic. These perceptions and convictions are evident from the urgency and comprehensiveness of his personal involvement with Algerian affairs in the period immediately following his return to power.

After completing the legal niceties in Paris, de Gaulle went straight to Algeria—the first time a French premier had traveled to Algeria since Mollet made his ill-starred visit in February 1956. On June 4, he appeared on the balcony of the Government General building, arms raised in a V for victory sign under a large banner of the Committee of Public Safety. If at that moment his first words, "I have understood you!" convinced the crowd of two hundred thousand pieds noirs to trust him, still their chants of "Soustelle, Soustelle" and "Algérie française" were louder than cries of "Vive de Gaulle."[134]

Intégration and *Algérie française* were the code words by which the pieds noirs and their political leaders separated friends from enemies. Neither term appeared in de Gaulle's "I have understood you" speech. His resistance and obvious irritation at constant pied noir demands that he use these phrases fueled suspicions among the ultra leaders and the officers associated with the Committees of Public Safety. They complained bitterly that Pflimlin, Mollet, Pinay, and other symbols of the "old regime" had been included in de Gaulle's cabinet, while Soustelle and Delbecque had been excluded. They began to wonder whether de Gaulle's view of the future was considerably different than theirs.[135]

While in Algeria de Gaulle rejected attempts to characterize his assumption of power as the beginning of an ongoing revolution—a revolution that would not only erase all possibility of separation between Algeria and France, but would destroy as well the political parties on the mainland whose leaders had shown themselves willing to contemplate that separation. In Bône, de Gaulle was confronted with an impassioned demand that all authority in Algeria be delegated to Salan, working through the network of Public Safety Committees, until "the regime of Parties" was entirely eliminated. He responded angrily:

> You gentlemen will *not* continue to make a revolution. Your job is to win over people's minds to national unity, to the reform of France, and to support for General de Gaulle, without trying to force his hand, and within the framework which I shall set down.
> . . . The Army must control everybody, and, in particular, it must control you. Do not force its hand; don't even look as though you were trying to do so.[136]

Upon his return to mainland France, de Gaulle was disturbed to learn that the umbrella group representing all Committees of Public Safety in

Algeria had passed a resolution calling for just the sort of "continuing revolution" he had so vigorously denounced and thanking him for his unequivocal commitment to the full "integration" of Algeria into France— a commitment he had carefully avoided making. That ranking officers had participated in the drafting and passage of this resolution, and that Salan had apparently approved it, only made the nature of the threat clearer. Although he rebuked Salan, he was not at all certain how far he could go in enforcing his will on the army. He had made clear his preference that officers remove themselves from the Committees of Public Safety but prudently refrained from ordering them to do so, and they did not.[137]

De Gaulle himself was soon convinced that tensions over his refusal to espouse the Algérie française orthodoxy were part of what would be an intricate war of maneuver for control over the regime he was in the midst of establishing.[138] In August, de Gaulle announced that he and not Soustelle, as the ultras continued to hope, would assume ministerial responsibility for Algeria. Wishing to avoid a premature confrontation, however, de Gaulle used a variety of symbolic maneuvers to reassure the ultras while the institutional structure he would require to defeat them was being consolidated. Over the objections of his Socialist ministers, he brought Soustelle into the cabinet in July as minister of information. Massu was made superprefect of Algiers. Algerian stamps were replaced by French stamps. If integration was not proclaimed, de Gaulle did ceaselessly emphasize that all Algerians, Muslim or European, were henceforth to be considered "complete Frenchmen." Bastille Day was allowed to become a kind of apotheosis for the men of May 13. Half a million Parisians cheered Salan and Massu as they led paratroopers and harkis marching down the Champs Élysées, even as Salan had predicted on May 21. Soustelle and his enthusiastic network of Algérie française activists were enlisted in the campaign for a massive yes vote in the September referendum on the draft constitution for the Fifth Republic, whose fifth article made the president of the republic (that is, de Gaulle) "the guarantor" of the integrity of the national territory. By positioning himself to appear to both sides of the Algeria debate as the only politician capable of implementing their ambitions (for disengagement or integration), and by not categorically committing himself to either approach, de Gaulle was able largely to eliminate Algeria's future as an issue in the September referendum which approved the Fifth Republic's constitution, in the November legislative elections which gave his supporters a massive majority in the new Parliament, and in his own election as president in December.

To help maintain calm in Algeria until the new regime was established, de Gaulle made four more visits there between June and December 1958. During these visits he paid more attention to the Muslims than to the pieds noirs, but an even larger proportion of his time was spent with the army, especially with junior officers in the field. His public praise of the army was fulsome and regular. In private he told the soldiers of his expectations—the army would be required to win a thorough military victory over the FLN. It would henceforth, however, stay out of politics. In October de Gaulle finally ordered all military officers to withdraw from Committees of Public Safety. In a speech in Constantine he described a plan for sweeping economic reforms that would raise Algeria's living standards to those of the metropole. To the ultras de Gaulle was sounding suspiciously solicitous of Muslim needs; couched in semi-integrationist language, however, these reforms, and de Gaulle's stress on the "Frenchness" of all Algerians, could also be interpreted in a reassuring mode. He also advanced an eloquent but enigmatic appeal for a "peace of the brave," to be signaled by the raising of white flags by rebel units and the initiation of some sort of contact with FLN representatives. All this activity, in the midst of the referendum campaign and the legislative elections, helped obscure the transfer from Algeria of fifteen hundred officers of the rank of major and above whose involvement in the May 13 movement and whose activities in the Committees of Public Safety suggested they would not abide by de Gaulle's strictures against military involvement in politics.[139] When Salan failed to implement de Gaulle's orders that Muslim candidates favoring independence be allowed to participate in the November legislative elections, he too was removed from the scene—"kicked upstairs" into the honorific post of military governor of Paris.

In January 1959 the regime was in place, with de Gaulle installed as the first president of the Fifth Republic. Chief of his cabinet was Michel Debré—whose Algérie française credentials were impeccable, but whose first loyalty was to de Gaulle. Under Soustelle's direction the unofficial "Gaullist" party, the UNR or Union pour la Nouvelle République, achieved an absolute majority in the new Assembly, although de Gaulle had prevented Soustelle from being chosen its president.[140] In Algeria, Salan had been replaced in December by Paul Delouvrier, a skilled administrator whose assignment as "delegate-general" was to assume responsibility for civil authority and the implementation of those aspects of the Constantine Plan for which funding was available. In the spring and summer of 1959 Maurice Challe, named commander in chief of French forces in Algeria, launched an unprecedentedly successful campaign to destroy FLN formations in the outlying regions of Algeria where they were still active. This accorded well with de Gaulle's plans. The army should be given much to do, he told his cabinet, "they will think less."[141]

In fact de Gaulle himself paid only minimal attention to Algeria during the first half of 1959. The "peace of the brave" offer had helped avoid a damaging UN debate, but had been rejected out of hand by the FLN as an attempt to call surrender by another name. Although Debré was allowed to make speeches pronouncing France's will to remain sovereign over Algeria, in his own statements on the subject de Gaulle seemed content to repeat formulas which in elegant but unmistakably contrived ways portrayed Algeria's future as "with France" and therefore neither certainly ruled by France nor completely autonomous from it. Angry at de Gaulle's refusal to declare forthrightly for integration, disturbed by the clemency extended to thousands of FLN prisoners, and worried because of his implicit willingness eventually to honor the political preferences of Algerian Muslims, Europeans in Algeria boycotted anniversary ceremonies on May 13, 1959, and proclaimed it a day of mourning. But de Gaulle's continued popularity in metropolitan France and the success of his economic initiatives encouraged him to believe he could overcome regime threats which he knew more direct attempts to solve the Algerian problem would bring to the fore.

Crossing the Regime Threshold, September 1959–June 1961

The Policy of Self-Determination

In September 1959, with the Fifth Republic operating smoothly and Algeria again slated for debate at the United Nations, de Gaulle made his first serious effort to move the Algerian problem through the regime threshold (from point H to point I on Fig. A-3 in the appendix). After intensive discussions with his Algerian affairs advisers, he decided to define publicly Algeria's separation from France as an acceptable possibility by presenting it as comparable to Guinea's separation from France (following its rejection of the Fifth Republic Constitution) a year earlier. He took this step with full awareness of the risks of regime destabilization it would entail. General Ely, reinstated after his May 1958 resignation as chief of the general staff, warned de Gaulle that Algerian independence was "incompatible with the French state of mind" and predicted that if Algeria were accorded independence, civil war would likely break out in France.[142]

Prior to his speech on Algerian self-determination, and with Operation Resurrection still fresh in his mind, de Gaulle gauged Army sentiment by making a sixth Algerian trip, featuring an extended tour of the officers' messes. In these conversations he stressed the need for successful pacification and for strict obedience to civilian authority. He also explained his view that global transformations had made it impossible for European countries to rule former colonies without their consent and told the officers that the mission of the French army was much larger and more invigorating than fighting in the wadis and mountains of North Africa. It was inevitable, he told them, that Algerians would choose their own future. Partly as a result of these conversations de Gaulle gained confidence in his ability to separate the mass of the army from extreme Algérie française elements in the military and among the pieds noirs.[143] In a special broadcast to the nation on September 16, 1959, he solemnly announced France's acceptance of the principle of Algerian self-determination, to be implemented, eventually, by a referendum in which three choices would be presented—Frenchification (de Gaulle's term for integration), autonomy (i.e., association with France), or secession from France (independence). The next day his foreign minister, Couve de Murville, invited the FLN to send representatives to France to discuss the terms of a cease-fire which would make a choice among these options possible.

Even with no immediate prospect of holding the Algerian referendum, and despite his own obvious preference for "association," de Gaulle's commitment to the principle of self-determination and his government's official willingness to negotiate with the FLN provoked French Algeria partisans, both civilian and military, into active efforts to overthrow the new regime. In Algeria, Colonel Jean Gardes, head of the psychological warfare department of the army, sought immediately to organize a challenge to the regime.[144] Soldiers in Algiers put up posters declaring "Algérie française forever!" Alphonse Juin, France's only living marshal, declared his personal opposition to the principle of self-determination. On September 19, Georges Bidault, Pascal Arrighi, Jean-Baptiste Biaggi, and Colonel Thomazo founded the Rassemblement pour l'Algérie française (RAF), dedicated to "fighting for victory for Algérie française."[145] On September 27, a congress in Paris of seven hundred officers, representing the ten regions of the National Union of Reserve Officers, passed vehement resolutions concerning Algeria. Safeguarding Algérie française was described as "the most imperative concern ... among [our] permanent missions of national defense." The Algerian departments were "an integral part of France and the Army has taken its oath," the officers declared, "that they will remain so."[146]

Civilian ultras who played central roles in May 1958 were now in communication with Gardes and other angry officers in Algeria. Along with elements of Bidault's RAF, veterans' organizations in Algeria, Indépendant party deputies, former Poujadists, and General André Zeller, chief of staff of the army, they developed plans for Operation Veronique.[147] Its objective was to convince de Gaulle to appoint Bidault as prime minister and abandon his self-determination policy or, failing that, to rule France and Algeria through a military junta. The plan was for a protest walkout by one hundred Algérie française deputies, who would accuse the de Gaulle government of treason in its policy toward Algeria. This was to be accompanied by assassinations and other destabilizing activities in Paris and Algiers. If the army were not then called on to intervene to maintain order, and if de Gaulle refused to replace his government and abandon his Algerian policies, teams of commandos would seize the Palais Bourbon and the residences of the prime minister and the president. De Gaulle would then be forcibly returned to Colombey. *L'Année Politique* called the conspiracy the "first serious crisis" of the Fifth Republic.[148]

De Gaulle learned of the plot from General Ely, who warned him that the army as a whole would "pass into dissidence" unless it were reassured against the possibility of political negotiations with the FLN or a referendum it could not "control." Although Bidault was arrested, de Gaulle drew back from a decisive test of strength with the army. Summoning Challe to Paris, de Gaulle told him to explain to the army that he, de Gaulle, had been misunderstood—a "French solution" to the Algerian problem was his own desire, no *political* negotiations with the FLN were intended, and the referendum would "of course" be overseen by the army, which would itself remain in Algeria.[149] Challe returned to Algeria and convinced the army, including Massu, to abandon Operation Veronique. On October 15, the effort sputtered to an end with a muted agitation in Paris, a boycott of the Assembly by the Algerian deputies, desertion of the UNR by Thomazo, Delbecque, Biaggi, and other Algerian ultras, and a mysterious assassination attempt against François Mitterrand. The next day the Assembly voted 441 to 23 to support the government in a question of confidence on its Algerian policy.[150]

The overwhelming vote made it obvious that incumbent-level challenges to de Gaulle, within the institutions of the Fifth Republic, could not possibly succeed. But de Gaulle, no less than his enemies, realized that parliamentary majorities were not yet decisive. What had been decisive in the regime's successful negotiation of the mini-crisis was the army's acceptance of de Gaulle's reassurances. "General de Gaulle has implicitly admitted," remarked the *Economist* several months later, "that in the crucial Algerian question the mood in the officers' messes is more important to him than that prevailing in the lobbies of the Palais Bourbon."[151]

The Barricades Rebellion

The regime threshold had not been crossed. The dangers associated with any attempt to do so had been made apparent. But de Gaulle was ready to try again. On November 1, 1959, the first Congress of the Union for the New Republic committed itself to work against the secession option, but defeated Soustelle's resolution calling for the integration of Algeria. Instead the new Gaullist party affirmed its "total confidence" in de Gaulle's efforts to end the Algerian War. On November 10, de Gaulle reaffirmed his commitment to self-determination in terms that rekindled military suspicions that the army would not be allowed to "control" the voting and that the FLN would be permitted full freedom to mobilize the Muslim population on behalf of independence. To the pieds noirs De Gaulle's message was blunt: "You, the French of Algeria, who for generations have done so much, if one page has been turned by the great wind of history, well, it is up to you to write another. Let there be a truce to vain nostalgia, vain bitterness, vain torments; take the future as it comes."[152]

De Gaulle's words spurred both officers and civilian ultras in Algeria toward yet another revolt. Only two officers who had been associated with the May 13 movement in Algeria remained there in the fall of 1959—Massu, superprefect of Algiers and deputy to Challe, and Jean Gardes. Along with Gardes, two colonels devoted to French Algeria—true believers in *la guerre révolutionnaire,* and furious at de Gaulle—held key positions: Antoine Argoud, Massu's chief of staff, and Yves Godard, chief of security and Gardes' predecessor as head of psychological warfare operations. These three colonels—along with Lacoste-Lareymondie, a deputy with close ties to Indépendant party leader Roger Duchet; Yves Gignac, head of the Indochina and French Union Veterans Organization; and Generals Jouhaud and Zeller—were at the heart of the "November plot," intended for implementation during a scheduled visit by de Gaulle to Washington, D.C., in spring 1960. Disruptions and the seizure of buildings in Algiers and Paris would be arranged, calling into question the unity of the army. The plotters calculated that to preserve that unity and prevent civil war, de Gaulle, if he chose to return from America, would be forced to accept creation of a *pur and dur* Sixth Republic, which would carry out their program of integration and pacification with full rigor.[153]

The colonels were in close touch with Joseph Ortiz, the Algiers café owner who had played an active role in May 1958, and two other ultra activists, Dr. Jean-Claude Perez and Jean-Jacques Susini (Lagaillarde's replacement as head of the Algiers Student Federation). These three had emerged as the most influential leaders of the pieds noirs in Algiers. In November 1958, Ortiz had created the Front National Française to subsume the Group of Seven and most of the other pied noir activist organizations. Reaction to de Gaulle's September self-determination speech helped swell FNF ranks. In January 1960, French intelligence estimated the group's membership at 13,500.[154] Its emblem was the Celtic Cross, easily recognized as the symbol of the outlawed fascist group Jeune Nation.

Assisted by the sympathetic colonels of Algiers and the careful ignorance of Challe and Massu, Ortiz had also developed a well-armed, uniformed force of FNF volunteers. Added to these were the Unités Territoriales de Choc, an elite force of 1,200 men drawn from the pied noir militia. By late 1959, the Territorial Units in Algiers included 25,000 men, now organized within the Interfédération—a framework established under the guidance of Colonel Gardes to link 100,000 militiamen from European communities throughout Algeria. The secretary-general of the Interfédération, Captain Marcel Ronda, was also head of Ortiz's semisecret volunteer force. Ortiz used the UT de Choc, and his contacts within the larger UT formations, to give a military cachet to the FNF. In December 1959, Ortiz provided Bidault, and the RAF meetings he attended in Algiers, with a disciplined array of 1,500 security guards.[155]

The extent to which the civilian ultras were aware of the colonels' plans to revolt in spring 1960 is not clear, but events soon pushed them into their own insurrection, disrupting the original scenario but confronting the regime with another failed, but considerably more substantial threat to its survival than Operation Veronique.

Late in December de Gaulle composed a handwritten memorandum to an unnamed officer of high rank in Algeria. Admitting that France enjoyed a "crushing military superiority," he nonetheless labeled as a "dreadful mockery" the army's high-flown "integrationist" claims that the Muslims wished to be French. "To delude oneself," he continued, "with the idea that the political solution is integration or Frenchification, which is and can only be our domination by force—what the people in Algiers and a number of soldiers call *l'Algérie française*—is a lamentable stupidity.... It is simply mad to believe that our forced domination has any future whatsoever."[156]

General Massu's reaction was intemperate but honest. In an interview he accused de Gaulle of becoming "a man of the left," of betraying both Algeria and the army. He warned that the army had installed de Gaulle and had the power and the authority to replace the Fifth Republic. He himself, Massu declared, "and the majority of officers in a position of command, will not execute unconditionally the orders of the Head of State."[157]

De Gaulle summoned Massu to Paris for a personal rebuke and subsequent transfer to a mundane post on the mainland. Immediately Challe warned de Gaulle that if Massu were not allowed to return to Algeria, "the unity of the army might break if riots erupted." He predicted, "Blood will flow in Algiers!" and threatened to resign. Ignoring Challe's resignation threat, and despite similar warnings of disaster from Delouvrier, Debré, Ely, and Guillaumat, de Gaulle stuck by his decision to sack Massu.

He indicated he was ready for a decisive confrontation. "Let it come," de Gaulle told Challe, "the army is true to me, with the exception of some malcontents. If it is necessary to use force, you will use it. You are the master of your means."[158]

Among Europeans in Algeria, Massu's recall ignited an already super-charged political environment. FNF members and other activist groups were advised to arm themselves. Ortiz and Martel claimed they enjoyed sufficient military support to prevent "the abandonment of French Algeria, even if a government of treason gives the order." An angry telephone call from Massu to Antoine Argoud gave ultra leaders to understand that the army would not intervene against them.[159] So began Barricades Week.

On January 23, Ortiz and his FNF organized a general strike and dem-onstration as a springboard for a repeat of May 13. Although Colonel Argoud and other army commanders (with their plans for the spring in mind) argued against its timing, Gardes actively involved himself. The Tenth Parachute Division, commanded by General Gracieux and known for its sympathy with and personal ties to the European population of Algiers, was recalled from its Kabylian campaign to preserve order in the city. On the night of January 23–24, Lagillarde (now a member of the National Assembly) sought to upstage Ortiz by setting up barricades in the university district. Hundreds of armed militiamen, having deserted from the UTs, joined Lagaillarde behind fortified barricades, while thou-sands more gathered in the city. On January 24, a general strike completely shut down the city of Algiers.[160] During the afternoon a demonstration was held in the Plateau des Glières, where Ortiz had established his head-quarters—in the offices of the UT Interfédération.

When the army ordered the demonstrators to disperse, they refused and instead erected barricades to complement those of Lagaillarde in the uni-versity area. Challe then sent two regiments of paras from the Tenth Division and one regiment of gendarmes to sweep away the barricades and disperse the crowd. But the commanders of the para regiments, overtly sympathetic to the activists, failed to move according to plan. When the gendarmes arrived, tear-gas grenades were fired and fighting erupted. The gendarmes were carrying unloaded weapons, as per regulations, and suf-fered heavy casualties. When the fighting ended, 14 gendarmes were dead and 123 were wounded, along with 8 demonstrators dead and 24 wounded. The next day de Gaulle denounced the revolt as a "stab in the back for France," expressing his confidence in Delouvrier and Challe, and committing himself and his government to achieve in Algeria "a solution which would be French." But he gave no indication of what his specific response to the barricades would be. "As for myself," he concluded, "I will do my duty."

While the pieds noirs rallied to the cause of their "martyrs" and hoped the paras' obvious sympathy would result in a recapitulation of May 13th, orders were sent from Paris to bring an end to the rebellion. At their headquarters in Algiers, however, General Challe and General Crépin (Massu's replacement) were told by the activist colonels, and General Gracieux, that orders to fire on the demonstrators would result in a crisis of discipline—that regimental officers and soldiers would not obey their superiors and that heavy street-fighting would likely break out in the wake of such orders. Therefore, instead of issuing instructions to clear the barricades, Challe reached an agreement with Ortiz to allow them to remain in place in return for a guarantee that no public buildings would be seized. Throughout the day on January 25, Ortiz and his men addressed enthusiastic crowds in the Plateau de Glières. Those behind the barricades took heart from the obvious goodwill of the paratroopers, who fraternized freely with them, in clear violation of the spirit if not the letter of the "state of siege" declared by Challe.

In cabinet discussions some ministers advised the government to insist on strong and immediate military action against "the rebellion," as de Gaulle himself was to refer to it in his televised speech to the nation on January 29. But Debré and others were unconvinced of the army's willingness to obey orders and feared the consequences of a split in the armed forces. Nevertheless, on the evening of January 25, de Gaulle sent Debré and Armed Forces Minister Guillaumat to Algiers with instructions to bring an end to the disturbances, by whatever means necessary, within twenty-four hours.

On January 26, Marshal Juin and Generals Zeller, Salan, and Miquel made it known that they would publicly announce their opposition if orders to fire on the demonstrators in Algiers were given.[161] Meanwhile, in Algiers, Debré and Guillaumat met with the military and civilian authorities and made a personal tour of the barricades. While Challe counseled patience, General Gracieux offered himself for arrest when told that the president of the republic had ordered removal of the barricades, by any means, within twenty-four hours. A dozen colonels and regimental commanders then met with Debré and warned him in stark terms against using force to disperse the demonstrators. The result, they said, would be between seven hundred to a thousand deaths; they added that they would refuse to command their troops to open fire on French crying Algérie française. On behalf of the group, Argoud demanded that de Gaulle abandon self-determination by making an unequivocal commitment to Algérie française or accept either Challe or a military junta to replace him.[162] If de Gaulle wanted to remain in power, Argoud insisted, he would also have to increase by a hundredfold the resources committed to the Algerian War and put an end to the "demoralization campaign" he accused the metropolitan press of waging.[163]

Upon his return to Paris, Debré tried and failed to convince de Gaulle to accept the demands of the Algiers colonels or at least solmenly affirm the government's commitment to maintain Algeria as French. Debré then offered his resignation, which de Gaulle also refused. The most Debré was allowed was to make a speech condemning the uprising and employing the term "French land" to refer to Algeria. Instead of making concessions or demanding immediate steps to end the episode by force, the government adopted a policy, by design or default, of wait and see. The men behind the barricades were left hoping that the army would swing behind them, but fearing that without army support their essential powerlessness would be exposed.

On January 27, Challe spoke to the people of Algiers, calling for order while declaring that "the French army is fighting to see that Algeria remains French indefinitely." Despite his loyalty to the integrationist view, however, Challe had refused entreaties by the colonels to join the insurrection. He left Algiers on January 28 to set up a temporary headquarters, along with Delouvrier, in a nearby air force base. This forced Gracieux and the activist colonels to escalate the revolt on their own authority or admit to the pieds noirs that the army would side with de Gaulle. Despite the virtual unanimous support offered the rebels by the European population of Algiers, the ultras' inability (without the army's active complicity) to fill the power vacuum in the city or effectively challenge the government in Paris left them increasingly discouraged.[164] With soldiers loyal to the government arriving in Algiers to replace the Tenth Parachute Division, militiamen began melting away, preferring to rejoin their units rather than face charges of desertion.

By January 29, leaders of the rebellion were seeking a negotiated end to the stalemate which would "commit the government more firmly to the doctrine of Algérie française."[165] But the government refused all such suggestions. In the evening of January 29, de Gaulle addressed the nation. Wearing his general's uniform, he demanded the obedience of every soldier, warning that even passive association with the rebels would be penalized. But he also expressed his confidence in General Challe and stressed the army's mission to achieve victory over the FLN—"to liquidate the rebel force which is seeking to drive France out of Algeria." He also promised the army that when the time came for the self-determination referendum, "it will be your responsibility to guarantee the complete freedom and sincerity of this vote." While emphasizing his unaltered commitment to the principle of self-determination, de Gaulle tried to encourage belief in the possibility that he and his government would work for "integration" rather than "association."

> Frenchmen of Algeria, how can you listen to the liars and the conspirators who tell you that in granting a free choice to the Algerians, France and De Gaulle want to abandon you, to pull out of Algeria and hand it over to the Rebellion? . . . How can you doubt that if, one day, the Muslims should freely and formally decide that tomorrow's Algeria is to remain closely tied to France, nothing would cause more joy to the fatherland and de Gaulle than to see them choose, among the solutions, that which would be the most French?[166]

Metropolitan opinion rallied strongly to de Gaulle, and officers who had been sitting on the fence committed themselves to the government. Fraternization between soldiers and the barricades' defenders ceased. On February 1, after an amnesty had been declared for all but the "chiefs of the rebellion," the last of the barricades was abandoned.

Perceptions of the Fifth Republic at Risk

Reporting immediately after the events, C. S. Sulzberger described de Gaulle's position as "like that of Asquith, faced at Curragh in 1914 with the mutiny of a British army commanded by generals sympathetic to North Irish insurrectionists."[167] Six months later Philip Williams described the attitude of army officers in Algeria as akin "to that of Gough's cavalry officers who, in 1914, resigned their commissions rather than coerce Ulster—and so in effect vetoed certain possible lines of policy."[168] Many of the obvious differences in the two cases are discussed in Chapter 8, with Asquith's embarrassment contrasted with de Gaulle's exploitation of the crisis. But the similarities are striking: settlers posing an organized challenge to the authority of the regime were able to elicit enough support in the armed forces to deter the direct use of military force against them. In both cases, moreover, the policy preferences and normal partisan concerns of governing elites were overshadowed by perceived threats to regime integrity.

The perceived seriousness of the barricades crisis was reflected in the range of extraordinary security measures put into effect by various ministries. Publication of four newspapers—two on the extreme right and two on the extreme left—was suspended. Travel to Algeria was halted, and news from there was heavily censored. All public meetings were banned.

Eighty arrest warrants were issued against the leaders of right-wing, ultranationalist, and veterans' organizations, including the RAF. One hundred and fifty loyal CRS (Compagnies Républicaines de Securité) men were brought to the Élysée Palace to guard de Gaulle against kidnapping or assassination.

In the shocked aftermath of the bloodshed in Algiers, which was the first time the "forces of order" had suffered substantial casualties at the hands of the Algiers ultras, few on the mainland thought to critize the government for high-handedness or panic. Throughout the country, opinion swung behind the government, demanding whatever steps were required to maintain "republican legality." In the major cities ad hoc groups arose with names such as the Committee to Support General de Gaulle in the Defense of the Republic. A petition formulated by the Club Jean Moulin, a collection of high-ranking civil servants, called on the president to "defend the authority of the state" and received three hundred thousand signatures in twenty-four hours. Telegrams of support from over 1100 municipal councils and tens of thousands of letters from public organizations and individuals flooded the Élysée Palace.[169] The peasants whose demonstrations had preoccupied French public opinion in the first weeks of January allowed their agitation to subside. Every party of the center and left condemned the revolt in Algiers and affirmed its support of de Gaulle. The large Communist-controlled unions effected a one-hour general strike to protest the ultra action and support self-determination for Algeria. Even Mendès-France became a "Gaullist for the occasion."[170] Only ex-Poujadists, such as Jean-Marie Le Pen, Algerian deputies, and extreme right-wingers such as Jean-Louis Tixier-Vignancour expressed unreserved support for the insurgents. Although the Indépendant party's central bureau, under the influence of Roger Duchet, expressed sympathy for those behind the barricades and urged de Gaulle to reassure them that France's "territorial integrity would be safeguarded," Paul Reynaud and other Indépendant leaders dissociated themselves from the resolution and criticized the party bureau for having fallen under the sway of the ultras.[171]

What lay behind this massive "civic mobilization" was not enthusiasm for the substance of de Gaulle's Algerian policy, but fear that an alliance between the ultras and the army was jeopardizing the Fifth Republic and threatening France once more with turmoil, widespread political violence, and the specter of authoritarianism. Indeed the Europeans of Algeria *were* trying to recapitulate the movement of May 1958, to create a sense among the great mass of French people that political stability in France could not be achieved unless French Algeria were assured of its future. But having gained confidence in the direction of French affairs under the Fifth Republic, metropolitan opinion was worried about the army's threat to the new regime and cared little for pied noir complaints that de Gaulle's policy would eventually lead to the abandonment of Algeria.[172]

If anything, government ministers were more worried than the public that the army would either join the insurgents or break apart.[173] Delouvrier's state of mind had been made embarrassingly public in an unauthorized and nearly hysterical radio appeal to the men on the barricades. On the return flight to the mainland, Armed Forces Minister Guillaumat bemoaned his loss of authority over the armed forces and told Debré he would resign. When the retired General Guillebon, a veteran Gaullist and director of the polytechnique, was asked to accept the post of Minister of the Armies, he responded with conditions that reflected his own sense of how precarious was the loyalty of the army and the future of the regime. He would accept the position only if "there would be no orders to fire on patriots; Massu would be returned to Algiers; and the army would be promised that neither Algeria nor the Muslims would be abandoned."[174] In his speech to the National Assembly on the day after the barricades were evacuated, Prime Minister Debré's relief was evident. Having, during the crisis, been reduced to tears and talk of suicide in front of his ministers, he now described the revolt as a direct challenge to the state and an ordeal that had raised fears of "the beginning of a civil war."[175]

There is also ample evidence of de Gaulle's own regime-level concerns—his view that both during and after the week of the barricades the integrity of the Fifth Republic was at stake. Immediately following the crisis de Gaulle asked the National Assembly for the special legislative powers available to the executive branch under article 38 of the Constitution. According to Bernard Tricot, his Algerian affairs adviser, that request (which was overwhelmingly approved) was not de Gaulle's initial preference. Only after being persuaded by Tricot did de Gaulle decide not to invoke the more drastic provisions of article 16—enabling the president to take over the full powers of the republic when "the institutions of the Republic ... are threatened in a grave and immediate manner and when the regular functioning of constitutional governmental authorities is interrupted."[176] Although de Gaulle told his ministers that he was certain the army would back him, and that the crisis would be resolved successfully without concessions to the rebels or their supporters in the army, he knew the army was close to open revolt and took some steps to appease it. De Gaulle responded to Challe's warnings of explosions in Algeria and his threat to resign (following Massu's recall) by satisfying two long-standing demands of the officer corps: henceforth FLN "terrorists and spies" could be subject to "summary justice," and "no direct negotiations would be undertaken with the FLN."[177] In striking contrast to his usual formality and studied aloofness, de Gaulle agreed on January 26 to meet during dinner with two of the most extreme of the Algiers colonels, who bluntly insisted that he proclaim himself in favor of Algérie française.[178] The next day he chose not to contradict Challe's declaration, broadcast over Algiers radio, that the French army was fighting to see that "Algeria remains French indefinitely,"[179] and carefully avoided issuing unequivocal orders to the army to reduce the barricades by force. Even in his speech to the nation on January 29, when the threat to his authority had already substantially lessened, de Gaulle was conciliatory—promising never to negotiate "the political destiny of Algeria" with the "rebel organization," and describing self-determination as "the only means by which the Moslems can themselves cast out the demon of secession."[180]

In February 1960, Raymond Aron commented that although the conspiracy of the Algerian ultras had failed and the army had, in the end, followed the orders of the chief of state, "it remains that a fraction of the officer corps did sympathize with the insurrection, [and] that the authority of General de Gaulle was publicly challenged for many days. After the crisis, the institutions of the Fifth Republic looked more precarious than ever.... France is still in a half-revolutionary crisis without an accepted regime."[181]

De Gaulle had won a battle but was not yet victorious in the war of maneuver, and he knew it. Early in February he reshuffled his cabinet. Those ministers who had expressed sympathy with the rebellion were dismissed (Soustelle and Cornut-Gentille), while Guillaumat was removed from the Armed Forces Ministry. An Algerian committee of de Gaulle's closest advisers was created, responsible for all policies concerning Algeria. The Territorial Units, which had played such a central role in the insurrection, were disbanded and the "psychological bureau" was dissolved. Lagaillarde, Sérigny, and other ultra ringleaders who did not go into hiding were arrested. The army newspaper *Le Bled* was relocated from Algiers to Paris. Many of the civil powers and responsibilities that had been transferred to the army were returned to civilian prefects and subprefects. Within three months, nine generals known for their opposition to de Gaulle's policies and their involvement in or toleration of the events of January 1960 were deprived of their Algerian commands and transferred. Also recalled were Colonels Gardes, Argoud, Godard, Bigeard, and Broizat. General Jouhaud was discharged from his post as air force chief of staff. In February Challe himself was informed he would be recalled, and in April he was transferred from Algeria to a NATO post. Challe was replaced by General Crépin—a man unpopular with the army but known in Paris for his hostility to mixing politics with military matters. By the end of 1960, hundreds more officers were recalled from Algeria and stationed elsewhere in France, Germany, or Africa.[182]

The Generals' Revolt, April 1961

Soon after the February 1960 cabinet shake-up, de Gaulle warned his ministers that negotiating an end to the Algerian War would be "an ugly business" and advised them to "hang on to the mast, because the ship is going to rock."[183] Fifteen months later one more regime crisis would arise from the Algerian debacle—the last time fears for the survival of the Fifth Republic figured more prominently than normal policy and partisan consideration in the determination and implementation of Algerian policy. In April 1961, Generals Challe, Salan, Jouhaud, and Zeller led a revolt engineered by the activist colonels transferred from Algeria after the Barricades Rebellion. Their aim was to defeat the FLN by seizing control of the army in Algeria and then use their success, and allies in the metropole, to overthrow de Gaulle and establish a new regime dedicated to and capable of sustaining French sovereignty in Algeria.

In the first half of 1960, however, many officers and Algérie française partisans hoped that another showdown would not be necessary—that de Gaulle had been sufficiently shaken by the events of January, and the threat to army unity associated with them, to have abandoned his intention of granting genuine self-determination to Algeria. Late in February the government began a vigorous campaign of prosecution and harassment of FLN sympathizers in metropolitan France. In March de Gaulle concluded another tour of officers' messes in Algeria with the obscure prediction of an "Algerian Algeria bound to France." But to many of his interlocutors, and according to the reports of the one journalist allowed to accompany him, de Gaulle's main message seemed a reversal of his Algerian policy, a swing toward full support for the army's pacification campaign. His language was closer to that of the integrationists than any he had used since May 1958. Among the remarks he made to officers while in Algeria were the following:

There will be no Dien Bien Phu in Algeria. The insurrection will not throw us out of this country. Pacify. There is time. No need to be hustled.[184]

The independence demanded by Ferhat Abbas and his gang is a farce, a monstrosity...misery, a reduction to beggary, catastrophe....When the Algerians will be able to choose, I do not think they will choose that. France must not leave. She has the right to be in Algeria. She will remain there.[185]

Algeria must not be separated from France. It is of the nature of things that Algeria be bound to France. Under what form? I do not prejudge that. That will depend upon the situation of the world and the vote of the population.[186]

Independence is a pleasantry.... You will still be in Algeria one hundred years from now.[187]

Popular Republicans, Mendèsistes, Socialists, and other supporters of Algerian self-determination attacked the government for giving up on its own policy of self-determination. They accused de Gaulle of deferring to the preferences of the ultras out of fear of another military rebellion.[188] Secret contacts between the government and FLN leaders from inside Algeria were taking place, however. Playing on the "external" rebel leadership's fear that "internal" commanders might sue for a separate peace, de Gaulle set the stage for a public invitation to the Gouvernement Provisoire de la République Algérienne (GPRA), on June 14, 1960, to engage in direct negotiations "in order to find with them an honorable end to the fighting."[189] For the first time, the FLN leadership responded positively. A delegation was sent to France to lay the groundwork for the talks. When the French made it clear that discussions could only pertain to arranging a cease-fire and that no real bargaining would be permitted, the effort collapsed.

But the negotiations in June were only the first of de Gaulle's signals to the FLN of his desire to reach a mutually agreeable end to the fighting and to French public opinion that a negotiated end to the war would be based on Algerian independence. Once more he chose to risk serious challenge to the Fifth Republic in order to get France out of Algeria.[190] In a September news conference de Gaulle described two and only two possible futures for Algeria: "secession, through rupture from France, or association, in amicable union with her." The Frenchification or integration option, which he had included a year earlier in his list of possible futures for Algeria, was omitted.[191] In a television broadcast on November 4, he made his position considerably more explicit. He solemnly portrayed "an Algerian Algeria ... an emancipated Algeria ... an Algeria which ... will have its own government, its own institutions, its own laws" as the objective of his government. Abandoning previous language which limited the FLN's role in negotiations to discussions of a cease-fire and surrender of arms, he now invited the "leaders of the external organization of the rebellion ... to participate in discussions regarding the organization of a future referendum." He even predicted that though it had never existed in the past, an Algerian republic would one day emerge.[192] A week later his cabinet announced plans to hold a referendum in France and Algeria in which the French public would be asked to approve the policy of self-determination and the government's intention to promulgate a new Statute of Algeria which would provide the legal framework for a future Algerian referendum.

The referendum on self-determination was held on January 8, 1961, after an intensive personal campaign by de Gaulle which included three nationally broadcast speeches, a threat to resign if the proposal were defeated, and a five-day trip to Algeria. In his speeches de Gaulle likened the referendum to the previous fateful occasions on which he had appealed to the people of France: while reestablishing the republic immediately following liberation, and while urging approval in September 1958 of the Fifth Republic's constitution. He stressed his unconditional willingness to "receive the representatives of those who are fighting us" and repeated his willingness to engage in political negotiations with "the leaders of the rebellion."[193] He promised peace and self-government in Algeria if he received a massive and positive response to the referendum. A weak or negative response, he said, would cause the downfall of much that he had achieved and trigger renewed subversion and political instability.[194]

During his trip to Algeria de Gaulle pointedly avoided the cities where the European populations were concentrated. He met and spoke mainly with Muslims. The settlers made their attitudes clear, however, by riots in Algiers and Oran, a five-day general strike, and no less than four assassination attempts.[195] In European areas the police were reinforced by thousands from metropolitan forces and by army units comprised predominantly of draftees (considered more loyal to the regime than the professional army), indicating how seriously the government took pied noir opposition to its policies. These measures helped insure the riots were contained, but only after tear gas and light tanks were used to break up the crowds and destroy makeshift barricades. In the course of the crackdown two pieds noirs were killed and hundreds more injured or arrested.

The most stunning aspect of de Gaulle's visit, however, was the FLN's successful organization of mass demonstrations in Algiers—demonstrations by middle class Muslims in favor of an FLN-led independent Algeria. The mobilization of so much support, under the guns of the French army and in a city from which most pieds noirs believed the FLN had been totally uprooted, was a devastating blow to ultra claims that genuine pacification would make "integration" and "fraternization" between Muslims and Europeans a reality.[196] There was no longer any question about the result of a referendum on Algeria's future if a genuinely free ballot were allowed.

On January 8, 1961, de Gaulle received the massive *oui* he had requested, amounting to over 72 percent of the votes cast. Accordingly, he proclaimed, his Algerian policy would be implemented "without reserve in its spirit as in its letter."[197] The December pro-FLN demonstrations in Algiers had meanwhile convinced de Gaulle to cast aside earlier plans to pursue a new statute for Algeria, as envisioned in the referendum. Abandoning ideas about developing an alternative to the rebel leadership (a "third force"), his government instead made direct overtures to the FLN. De Gaulle's accelerating movement toward public acceptance of a fully independent, FLN-governed Algeria was also reflected in statements revealing his attitude toward Algeria as increasingly "Cartiérist." At an April 11 press conference he spoke in brutally frank terms: "Quite simply, Algeria costs us, to say the least, more than she is worth to us.... And that is why, today, France considers with the greatest composure a solution such that Algeria would cease to be a part of her domain."[198]

For metropolitan politicians committed to Algérie française, pieds noirs, and many army officers, de Gaulle's Algerian policies from June 1960 to April 1961 were felt as a series of shocks. Those officers who had accepted at face value de Gaulle's post–Barricades Rebellion assurances to the army (i.e., that no political negotiations with the FLN would be undertaken and that the army, in pursuit a military victory, would remain in Algeria for a long time) were enraged. They were now convinced that the government meant to break solemn promises of protection offered by the army to "loyal Muslims," especially the *harkis*. The response of Algérie française partisans to what they perceived as de Gaulle's lies and betrayals was fragmented but familiar. Publicly and clandestinely ex-Poujadists, veterans' organizations, reservists, and officers transferred from Algeria by de Gaulle organized to block the "surrender" of French Algeria by destabilizing the Fifth Republic and replacing de Gaulle. In Parliament the former Poujadist, now Indépendant deputy, Jean-Marie Le Pen failed in his effort to attain Lagaillarde's release from prison based on his parliamentary immunity. But the proposal, which enjoyed the active support of both the veterans' and reservist organizations, received 165 votes in favor (compared to 268 votes against)—the most substantial opposition vote on an Algeria-related issue since the creation of the Fifth Republic.[199]

The most significant political mobilization against de Gaulle's policy of disengagement from Algeria came from Soustelle and the Fourth Republic leaders who had been most closely associated with Algérie française. After Soustelle's ouster from the UNR for opposing Algerian self-determination, and while under constant surveillance, de Gaulle's former information minister founded a propaganda organ for French Algeria—Centre d'Information sur les Problèmes de l'Algérie et du Sahara—and began writing again for the journal he had founded in 1957, *Voici Pourquoi*. He was joined in his efforts by the former premier and Resistance chief Georges Bidault, who railed against de Gaulle's idea of Algérie algérienne, which he said was contrary to the constitution. Resistance to it he likened to resistance to the Vichy regime. Bidault condemned de Gaulle's June 14 offer of negotiations with the FLN as "possibly tantamount to treason."[200]

Soustelle, Bidault, and Duchet (leader of the Algeria diehards among the Indépendants) were the moving forces behind the Vincennes Committee, a broad-spectrum, non-Gaullist descendant of the USRAF whose manifesto denounced surrender to terrorism, condemned any sort of negotiations with the "totalitarian" FLN, and proclaimed "the maintenance of Algeria within the French Republic" as the only solution. Established in June 1960, the Vincennes Committee linked right-wing groups and ultras, including the group Jeune Nation, Pascal Arrighi, and Léon Delbecque, to mainstream politicians. Among the signatories to the Vincennes manifesto were Soustelle, Bidault, Cornut-Gentille, Bourgès-Maunoury, Lacoste, Lejeune, and Morice. Its inaugural meeting was attended by thirty-five deputies and two hundred important figures from universities, business, labor unions, and the civil service.[201]

In November, politicians and others associated with the Vincennes group denounced the scheduled referendum in regime-challenging terms. Duchet predicted that de Gaulle's "*Algérie algérienne* risked leading Algeria into chaos and dividing France." Bidault declared his "total opposition" to de Gaulle, describing the referendum as "execrable, worse than ever; it is unacceptable and will not be accepted." Marshal Juin explained his refusal to march in the Armistice Day parade, "despite a fifty-year friendship with General de Gaulle," by publicly condemning the president's Algerian policy. Juin believed that "to abandon our Algerian brothers ... to conceive that Algeria, in the end, would be excluded from the body of the Republic, imperils France, Europe and the free world."[202] On April 18, 1961, Soustelle, Bidault, and other prominent members of the Vincennes Committee issued an "appeal to the French people" which accused de Gaulle of "defeatism" and of being criminally responsible, under the constitution, for endangering the "the integrity of the national territory."[203]

In Algeria itself the settlers reacted to de Gaulle's overtures toward negotiations by forming the French Algerian Front (FAF) to replace the now banned French National Front. Its purpose was plain: to repeat the uprising of January 1960, but to achieve the outcome of May 1958. By the end of 1960, French security credited the organization with two hundred thousand members in Algeria alone. After de Gaulle's speech on November 4, with its reference to the eventual emergence of an Algerian republic, the FAF joined General Jouhaud in a conspiracy to assassinate the president during de Gaulle's trip to Algeria in December. Although Jouhaud's poor planning led to the collapse of the plot, the general strike and violent riots that marked de Gaulle's visit were the work of the FAF.[204]

The putsch of April 1961, however, was purely a military affair. Despite the systematic dispersal of officers implicated in the Barricades Rebellion, the activist colonels and their sympathizers remained in touch with one another and remained committed to preventing French disengagement from Algeria. These men had no faith in de Gaulle's promises during his "tour of officers' messes," and as early as March 1960 they were once again contemplating a coup d'état. The lesson they had drawn from the events of January was that the civilian ultras in Algiers were bumbling amateurs and that a revolt could succeed only if it remained strictly under the control of the military.[205] Some also embraced the logical extension of their analysis—that French political life would have to be reorganized according to the dictates of *la guerre révolutionnaire,* and that republican democracy would have to be supplanted by a form of national-military rule.[206]

Raoul Salan responded to de Gaulle's September news conference with a dramatic communiqué directly challenging the legitimacy of any government or regime which sought to end French rule in Algeria. "It is not within the power of any authority," Salan declared, "to decide upon the relinquishment of a part of the territory where France exercises her sovereignty."[207] He was immediately summoned to Paris, reprimanded, and ordered not to return to Algeria. Under constant surveillance by the Sûreté, Salan left France in October and established his headquarters in Spain. There he was joined by Susini, Lagaillarde, and other fugitives who had played leading roles in the Barricades Rebellion. These men became the founding chiefs of the Organisation Armée Secrète (OAS)—a terrorist organization of pied noir ultras dedicated to defeating de Gaulle's self-determination policy by any means.

The Generals' Revolt of April 1961 was carefully organized by the activist colonels—including Argoud, Godard, and Gardes—who had been banished from Algeria, but who met clandestinely between January and April 1961 at the War College in Paris.[208] De Gaulle's success in the referendum of January 8 had convinced them that Algeria was lost unless the Fifth Republic could be overturned. When, in March 1961, commanders in Algeria received secret orders to prepare for a cease fire, the colonels were sure that a united army would rise in revolt against the regime once the paratroop and Foreign Legion regiments made the first move. With firm commitments of support from the commanders of the Foreign Legion's First Paratroop Regiment, stationed near Algiers, they lacked only a popular leader. Challe, the most successful commander in chief the French had had in Algeria, was the ideal candidate. He had resigned in protest against de Gaulle's Algerian policies in January 1961, following the referendum, but had resisted the colonels' blandishments to assume a leadership role in their revolt. Then, in an angry reaction to de Gaulle's April 1961 remarks about Algeria costing France more than it was worth, Challe changed his mind. Along with Generals Jouhaud, André

Zeller (a former army chief of staff), and Salan, Challe agreed that within two weeks the army would seize Algeria.[209]

In the early morning hours of April 22, the First Paratroop Regiment seized every strong point in Algiers, including the radio station and the headquarters of both military and civilian administrations. Gendarmes manning barricades hastily erected by the authorities refused to fire on the paratroops. General Fernand Gambiez, who had recently replaced Crépin as commander in chief of French forces in Algeria, was arrested, as were Jean Morin, who had taken Delouvrier's place six months earlier, and Minister of Public Works Robert Buron, who was visiting Algiers. Approximately 7,000 soldiers, chiefly from four paratroop and Foreign Legion regiments, rallied to Challe's banner, helping him establish control of central Algeria. Civilian demonstrations and a mutiny by Legion paratroops forced General Henri de Pouilly to abandon his headquarters in Oran. Colonels Argoud and Gardy arrived to take charge of the city. In Constantine, Challe and the colonels elicited reluctant support from General Gouraud.

Meanwhile Algiers radio (renamed, significantly, Radio France) announced that General Challe, supported by Generals Jouhaud, Zeller, and Salan, had assumed control of the army in Algeria, that all civil powers had been transferred to the military command, and that a state of siege was in force. Communiqués described the action as having been taken "in order to keep our oath, the army's oath, to keep Algeria, so that our dead may not have died for nothing... *Algérie française* is not dead. There is not, there will not be, there never will be, an independent Algeria. Long live *Algérie française* so that France may live!"[210] Challe made the fundamental nature of his challenge to the Fifth Republic explicit in a radio broadcast on the morning of the coup: "The command reserves the right to extend its action to the metropole and re-establish a constitutional and republican order which has been gravely compromised by a government whose illegality must be obvious in the eyes of the nation."[211]

Ever since the end of Barricades Week de Gaulle had expected that his policies toward Algeria would trigger renewed challenges to the Fifth Republic. Early in spring 1961, intelligence reports submitted to Prime Minister Debré identified hundreds of officers (including forty generals) as "unreliable" in the event of a coup attempt.[212] Nonetheless the government in Paris was shocked by the April putsch. Challe had a reputation as a sensible, careful man and an oustanding general. His participation led many high government officials to believe the revolt might succeed and led others to indicate their readiness to accept terms from the quartet of generals rather than forcibly resist their demands.[213]

Unsure of the extent of the army's response to Challe's appeal, de Gaulle sent Minister of Algerian Affairs Louis Joxe and Chief of Staff General Jean Olie to Algeria to serve as a rallying point for loyal units. Ultra officers serving with French armored units in Germany were put under guard. When bombs exploded at the Paris airport and in the train station, the city was placed under a state of alert and travel sharply curtailed. Rightwing activists, both civilian and military, were arrested.[214] Outmoded tanks were driven or towed into position around key points, to defend them, supposedly, against an attack from Algeria.

During the evening of April 23, de Gaulle addressed the nation on television. Again wearing his general's uniform, he scathingly condemned the insurrection as an "odious and stupid adventure" led by "a handful of retired generals...partisan, ambitious, and fanatic." He ordered every soldier to "bar the route to these men" and forbade any soldier from executing their orders or accepting their command. Then he invoked article 16 of the constitution, giving himself virtually dictatorial powers, and made an unusually emotional appeal for support from the French public.

> In the face of the misfortune which looms over the country and of the threat that hangs over the Republic...I have decided to put into force Article 16 of the Constitution. As of today, I will take, if necessary directly, the measures that will appear to me to be required by the circumstances.
>
> In this way, I confirm myself in the French and republican legality which was conferred upon me by the nation and which I will maintain no matter what happens until the end of my term, or until I lack either force or life...
>
> Frenchwomen, Frenchmen, help me![215]

If de Gaulle appeared somewhat more aroused than usual, many in the government were in panic about their obvious incapacity to resist an invasion by well-equipped, combat-ready units from Algeria. After de Gaulle's speech, Prime Minister Debré appeared on national television to announce that the insurrectionary generals intended to launch an airborne assault on Paris. Somewhat pathetically, he asked Parisians to mass themselves at the airfields to convince the paratroopers of the error of their ways. Although Communist demands that weapons be distributed en masse to the civilian population were refused, reservists were called up and fifteen hundred UNR militants, Resistance veterans, and other volunteers were organized as an emergency militia.

By Monday, April 24, it was clear the revolt would fail. Around the country, Vigilance Committees formed, uniting representatives of all political parties (except the Indépendants) in opposition to the revolt.[216] A nationwide, extraordinarily effective, one-hour general strike showed how massive was popular opposition to the insurgents. Navy, air force, and even many professional army officers had remained loyal or at least stayed on the sidelines long enough to let de Gaulle's resolute words take effect. Transport planes intended to carry the invasion force were instead flown empty from Algeria to bases in southern France. Most soldiers in Algeria refused to accept orders issued by officers identifying with the putsch. Impressed by de Gaulle's authoritative claim to their loyalty, the *contingent* (the nonprofessional army) ignored Challe's promise that draftees would be sent home, to be replaced by a reconstituted pied noir militia. All over Algeria, war-weary conscripts engaged in sit-down strikes, slowdowns, and other forms of largely nonviolent resistance to the efforts of the putsch-ists. The next day Challe surrendered. Zeller was arrested ten days later. The First Paratroop Regiment was returned to its base and disbanded.[217] Salan, Jouhaud, and other ultras went underground.

Aftermath: The Algerian Problem Relocated

Within a month after the collapse of the putsch, public peace talks between France and the FLN began in Evian. Although officially suspended in July, the negotiations proceeded in secret, amid French threats to par-tition Algeria, or withold economic assistance, or both. But de Gaulle was bluffing. While his negotiators were seeking to retain control of the Sahara, or at least privileged access to its natural resources, and to secure firm guarantees for the rights, political representation, and property of the pieds noirs, substantial numbers of French troops were already being withdrawn. The Algerian nationalists remained adamant. Gradually the French gov-ernment gave up its demands. In February 1962, agreement was reached on the terms of transition to an independent and united Algeria. A cease-fire went into effect on March 19, 1962. Referendums, in France in April 1962 and in Algeria in July 1962, gave overwhelming approval to the treaty. On July 3, de Gaulle formally recognized the sovereign Republic of Algeria.

The two sides were drawn toward each other by an intensive OAS campaign of terror, in both France and Algeria, and against Muslims and European supporters of de Gaulle's government. From the summer of 1961 to June 1962, the OAS killed 2,360 people in Algeria and wounded another 5,418. Daily bombings, repeated assassination attempts, and other acts of terrorism spread. Combined with counterterrorism by the FLN, and severe repression of demonstrations and disturbances in Algeria and in France, the OAS campaign made the last year of the war an unnerving one in France and the bloodiest of all in Algeria's largest cities.[218]

Throughout this period Algeria remained a highly salient issue in French political life, but in the months following the putsch attempt it was obvious that the scale of the disruption which French political elites anticipated would accompany disengagement from Algeria had changed. In terms of the diagram presented in the Appendix as Figure A-3, the Algerian problem was now located near point I, where only incumbent-level threats were present, rather than around point H, where regime threats were highly salient. The regime threshold, in other words, had been crossed in the state-contracting direction. Now policies would be implemented at higher or lower costs; de Gaulle and other Fifth Republic politicians would emerge with more or less credit and clout in "post-Algeria" political comptetition; but the regime was no longer perceived to be in danger. No matter how vicious OAS terrorism was, and how completely its fugitive leadership rejected the legitimacy of the treaty signed in March 1962, few French politicians entertained seriously the possibility that the fanatics of the OAS and their killer squads of Delta Commandos, or even Bidault and Soustelle (both of whom, in exile, defended the OAS), were capable of putting the stability of the Fifth Republic at risk.

Once again de Gaulle conducted a purge of army officers suspected of disloyalty or reluctance to abide by the government's unfolding Algerian policy. This time, however, the purges were not accomplished by transfers, affectations of presidential approval, or "promotions." The trials of the Barricades defendants had been long and involved, with only one officer prosecuted; he was acquitted. After the failed putsch of April 1961, however, de Gaulle used the full powers of article 16 to ensure quick trials and harsh punishment for the rebellious military men. Fifteen generals and more than two hundred other officers were imprisoned. Challe and Zeller each received fifteen-year sentences. Those who had gone underground were condemned to death in absentia.[219]

Despite the intensity of OAS terror, de Gaulle was now confident that the war of maneuver was over, that residual support within the army for another putsch attempt was insufficient to pose a realistic threat, and that the OAS could be dealt with as a police and not a political problem. Referring to the failed putsch in his memoirs, de Gaulle observed: "The collapse of this escapade henceforth rid men's minds of the specter of an Army move to take over the State or at least force it to maintain the status quo in Algeria."[220]

The disappearance of credible threats to the regime and the qualitative change in his government's evaluation of the political landscape associated with it were reflected in de Gaulle's decision, after April 1961, *not* to travel to Algeria to feel the pulse of the officer corps or reassure it against the worst of its suspicions. This decision contrasts sharply with the pattern of his visits to Algeria for these purposes in July 1958, following the insurrection that brought him to power; in August 1959, before announcing his self-determination policy; and in March 1960, following the Barricades Rebellion. To make the point of the army's political subordination as clear as possible, de Gaulle summoned to Strasbourg, in November 1961, four thousand officers from throughout France and Algeria. In his address to the assembled officers, de Gaulle removed all shading and ambiguity from his intention to grant independence to Algeria.[221] He scolded them for thinking that it was ever possible to "make things be what one desires and the contrary of what they are." The army had important national missions in Europe and the world, but it had no political role whatsoever. "When the state and the nation have chosen the way," he concluded, "military duty is clear. Outside these limits there can be only—there are only—lost soldiers."[222]

With the army removed from the antiregime struggle, the European settlers of Algeria, who for a century had been at the center of policy determination and political competition over the fate of Algeria, and who in the aftermath of the April revolt gave effective and outspoken support to the OAS, also ceased to be an important factor in the political equation that de Gaulle, his ministers, and his advisers were seeking to solve.[223] Whether OAS terrorism weakened the French bargaining position (by undermining efforts to secure meaningful guarantees for the European population) or strengthened it (by convincing the FLN that only a negotiated settlement would give them control of the whole country), the weight of OAS influence could be measured on the margin. Few if any metropolitan observers suggested it could prevent an agreement or effectively challenge the legitimacy of France's decision to disengage.[224]

Even the pieds noirs came to recognize this reality. The OAS still enjoyed broad and enthusiastic support in the European neighborhoods of Oran and Algiers. By fall 1961, however, Europeans in Algeria valued OAS efforts not because they seriously thought a new regime might be established in Paris, but because they hoped to achieve a better bargaining position with the future nationalist government of Algeria. Others imagined a coastal strip between Algiers and Oran emerging suddenly as a kind of pied noir South Africa, or Israel.[225] In any case, before the referendum on independence the OAS itself abandoned the struggle. In April 1962 Salan was arrested. On June 1 a truce went into effect—a truce reached through direct negotiations between the Algiers branch of the OAS and the FLN.

After April 1961, one of the only politicians in France who still spoke as if the Fifth Republic was in danger of a right-wing takeover was Pierre Mendès-France. Since the Barricades Rebellion he had castigated de Gaulle for not moving faster toward Algerian independence. Beginning in September 1961, he sought to make a political comeback by declaring de Gaulle incapable of making peace, denouncing the "Algerianization" of France by OAS terrorism, and predicting the near-term collapse of the Fifth Republic and the departure of de Gaulle from the political scene. Mendès-France therefore advocated establishing an "interim government." His otherwise sympathetic biographer observes that this Quixotic campaign for "a democratic succession to the collapsing Fifth Republic" produced "widespread surprise.... Cassandra had never been in better form; his arguments had never seemed more striking; and the facts had never managed so wickedly to contradict him."[226]

Indeed, far from being preoccupied with the danger of a collapsing regime, Socialist, Radical, and Independent politicians complained that de Gaulle was exaggerating the danger to the republic in order to maintain article 16's provisions in force and thereby prevent Parliament from expressing dissatisfaction with many of the government's policies. Early in 1961, Mollet declared the Socialist party's unwillingness to participate in a Gaullist government, "except, of course, if the nation or the Republic was subject to a mortal threat."[227] Compared to Mollet's position from late 1957 to the end of 1960, when he advocated Socialist participation in government coalitions precisely because republican regimes were thought to be threatened, this position shows that in 1961 he perceived the Fifth Republic was no longer at risk. Mollet and the Socialists did rally to de Gaulle during the putsch and did support the invocation of article 16. But once they considered the crisis to have passed (late June or early July), they demanded its provisions be lifted. By the end of 1961 and early 1962, the SFIO was engaged in a full-scale effort to rouse the left toward creating an alternative to a Gaullist government—within the institutions, however, of the Fifth Republic. Such oppositional activities, and a general "invigoration" of political parties observed by *L'Année Politique* in the second half of 1961, indicate the substitution of incumbent-level concerns for regime concerns on the agendas of French political elites.[228]

Although de Gaulle judged the "regime crisis" which justified article 16's invocation to have passed much earlier, it was not until late September that the article's application was finally lifted. By then, explained de Gaulle in a speech on October 3, the alarm associated with the events of April "appeared to have died down." In fact by late September, intensifying resentments in the Assembly endangered the continuation of the Debré government. These *incumbent-level* interests convinced de Gaulle to acquiesce in demands for an end to article 16's enforcement.[229] Complicating an analysis of this period, however, one of these interests was the political benefit de Gaulle derived from a general perception of the situation as posing a choice between himself, on the one hand, and chaos, on the other.

De Gaulle alluded to this chaos as either the violent disorder evoked by OAS outrages or the political disorder (associated with the Fourth Republic) which would be unleashed if, in his stead, the jealous competition of political parties was again allowed to become the center of French political life. De Gaulle's continued use of this rhetorical device and his exploitation of public apprehensions engendered by a series of failed assassination attempts met with increasing exasperation from politicians anxious to compete for influence within the institutions of the Fifth Republic and disadvantaged by what they now considered an *artifically* constructed view of the regime in danger—the choice of de Gaulle or chaos.[230]

Conclusion

In this chapter I have examined the difficulty experienced by successive French governments in translating generalized desires to be rid of the Algerian incubus into policies that could be sustained by risking governments and careers rather than regimes. Explaining how this transition was accomplished, in comparison to the British-Irish case, is the task of the next chapter, but a subsidiary question can be answered now. An apparent discrepancy exists between the historical burden of the Algerian problem for France, and the apathy with which the problem's denouement was experienced. In view of the length of the struggle in Algeria and the horror of its conclusion, many observers have commented on how mild was metropolitan reaction was to France's final departure from the country, and how suddenly and completely the Algerian problem vanished from French political life.[231] Similar observations have been made in connection with the virtual disappearance of the Irish question from British politics after the implementation of the Anglo-Irish treaty and the Irish government's victory (with British assistance) in the Irish Civil War in May 1923.[232] These discrepancies are explainable by what both Chapters 6 and 7 have shown, that in each case the decisive transformation occurred when the problem was relocated across the regime threshold, not when disengagement per se was accomplished. In each case the forces necessary to accomplish the prior change in the scale of the problem were so much larger than those required to formulate and enforce an actual decision to disengage that the process of disengagement itself, however bloody and costly, was *politically* anticlimactic.

The Evian agreement reached between the French government and the FLN was approved virtually without debate by both the French cabinet and the Parliament in February 1962. In an April 8 national referendum on granting independence to Algeria, 91 percent of French people casting valid ballots approved. Two weeks later de Gaulle marked the end of one political era and the beginning of another by replacing Prime Minister Michel Debré (whose credentials as an Algerian ultra had helped de Gaulle fight and win his war of maneuver) with a technocrat—Georges Pompidou. The reemergence of incumbent-level competition was illustrated by the resignation of Pflimlin, Schumann, and three other MRP ministers on an issue having nothing to do with Algeria.[233] Six months later the National Assembly demonstrated its own recognition that "normal" political struggles could now be joined, without fearing for the collapse of the regime, by voting the Pompidou government out of office on the first successful motion of censure to be advanced since the establishment of the Fifth Republic.

But if political life was returning to "normal" in France, Algeria, in the months prior to independence, plunged toward anarchy. The significance of the Algerian problem in metropolitan French politics, from a regime-threatening to an "ordinary" incumbent-level issue, is unmistakably evident in 1962 in the political marginality of levels of violence and disorder among the pieds noirs which far exceeded those that shook the Fifth Republic in January 1960. In a desperate effort to elicit Muslim reprisals that might force France to abandon the treaty, the OAS unleashed a hurricane of violence. During this period it was not unusual for twenty or more civilians to be killed in a single day's collection of shootings and bombings. In response to direct and repeated OAS attacks on French soldiers, the army undertook an unprecedentedly brutal crackdown on pied-noir neighborhoods concealing OAS operatives. In Algiers, on March 23, twenty thousand French troops, using heavy machineguns, tanks, and strafing fighter planes, attacked the pied noir neighborhood of Bab-el-Oued. A violent siege continued for three days until the area was subdued. Fifteen soldiers were killed and 70 wounded. The known casualties among neighborhood residents were 20 killed and 80 wounded. On March 26th, the OAS sponsored a march in defiance of the government's ban on Algiers demonstrations. Shots fired by OAS provocateurs against jittery French troops triggered a massacre. At least 65 European men, women, and children were killed or fatally wounded in the fusillade; 200 more were injured. As Algerian independence approached, the OAS shifted to a scorched earth policy, deliberately destroying as much valuable property and public facilities as possible. In April and May a massive exodus of pieds noirs began, leading to the resettlement of almost eight hundred thousand of them in metropolitan France. The French departure also resulted in the slaughter of tens of thousands of Muslim *harkis* by vengeful nationalists.

Despite these bloody upheavals, in which many more French citizens were killed by Frenchmen than in 1958, 1960, and 1961 combined, implementation of de Gaulle's policy of separation from Algeria proceeded without concern for the integrity of the regime. A state-contracting threshold effect is thus apparent in the sudden and drastically less serious disruption within France associated with government responses to extra-constitutional mobilization in Algeria.

CHAPTER EIGHT

Regimes at Risk: Rescaling the Irish and Algerian Questions in Britain and France

Wars of position are fought over beliefs and expectations that can enshrine and protect the legality of regimes and the governing coalitions that rise to power within them. Wars of maneuver are fought over the nature of these regimes, especially the stipulated rules for legal political competition and control of the mechanisms for their enforcement. Struggles in Britain and France surrounding the ideological hegemony threshold were struggles over beliefs and expectations determining whether and in what form the "questions" of Ireland and Algeria would emerge onto metropolitan political agendas. These were described in Chapters 3 and 4 as wars of position. Chapter 5 then drew on Gramsci's observations about the determinants of such struggles to guide comparative analysis of the two cases.

From 1912 to 1914 in Britain, and from 1958 to 1961 in France, violence or threats of violence, by settlers and important segments of the metropolitan political class, countenanced or supported by substantial elements within the military, led governing elites to be more concerned with the stability of their respective regimes than with the future of their particular governments. In Chapters 6 and 7 these struggles, surrounding passage of the regime threshold in the state-contracting direction, were described as wars of maneuver. Parallel to Chapter 5's discussion of wars of position, this chapter is devoted to the comparative analysis of these wars of maneuver, seeking as far as possible to establish plausible explanations for similarities and differences. A central argument is that de Gaulle's relatively high-risk, big-stake strategy for crossing the regime threshold had dramatically different consequences for France and for French disengagement from Algeria than did the low-risk, less ambitious strategies chosen by Asquith, and adhered to by Lloyd George, for Britain and for British disengagement from Ireland.

Analyzing Wars of Maneuver

Despite his close involvement in Communist party politics, Gramsci's intellectual interest was focused much more saliently on the role of hegemonic ideas and the "organic crises" surrounding their construction and breakdown than on "assault" operations, to seize or protect state power, associated with wars of maneuver. Questions of intellectual taste aside, it must be remembered that most of Gramsci's theoretical writing was done while confined in Mussolini's prisons (following that political entrepreneur's own successful war of movement against the liberal Italian state). Presumably Gramsci was more constrained by prison censorship from writing about mechanisms to overthrow established regimes than about the latent political function of different forms of consciousness. The scattered comments he does make on wars of maneuver are somewhat confused. At times Gramsci characterizes them as preceding wars of position. At other points the overthrow of hegemony is seen to set the stage for the seizure of state power.[1]

Although Gramsci provides no coherent theory of wars of maneuver, the very notion of sequence, in the relationship between struggles over regimes and struggles over presumptive conceptions designed to protect those regimes, is of tremendous importance. In Gramsci's scheme such struggles divide the histories of states into stages dominated by different forms of political competition.[2] Focused on one key dimension of political conflict—the boundaries of the state—the two-threshold, three-stage model used in this study envisions the possibility of moving *either* from a war of position to a war of movement (e.g., British struggles over Ireland from 1834–43 to 1912–14) or from a war of movement to a war of position (e.g., the intent of Algérie française partisans after they successfully overthrew the Fourth Republic in 1958).

The most fruitful of Gramsci's comments about wars of maneuver pertain to what he characterizes as "Caesarist" or "Bonapartist" strategies and the patterns of authority associated with them. "Caesarism," according to Gramsci, tends to emerge during those "historico-political situations" when forces in conflict "balance each other in a catastrophic manner." Under such circumstances, during a "struggle to constitute (or reconstitute) an organic equilibrium," and when the overthrow of constituted authority and even civil war are threatened, "a great personality is entrusted with the task of 'arbitration.' "[3] Although coalition governments can adopt an essentially Caesarist strategy (i.e., one that bases claims to authority on overarching appeals for national salvation and unity), Gramsci suggests that such coalitions typically produce or fall victim to some "great, 'heroic,' and representative personality."[4] Thus conceived, Caesarism can be viewed as a strategy for avoiding or ending a war of movement. In that context it can be understood as a technique for moving "backward" across the regime threshold—transforming a regime-threatening problem into an incumbent-level concern.

Keeping in mind the roles played by Lloyd George and de Gaulle, we see that in both the British-Irish and French-Algerian cases, Caesarist elements were prominent in the negotiation of the regime threshold, the implementation of disengagement policies, and the stabilization of relations between metropolitan cores and historically subordinated territories. This accords with conventional views that democratic states require strong or charismatic leaders for the solutions of peculiarly difficult problems. But the substantial differences in outcomes between the two cases suggest the need for a more finely grained analysis of these wars of maneuver than Gramsci's Caesarist imagery can provide.

The model of state-building proposed in this study envisions a Guttman-scale process in which more fundamental levels of institutionalization are reached by passing thresholds beyond which new and qualitatively different kinds of disruption become associated with efforts to reverse the process. State contraction, in zones near but to the right of either threshold, may thus be said to involve an "unpacking" or "rescaling" of the problem—entailing "backward" movement through, or against the grain of, either threshold. In the following section, four logically distinct but not mutually exclusive mechanisms for shifting the location of regime-threatening problems to the left of the regime threshold are advanced. In addition to Gramsci's ideas, these "rescaling mechanisms" are related to concepts developed by Juan Linz in his study of democratic regimes confronted with "unsolvable problems," by Albert O. Hirschman and Samuel Huntington in their consideration of strategies used by "reform-mongering" leaders seeking to accomplish large-scale transformations, and by Gabriel Almond and his collaborators in their examination of coalition-building in crisis situations.[5] In different combinations, these mechanisms offer a satisfying account of and a partial explanation for the pattern of differences and similarities in the British and French episodes of state contraction considered in Chapters 6 and 7. The balance of the explanation is provided by comparing the choices made by leading politicians and the variation in the distribution and mobilization of resources among governing elites, settlers, metropolitan opposition groups, and nationalist rebels.

Four Rescaling Mechanisms

Decomposing the Problem

If disengagement from a particular territory raises threats to regime stability, one way to proceed toward that objective while lowering or eliminating risk to the regime is to separate either the territory or the process of disengagement into parts. By thus "decomposing" the problem, a "partial disengagement" (either temporary or permanent) might be achieved which would arouse only incumbent-level opposition. The remaining portions of the territory or the process might or might not trigger regime-level opposition to further movement toward disengagement, and might or might not be further decomposable. Regardless, however, a regime-risking showdown would be avoided, new circumstances created, and possibly useful precedents established.

Although not specified in the context of disputes over efforts to reshape the territorial extent of the state, decomposition is in effect what Huntington recommends in his analysis of "reform-mongering." He portrays elites, such as Kemal Attaturk, as fearful that direct pursuit of the comprehensive transformations they desire would produce regime-destroying opposition by alliances formed among widely divergent groups. Each of these groups, argues Huntington, might well feel sufficiently threatened by some aspect of the reform program to prefer challenging the regime to accepting the program. Therefore, as Attaturk demonstrated, reform-mongering has better chances of success if the transformational project is broken into pieces associated with discrete policy changes in specific spheres. Implemented serially (and suddenly), this "combination of a Fabian strategy with blitzkrieg tactics" is depicted by Huntington as capable of fragmenting potential opposition and defeating each segment in turn rather than forcing the "state renovator" to confront possibly overwhelming opposition from a lowest common denominator alliance.[6]

Recomposing the Regime

In Linz's analysis, "unsolvable problems," or "practically unsolvable problems," are cited as circumstances likely to threaten democratic regimes with breakdown. Indeed for Linz the very definition of an unsolvable problem is that the strain associated with it cannot be alleviated by any coalition of forces for whom loyalty to the regime takes precedence over preferred solutions to the problem.[7] Linz identifies disputes over the proper boundary of the state, and the inclusion or separation of peripheral territories, as particularly salient examples of problems liable to become "unsolvable" and to produce regime-threatening crises. But bold and perceptive leaders, he argues, can negotiate such crises and avoid regime breakdown by guiding processes of reequilibration or "regime transformation." For him, "reequilibration occurs in the presence of the readiness of the electorate to approve the regime transformation or change, an approval conditioned by trust in the new regime's capacity to solve the unsolvable problem that precipitated the final crisis."[8]

Linz's emphasis here is not on decomposing the problem, but on recomposing the regime. In his focus on the intractable balance of opposing forces leading to the threat of regime breakdown, and on the trust one must place in leaders of a redesigned regime to achieve a crisis-ending solution to the previously "unsolvable problem," he echoes Gramsci's characterizations: of "forces balancing each other in a catastrophic manner" and of the tasks of reconstitution and arbitration "entrusted" to a Caesarist figure.

Recomposition of the regime is thus another possible method for crossing the state-contracting threshold, for rescaling a regime-level problem into an incumbent-level problem. The theoretical basis of such a strategy is the reconstitution of authority relations. By centralizing authority to make crucial choices and substantially restricting access to the decision process, such a reconstitution can broaden the range of policies capable of being endorsed by state institutions. Whether officially acknowledged as a change in regime or not, the stalemate produced by the domination of negative majorities can thereby be overcome. Meanwhile, risks of extralegal challenges may be more easily managed due to whatever enhanced loyalty and expectations of success the Caesarist leader can elicit, and to the mobilization of residual support among those whose fear of regime collapse or destabilization exceeds their displeasure over decisions leading to disengagement.

Change in Utility Functions

Neither problem decomposition nor regime recomposition necessarily entails change in the individual preferences of metropolitan politicians or citizens. Assuming stable preferences, problem decomposition is a strategy for changing the question to which those preferences are applied, while regime recomposition is a strategy for making the preferences of some more determinative than those of others. But people can and do change their minds. Impressive events or persuasive arguments can strip an "unsolvable problem" of its regime-threatening aspects by effecting substantial changes in both absolute and relative preference orderings.

Gramsci's entire approach to politics is as a process of "political education," with intellectuals and "progressive" leaders providing their publics with workable assumptions about political conditions and teaching them how best to pursue their interests based on those assumptions. Likewise, though Linz describes leadership as "a residual variable," his crucial case of reequilibration (France's movement from the Fourth to the Fifth Republic) is analyzed almost wholly in terms of de Gaulle's exercise of political leadership.[9] According to Linz, people can be taught to make sensible choices, and effective democratic leaders (such as de Gaulle) are those capable of educating their supporters to lower expectations in specific areas and rearrange their preferences within an expanded structure of values.

In the British-Irish and French-Algerian cases, utility function change can be evaluated as a factor contributing to disengagement by searching for shifts by strategic groups, or in public opinion, which suggest relatively drastic changes in valuation of a British-ruled Ireland or a French-ruled Algeria.

Realigning Coalitions

The fourth rescaling mechanism presumes neither problem decomposition, regime recomposition, nor change in preferences. A situation of stalemate, whether in the midst of a regime crisis or simply in the context of ordinary, incumbent-level competition, might always be broken if one or more segments on one side of the political divide become convinced that a different set of alliances, with groups on the other side, would be a more efficacious route to their distinctive objectives. Although the polarization of political competition characteristic of wars of maneuver makes such shifts less likely than the more fluid patterns of interaction which normally prevail in democratic states, the presence of groups with strong commitments on issues orthogonal to the substantive question(s) perceived by most competitors as crucial, charismatic leadership, and/or the appearance of an overarching external threat, could provide the basis for dramatic realignments.

In *Crisis, Choice, and Change,* Gabriel Almond, Scott Flanagan, Robert

Mundt, and their collaborators seek patterns in the progress and outcome of political crises—patterns describable in terms of four kinds of conceptual approaches. One of these approaches is variably referred to as game theory, coalition theory, or rational choice theory.[10] Its distinctive contribution is described as the systematic appraisal of how choices among possible winning coalitions can influence the outcome of regime-threatening crises. By distinguishing winning coalitions from potential, effective, or preferred coalitions and by emphasizing the impact of polarization during crisis situations on choices among potentially winning coalitions, scenarios of "depolarization" and crisis resolution can be mapped.[11]

Brian Barry's detailed consideration of this work suggests that when two complementary coalitions each represent possibly winning coalitions, civil war is threatened. Using language which corresponds closely to Gramsci's description of the stalemate between opposing blocs likely to produce wars of maneuver, Barry asserts that a polity wherein such an alignment prevails can no longer be considered "operationally constitutional."[12]

In wars of maneuver over possible disengagement from closely held peripheral territories, formation of a stronger new "winning coalition" would not eliminate risks of regime breakdown. As with regime recomposition, however, an appropriate coalition realignment would make it more likely that governing elites favoring disengagement would not be deterred from attempts to cross the state-contraction threshold by pursuing decisive policies.

Crossing the Regime Threshold in Britain and France

The Ulster Crisis and the Decomposition of the Irish Question

In 1912 and 1913, Churchill had been among those ministers most desirous of accepting the decomposition of the Irish problem as a means of avoiding a regime crisis. As that crisis reached its climax in March 1914, he was the leader of those seeking to sharpen it as a means of destroying the political base of the antiregime coalition. Churchill's turnabout corresponded to a similar movement in Lloyd George's thinking. At a closely guarded dinner meeting in November 1913, Lloyd George had proposed to four key members of the cabinet—Asquith, Crewe, Haldane, and Grey— the *temporary* exclusion of heavily Protestant Ulster counties. The purpose of this serial decomposition strategy was to "knock all moral props from under Carson's rebellion, and either make it impossible for Ulster to take up arms, or if they did, put us in a strong position with British public opinion when we came to suppress it."[13]

Asquith's March 9 proposal for a six-year exclusion amendment (an option to be exercised by any county choosing, in a plebiscite, to do so) was perfectly consistent with this strategy. Clearly it was an attempt to isolate Milner, Bonar Law, Carson, Craig, and the UVF from the sympathy of British public opinion by removing from the establishment of a Home Rule Parliament in Dublin the drama of physically having to overcome loyalist resistance in Ulster. Warnings of resistance were made to appear all the more unreasonable, and illegitimate, because such appeals for spilling British blood would pertain to a situation (automatic inclusion within the jurisdiction of the Dublin Parliament) not due to arise until after two national elections would allow the arrangement to be scuttled by a new government. When Carson took the bait by refusing the offer out of hand, the government, or at least Churchill, Seely, and other members of the cabinet's Irish Committee, thought the time had arrived for decisive action.

This was the setting for Churchill's March 14 speech at Bradford in which he sought to rally public opinion in preparation for a violent showdown over home rule in Ireland. Churchill began by portraying Asquith's offer for a six-year exclusion as more than any opponent of Irish home rule could legitimately demand of a government legally empowered to enforce home rule over the entire island.

> What are we to say of persons, professing to be serious, who are ready, so they tell us, to shed the blood of their fellow men, all because they won't take the trouble to walk into the polling-booth and mark a voting paper?
> . . . After this offer has been made any unconstitutional action by Ulster can only wear . . . the aspect of unprovoked aggression, and I am sure and certain that the first British soldier or coastguard, bluejacket, or Royal Irish Constabulary man who is attacked and killed by an Orangeman will raise an explosion in this country (cheers) of a kind they little appreciate or understand, and will shake to its very foundations the basis and structure of society.[14]

Churchill cast Ulster Protestants and their die-hard British supporters as violent, dangerous men, engaged in a "treasonable conspiracy" to defy British democracy, wreck British institutions, and kill British soldiers for their narrow and fanatic beliefs. Faced with such a challenge, and in defense of the supremacy of the will of Parliament, the government, declared Churchill, was willing to shed a good deal of Ulster Protestant blood: "Bloodshed, gentlemen, no doubt is lamentable. I have seen some of it— more perhaps than many of those who talk about it with such levity. (Hear, hear.) But there are worse things than bloodshed, even on an extreme scale."[15]

In terms of the four rescaling mechanisms presented above, the strategy developed by Lloyd George and articulated by Churchill employed serial decomposition as a tactical device to shape the dimensions of a regime crisis—a crisis that would be exploited rather than avoided. The key element in this strategy, however, was not problem decomposition but the mobilization of new political resources to be made available by the regime crisis itself. These resources, in the form of widespread "patriotic" support for national institutions and British soldiers under fire, and fear of continuing civil and economic dislocations, would be used to construct a Caesarist bloc—a realignment of political forces based on change in the kind of preferences the British public (including large numbers of Conservative party voters) would perceive as relevant to judging government efforts to contract the state. "Mr. Bonar Law says in effect if there is civil war in Ulster it will spread to England too," Churchill stated. I agree with him. I go further. Once resort is had to violence by the leaders of a great British party Ulster and Ulster's affairs will dwindle to comparative insignificance." Thus would the regime crisis be used as an opportunity to redefine the issue in the mind of the British public, to encourage the substitution of higher-order preferences for whatever specific sympathies Britons might have for "kith and kin" in Ulster.

> This will be the issue—whether civil and Parliamentary government in these realms is to be beaten down by the menace of armed force. Whatever sympathies we have for Ulster we need have no compunction here. It is the old battle-ground of English history. It is the issue fought out 250 years ago on the field of Marston Moor. From the language which is employed it would almost seem that we are face to face with a disposition on the part of some sections of the proprietary classes to subvert Parliamentary government, and to challenge all the civil and constitutional foundations of society. Against such a mood, wherever it manifests itself in action, there is no lawful measure from which the Government should shrink, and there is no lawful measure from which this Government will shrink.[16]

Churchill intended to follow up this speech with arrests and troop movements that would provoke UVF violence and set the stage for a military crackdown in Ulster. If substantial resistance was offered, political and legal justification would exist for the forcible dissolution of the UVF and its British support groups, accompanied by prosecution on charges of sedition of Carson, Milner, Bonar Law, and others. From heros and respected political leaders, they would be reduced to criminals. It was a risky strategy. It meant calling the bluff of the antidisengagement coalition, raising real and pervasive fears of violent disorder, and then using those fears to reduce British sympathy for demands that Ulster be given special treatment based on the "loyalty" of its Protestant Unionist inhabitants. If the strategy was successful, home rule would have an excellent chance of being effected over the whole of Ireland. If unsuccessful, the strategy would result in bloody confrontation, a divided army, and an open-ended struggle over the integrity of the post–Parliament Act constitutional order. The record shows that these were not risks Asquith was prepared to run.

Asquith at least tentatively endorsed some version of this strategy, but backed away from it when confronted with evidence of army unrest. He had appointed General Nevil Macready as, in effect, military governor of Belfast. Macready was known for his effective use of troops to quell disturbances among striking miners and for his antipathy toward the Ulster Unionist movement. Asquith also presided over meetings at the War Office of Churchill's cabinet subcommittee on Ireland, during which the coming confrontation was discussed in detail. As a result of these meetings, orders were issued for the dispatch of three battalions into Ulster, despite clear warnings from Paget (commander in chief in Ireland) that serious trouble in Ulster would result, including UVF attempts to prevent the railroads from being used to carry his soldiers. Paget was promised "as many troops as he needed 'even to the last man,' " while Churchill offered naval transport as an alternative to the railroads. Indeed, whether or not Asquith was aware of it, as first lord of the admiralty Churchill was deploying a fleet not only for logistical purposes or intimidation, but also for bombardment of Ulster fortifications.[17]

Instead of gambling on the army's loyalty and the ability of his government to rally public opinion, Asquith retreated. As reported in Chapter 6, the prime minister responded to the resignation of the Curragh officers, and to threats of disobedience elsewhere in the military, by in effect renouncing armed force to impose the terms of the Home Rule Bill on Ulster. The question of whether Churchill's strategy would have worked cannot be answered definitively. However reluctant the officers at the Curragh were to obey orders that would likely have led to bloodshed in Ulster, the incident could well have been handled in a way that would have preserved military options against the UVF.[18]

By preserving ambiguities, reinterpreting proposals, and avoiding decisive engagements, Asquith displayed his mastery of the British political game as played in the halls of Parliament and around the cabinet table.[19] Although unsurpassed in the subtle shadings of incumbent-level partisanship, Asquith was incapable of rousing the public with dramatic gestures or clear-cut propositions, and was unprepared for the bold strokes and high risks associated with wars of maneuver.[20] His subsequent failure to inspire the British public, organize the national economy on a war footing, or bring quarreling generals to heel over policy on the western front led to his fall from the premiership in the middle of the First World War. In retrospect, his shortcomings as a leader of a nation at war suggest how thoroughly inappropriate Asquith was, personally, for the role in which he was cast by Churchill's Irish strategy in March 1914. Instead it was Churchill, ordered to return the navy ships he had assembled to their bases and call off his plans for a systematic investment of Ulster, who was required to play a role defined by Asquith—that of misunderstood minister—indignantly denying there ever existed a "pogrom plot" against Ulster and repudiating the "hellish insinuation" that his purely precautionary steps had been designed as a deliberate provocation.[21]

The Basis of De Gaulle's Caesarist Strategy

A Recomposed Regime. The Constituent Assembly's opposition to de Gaulle's constitutional views (and to the advantages he would enjoy within a system designed according those views) was so intense that early in 1946 de Gaulle resigned as head of the provisional government and withdrew from ordinary political competition. As most expected, the Fourth Republic Constitution systematically benefited the existing political parties. Thanks to proportional representation and complex arrangements governing runoffs in fragmented constituencies, parties able to gain a small but significant percentage of the national vote were assured of representation in the Assembly. The Assembly itself was empowered to choose both the prime minister and the president. The president was a figurehead, but even the prime minister's powers were severely limited. Legislation proposed by the government was amended if not redrafted by parliamentary committees before its discussion on the floor. Both the prime minister and his cabinet were creatures of the Assembly—elected to it, approved by it, and subject to sudden dismissal following a failed vote of confidence. The institutional superiority of the Assembly over the government was expressed in the fact that it could dismiss one government and form another without calling new parliamentary elections.

As shown in Chapter 7, the result of this system was a fractionated Parliament and a series of short-lived governments based on negative majorities, most of which were incapable of sustaining bold initiatives in controversial areas, especially toward the most difficult problem of all—the future of Algeria. The shortcomings of the constitution were widely acknowledged. Attempts to strengthen the executive and rein in the power of the Assembly were made by every prime minister, from Mendès-France to Pflimlin. But one consequence of the system as established by the 1946 constitution was the inability of each of these governments (with the interesting but irrelevant exception of Pflimlin's three-week ministry) to agree on the specifics of any one constitutional reform project. As a result, every one of the attempts between 1954 and 1958 to reform the constitution— to achieve a partial recomposition of the regime—failed.[22]

Instead of a partial regime recomposition, which might have alleviated some of the pressure on Fourth Republic institutions, tensions accumulated, leading to the crisis of 1958, the collapse of the Fourth Republic, and a redesign of Republican institutions which accomplished a radical rearrangement of the regime.[23] The constitution of the Fifth Republic, drafted by de Gaulle's closest advisers, accomplished a massive shift of authority from the Assembly to the government, especially the president. Elected by a college of local and regional notables (changed to direct election by universal suffrage in October 1962), the president (not the Assembly) was empowered both to choose and dismiss the prime minister and, once every twelve months, to dissolve Parliament. All powers not specifically delegated to Parliament were reserved for the government, which meant, in effect, the president. Centralization of power was also achieved by constitutional provisions requiring the Assembly to debate the government version of bills, enabling promulgation of government-supported legislation unless opposed by an absolute majority of the Assembly, permitting the president to appeal directly to the people through referenda of his own choosing, and allowing the president, in times identified by him as national emergencies, to rule by decree. Parliamentary influence was further reduced, and the cabinet's reliance on the president further reinforced, by the rule that neither the prime minister nor any other minister could hold seats in the Assembly.[24]

Against the background of the collapsing Fourth Republic, France's embrace of a strong leader and a centralized authority system is often cited as an instance of Bonapartism. Indeed the rise of a Caesarist figure in times of great national distress or deep divisions is a recurring theme in French history. The first and second empires were both constructed around such men—Napoléon Bonaparte and Napoléon III. Clemenceau played this role during World War I; both Pétain and de Gaulle did so in World War II. But the man on the white horse has not always succeeded. In 1887, General Georges Boulanger failed in his effort to translate popularity as a military leader into the overthrow the Third Republic. In 1934, ex-President Gaston Doumergue was put forward, with only limited success, as a "national arbiter" who might steer France clear of the catastrophe that violent clashes between right and left seemed to portend.

One crucial factor in de Gaulle's Caesarist success was his cultivation of a crisis disruptive enough to make comprehensive regime recomposition possible. Alexander Werth draws an instructive comparison between Doumergue's brief attempt to transform the Third Republic into a presidential-style regime and de Gaulle's experience as founder and ruler of the Fifth Republic. In February 1934 the elderly Doumergue was called upon, following severe riots in Paris, as a symbol of "national reconciliation." He agreed to form a government. Once installed, he and some of his ministers thought to at least partially recompose the Third Republic—to increase executive power and reduce tensions between left and right by shifting authority from the Assembly, and the cabinets it produced, to the presidency. But the proportions of the crisis that had brought him to power were not large enough to create fears capable of displacing the partisan oppositions Domergue intended to stifle. Doumergue's government was soon toppled by an "anti-fascist" alliance of Socialists and Communists who went on to win power in 1936 under the banner of the Popular Front.[25] Werth comments that unlike Doumergue, who was ready "to be used as a mere expedient to relieve the temporary headache of the Republic," de Gaulle waited for a crisis of much greater proportions to materialize. In that context he could expect and was granted "a free hand to 'rebuild the State,' "[26] thereby enabling the charismatic potential of his Caesarist figure to be realized.

Notwithstanding his shrewdness, sense of timing, and tactical flexibility, it is de Gaulle's charisma that virtually all observers have regarded as the sine qua non of his success as the founder of the Fifth Republic and the engineer of France's separation of Algeria. His adroit and highly personal appeals for public support in the midst of the 1960 and 1961 crises showed de Gaulle superbly qualified to play the Caesarist role his regime had been designed to assign him. We have seen in Chapter 7, however, that his qualities of leadership were not politically relevant; indeed they hardly seemed present as a factor in French political life until the regime crisis of 1957–58 sharpened French frustrations with the inadequacies of the Fourth Republic, prompting fears of both chaos and fascism.

In fact it was not only the severity of the crisis bringing him to power, but the new rules for political competition enforced within the recomposed regime, which unleashed the political potential of de Gaulle's charismatic appeal to masses of French people.[27] In his preface to Alfred Grosser's 1965 study of foreign policy under the Fifth Republic, Stanley Hoffmann noted how different Grosser's examination of this topic was from his earlier investigation of foreign policy under the Fourth Republic. Grosser's study of the Fifth Republic's foreign policy, Hoffmann observed, "does not contain a systematic analysis of the political forces: parties, institutions, pressure groups, press, etc. The reason is obvious: foreign policy under the Fourth Republic was the product of a complex bargaining process; foreign policy in the Fifth Republic is the expression of one man's vision, will, and statecraft."[28]

The institutional structure within which French foreign policy in general, and French policy toward Algeria in particular, could be transformed as Hoffmann describes was the product of the 1958 constitution. The pattern of authority relations it helped bring about corresponded closely to the way de Gaulle had wanted power to be organized in the regime founded in 1946. It is no exaggeration to describe the Fifth Republic as a polity organized to make de Gaulle's skills and those resources which he commanded, especially the trust and diffuse support of wide sectors of metropolitan public opinion, relatively more important than the resources commanded by his political opponents (coherent party organizations, the ability to launch coup attempts, and the capacity to put tens of thousands of violent demonstrators into the streets of Paris and Algiers).

Serial Decomposition, Realignment, and Pedagogy in the Fifth Republic. If the institutional transformation of the French state that is connoted by the term "regime recomposition" was a necessary condition for France to leave Algeria, that is, for the strategic contraction of the French state, it was certainly not sufficient. Centralization of state authority meant that policies designed to support Algérie française could have been as well protected from metropolitan opposition as were disengagement-oriented policies. After all, the idea of a *pur and dur* regime as well as the return to power of a strong leader (de Gaulle) were favored by the colonels, the ultras of Algiers, and Soustellian Gaullists precisely because these partisans of Algérie française believed a more authoritarian political regimen was necessary to marginalize antiwar sentiment (in the press and in Parliament) and bring the conflict in Algeria to an integrationist conclusion. Michel Debré, who served as justice minister in de Gaulle's government from June to December 1958, and as prime minister, from 1959 to 1962, as well as General de Beaufort, de Gaulle's chief adviser on military affairs until his resignation during Barricades week, were both ardent proponents of Algérie française.

Explaining both the relocation of the Algerian problem across the regime threshold and the implementation of a withdrawal policy requires consideration of how de Gaulle exploited the opportunities created by regime recomposition to move France toward disengagement from Algeria rather than to revitalize efforts to incorporate it. This, in turn, requires analysis of de Gaulle's subsidiary use of the other rescaling mechanisms: realignment, utility function change, and (serial) decomposition.

De Gaulle backed away (several times) from decisively confronting his opponents over attempts to cross the regime threshold. His decision to avoid a showdown with Massu, Salan, and Soustelle in the second half of 1958, his reassurances to military commanders in October 1959 (which helped prevent Operation Veronique from coming to fruition), and his tour of the officers' messes in March 1960 (following the Barricades Rebellion) were calculated retreats. But these retreats were tactical, not strategic. At no point did de Gaulle, as Asquith did in summer 1914, forswear the use of state power as a means of enforcing state contraction. Each of his retreats was followed by substantially more explicit and "advanced" formulations of his intentions toward Algeria. The climax of this process was reached in April 1961, when a direct collision with the military high command resulted in the relocation of the Algerian question across the regime threshold.

This interpretation of de Gaulle's strategy requires a view of his leadership as more Machiavellian than empirical, as based, for all its tactical flexibility, on a deliberate plan to end France's rule over all of Algeria— a plan whose main outlines, at least, must have been relatively clear to de Gaulle himself in 1958.[29] Although in his memoirs de Gaulle portrays himself as having had "no strictly pre-determined plan" as to "the precise details, the phasing and timing of the solution," he describes "the main outlines" as having been "clear in my mind"—negotiations based on battlefield successes, acceptance of the principle of Algerian national self-determination, and abandonment of Algérie française as a "ruinous utopia." According to this formulation, his aspirations for Algeria had been reduced to a vague "hope." He "hoped to ensure that, in the sense in which France had always remained in some degree Roman ever since the days of Gaul, the Algeria of the future... would in many respects remain French."[30]

As de Gaulle well knew, in 1958 an Algeria as French as France still was "Roman" was not what partisans of Algérie française had in mind when they demanded "de Gaulle au pouvoir."[31] Accordingly, in his memoirs de Gaulle also portrayed himself as aware of the need to camouflage his ultimate intentions until his regime was solidly established, until *military* victories over the FLN had been achieved, and until processes of political education in France had reached fruition. Once his political supremacy over the army, the settlers, and metropolitan diehards had been established, domestic political criticism of "abandonment" could be isolated and overcome.

> I should have to proceed cautiously from one stage to the next. Only gradually, using each crisis as a springboard for further advance, could I hope to create a current of consent powerful enough to carry all before it. Were I to announce my intentions point-blank, there was no doubt that the sea of ignorant fear, of shocked surprise, of concerted malevolence through which I was navigating would cause such a tidal wave of alarms and passions in every walk of life that the ship would capsize.[32]

Of course such retrospective and self-serving analyses portraying de Gaulle as unusually perspicacious, not to say clairvoyant, cannot be taken at face value. What is impressive is that de Gaulle's worst detractors, those partisans of French Algeria who have reviled him for his betrayal of their dreams and his promises, agree with de Gaulle's own account, even though by doing so they are forced to admit their own lapses of judgment. Jean-Louis Tixier-Vignancour, serving as Raoul Salan's lawyer at the latter's trial for treason in 1962, described de Gaulle as having "come to power with the intention but not the strength to give Algeria its independence. Thus to arrive at the goal, he had usurped the force of Algérie française and tricked all but a handful of his closest collaborators ... by practicing his duplicitous gradualism."[33] According to Soustelle in 1962, de Gaulle had inaugurated an Algerian policy in June 1958 whose "trickery was so skilled, so gradual (at least at the beginning), camouflaged with such astuteness, that it was difficult to penetrate."[34]

In the final analysis, however empirical were de Gaulle's tactical responses to the unfolding situation, three basic elements of his Machiavellian self-description may be considered well established—his early acceptance of an open-ended process of French disengagement from Algeria, his decision to camouflage that acceptance, and his perception of the regime-challenging nature of the threats he would have to overcome before consummating the disengagement process. By serially decomposing the process of disengagement from Algeria into conceptually discrete steps, no one of which offered his opponents among the colons or within the military a politically suitable basis for mobilizing large-scale metropolitan opposition, and by preserving as long as possible the image of a leader who *might* be devoted to keeping Algeria French, de Gaulle minimized the seriousness of the challenges his opponents could raise against him.[35]

The staggered unfolding of de Gaulle's intentions toward Algeria, what Soustelle meant by de Gaulle's "duplicitous gradualism," marked de Gaulle's *tactical* use of serial decomposition to fragment a regime-threatening coalition. Its purpose was similar to that of temporarily excluding Ulster in the scheme developed by Lloyd George and Churchill in late 1913 and early 1914. By endorsing the principle of unfettered Algerian self-determination while condemning the "secession" option and promising French army "supervision" of the balloting, by prosecuting the war with full vigor while reinterpreting the meaning or importance of victory, and by exploiting public fear and distress in the midst of regime crises *operationally* precipitated by the extraconstitutional activities of his opponents, de Gaulle isolated, neutralized, and then marginalized pieds noirs, metropolitan partisans of Algérie française, and, finally, the generals.[36]

Unlike Asquith, however, de Gaulle never allowed decomposition of the process of disengagement to be replaced by decomposition of the objective of that process—withdrawal of French sovereignty from all of Algeria. Despite de Gaulle indirectly encouraging the French to think about the partition of Algeria as a possible result of his policies, the centerpiece of his strategy for state contraction was to rely on recomposing the French regime to create political conditions within which a spatially undecomposed Algerian problem could be relocated across the regime threshold, and then solved. Those political conditions were a major realignment of French political competition, featuring a dominant centrist party whose internal unity was *not* based on uniformity of opinion about Algeria, and a substantial decline in the value that many French placed on their country's rule of Algeria.

The 1958 elections were the first held under the terms of the Fifth Republic Constitution. They produced a disciplined Gaullist party (the UNR) large enough to dominate the National Assembly. The parliamentary presence of the Communist party was reduced to irrelevance, thereby depriving the center-left parties favoring Algerian disengagement of any alternative to cooperation with the Gaullists.[37] De Gaulle's appeal to French nationalist sentiment, his incontestable credentials as a *resistant,* and his ability to elicit support from both clericalists and anticlericalists also made the MRP's program somewhat redundant. It won only 10 percent of Assembly seats in the 1958 elections and disappeared as a separate organization after the 1963 elections. The Poujadists vanished even more quickly, partially because of changed economic conditions, but also because in the Fourth Republic's demise they had lost a necessary target for the populist anger they expressed and exploited. Most important of all, a fundamental split developed among the Indépendants—the large conservative party that had given solid and decisive parliamentary support to every initiative since 1954 it considered inconsistent with permanent French sovereignty over Algeria.

In the 1958 elections the Indépendants raised their percentage of the popular vote and the size of their representation in the Assembly. The new rules of Fifth Republic politics, however, and the size of the Gaullist bloc of deputies meant that their party could no longer bring down any government of which it was not a part. Forced to choose between participation in cabinets and a hardline toward Algeria, the party could not hold itself together. A minority of its top leaders, led by Roger Duchet and the party center, remained wedded to Algérie française. This faction's telegram of solidarity with those manning the barricades in January 1960 embarrassed and angered the bulk of the party. After the Generals' Putsch attempt, Duchet was forced to resign as secretary general of the party. Indépendant parliamentary leaders, such as Antoine Pinay and Valéry Giscard d'Estaing, traded their acquiescence in de Gaulle's Algerian policy for ministerial posts in Fifth Republic governments. They, and most other Indépendant politicians, allowed their fear of instability, their desire to serve in the cabinet, and their need to compete for moderately conservative voters attracted to the new Gaullist party to overrule their waning enthusiasm for the Algerian War.[38] Thus was a major realignment of French metropolitan politics achieved, eliminating the stalemated confrontation on Algeria between antidisengagement and disengagement-oriented blocs, which had paralyzed the Fourth Republic.

Algerian ultras and army officers ready to carry out a coup d'état were severely disadvantaged by the absence of a weighty metropolitan political organization committed as strongly as they were to maintaining French Algeria. The banner of Algérie française attracted no large political party or organization whose leadership might have presented itself as an alternative to de Gaulle or to the Fifth Republic. Pinay, the leading Indépendant contender for the presidency, was coming to the conclusion that the war in Algeria was a waste of resources.[39] Soustelle's only party links were to the UNR, which he had founded but which subsequently rejected him. Bidault was cut off from what remained of the party he had formerly led, the MRP, by its acceptance of Algerian self-determination. None of the other figures on the Vincennes Committee had the political stature or experience to be considered serious candidates for president of the Fifth, or any other, Republic.

Realignment within the institutions of the new regime thus played a key role in their preservation. Faced with massive public displays of support for de Gaulle—during the Barricades Rebellion in January 1960, in the results of the January 1961 referendum on Algerian self-determination, and during the Generals' Revolt of April 1961—the settlers and the professional army were deterred from employing all their resources (including invasion of the mainland) by the prospect of wielding power over a hostile metropolitan population. On the tactical level it was this shift in the balance of expectations about available options for governing France which permitted de Gaulle to be as patient as he was in January 1960 and April 1961. His confidence that he could rally public opinion to his side forced his opponents to take the politically costly initiative of breaking the newly established rules for political competition. The ultras, and especially the rebellious Army commanders, were thus compelled to assume the burden of proof that they had the means and the will to rule France without de Gaulle and without a large, established metropolitan political organization.

To build support for his Algerian policy and defend his regime against the challenges he expected its implementation to trigger, de Gaulle relied not only on the French public's deference to his opinions. He also sought to substitute his own views of the Algerian question for the ones that still prevailed, in 1958, among those members of the electorate in the center, and to the right of center, of French politics. The same staggered presentation of less ambiguous, less tortuously phrased constructions of his plans and preferences, which serially decomposed the problem of disengaging from Algeria, thereby depriving his opponents of early and convenient opportunities for resistance, was also part of a sustained effort to change French attitudes toward Algeria.

Of course de Gaulle was not the only contributor to the pedagogical process. In the final years of the Fourth Republic, books and articles about torture framed the war as an ethical question. These issues attracted the attention of many French intellectuals to the problem of the Algerian conflict's relationship to democracy in metropolitan France, but never generated a mass base for the moral critique of the Algerian War which was widely accepted within the intelligentsia.[40]

In the first years of the Fifth Republic, French intellectuals displayed a new willingness to draw uncompromising conclusions about the moral status of French verses Muslim claims in Algeria. The Jeanson network, organized to assist the FLN in its "just resistance" to French oppression, raised fundamental questions about the forms opposition to the Algerian War could legitimately take. In September 1960, 121 of France's leading noncommunist intellectuals issued a manifesto in support of conscientious objection to serving in the armed forces, desertion from the ranks, and even aid to the FLN. These activities helped shift the center of gravity of French opinion toward disengagement. Although the government prosecuted the Jeanson network and banned publication of the manifesto, it drew back from filing charges against the manifesto's signatories.[41]

In general the leading French newspapers followed government policy toward Algeria and their sense of what public opinion would tolerate, rather than trying to change the policy or shape public opinion. As Raoul Girardet points out, at the end of 1954 both *Le Populaire* (the official newspaper of the Socialist party) and *Le Figaro* (associated with the Indépendants) published editorials affirming the nation's "irreducible will to maintain Algeria within France, emphasizing that self-determination would mean secession and represent a mortal danger to the national community." In 1962, just prior to the Evian Accords, both newspapers published similarly impassioned endorsements of government policy (to recognize Algerian independence) as "conforming to the requirements of reason and the necessities of national interest."[42] Between 1956 and 1959, France's large circulation newspapers were inclined to do no more than report the *existence* of Cartiérist critiques of Algerian policy (in "reviews of the press") or print letters to the editor raising similar points.[43] In 1957,

Le Figaro rebuked its own writer, Raymond Aron, for both the mode of his analysis and his conclusions in *The Algerian Tragedy*. Despite some warnings of the need to reevaluate French policies toward Algeria, *Le Monde* maintained (until spring 1961) a "habitual optimism," shifting its editorial line to follow de Gaulle's gradually developing public position.[44]

In 1958 only leftist newspapers such as *L'Express, Le Populaire* and *Témoignage Chrétien* were offering forthright criticism of the war. But their readership was small and insulated from most sectors of French society. As noted, before 1958 the most dynamic sectors of the French business community were Cartiérist in their attitude toward French colonies, but these circles were slow to apply their analysis (in public at least) to Algeria. In early 1959, however, a key French business journal, *Les Echoes,* published an article opposing the Algerian war as an intolerable burden on the French economy. The war cost France, according to *Les Echoes,* 1,200 billion francs per year plus 120 billion francs in new investments. *L'Express,* which had disagreed with Aron in 1957 when he raised similar arguments against continuing French rule of Algeria, now hailed the article in *Les Echoes* as a "new sign of the evolution of thinking among the controllers of the French economy."[45]

By 1959 the French Catholic church had also moved away from strong support of the war. Signals from the Vatican that its missionary activities in the third world were now more likely to be enhanced by endorsing the right of Asian and African peoples to self-determination than by clinging to a dying colonialism were increasingly interpreted by French Catholics as applying to Algeria. Although divided on the issue, many bishops and priests in France spoke out against torture and other abuses and in favor of reaching an accommodation with Algerian Muslims that would set the stage for French withdrawal.[46]

In the final analysis, however, it was de Gaulle's own determined efforts that were the motor behind substantial change in the publicly displayed attitudes of metropolitan Frenchmen. Virtually all of de Gaulle's public utterances were consistent with a pedagogical strategy based on calculated ambiguity and a slow revelation of how few were the constraints he was willing to accept in finding a way out of Algeria.[47] In retrospect it is clear that de Gaulle's post–May 1958 remarks about Algeria were almost always more important for what they implied about the possibility of future movement toward disengagement than for their specific content (which was often irrelevant, vague, or tautological). For example, the procedures for establishing contact between the FLN and France, suggested in his October 1958 "peace of the brave" speech, were immediately rejected by the guerrillas as tantamount to capitulation. However, the tribute de Gaulle paid to the courage and honor of the "men of the insurrection" encouraged the French to change their expectations about what sort of relationship France might eventually have with those who previously had been officially referred to only as criminals and terrorists.

In his self-determination speech of September 1959, de Gaulle vehemently rejected and even ridiculed the idea of Algeria's "secession" from France. But much more important than his specific comments was the way they were framed. He chose to substitute an awkward and obviously inappropriate-sounding neologism—Frenchification—for the traditional, emotion-laden slogans of Algérie française or *intégration*. He thereby reduced the most enthusiastically supported vision of French victory to the status of one among several options (and not even the preferred option) for Franco-Algerian relations. Moreover, by simply mentioning separation as an outcome of the war that France would survive with her security and honor intact, he prompted others to debate the possibility on its merits. By stressing the disaster that secession would bring for the living standards of Algerian Muslims, instead of for metropolitan France's own interests, he strengthened those who contended that the costs of holding Algeria had, or soon might, exceed the advantages of continuing to enforce French sovereignty there.

In his January 25, 1960, address to the nation during Barricades Week, de Gaulle refused to use the phrase "French Algeria." Instead he characterized France's task in Algeria as "assuring the triumph of a solution that is French." As Grosser points out, "this statement could mean either '*Algérie française*' or 'It is unworthy of France not to give independence to a dominated country.' "[48] The point is that such ambiguity was calculated to encourage thinking and arguments about Algeria's future framed in terms of what was, in fact, "worthy" of France, rather than in terms of what would be required to achieve the particular image of French-Algerian relations contained in the slogan of Algérie française.

Thus de Gaulle sought gradually, but fairly steadily, to broaden the number of outcomes deemed consistent with French "grandeur," to raise questions about Algeria's value to France, and, finally, to create and strengthen beliefs that France would be better off without having to rule Algeria. This entailed implicit acceptance of the two major critiques of postwar French overseas policies offered by leftist French intellectuals: (1) the "relativist" rejection of Western (i.e., French) culture as the standard against which the maturity and value of native peoples (and their cultures) should be measured; and (2) the "realist" contention that decolonization (including the relinquishment of Algeria) was not only inevitable but also in France's economic and diplomatic interest. Before 1958, as part of his war of position against the Fourth Republic, de Gaulle and many of his supporters used these critiques as a foil to highlight his own virtues and suggest the degredation of the regime that seemed as though it might be responsive to them. In his war of maneuver against those who sought to do to the Fifth Republic what he had done to the Fourth, de Gaulle promoted precisely these critiques in an effort to reduce to a small minority those French strongly committed to Algérie française.

De Gaulle's stress on the notion of Algeria's distinctive "personality," his substitution of the phrase "Algerian Algeria" for "French Algeria" as the emblem of that country's future, and his endorsement of self-determination for a third world people not yet fully assimilated into French culture echoed the "relativist" critique—ideas that had been politically marginalized under the Fourth Republic when advanced by Jean-Paul Sartre, Claude Bourdet, Jacques Berque, François Mauriac, and Claude Lévi-Strauss. The "realist" critique was reflected in Gaulle's attempt to decrease Algeria's salience for those French concerned about France's future. In doing so he relied on Cartiérist analyses of French colonialism developed within the French business community. For example, the significance of de Gaulle's announcement, in October 1958, of his sweeping Constantine Plan for the economic rehabilitation of Algeria can only be appreciated within the context of Raymond Aron's 1957 book applying Cartiérist thinking to Algeria (discussed in Chap. 4). Aron's calculations were based in part on information contained in the Maspetiol report of 1955 which documented how abysmal were the living conditions of the mass of Algerian Muslims and how enormous were the sums required to carry out Soustelle's program of *intégration*.[49] In this light it can be seen that the sheer economic impossibility of implementing de Gaulle's Constantine Plan for the development of Algeria was perhaps the most important reason for its announcement—de Gaulle's desire to encourage those who appreciated the economic irrationality of France's Algerian policy to publicly make their case.

But de Gaulle had to make his argument more explicit before its logic became politically potent and before most managers, businessmen, and financial journalists, who privately opposed French rule of Algeria on grounds of economic irrationality, were willing to make their views known.[50] Not until after de Gaulle's articulation of self-determination as the basis for Algeria's future did Cartiér himself, in his 1960 book *Algeria without Lies,* finally apply his earlier analysis of colonialism to Algeria. He now contended that Algeria was, and would continue to be, an economic drain on France. Cartiér characterized as inevitable the decline of France's position there, describing European settlement in North Africa as "probably an error from the start."[51]

De Gaulle was not a Cartiérist himself, but a French nationalist in the tradition of Louis XIV and Napoléon, oriented toward achieving French leadership in Europe and opposed, as Ferry's critics had been in the 1880s, to imperialist adventures which distracted France from her continental vocation.[52] Nevertheless, in spring 1961 de Gaulle used the prohibitive cost of realizing *intégration,* combined with the burden of the continuing military conflict, as a basis for his own public adoption of a severely Cartiérist approach to Algeria: "Algeria costs us—that is the least we can say—more than she is worth . . . decolonization is our interest, and therefore our policy."[53] If de Gaulle's use of profit-and-loss terminology was unnatural, and oddly discordant with the grand style characteristic of his rhetoric, still it had a purpose. His blunt statement appears to have provided decisive encouragement for *France-Observateur, Le Monde,* and *Le Figaro,* newspapers that had largely avoided publishing Cartiérist analyses of the Algerian question. Between April and September 1961, they each published numerous articles applying "the logic of the accountant" to the problem of Algeria and endorsing disengagement.[54]

De Gaulle never seriously attempted to persuade the pieds noirs to support self-determination in Algeria. He did, however, expend considerable energy in seeking to change the values and expectations of the army. While praising its military "victories" in Algeria, he portrayed the Army's achievements, and "pacification" in general, as nothing more than ancillary contributions to a political settlement with the Algerian Muslims. In February 1960 France detonated her first atomic bomb. Again and again officers were told that in the nuclear age, the mission of the French army was considerably grander and more exciting than policing villages and casbahs or flushing guerrillas out of mountain hideouts. These were the operational preoccupations of the army in Algeria, most of which de Gaulle contemptuously dismissed as "boy scout" activities.[55] De Gaulle encouraged commanders to envision an "atomic army," based on the most sophisticated technology available, built around France's own independent nuclear strike force, whose mission would be to reestablish France in the front rank of world power.[56] There are few signs that these arguments made much of an impression on officers whose entire careers were based on their achievements in Indochina and Algeria, but they did provide an alternative framework within which new officers, and those based in Europe, could see the end of French rule in Algeria as an exciting beginning and a potential basis for boosting their careers.

The pedagogical success de Gaulle enjoyed was reflected in what Raoul Girardet calls a "decisive displacement of the national *consensus.*" It was the state, he argues, which had overcome French anticolonialist inhibitions in the late nineteenth and early twentieth century, and it was also the state, personified by Charles de Gaulle, whose efforts were responsible for public acceptance of decolonization in general and withdrawal from Algeria in particular. "More or less from the end of 1960," he continues, "the State was deliberately using all the weight of its authority, all the power of coercion, and the pressures of persuasion it had at its disposal to orient opinion toward a view very different from that with which the government had always sought to engage it."[57]

Contrary to Girardet's image, however, the "education" of the French public, which de Gaulle spurred and in which he actively participated, did not occur within an unchanging French state. The recomposition of the regime and the massive political realignment that redesign made possible were necessary components of a rescaling strategy featuring pedagogically induced change in value preferences about Algeria as an important, but subsidiary mechanism in the process of state contraction.

Lloyd George's Caesarism

Realignment without Recomposition. Both the UNR-supported government of Charles de Gaulle and the Lloyd George coalition between Liberals and Unionists were the result of substantial political realignments. Dominant centrist blocs replaced polarized competition over whether or not to contract the territorial scope of the state. Each "Caesarist bloc" relied heavily on the charismatic appeal of its respective architect, whose leadership was widely deemed essential to overcome a protracted national emergency.

However, the impetus for creating these blocs as well as the consequences of their formation were quite different. In France a regime crisis led toward, and was exploited to produce, regime breakdown. The rescue of the state from the chaos which seemed to threaten it produced new political capital. These resources—trust in de Gaulle's judgment, fear of the consequences of his absence, and hope for the consummation of his promises—were used effectively to recompose the regime. The calculated intent of recomposition was to change the rules of political competition so as to enhance the discretion of a centralized authority structure over all areas of public life, including the substantive question of Algeria's future. The realignment of political forces evident in the outcome of parliamentary elections and referenda, and de Gaulle's willingness to risk and ability to withstand repeated regime crises reflect the success of this strategy. Together with the pedagogic campaign described above, they permitted the relocation of the Algerian problem across the regime threshold.

In Britain, on the other hand, the regime crisis was defused before breakdown occurred. Plans for regime recomposition, harbored by Milner and other Unionists associated with him, were never given an opportunity to become politically relevant.[58] By accepting some sort of Ulster exclusion (in principle, if not in detail) and by closing ranks in the face of a major external threat to the state (war with Germany), Unionist and Liberal leaders relocated a decomposed Irish question across the regime threshold and formed the basis for a realignment whose origins insured both the continuation of the regime and the eventual partition of Ireland.

Absent the political capital that might have been available had the Ulster crisis been allowed to develop as Churchill had intended, and without any significant change in the rules of political competition, Lloyd George was incapable of freeing himself from the Unionist party's veto over disengagement from all of Ireland—a veto it had acquired as a result of its victory in the prewar showdown. The fact is that the scope of Lloyd George's Caesarist authority was considerably narrower than that of de Gaulle's in the Fifth Republic. It was based very specifically on his value to the Unionists as a wartime leader.

In April 1915 Asquith bowed to public pressure, and the promptings of those within his own party dissatisfied with the conduct of the war, and agreed to form a coalition government with the Unionists. As described in Chapter 6, Lloyd George (with Unionist backing) pushed Asquith from the premiership in December 1916 and remained in office until October 1922. His personal success was based on a significant realignment of British political life. Using his Caesarist-style leadership, he formed a coalition between the right wing of the Liberal party (the "Ginger," or "Lloyd George" Liberals) and the great bulk of the Unionist party. In its composition, if not in its form and durability, this political bloc resembled the dominant, "national-fusionism" party it had long been Lloyd George's ambition to create. But apart from his conduct of the war, Lloyd George never had the freedom to act without consideration of immediate partisan political implications that de Gaulle enjoyed.

For British Conservatives Lloyd George was not a naturally attractive figure. His inelegant manner and plebeian origins were distasteful enough, but his populist, welfare state politics were worse. As chancellor of the exchequer Lloyd George had been the originator of the great budget crisis of 1909. His People's Budget sought to tax the wealthy to pay for social programs. For this he was vilified by the Unionist party as a destroyer of private property. He was also held primarily responsible for loss of the Lords's veto in 1911—the issue having been joined as a direct result of the upper chamber's rejection of the 1909 budget, which the House of Commons had passed overwhelmingly.

In 1916, Unionists threw their support to Lloyd George because they saw in him the only political leader able to mobilize British resources for total war. No one else seemed to have the energy, stature, and popularity necessary to discipline recalcitrant commanders and elicit the sacrifices from British working people necessary to fight the war through to victory. But it would have been considerably more difficult, and perhaps impossible, for Bonar Law, Carson, Milner, Birkenhead, and other Conservative leaders to have swung behind Lloyd George if the Irish problem had remained the great defining issue it had been, between Liberals and Unionists, from 1886 to 1914. If achieving an Irish settlement was not a part of the tacit agreement on which the success of the wartime coalition was based, it *was* accepted that pursuit of such a settlement would be limited by the requirement that Protestant Ulster be effectively excluded from the jurisdiction of a Dublin Parliament. Even granted this condition, agreement within the coalition could not be reached over the exact terms of an Irish settlement. As shown in Chapter 6, negotiations on the Irish problem in the summer of 1916, the Irish Convention (summer 1917 to spring 1918), and policies during the Anglo-Irish War (1918–21) put significant strains on Lloyd George's personal political standing and the integrity of coalition cabinets. In response to these incumbent-level difficulties, he drew back from pressing for Irish solutions until he judged, in June 1921, that the coalition on which his political ascendancy depended would survive their implementation and that he himself would profit thereby.

Thus the political capital Lloyd George amassed in the course of leading Britain to victory over Germany was never available, or at least never perceived by him to be available, for objectives that fell substantially outside the scope of the war effort or beyond the bounds of Unionist preferences. Not until mid-1921 did Lloyd George pursue disengagement from most of Ireland with real vigor. By then the exasperating difficulty of containing the Irish rebellion had combined with the sobering experience of the world war to change the relative value Unionists placed on British rule of a united Ireland. Only then was hammering out the exact terms of Ulster exclusion a task from which Lloyd George perceived he might profit, and only then was disengagement implemented.

In France, once the substantively undecomposed Algerian problem had been moved across the regime threshold, only a single tumultuous year of negotiating the exact terms of disengagement preceded the evacuation of the Europeans and French recognition of Algerian independence. In contrast, seven years lay between crossing the regime threshold in Britain and implementing a decomposed solution to the Irish problem.

The Irish Problem Decomposed

However slow it was in implementation, decomposition of the Irish problem (rather than regime recomposition) was the political basis of Lloyd George's Caesarist bloc. Excluding portions of Ulster as a means of avoiding a regime-threatening confrontation was first publicly proposed by a Liberal backbencher, T. C. Agar-Robartes, in June 1912. Four months earlier, it will be recalled, the Cabinet had rejected a proposal by Churchill and Lloyd George that to avoid a confrontation with the Unionists, parts of Ulster be temporarily excluded. But most Liberals still made light of the possibility of a regime-threatening crisis. Very few were willing to compromise on their traditional commitment to home rule for all of Ireland. Most opposed any sort of Ulster exclusion as a needless concession to Ulster Protestant bigotry and bombast. Agar-Robartes's amendment to the third Home Rule Bill was accordingly rejected.

Initial Unionist reaction was also hostile. But Unionist responses to the idea of separate treatment for "Loyal Ulster" were also colored by the realization that the general public would refuse to sympathize with Ulster Unionist resistance unless the object of that resistance were Ulster itself, and no more than that. Therefore, while continuing to oppose creation of any Dublin legislature, most Unionists avoided categorical denunciations of an Irish settlement based on the exclusion of Ulster from its terms. Some began treating it as a bad idea, but one that might be preferable to civil war and against which, at least, they would confine themselves to constitutional forms of agitation.

Another approach, adopted by Carson in 1912, was to demand that all of Ulster, including its three heavily Catholic counties, be excluded from the Home Rule Bill—an attempt to scuttle the proposal by making it as impractical as possible. By fall 1913, however, both Carson and Bonar Law were privately making known their willingness to accept six-county exclusion as the basis for a settlement. While willing to compromise on the extent of the area of Ulster to be excluded, they insisted that the exclusion be made permanent. That was the brunt of Bonar Law's proposal to Asquith during their secret meetings in December 1913. Although squabbles continued over the fate of mixed Catholic-Protestant areas in Counties Fermanagh and Tyrone, these were due mainly to the refusal of the Liberals and the Redmondites to accept arrangements guaranteeing the *permanent* exclusion from home rule of whatever area might be demarcated. Exclusion, followed by automatic inclusion in six years, unless Parliament were in the interval to change the law, was as far as the Liberals and their Irish allies were willing to go. Six-year exclusion, followed by continued exclusion of those counties voting to remain outside the Home Rule Parliament's jurisdiction, was as much as the Unionists were willing to concede. This was the specific point at issue in Unionist rejection of Asquith's offer of March 9, 1914, which preceded the Curragh episode and the Larne gunrunning. It was also the main reason for the failure of the Buckingham Palace conference in July 1914.

When war erupted in August 1914, the two sides agreed to postpone their struggle over the Irish problem. When the problem resurfaced, after the Dublin Rising in April 1916, it was found to have been effectively transformed. From whether or not to create an Irish legislature for the whole island—the question that had pitted Unionists against Liberals for a generation and a half—the Irish question had been decomposed into two parts. The first of these was the problem of reaching agreement on the modalities for excluding the overwhelming majority of Ulster Protestants from Dublin's jurisdiction. The second was the extent of independence to be granted Irish nationalists in the balance of Catholic-dominated Ireland.[59]

From 1916 to 1921, both of these issues were contentious. Until convinced in 1918 that some sort of Dublin legislature was inevitable, Protestant Unionists in the south of Ireland strongly resisted the exclusion of northeastern Ulster as the basis for an Irish settlement. Meanwhile the displacement of Redmond's Irish Parliamentary party by Sinn Fein and the Irish Republican Army, and the abstention of Sinn Fein deputies from the House of Commons, deprived Lloyd George of parliamentary support for Irish home rule. The radicalization of Irish nationalism, by making more apparent Irish demands for a thoroughly independent republic, also renewed Unionist opposition to disengagement from any part of Ireland.

Despite these difficulties, neither version of the post-1914 decomposed Irish question ever emerged as a regime-threatening problem. Neither, that is, was divisive enough to raise fears about regime stability or even to prevent alliances and coalitions among politicians with outstanding differences on the terms of Ulster exclusion or the extent of autonomy to be granted to Dublin.

Disengagement without Pedagogy. During the Anglo-Irish War (January 1919–July 1921) Lloyd George took few political risks. In public he adopted a hardline against negotiations with Sinn Fein and in favor of victory over the "murder gangs." Only by waiting for events, public pressure, and the rising costs of military repression to convince his Unionist colleagues of the need to compromise did he finally succeed in implicating the Conservative party in a policy of disengagement from most of Ireland. By not seeking to persuade British Conservatives to see disengagement as a positive outcome, or at least as inevitable, Lloyd George minimized opportunities for rivals on his right (especially Bonar Law) to use the Irish question to replace him. Moreover, by insisting, even at the risk of a renewal of fighting, on the Irish Free State's formal recognition of the authority of the British Crown, he sought to enhance his coalition's long-term prospects by making the Irish settlement consistent with a reformed, but still vigorous British Empire. All this represented a parochial but politically prudent strategy. When Lloyd George finally did enter negotiations with the IRA, he could be confident that the public's yearning for an end to the bloodshed, and the involvement of leading Unionists in the Anglo-Irish negotiations, would give him the whip hand over die-hard opponents of any Irish settlement.

Of course Lloyd George's political profit and the composure, not to say enthusiasm, with which the Anglo-Irish treaty was greeted in Britain came at a price. The price was paid by the Irish, mainly the Catholic Irish. The casualties they suffered during the two and a half years of the Anglo-Irish War, in addition to the even heavier losses and deeper emotional scars endured during the Irish Civil War, were due directly though not solely to Lloyd George's decision to take as few political risks as possible in achieving an Irish settlement. Aside from using his talents and his authority to begin negotiations earlier, he might (during the negotiations) have focused the desire of the British public for a settlement on the refusal of Ulster Protestants to compromise on the fate of Fermanangh and Tyrone (counties where Catholics were a narrow majority). He could certainly have insured that the boundary commission would operate to achieve a border between northern and southern Ireland more in keeping with the pattern of nationalist and loyalist habitation. He might even have led British opinion to see the practical irrelevance of arcane language in the treaty which required leaders of the Irish Free State to swear, or appear to swear, allegiance to the Crown—a condition of the treaty which, more than anything else, triggered the civil war.[60]

However, just as Lloyd George did not attempt to "educate" British opinion toward a more generous Anglo-Irish treaty—one that might have been more quickly attainable and less likely to have precipitated an Irish civil war—so too had he not relied on pedagogy but on the sheer dimensions of the slaughter during World War I, and on shifts in the international landscape associated with it, to achieve a broad shift in British attitudes. By the end of the war with Germany, the British public was weary of war and sick of casualty lists.[61] Certain traditional arguments against Irish separatism—that the Irish were incapable of ruling themselves and that an Irish state would endanger vital security interests of Great Britain—no longer carried much weight in a world governed by the spirit if not the letter of the Fourteen Points, and where Anglo-American military supremacy over any combination of enemies seemed absolute. Additionally, Britain's military dependence on the United States during the war had changed to economic dependence in the years immediately afterward. If satisfaction of Irish nationalist ambitions was necessary to gain U.S. favor, and if securing U.S. loans was necessary to stave off Bolshevism, the demands of Irish nationalists could certainly be reevaluated.

Thus did the experience of the war, and the very different kind of international environment Britain encountered in its aftermath, help reduce the value Britons placed on their country's continued rule of Ireland. By 1921 these changed preferences gave Lloyd George the assurance he had wanted that objections by Unionist diehards would not pose a serious threat to his political fortunes, that is, as long as Ulster Protestants remained within the United Kingdom and the prestige of the British monarchy were preserved.

Summaries and Comparison

The relocation of the Irish problem from point C, across the regime threshold, to point D on Figure A-2, and of the Algerian problem from point H, across the regime threshold, to point I on Figure A-3 were described in Chapters 6 and 7 and analyzed in this chapter. The processes involved in accomplishing those transitions can now be summarized and compared as different combinations of the four rescaling mechanisms.

A partial recomposition of the British regime (removal of the House of Lords veto) encouraged a direct attempt to cross the regime threshold (the third Home Rule Bill). This triggered a regime crisis (1912–14) which led governing elites (beginning in late 1913) to seek to avoid future regime threats by decomposing the Irish problem (private and then public offers from Asquith for temporary Ulster exclusion). When the anti–home rule alliance (among British Conservatives, Ulster Protestants, and a substantial portion of the officer corps) insisted on the principle of permanent exclusion and mobilized for a regime-threatening showdown on that issue, the government again retreated—entering a bargaining process over the exact manner in which the Irish problem would be decomposed that lasted until the Anglo-Irish treaty was signed in December 1921. The ultimate result of that bargaining process was the grant of virtual independence to most of Ireland and full satisfaction of demands by Protestant Unionists in the six northeastern counties. This rigidly decomposed outcome was shaped by three factors. One of them was Sinn Fein and the IRA's domination of the Irish nationalist movement. The ascendancy of these groups was based on the disappearance of the Irish Parliamentary party, which could not survive the retreat of its British allies from the Home Rule Bill and their insistence on the permanent exclusion of most of Ulster. The two other factors were the realignment of Lloyd George Liberals into a Unionist-dominated Caesarist bloc (Lloyd George's wartime and postwar coalitions), and wartime transformations in British utility functions, that is, preferences and perspectives on economic, military, and political aspects of the Irish question.

From 1954 to 1958, the Fourth Republic was severely weakened by its inability to produce a government capable of either ending the Algerian War or beginning negotiations toward disengagement from Algeria. Despite repeated attempts to enact constitutional reforms, the regime failed to recompose itself in a fashion that might have allowed it to prevent, or survive, the crisis of 1958. Exploiting the "unsolvable problem" of Algeria, an alliance among colons in Algeria, substantial portions of the French officer corps, and antiregime politicians in the metropole successfully challenged the authority of the regime and replaced it with de Gaulle's Fifth Republic. The recomposition of the regime which de Gaulle undertook centralized power by shifting the locus of authority from the Assembly to the executive. It also created electoral conditions which fostered a realignment of political competition, giving rise to de Gaulle's own Caesarist bloc—based on a dominant "Gaullist" party (the UNR). Opponents of de Gaulle's Algerian policy were kept off guard by the serial decomposition of the Algerian problem, accomplished by separating vigorous prosecution of the war from gradually less ambiguous overtures to negotiate toward Algerian independence. These latter measures were accompanied by sustained efforts to "educate" French opinion in regard to France's "true" interests—especially the relative unimportance of Algeria (as de Gaulle saw it) for France's future and its "grandeur." Although de Gaulle's policies triggered a series of regime challenges by elements of the coalition that had brought him to power, within the recomposed regime most supporters of Algérie française in the right-wing Indépendant party saw no political profit in opposing de Gaulle. Accordingly, neither the pieds noirs (in 1960) nor the professional army (in 1961) could draw significant public support for their antiregime activities in France itself. Drawing strength from the public anxieties produced by each successive failure to overthrow the Fifth Republic, de Gaulle moved the Algerian problem across the regime threshold without decomposing it spatially. The result was a relatively short, tumultuous, but complete disengagement of France from all of Algeria.

Comparative analysis of these two cases draws attention to certain key similarities. Both represent wars of maneuver fought to state-contracting conclusions. In both cases, crossing the regime threshold was preceded by crises precipitated by government efforts to move toward disengagement from the peripheral territory. During these crises, settlers, metropolitan conservatives, and army officers made joint extraconstitutional challenges to legally promulgated government policies. In each case territorial disengagement followed the crossing of the regime threshold. In both cases this disengagement ended violent struggles between the metropole and nationalists in the former outlying territory. In both cases as well there was a drastic reduction in the internal political salience of historically prominent issues concerning the status of these territories.

Undoubtedly the most significant difference in outcomes between the two cases was France's complete disengagement from Algeria in contrast to Britain's disengagement from the "southern" twenty-six counties and the retention, within the United Kingdom, of the six northeastern counties.[62] Other major differences between the two cases include the collapse of one French regime in the course of the war of maneuver, compared to the survival of the British regime; the absorption of substantially heavier dislocation costs by Europeans in Algeria, compared to Protestants in Ireland; and the eruption of an Irish civil war over the terms of British disengagement, compared with the difficult, but relatively straightforward assumption of power in Algeria by the FLN. These differences form a pattern, traceable primarily to the prominence of problem decomposition in the British case and regime recomposition in the French case. These mechanisms were the centerpieces of distinctive strategies of state contraction. Their use and effect reflected both elite choices and differences in the balance of forces among the protagonists—differences linked to prior characteristics of the two political systems.

Wars of maneuver, like all wars, are strategic conflicts whose outcomes are constrained by the resources available to the protagonists and the effectiveness with which they are used. Comparing strategies and decisions that were adopted or rejected by Asquith, Churchill, de Gaulle, and Lloyd George accentuates aspects of strategy, choice, and leadership style when explaining differences in outcome between Britain and France. The most important choices were Asquith's decision to retreat from confrontation with the anti–home rule coalition in 1914, versus de Gaulle's repeated decisions to confront the anti-disengagement coalition, despite the immediate threats to Fifth Republic stability he knew would result. But analysis of wars of maneuver entails consideration of prevailing constellations of power as well as of the techniques with which available resources are manipulated. The particular combinations of rescaling mechanisms through which the Irish and Algerian questions were transformed, from regime-threatening to incumbent-threatening problems, reflect prior differences in the relative weight of key political groups and the timing and extent of pressure exerted by nationalist rebels. These factors, along with important differences in geography and international context, made certain choices more likely than others and help explain why specific policies or gambits employed by actors in one case had consequences substantially

different from the results of similar maneuvers adopted by their counterparts in the other case.

Ulster Protestants versus Pieds Noirs

The Protestants of Ireland were a larger proportion of the total Irish
population than were the Europeans as a proportion of the total Algerian
population. Irish Protestants were also more teritorially concentrated than
were the pieds noirs. In 1911, approximately 1.1 million Protestants lived
in Ireland, 25 percent of the island's population. Seventy-eight percent of
Irish Protestants lived in the nine counties of historic Ulster, concentrated
particularly in the six northeastern counties that became Northern Ireland
under the terms of the Partition Act of 1920 and then the Anglo-Irish
treaty of 1921. In this area Anglicans, Presbyterians, and Methodists (virtually all loyalists) made up 60 percent of the population, while 37 percent
were Roman Catholic (virtually all nationalists). In the city of Belfast,
Catholics numbered only 24 percent of the population. In the twenty-six
counties of what would be "Southern Ireland" under the terms of the
Partition Act (and then the Irish Free State under the terms of the Anglo-
Irish treaty), Protestants were wealthy and influential, but represented only
just above 9 percent of the population.[63]

In 1960 the European population of Algeria was approximately 10
percent of the total. In 1954, 80 percent of Europeans lived in urban
centers, located mainly along the coast. European preferences for urban
life-styles had reversed an early emphasis on rural settlement patterns for
nineteenth-century immigrants from Alsace and Lorraine. In the late 1950s
the urbanization of the European population was made virtually complete
by the constant fear of FLN attacks against European farms and neighborhoods in rural districts. Nevertheless, the pieds noirs were not as com-
pactly situated as were the bulk of Irish Protestants. In 1960 there was
still a slim European majority in the city of Oran. But a major influx of
Muslims from the rural areas into cities and towns produced a non-
European majority in the city of Algiers and increased it in every other
major urban area except Oran.[64]

The various proposals for partition that were suggested envisioned establishing "French Algerian" enclaves centered around the coastal area
between Algiers and Oran. But even assuming the *regroupement* of up to
two million Muslims and Europeans, estimates of the population balances
in these variously shaped versions of "French Algeria" anticipated a population of no more than 50 percent European (in the smallest of the
projected enclaves, and under the most "optimistic" conditions) versus

probable proportions of Europeans ranging from 45 percent to 21 percent in progressively larger enclaves.[65]

In contrast, the comparative concentration of the Irish Protestant population, as well as its local majority, religious homogeneity, and the powerful sense Ulster Protestants had of themselves as a distinct historical community help explain why the Ulster Unionist Council and the Ulster Volunteer Force emerged as such disciplined and effective political and paramilitary organizations. Able to mobilize hundreds of thousands of men and women for regular and extraordinarily well-controlled demonstrations of political resolve, Carson and Craig could impress upon British politicians and British army officers the impossibility of using the regular judicial system against them, as well as the likelihood of violent Ulster resistance to any use of armed force. Moreover, they could send these signals without engaging in politically dangerous provocations. In contrast to the Algerian case, this ability put the onus of initiating hostilities, and the image of provocateur, on the government.

In Algeria, for cultural as well as demographic and geographical reasons, the pieds noirs were less well equipped to organize themselves for sustained political confrontations. Like Ulster Protestants, who received enormous amounts of money from Belfast industrial tycoons and shipping magnates, the Europeans of Algeria had access to the resources of a small number of fabulously wealthy colon families. But the organizations that arose among the pieds noirs during the Algerian War were seldom independent of metropolitan political parties or interests.[66] Those that were independent often were led by students, demagogues, and streetwise adventurers who had little following beyond their own immediate circles of supporters and virtually no standing in France itself. Although able to mobilize substantial sections of the European population for protest strikes, violent or semi-violent demonstrations, and short bursts of enthusiastic political activity, these groups were never capable of defending any area of Algeria larger than a neighborhood against the FLN. While the barricades constructed in January 1960 gave sympathetic army units pause when issued orders to effect their removal, the undisciplined and murderous pied noir attack on the gendarmes was a provocation tailor-made for de Gaulle in his effort to rally public opinion in defense of the Fifth Republic.

If the geographical concentration and cultural distinctiveness of Ulster Protestants help account for their political effectiveness, however, they also help explain why the Protestants' success was limited to the six northeastern counties. From 1886 to 1911, Protestant Ulster mobilized on behalf of all loyalists in Ireland, including those in "Southern Ireland." But this changed, despite protests from southern Irish Protestants that they were being abandoned, and despite Carson's own origins as a native of Dublin.

The legislative progress of the third Home Rule Bill and the sharpening of the regime crisis associated with it led the British public and British political elites to distinguish between versions of the Irish question that were "unsolvable" and those that were merely very difficult. Such distinctions first became important in proposals for some form of Ulster exclusion which appeared with increasing regularity and support from 1912 onward—proposals that, as we have seen, Unionist leaders in Ulster and in Britain found it prudent not to reject in principle. In this way the qualitatively different kind of antidisengagement struggle Protestant loyalists were able to wage in Ulster, compared with what they could carry on or credibly threaten in the rest of Ireland, gave rise, in the image of some form of Ulster exclusion, to the kind of "focal point" for compromise that Thomas Schelling described—a conspicuous point of possible agreement leading to a convergence of expectations. The six-county exclusion—constituting an apparently available, well understood, and minimally satisfactory escape from an increasingly disturbing regime crisis—was just such a point, at least in the bargaining carried on among Liberals, Unionists, and Ulster Protestants.[67] The emergence of some form of Ulster exclusion as such a focal point encouraged government policies of decomposition as the path of least resistance and made it relatively more difficult for those (such as Churchill in 1914) willing to accept higher risks of regime destabilization in return for a more comprehensive disengagement from Ireland.

As British politicians had been the first officially to suggest some form of partition as a solution to the 1912–14 home rule crisis, so were metropolitan French the first to suggest it as a solution to the Algerian question. Proposals for what was called a "Palestinian" solution (i.e., the partition of Algeria, as Palestine had been partitioned) were published in *Le Monde* as early as May 1956. Germane Tillion mentioned (and bitterly condemned) the idea in her influential book *L'Algérie en 1957*.[68] In February 1957, three Radical deputies presented a plan to divide Algeria (apart from the Sahara) into a French Algerian province and two "autonomous" Muslim entities—the Autonomous Republic of Constantine in the east and the Autonomous Territory of Tlemcen in the west—a plan condemned as "odious and absurd" by the conservative press.[69] Not until 1961 did partition receive systematic attention. In that year Alain Peyrefitte, one of several Gaullist deputies who expressed support for the idea, published four articles in *Le Monde* explaining the various ways Algeria could be divided and arguing that it could be accomplished to France's advantage whether the FLN agreed or not.[70] But even this most systematic study of the idea of spatially decomposing the Algerian problem took as its point of departure the refusal of all parties concerned—metropolitan French, Algerian Muslims, and Algerian Europeans—to take partition seriously. Why, asked Peyrefitte, was there a "taboo" on the very suggestion that Algeria might be divided? It was almost, he complained, as if the French were "hypnotized" against rational consideration of its advantages and disadvantages. Perhaps, he argued, this was due to the success of FLN and extreme right-wing propaganda, which insisted on interpreting the problem in "all or nothing" terms.[71]

Indeed, despite Peyrefitte's efforts, the notion of dividing Algeria into an independent Muslim state (in the center and east of the country) and a smaller Algérie française based along the northwestern coast elicited no substantial support—never among Algerian Muslims, and only tentatively and very late in the day (autumn 1961) among the pieds noirs. Pied noir organizations eschewed any talk of partition until the last desperate months of French presence, when the OAS itself broached the idea.

What attention was paid to Peyrefitte's articles and book was mainly due to the belief he was echoing one side of de Gaulle's thinking. Beginning in spring 1961, and occurring most frequently in the fall of that year, de Gaulle made a number of references to the *regroupement* and defense of Europeans in Algeria as unilateral steps France might take if the FLN remained obdurate in its demands for unconditional French withdrawal and Algerian control of the Sahara. In contrast to Ulster exclusion proposals made by Lloyd George and Churchill, and put forward to the cabinet as early as winter 1912, these remarks by de Gaulle were not part of a strategy to defuse the regime crisis by decomposing the problem. By this time, as shown in Chapter 7, the regime threshold had been crossed. By all accounts, de Gaulle's encouragement of expectations that partition might be effected was part of a bluff—an unsuccessful tactic intended to create the appearance of a French option, and to exploit FLN fears of an OAS seizure of power in European areas. With this bluff he hoped to elicit more flexibility from the rebel leadership in negotiating French control of the Sahara and guarantees for Europeans in an independent Algeria.[72]

The contrast between Irish Protestant willingness (by 1918, even among some Protestants in the south of Ireland) to explore and finally accept partition as a minimally satisfactory arrangement versus the virtual refusal of Europeans in Algeria to even take the idea seriously reflects a larger difference in the patterns of historical ambition, success, and failure displayed by the two settler communities. From establishment of the English Pale of Settlement in the twelfth century to the 1790s, English and Scottish settlers in Ireland had undermined or prevented recurrent attempts by British governments to grant equal property and equal political rights to

Gaels or Catholics. But the incorporation of Ireland into the United Kingdom in 1801 set the stage for more successful challenges to the entrenched domination of Ireland by British settlers.

As part of the bargain that led Irish Catholic elites to accept the formal annexation of Ireland, Prime Minister William Pitt promised the Act of Union would provide the Irish with equal rights, regardless of religion. Irish Protestants, who had opposed annexation precisely because it would offer new political opportunities to Irish Catholics, then reversed their field, declaring eternal fealty to the Union while opposing Catholic emancipation on the grounds that Irish Catholic loyalty to the Union could not be assured.[73] In part because of opposition by the Protestant Ascendancy and the Orange Order, it took Catholics nearly thirty years to achieve the right to sit in Parliament, another forty to disestablish the Irish (Anglican) church, and another decade after that before Irish Catholics enjoyed truly equal access to the British political system.[74] But as a result of incorporating Irish Catholics into the British political system, and the slow success of these struggles for Catholic rights, the Protestants of Ireland—both the Anglican, Dublin-based Ascendancy, and the Presbyterians and Methodists of Ulster—were constrained to abandon formerly sacrosanct political positions regarding land reform, the Irish church, and, finally, the existence of some sort of Dublin legislature. They did so out of a grudging realization that to secure their most vital interests (their property rights and political control over areas of Ulster where they were a majority), ambitions to prolong other privileges and more complete forms of political domination would have to be sacrificed.

These lessons in retrenchment and political adaptation were never learned by the pieds noirs. They and their representatives in Paris enjoyed a virtually unbroken string of successes in their effort to block reforms designed to enfranchise Algerian Muslims and encourage their participation in French political life. Compared to Britain, from the late eighteenth to the mid-nineteenth century, regimes produced by the French political system appear to have been substantially more vulnerable to the single-issue-movement tactics of the settler lobby, and less able to prevent the local administrative apparatus from falling under effective settler control.[75] By hailing severe French repression at Sétif in 1945 as the only appropriate response to Muslim dissatisfaction, and by helping to prevent the organization of any mass attempt by Algerian Muslims to express aspirations or redress grievances through constitutional means, the Europeans of Algeria drove potential leaders of a Muslim constitutionalist movement into the arms of revolutionary organizations such as the FLN. Ferhat Abbas is the obvious example, but his career is emblematic of the fate of many

Algerian Muslims—students, professionals, and army veterans—in the 1920s, '30s, '40s, and '50s.

Irish Nationalism versus Algerian Nationalism

When compared to the consequences of the more complete historical success of French settlers in Algeria in blocking reforms of benefit to Muslims, Irish Protestant failure to prevent Irish Catholics from entering the British political arena seems to have had a most dramatic impact on the character of Irish nationalism and the flexibility of its leadership. When the possibility of territorial compromise in Ireland arose, a long tradition of gradualist bargaining made the idea minimally acceptable, if not attractive, to the mainstream of the Irish nationalist movement. An extraordinarily dense array of constitutional nationalist organizations offering places, honor, and status to all manner of Irishmen was available to attach individual interest to a program of political compromise.[76] In Algeria, by contrast, Muslim nationalists had no hallowed tradition of leaders such as O'Connell, Parnell, and Redmond—whose political successes were built from exploiting available compromises as stepping-stones to more fully satisfying arrangements. Public organization was a scarce commodity among Algerian Muslims. French, and especially pied noir, efforts to atomize native society had been extraordinarily successful. In Algeria, therefore, unlike Ireland, no network of nationalist organizations existed able to link vested interests to adaptive compromises. For the FLN leadership itself, only complete elimination of French authority from Algeria could serve as a basis for political survival during and after the fighting.

Of particular importance to the character of revolutionary nationalism in Ireland as compared to Algeria was implementation of land reform (including land redistribution) in Britain, compared to its virtual absence in Algeria. Although early Gladstonian land legislation was inadequate, it did set important precedents for tenant farmers. It was also the demonstrable result of pressures exerted by Irish constitutionalist nationalism. The principle having been established by the Liberal–Irish Home Rule party alliance, the Unionist party itself eventually sponsored the most significant measures of agrarian reform. This legislation, by the early 1900s, turned tens of thousands of essentially landless peasants into small proprietors, determined above all else to protect the property they had finally gained.

This solution to the agrarian problem sharply reduced the prospects for Irish socialists in the towns and cities to combine with the "physical force" men of the IRB as leaders of an Algerian-style peasant revolution against British-Protestant control of Ireland.[77] The most "advanced" elements in the Irish nationalist movement were middle-class Catholics, and the most important leaders of Irish nationalism in the early twentieth century, from Redmond and Dillon of the Irish Parliamentary, to Griffith, Cosgrave, and the pro-treaty majority in Sinn Fein, to Collins and de Valera of the IRA, were (despite differences of style and emphasis) bourgeois nationalists. As such they were ready, in the final analysis, to prefer the consolidation of political independence in most of Ireland to the price, and the risks, of fighting to the end for the whole island. All were prepared, by the end of their careers, if not at the beginning, to negotiate the terms of British disengagement from Ireland and even to accept the exclusion of predominantly Protestant sections of Ireland from the immediate jurisdiction of the Irish political system they sought to create.[78]

In Algeria, however, a century of land expropriations, sabotaged reform efforts, and brutal techniques of suppression had pulverized Muslim peasant society. Rapid increases in the Muslim population combined with ownership of most agricultural land by Europeans to create an ever-worsening shortage of land among the peasant masses, leading to growth of a restless class of underemployed, impoverished agricultural workers. Yet not until 1956 was even a small-scale land distribution scheme put in place.[79] In the 1920s and 1930s the Muslims had tried to establish a representative political organization based on professionals and locally elected officials. The constitutionalist movement foundered, however, when virulent pied noir opposition killed the Blum-Violette package of reforms.[80] The chiefs of the rebellion repeatedly promised their recruits that "all colonial assets would be expropriated and redistributed."[81] They established their credibility not through mass political organization or achievement of satisfying measures of land reform, but by violence. They relied on violence, and the animosities triggered by French/pied noir over-reaction, to displace their rivals, and on both violence and uncompromising demands for independence to build legitimacy and insure their continued domination of the nationalist movement.

In contrast to the flexible leadership provided at crucial points by Sinn Fein, the IRB, many IRA commanders, and by the Dail Eireann, the top echelons of the FLN were composed of an uncompromising revolutionary elite, purged repeatedly of anyone suspected of being willing to reach a modus vivendi with the French.[82] This meant that candidates for leadership among Algerian Muslims, including Ferhat Abbas, had no history of successful constitutional activity and no historical basis for expecting, or persuading other Algerian Muslims, that even halfway satisfactory arrangements could be made with the French government or the Europeans of Algeria. Indeed the FLN's own ability to enforce whatever small compromises its negotiators might have been willing to accept was itself very limited.

On the mass level the contrasts are equally vivid. In Ireland a relatively bloodless nationalist struggle in the early twentieth century was centered in the towns and cities and supported by small proprietors in the rural areas. In Algeria a very bloody revolution was organized in the rural areas, by "small holders almost able to make ends meet," and backed by landless pauperized masses.[83] While Irish Catholic peasants participated in a struggle combining well-understood traditions of limited agrarian violence and constitutional nationalism, Algerian Muslims gave their support to an exceedingly violent, prolonged, and radically new form of revolutionary mobilization—a struggle that spread only gradually from rural to urban areas.[84]

The political role of organized religion among the Catholics of Ireland and the Muslims of Algeria also differed markedly, and for similar reasons. Under the terms of the Union, the Catholic church in Ireland was liberated from the severe restrictions from which it suffered during the eighteenth century. With Catholic emancipation, the church supported constitutionalist efforts to achieve land reform and home rule. During World War I it took a firm anticonscription line but continued to exert a restraining influence over tendencies toward extreme positions and violent revolution. In Algeria, on the other hand, the failure and disappearance of the reformist Ben-Badis movement of the 1930s, and the outright collaboration of many ulama with the French, removed organized religion as a break on the inclinations of the FLN leadership (and their predecessors in various radical nationalist groups) toward violent revolution. But Islamic motifs and sentiments were still more salient than any others among Algerian peasants. Under these circumstances, secular revolutionaries were able to appropriate the Muslim identity shared by Berber and Arab Algerians and use it for purposes of national mobilization and social revolution.[85]

Metropolitan Opponents of Disengagement in Britain and France

If comparing dialectical relationships between settler political action and native mobilization helps explain why problem decomposition was crucial in Britain and not in France, comparing the basis for settler alliances with metropolitan opponents of disengagement helps explain why regime recomposition was central in France and not Britain. As noted in Chapter 6, alliances between Irish Protestants, British Unionists, British army service organizations, and military officers were necessary for the UVF's successful campaign to defy the Home Rule Bill because these alliances created the specter of armed and bloody resistance. Chapter 7 traced the decisive importance of alliances established by civilian ultras in Algeria with Gaullist politicians from the mainland, veterans organizations, and sympathetic army officers—alliances which led directly to the collapse of the Fourth Republic. Similar but looser alliances among Algerian ultras, disaffected colonels and generals, and metropolitan partisans of Algérie française were the background to Operation Veronique, the Barricades Rebellion, the abortive antiregime conspiracy of December 1960, and the Generals' Revolt of April 1961.

Upon examination, however, these apparently similar alliances entailed different kinds of partnerships and were based on very different premises. In the British-Irish case, Ulster Protestants received enthusiastic and virtually unconditional declarations of support from the entire leadership of a united opposition party—the Conservatives. This well-organized party had slipped from the dominant position it enjoyed from 1886 to 1906, but it still conceived of itself as the "natural" governing party. Its success under Prime Ministers Salisbury and Balfour was due in large measure to the electoral coalition it created, based specifically on opposition to home rule for Ireland—hence incorporation of the term "Unionist" in the party's official appellation. In the aftermath of three successive electoral defeats (January 1906, January 1910, and December 1910) and passage of the Parliament Act in 1911, many in the party saw their only chance for returning to power as resting upon a revival of the great controversy over Ireland's status from which British Conservatives had previously benefited so spectacularly.[86] Although Bonar Law had a personal attachment to Ulster, the elegant aristocrats who dominated the party leadership (Balfour, Austin Chamberlain, Birkenhead, and Curzon) felt more distaste than affection for the dour Presbyterians of Ulster and the blunt, ruthless approach to politics of their representatives (Carson and Craig). On the other hand, the Tory elite saw in Ulster's loyalist activism, in its unsubtle appeals to anti-Catholic sentiment, and in its emphasis on discipline and standing firm for Crown and country a political path to victory over the Liberals. Even more, their frustration with the Liberal–Irish nationalist alliance's ability to overturn what they considered the country's "ancient constitution" (stripping the House of Lords of its veto and instituting progressive taxation) led the Conservatives to tolerate and even support the extraconstitutional aspects of Protestant Ulster's campaign. This support was meant to highlight what they wanted the electorate to see as an illegitimate Liberal alliance with Irish nationalists, foster an image of Britain as ungovernable by Liberals, and prompt a desire to return the country to the

Conservatives, who might then mend the broken constitution and reestablish political stability.

Both Ulster Protestants and British Unionists were willing to threaten a regime crisis in order to block the third Home Rule Bill and reverse the fortunes of the Conservative party. Although Milner entertained more revolutionary ambitions, neither the UVF nor the British Unionist party, nor the army officers whose pro-Ulster and Unionist sympathies made the Curragh episode possible, aspired to recompose the regime, that is, to replace the constitutional monarchy or inaugurate a substantially different version of it. In France, however, during both the Fourth and the Fifth republics, the Algerian question provoked explicit efforts to recompose the regime. During the last year of the Fourth Republic, Gaullists, the pieds noirs, and the professional officer corps of the army were convinced that their overlapping objectives (to return de Gaulle to power, to preserve European domination in Algeria, and to avoid another humiliating defeat) could only be accomplished by overthrowing and replacing the regime. When the direction of the Fifth Republic's policies toward Algeria became apparent, a similar, albeit weaker, alliance remerged—among metropolitan partisans of Algérie française, angry generals and colonels (including the *pur et dur* afficianados of *la guerre révolutionnaire*), and the pieds noirs. Like its predecessor before May 1958, this alliance was based on a common belief that a regime change, and not simply a regime crisis, was necessary to fulfill the varied goals of its partners.

In Britain the Unionist party was, ultimately, the dominant force in the anti–home rule alignment. When the outbreak of the Great War forced the Conservatives to accept Liberal leadership in a great patriotic struggle, it also gave them a route back to power that did not require the continuation of the controversy over Ireland. Unionism thereupon ceased to be the party's guiding principle. Though strong commitments to six-county Ulster exclusion remained, Conservatives were no longer willing to fight hard to prevent home rule, or even more generous forms of political autonomy, from being granted to the rest of Ireland.

Likewise, the Gaullists were the dominant force within the coalition that overthrew the Fourth Republic. Unlike the prewar Unionists, however, the Gaullists were thoroughly committed to reconstructing the regime. The largest party on the French right during the Fourth Republic, the Indépendants, was splintered and bereft of effective central leadership. Uncertain of its attitude to both the Fourth Republic and de Gaulle, it exploited the Algerian issue to its electoral advantage before 1958 and continued to emphasize the issue for the first two years of the Fifth Republic. But the party's weakness was revealed in its leadership's inability to fasten on any intermediary, realistic approach to Algeria, such as the idea of partition might have provided. When de Gaulle's Algerian policies, and his threat of "chaos or me," forced Indépendants to choose between risks of further regime instability and honoring their former commitments to French Algeria, the large majority of party leaders threw their pied noir allies overboard.

During the Fifth Republic, the pieds noirs and especially the professional army were the key players in challenges launched against the Fifth Republic on behalf of Algérie française. Although increasingly suspicious of one another, between 1959 and 1961 these two groups were committed to overthrowing the Fifth Republic and showed the same determination as the Gaullists had displayed in 1957 and 1958. On the other hand, Bidault, Soustelle, Morice, Duchet, and other metropolitan politicians with at least some ties to the institutions of the Fifth Republic played a relatively minor role in the movement to keep Algeria French. Thus during both the Fourth and the Fifth republics, the commanding positions within the antidisengagement alliances were held by groups whose fundamental ambitions could only be achieved through regime recomposition. By contrast, in Britain the center of gravity in the antidisengagement coalition was occupied by the Conservative-Unionist party, whose leaders rallied around the regime during wartime and who could reasonably anticipate a return to power as a result of normal political competition within its institutions. In this context, decomposing Ireland rather than recomposing the British regime became an eminently acceptable outcome, if an inelegant one.

Thus the central role of regime recomposition in France and problem decomposition in Britain as mechanisms for rescaling the Irish and Algerian problems can be traced to the strategic choices of key metropolitan politicians, the historical consequences of different patterns of settler-native competition, and the premises which linked somewhat differently weighted antidisengagement forces together to present both states with regime crises.

Payoffs and Prices in Wars of Maneuver: Conclusions about the Conservation of Suffering, Political Advantage, and Political Risk

Wars of maneuver can punctuate the history of state institutions in ways that effect long-lasting changes in their shape and operation. Who wins these contestations and by what means determine the substance of those changes and the distribution of pain and profit among the survivors and their political descendants.

From the perspective of the French republic—not the First, Second, Third, Fourth, or Fifth, but from the perspective of the long struggle in France to institutionalize republican democracy as a substitute for the ancien régime—the Algerian War was a boon. Ever since the revolution of 1789, republican regimes had faced severe difficulties reconciling a legacy of centralized authority with deep ideological divisions over the role of the state and a diffuse, but sustained belief that appreciating the substance of the general will, and not bargaining a series of awkward but workable allocative arrangements, was the only legitimate mode of political participation.[87] Combined with geostrategic overextension and vulnerability, the tensions arising from these longstanding conditions of French politics doomed four versions of la République française and help explain why not one of them (until 1958) was succeeded by another.

The Algerian crisis of 1958, engineered by the Gaullists, the pieds noirs, and the army, but based ultimately on the disruption caused and the sacrifices endured by Algerian Muslims, provided the impetus for reconstructing the most successful republican regime in French history—the Fifth Republic. More than any other postrevolutionary French regime, the Fifth Republic's mix of executive power, popular participation, and legislative restraint has provided a stable, flexible, and legitimized basis for bargaining-oriented participation.[88]

But as I have emphasized, another key ingredient in the stable, and stabilizing, outcome of the French-Algerian relationship was a willingness by de Gaulle to take large risks for potentially very large payoffs—a bold approach to political life that differentiates him as sharply from Asquith and Lloyd George as it does from all Fourth Republic politicians (including Mendès-France). To preserve the possibility that he might be able to reconstruct the French regime in a comprehensive fashion, de Gaulle risked oblivion by steadfastly refusing to play the game of Fourth Republic politics. Once called upon to implement his vision of regime recomposition, he preferred successive, regime-threatening confrontations to compromises on the institutionalization of presidential power or the disengagement of France from Algeria—compromises that might ultimately have saddled the Fifth Republic with burdens it could not bear in his absence.

Aside from deriving at least temporary sustenance from the "routinization" of de Gaulle's charismatic authority, the Fifth Republic also benefited enormously from the completeness with which the governments it produced removed the Algerian question from the French political agenda. De Gaulle used the popularity he enjoyed as a result of the end of the conflict not only to gain another term as president but to promulgate an amendment to the constitution providing for the direct election of the

president. Thus he prevented France from returning to the kind of legis-
lature-dominant system many politicians and Assembly deputies began to
argue for once the Algerian "emergency" had ended.

The leaders of the FLN, especially of the external army, also benefited
from de Gaulle's sharp-edged pursuit of regime recomposition, rather than
problem decomposition, as the primary route to disengagement from Algeria. First, the ruthlessness with which Fourth and Fifth Republic governments prosecuted the military conflict against guerrilla commanders
located inside Algeria eliminated the external leadership's most serious
rivals. Second, and even more important, the readiness (and ability) of the
Fifth Republic government in 1961 and 1962 to effect a total French
withdrawal from Algeria provided the revolutionary leadership with un-
compromised national independence throughout the entire territory of
Algeria (including the oil- and gas-rich Sahara).

Though this achievement did not prevent violent feuds, a military coup
in 1965, failed development policies, or a potent Islamist challenge, the
national solidarity produced by collective suffering and triumph was a
dependable basis for nearly three decades of rule by the political class
which the revolution produced. In view of the disorganized state of Algerian Muslim society in the aftermath of the war and the havoc wreaked
on Algerian institutions and infrastructural facilities by vengeful, departing pieds noirs, this solidarity was itself an impressive achievement. The
surviving leaders, and the middle-class and professional elements who
attached themselves to the new government at the achievement of independence, were the first countrywide, indigenous political leaders to enjoy
mass recognition and support since the defeat of Abdel-Kader's tribal
resistance movement in 1847. Had French governments crossed the regime
threshold by using a mix of strategies more similar to those employed in
the British-Irish case, which forced the Irish into humiliating compromises,
prospects for the rapid crystallization of an accepted national leadership
would have been substantially reduced.[89]

Except for the long-suffering Muslim masses, the settler community in
Algeria paid the highest price for de Gaulle's success. The settlers' historic
wager, that their links to France could give them the resources necessary
to forever marginalize Muslim political demands, was lost. The result was
that all efforts to achieve meaningful guarantees for their future in Algeria
failed. In one of the most rapid and comprehensive evacuations of its kind,
over 90 percent of the Europeans living in Algeria at the end of 1961
became refugees by the middle of 1962—their homes, livelihoods, and
culture destroyed by forces whose extremism their own intransigence had
helped produce.

The very different strategy of disengagement followed by Asquith and

Lloyd George, from 1914 to 1921, resulted in a correspondingly different array of political consequences. Unlike de Gaulle, Lloyd George did not entertain the ambition to remake the British regime. He did, however, want very much to achieve a sweeping realignment of British political life within the existing regime. The "national fusionist" party he aspired to lead would not only prolong his own political preeminence but allow the British state to shed nineteenth-century problems (such as that of Ireland) which continued to burden its political life, to reallocate resources in pursuit of a more egalitarian, "efficient" national economy, and to conduct a forceful foreign policy capable of preserving Britain's world-power status while managing change in imperial affairs. World War I provided Lloyd George with opportunities to achieve a substantial proportion of these goals. But his fall from power in 1922 reflects his failure to achieve as thorough a realignment of political competition as he had sought, that is, the submergence of his Unionist and Liberal supporters within a new, majority political party of his own making.

The French case suggests, but it cannot prove, that had the Ulster crisis of 1914 been allowed to develop into a bloody confrontation, Lloyd George, or perhaps Churchill, might have enjoyed an earlier opportunity to replace Asquith. In such circumstances, either might have used his talents to exploit intensified fears of internal disruption and external threat for achieving grander ambitions, including enforcement of home rule over all of Ireland. In any event, the burgeoning regime crisis of early 1914 was defused by the decomposition of the Irish question. This mode of rescaling the problem preserved the prestige of the Unionist leadership. While making the Unionist party available for a wartime coalition led by Lloyd George, the Conservatives were also left strong enough to resist the prime minister's efforts to dissolve their party in favor of a "national fusionist" framework. By preserving the autonomy of their political organization until the end of the wartime emergency, and then until disengagement from southern Ireland, Bonar Law and his allies were in position in 1922 to oppose and defeat both a shattered Liberal party and an isolated Lloyd George.[90] Although Lloyd George remained active in British political life until the 1940s, he never returned to center stage.

Only the Protestants of the six northeastern counties of Ulster benefited more than the Conservative party leadership from the denouement of the 1914 regime crisis. The separate Parliament established for Northern Ireland by the 1920 Partition Act and the terms of the 1921 Anglo-Irish treaty, which left the area alloted to Northern Ireland intact, afforded the Protestant-Loyalist majority of that area virtually untrammeled dominion over the Catholic-nationalist minority. Not since the mid-eighteenth century did Protestants in Ireland enjoy as much freedom to organize their affairs at the expense of Irish Catholics as did Northern Ireland's Protestant community from 1922 to the mid-1960s. Nor did the Protestants in the twenty-six counties of the Irish Free State suffer very much. Irish nationalist anxieties to prove their faithfulness to the ideal of an Irish nation-state which included Protestants, in combination with the small numbers and the accommodativeness of southern Irish Protestants, made Protestant life in the new state a comfortable one.[91]

In contrast to Irish Protestants, Irish nationalists (i.e., Catholics) paid a very high price for Britain's embrace of decomposition as the centerpiece of a disengagement strategy. In the first years following the Anglo-Irish treaty, the Catholics of Northern Ireland suffered from repeated and violent attacks by Protestants anxious to reduce the size and self-confidence of the Catholic-nationalist minority in the six-county area. In southern Ireland the result of decomposition was civil war.[92] The pro-treaty majority within the provisional Irish Parliament (the Dail Eireann) accepted both the exclusion of the six counties and a nominal oath of fidelity to the Crown as the price of avoiding risks of military defeat in a continued war and on the basis of beliefs (typical of mainstream Irish nationalists) that compromises with Britain could be used as stepping-stones to more complete fulfillment of nationalist objectives. Thus Michael Collins, who served as commander in chief of the Free State army during the Civil War, described the results of the treaty, not as freedom, but as "freedom to achieve freedom."

With substantial British military assistance, but at a cost in Irish lives which greatly exceeded the cost of the Anglo-Irish War itself, the pro-treaty forces subdued their anti-treaty opponents (led by de Valera himself). In 1927 de Valera and his party, Fianna Fail, took the oath (while dismissing it as an "empty formula") and entered political life in the Free State. Five years later he became president. A new constitution, promulgated in 1937, effectively severed the state's tenuous connection to the British Empire. In 1949 the Dublin government officially declared itself the government of the Republic of Ireland. Despite this progression from "free state" to "republic," bitter memories of the civil war, anger over continued British-Protestant domination of Northern Ireland, and the violent agitation and terrorism of remnants of the anti-treaty wing of the IRA burdened the Dublin government with lawlessness, assassinations, and challenges to its authority.

If, in the Algerian case, the way France negotiated the regime threshold helps explain why a state-building elite of any sort was available upon independence, in the Irish case the way that Britain negotiated the regime threshold helps explain why as well-institutionalized a national movement as Ireland's, and one blessed with as many talented and respected leaders, had as many difficulties as it did establishing a stable and legitimate political order.

In relatively mild form, political life in the Republic of Ireland continues to be afflicted by virtually unrealizable, but virtually unrenouncable, irredentist ambitions. From the perspective of the last seventy years, however, and especially following the violent transformation of the failed Catholic civil rights movement in Northern Ireland in 1968, it is also apparent that Ulster Protestants, and the British government itself, continue to pay the price of having enjoyed a relatively easy escape from the regime crisis of 1914 and, concomitantly, of having forced the Irish nationalists to bear the political burden of compromise in 1921.

No one can know for certain whether a Churchillian crackdown on Protestant Ulster in March 1914 or earlier would have led to either the evacuation of the Protestant majority or a grudging acceptance by most non-Catholics of a gradually harmonious power-sharing arrangement (such as "home rule" for Protestant Ulster, within a united Ireland).[93] It would be reckless to assert that substantial bloodshed would not have occurred or to suggest that some Protestants would not have turned to terrorist methods. But had the regime threshold been crossed without the spatial decomposition of the Irish problem, both the Anglo-Irish War and the civil war might well have been avoided. Such an outcome would also have relieved Northern Irish Catholics from Protestant domination, reduced the likelihood and intensity of cyclical violence over the fate of the six counties, and spared Britain the chronic political distress, economic cost, and international obloquy associated with its continued rule of Northern Ireland.

PART IV

Applications to Israel
and Other Cases

This book began with an examination of the debate in Israel over opposing "inexorable logics"—the so-called irreversibility of Israel's absorption of the West Bank and Gaza Strip versus the so-called inevitability of Israeli disengagement from those territories. Along with the manifest variability in the shape and size of territorial states in contemporary Europe, Asia, and Africa, the confusion of the protagonists in the Israeli debate was used to uncover the inadequacy of designating a state's territorial composition as a part of its definition, that is, as a "given," and the importance of conceiving state expansion and contraction as instances of political institutionalization. Using a two-threshold model of institutionalization (state-building) and de-institutionalization (state contraction), I plotted the evolution of the British-Irish and French-Algerian relationships and developed hypotheses about transitions across the two thresholds, in either direction.

By returning to the Israeli-Palestinian case, the model and the hypotheses associated with it can now be put to work. Chapter 9's task is to plot the Israel–West Bank/Gaza Strip relationship according to the same categories applied to Britain and Ireland (Chaps. 3 and 6) and France and Algeria (Chaps. 4 and 7). In Chapter 10 I draw directly on the two European cases, as well as on hypotheses developed in Chapters 5 and 8, to analyze wars of maneuver and position over the relationship between the State of Israel and territories of the Land of Israel and evaluate the plausibility of different ways to stabilize that relationship. In a final chapter the broader implications of the entire work are discussed.

CHAPTER NINE

Israel and the West Bank and Gaza Strip: Tracing the Status of a Changing Relationship

Israel's victory over Egypt, Syria, and Jordan in June 1967 was a watershed in the Arab-Israeli conflict. In its aftermath, Arab leaders began fashioning policies and adopting attitudes toward Zionism which presumed the long-term presence of a Jewish state in the Middle East. In Israel itself the conquest of Sinai, the Golan Heights, and especially the West Bank and the Gaza Strip set off a revival of religious enthusiasm and Zionist sentiment. As a result, an issue was placed squarely at the center of Israeli politics which before the state's establishment in 1948 had defined the fiercest and most sustained debate within Zionism. Was, or was not, Jewish sovereignty over only *a portion* of the Land of Israel (i.e., partition) a legitimate end to Zionism's geopolitical career?

The Renewed Struggle over the Shape of the State of Israel

In the two decades of independent statehood preceding the Six Day War, Israeli politics had been dominated by competition among rival leaders and factions within the Labor Zionist movement. The "activist" or militantly irredentist wing of Labor Zionism had largely traded its espousal of territorial maximalism for opportunities to share with the dominant Mapai (Labor) Party in governing the country. The religious parties, preferring political spoils to political messianism, became Labor's junior partner. Herut and other Land of Israel–oriented groups were marginalized within a State of Israel whose politics revolved around issues of security, economic progress, and processes of social adjustment. The liberation or redemption of biblically promised territories or religious commitments to advance the coming of the Messiah through political action were ideas that virtually no one discussed as politically significant.

A crucial feature of this political landscape was the hegemonic status achieved by the armistice lines of 1949—the Green Line (movement from point J to point K on Fig. A-4 in the Appendix). Not only the vast majority of Israeli citizens (both Jewish and Arab) but virtually the entire non-Arab world accepted Israel's 1949 boundaries—bigger than the United Nations's Partition Plan borders, but considerably smaller than any historically based description of the Land of Israel—as the Israeli state's permanent and legitimate frontiers. According to the most comprehensive study of the subject, between the Sinai campaign in 1956 and the 1967 war there was in Israel "no public discussion of the possibility of changing the borders."[1] Although the anthems and the official documents of Menachem Begin's Herut party proclaimed loyalty to the Revisionist dream of a Jewish state throughout the entire Land of Israel (including both banks of the Jordan River), by 1965 the party responded to the disinterest and skepticism of Israeli voters by paying only lip service to its traditional irredentist demands.[2]

But as exaltation and amazement after the June victory replaced the fear and depression that had preceded it, the limits placed on the geographic shape of the Israeli state by the Green Line lost their hegemonic status. The dramatic expansion of Jewish control over the very heart of biblical Israel brought the question of Israel's rightful size and shape back to the center of its political life. Mythologies of the Land of Israel and the emotions, appeals, and symbols associated with *geulat haaretz* (redemption of the Land) and *Eretz Yisrael hashlema* (the completed Land of Israel) could once again be mobilized on behalf of expansionist political programs, affording unprecedented opportunities for Revisionist and religious Zionism to unseat the Labor party from its traditionally dominant position.

The Six Day War thus set the stage for a war of position over the shape of the state. The common ideological core of the various hegemonic projects advanced by Israeli annexationists has been their determination to transform the extension of Jewish sovereignty over the whole Land of Israel into a collectively recognized purpose of the state, a purpose just as central to its identity as maximizing Jewish immigration (the "ingathering of the exiles"—*kibuttz galuyot*). In response, anti-annexationists were forced to defend and promote their no longer hegemonic conception of the state and its territorial composition. In contrast to the expressivist, consummatory norms invoked by those favoring absorption of the captured territories, anti-annexationists have advocated fundamentally instrumental approaches, denying that the principle of the unity of the Land of Israel should stand prior to the principle of the State of Israel or the interests of its citizenry. Within this discourse, secular, territorially pragmatic, ethnocentric, but largely liberal interpretations of Zionism were highlighted—approaches associated since the mid-1930s with the mainstream of the Labor Zionist movement.

The war of position that developed over the shape of the Israeli state can be divided into two stages. From 1967 to 1977, ideological and political entrepreneurs from each of the three main streams of Zionist political life—Labor Zionism, Revisionism, and religious Zionism—refashioned available ideational resources to develop hegemonic projects centered on the substantial expansion of the boundaries of the state. In 1977 an annexationist alliance among these groups, led by Revisionists (the Likud), took power and embarked upon a wide-ranging effort hegemonically to institutionalize beliefs that the size and shape of the State of Israel corresponded to a conception of the whole Land of Israel which included as its irreducible core all the territory of Palestine between the Jordan River and the Mediterranean Sea.

August 1967 saw the emergence of the Movement for the Whole (Completed) Land of Israel. Predominant among its organizers were followers of Yitzhak Tabenkin—the ideological leader and political mentor of "activist" Labor Zionism. Before the June war Tabenkin had largely abandoned irredentist appeals, but afterward he characterized the war as a continuation of the 1948 War of Liberation, arguing that maintaining the newly won unity of the whole Land of Israel was the only chance for "true peace" and the only acceptable basis for Zionism.[3] Joining the Tabenkinites in this organization were veterans of the Irgun and Lehi underground, and some religious intellectuals influenced by the messianic, mystical Zionism of Rabbi Abraham Isaac Kook—first chief rabbi of Palestine under the British mandate. In the movement's credo, the principle of the entire Land of Israel replaced the idea of a "normal" Jewish state intent on accommodating itself to its neighbors as the core principle of Zionism. "No government in Israel," it declared in its manifesto, "is entitled to give up this entirety, which represents the inherent and inalienable right of our people from the beginnings of its history.[4]

With Begin's rise to power in 1977, the Movement for the Whole Land of Israel dissolved. Most of its members joined the Likud, and various ultranationalist parties allied with Likud or blended into Gush Emunim—the settlement-oriented, mass-based fundamentalist movement.[5] Gush Emunim (Bloc of the Faithful) was officially founded in 1974 by students of Rabbi Tzvi Yehuda Kook, Abraham Isaac's son. Most of these religious and political activists had emerged after the Six Day War as the angry young guard of the National Religious party, bent on moving its place-holding leaders aside and substituting redemptionist zeal and irredentist enthusiasm for their patronage-based politics.

Rabbi Tzvi Yehuda Kook's transmission of his father's message offered the future leaders of Gush Emunim, and the generation of religious youth they came to represent, a distinctive and inspiring version of Zionism, emphasizing the imperative of reclaiming all the Land of Israel as the decisive step toward messianic redemption. Before the Six Day War, his passionate speeches about redeeming "every clod of earth" of the Land of Israel seemed irrelevant, and even absurd, to those outside his small circle of devotees. After June 1967, however, hundreds, thousands, and then tens of thousands of religious youth were persuaded of his prophetic gifts. Upon Begin's election to the premiership in 1977, the new prime minister publicly acknowledged Gush Emunim's political importance by first praying at the western wall and then kneeling in homage before Tzvi Yehuda himself.[6]

As Likud leaders were well aware, the hegemonic project of Gush activists was enormously more ambitious than their own. Gush's ambition was to eliminate secular Zionism (including Revisionism) as a candidate for hegemonic status in Israel and to replace it with their own militantly religious conception of Zionism's nature and purpose. In the meantime, however, Gush Emunim shared with Revisionist Zionism, and with the activist school of Labor Zionism, a primary commitment to expanding the geographical contours of the state. For Gush Emunim's secular allies, this commitment was itself of ultimate importance. For Gush Emunim it was crucial as the decisive stage in a world-historic and divinely ordained "process of redemption" (*taalich hageula*).[7]

By bringing to fruition an alliance of Revisionism and Jewish fundamentalism, the Labor party's stunning defeat in the May 1977 parliamentary elections marked the beginning of the second stage in the war of position which had begun a decade earlier. Despite the relative unimportance of the territorial issue in the 1977 campaign, the outcome of the election and subsequent Likud victories brought to power men and women committed above all else to reshaping the state in conformance with norms of integralist, irredentist nationalism and activist messianism. Politicians were elevated to the premiership—Menachem Begin and Yitzhak Shamir—whose entire careers were based on uncompromising commitments to Jewish sovereignty over the entire Land of Israel. In September 1983, shortly after he assumed the post of prime minister in the wake of Begin's resignation, Yitzhak Shamir clearly stated his view of the struggle over the whole Land of Israel as a war of position, as a conflict over values so precious and absolute that normal political competition, including elections or referenda, could simply not be allowed to determine the outcome. The fight over "partition," Shamir told a sympathetic journalist,

> has become, indeed, an ideological war.... The wholeness of the country is founded on the annals of the people of Israel. One should never forget that changes do take place in democratic elections, but this subject—involving the borders—is substantive, historic. The question of Eretz Yisrael is topical every 4 years during the elections, because people must adopt a stance. But beyond that, no election campaign will make a decision that would affect the following generations on a subject that forms the basis of Zionism. Eretz Yisrael is above any decision in elections because it constitutes the basis of Zionism.[8]

In the first decade of the war of position that followed the 1967 war, a set of hegemonic conceptions which had protected the power of the Labor establishment for two decades was displaced. After 1977, those whose ideas had been trivialized by formerly hegemonic notions sought to do the same to their anti-annexationist opponents. Begin's objective was nothing less than the hegemonic establishment of a new Zionist paradigm, supported by a new history of the independence struggle, a new relationship between religion and politics, and a new emphasis on the people, Bible, and Land of Israel rather than on the boundaries, citizens, and laws of the state of Israel. The heroes and honored myths of one Zionist subculture represented the villains, falsehoods, jealousies, and bombast of the other.[9]

The definitive focus of this transformation was the government's explicit determination to make permanent Israel's control of the West Bank and Gaza Strip, thereby implementing Jewish rule throughout the western Land of Israel, that is from the Jordan River to the Mediterranean Sea. From 1977 to the end of the second Likud government in 1984, and during the third Likud government (1990–92), the beginning and the end of government policy was to create conditions that would incapacitate any future government's effort to disengage from these territories. Abandoning the relatively small-scale policies of settlement and de facto annexation implemented by previous Labor-led governments, Begin's governments undertook a wide-ranging, multifaceted campaign to encourage Jews to settle in all parts of the territories, encourage Arabs to emigrate from them, and strip as many legal, administrative, and psychological meanings as possible from the pre-1967 Green Line.[10]

Gush Emunim was the spearhead for Likud settlement policies and the political guardian of its support among large segments of the religious population. But its ideology was too elaborate and extravagant to provide formulas which the majority of Israelis could accept as the "common sense" of their political beliefs. Since the Likud had not produced theoreticians whose work could be used to rationalize its state-building ambitions to the taste of contemporary Israeli Jews, its governments relied on the thinking of disciples of Yitzhak Tabenkin, Berl Katznelson, disillusioned admirers of Ben-Gurion, and other Land of Israel–oriented Labor Zionists for formulas to anchor Israeli rule of the territories on a hegemonic basis. These formulas advance transcendental understandings of Jewish rights to the whole Land of Israel. They elevate an exclusivist and romantic interpretation of the Jewish nation's collective memory to the status of a first principle, treating the Bible and its promises as "holy" without, however, acknowledging the existence of God.[11]

On the popular level it was Moshe Dayan who was mainly responsible for developing a strategy for victory in the annexationists' war of position. Chief of staff in the mid-1950s, minister of defense during the Six Day War, Dayan split from the Labor party in 1977 and accepted Begin's offer to be foreign minister in the first Likud government. Dayan's importance to the Likud flowed from his traditional links to the Labor party establishment (his father had been among the founders of Mapai), his status as Ben-Gurion's preferred heir, his charismatic appeal to broad sectors of the Israeli population (at least before 1973), and his politically expedient preference for accomplishing territorial expansion by "creating facts" rather than through formal declarations of annexation.

Two months after the Six Day War, Dayan spoke at a reinterment ceremony for Jews killed in 1948 defending the Jewish quarter of Jerusalem's Old City. Dayan hailed the return of the Jewish nation to its heartland in tones that signaled abandonment of his Ben-Gurionist heritage and his embrace of an irredentist ethos. He intoned, "We have returned to the Mount, to the cradle of our nation's history, to the land of our forefathers, to the land of the Judges, and to the fortress of David's dynasty. We have returned to Hebron, to Shechem [Nablus], to Bethlehem, and Anatoth, to Jericho and the fords over the Jordan."[12]

Dayan considered hegemonic incorporation of Judea, Samaria, and the Gaza District possible after twenty to thirty years of Israeli state-building. His strategy was to create networks of "facts"—facts that would cumulatively prevent smaller conceptions of the shape of the state from appearing to be right or even possible. He characterized his approach as "in opposition to those who fear that this will 'bind our hands' . . . I favor facts that will bind hands; not only ours—also those of the other side, and the hands of reality."[13] He advocated settlements in the territories, economic ties spanning the Green Line, and adjustments in prevailing legal and administrative arrangements, not for their own sake, and explicitly not for security purposes, but to make the point that "there is nothing sacred about the previous map from 1948" and to contribute to the creation of a new psychological reality.[14] A way had to be found, Dayan argued, to bring an end to questions raised by Israelis which "explicitly or implicitly challenge our right to this land." The key element in this transformation of public discourse would be the reconstructed "will and faith" of the Jewish people.[15] Dayan believed that *"If we are able to unite around this idea in this spirit—in our behavior, within the Jewish public in Israel and within the Jewish people as a whole—we will be able to face this challenge of determining the map,* the territory, and the borders of security for the state of Israel."[16]

Despite his best efforts, Dayan failed to convince the Labor party to adopt "creeping annexation" as the guiding principle of its policy toward the territories. Blamed by many Israelis for casualties suffered in the 1973 war, Dayan resigned as defense minister in 1974. As noted, he joined the Likud government as foreign minister in 1977. Indeed, absent the religious imagery commonly employed by Begin and other leaders of the Likud and the National Religious party, Dayan's perspective corresponded quite well to the overall objectives and the modus operandi of the Likud leadership. In December 1982, Yitzhak Shamir, who served as prime minister in four different Likud-dominated governments, publicly indicated his understanding of the requirements of hegemonic construction as Dayan had described them. Then Foreign Minister Shamir told a meeting of young Herut activists that they should refuse to respond rationally to arguments about the merits of the case for keeping the territories under Israeli rule. To do so, he suggested, would imply that some sort of conditionality was attached to the enlarged shape of the state and thereby postpone the elimination of such arguments from public debate. "We, members of the national movement," he continued, "must drive into every youth and Jew, this deep, simple, and elementary realization that Eretz Yisrael is ours. Why? Because, without any justifications or explanations, it is [*kacha zeh*]."[17]

The settlement campaign was the centerpiece of the Dayan–Likud–Gush Emunim strategy for absorbing the territories. Although economic and military rationales were commonly invoked, the campaign's ultimate purpose was to set in motion more fundamental ideological, cultural, and psychological processes. Accordingly, the drastic increases in expenditures on settlements between 1978 and 1983 (described in Chap. 1) were accompanied by policies in the educational, broadcasting, judicial, and administrative spheres designed to accelerate the disappearance of the Green Line from the practical life and ordinary language of all Israelis. Under Dayan's influence the Ministry of the Interior had ordered as early as

February 1968 that the West Bank be referred to in official pronouncements as "Judaea and Samaria." Use of the term "enemy territory" to
refer to the occupied areas was also prohibited.[18] By 1969 the government
eliminated the Green Line from all official maps of the country.[19] After
coming to power the Likud changed the government's terminology for
settlement in the occupied territories, substituting the term *hitnachlut*
(evoking biblical injunctions and promises to "inherit" the land through
settlement) for *hityashvut*, an emotionally neutral term.[20]

Early in his second term, Prime Minister Begin condemned Israel state
radio as "anti-Zionist" and likened its director to an official of the British
mandatory regime. Thereafter use of the terms "occupied territory" and
"West Bank" was forbidden in news reports. Television and radio journalists were effectively banned from initiating interviews with Arabs who
recognized the PLO as their representative.[21] Early in 1983 the Television
Board ruled that settling the West Bank and Gaza strip no longer constituted a "subject of public controversy," thereby permitting stations to
broadcast advertisements for settlements as "public service announcements." It also began enforcing a ban on generic terms (such as "personalities"—*ishim*) to refer to PLO members unless the terms employed clearly
labeled them as terrorists.[22] In 1980 and 1986 laws were passed outlawing
any nonscholarly meetings between Israelis and PLO-affiliated Palestinians,
whether in Israel or abroad, banning expressions of support for the PLO
(including representations of the Palestinian flag), and declaring as ineli-
gible for participation in parliamentary elections any political party not
recognizing Israel's character as "the state of the Jewish people."

This effort to establish its own ideological position as bounding what
would be considered legitimate was reflected in the rhetoric of Likud
politicians and in the party's tactics in the 1984 election campaign. During
the 1984 and subsequent campaigns the Likud and its allies began promoting themselves as comprising *hamachane haleumi* (the national camp).
By so doing they reversed Ben-Gurion's campaign of hegemonic ostracism
against the right by suggesting that those who questioned the principle of
Eretz Yisrael hashlema, including the Labor party, were no longer fit to
be considered members of the national community.[23]

To further the absorption of the territories into the consciousness of
what Israelis considered their state, and not alien, "occupied" areas, the
Arabs who lived there were redesignated and the system of administrative
controls over them reconceived. Official planning documents for the future
of the territories referred to the non-Jewish residents of these areas, who
in fact comprised overwhelming majorities of their populations, as "the
minorities"—the term traditionally favored by Israeli governments for Arabs living within the boundaries of the state. In 1978 Prime Minister Begin

and other cabinet ministers regularly began referring to Palestinian Arabs within the territories along with Arab citizens of Israel as "Arabs of the Land of Israel." In November 1981 the administrative apparatus that governed Arab affairs in the territories was, in name at least, replaced by a "civilian administration" with "coordinators" and "administrators" substituting for "military governors" and their subordinates. These personnel were backed up not by a separately constituted "military government" for the occupied territories but by army units designated by the overall command structure of the Israel Defense Forces—the Central Command for the West Bank and the Southern Command for the Gaza Strip.[24]

A wide variety of measures was taken to foster perceptions by the settlers and other Israelis that life in the territories was governed by the same norms and expectations as prevailed within the Green Line. In 1979, under the rubric of the Ministry of the Interior, the areas were divided into "administrative regions" within which regional councils composed of representatives of Jewish settlements (but not of Arab towns and villages) were given authority for planning activities, zoning regulations, self-administration, and enactment of ordinances.[25] Early in 1983 both settlements and Arab municipalities were hooked up to the Israeli telephone and electricity grids. An expensive road-building program was begun, emphasizing highways that would bypass Arab localities, thereby linking Israeli commuters in West Bank settlements to their jobs in the coastal plain while encouraging perceptions of the landscape as no more "Arab" than any other part of the country. Subsidies equal to twenty times its ticket sales were also granted to the Egged Bus Company for providing regular service to and from Jewish settlements in the West Bank.[26]

In December 1980, municipal courts for Jewish inhabitants of the territories were inaugurated, making it unnecessary for Israeli citizens to appear before local Arab courts enforcing the military government's interpretation of Jordanian law. But the accelerated flow of settlers to the territories brought a host of tangled legal and administrative issues to the surface. Ranging from tax evasion to vigilantism, these "technical problems" were exploited to justify standard clauses in all new Israeli legislation which provided that Israeli citizens living in the territories should be treated under the law "as if they were living within Israel." In January 1984, the Knesset attached to its routine extension of the Emergency Regulations a clause enabling the justice minister, with the approval of the Knesset Constitution, Law, and Justice Committee, to apply any Israeli law he might deem fit to Jewish settlers in the West Bank and Gaza Strip. In light of Israel's commitment under the 1978 Camp David Accords not to impose Israeli sovereignty over these areas until after negotiations on their future had taken place, such discrete, "technical" responses to administrative and

legal "anomalies" provided convenient, "natural" opportunities to promote state expansion without confronting directly an international consensus opposed to outright annexation.[27]

The long-run purpose of these policies was to transform Israeli beliefs,
allegiances, and interests—to reshape the cognitive map of Israeli to con-
form with an image of the country which included the territories as no
different from other regions of the state. If this were accomplished, all
future governments would be prevented from publicly entertaining "land
for peace" options with respect to the West Bank and Gaza Strip. In terms
of the framework presented in this study, pursuit of this aim has been an
effort to establish on a hegemonic basis a new conception of the shape of
the Jewish state—to push the problem of what to do with the West Bank
and Gaza Strip not only past the regime threshold, but past the ideological
hegemony threshold as well.

The Trajectory of the West Bank/Gaza Strip Problem in Israeli Politics

After approximately a dozen years of movement within the incumbent
stage of the state-building process, the relationship between Israel and the
West Bank and Gaza Strip crossed the regime threshold. In other words,
within the Israeli political class the implications of state contraction for
the integrity of the regime were added to perceptions and calculations
about partisan advantage. The location of the problem of the size and
shape of Israel, that is to say, the degree of institutionalization of the
territories' integration into the Israeli state, has subsequently oscillated
between the regime and ideological hegemony thresholds.

Establishing that this in fact has been the trajectory of the West Bank/
Gaza Strip problem in Israeli politics requires demonstrating the following
three things. First, I show that between 1967 and 1977 Israeli elites who
favored territorial compromise were politically constrained from pursuing
that objective by incumbent-level concerns, and *not* by fears of extralegal
threats to the stability of the parliamentary regime or the legitimacy of
state authority. Second, I demonstrate, with converging streams of evidence, that by 1983 Israeli elites and the attentive public believed that the
norms and legal framework of Israeli democracy would no longer constrain
opposition to policies leading toward territorial compromise, that such
policies might well trigger extraconstitutional and even violent reactions,
and that leaders inclined toward disengagement would be obliged to cope
with threats to the regime as well as manage risks to their careers, parties,
or coalitions. Third, I show that even during their most successful period,

between 1984 and 1987, Israeli annexationists were unable to move the status of the territories across the ideological hegemony threshold in the state-building direction—unable, in other words, to replace arguments over the future of the West Bank and Gaza Strip with presumptions.

Incumbent-Level Aspects of the Struggle, 1967–1977

We have already seen how great was the political impact of the Six Day War on Israel. But the war also had enormous consequences in the Arab world, without which Israel would not have been as torn as it has been over whether to engage in a territories-for-peace deal with its traditional enemies. A great consequence of the war was the apparently mortal blow it dealt to the "myth of the second round"—the idea, popular in the Arab world between 1948 and 1967, that if only the Arab states were given one more chance to defeat Israel the 1948 disaster would be shown to have been a fluke. According to this view, the Zionist problem could be solved by forcibly liquidating Jewish political power in the Middle East. The decisiveness of Israel's victory in the Six Day War, along with a growing belief in Israel's nuclear capacity, drove this kind of thinking to the margins of Arab political debate—especially within the states bordering on Israel.

In November 1967, Jordan and Egypt accepted United Nations Security Council Resolution 242, "guaranteeing the territorial inviolability and political independence of every state in the area and their right to live in peace within secure and recognized boundaries." From 1967 to 1971, groups of Palestinian leaders in the West Bank offered to represent the population of the area in negotiations with Israel which would lead to Israeli withdrawal from the occupied territories, autonomy, or establishment of a nonbelligerent Palestinian state.[28] In 1971, Egypt's new president, Anwar Sadat, publicly announced his willingness to make peace with Israel and offered to sign an interim agreement based on Israeli withdrawal from the eastern bank of the Suez Canal. In 1972, President Hafez el-Assad announced Syria's acceptance of Resolution 242 as a means for achieving Israeli withdrawal from the occupied territories and the national rights of the Palestinians. Aside from repeated secret meetings with Israeli cabinet ministers, in March 1972 Jordan's King Hussein offered to reach a modus vivendi with Israel on the basis of a Hashemite federation that would include a Palestinian homeland comprised of the West Bank and Gaza Strip. In the aftermath of the October (Yom Kippur) War in 1973, King Hussein also expressed interest in an interim agreement based on Israeli withdrawal from a portion of the West Bank near the Jordan River.

The conditions and ambiguities surrounding Arab offers and trial balloons complicated Israel's response to them. Nevertheless, the contrast between unambiguous Arab commitments to achieving military victory before the Six Day War and ambiguous Arab commitments to nonbelligerency after June 1967 marked a fundamental transformation in the center of gravity of Arab opinion.[29] This change was the basis for a series of peace initiatives by the Great Powers and the United Nations, including the 1968 efforts of the Big Four, the Rogers Plan advanced by Secretary of State William Rogers in 1969 and 1970, Gunnar Jarring's mediation mission on behalf of the United Nations between 1968 and 1970, and Henry Kissinger's attempts to broaden the scope of the 1974 disengagement-of-forces discussions (between Israel and Syria and Israel and Egypt) to include Jordan.

None of these initiatives was warmly received by Israeli governments. On the second day of the 1967 war, Prime Minister Levi Eshkol announced that Israel sought only peace and entertained no territorial ambitions. A few days after the war, Israel's representative told the United Nations that "everything is negotiable" and that in return for peace treaties with her Arab neighbors Israel was prepared to withdraw from virtually all of the territories occupied during the conflict. By midsummer, however, Israeli leaders began to specify certain portions of the territories which for strategic or emotional reasons would under no circumstances be returned to Arab rule.

In their cautious responses to Arab overtures and these peace initiatives the Israeli governments of Premiers Levi Eshkol (1967–69), Golda Meir (1969–74), and Yitzhak Rabin (1974–77) reflected the deep-rooted suspicions and fears that most Israeli Jews entertained toward anything connected to their security. The Six Day War occurred just twenty-two years after the Nazi Holocaust. Israel's international isolation in the weeks prior to the Six Day War, during which Syrian, Egyptian, and other Arab leaders proclaimed that the day of Israel's destruction was at hand, lent powerful support to the natural inclination of Israelis to take threats of annihilation seriously and to reject any "guarantee" of security other than that which could be achieved through the deterrence or direct application of their own military power. Nevertheless, many Israelis feared the consequences of incorporating masses of Palestinians living in the West Bank and Gaza Strip and were hopeful that most of the territories could be traded for a peace settlement.

When it came to the extent of allowable territorial concessions, however, Israeli public opinion and Israeli political leaders were extraordinarily divided. Even so, no Israeli government between 1967 and 1977 ever feared that a policy of territorial compromise might trigger substantial threats to the integrity of the parliamentary regime. Instead, fears of splitting the coalition or the major parties that comprised the coalition, that is incumbent-level factors, inhibited virtually every government during this period from pursuing negotiating opportunities or restraining settlement activity with the vigor that many in successive cabinets desired. Hence the location of the problem of the disposition of the West Bank and Gaza Strip can be depicted, from late 1967 to the Likud victory in the May 1977 Knesset elections, as moving toward but remaining to the left of the regime threshold (point L to M on Fig. A-5).

The importance of incumbent-level constraints on Israeli 1967–1977 policy toward the territories as well as the absence of regime-level concerns among Israeli political elites immersed in struggles over these policies are apparent in policies sponsored by the 1967 national unity government until its demise in mid-1970, and by the Labor party and the governing coalitions it subsequently organized between 1970 and 1977. Referred to often as a policy of "deciding not to decide," this response to Arab and international suggestions for movement toward new political arrangements and territorial withdrawals was characterized by vague formulations, stipulations of what Israel would *not* accept as part of a negotiated settlement, avoidance of official endorsement of any explicit commitment to withdraw eventually from parts of the West Bank and Gaza Strip, and postponement of direct and public consideration of pointed questions. The most thorough available study of the link between Israeli domestic politics and foreign policy in this period explains the pattern of "deadlock and immobilism in Israeli foreign policy" not only by differences of opinions between the parties that made up successive coalition governments, but also by "deep divisions of opinion *inside* each of the major parties... [which] deprived successive coalition governments of a workable consensus and prompted them to avoid decision—thereby preserving the unity of their ranks."[30] Meanwhile, occupation policy was designed to prevent the emergence of a central and recognized Palestinian leadership that could serve as a candidate for negotiations. Discouragement of Palestinian initiatives was accompanied by systematically pessimistic constructions of overtures from the Arab states and the international community. Fragile alignments were thereby protected from the strain of arguing over how to respond to viable opportunities for negotiating a "territories for peace" agreement.[31]

The most important aspect of the national unity government formed on the eve of the Six Day War was Begin's presence—the first time in its forty-year history that the leader of Revisionist Zionism had been allowed entry into the governing coalition of the Zionist movement or the Israeli state. Begin's appointment as "minister without portfolio" was a major contribution to rehabilitating his public image—from that of a violent and dangerous demagogue to a responsible political leader. His presence in the government, along with the voices of ultranationalists within the National Religious party, the traditional preferences of "activist" elements within the Labor Party, and Dayan's influence, made it impossible for the cabinet to remain united behind its initial proclamations indicating readiness for sweeping territorial concessions on all fronts in return for peace.

The repeated response of the Labor leadership to the specter of a Dayan-Gahal-NRP government was to avoid situations, especially peace negotiations, which would have led to a confrontation with Dayan and his allies. Accordingly, any ambiguity in negotiating opportunities was construed as compelling justification for rejecting them. Instead, emphasis was placed on achieving formal peace treaties. Israel's commitment to peace was expressed officially in vague formulas emphasizing withdrawal to "secure" or "defensible" boundaries. Meanwhile, a number of paramilitary settlements were established in the West Bank, while various measures of economic integration were implemented—measures sponsored by Dayan's Defense Ministry and the military government it supervised. In general, Israeli governments between 1967 and 1977 acted as if their official policy were guided by the principle of "territorial compromise," even as policies of settlement, economic integration, and political repression were implemented which supported the Dayan approach of de facto incorporation of all the West Bank and Gaza. The result, as Dayan himself remarked in October 1967, was a government "reluctant to state its position on peace proposals [because] it had no policy in this regard."[32]

The national unity government formed in 1967 was reconstituted after the 1969 elections, a coalition largely made possible by its "decision-not-to-decide" policy toward the territories. The arrangement held until the summer 1970, when the United States brokered a cease-fire agreement between Egypt and Israel to end the costly "war of attrition" over the Suez Canal. Washington provided a package of armaments, guarantees, and threats, which convinced Prime Minister Meir and her Labor party ministers in July 1970 to accept the cease-fire, including formal acceptance of United Nations Security Council Resolution 242 "in all its parts." This meant, according to Meir's own interpretation, that in principle Israel was prepared for withdrawal from territories on *all* fronts.

Meir's acceptance of Resolution 242 was made in full recognition that the cost would be Begin's exit from the cabinet and the collapse of the national unity government. Begin had made his conditions for remaining in the cabinet clear. Meir had coaxed Begin into remaining in the cabinet in May 1970, by hedging her announcement of Israeli acceptance of Resolution 242 and by permitting Gahal deputies to abstain on the relevant parliamentary vote. No such arrangements were offered, or solicited, in

July. So Gahal (the Herut-led bloc that preceded establishment of the Likud) exited from the government, leaving the National Religious party holding the government's coalition majority in its hands and sharpening the threat of coalition collapse.[33] What is important to observe, however, in establishing that the question of the territories was located to the left of the regime threshold in 1970, is that aside from Begin's threat to breakup the national unity coalition if the terms offered by the United States were accepted, neither he nor his party challenged the authority of the government to act as it did. Nor, prior to their decision, did the possibility of such a challenge enter into the calculations of Labor party leaders.[34]

Confidence in the apparent invincibility of Israel's military position and the strong desire to avoid exposing disagreements within the coalition and within the Labor party influenced Israel's negative responses to Egyptian President Anwar Sadat's 1971 plan for an interim agreement in the Sinai and to King Hussein's "Hashemite Kingdom" plan in 1972.[35] These factors, combined again with Dayan's popularity and fears that he might mount an independent challenge to the Labor party, also explained adoption in April 1973 of the Galili document, which expanded the government's commitment to policies of de facto annexation, including approving one of Dayan's pet projects—construction of a port city (Yamit) in northeastern Sinai.

The most striking evidence of the incumbent-level determinants of Israeli policy toward the future of the West Bank occurred after the Yom Kippur War of October 1973. In July 1974, Prime Minister Yitzhak Rabin overruled the advice of his foreign minister, Yigal Allon, and rejected Henry Kissinger's offer to mediate peace negotiations between Jordan and Israel based on Israeli withdrawal from the strategically unimportant town of Jericho. As had Golda Meir before him, Rabin had secured the participation of the National Religious party in his coalition by promising that no decisions about the future of the West Bank and Gaza Strip would be taken without first calling new elections. Rabin also feared the Labor party could split apart if open debate on the Palestinian question were allowed.[36] This was the last serious opportunity to move toward an Israeli-Jordanian or Israeli-Palestinian-Jordanian settlement of the West Bank question before the fall of Rabin's government in 1977.

Crossing the Regime Threshold in the State-Building Direction, 1977–1984

Rabin's mid-1970s Labor government was the last Israeli cabinet that could contemplate policies of territorial compromise in the West Bank and

Gaza Strip without calculating the implications of such a policy for the stability and legitimacy of the legal-political order. This substantial shift toward incorporating the territories into the state of Israel was the direct result of policies of de facto annexation pursued by the first and second Likud governments, in partnership with its extragovernmental allies, especially Gush Emunim.[37] The intent of their efforts had been to advance the integration of the territories beyond the ideological hegemony threshold. As I demonstrate below, they did not achieve this objective. By the mid-1980s, however, their efforts had had a substantial enough demographic, cultural, psychological, and political impact to push the problem of withdrawing from the West Bank and Gaza Strip beyond the regime threshold.

Since the events are so recent, since the issues involved continue to occupy the center of Israeli political life, and since many of the politicians whose behavior and calculations are of interest are still active, detailed memoirs and monographic materials concerning the private calculations of key actors are unavailable. Nevertheless, converging streams of evidence clearly indicate that the crossing of the regime threshold in the state-building direction, marking a discontinuous change in the level of disruption which politically attentive Israelis expected to be associated with contraction of the state's jurisdiction, took place between 1982 and 1984.

Beginning in 1980 a series of events indicated that the regular, legal institutions of political competition were unlikely to be able to contain the struggle among Israelis over the disposition of the territories. In May 1980, two West Bank Arab mayors were maimed in car bombings carried out by Jewish vigilantes. Shortly afterward, Avraham Achitov, head of the Shin Bet (Israel's internal security service), resigned in protest against obstruction by Prime Minister Begin and Chief of Staff Rafael Eitan of his investigation of the incident and the refusal of requests to arrest Gush Emunim leaders or infiltrate groups affiliated with it which were suspected (rightly so as it turned out) of responsibility for the bombings and of participation in other terrorist activities.[38] In July 1980, fourteen law professors petitioned the attorney general demanding a comprehensive investigation of collusion among Likud ministers, right-wing army officers, and settler vigilantes. A commission to study the problem was appointed in May 1982. Its heavily censored report attributed a widespread pattern of disrespect for the law and lackadaisical investigation of settler violence against Arabs to political pressures emanating from the highest echelons and to the sentiments of top-ranking military authorities.[39]

In April 1982, clashes occurred between Israeli soldiers ordered to evacuate the Sinai settlements and Gush Emunim settlers. Six weeks later Israel invaded Lebanon. The strategic objective of the war, as explained by Begin,

Eitan, and Defense Minister Ariel Sharon, was to shatter the national morale of the Palestinians and eliminate effective Arab opposition from within the West Bank and Gaza Strip to Israeli absorption of these areas. As casualties mounted, an unprecedented antiwar movement developed within Israel whose participants included some soldiers who refused to enter Lebanon. By early 1983, virtually the entire anti-annexationist camp was condemning the Begin government for using the Israeli army to achieve political objectives not supported by a national consensus. It was against this background, in February 1983, that a grenade was thrown by a Kahane supporter during a Peace Now demonstration in Jerusalem. One demonstrator, Emile Grunzweig, was killed. Eight more were wounded, including Avram Burg, son of the minister of the interior.[40]

In late 1983 and early 1984 a wave of violence against Muslim and Christian targets was conducted by a shadowy Jewish group calling itself Terror against Terror. In spring 1984, dozens of Gush Emunim activists were arrested as members of an organized underground terrorist network responsible for the car bombings of the Arab mayors, the deaths of eight Arab students in a machine-gun and grenade attack on the Islamic College in Hebron, and a series of unsuccessful sabotage operations against Muslim shrines on Jerusalem's Temple Mount (the Haram el-Sharif). The arrests were made just prior to implementation of a plot by the underground network to blow up several buses filled with Arab passengers.[41]

These developments, combined with the rapid expansion of settlement in the territories, gave credibility to regime-challenging warnings that Gush Emunim leaders had issued at various times since the mid-1970s—declarations that no government engaged in a policy of territorial compromise in the West Bank and Gaza could be considered legitimate and that the group would resist such a policy by whatever means necessary to prevent the return of parts of the Land of Israel to "foreign rule."[42] Expectations that any struggle over "Judea, Samaria, and the Gaza District" would draw support from the leaders of annexationist political parties, including the Likud, were strengthened by the Likud government's encouragement of Gush Emunim's struggle against its own decision to withdraw from Yamit (the heavily settled northeastern corner of Sinai), the freedom from prosecution enjoyed by hundreds of violently protesting settlers at Yamit when it was evacuated in 1982, and the vigorous support of Likud and NRP ministers for granting amnesty to Gush Emunim terrorists arrested in spring 1984.[43]

A wave of concern for the ability of Israeli democracy to withstand the pressures generated by deep divisions over policies toward the territories and their Arab inhabitants was set off by the growing popularity of Rabbi Meir Kahane, who advocated a theocratic state and the expulsion of all

Arabs from the Land of Israel. Although he had failed in previous attempts to gain a seat in Parliament, in 1984 he was elected. Polls in 1984 and 1985 showed increasing popular support for Kahane and much higher levels of public approval for his message, suggesting that public opinion would not be an effective barrier to right-wing challenges to governmental authority.[44]

These developments led Israeli academicians to begin focusing their scholarship and public commentary on the regime-threatening potential of the struggle over the future of the territories. Shortly before his death in 1980, Israel's leading historian and an authority on European totalitarianism, Jacob Talmon, published a lengthy open letter to Prime Minister Begin. "Extra-parliamentary bodies have been established," wrote Talmon, "which see themselves as bearers of national destiny and saviors of the people, and thereby entitled to their own laws and imperatives." "The rule of law and order," he warned, "is on the point of collapse." Talmon pleaded for a reversal of annexationist policies in order to avert what he characterized as "the danger of civil war hovering over us."[45]

A similar view, citing fears of intra-Jewish violence and the breakdown of parliamentary democracy as incumbent-level consequences of disengagement policies, appeared in Meron Benvenisti's annual reports on the status of the West Bank. From 1981 to 1983, he justified his irreversibility thesis by emphasizing the weight of accumulating incumbent-level pressures to block any possible movement toward withdrawal from the West Bank and Gaza Strip. One hundred thousand settlers in the territories, he had argued, would represent "four or five marginal seats in the Knesset ... an effective barrier to any political alternative espousing the principle of territorial compromise."[46] However, in Benvenisti's report on the status of the West Bank in 1984 and 1985, he cited the threat of civil war as another crucial obstacle to Israeli withdrawal from the West Bank and Gaza Strip. Prime Minister Shimon Peres, wrote Benvenisti, "has to contend not only with Shamir and Sharon, but also with the hawks in his own [Labor] party, and beyond them, with the specter of a Jewish civil war, the ultimate enormity in Jewish eyes."[47] By the mid-1980s almost all Israeli social scientists studying the problem of Israel's future relationship to the territories either framed their research around questions pertaining to the vulnerability of the democratic order to extralegal challenges, should a government ever move toward withdrawal, or qualified their findings with the caveat that exercising withdrawal options might well produce organized threats to the stability of the regime, uncertainty as to the unity of the army, and even civil war.[48]

In Israel in the 1980s, as in France in the 1950s, the willingness of polling organizations (or the scholars and politicians who hired them), to pay for polling on particular topics is a reliable indicator of when the political class believes the questions asked have become politically relevant. It is therefore instructive to note that it was in the early 1980s that Israeli pollsters began regularly to ask questions about support for various "antidemocratic" measures. In a PORI (Public Opinion Research Institute) institute poll sponsored by *Haaretz* in July 1980, Israeli Jews were asked whether they "favored or opposed a Jewish terrorist system in the hands of nongovernment Jewish organizations as a reaction to hostile activities of the Arabs of the occupied areas?"[49] In 1983 the Hanoch Smith Institute began asking respondents whether they "supported anyone who acts to get Arabs to leave Judea and Samaria."[50] In February 1983, Mina Tzemach of the Dahaf polling organization was hired by the weekly *Koteret Rashit* to probe public views on whether Peace Now and Gush Emunim, among other organizations, should be outlawed.[51] In December 1983, the *Jerusalem Post* commissioned the Modi'in Ezrahi Research Institute to evaluate public support for creation of "a Jewish group to fight terror with terror."[52] Monitin characterized that 23 percent of the Jewish population which its polls showed supported Kahane's ideas either in full or in part as "the scope of potential support for Israeli fascism."[53] Apart from the actual results of these polls, which showed levels of support for these measures ranging from one-quarter to one-half of the Jewish population, the fact of the surveys themselves indicates the presence of elite calculations about threats to the stability and democratic character of the regime.

Much of the scholarly research which lay behind or was based on these polls was framed by the question of whether changes in Israeli public opinion could provide a diffuse basis of political support for challenges to the legitimacy of the regime.[54] In his study of Israeli political participation, Gadi Wolfsfeld found a significant rise in the number of illegal protest activities between 1979 and 1984. During this period, according to Wolfsfeld, "30% of all acts of protest were illegal, 23% of all protest acts involved some type of public disorder, and 15% included some act of violence." Wolfsfeld's findings also indicate a substantial reluctance on the part of the government and the police to apprehend and prosecute lawbreakers motivated by right-wing political sympathies. Echoing the findings of other Israeli scholars working on similar questions, Wolfsfeld concluded his study with a warning of what he saw as the emergence of "an alarming contempt for the rule of law, and even a potential danger to the stability of democracy in Israel."[55] The proliferation of editorials, commentaries, and public exhortations in the early 1980s concerning the effects of extreme polarization over the West Bank/Gaza Strip/Palestinian Arab question on the integrity of democratic institutions and the rule of law also indicates that the regime threshold was passed about this time.[56]

A content analysis of *Jerusalem Post* editorials shows that in the period 1977–80 only one editorial warned of possible civil war or the violent breakdown of democratic institutions in connection with the dispute over the occupied territories. In the period 1981–84 the same newspaper published thirty-nine such editorials.[57]

A final stream of evidence available for timing the addition of regime threats to incumbent threats as inhibitors of territorial compromise is the introduction of visions of civil war and regime breakdown into the discourse of politicians on both sides of the great debate over the territories. In 1980, Deputy Prime Minister Yigal Yadin, who was known to oppose Begin's policies of de facto annexation, explained the controversial decision to align his centrist Democratic Movement for Change with the Likud by arguing that "if the Labor Party returns to the government, a civil war is possible."[58] In May 1982 and again in a major speech marking the opening of the fall 1982 Knesset session, Prime Minister Begin accused Peres and other Labor party politicians of not only imagining that a civil war would occur, but of hoping it might. Begin cited an article by a Labor party activist which warned of civil war. Begin accused the Labor party of encouraging an atmosphere of impending domestic catastrophe in order to frighten Israelis into turning against the Likud government's commitment to the whole Land of Israel. In his response, Labor party chief Shimon Peres vehemently, albeit somewhat disingenuously, denied the accusations. "I do not know even one person," he said, referring to the confrontation at Yamit, "who even conceived of such an expectation of blood, Jewish blood."[59] After the killing of Emile Grunzweig in February 1983, however, even prominent Herut politicians acknowledged the possibility of serious intra-Jewish political violence.[60]

The intensity of political antagonism was repeatedly manifest on the floor of the Israeli Parliament, where deputies from opposing blocs described each other as living on different planets and vowed to confront each other "Steel against steel, missile against missile."[61]

Exchanges in the Knesset are famous for their vitriol, but by 1985 the idea that the question of what to do with the territories might erupt in a violent conflict between Jews had become an unsurprising element in public discussion. In June 1985, when Peres was asked whether he feared that struggle in Israel over the territories question might lead to "collapse of systems that were considered to be sacred, perhaps even to the point of, heaven forbid, civil war," he responded quite differently than he had three years earlier. Instead of denying he knew anyone who could imagine such a possibility, or casting doubt on the reasonableness of the interviewer's question, Peres justified Labor's participation in a national unity government with the Likud as a means of avoiding the threats to regime stability he was now publicly ready to characterize as real. "I am very disturbed, as you are," Peres told the interviewer, "by the matter of polarization. What is the solution? I say that the solution is to guard the nation's unity, to also guard unified frameworks and, from this aspect, I think the national unity government, with all its problems, is contributing to the nation's unity.... This is a contribution of prime importance, in a situation of polarization."[62]

Even the president of Israel, whose functions are almost exclusively honorific and ceremonial, began taking an active and highly visible role in support of what both President Yitzhak Navon, from 1983 to 1984, and President Haim Herzog, beginning in 1985, publicly characterized as a severe threat to the integrity of Israeli democracy arising from polarization over the issue of the territories and the violent anti-Arab sentiments aroused by right-wing demands for mass expulsions of Arabs. In 1983 the president's office began sponsoring a variety of "education in democracy" programs for Israeli youth. In contrast to the platitudes traditionally offered by Israeli presidents in their Independence Day and Jewish New Year speeches, Presidents Navon and then Herzog, in 1983, 1984, and 1985, made pointed warnings about the dangers of extreme polarization and the threat of a breakdown of Israeli democracy.[63] In preparation for the celebration of Israel's fortieth anniversary, President Herzog invited a collection of Israeli leaders to re-sign the Israeli Declaration of Independence, thereby reaffirming the country's commitment to democracy and to equal rights for all citizens regardless of race, nation, or religion.[64]

The converging streams of evidence presented here indicate that with respect to the West Bank and Gaza Strip, the regime threshold was passed, in the state-building direction, between 1982 and 1984. Since that time no Israeli politicians, including those anti-annexationists who came to power with Yitzhak Rabin in July 1992, have been able to assume that legally promulgated policies of territorial compromise could be pursued effectively without managing severe strains on the regime as well as the government. As noted in my consideration of the British-Irish and French-Algerian cases, however, movement across state-building thresholds entails accumulating obstacles to disengagement, *not* replacing one kind of obstacle with another. The location of the problem of the status of the peripheral territory to the right of the regime threshold thus does not mean that incumbent-level competition ceases to motivate politicians, that regime threats continuously present themselves, or that regime threats henceforth appear as the most salient aspect of competition over the fate of the territory. In the British and French cases, when struggles over the disposition of Ireland and Algeria were located between, but not near to, the regime and ideological hegemony thresholds, political competition was dominated by incumbent-level concerns. In both cases the latent threats to the regime which the location of these problems posed were made manifest only when competition at the incumbent level produced governing coalitions with the potential to move toward disengagement. In Britain this regime crisis developed after the elections of 1910 had produced a coalition joining the Liberal and Irish nationalist parties and after passage of the Parliament Act in 1911 had removed the Lords's veto. In France the regime crisis emerged in early 1958 when increasingly precarious governments within the Fourth Republic became unwilling and/or unable to reassure partisans of French Algeria that disengagement from Algeria would not be sought. In the French case, when the campaign to establish Algérie française was at its zenith, from early 1955 to mid-1957 (i.e., when the location of the problem approached but did not pass the ideological hegemony threshold), struggles over the rules of public discourse concerning Algeria dominated the scene, rather than fears for the integrity of the regime, or calculations of partisan advantage.

In the Israeli case, the prominence of calculations about the regime-threatening consequences of withdrawal from the territories has ebbed and flowed. In early 1985 and 1990, when Shimon Peres as prime minister, and then as Labor party leader, appeared poised to move quickly toward a settlement based on territorial withdrawals, regime threats and calculations about how to cope with or avoid them moved into the spotlight. These concerns faded in 1986, the last year of Peres's term as prime minister, as his anti-annexationist policies appeared to be effectively stymied and as the date of Shamir's assumption of the premiership neared. The absence of public discussion of regime-level issues during the 1992 campaign can be attributed to widespread belief that the election would produce another national unity government. However, discussion of armed resistance to either autonomy or territorial concessions appeared almost immediately after the announcement of a Labor party victory in the June 1992 elections.[65]

State-Building Stalled, 1977–1992

Since the first Likud government in 1977, state-building efforts by Israeli annexationists inside and outside the government have moved the problem of the relationship between Israel and the West Bank and Gaza across the regime threshold. But these efforts have not succeeded in establishing the idea of the whole Land of Israel, or the expansive shape of the state which corresponds to it, as hegemonic within Israel itself. Presumptions have never removed arguments over the future of these areas from the discourse of leading politicians. In other words, the problem has not been relocated across the ideological hegemony threshold.

On the other hand, the intensity and precise terms of debate have varied significantly. In the early to mid-1980s, this variation led some observers of Israeli society to argue that religious Zionism, the principle of the whole Land of Israel, and integral nationalism were in the process of supplanting the secular/rational ethos of Israel as a social democracy.[66] Despite careless formulations and the impression created by exaggerated summaries of their work, none of these scholars claimed that the idea of the whole land of Israel actually became hegemonic inside of Israel. More precise assessments of the ideological, psychological, and cultural success of what was variously termed New Zionism, Neo-Revisionism, or Gush Emunim's redemptionist "fundamentalism" acknowledged the "war of position" waged by the Likud and Gush Emunim to establish a new interpretation of Zionism as hegemonic, but argued that this campaign had not succeeded.[67]

Diachronic analysis of polling data and consideration of the changing language of political debate support the view that following the Six Day War and the breakdown of the hegemonic conception of the 1949 armistice lines as Israel's boundaries, no image of the size and shape of the Israeli state has enjoyed ideological hegemony. It is still possible, however, that a consensus of sorts did form, if by "consensus" one means a nearly unanimous belief, but minus the implication that challenges to it are inconceivable. Even so, contrary to repeated claims of Likud politicians and other annexationists, whatever "national consensus" may have existed against a Palestinian state, negotiations with the PLO, or compromise on the status of expanded East Jerusalem, all but the latter had certainly disappeared by the late 1980s.[68]

Signs of significant expansion in the parameters of public discourse regarding the PLO and a Palestinian state appeared in 1976 and 1977, following discussions among U.S., Soviet, and Israeli diplomats of the possibility of including PLO representatives in a reconvened Geneva conference. In March 1977, Yehoshafat Harkabi, former chief of Israeli military intelligence, published a long article indicating his openness to the possibility that the PLO might evolve into a viable negotiating partner and that establishment of a Palestinian state in the occupied territories might be the basis for an Arab-Israeli peace. Only two years before, Harkabi had rejected the idea of a Palestinian state in the territories as an impossibility. The significance of Harkabi's views is linked to his role as Israel's leading propagandist in the late 1960s and early 1970s, when he portrayed the Arab world, and especially the PLO, as dedicated unreservedly to the destruction of the State of Israel.[69]

Survey data show clearly that from the end of 1976 to 1991, between

30 percent and 60 percent of Israel's Jewish population was willing to accept negotiations with the PLO. The questions used in these surveys almost always included stipulations that the PLO would recognize Israel, renounce terrorism, and/or accept UNSC Resolution 242.[70] By spring 1990, whether to negotiate with the PLO had become such a widely debated and routinely posed question in Israel that survey researchers decided it was no longer appropriate to pose the issue as conditional upon the PLO meeting one condition or another. Instead, explaining a questionnaire used in May 1990, they "preferred to omit these speculative constraints and ask directly about the readiness to negotiate with the PLO at present." They reported that 40 percent of Israeli Jewish respondents answered affirmatively.[71]

At the elite level, as early as February 1985, Minister without Portfolio Ezer Weizman publicly refused to rule out negotiations with the PLO.[72] In March 1985 an editor of the *Jerusalem Post* published a long article describing as "utter nonsense" the claim that there had ever been a "national consensus [that] Israel will not talk to the PLO."[73] In fact, in 1985, even Likud politicians drew back from declarations that negotiations with the PLO were opposed by all Jewish Israelis. Instead Shamir and Sharon accused Shimon Peres and other dovish-liberal politicians of supporting such negotiations. By making these accusations against mainstream politicians, they acknowledged that a consensus against negotiations with the PLO no longer existed. Instead they were forced to retreat to the argument that only by purging Israeli political life of doubts about Jewish rights to the whole Land of Israel and of opinions tending to legitimize the PLO would the country be able establish permanent rule over the territories. This educational effort, to build a consensus and then establish it as hegemonic, was portrayed as the main task of confronting those "faithful to the Land of Israel."[74]

Anti-annexationists in Israel were deeply disappointed that Shimon Peres's term as prime minister in the rotational national unity government ended in October 1986 without beginning "territory-for-peace" negotiations. A mood of depression settled on the "peace camp" from late 1986 to the beginning of the intifada (Palestinian uprising) in December 1987— a mood similar to what it experienced in 1983 and early 1984, following the second Likud government's sharp acceleration of settlement of the territories.[75] Discussions began again over whether energies would be better spent improving living conditions for West Bank and Gaza Palestinians rather than on efforts to end the occupation.[76]

Conversely, the mood in the annexationist camp soared. The Likud's message was that the historic battle over the integrity of the Land of Israel was virtually over. It might take a while for many doves to accept the new parameters of political life, but with Israelis treating the territories, for purposes of transportation routes, recreation, and habitation, as no different from any other part of Israel, it was time to move on to new issues and new challenges. With confidence regained in their ability to block any attempt to move Israel toward disengagement from the territories, annexationists replaced strident characterizations of their opponents with gentler formulations. In 1984 and 1985, while Peres was prime minister, avant-garde commitments to assert Jewish rights on the ancient Temple Mount and even to replace Muslim shrines there with a rebuilt Temple had been primary objectives of Gush Emunim activity. The campaign, employing slogans such as "Messiah Now" and photomontages of Jerusalem as it would appear with a rebuilt Temple instead of the Muslim shrines, was supported by a variety of religious leaders and right-wing politicians both as a means of accelerating the advent of the Messiah and of sabotaging prospects for peace negotiations. But talk about the Temple and the Messiah, and about removing the Muslim "abominations" (Gush Emunim's term for the Mosque of el-Aksa and the Dome of the Rock), frightened most Israelis, no matter what their political inclinations. Following Shamir's assumption of the premiership in October 1986, Gush Emunim and other Temple Mount enthusiasts from the Likud, Tehiya, and the Chief Rabbinate drew back from these sensitive issues to encourage consolidation of a broad national consensus.[77]

Indeed the entire debate in Israel over withdrawal from the territories faded somewhat in late 1986 through 1987, but the progress made by the Likud and its allies in fostering the impression of the permanence of Israeli rule of the territories was short-lived. The intifada, which erupted in December 1987, caused the question of the territories as well as associated debates over the PLO and a Palestinian state to burst back on the Israeli political scene.[78] In fall 1988, surveys designed to identify the beliefs forming the basis of the "Israeli national consensus" showed that on the shape of the state there was no consensus whatsoever. Gideon Doron commented, "If there exists a consensus in Israel, it is only on an extremely basic level, connected to security matters and to Zionism. When we pass to the means to accomplish these goals the consensus vanishes."[79]

The extent to which mainstream politicians were no longer constrained to deny their contemplation of a Palestinian state or negotiations with the PLO as plausible options is reflected in formulas used by Labor party leaders to answer questions on this subject in spring 1988. Shimon Peres said he would not negotiate with the PLO, "not because of the organization or its leaders' past, but because they want to establish a Palestinian state with an army equipped with Soviet weapons 100 meters from Jerusalem." He expressed "doubts whether it is possible to negotiate with the PLO because the organization is divided, and until Arafat can prove that the PLO can make decisions, there is no chance of him convincing us that he can make decisions in the name of the PLO."[80] Responding to a question by an Egyptian reporter, Yitzhak Rabin characterized the Labor party's position as "*currently* against the establishment of a Palestinian state between Israel and Jordan."[81] Thus did both Peres and Rabin shift from principled to contingent rejections of a Palestinian state and negotiations with the PLO. By so doing they revealed their calculations that neither topic was beyond the pale of discussion in Israeli politics.

Labor's allies on the dovish-liberal side of the spectrum were considerably bolder than either Peres or Rabin in breaking the old taboos. Following King Hussein's formal disengagement of Jordan from the West Bank, in summer 1988, the leaders of the Civil Rights Movement, Mapam, and Amnon Rubinstein's Shinui (Change) party formally called on the government of Israel to announce its readiness to negotiate with the PLO once the PLO renounced terrorism and recognized the state of Israel.[82] In September the Foreign Ministry's director general Abraham Tamir, a leader of Weizman's short-lived Yahad party, told Jewish leaders in New York City that "Israel would have to get used to the idea of negotiating with the PLO."[83] By the end of the year the large, consensus-oriented Peace Now movement also shifted its public stance. Peace Now's traditional strategy has been to remain perfectly acceptable to middle-of-the-road Israelis. Accordingly, for years it muzzled its leaders' preferences for negotiations with the PLO. In December 1988, following Arafat's Geneva declaration and the United States–PLO dialogue, Peace Now publicly expressed its support for negotiations with the PLO and its "unequivocal recognition of the Palestinian people's right to national self-determination."[84] In 1989, General Amnon Shahaq, chief of military intelligence, publicly characterized the PLO as the only viable Palestinian leadership in the territories.[85] More importantly, mainstream Labor leaders with ambitions to lead their party and their country, such as Moshe Shahal, Uzi Baram, and Mordechai Gur, began to call explicitly for negotiations with the PLO. Meanwhile Shimon Peres and even Yitzhak Rabin edged ever closer to public declarations and formulas corresponding to private indications of their belief in the necessity of doing so.[86]

The loss of ground suffered by the annexationist hegemonic project is also evident in the Likud's failed attempt, early in 1989, to pass a Knesset bill extending to parliamentary deputies the 1986 ban on contact by Israelis with PLO members. In a February 1989 survey of 113 of 120 members of Israel's Parliament, 21 indicated they were willing to carry on a dialogue with Arafat. Twenty-seven deputies refused to answer the question.[87] The following month a survey of Likud leaning voters indicated that 49 percent were prepared, under the usually stated conditions, to talk to the PLO.[88] A January 1990 poll of Israel's urban Jewish population reported that whatever their preferences, 50 percent of respondents believed that "eventually we will have to negotiate with the PLO"; another 12 percent thought it was a possibility.[89]

Early in 1989, Yitzhak Shamir was reliably reported to have abandoned any hope of advancing Israeli rule over the territories toward hegemonic status. Instead he reconciled himself to a struggle against a further weakening of Israel's hold on the areas—"passing the banner to the next generation without a change in the situation."[90] Meanwhile even he felt constrained by the changing contours of Israeli public opinion to defend his opposition to negotiations with the PLO, not in principle but on instrumental grounds. Searching for a more limited but convincing characterization of a "national consensus" with which to anchor his views, Shamir focused on opposition to a Palestinian state. He argued, "We don't want to negotiate with the PLO. . . . What does the PLO want? a Palestinian state, immediately. But we say we oppose a Palestinian state, this is the national consensus. So what will they talk to us about?"[91]

But as I have already suggested, even this minimalist characterization of the "national consensus" was untenable. Using questions that asked if respondents would find it acceptable if a Palestinian state were established in the West Bank and Gaza Strip as part of a comprehensive peace settlement, Israeli pollsters found on average that 25 percent of Jewish Israelis responded affirmatively.[92] Other polls showed that comparable or higher proportions considered it likely that such a state would be established. Between 1971 and 1981 the proportion of Israeli Jewish respondents who held the opinion that there was a "minimal chance" or a "good chance" for a Palestinian state to be established within ten years decreased but remained substantial, moving from 41.7 percent to 36.2 percent.[93] In June 1988 a poll investigating the impact of the intifada on beliefs about the likelihood that a Palestinian state would be established showed that 55 percent of those leaning toward the Labor party and its dovish Liberal allies believed it more likely, while 45 percent believed it less likely. For those identifying with the Likud or its hawkish allies, 34 percent deemed a Palestinian state more likely, while 66 percent thought it was less likely.[94] In September 1988, Shlomo Lahat, the Likud mayor of Tel Aviv, said publicly that he believed a Palestinian state to be "inevitable."[95] Far from depicting the emergence of a Palestinian state in the West Bank and Gaza Strip as an impossibility or an absurdity, leading figures within the annexationist camp began warning that "establishment of a second Arab-Palestinian state in Eretz Yisrael" would be the "inescapable" result of even a small misstep in the government's policy toward arranging or refusing entry into U. S.-sponsored peace negotiations.[96]

Of course on the fundamental question of willingness to withdraw from the occupied West Bank and Gaza Strip, literally hundreds of polls have revealed a pattern of division among Israeli Jews that has remained remarkably stable. Depending on exactly how the questions have been phrased and on the particular character of events that preceded each survey, the vast majority of polls has shown that 35 percent to 55 percent of respondents oppose trading any territories for peace, while percentages of respondents within roughly the same range indicate willingness to trade most or all of the West Bank and Gaza Strip for a peace agreement ending the Arab-Israeli conflict. During the height of political discontent in Israel, during the prolonged government crisis of spring 1990, a representative poll showed 41.1 percent favoring a Likud-based government and 40.0 percent favoring a Labor based government.[97] In another typical poll, taken after the Gulf War in early 1991, 49 percent of Israeli Jews found the "principle of 'territories for peace' acceptable" while 49 percent found it "unacceptable."[98]

A detailed survey of Jewish Israeli attitudes conducted at the beginning of the intifada, in December 1987 and January 1988, reveals both the difficulties of depending on any one poll for a precise picture of opinion on the territories question, and the intractable evenness of the division between two fundamentally different views. Presented with three options for a "long-range solution" for the territories, 32 percent chose "willing to give up the territories"; 28 percent chose "annexing the territories"; and 40 percent chose "leaving the situation as is." When the 40 percent who chose the third option were then asked to choose between the first two alternatives, 39 percent of these chose territorial compromise and 61 percent chose annexation. According to these two questions, therefore, the overall proportion of those willing to endorse (however reluctantly) either territorial compromise or annexation was 45 percent for territorial compromise and 55 percent for annexation. Another question in the same survey, however, asked whether refusal "to return territories of the Land of Israel is a principle not to be challenged under any circumstances." Here the responses were almost exactly the same, but in reverse: 46 percent chose "certainly agree" or "agree," while 54 percent chose "certainly disagree" or "disagree."[99]

The one exception to this even division of sentiment regards the future of expanded East Jerusalem. Within a month after the Six Day War, a complex series of new laws and administrative orders empowered the government to extend the jurisdiction of the West (Israeli) Jerusalem municipality to include a seventy-five-square-kilometer portion of occupied territory. The line demarcating the boundary of this area corresponded to no previous conception of Jerusalem's city limits. Stretching around West Jerusalem in an arc, from Bethlehem in the south to Ramallah in the north, it encompassed the lands of a dozen West Bank villages but excluded, wherever possible, their populations. In the center was the heavily populated Jordanian municipality of East Jerusalem, including, as a tiny proportion of the total area, the Old City and its holy shrines.

In sharp contrast to divisions within Israel over settlement of the rest of the occupied territories, no important groups of Israelis protested the massive influx of Jews into new neighborhoods in expanded East Jerusalem. The number of Israelis in these settlements has, since the late sixties, exceeded the total of Jewish settlers in the balance of the West Bank. In 1992 approximately 135,000 Jews lived in expanded East Jerusalem, compared with approximately 108,000 in the West Bank exclusive of this area. Since 1967, Arabs in expanded East Jerusalem have had the legal status of permanent residents of Israel, not residents of occupied territories. Accordingly, while they do no have the right to vote in parliamentary elections, they have the right to vote in Jerusalem municipality elections.

In July 1980 the first Begin government promulgated the Basic Law on Jerusalem, which officially declared that "united Jerusalem" was Israel's permanent capital and that Israel exercised exclusive sovereignty over it.[100] Although the law had no practical implications, it had considerable symbolic and political importance. It forced politicians who may have secretly harbored a willingness to share Israeli sovereignty over the city to choose between the risks of arguing explicitly for the preservation of this option, on the basis of a hypothetical possibility that some day it would be crucial to making peace, and the safety of acquiescing in a "patriotic" declaration, knowing that the law would some day be used against efforts to consummate an Arab-Israeli peace agreement based on territorial compromise.

But the emphasis placed on the Jerusalem issue by the Likud governments had another, wider purpose. Massive expropriations of Arab land for the construction of new Jewish neighborhoods, regular declarations treating the entire arc of expanded East Jerusalem as if it were as historically and religiously important to the Jewish people as the southeastern portion of the Old City (containing the Temple Mount, Wailing Wall, and Jewish quarter), transfer of most government offices from the western side of the city to the eastern, and insistence for a while that foreign diplomats (including Egyptian peace negotiators) meet with their Israeli counterparts in East Jerusalem were steps designed to exploit broad public support in Israel for rule of "united Jerusalem" as a means of raising significant hurdles for political or diplomatic progress toward territorial compromise of any kind.

For the Likud, the political logic of fetishizing Jerusalem is clear. It is easier to fight over "Jerusalem" than over Nablus and Gaza. Israel's annexationists appreciate the difficulty of preventing at least a slim majority of Israelis from supporting a trade of occupied territory for lasting peace. They also know that eventually they must establish Israel's permanent control of these areas as a hegemonic fact of Israeli political life. Meanwhile, they realize that no Arab partner will sign a comprehensive peace agreement that permits Israel to maintain exclusive sovereignty over expanded East Jerusalem. Therefore if the permanent absorption of "united Jerusalem" can be established as a hegemonic belief, the failure of almost any negotiating initiative can be insured, thereby giving settlement and other components of de facto annexation in the rest of the occupied territories time to accomplish their political, cultural, and psychological objectives.[101]

The campaign to identify the greatly expanded municipality as an icon of Jewish yearning for "Zion and Jerusalem" has had a substantial effect. Although the question is still asked in many surveys of public opinion, withdrawal or political compromise over this portion of the occupied territories is not an option which more than 10 percent of Israeli Jews have ever been willing to accept. But if a consensus against compromise on the future of expanded East Jerusalem does exist, beliefs in the permanence of Israeli political control there have not achieved hegemonic status.[102] This was apparent during the mid-1980s in occasional remarks by center and left-of-center politicians that compromises were possible on the Jerusalem question once all other issues had been addressed.[103] In July 1988 the Civil Rights Movement, headed by Shulamit Aloni, presented a new political platform describing Jerusalem's status as "open for negotiation."[104] The ordinary language of politicians includes references such as "East Jerusalem . . . and the rest of the territories."[105] The official *Statistical Abstract of Israel* also still considers it necessary to note that its listing of the state's surface area represents the "Area of Israel according to 1949 Armistice Lines, including East Jerusalem."[106]

More significant in marking the absence of ideological hegemony on the future of East Jerusalem were right-wing attacks on anti-annexationist politicians for being insufficiently committed to maintaining permanent and exclusive Israeli sovereignty over the "united capital." These were especially prominent during the debate in early 1990 over whether Palestinians residing in East Jerusalem could participate in negotiations to develop "modalities" for elections in the occupied territories. They were associated with a failed Likud effort to use a reference, by U. S. president George Bush, to East Jerusalem as "occupied territory" in order to deter or prevent the Labor party from unseating the government within which it was only a junior partner. Likud and other annexationist politicians condemned the Labor party and its supporters for agreeing to negotiate with East Jerusalem residents or permit them to vote in proposed elections, warning that Labor and its allies were undermining Israel's prospects for maintaining control of the eastern portions of the city. Such a warning implied a calculation that the Israeli public could contemplate and was worried about the possibility of a redivision of the expanded city, signaling that the campaign to make change in the city's official status appear absurd had failed.[107]

When Shimon Peres defended himself and his party against these attacks, he acknowledged that an overwhelming majority of Israeli Jews supported the idea of a "united city" serving as Israel's capital. But while he wrapped his position in the language of the consensus, he was careful to include the principle that the geographical definition of the city, its boundaries, were subject to change by government decision. He remarked, "There are no differences of opinion on the issue of Jerusalem. . . . Israel's capital, *within borders decided by the Government of Israel,* will remain a united city where Israeli law will prevail, where autonomy will not be imposed—an eternal capital of Israel."[108]

Two weeks later the Knesset passed a resolution, introduced by a hawkish Labor parliamentarian and supported by all the parties to the right of Labor, reaffirming that "united Jerusalem is under Israeli sovereignty and there will be no negotiations on its unity and status." The purpose of the resolution was identical to that of the Jerusalem law, to force Israeli politicians to go on record against any compromise regarding expanded East Jerusalem which might facilitate a more general territorial compromise. Tellingly, however, only forty-five deputies voted for the resolution. Four voted against, but the rest (seventy-one) either absented themselves from the balloting or abstained.[109] That presumptions of permanent Israeli sovereignty in East Jerusalem were under severe attack was also apparent in the "basic guidelines" which both the Labor party and the Likud offered for the government each hoped to lead after the collapse of the 1988 national unity coalition. One provision within each set of guidelines was devoted to Jerusalem. Each militantly asserted what apparently seemed impossible to take for granted—that "Jerusalem is one indivisible city under Israeli sovereignty."[110]

Conclusion

In this chapter I have traced the trajectory of the boundary question in Israeli politics—the question of how much of the Land of Israel should be included within the State of Israel. That trajectory can now be summarized. (The points listed refer to those displayed in Figs. A-4 and A-5 in the

Appendix.) Before 1967 an ideologically hegemonic view of Israel as bounded by the 1949 armistice lines had been constructed (movement from point J to point K). The Six Day War, however, resurrected the irredentist dimension of Zionism and gave new life to counterelites associated with the ideal of the Eretz Yisrael hashlema. For a decade after the war, increasingly weighty incumbent-level considerations dominated Labor government decision-making about policies toward the territories and toward international and Arab initiatives to negotiate peace agreements based on territorial compromise (movement from point L to point M).

In 1977, however, the annexationist camp took control of the government. Using the resources at its disposal the Likud began a far-reaching campaign of de facto annexation. Borrowing state-building slogans and techniques from "activist" Labor Zionists, and forging a thorough-going alliance with messianically oriented religious Zionists (Gush Emunim and the National Religious party), the first and second Begin governments massively increased Israeli investments in the territories, triggering a large increase in the number of Jewish settlers in the occupied territories. By signing a separate peace with Egypt, Begin removed an important incentive for Israelis to solve the West Bank and Gaza problem to the satisfaction of the Palestinians. Although his government's 1982 war on the PLO in Lebanon did not have the desired effect of eliminating Palestinian loyalty to the PLO or hopes for a state in the West Bank and Gaza Strip, by the time Israeli troops had completed their withdrawal from the mountains of Lebanon, the issue in Israeli politics of what to do with the occupied territories had crossed the regime threshold (movement from point M to point N). Since 1983, worries that movement toward withdrawal from the West Bank and Gaza might trigger a regime crisis have been added to incumbent-level considerations in the minds of anti-annexationist Israeli politicians.

But although the annexationist camp institutionalized Israeli rule of the West Bank and Gaza at the regime level, although its efforts blurred the Green Line and reduced its political salience for most Israelis, although a "consensus" was constructed that expanded East Jerusalem would not be separated from the state of Israel, Israeli annexationists did not and have not succeeded in institutionalizing absorption of the territories at the hegemonic level. Even at the peak periods of the fortunes of the annexationist camp—in 1983–84, 1987, and 1990–91 (point O)—presumptions never replaced arguments in public discussion of the political future of the territories. Indeed, with the outbreak of the intifada in December 1987, the entire debate shifted back, away from the conditions under which Israeli disengagement should or could take place, to an unprecedentedly heated and extreme competition between Labor and Likud for control of the government—a pattern of incumbent-level competition in late 1989 and early 1990 which substituted the threats and fears associated with a war of maneuver for the rhetoric of hegemonic construction, characteristic of a war of position, which predominated from 1986 through the end of 1987 (movement from point O to point P). Even the separable question of the fate of expanded East Jerusalem moved noticeably away from the ideological hegemony threshold (point Q to point R).

By the 1990s it was clear that to remove the question of how to dispose of the West Bank and Gaza Strip from the agenda of Israeli politics, one of two things would have to occur. Either the annexationist camp would have to win a war of position and establish as hegemonic a belief that the State of Israel contains the whole of the (western) Land of Israel, or the anti-annexationist camp would have to win a war of maneuver, stripping the question of its regime-threatening aspects in preparation for implementing extensive withdrawals in exchange for peace agreements. The task of the following chapter is to evaluate prospects for either of these outcomes, based on the conditions and strategies identified as central to the explanation of patterns in the British-Irish and French-Algerian cases.

CHAPTER TEN

Hegemonic Failure and Regime Crisis in Israel

Hegemonic Breakdown and Construction in Israel: Comparisons with Britain and France

In Part I, analysis of wars of position produced explanations for the fate of hegemonic projects regarding Ireland and Algeria. These explanations were based on the interaction of three variables, summarized as the presence or absence of (1) severe contradictions between the conception advanced as hegemonic and the stubborn realities it purports to describe; (2) an appropriately fashioned alternative interpretation of political reality capable of reorganizing competition to the advantage of particular groups; and (3) dedicated political-ideological entrepreneurs who can operate successfully where fundamental assumptions of political life have been thrown open to question, and who see better opportunities in competition over basic "rules of the game" than in competition for marginal advantage according to existing rules. Now, on the basis of the previous chapter's analysis of the Israeli case, we can see whether establishment of the 1949 armistice lines as ideologically hegemonic boundaries (1957–67), breakdown of the hegemonic status of these borders (1967–77), and the failure (thus far) to establish annexationist definitions of the state as hegemonic are explainable by apposite configurations of the three variables identified as decisive in the British-Irish and French-Algerian cases.

Establishing Hegemony of the 1949 Armistice Lines

In 1949 the State of Israel could lay convincing claim to having been established according to Zionist myths and to having achieved the central objectives of classical Zionism. Jewish independence in the Land of Israel had been attained and enjoyed wide recognition in the international community. Distinctive social, scientific, cultural, and economic achievements were a source of both pride and reassurance. Zionism had created, or revived, a new Jewish personality and, perhaps, a model society. Enough of "Jerusalem" lay under the state's control for the Israeli government proudly to declare the city as the capital of the country. All Jews, anywhere in the world, enjoyed rights to citizenship upon arrival within the borders of the Jewish state. Nor did any outside power exercise limits on Jewish immigration.

Though small by many standards, the state included undeveloped areas in the Galilee and the Negev and had sufficient room to accommodate as many immigrants as could be expected to arrive. Israel also corresponded, within the 1949 boundaries, to an effectively enforced legal state of affairs that established orderly life, relative security, and relative prosperity on one side of its boundaries, in contrast with danger, squalor, and disorder across them, in "enemy territory." With the flight and expulsion of seven-eighths of its Arab population during the 1948 war, Israel was also relatively homogeneous from a demographic point of view. Eighty-five percent of Israel's inhabitants were Jewish; virtually all were citizens. In these ways belief in the permanence and appropriateness of Israel's 1949 borders cannot be seen as standing in severe contradiction to psychological, ideological, legal, or existential realities.

Of course the 1949 lines were far from "historical" or "natural" boundaries. In fact, as demarcated by the conclusion of hostilities in 1948 and 1949 and as ratified in the armistice agreements of 1949, the Green Line separated the State of Israel from most biblically significant portions of the Land of Israel. This was the biggest problem facing the Green Line as a candidate for hegemonic status. It was also, however, its most significant advantage to the political elites most closely associated with the founding of the state it delimited.

The hegemonic belief in the armistice lines as bounding the geographical shape of the political community was thus quite obviously a constructed belief, requiring political entrepreneurs capable of packaging an appropriate mix of symbols and appeals to promote and establish it on a hegemonic basis. Both Ben-Gurion and the Mapai party (along with its successor, the Israeli Labor party) benefited enormously from the removal of irredentism from respectable Israeli political discourse. Ben-Gurion's ardently promoted formula of *mamlachtiut* (étatisme) disadvantaged his personal and political rivals by enshrining the State of Israel itself, its military and governmental institutions, its geographical frontiers, and its economic and cultural accomplishments, as the culmination of Zionism and the permanent framework for the expression of Jewish nationalism. Taking into account both passionate ideological attachments to the idea of the whole Land of Israel present within every major segment of the pre-1948 Zionist movement, as well as the military superiority enjoyed by Israel over both Jordan (in the West Bank) and Egypt (in the Gaza Strip), it is easy to appreciate how great a political achievement was the pre-1967 exclusion of the territorial issue from the Israeli national agenda. Each of the three most important threats to Ben-Gurion/Mapai dominance of Israeli politics—militant Labor Zionist activism, Revisionism, and, *in potentis*, messianic religious Zionism—was thereby deprived of a defining issue without which claims to national leadership were difficult to justify.[1]

Breakdown of the Green Line as a Hegemonic Conception

In the British-Irish case, British rule of Ireland as a part of the United Kingdom emerged as a problematic issue in British politics. Memories of the Great Famine, Fenian terrorism, and nationalist organized land wars in Ireland produced a severe discrepancy between palpable realities and the claims of the previously hegemonic belief,—that Ireland was as fully and integrally a part of the United Kingdom as was Wales or Northumbria. New visions of Ireland's proper political status, woven from historicist, social Darwinist, and imperialist themes prominent in Victorian culture, were available to interpret this discrepancy in satisfying ways. Finally, political elites, including Gladstone, Salisbury, Chamberlain, and Randolph Churchill, saw exciting and extremely profitable political opportunities in the public problematization of Ireland's future political status.

The 1967 war in Israel produced a comparable set of conditions within Israeli politics. These, in turn, broke down the previously hegemonic conception of Green Line Israel, and prompted emergence of the issue of whether the West Bank and Gaza Strip would be considered and absorbed as integral parts of the state.

The severe discrepancy that was a direct consequence of the Six Day War was the extension of control and jurisdiction of the Jewish state over territories that formed the heartland of biblical Israel. Significant sites within the West Bank included the city of David in Jerusalem, the remnant of the ancient Temple courtyard (the Wailing, or Western Wall—also in

Jerusalem), the city of Hebron (where, according to Genesis, in the cave of Machpelah, are buried Abraham, Sarah, and Isaac), the tomb of Rachel in Bethlehem, the place of Jacob's dream, in Beth-El, and Joseph's tomb in Nablus (biblical Shechem). It was impossible to deny the genuine emotional and ideological attachments to these areas and to the idea of resuming Jewish life in and near them by the same sort of "pioneering" settlement activity that had been, according to established Zionist mythology, largely responsible for the renaissance of the Jewish people and the establishment of the state.

Before 1967 the separation of the West Bank from Israel had been profitably treated by Ben-Gurion and Mapai as a necessity made into a virtue. Between 1949 and 1967, an onerous burden of proof lay on the shoulders of the irredentists. Although for a time they tried, they failed completely to persuade Israelis that until the entire Land had been liberated, the state established in 1948 could be neither secure nor honored as the culmination of Jewish nationalist aspirations. Once Israel's control of biblically significant portions of the Land of Israel had been accomplished, however, once Jewish settlement of these territories had begun, and once their Arab population had been coerced into relative docility, the burden of proof shifted dramatically. In the years following the Six Day War, and certainly by the Yom Kippur War in 1973, the burden had come to rest on the shoulders of those Israelis who argued that the restricted and "artificial" borders which had "invited attack" were both virtuous and necessary.[2] A gross discrepancy had thus appeared—a severe contradiction between professed commitments of Zionism and the state of Israel to the Jewish people's security and biblical heritage, and official boundaries and legal demarcations which treated mythically peripheral areas as core territories and mythically central and security-significant areas as dispensable, even burdensome "occupied" territories.

In the British-Irish case new ideas about culture and politics achieved prominence between 1860 and 1885. As shown in Chapter 5, these ideas provided formulas with which to recast the British-Irish relationship in ways that could, without insulting the amour propre of the British public, explain the gross discrepancy between an old hegemonic conception and severely contradictory realities. In the Israeli case the ideas that emerged after 1967 to recast the relationship between the State of Israel and the Land of Israel were not new. They were latent formulations resting within the repertoire of Zionism. Until a severe contradiction arose, however, between hegemonic views of the shape of the Israeli state and "stubborn realities," they could not be used to promote the political interests of those who could most credibly articulate them.

Not long after June 1967, Revisionist, religious, and activist Labor Zionist political entrepreneurs realized how fundamentally the outcome of the war had changed the contours of the political terrain. By emphasizing instead of suppressing irredentist sentiments, they could launch a war of position over the proper conception of the State of Israel—a struggle whose outcome promised opportunities to remove the chiefs of the Labor party from the commanding heights of the polity and replace them with their own candidates for national leadership. Just as the leaders of the British Conservative party and of the Radicals used problematization of Ireland's status to shift the focus of British politics from politically inconvenient class issues to questions of national prestige and to the passions and prejudices of urban workers, and just as de Gaulle found in the image of France retreating from Algeria an ideal way to exploit his reputation as the champion of French greatness against the party politicians of the Fourth Republic, so too did those who had suffered at the hands of Mapai see in the problematization of Israel's boundaries an issue with which to reverse their political fortunes.

Revisionists had always celebrated a Jewish state whose territorial expanse would correspond to the world-historic destiny and regional if not global power potential they ascribed to the Jewish people. The results of the 1967 war seemed to confirm that the path to national greatness lay in territorial expansion and the elevation of those who had been most faithful to this principle (i.e., the Revisionists) to national leadership. With the expansion of the territory controlled by the Jewish state an accomplished fact, Menachem Begin's record of espousing this expansion could no longer be used as convincing evidence that he was too reckless to be trusted with the premiership. Using his impeccable credentials as a whole Land of Israel loyalist and his substantial oratorical talents, Begin donned a yarmulke (orthodox Jewish head covering) and made religiously traditionalist, populist, and hardline anti-Arab appeals to Israel's emergent oriental Jewish plurality.

Leaders of the militant "young guard" faction of the National Religious party also found in the territories issue a road to national prominence and eventual control of the NRP. They envisioned a geographically "completed" State of Israel acting as the instrument and sign of a culminating messianic-redemptive process. The results of the war were interpreted as a giant step forward in the process, a process that could be facilitated by political leaders sensitive to the cosmic implications of policies to be implemented in and toward the territories. Exploiting their intimate links to Rav Tzvi Yehuda Kook and their instrumental role in establishing and supporting Gush Emunim, these men tapped a painful sense of inferiority and unfulfilled mission experienced by a generation of religious Zionist youth. They represented young orthodox Israelis who were proud to have served in the army for the first time in substantial numbers during the 1973 war and who were anxious to prove their worthiness by winning the whole Land of Israel for the Jewish people, as the previous secular-sabra generation had won Jewish statehood.

The third group of political entrepreneurs to raise the banner of the whole Land of Israel were hundreds of second-echelon personalities within the Labor Zionist apparatus—"activists" who had been forced to lay aside their territorial maximalism in order to participate in governing the country and who had, even so, never achieved positions of supreme leadership in the military or civilian branches of the state. They saw in the post-1967 resumption of settlement and pioneering activities in the West Bank and Gaza an opportunity to revive the slumbering national genius of the Jewish people and trigger new waves of immigration, making Zionist ideology and "pioneering" commitment again respectable instead of a favorite subject for satire. They explained the powerful emotional response of Israeli Jews visiting East Jerusalem and other portions of the territories as an expression of the normalness of the Jewish people's existential attachment to their patrimony and as a mystical but organic bond that would build and redeem the Jewish people while the people themselves built and redeemed the land.[3] This group was the animating force behind the Movement for the Whole Land of Israel (established in August 1967). After its demise, the ascendancy of the Likud, and the latter's alliance with the National Religious party, the more ambitious and daring elements within the activist wing of Labor Zionism chose one of three paths. They either joined Gush Emunim as nonreligious fellow travelers, supported Moshe Dayan in his alliance with the Likud, or formed small ultranationalist parties such as Tehiya (1979), Tzomet (1983), and Moledet (1988). These latter parties have seen themselves as candidates for national leadership and hope to achieve it by an uncompromising commitment to the whole Land of Israel, a sharpening conflict with the Arab world (including the "transfer" of large numbers of Palestinians out of the country), and the need, eventually, to establish a *pur et dur* regime capable of protecting Israel's sovereignty and security within its enlarged borders.

In the Israeli case, then, a gross discrepancy materialized after the 1967 war between the previously hegemonic image of the constricted shape of the state and the realities of effective state control over the greater Land of Israel. This condition, favoring hegemonic breakdown, was accompanied by alternative and compelling interpretations of the proper domain for the exercise of Israeli sovereignty. It was reinforced by the presence of strategically placed, ambitious counterelites able to benefit greatly from fighting a war of position. The configuration of these three variables is the same as that advanced to explain hegemonic breakdown in the British-

Irish case. My findings about hegemonic breakdown in Israel are thus fully consistent with my analysis of breakdown in the hegemonic status of mid-nineteenth-century British conceptions of Ireland as an integral part of the United Kingdom. Although this correspondence cannot, of course, confirm the validity of the general hypotheses, it lends them substantial support.

Failure to Establish a Hegemonic Conception of the Whole Land of Israel

Despite the best efforts of the three groups identified above to build a hegemonic conception of the greater Land of Israel, their fate has remained controversial. Few politically active Israelis have chosen to speak (for more than a few weeks or months at a time, at any rate) as if the fate of the West Bank and Gaza Strip were no longer an issue in Israeli politics, that is as if these areas had been absorbed as completely into Israeli beliefs about the shape of their state as had beliefs about the Galilee or the Negev. What accounts for the failure, to date, of hegemonic construction in the post-1967 Israeli case?

In Chapter 5 I hypothesized that the *presence of only one* of three appropriate conditions would be *sufficient* for an existing hegemonic belief to be *defended* successfully. The three conditions (simply the obverse of those relevant to explaining hegemonic breakdown) were (1) reasonable correspondence between the substance of the hegemonic belief and realities purportedly described by it; (2) unavailability of alternative but reassuring accounts of those realities; and (3) absence of ambitious political elites able to benefit greatly from challenging hegemonic beliefs. To explain *breakdown* of a hegemonic conception, I hypothesized that *each* of three appropriate conditions (again, the obverse of those useful in its defense) would be *necessary*. A successful defense occurred in Britain (1834 and 1843). Breakdown occurred in Britain (1867–85) and in Israel (1967–74). We have seen that each of these cases of defense and breakdown is consistent with the hypothesized implications of different combinations of the three conditions (or their absence).

As my explanation for the breakdown of the hegemonic conception of Ireland's status within the United Kingdom provided an analogous explanation for the breakdown of the Green Line's pre-1967 hegemonic status in Israel, so too does consideration of the same group of variables after 1967 explain the failure of a new program of hegemonic construction— the State of Israel as the whole Land of Israel. This failure is analogous to the failure of partisans of *la plus grande France* to establish the French

Union or Algérie française on a hegemonic basis within metropolitan France.

To explain the *establishment* of a belief as hegemonic, as occurred in Israel with respect to the 1949 armistice lines (1957–67), I hypothesized (in Chap. 5) that at least one of the appropriate conditions would be necessary. This is, of course, a rather weak claim. Nevertheless it is supported by the Israeli case in the pre-1967 period, where I have suggested how effectively Ben-Gurion was able to marginalize elites offering competing constructions of the state established in the borders of 1949. On the other hand, consideration of the French case vis-à-vis Algérie française, together with the Israeli case regarding annexation of the West Bank and Gaza Strip, suggests that building a new hegemonic conception may require more than the presence of just one "appropriate" condition.

Failure of the first, pluralist and democratic version of the French Union can be explained not only by the gross discrepancy between the lofty visions espoused by its native and metropolitan exponents and the prevailing realities of oppression and prejudice, but by the absence of strategically placed elites able to benefit greatly from campaigns to establish the "Union of free consent" as a hegemonic image of France. The second, hierarchical version of the French Union, the "Union of tutelary subordination," that was incorporated into the constitution of the Fourth Republic, did have important political elites associated with it—such as Bidault and even de Gaulle, to an extent. But France's weakened international position and the pressures toward decolonization throughout "overseas France," including violent struggles in Indochina and Madagascar and severe unrest in black Africa, North Africa, and the Levant, fatally controverted official claims of natural and permanent French leadership over grateful yellow, brown, and black peoples.

Only the third postwar hegemonic project, portraying the metropole plus Algeria as "France," enjoyed some real prospect of success. By 1956 and 1957, opposition leaders such as de Gaulle and Poujade, governing party chiefs such as Mollet and Bourgès-Maunoury, Conservatives such as Duchet, the colon leaders in Algeria, and a majority of high-ranking officers in the French army, saw in the formula of Algérie française a key element in satisfying their personal and political objectives. Drawing on the long history and great size of European settlement in Algeria, the country's relative proximity to the hexagon, and the powerful sense that France needed Algeria and the resources of the Sahara to reestablish its status as a great power, an elaborate and, for most French people, persuasive conception of Algeria as a prolongation of France was developed. However, despite the army's eventual military success in eliminating the threat of an FLN battlefield victory, the tremendous discrepancies between the resources required to defend and maintain French control over Algeria and the political and economic capacities of France under the Fourth Republic prevented the idea of Algérie française from ever being established as the common sense of French political life.

A somewhat similar though not identical array of forces seems present in the Israeli case, especially since the early 1980s. The predicament arising from this state of affairs is also similar. The basis for an alliance of settlers, Revisionists, religious Zionists, and militant segments of the Labor Zionist movement is their uncompromising commitment to build the West Bank and Gaza Strip into the Israeli state as thoroughly as possible. The ideological and cultural basis for this alliance blends religious, security-related, and integral nationalist motifs. They combine within a hegemonic project that has inspired a large proportion of Israel's Jewish population to believe the exercise of Jewish political rights in and over Tel Aviv can be no more valid or secure than the exercise of those same prerogatives in and over Hebron, Ramallah, expanded East Jerusalem, and Gaza.

Although this political bloc is strong enough to have controlled the Israeli government for all but two and a half years between 1977 and 1992, it has not succeeded in establishing its annexationist program as hegemonic. Despite massive settlement activity and sometimes convincing images of irreversible incorporation, the controversy over what to do with the territories has continued. The biggest obstacle to hegemonic construction has been the vast Arab majority in "Judea, Samaria, and the Gaza District," specifically the severe contradiction between the presence of the angry and sometimes violent opposition of nearly two million noncitizen Arabs and claims that these portions of the Land of Israel had been transformed into integral parts of the state of Israel. The strategic problem confronting their hegemonic project was clearly recognized by many Gush Emunim leaders at the end of 1986. As an editorial in *Nekuda* stated,

> We must all understand that the struggle for the completeness of the Land will be won after the great majority of the public in this country supports the idea with active political support. To attract this kind of support we must persuade the public to believe what we believe, that our idea is eminently practical....
> The key question, perhaps the question of questions, that the wider public requires us to answer, bears upon our ability, as a people and a state, to establish a quiet and normal sovereignty in Judea, Samaria, and Gaza, despite the fact that Arabs living there still comprise an unchallenged demographic majority.[4]

These words were written as an immediate response to scattered attacks of Arabs on Jews in the occupied territories. One year later, however, the memory of such sporadic outbursts was wiped away by the eruption of the intifada—the Palestinian uprising and civil rebellion which began in December 1987. Although Jewish casualties of the uprising were relatively light (thirteen soldiers and thirteen civilians killed between December 1987 and February 1991), they represent, along with the severe economic dislocations and international outcry associated with Israeli repressive measures, an order-of-magnitude increase in the costs Israel had to pay for maintaining its hold over the West Bank and Gaza Strip. Instead of the usual scattered array of small units, the Israeli army was forced to deploy tens of thousands of soldiers to disperse demonstrations, break strikes, enforce curfews and school closings, patrol refugee camps, build and guard large new detention centers, and prevent popular committees from making villages and towns into zones of "liberated Palestine." To permit new recruits, who had been transferred en masse to the territories, to continue their training, the defense ministry increased the average length of annual reserve duty from thirty to sixty days. Without workers from the territories, construction was brought to a standstill on hundreds of projects throughout the country. In the first four months of the intifada, according to government sources, the Israeli economy lost approximately $350 million. This figure stood at $500 million for all of 1988, equaling 1.4 percent of Israeli's GNP, and more than $1.1 billion by December 1989.[5]

The intifada resulted in very heavy casualties among Palestinians. According to an Israeli human rights group Btzelem, Israeli soldiers killed 750 Palestinians in the territories from the beginning of the uprising in December 1987 to the end of February 1991. During the same thirty-nine-month period, 37 Palestinians were killed by Israeli civilians (usually settlers) and 349 Palestinians were killed by other Arabs, under conditions of general lawlessness or "on suspicion of collaborating with the authorities."[6] Between December 1987 and October 1989, according to Btzelem, 60,000 Palestinians were arrested, leading to a widely publicized breakdown in the military government's legal system.[7] The Likud minister of justice announced that in the first two years of the uprising, 350 Arab homes had been demolished, 60 people deported, and 40,000 placed in administrative detention (i.e., without indictment or trial)—practices Israel had largely abandoned in the years preceding the intifada.[8] In September 1990 the Israeli army released its own comprehensive set of statistics showing that 13,100 Palestinians had been wounded in the first one thousand days of the uprising, compared to 2,500 Israeli soldiers and 1,100 Israeli civilians.[9] Palestinian sources reported much higher casualty levels, showing that more than 100,000 Palestinians suffered serious injuries during the first three years of the uprising.[10] Whatever the exact figures, the political costs Israeli annexationists were forced to pay as a result of the harsh and prolonged crackdown were substantial. No longer could the government claim to have achieved conditions of "coexistence" between Jews and Arabs in the territories. It was also confronted with what one Israeli cartoonist depicted as the virtual "resurrection" of the Green Line, not only in the minds of ordinary Israelis but also among stalwarts within the annexationist camp.[11]

One of the most reliable signs that the annexationist camp realized early on how dramatically the intifada had impacted on their hegemonic project was the strained but untiring efforts by Arik Sharon and other Likud and Gush Emunim leaders to portray the intifada as waged against Jews on *both* sides of the Green Line. To the extent that solidarity activities and sporadic violence of Israeli Arab citizens of Israel, within the Green Line boundaries, could be construed as equivalent to the massive unrest within the territories themselves, the annexationist camp could use the intifada to advance their hegemonic project, to convince Israeli Jews that no viable distinction could be made, by Arabs or Jews, between territories ruled by Israel before 1967 and those acquired as a result of the Six Day War.[12]

Indeed the contradiction between annexationist claims that the Green Line had been erased, and the categorical differences between life within "Israel proper" and life within the intifada-ruled West Bank and Gaza, was impossible to ignore. Even in areas within Israel proper most heavily settled by Arabs, and where numerous rock-throwing incidents were reported, Jewish inhabitants made clear their own sense of the existence and practical importance of the Green Line by insisting that a security fence be built along it, regularly patrolled by the army, to shield their settlements from intifada-related sabotage and violence spilling over from the West Bank.[13] During periods of particularly intense intifada activity or following bloody acts of terrorism, these realities have led many annexationist leaders to abandon the principle of the erasure of the Green Line in favor of measures to seal off "the territories" and their inhabitants from "Israel," both to punish the Palestinians and to protect Israelis from them. Even Arik Sharon's ordinary language showed how alive and well the Green Line was in his cognitive map as a demarcation of "Israel." Demanding that thousands of West Bank and Gaza Arabs who had been living inside Israeli Arab villages be sent back to their homes in the occupied territories, Sharon warned that if this were not done, "control of a significant slice of Israel's territory" would be lost.[14]

Prospects for a New Hegemonic Conception of Israel's Borders

British rule of all of Ireland and French rule of Algeria are ideas no longer advanced by any serious contender for political power in Britain or France. In Israel, efforts to incorporate the Palestinian territories into the State of Israel on a hegemonic basis are continuing. What are the requirements and prospects for success?

Traditionally, one of the most important resources available to Israeli annexationists has been the identification of the territories as vital security assets. Security arguments were also of enormous salience to British elites contemplating Ireland's status in the eighteenth and nineteenth centuries and to French military experts discussing NATO requirements in North Africa after 1945. But changing circumstances substantially lessened Ireland's importance for British security after World War I; they also lessened the credibility of French claims in the 1950s about the vital military importance of holding on to Algeria. In like manner, Israeli thinking about the security significance of the territories has been affected by the moderating trend in the foreign policies of most Arab states and the acquisition of long-range missiles and unconventional warheads by Iraq, Syria, and Iran.[15] For annexationists out to create hegemonic presumptions about the territories rather than contingent commitments, their diminishing security significance has highlighted the importance of providing an ideological (Zionist, historicist, or religious) underpinning to the state-expansion process.

Indeed the historical, ideological, and emotional links between Israel's Jewish majority and the disputed territories *are* strong and widely shared. Also significant is that there are no geographical barriers separating pre-1967 Israel from the West Bank and Gaza Strip. Hence the "map image" of the country as including the occupied territories is at least as appealing and "natural" (probably more so) than the shape of the state within the Green Line boundaries. Certainly no body of water, such as the Irish or Mediterranean Sea, exists to inhibit the establishment of routinized contacts between "core" and "periphery."

From the point of view of hegemonic construction, however, these advantages are unlikely to be decisive. The failure of governing elites in Britain and France to defend or establish the hegemonic status of enlarged visions of their states suggests the importance of another factor. In each case hegemonic failure was directly linked to the intense and pervasive dissatisfaction of indigenous inhabitants of those territories targeted for absorption into the state-building core. Sustained opposition by Irish Catholics and Algerian Muslims produced gross discrepancies between claims of integration advanced as part of expansive hegemonic projects and radical differences between conditions of life in the outlying territories and conditions within the state-building core.[16] In the Israeli case the 1949 boundaries of the state were hegemonically established, but only after forcible evacuation of Arabs during the 1948 war had reduced the Arab population of the area within those boundaries by 85 percent. By contrast the West Bank and Gaza Strip are inhabited by large and cohesive Arab populations.

With annexationist elites and attractive, expansionist ideological appeals available, the key to successful incorporation of the territories into the Israeli state will be elimination of the gross discrepancy between *expectations* of continuity between different parts of the national domain and *realities* of sharp discontinuities. Since these discontinuities are mainly expressions of the presence and antagonistic sentiments of the Arabs of these areas, the model of hegemonic construction offered in this study (supported by analysis of the British and French experiences) leads to the conclusion that to establish a hegemonic conception of the State of Israel encompassing the whole Land of Israel, annexationists must either satisfy the Palestinian Arabs of the West Bank and Gaza Strip or remove them. These are the two conditions under which the ideological hegemony threshold can be crossed, entailing a qualitative change in the collective perception of these areas as just as irreversibly and unproblematically integrated into the Israeli state as are any other regions of the country.

To be sure, many Israelis believed, before the intifada, that the enormous coercive potential of the Israeli army, the careful surveillance of potential troublemakers, and the economic benefits accruing to Palestinian workers commuting into Israel were sufficient barriers to the expression of political resentments or nationalist frustrations festering beneath the surface. A public opinion survey conducted by the Jaffee Center for Strategic Studies in 1986 reported that 93 percent of respondents "were convinced Israel would be able to deal with a revolt of the Arabs living in the territories."[17] Those concerned about the uneven rates of natural increase between Arabs and Jews, and the specter of an Arab majority crystallizing within the country over a twenty-to-thirty-year period, predicted and then welcomed the massive immigration of Soviet Jews as an effective solution to the "demographic problem." The general view, often stated explicitly by then Prime Minister Shamir, was that the Arab-Israeli conflict in general and the Palestinian problem in particular were not "burning" issues requiring urgent or imaginative consideration by the Israeli government.

In the territories, however, vast changes were occurring, unbeknown to most Israelis and unappreciated by those aware of them. A generational shift, associated with greater militancy among better-educated, under-employed nationalists and Muslim fundamentalists, had removed virtually all the traditional elites with whom the Israeli authorities had enjoyed a working semi-collaborative relationship. Large numbers of youthful nationalists were inspired by hundreds of PLO activists released by Israel as part of its 1985 prisoner exchange with Ahmed Jibril. Armed with a sophisticated understanding of Israel and appreciating the kind of pressures to which it would be sensitive, they had forged a thick network of associations and organizations. With assistance from the PLO on the outside, these had been gradually built up as a nonmilitary infrastructure of a Palestinian "state on the way."

For Israelis, eruption of the intifada, so unexpected, so resilient, and from so narrow a resource base as existed within the Palestinian community, was a great shock. Even if the army could stamp out large-scale disturbances, it could not prevent stone throwing and other forms of harassment from making the West Bank and Gaza Strip into zones of personal insecurity for Israelis. With no confidence that future uprisings could be deterred, images of returning to the status quo ante quickly disappeared, even from most discussions within the annexationist camp. What had been, prior to the intifada, a rather popular option on opinion surveys regarding preferred policies for the future in the territories, namely, "maintaining the status quo," lost almost all its support, at least during the first two and a half years of the intifada.[18] No longer did Israeli government officials, or other advocates of maintaining Israeli rule over the West Bank and Gaza Strip, characterize the occupation as "benign," blame disturbances in the territories on PLO "troublemakers" or agitators, or argue that the Palestinians there were not demanding independence from Israel.[19] Five years after its initial outburst, though the intifada may have faded away as a coordinated array of strikes, committees, and demonstrations, the depth of the anger it expressed and generated, and the mobilization of virtually the entire society in acts of resistance it produced are understood by the vast majority of Israelis to mean that ruling the Arabs of the territories will require repeated use of harsh, sustained, and politically costly repressive measures.

The expectation that Palestinian Arab discontent will continue to disrupt all efforts to promote images of "normal" life for Jewish Israelis in the West Bank and Gaza Strip is strengthened by comparing international support for Palestinian demands with the kinds of international support enjoyed by Irish nationalists in the late nineteenth century and Algerian rebels in the 1950s. The long process of Irish political mobilization that helped break the hegemonic conception of Ireland as an integral part of the United Kingdom moved from the Fenian terrorism of the late 1860s and early 1870s, to the Land League and the Land War of the late 1870s and early 1880s, to the appearance of a disciplined, countrywide nationalist party under the leadership of Parnell and Redmond. Important elements in each of these waves of Irish discontent were the funds, political support, and conspiratorial leadership provided by the Irish Republican Brotherhood, the Clan na Gael, and the large population of Irish Catholics in the United States who rallied around these groups in support of whatever demands for land or independence their brethren in Ireland were willing to make. Although hardly decisive, the Irish lobby in the United States encouraged the U.S. government to make some diplomatic efforts on behalf of more considerate British treatment of Ireland, efforts which interfered with Unionist promotion of the idea of Ireland as a strictly domestic affair.

The FLN's revolutionary struggle against French rule of Algeria, which played a crucial role in the failure of the Algérie française hegemonic project, was even more reliant on international support than was the mobilization of Irish discontent in the late nineteenth century. Nasser's Egypt in particular was a vital source of arms, encouragement, training, and funds in the early years of the struggle. Eventually Morocco and Tunisia served as key training and staging areas for the Algerian Liberation Army and as safe havens for the FLN's "external" leadership. In the international arena as a whole, and in the Soviet bloc in particular, diplomatic and material assistance for the struggle was readily available. The great wave of decolonization that swept Asia, Africa, and the Middle East in the fifteen years following World War II, sponsored and legitimized by U.N. support for the principle of national self-determination, eventually forced France's NATO allies, including the United States, to pressure France to withdraw from Algeria. Even before significant international leverage was brought to bear against the French government in early 1958 and before explicit resolutions were passed in the United Nations in support of the Algerian rebels, attempts by the Faure, Mollet, and Bourgès-Maunoury governments to treat Algeria as if it were an integral part of France were substantially harmed by the need regularly to defend French rule of Algeria, at the United Nations and in the pages of the international press on an instrumental, utilitarian, or legalist bases.

In the Palestinian case, the range of international support available for the struggle to end Israeli control of the West Bank and Gaza Strip is broader and deeper than in either the Irish or Algerian cases. For forty-five years the United Nations Relief and Works Agency has fed, cared for, and educated millions of Palestinians in refugee camps throughout the Middle East, including inside the West Bank and Gaza Strip. Excepting Iran, Sudan, and Libya, every county in the world has endorsed the principle of trading "territories for peace." United Nations Security Council Resolutions 242 and 338 have enshrined the principle of "the inadmissibility of the acquisition of territory by force" as the basis for almost all serious diplomatic efforts to resolve the Arab-Israeli conflict. The Arab and Muslim countries regularly treat the Palestine question as the most pressing foreign policy issue on their agendas. The Security Council and General Assembly of the United Nations, the European Community, and dozens of other international organizations have regularly condemned Israeli government policies of settlement, land expropriation, discrimination, and refusal to address the Palestinian refugee problem. Israel's announced annexation of expanded East Jerusalem, with its shrines and pilgrimage sites for billions of Christians and Muslims, is rejected by virtually the entire world, insuring global interest in any protests or violence that occur in the "holy city."

Though the PLO's diplomatic fortunes wax and wane with notorious frequency, it enjoys a recognized position on the international scene as the "sole legitimate representative of the Palestinian people." The Palestinian problem itself has become a fixture of contemporary international politics. Increasingly Palestinians are seen as victims of Israeli intransigence, fanaticism, or paralysis rather than as perpetrators of bloody and unnecessary acts of terrorism. In countless international fora, the broad consensus that settlement of the Arab-Israeli conflict will require a "just solution to the legitimate national rights of the Palestinians," and that it will require a Palestinian state based in the West Bank and Gaza Strip, compels Israelis, whether annexationists or not, to defend their country against those who use continued occupation and repression to question Israel's commitment to peace, democracy, and humane values.

Israel is also a smaller country than either Britain or France and relatively more dependent on networks of economic, technological, political, military, and cultural links to every continent. Because of Israel's thoroughgoing involvement in the international system, neither the government of Israel nor Israelis can avoid confronting the worldwide refusal to view incorporation of the territories into Israel as acceptable, let alone proper, natural, or commonsensical. Whether or not the force of international opinion, the exertions of diplomats, or the threat of economic sanctions could ever remove Israel from the territories, the international context of Israeli state expansion is such that Palestinian opposition from within the territories, as long as it exists, will find sources of support and encouragement for its effective expression. This is yet another reason to expect that Israeli policies of de facto annexation will *not* eliminate Israeli perceptions of a gross discrepancy between life on either side of the Green Line.

Therefore crossing the ideological hegemony threshold in the statebuilding direction will require a substantial change in Israeli policies. Israel must either offer West Bank and Gaza Palestinians arrangements capable of eliciting their acquiescence in the absorption of those territories into Israel or accomplish the wholesale removal of Palestinians from those territories. A deal with the Palestinians would remove the source of mass discontent which would otherwise sustain prolonged resistance struggles. Removal of the Palestinians could mobilize Arab and world opinion so violently against the Jewish state, regardless of its borders, that demands for Israeli disengagement from the West Bank and Gaza Strip in return for peace, demands supportable now by many, perhaps most Israelis, would be displaced by demands for Israel's isolation and defeat which no Israeli Jews could entertain.

Even in comparison with British and French stances toward the natives of Ireland and Algeria, however, Israel would seem unlikely to be able to promote a formula for incorporating the target territories which would remove the basis for sustained opposition from their indigenous inhabitants. As in the two European cases, Israel has settled the territories with its own nationals, who in large measure have been self-selected for ideological and cultural perspectives, political ambitions, and economic interests that encourage them to oppose extending local Palestinians any substantial protection of property or political rights. In 1992 the proportion of Jews to Arabs in the West Bank (including expanded East Jerusalem) and the Gaza Strip was approximately 12 percent, roughly equal to the proportion of Europeans in Algeria to Muslims in Algeria in the 1950s, though somewhat less than half the proportion of Protestants to Catholics in early twentieth-century Ireland.

To be sure, despite the opposition or sullen acquiescence of Irish Protestants and pieds noirs, both British Unionists in the 1890s and early 1900s and Soustellian integrationists in the mid-1950s promoted expensive projects to foster native loyalties to Britain and France rather than to Irish or Algerian nationalism. In Ireland, Balfour sought to "kill home rule with kindness." Soustelle's plan, and the official policy of French governments from Faure and Mollet to de Gaulle, was to extend massive economic aid and equal political rights to Algerian Muslims in order to drain the independence movement of mass support. But French investments and political reforms made hardly a dent in popular support for the independence struggle, and although far-reaching land redistribution schemes were implemented in Ireland, from a political point of view both these efforts were classic cases of "too little too late."

There are cultural and historical reasons to believe, and evidence to suggest, that Israeli emulation of these efforts will fail, on the political level at least, even more spectacularly. In Britain and France the *formal* legitimizing myths standing behind state claims of authority over both populations and territories included primary commitments to citizenship and political equality for all adults (or adult males). Neither the British nor the French states were, officially and legally, envisioned as representing the interests of one nationally or religiously distinct body of citizens to the exclusion of Irish Catholics or Algerian Muslims. No matter what the real obstacles raised by prejudice, differential mobilizational capacities, or de facto discrimination, the images of Britain and France sponsored by those who sought hegemonic integration of Ireland and Algeria included the *eventual* attainment of social and political equality for their majority populations within a larger British or French political community. Annexationists in Israel, on the other hand, regardless of differences among them on a variety of issues, agree that the state into which the West Bank and Gaza Strip are to be incorporated is, and will always be, a Jewish-Zionist state—a state with a mission to serve and represent the interests of the Jewish people; a state within which formal citizenship, even if granted to the Arabs of the territories, would mean less for determining access to status honor, political power, and economic resources (such as land, water, and employment) and more for enforcing their identity as non-Jews. Nor, consistent with Judaism's norms against proselytization, have any elements within the annexationist camp suggested that eventually the Arabs of the territories, along with the Arab citizens of Israel proper, could be assimilated into the Jewish population through conversion or intermarriage.[20]

Furthermore, Palestinian Arab national consciousness is, if anything, even more completely defined in opposition to Jewish Israelis than was Irish national consciousness in opposition to Britons, or Algerian national consciousness in opposition to the French. After a hundred years of Arab-Jewish conflict in Palestine/the Land of Israel, conducted almost entirely within an international and Middle Eastern political culture recognizing national identities as the only ones constitutive of internationally accepted rights to territory, the national consciousness of Palestinian Arabs as separate from, not to say intrinsically opposed to, Jewish nationalism seems at least as unlikely to fade as was Irish nationalism in the early twentieth century or Algerian nationalism in the 1950s.[21]

It is therefore unsurprising that halting attempts by various Likud governments to strike a bargain with credible Palestinian elites in the territories have either failed miserably or been withdrawn as soon as some Arab interest was displayed. Between 1979 and 1981 the first Begin government conducted negotiations over "full autonomy" for the West Bank and Gaza Strip Arabs with the United States and Egypt as part of the Camp David "Framework for Peace." Whatever small degree of interest some Palestinian notables had in the formula evaporated when the Likud's highly restricted definition of "full autonomy" became known.[22]

Subsequently some efforts were made to cultivate village notables and heads of clans in rural areas of the West Bank who might help isolate the PLO and provide a nonpolitical basis for cooperation with Israel. The Village Leagues, as they were called, however were dissolved as soon as their leaders began making political statements, such as publicly identifying themselves as Palestinians, demanding recognition of the PLO, and endorsing U.S. peace initiatives.[23] In response to the intifada the Likud again offered to discuss an arrangement with the Palestinians based on "interim autonomy," which was the basis for Shamir's participation in talks with Palestinian representatives following the Madrid peace conference. After the Likud's defeat in the 1992 Israeli elections, however, Shamir publicly admitted that he had never contemplated offering Arab inhabitants of the territories any arrangements they might have found acceptable. "I would have conducted the autonomy negotiations for ten years," he said, "and in the meantime we would have reached half a million Jews in Judea and Samaria."[24] As Shamir himself plainly understood, Palestinian political mobilization in the territories is so broad and intense, and the rejection by Israeli annexationists of Palestinian claims so absolute that no basis exists (or is likely to exist) for negotiating mutually acceptable arrangements between annexationist Israeli governments and Palestinians.

In light of the dismal prospects for removing, obscuring, or safely containing Palestinian discontent, it should not be surprising that removing the Palestinians themselves has crystallized as the preferred option of Israelis committed to the hegemonic institutionalization of Jewish rule throughout the whole Land of Israel. Since the mid-1980s, the idea of transferring Arabs en masse out of the country, whether through offering financial inducements, exerting indirect pressures, or implementing state-supervised coercion, has passed from the realm of the unthinkable to the plausible, and from the plausible to the policy of choice for a plurality if not a majority of annexationists. A particularly elaborate survey conducted in 1986 asked respondents to indicate which of ten different options for dealing with the territories and their Arab populations were both favored and found acceptable. The most extreme option in the annexationist direction was outright annexation plus expulsion of all Arabs. Of all the ten options, this option was deemed acceptable by more Israeli Jews than any other (42.9 percent). A plurality (29.7 percent) chose the same option as the one they most favored.[25] Beginning in spring 1989, the Hanoch Smith Institute reported a sharp increase in support for "transfer"-type solutions. Between May and November 1989 the percentage of Jewish Israelis answering yes to the question "Are you prepared to consider the deportation of Palestinians if a way is not found to make peace?" rose from 38 percent to 52 percent.[26]

The individual most closely identified with popularizing the expulsion of Arabs as a solution to Israel's demographic and political problems was Rabbi Meir Kahane (assassinated in New York City in 1991). Kahane demanded that every Arab in the country either leave or sign a form renouncing all claims to citizenship or any other form of national or political rights. His successful 1984 campaign to enter the Knesset was based on two slogans: "Let me deal with them!" and "I say what you think!" While a member of Knesset he introduced legislation forbidding sexual intimacy between Jews and non-Jews and banning all non-Jews from living within Jerusalem.[27]

The Likud and its "respectable" allies on the fundamentalist and ultranationalist right were disturbed by Kahane's popularity but open to his message. While helping to ban Kahane and his followers from subsequent elections, they began indicating their own support for, or refusal to rule out, the mass "transfer" or "repatriation" of Arabs.[28] In 1985, books and articles describing the evacuation of Arabs from the country as humane and fully compatible with Zionist principles began appearing on publishing-house lists and in the journals and newspapers associated with Herut, its ultranationalist allies, and Gush Emunim.[29]

In October 1987, Yosef Shapira, a National Religious party cabinet minister closely identified with Gush Emunim, proposed a program of $20,000 grants for all Arabs willing to leave the Land of Israel and permanently renounce the right to return. A survey of 120 rabbis who participated in an antiterrorism conference in a West Bank settlement in 1987 showed that 62 percent believed "the foreigners" should be encouraged to emigrate while 15 percent supported forcible expulsion.[30] At the beginning of 1988 a survey of two thousand members of Herut's central committee showed that 41 percent of respondents favored "a transfer (of the Arab population outside the boundaries of Eretz Yisrael)... if the demographic situation in Judaea, Samaria, and Gaza worsens."[31] Only after months of intifada, however, did leaders of Herut, Tehiya, Tzomet, and Gush Emunim speak publicly of their support for various schemes of population transfer. In 1988 the new Moledet (Homeland) party based its appeal entirely on its commitment to engineer the departure of all Arabs from the territories.[32]

Many Irish historians describe the purpose of Britain's laissez-faire policies in Ireland during the Great Famine of the 1840s as designed to reduce drastically the island's Catholic population. Some small attempts in French Algeria were made, in the late nineteenth and early twentieth centuries, to encourage Muslim emigration. Neither case, however, provides a useful basis for evaluating the plausibility of an Israeli-sponsored evacuation of Arabs from the occupied territories. Though no one can know what exactly the response of the anti-annexationist camp would be to a government-ordered policy of transfer, some Peace Now leaders have declared that policies of mass deportation would trigger explosions within the army caused by refusals to follow orders and by violent resistance. Indeed even many annexationists, citing political and logistical problems, have warned

that however attractive "transfer" options may appear, they have no realistic chance of implementation.[33] The only scenarios entailing mass expulsions depicted by observers as plausible are those associated with major
wars in which large-scale fighting erupts in or near the West Bank. It seems
best, therefore, to assume that deportations will not take place on a scale
able to reduce significantly the size of the Arab population of the territories
and thereby eliminate the basis for a "gross discrepancy" between life in
Israel proper and life in the occupied territories.

The inability of Israeli annexationists to either satisfy the Arabs of the
territories or remove them means it is unlikely the annexationists will be
able to construct a hegemonic view of the whole Land of Israel. This is a
judgment about the implausibility of an annexationist victory in a war of
position—a victory necessary to relocate the question of the fate of the
occupied territories across the ideological hegemony threshold and thereby
remove it from the Israeli political agenda. Certainly a state-building victory in a war of position seems at least as unavailable to Israeli annexationists as it was to partisans of Algérie française in France or to supporters
of various schemes for a "Greater Britain," or a reconsolidated Union, in
late nineteenth century Britain. But if Israeli annexationists are unable to
win a state-building victory in a war of position, then the problem of the
occupied territories will continue to burden the Israeli polity unless anti-
annexationists can win a state-contracting victory in a war of maneuver.

Prospects for State Contraction in Israel

From 1983 to at least the early 1990s, Israel's relationship to the West
Bank and Gaza, as a problem in Israeli politics, has been located to the
left of the ideological hegemony threshold, but to the right of the regime
threshold. The Israeli-Palestinian relationship during these years should
therefore be expected to resemble the British-Irish relationship between
1886 and 1914 and the French-Algerian relationship between 1946 and
1961. In this location, according to analysis of the European cases, changing domestic and international constellations of power can be expected to
produce repeated opportunities for elites favoring state contraction to fight
a war of maneuver against those willing to challenge the regime itself
rather than permit disengagement from the target territories. What then
do the patterns discovered during analysis of wars of maneuver in Britain
and France over disengagement from Ireland and Algeria suggest about
the circumstances under which such struggles are likely to erupt in Israel,
the relative plausibility of different strategies for "rescaling" the problem

which are available to Israeli anti-annexationists, and the prospects for their success?

An Israeli War of Maneuver in Comparative Perspective, 1988–1990

Labor's ouster of Likud in the 1992 elections gave anti-annexationist elites new opportunities to contract the state. To exploit these opportunities, however, decision makers will confront crucial questions about the likelihood of decisive engagements in a war of maneuver over withdrawing Israeli authority from the West Bank and Gaza Strip and the strategies and circumstances that could help avoid or win such engagements. An excellent opportunity to address these questions, by tapping my analyses of British and French wars of maneuver regarding Ireland and Algeria, is provided by the crisis in early 1990 surrounding the fall of the second Likud-led national unity government and the desperate and prolonged attempts by Peres and Shamir to form narrow governments of their own. This was not the first time that annexationist threats to state authority were made in connection with the dispute over the territories, but it was the first time that such challenges, and public fears about the possibility of regime failure, played an important role in the political calculations of Israeli political elites.

I noted in Chapter 5 that not until the political status of Ireland had been problematized did regime-level barriers to British disengagement from Ireland become visible. Even so, threats to the regime associated with movement toward the separation of Ireland from Britain did not manifest themselves except when governments committed to such a policy sought to implement disengagement policies or appeared poised to do so. The climactic phase of this war of maneuver was reached in the years between the Parliament Act's elimination of the House of Lords veto in 1911 and the outbreak of World War I in September 1914.

This decisive political battle was prefigured by minor skirmishes in 1886 and 1892. Before the defeat of Gladstone's first Home Rule Bill by the House of Commons in 1886, Ulster Unionists, drawing encouragement from Randolph Churchill, reacted with defiant gestures, violent rhetoric, and rudimentary preparations for armed resistance. Six years later Gladstone's rise to the premiership, in alliance with the Irish nationalists, resulted in passage of his second Home Rule Bill by the Commons. As we have seen, this success roused both Irish Protestants and British Conservatives to a wider-ranging, more explicit, and more coherent mobilization along regime-challenging lines than had occurred in 1886. With the crushing defeat of home rule in the House of Lords in 1893, however, the regime-threatening dimensions of the Irish problem were again submerged beneath the froth of "normal" British political life. Landslide election victories by the Unionists in 1895 and 1903 and by the Liberals in 1906 made Irish nationalists irrelevant for coalition formation, while the certainty of rejection by the Lords assured Unionists that even passage of a Home Rule Bill by the House of Commons would not result in Irish political autonomy. However, when two elections in 1910 produced razor-thin margins between the Liberal and Unionist parties, the Irish nationalists were once again able to bring their issue to the fore. After passage of the Parliament Act in 1911, both Irish and British Unionists confronted the real prospect of an authoritative decision to separate Ireland, in most significant respects, from the British state. These were the circumstances, prefigured in 1886 and 1892, that led to the full-scale, regime-challenging mobilization of Ulster Protestants and British Unionists.

The fierce war of maneuver analyzed in the French case had its climax in the overthrow of the Fourth Republic, while Pierre Pflimlin was premier, and strong but unsuccessful challenges to the Fifth Republic in 1960 and 1961. As in the British case, this decisive engagement in the struggle over Algeria's relationship to France was prefigured by earlier, milder confrontations. In summer and fall 1955, Prime Minister Faure's government was induced to recall its resident minister from Morocco, abandon its reform program, and escalate coercion in Algeria. These steps were taken in direct response to mass resignations by French officers in Morocco and violent threats of revolt by European settlers supported by right-wing metropolitan critics of the both the government and the regime. All three groups were reacting to what they sensed was a weakening commitment to maintaining the French protectorate in Morocco and French sovereignty in Algeria. The regime survived, but Faure's government collapsed. Following new elections in January 1956, Mollet's Socialist-led, "Republican Front" government was faced with violent riots by the pieds noirs of Algiers. With the Moroccan debacle fresh in his mind, Mollet drew back from what had seemed to be the inclination of the Socialists to implement sweeping changes in France's Algerian policy. The relatively long tenure of Mollet's government and the temporary alleviation of explicit threats to the regime were due, above all, to its partnership with partisans of Algérie française and strict adherence to the rhetoric and military policies demanded by them.

By late 1957, however, economic distress, international pressures toward negotiations with the FLN, and an increasing inclination among politicians in the center and on the left to entertain Algerian self-determination as an acceptable option made forming a stable government committed to Algérie française seem a doubtful prospect. Potent threats to the regime quickly reemerged. Neither Gaillard's ministry nor Pflimlin's could withstand the virulent and sustained attacks. Antiregime mobilization and conspiracies within the army, among the Europeans of Algeria, and within the Gaullist movement brought down both these short-lived governments and the Fourth Republic itself.

In Israel no war of maneuver has yet been fought to a conclusion, but some skirmishing has occurred. As in the British and French cases, the production and severity of regime crises in Israel appear directly linked to the emergence of constellations of political power, suggesting that a winning coalition of state contractors is taking, or is about to take, legal-authoritative decisions to disengage from the territory(ies) in question.

When the Peres-led version of the rotating national unity government tried in 1985 to engineer a deal with King Hussein and the PLO, right-wing politicians and settlers loudly declared their unwillingness to accept the authority of the Knesset to loosen Israeli ties to the territories. Accompanying some of these declarations were threats to take up arms, if necessary, against the government. According to an official pronouncement by the Gush Emunim—controlled Association of Jewish Local Councils in Judea, Samaria, and the Gaza District (Yesha), Peres's plans and proposals were "a prima facie annulment of the State of Israel as a Zionist Jewish state." The leaders of the settlements characterized any return of territory to foreign sovereignty as an "illegal action" and declared that they would treat "any regime in Israel which perpetrates [this crime] as an illegal regime, just as de Gaulle treated the Vichy government of Marshal Pétain . . . which surrendered most of France's historic territory." A petition for signature by masses of Israelis was prepared, addressed to the prime minister, declaring that "any Israeli government which hands over the sovereign governance of Jerusalem, Judea, Samaria, Gaza, or the Golan, in whole or in part . . . will be considered by me to be illegal, and I shall not recognize it."[34] Members of Knesset belonging to the Land of Israel lobby endorsed the Yesha Council's declaration.[35] While Attorney General Yitzhak Zamir criticized it as "political criminality" and "seeds of a catastrophe which will lead to a civil war," Deputy Prime Minister and Foreign Minister Yitzhak Shamir condemned the attorney general, describing the resolution as part of the "political and ideological arguments in the country."[36] Aware of the political support enjoyed by the settlers, and the fact that they had approximately ten thousand weapons in their personal possession, Attorney General Zamir informed the defense minister that although the Yesha declaration was illegal, he advised not indicting its authors in order to avoid aggravating the situation. Then Defense Minister Yitzhak Rabin took the attorney general's advice and satisfied himself with a warning against issuing similar incitements against state authority in the future.[37]

But not until 1988, following the outbreak of the intifada and the expectation of new elections later that year, did the struggle over the fate of the territories begin to display itself clearly as a war of maneuver. The elections of that year again resulted in a stalemate between the two major camps. After lengthy and intense bargaining with ultra-orthodox parties, the Likud and the Labor party failed to form a narrow annexationist or anti-annexationist government. The result was another government of indecision—a second national unity government between the two major parties. In March 1990, however, the coalition broke apart under pressure from the intifada, vigorous U.S. diplomacy, and extreme unease within the Likud that the unity government was being dragged into real negotiations. With a lame-duck Likud-controlled government in power, Israel experienced a two-month political crisis which ended in May when the Likud finally succeeded in forming an extreme annexationist government, supported by fundamentalists, ultranationalists, the ultra-orthodox parties, and two renegade Labor party deputies.

From the outbreak of the intifada in December 1987 to the establishment of the narrow Likud-led government in May 1990, Israelis paid unprecedented attention to the question of the Palestinians, the costs of the occupation, and the options for the eventual disposition of the territories. For the first time Israelis from all walks of life were spending month after month directly exposed to the hatreds generated among Palestinians by prolonged occupation, the solidarity of an entire population in various stages of active and passive revolt, the often brutal methods used in response, and the fear and fury of Jewish settlers (directed at both soldiers and Palestinians). Returning home on leave or upon completion of their unit's reserve duty, men told family and friends about what they had seen and done in Palestinian towns, villages, and refugee camps, in army prisons, and in large, hastily constructed detention and punishment facilities. These personal reports for the most part corroborated what Israelis were hearing and reading every day in the Israeli press and in reports from hundreds of foreign journalists attracted to Israel by the uprising.[38] Travel to the territories by Israelis, for pleasure, house-hunting trips, convenience, or even to visit relatives, virtually ceased.[39]

Polarization among Israeli Jews over how the problem might be resolved, combined with the evenness of the split between those favoring annexationist versus anti-annexationist solutions, and repeated government crises provoked fears among annexationists that "irreversible" steps toward Israeli disengagement from the territories might be the result of any one setback or misstep. On the other hand, many anti-annexationists believed that if only their forces could be mobilized effectively, and if only they were prepared to be as ruthless as they perceived their opponents to be, they could form a government ready for serious negotiations and save the country from the disaster they identified with its continued rule over the West Bank and Gaza Strip.

Although not a decisive engagement, this juncture in the history of the relationship between Israel and the territories fairly resembles the acute phases of wars of maneuver in Britain and France, when both sides of the fierce dispute within the center viewed the problem of Ireland or Algeria as located just to the right of the regime threshold. Among Israelis during this period, the question of whether illegal political action would be decisive in determining Israel's future relationship to the territories became a central and explicit topic of political debate. Special attention focused on threats of revolt by armed settlers, anti-Arab provocations, terrorism and assassination threats directed at public figures, the politicization of the army, organized refusal by reservists to serve in the territories, a new savagery in public debate, and much worried discussion of the likelihood of civil war.

Settlers complained that Israeli reporters and officers characterized the intifada as a civil rebellion rather than terrorism or war. With support from all the right-wing parties, settler activists organized a furious campaign against Israeli journalists—People against the Enemy Media as it became known, with thousands of bumper stickers appearing throughout Israel. Virtually every night Israeli television and radio received hundreds of telephone calls complaining about the use of "unpatriotic" terminology. Violent attacks on journalists and camera crews became a regular feature of life in Israel, particularly in the aftermath of Arab attacks on Jews.

Minor clashes also occurred between army units and groups of settler vigilantes. Some resulted in injuries and arrests; some were brought to an end only following the army's use of tear gas. Bitter confrontations between settlers and soldiers were common. In several instances, IDF officers were insulted, spat upon, and even beaten by angry settlers who accused them of sympathizing with the Arabs and held them responsible for Jewish casualties.[40] Gush Emunim leaders went on a hunger strike in front of the prime minister's office to warn that pressures among the settlers and their supporters elsewhere in Israel were leading to a resurgence of a terrorist underground even more widespread than the one uncovered in 1984.[41]

In fact by 1989, private militias had already formed a semisecret underground network, based in the settlements, that was conducting regular, well-organized raids on Arab villages. These groups united Gush Emunim activists with the "nonideological" but frightened and often furiously anti-

Arab residents of the new West Bank towns. The new underground had a variety of objectives, including initiating retaliation and deterrent attacks on Arabs, patrolling roads, establishing and maintaining a Jewish presence in all areas of the West Bank (no matter how likely to provoke clashes with local Arabs), providing security for businesses and residents in Jewish settlements, and laying the political, administrative, military, logistical, and technical infrastructure for maximum resistance in the event of developments deemed threatening to the continuation of Jewish rule over the territories.[42]

Beni Katzover, a Gush leader living in the Nablus area of the West Bank and a member of Knesset for Tehiya, estimated that 75 percent of the (then) eighty thousand settlers in the West Bank and Gaza Strip would resist evacuation nonviolently, but that 5 percent would take up arms.[43] In a poll of settlers in the northern bulge of the West Bank, in November 1988, 26 percent said they would carry their resistance to evacuation as far as civil war.[44] In 1990 a book of questions and answers commonly asked of him was published by a prominent West Bank rabbi for use by religious settlers in guiding their understanding of and responses to the intifada. Included in the book were several questions about whether "it would be permissible to fight against army units sent to evacuate settlements" in the event of a government decision to withdraw from parts of the Land of Israel.[45]

Following the PLO's declaration of the "State of Palestine" in the West Bank and the Gaza Strip in fall 1988, hundreds of activists associated with Rabbi Meir Kahane formally and publicly declared establishment of the "State of Judea," with a flag, an anthem, stamps, and passports. The stated purpose of the organization was to operationalize its founders' condemnation of the State of Israel as "traitorous" and to seize control of any areas abandoned to Arab control. Included within its clandestine "security" branch were said to be reserve officers from elite units, including Shlomo Baum.[46] A shadowy group (or groups) linked to both Kahane and Tehiya called itself the Sicarii (after the band of assassins who killed Jews it considered traitors during Roman rule of Judea). The Sicarii specialized in arson attacks and bomb and murder threats against (Jewish) journalists, politicians, and other public figures accused of lowering national morale or favoring negotiations with the PLO.[47]

The outrage of the settlers and other elements within the ultranationalist and fundamentalist right, against the media and the army high command, was based in part on the fact that Israel's most prominent journalists, and the decisive majority of the upper echelons of the army, were drawn from social and political backgrounds (Ashkenazim, secularists, graduates of high-prestige schools, and kibbutzniks) strongly suggesting their anti-annexationist sentiments.[48] Indeed representatives of the general staff did publicly and repeatedly insist that a political solution to the problem was the *only* way to end disturbances in the territories, since the fundamental problem was political not military. The army's mission, as the leaders of the IDF construed it, was to "contain" the uprising in order to allow the political echelon to act and to negotiate without having to do so under the pressure of violence. Chief of Staff Dan Shomron compared the situation in the territories to that in Algeria during the French war there and observed that in such situations, absent a political settlement, order and stability could be restored only through starvation or mass deportation of the population.[49]

Contrary to the position of the general staff, the settlers, joined by rank and file activists within the Likud, leaders of ultranationalist parties outside of the governing coalition, and several Likud ministers willing to strain the principle of "collective cabinet responsibility," insisted that the IDF be ordered to fight the intifada as a war, that it define the uprising's liquidation as victory, and that it commit itself with the same determination and willingness to make sacrifices that it always did in order to achieve victory in war. During a Knesset committee meeting in April 1989, one Likud deputy, a former chief of Israeli military intelligence, accused Shomron of purposely refusing to end Palestinian unrest and of "forging the *intifada* with his own hands."[50] Repeatedly, in public comments offered from January 1989 to May 1990, Shomron went out of his way to emphasize that the army would disintegrate if ordered to "quell the uprising. ... This would lead to a rift in Israeli society and subsequently in the IDF, which encompasses the entire political spectrum in Israel. The moment the IDF stops operating within the national consensus—which includes people on the fringe who think differently—the IDF would weaken and tear apart."[51] It was in response to such remarks, reflecting not only Shomron's views but those of the large majority of senior commanders, that Uzi Landau, a leading Likud parliamentarian, called for a systematic purge of the army and the security services.[52]

Labor party leader Yitzhak Rabin, who was defense minister until the end of the second unity government in November 1989, stood by his policy of containing rather than defeating the intifada, despite vehement and not altogether inaccurate charges from the annexationist camp that he and other anti-annexationists were welcoming the continued revolt as a spur to their political objectives.[53] When the Likud assumed control again, with Moshe Arens as defense minister, there was considerable speculation that the standing orders to the army would change, that the order to treat disturbances as terrorism or aggressive war, and to liquidate rather than contain the uprising, would be given. The evidence strongly suggests that

Sharon was not appointed defense minister, and sweeping changes were not made in the standing orders for responding to the intifada largely because the cabinet doubted many IDF generals and colonels would obey a command to fight the uprising as a war entailing the mobilization of artillery and armor, wholesale expulsions, tens of thousands of fatalities, and the destruction of villages and towns.[54]

During the height of the intifada, midrank officers and ordinary soldiers were also affected by the politicization of army policy. The pressures which politicized the IDF and produced serious internal strains came from the anti-annexationist camp as well as from the right. Army service in the territories during the intifada was, at best, a frustrating experience. Combined with the violent techniques used to subdue, punish, and intimidate Palestinians and the unorthodox methods employed by secret "disguised" units operating with unclear lines of accountability, the army's modus operandi produced daily situations in which strict application of written orders would expose many soldiers and/or officers to potential prosecution.[55] Cover-ups and pressures to participate in cover-ups of "deviant" behavior became a regular part of military life.[56] In addition, political differences among soldiers and reservists, between enlisted men and midlevel officers, and between midlevel officers and the high command fostered distrust and caused operational difficulties. The upper echelons were particularly concerned about deteriorating standards, morale, and fighting ability associated with prolonged, brutalizing confrontations with civilians and about extremist and "antidemocratic" tendencies emerging among midlevel officers, more of whom were now drawn from previously underrepresented segments of Israeli society—Middle Eastern and North African Jews.[57] Yesh Gvul (There Is a Limit), an organization that supported soldiers who refused service in the Lebanon War, reemerged as one of dozens of new anti-annexationist groups embracing more radical critiques of the occupation than Peace Now or established political parties had traditionally articulated.

The violence of the Sicarii and the settler militias, the extreme but portentous posturing of the "State of Judea," and the increasingly obvious political strains within and upon the army appeared especially salient against a background of political immobilism and an explosive escalation in the rhetoric of debate. The editor of a serious right-wing journal quoted from *The Diagnostic and Statistical Manual of Mental Disorders* to prove that Shulamit Aloni and other "radical leftists" were certifiably psychotic.[58] West Bank settlers insulted high-ranking army officers by calling them "kapos."[59] One leader of Tzomet called Labor leader Yitzhak Navon, formerly president of the State, a "quisling."[60] Over 250,000 Israelis demonstrated at a massive Tel Aviv rally organized by Gush Emunim in March

1988. Prominent banners were raised decrying Shimon Peres as Israel's Neville Chamberlain and warning those who would "stab the Jewish state in the back."[61] Ron Nahman, mayor of the Ariel settlement, a Likud member of Parliament, and known previously for his insistence on building bridges to all sectors of Israeli society, said in February 1988 that eventually the problem of the Arabs would be solved by their wholesale expulsion in the midst of a war with the Arab states. "First of all, however, we must have a civil war in this country, to purify the blood of the people. Shulamit Aloni, Dedi Zucker, and their friends will be happier anyway in New York and Paris."[62] Similarly, from the podium of the Knesset, Tehiya member Geula Cohen used the names of three prominent liberal-dovish Knesset deputies when she condemned "all the Sarids, the Dedi Zuckers, and the Tzabans, who are victims of national AIDS, who have lost their immunity mechanism, and are full of germs and think that they will spread them among the people."[63]

Of course annexationists were not the only ones to contribute to the polarization of Israeli political life or to use such vitriolic language. In April 1988 the left-wing Mapam party refused to invite Prime Minister Shamir to the festive opening session of its decennial conference, while pointedly inviting Palestinian leaders from the occupied territories. Amos Oz is Israel's foremost living author and one of the most respected personalities in the anti-annexation camp. Before a large Peace Now rally in Tel Aviv in June 1989, Oz declared that

> A small sect, a cruel and obdurate sect, emerged several years ago from a dark corner of Judaism; and it is threatening to destroy all that is dear and holy to us, and to bring down upon us a savage and insane blood-cult. People think, mistakenly, that this sect is struggling for our sovereignty in Hebron and Nablus, that it wants the Greater Land of Israel, and this end justifies all the means at their disposal—including those dripping with blood. But the truth is that, for this cult, the Greater Land of Israel is merely a sophisticated ploy to disguise its real aims: the imposition of an ugly and distorted version of Judaism on the State of Israel.

Oz went on to justify his words as a warning that the left in Israel had its own "red lines," that it too cherished values more important than avoidance of civil war, and that its willingness to fight in the ranks of the armed forces was ultimately conditional. "These warnings must be sounded in unambiguous language," he stated, "we do not want the nation to be ripped apart—but under no circumstances whatever will we acquiesce in the transformation of our country into a monster. And we will not allow them to use us to serve as the fangs and claws of the monster." Oz challenged the Likud to "rehabilitate" the rule of law and the principle of humane treatment of Arabs. "If you do not do this at once, our blood is on your heads; and, at the end of the road, your own blood as well. You have been warned."[64]

Surrounded by such rhetoric, the public's affirmative response to a June 1989 poll is no surprise. Fifty-eight percent answered yes to the question "Could the exacerbation of domestic controversies lead to civil war?"[65] In September 1989, one of Israel's leading newspapers, *Hadashot*, responded to the bitter political atmosphere by commissioning a major polling organization to conduct a survey among Israeli Jews asking respondents to identify the "most hated person in the country." Two doves led the list—Shimon Peres (21.3 percent) and Yossi Sarid (16.9 percent)—followed by two leading hawks, Ariel Sharon (15.2 percent) and Meir Kahane (10.3 percent).[66]

During this period many private and public meetings were held between representatives of Gush Emunim and various peace groups with the express purpose of finding common ground and lessening fears of political violence between the two camps. None were successful.[67] In fact, questions about civil war and the likelihood of regime breakdown became a regular feature of interviews with politicians. In a joint interview in late 1989, dovish Labor MK Yossi Beilin and Likud leader Uzi Landau were asked questions about the paralysis of the national unity government and about chances that a violent right-wing challenge would materialize against a narrow Labor government's peace policy. Beilin argued in favor of dissolving the national unity government, despite the risks of regime threats and of a narrow right-wing government. Beilin argued that peace policies that avoided uprooting existing settlements would make civil war or intra-Jewish violence less likely, but expressed confidence that a Labor government would overcome outbursts if they did occur. Landau, on the other hand, encouraged the idea of such threats materializing and magnified their likely consequences. He emphasized that "history teaches us that many societies, when confronted with the need to take major decisions, have collapsed because of divisions and controversies." He cited the controversy over the Lebanon War as an indication of how imperiled the political system in Israel might be by the decision of a narrow Labor government to withdraw from territories. "I believe," he said, "that the danger of a split is so grave, and the prospect of Jews getting hold of each other's throats so frightening, that the effort to avoid a split is paramount." When asked whether he foresaw the danger of civil war or emergence of a left- or right-wing underground should a narrow government be formed, Landau promised that he personally would not participate in such activities. "But," he continued, "there is a danger that if a decision is made to withdraw from Judea and Samaria, there might be hundreds of thousands of Israelis taking the law into their own hands...a wise statesman will be careful to avoid such a situation."[68]

Some months earlier a prominent Hebrew University sociologist warned that settlers and right-wing militants were ready to challenge the authority of the state and had enough support from politicians and elite groups so that "a forced withdrawal from the territories or a deep economic crisis could lead to violent clashes within the organs of the state...a case of Yamit writ large and much more serious."[69] After an eight-month study of the options facing Israel in the territories, twenty-four Israeli national security experts concluded that the most salient obstacles to a settlement based on negotiated withdrawal from the territories were "the grave challenges" it would present "to the delicate fabric of Israeli society and to the very unity and integrity of the nation." Although the study group suggested that eventual establishment of a Palestinian state in the territories was in Israel's long-term national interest, they also concluded that a Knesset decision in support of such a policy would trigger sedition within the army, large-scale settler resistance, internecine bloodshed, political assassinations, and widespread anti-Arab provocations.[70]

My point here is not that Israel was on the brink of civil war or that the breakdown of central institutions was imminent. Nor am I arguing that the Israeli political situation in early 1990 was as explosive as the Irish crisis in Britain before World War I or the crises faced by two regimes in France from 1957 to 1961. What I do contend is that between the outbreak of the intifada in December 1987 and the establishment of a narrow right-wing government in June 1990, the Israeli public and Israeli elites substantially diverted their attention from incumbent-level competition and associated policy outcomes to threats and concerns about the regime within which that competition was nominally occurring.

Indeed the particular outcome of the crisis which dissipated Israeli fears of regime collapse or civil war, that is, formation of an unprecedentedly right-wing annexationist government, appears to have been a *direct* result of those fears. In March 1990, sixty members of Parliament announced their support for a Labor-led government, while the other sixty deputies announced support for a Likud-led government. Almost everything turned on Rabbi Eliezer Shach, the ninety-two-year-old leader of the Lithuanian branch of the non-Zionist ultraorthodox community.[71] What signals would he send to his followers in the small Flag of the Torah (Degel Hatorah) party and the Torah-Observing Sephardim (Shas), both of which he had helped found as part of longstanding rivalries within the *haredi* community?

On March 26, in a dramatic televised address delivered in a sports arena, Rabbi Shach affirmed his anti-annexationist beliefs but proceeded to vilify the kibbutz movement and other secular Israelis, virtually forbidding his followers to support any government organized by the Labor party. The door was thus open to a coalition of the Degel Hatorah and Shas with the Likud and its ultranationalist and fundamentalist partners. After some further dispute over attempts by both Labor and Likud to purchase the loyalty of certain of each other's Knesset representatives, Shamir succeeded in forming a Likud-fundamentalist-ultranationalist-ultraorthodox government which was voted into office by the Knesset on June 11, 1991.

Why did Shach renege on commitments his emissaries had made to Peres? Why did he go against his own consistently voiced opinions favoring withdrawal from the territories?[72] Why did he choose to emphasize the secular profanities of life among dovish kibbutzniks instead of the Messianic heresies associated with Gush Emunim? Four days before the speech was delivered, the answer to these questions was provided by sources identified as close to the nonagenerian rabbi. These sources predicted Shach would support the Likud because of his immediate concern to avoid the kind of internecine struggle which Jewish tradition says was responsible for the Roman destruction of Jerusalem. Under prevailing circumstances, they said, Shach would throw his support to Likud, fearing that "a government which does not include the Likud may lead to internal dissension and even bloodshed within the Israeli people, were it to make territorial concessions."[73]

The substantive intrusion of regime-level concerns into Israeli politics from 1988 to 1990 was triggered by the state-contracting influence of the intifada. But this order of magnitude in the disruptiveness of struggles over disengagement was present only because five years earlier the annexationist camp had succeeded in achieving a substantial institutionalization of its expanded image of the shape of the Israeli state. It had, in other words, succeeded in pushing the problem of the occupied territories past the regime threshold. This sequence of change and consequence[74] corresponds to expectations generated by my model as well as to patterns traced in the British and French cases. By examining responses of Israeli politicians to this crisis in light of the British and French experience with similarly located territorial problems (just to the right of the regime threshold), the likely role of different rescaling mechanisms and the plausibility of various scenarios for Israeli state contraction can be evaluated.

Israeli Strategies for Recrossing the Regime Threshold

Rabbi Shach's decision to back the Likud doomed desperate but promising Labor party efforts to negotiate the regime threshold with a rescaling strategy based initially on a dramatic realignment of Israeli politics. From late 1989 to June 1990, anti-annexationist politicians and opinion leaders believed there was a good chance they would have an opportunity to form a government without the Likud. Amid initial skirmishing in a war of maneuver I have argued was taking place at that time, they contemplated possible strategies for pushing the problem of the disposition of the occupied territories across the regime threshold in the state-contracting direction. The most serious initiative, and the one that came closest to success, was carried forward by Shimon Peres and the dovish Mashov faction of the Labor party. Believing it was perhaps his last chance to form a government under his leadership, Peres pulled out all the stops in pursuit of the votes in Parliament necessary to form a winning coalition. Once in power the government would implement a disengagement policy emphasizing serial decomposition (to deprive opponents of strategic opportunities for resistance), and pedagogy (to change the preferences of Israelis not ideologically committed to the whole Land of Israel project).

To build their coalition, Peres and his supporters targeted Arab and Communist Knesset deputies, the ultraorthodox parties, and even individual deputies within the Likud. If necessary, Peres was prepared to settle for a minority government, one that could survive votes of no confidence on specific issues by counting on different Knesset deputies from opposition parties to abstain or vote in the negative on different issues. It appears he intended to use his freedom of maneuver as prime minister in a narrow government to plunge Israel into a rapid and decisive diplomatic process whose stated objective would be agreement on transitional arrangements but whose actual goal would be a comprehensive settlement. While standing down regime threats from right-wing extremists, he would count on securing generous U.S. economic and political assistance. Once terms of a peace agreement based on withdrawal from the territories had been arrived at, he would call new elections, using the prospect of peace, strong international backing, and endorsement of his policy by the army high command to give him a victory large enough to turn issues of peace and territorial withdrawal into questions no longer capable of posing serious threats to the stability of the regime.[75]

This strategy required Mapam, Ratz, and Shinui—Labor's three dovish-liberal allies—to trade strong commitments against "religious coercion" and their opposition to extravagant government funding of religious institutions for ultraorthodox support in their struggle to take Israel out of the West Bank and Gaza. Demands from the religious parties Peres was ready to accommodate would have effectively extended the power of ultraorthodox rabbis to control intimate aspects of private life and enforce their interpretation of Jewish religious law on a wide range of other issues, including the sale of pork, the operation of public transportation, restaurants, and places of entertainment on the Sabbath, "indecent" advertising, and censorship of the arts. In addition to furthering the appointment of religious politicians to key ministerial and deputy-ministerial positions, these deals would have entailed allocations of huge new sums for distribution in their extensive patronage systems and even bribes, reportedly in the range of millions of dollars, to individual Likud parliamentarians whose votes, it was learned, could be had at the right price.[76] Despite the embarrassment of strengthening groups they typically condemned as "religious reactionaries," Mapam, Ratz, and Shinui agreed to follow Peres's lead and support any narrow government he could muster committed to trading the occupied territories for resolution of the Arab-Israeli conflict.

In the end Peres's efforts came to nought. He did get the agreement of the Arab parties and the Communists to support if not join his government, and he thought he had at least two of the three ultraorthodox parties on board. However Rabbi Shach was, as we have seen, unconvinced that Peres could contain domestic disruption within acceptable bounds, and so he opted for the Likud. Once Shach had made his decision, the political winds shifted strongly against Peres, who found himself no longer able to outbid Shamir for the "loyalty" of several renegade Likud and Labor Knesset members.

In fact it was not at all clear that Peres would have been able to carry out his game plan, even had Shach encouraged his followers to support Labor rather than Likud in spring 1990. Some Knesset deputies from the Labor party, and some ultraorthodox deputies indicated they would refuse to support any government that relied crucially on Arab votes in order to decide the fate of the territories.[77] In a local branch meeting of Labor party activists, Mordechai Gur argued for a return to a national unity government because in the context of what he characterized as "a crisis of the state," it was simply too dangerous to allow either a narrow right-wing or left-wing government to pursue its objectives. "As Rabin and I both say," he told his audience, "we have no spare state here, and no spare army."[78] Interviews in April, May, and June 1990 with a dozen Labor party central committee members and Knesset deputies suggested that at least one-third of the Labor party were unwilling to take the risks of regime breakdown that they believed *any* narrow government would face should it go beyond incremental measures and commit itself to withdraw from the West Bank and Gaza Strip. Referring to the prospect of a Peres government committing itself to a land-for-peace settlement, one Labor Knesset member from the hawkish wing of the party said that "anyone within a narrow government who would give an order that might not be followed would risk the very essence of the regime. They know it, and in the end would not risk it." Another Labor MK associated with the political center of the party agreed, saying that hundreds of officers would resign if ordered to evacuate the territories by a narrow government, and that they would be supported by armed settlers and political groups within Israel itself with easy access to weapons. Other Labor politicians closer to Peres believed that challenges to the authority of the government could and would be resisted successfully, and that the risks were in any case worth taking.[79]

The failure of several splinter rightist parties to pass the 1.5 percent minimum threshold for Knesset representation helped put the Labor party in a position to form a government in July 1992, even though the number of Jewish votes for annexationist parties (excluding the ultraorthodox) was equal to or greater than the number cast for explicitly anti-annexationist parties. In any event, the ability of the Labor party to win the June 1992 election on a platform that stressed its opposition to annexation was a substantial setback to the right wing's state-building ambitions in the territories. But as shown by the victory of the Liberal party in the 1910 elections, and the willingness of the Gaillard government to move toward disengagement from Algeria in early 1958, this incumbent-level victory should be seen as only the first step on a rocky, dangerous, and uncertain road toward state contraction.

Within the anti-annexationist camp the really crucial questions are if, how, and when to confront regime challenges. The debate over this question will be all the more intense because, although the dovish wing of the Labor party was strengthened by the result of internal elections in early 1992, Rabin's traditional sources of support in the party are drawn from circles that generally opposed Peres's narrowly based, high-risk realignment strategy. Also because of its reliance on Knesset deputies elected by Arab and ultraorthodox votes, Rabin's government is vulnerable to accusations of not representing a majority of Zionist Jews—comparable to the accusations leveled by Unionists against the third Home Rule Bill as the product of a "corrupt" bargain between Liberals and Irish nationalists. While ready to launch a process of serial decomposition, including negotiation of an interim autonomy agreement, Palestinian elections, and/or implementation of unilateral autonomy measures in the Gaza Strip, Rabin is not likely to move quickly or explicitly toward a permanent settlement based on a Palestinian state in the West Bank and Gaza. Although he has spoken openly about withdrawal from the Golan Heights, and has repeatedly expressed his desire to be rid of the Gaza Strip, as of this writing Rabin has avoided committing himself explicitly to territorial withdrawals in the West Bank by emphasizing that the question of drawing maps need not be decided until five years after the interim autonomy agreement goes into effect. As he has pointed out, this means that no territorial concessions will be made before new general elections.

To minimize the danger of the regime crisis Israel will experience in connection with movement toward state contraction, those who have been associated with Rabin in the past would prefer that he wait for a large centrist bloc to coalesce in support of such a policy. This rescaling strategy is based on a different kind of "realignment" and a gradual change in the preferences of non–ideologically motivated Israeli annexationists. It envisions a Labor-led bloc, or a new grouping dedicated to territorial compromise that would represent 70 to 80 percent of the Parliament. Such a large majority, it is argued, could form as a result of the rising costs of repressing the Palestinians, trust built up by the success of autonomy agreements, and the need to harmonize Israeli policies with the demands of the international community in general and the United States in particular. In this way, it is hoped, all but 10 percent of the settlers, and a smaller percentage of their supporters within Israel proper, would either support or feel compelled to accept the decision of the government.

This kind of a "fusionist" or "Caesarist" bloc is what materialized in both Britain and France—under Lloyd George and the Unionists after 1916 and under de Gaulle's leadership in the Fifth Republic. Neither of these cases suggests it as a plausible scenario for Israel, however. In the British case, the bloc crystallized only in the context of World War I, only after the Irish question had been radically decomposed, and only after the losses of the Great War had helped marginalize Irish matters in the minds of most Unionist politicians. Even then it also required for its achievement the singular talents and charismatic authority of David Lloyd George. In Britain, in other words, this sort of realignment was not an important element in rescaling the Irish problem, only in smoothing the way to a disengagement solution of an already rescaled problem.

In France, this fusionist-type realignment took shape within the contours of a regime specially recomposed to facilitate its crystallization and was heavily dependent on the charisma and leadership talents of de Gaulle. As Lloyd George's leadership gifts were made relevant in part by international crisis, so were de Gaulle's personal appeal and the integrity of the political bloc formed as a reflection of it, functions of the vividness of French beliefs that de Gaulle, Gaullist governments, and the Fifth Republic itself were the only alternatives to civil war over Algeria. More fundamental to de Gaulle's success than whatever "unique" qualities he possessed were the thoroughgoing recomposition of the French regime that accompanied his rise to power and the beliefs of most metropolitan supporters of Algérie française that severe threats to the stability of the legal order associated with continued struggle over the future of Algeria were an order of magnitude more important to them than their desire to keep Algeria French.

Accordingly, for Israelis who advocate a rescaling strategy based on a centrist coalition and a new national consensus, it is misplaced to bemoan the absence of a politician capable of performing the pedagogical or inspirational role associated with de Gaulle in rescaling the Algerian problem.[80] In their emphasis on great leadership or charismatic authority figures, they ignore the institutionally and situationally determined context of its successful exercise. That is, even if someone were present on the Israeli scene possessing the necessary talent, reputation, and flexibility, the decisive question would still be whether conditions enabling such a leader to exploit those assets either existed or could be engineered.

To be sure, a partial recomposition of the Israeli regime is now likely, involving direct election of the prime minister and some change in Israel's extreme version of proportional representation. By affording wider discretion to the prime minister and more security to governments he is able to form, such changes will tend to elicit a stronger leadership style more conducive to the use of charismatic appeals and political pedagogy than has been the case under the current system. However, because the great national debate over the territories is so polarized and so evenly balanced, and because the religious parties see a dire threat to their interests in any far-reaching change in the rules of the parliamentary game, only a very partial recomposition of the regime can be expected—not one capable of providing a basis for a large majority party, at least not until after the territories question is resolved or until a profound crisis over the territories effectively submerges that issue beneath concerns for the integrity of the regime.[81] My point is that the entire purpose of the pseudo-Caesarist realignment strategy designed by cautious anti-annexationists in Israel is to *avoid* sharp, regime-threatening, political struggles—struggles that could produce a powerful charismatic leader by setting the stage for drastic forms of political recomposition and/or by overshadowing preferences for territorial expansion with fears of severe societal disruption.[82]

In both Britain and France, contraction of the state across the regime threshold required a large surplus of political capital. Given the difficulties of accumulating such a surplus, it is not surprising that anti-annexationists have been increasingly explicit and insistent about their desire for stringent U.S. pressure.[83] By reducing economic and military assistance and the intimacy of U.S.-Israeli relations, or at least by explicit threats to do so, U.S. politicians could remove from the shoulders of Israeli politicians much of the burden of persuading Israeli annexationists or of imposing state contraction on unpersuaded Israeli state-builders.

While it is not inconceivable that the United States might play this deus ex machina role, neither the record of U.S. foreign policy in the Middle East nor consideration of the British and French cases suggests this as a likely scenario.[84] U.S. support for a territories-for-peace solution to the

Arab-Israeli dispute is clear. Washington is ready to finance, guarantee, and/or broker almost any agreement Israeli and Arab negotiators may be able to come to. At times U.S. diplomacy has displayed an unusually dogged commitment to fostering formal negotiations between Arabs and Israelis over the future of the West Bank and Gaza Strip. President Bush's policy of withholding loan guarantees from the Shamir government as long as it continued to construct settlements in the territories was a key factor in bringing the Labor party to power in 1992. It is doubtful, however, that the imperatives of U.S. domestic politics and the complex array of alliances and antagonisms in American–Middle East relations will ever lead a U.S. administration to shoulder the burden of enforcing concessions necessary to achieve a settlement.

In neither France nor Britain did external pressure play a significant role in the vital task of rescaling the problems across the regime threshold. In 1958, Anglo-American diplomacy and U.S. threats to withhold badly needed loans did help push the Fourth Republic over the precipice on which it was teetering. Subsequently international opposition to French policies in Algeria also influenced many French to change their attitudes. In Britain, U.S. sympathy and diplomatic support for the Irish struggle were used by Lloyd George during and after World War I to convince Unionists to soften their positions on terms to offer Irish nationalists.[85]

However, no evidence from either of these cases suggests that the territories problem in Israel can be rescaled without decomposing the problem, recomposing the regime, or drawing the necessary political capital from an intense regime crisis. Of course *spatial* decomposition of the territories, meaning some version of the Allon Plan, has traditionally been the dominant view among Israeli doves of the shape a peace agreement would eventually take. In all its various guises, the Allon Plan emphasizes a division of the West Bank and Gaza Strip, awarding Israel particularly salient areas, including the Jordan Valley, expanded East Jerusalem, and virtually all of the post-1967 Jewish settlements. The remainder of the territories, containing the great bulk of the Arab population, would be ruled by a Jordanian/Palestinian state based in Amman under the leadership of the Hashemite dynasty or a combination of Jordanian and Palestinian elements. In the 1988–90 crisis triggered by the intifada, however, spatial decomposition was rarely discussed. As annexationists had often pointed out, the Allon Plan had never been a practical basis for a settlement. Neither King Hussein of Jordan nor any other Arab state had ever indicated readiness to accept permanent Israeli rule of substantial parts of the territories. Intensive settlement of the West Bank and Gaza did not erase the Green Line, but it did erase the lines drawn within those areas by Allon Plan aficionados separating portions to be relinquished, with few or no

Jewish inhabitants, from those containing Jewish settlers and sites of strategic or historical significance, which were to have remained under permanent Israeli jurisdiction. The intifada increased the confidence of Palestinians to demand satisfaction of their national aspirations throughout the small parts of Palestine (the West Bank and Gaza Strip), which they now made plain they were willing to accept as their state. Correspondingly, the anti-annexationist camp in Israel has become increasingly willing to forego any substantial Israeli demands for permanent control of various parts of these areas, at least exclusive of expanded East Jerusalem. When Jordan announced in July 1988 that it was formally and effectively severing all its political ties to the West Bank and acknowledging the full authority of the PLO and the Palestinians of the occupied territories to decide the fate of those areas on their own, few Allon Plan loyalists could be found willing to argue in favor of its continued relevance.[86]

If spatial decomposition, that is, the Allon Plan, as a depiction of the final objective of Israeli state contraction has been of decreasing interest to anti-annexationists, serial or temporal decomposition, in which a more total withdrawal of Israeli authority would be achieved at the end of a phased process, has attracted increasing support. In January 1990, Shmuel Toledano[87] published a peace plan involving negotiations with the PLO and eventual establishment of a Palestinian state. His proposal for "peace in stages" received a 60 percent approval rating in surveys of Israeli Jews, the first time a majority of Israelis had ever been found to endorse a "two-state solution."[88]

The basis of Toledano's scheme was to assure the Palestinians at the outset that, five years down the road, a fully recognized, sovereign Palestinian state in the West Bank and Gaza Strip could be established. This would occur, however, only after the successful implementation of a stipulated timetable of interim arrangements and confidence-building measures. In the final stages, Israeli settlers would be given the choice of remaining in place as Israeli citizens, leaving, or becoming citizens of the Palestinian state. Although Toledano's plan explicitly ruled out transfer of expanded East Jerusalem to Palestinian sovereignty, the plan included provisions for separate supervision of the holy places, two sets of municipal elections, and two mayors (one Arab and one Jew).

Toledano's plan made a sovereign Palestinian state and the relative completeness of ultimate disengagement explicit, thereby challenging argument-persuadable Israelis to reexamine their preferences about acceptable outcomes. The serial decomposition aspect of the plan was its emphasis on a preimplementation basis for corroborating the workability of a Palestinian state solution. The prospect of a series of "tests" of Arab performance was meant to separate Israeli security concerns and visceral distrust of Arabs from their acceptance of the abstract principle of Palestinian statehood. By replacing spatial division (per the Allon Plan) with temporal division, the potential for flexibility existing within the Israeli Jewish population would be brought to the surface. Finally, by promising that settlements would not be dismantled and that not until close to the end of the process would their inhabitants have to choose whether to leave or stay, the scheme was designed to remove dramatic opportunities for annexationists to rally settler and wider Israeli support for regime-challenging opposition.

An important variation on the Toledano plan was advanced by the Jaffee Center for Strategic Studies. It too emphasized a combination of serial decomposition and preference change as a rescaling strategy, but with one crucial difference.[89] To cope with regime threats, the authors of the Jaffee plan were convinced that a disengagement-oriented government would need to be fundamentally deceptive about its real intentions, both in coming to power and in implementing its policies. To gain support among Sephardic Jewish supporters of the Likud, businessmen formerly identified with the Liberal party, and other non–ideologically committed groups within the annexationist camp, the schedule of transitional stages would be presented as a more rigorous test of Palestinian behavior, and as a guarantee of more Israeli prerogatives, than would actually be the case. In contrast to Toledano, the framers of the JCSS proposal did not depict a Palestinian state as either a guaranteed or likely outcome of even a fully successful process of "confidence-building measures" and transitional agreements, saying only that their plan did not "negate the possibility of the eventual emergence of a Palestinian state."[90]

This is not to say that the framers of this proposal did not believe in the ultimate necessity of this option, only that they judged it unwise to make that conclusion explicit. While describing their plan as a framework to encourage the evolution of change in "fundamental perceptions," and characterizing the process as contingent upon the achievement of change in these perceptions, the clear intent of the framers of the Jaffee proposal was to move the Israeli body politic toward circumstances under which the emergence of a Palestinian state solution could no longer be prevented. Thus the proposal was presented as a means of creating political and diplomatic dialectics with a very definite, but *publicly* unanticipated consequence—the reconciliation of enough Israelis to a Palestinian state so that the government in power in Israel would be able to withstand the challenges to its authority that would most likely erupt in response.[91]

Consideration of the British and French cases suggests that a serial decomposition/change-of-preferences strategy is not by itself likely to bring victory in a state-contracting war of maneuver. In both cases this combination of rescaling mechanisms was present, but only as partial or failed strategies. De Gaulle used serial decomposition to deprive his opponents of strategic opportunities for mobilizing regime threats against the "abandonment" of Algeria. But this occurred during the first years of the Fifth Republic, after the centerpiece of his rescaling strategy—regime recomposition—had been accomplished. In Britain attempts to employ serial decomposition, by implementing home rule in most of Ireland followed by its implementation in Ulster some years later, failed to prevent regime-threatening mobilization. Instead the government accepted a radical spatial decomposition of the Irish problem as a means of avoiding a more severe or prolonged regime crisis. Persuasion was not an important factor during the Ireland-related war of maneuver in Britain prior to World War I.

Thus an approach based on this combination of rescaling mechanisms (i.e., one which did not rely on spatial decomposition) would appear to require those promoting disengagement to find some other source of surplus political capital with which to weather even the diminished regime crisis likely to ensue. With this in mind, the most promising route to an anti-annexationist victory in a war of maneuver might well be that pursued, in part at least, by Shimon Peres and his colleagues in spring 1990. Its salient elements comprised a sequential rescaling strategy: entry into deceptively framed negotiations to serially decompose the process of disengagement; reliance on a narrow coalition to precipitate a serious but manageable crisis or crises; exploitation of the confrontations with annexationist extremists to redefine the issue as regime stability, the rule of law, and respect for the army rather than territorial withdrawal; and finally, isolation and defeat of regime-challenging opponents of state contraction and their supporters.

As it was in the French case, and as it well might have been in the British case if Churchill had had his way in 1914, the source of needed political capital would be the tension generated by regime threats and the prerogatives accorded the government for resisting them. In Israel the idea would be to use actions by settlers or other opponents of state contraction, such as anti-Jewish terrorism, large-scale anti-Arab provocations, assassinations of political leaders, or attacks on soldiers, to justify tough measures. These might include a partial military mobilization, declaration of a state of emergency, arrest of opposition leaders, proscription of political and paramilitary organizations among the settlers and their supporters, strict press censorship, and so forth. In such a context, the government would have an excellent chance to mobilize public sentiment in support of state contraction by identifying the successful implementation of required policies as validation of the state itself and as support for legal authority threatened by civil war and institutional collapse. Talented leaders could also capitalize on the crisis by cultivating an image of courageous leadership acting decisively at a historic juncture to save the state from fanatic oppositionists.[92]

In Israel there are several reasons to think that this kind of high-risk, crisis-prone strategy, testing loyalties to the integrity of the regime against ideological commitments to the whole Land of Israel, would stand a better chance of contracting the state across the regime threshold than the broadly similar efforts of Churchill and Asquith in March 1914 (which failed) or even those of de Gaulle from 1959 to 1961 (which succeeded).[93] Although the contribution Israeli settlers are capable of making to a regime challenge on the issue of territorial withdrawal from the West Bank and Gaza might be more substantial than that of the Europeans of Algeria, it would be less weighty than that of the Protestants of Ireland. Israelis in the occupied territories, excluding the Jewish population of expanded East Jerusalem, are a proportion of the total Israeli Jewish population that is just a bit smaller than that comprised by the Irish Protestant population in relation to the population of Britain but about 20 percent larger than the European population of Algeria relative to the metropolitan population of France.[94]

Of course equivalent population proportions would not directly translate into equivalent political potential in the context of a war of maneuver. Any regime challenge emanating from the West Bank and Gaza settlers would be spearheaded by Gush Emunim, in cooperation with activists and politicians within the fundamentalist and ultranationalist parties to the right of Likud. Unlike the rather ad hoc organizations that emerged among the pieds noirs during the first years of the Fifth Republic, Gush Emunim contains an extremely talented and experienced elite, thousands of zealous adherents, and a proven track record of sustained, disciplined political mobilization. This elite has wide-ranging political experience, giving it the self-confidence to view itself as capable of leading the state. It has intimate knowledge of and close contacts with the leadership of the National Religious party and all the parties to the right of the Labor party. Its ideological appeals are capable of justifying extreme measures to its followers and to a large proportion of the inhabitants of non-Gush-affiliated settlements. Depending on specific circumstances, these appeals have the potential to rally active support from 20 percent to 30 percent of Israeli Jews.

Although not nearly as formidable a force as the Ulster Volunteers, and although not as numerous as the pied noir militia (the Territorial Units), settlers in the occupied territories have organized well-armed paramilitary and terrorist groups. Together they possess a dense communications network, enough small arms and ammunition to supply ten thousand to fifteen thousand resistants, and a logistical and organizational infrastructure capable of being used effectively against Arabs or anti-annexationist Jews, or to "up the ante" considerably for any government inclined toward confrontation over the future of the territories. As in the French-Algerian case, many of those active in these groups, along with other settlers, have under different Likud governments and chiefs of staff been integrated into a "civil guard." By carrying out security functions for the army in the West Bank and Gaza Strip, these individuals serve their political objectives while performing their reserve duty and achieve a politically useful blurring of boundaries between legally sanctioned patrols and paramilitary activities not sanctioned by legally constituted authorities.

The compactness, leadership, and political sophistication of Gush Emunim settlers suggest that their contribution to a regime crisis might be more substantial than that of the Europeans of Algeria. No Israeli government is likely to experience the relative ease with which de Gaulle outmaneuvered the pieds noirs, first convincing them that he was their savior, then goading European firebrands into the Barricades Rebellion, and subsequently using terrorist (OAS) excesses to eliminate most if not all metropolitan French sympathy for the Europeans of Algeria. Still, the settlers in the occupied territories do not match the solidity, discipline, and elaborate preparation for armed resistance and self-government manifested by Ulster Protestants, at least in the years 1911–14. Therefore, two of the difficulties facing the Asquith government in 1914 are not as likely to be present in the Israeli case, namely, a settler population so firmly united behind its leadership that government threats of confrontation can neither shake its determination nor spur settler extremists to engage in politically disastrous actions.

Geography is an important factor that will likely reduce the willingness of large numbers of West Bank and Gaza settlers to rally behind a violent challenge to the regime, even if faced with an explicit government policy of relinquishing the territories. Because Ireland and Algeria are separated from Britain and France by substantial bodies of water, the Protestants and Europeans in those territories had good reason to believe that political separation from the metropole would mean a transformation in their entire way of life, including, for most, a significant decline in their standard of living. Jewish settlers in the occupied territories, on the other hand, precisely because of the contiguity between Israel proper and the West Bank and Gaza Strip, know that even if they are forced to evacuate the territories and return to homes within the Green Line, they will move only a short distance, maintaining life-styles and employment opportunities that would be only marginally less attractive, and possibly even more attractive, than those to which they are now accustomed in their settlements. In other words, one ingredient in the political effectiveness of regime challenges by settlers in Ireland and (especially) Algeria, belief by the great majority of settlers that their standards of living would be drastically reduced if the indigenous majority were accorded self-determination, is not present in the Israeli case. Indeed if the compensation offered Jewish settlers in the event of evacuation were even a substantial fraction of the funds made available to Yamit settlers in 1981 and 1982, most settler families would experience an absolute improvement in their economic situation.

In Chapter 8 the distribution of power within the antidisengagement coalition was identified as a key variable helping to explain differences in outcomes in the wars of maneuver fought in Britain and France over Ireland and Algeria. It was noted that the Unionist party in Britain fully and completely committed itself to the regime-threatening strategy of Carson and the Ulster Volunteers. Its very name connoted its fundamental commitment to maintaining British rule of Ireland, but even that objective was subordinate to its desire to return to power within a stabilized, not recomposed, regime. These characteristics were cited as contributing to a problem-decomposition-based outcome in Ireland.

In France, on the other hand, recomposition of the regime was itself the highest priority of the Gaullists—the senior partner within the antidisengagement coalition that overthrew the Fourth Republic. But as many suspected even in 1958, and as everyone appreciated soon afterward, only a minority of Gaullists were committed to Algérie française in a fundamental way. Certainly de Gaulle was not. This helped explain why regime recomposition was so much more salient as a rescaling mechanism in the French case than the British. The relative fragmentation of the main conservative party in France (the Indépendants) and its nature as a collection of notables with traditional and highly localized bases of support were reflected in the decision of most of its leaders to sacrifice what were, in fact, relatively casual commitments to French rule of Algeria in return for maintaining positions of status within de Gaulle's Fifth Republic. Of particular note is the decision of most of these *modéré* leaders in 1960–61 to rally behind legally constituted authority when confronted with revolts by settlers or army officers or with the prospect of civil war. Even more than the Unionists of Britain, the Indépendants of France were committed above all else to preserve a coherent central authority and respect for legal institutions upon which they relied to protect their wealth and status.

Of course the Likud has resembled British Unionists, French conservatives, and Fourth Republic Gaullists in its use of the problematic future of outlying territory(ies) to gain and maintain political power by fully identifying itself with campaigns to prevent disengagement. In doing so the Likud followed the direction of its organizational core, the Herut (Revisionist) movement. Herut's ancien leader, Menachem Begin, was a true believer in the principle of the whole Land of Israel, especially as implemented west of the Jordan River. His personal commitment to the state-building enterprise in the territories as well as the commitment of his successor, Yitzhak Shamir, exceeded in intensity and sincerity the commitments of all the top British Unionists for maintaining Ireland within the Union, and the commitments of the vast majority of Gaullist and *modéré* leaders for preserving of Algérie française. Most of those forming the traditional core of Herut—followers of Jabotinsky, graduates of the Betar youth movement, or veterans of the Irgun—share these undeviating beliefs in the imperative of enforcing Jewish sovereignty over those portions of Eretz Yisrael that fell under Israeli jurisdiction following the Six Day War.

In the meantime the Likud has changed and continues to evolve. The businessmen who joined the Likud from the old Liberal party are notorious for their opportunism and are certainly no more likely than most Indépendant notables were to risk their property, status, and influence by supporting a violent challenge to regime authority on behalf of integralist or fundamentalist religious principles of territorial "completeness." Many other positions of influence in the party are now held by development town mayors and other representatives of the Sephardi community who voice the same slogans as Herut veterans but who entertain and represent ambitions for political, social, and economic advancement which play a much more determinative role in their thinking. It has often been noted, for example, how small is the proportion of Sephardi Jews within the ranks of Gush Emunim and its settlements in the territories, how weak is their identification with the settlers, and how unimportant to their political preferences are appeals to maintain the "completedness" of the Land of Israel.[95]

Support for legally constituted authority was the choice made by most Indépendant politicians and their traditional supporters in France during the Fifth Republic. Once the six-county decomposition of the Irish problem had been guaranteed, this was also the choice made by virtually all British Unionists. Since recomposition of the regime has never been an objective of Herut or Likud, and since its electoral strength is drawn from a wide range of practical interests, prejudices, and affiliations unconnected to the fate of the territories, there is no reason to expect that the Likud would in toto embrace a violent or even illegal challenge to the regime. On the other hand, substantial elements within the Likud, especially those long identified with the Herut movement, are likely to follow the course adopted by Soustellian Gaullists and the minority of modérés and MRP militants who followed Duchet and Bidault. These elements will likely endorse and even join a regime-challenging resistance movement. Together with activists within the ultranationalist and fundamentalist parties and Gush Emunim settlers, they would be willing to risk regime disintegration rather than accept substantial movement toward disengagement.

The single most important element distinguishing the constellation of forces likely to determine the course and outcome of a regime crisis in Israel from conditions prevailing in Britain and France is the position of the high command and officer corps of the armed forces. In March 1914, sympathy for the Ulster Volunteers within the British officer corps was evident in the organized refusal by scores of officers in Ireland to carry out orders they believed were designed to lead to the imposition of home rule on Ulster. As noted in Part III, Britain's most prestigious retired generals participated in the organization and command of Ulster resistance forces. Sir Henry Wilson, director of military operations in the office of the chief of staff, systematically connived with Milner, Carson, and the other leaders of the Unionist regime challenge. Support for the "mutineers" at the Curragh by the officers at Aldershot military base near London created the strong impression that the army could disintegrate if ordered to force home rule on Ulster. This evidence suggests that even if Churchill's plan to provoke an Ulster Volunteer attack on British forces had worked, and even if enough units would have remained loyal to deliver a crushing military and political blow, this outcome could not have been entertained by Asquith as more than an informed and optimistic judgment. De Gaulle's careful policy toward the French army, mixing solicitousness, deceit, and reassurance with repeated purges, reflected his judgment that as of late 1958, most of the high command of the French army, a substantial proportion of the officer corps, paratroop and legionnaire regiments stationed in Algeria, as well as important veterans organizations were fully prepared to challenge him and the Fifth Republic over the principle of disengagement from Algeria. The recalcitrance of many officers in January 1960 and the army revolt of 1961 bore out his suspicions. To overcome opposition to his policy from the military, de Gaulle sought not only to isolate Algérie française officers from sources of political support within French society but also to divide the French army horizontally. In May 1961, de Gaulle successfully appealed to conscripts, over the heads of their officers, to obey the law as he and the Fifth Republic defined it and to refuse participation in the revolt.

For any Israeli government contemplating a policy likely to lead to confrontation and an annexationist-inspired regime challenge, the risks of military insubordination by a dangerously large segment of the IDF high command would be small compared to those faced by Asquith as a result of Churchill's gambit or compared to those de Gaulle did accept, and survive, from 1958 to 1961. Of course the IDF would be strained by orders to crack down on right-wing militants and cordon off or evacuate settlements. But unlike the French army, with its paras and legionnaires, or the British army, with its strongly pro-Unionist political ties and its abundance of high-ranking Irish-Protestant officers, the IDF does not contain elite units, or any units, with a particular political coloration. The segment of Israeli society that is significantly overrepresented in the army's high command is the kibbutzim, whose members vote overwhelmingly for the Labor party and its left-wing/dovish allies. Though political authorities set upon a policy of confrontation with the annexationist right might well be concerned with reactions within the ranks, and will certainly expect difficulties with substantial numbers of middle-level officers, they would be unlikely to worry about a politically motivated defection of integrated units led by well-known and popular commanders.[96]

In both Churchill's plan and de Gaulle's actions, however, the decisive element was not the ability to withstand regime-threatening crises, but the mobilization of substantial new bases of positive support arising from them. By accepting the risks of bringing the latent regime challenge out into the open, each hoped to treat the crisis that would result not as a problem but as an opportunity. The accumulation of enough political capital to push the problem of state contraction past the regime threshold was to be accomplished as a result of the fears engendered among most British and French citizens, and their impulse to seek, above all else, reassurance that their lives and property would not be jeopardized by civil war or political disarray. In similar fashion, those in Israel who might try such a strategy will need to push the annexationist camp just as hard as Churchill and de Gaulle pushed their enemies in the wars of maneuver in which they were engaged. As noted earlier, provocations by extremists which would result could enable a determined government to identify the stability of ordinary people's lives, and the most valued institutions of the society, including the army, as at risk. This in turn could justify far-reaching measures to isolate the leadership of the annexationist camp and impose emergency constraints against rights of assembly and speech that might include banning threatening political parties or groups.

Indeed most oriental Jews who have voted regularly for the Likud and its allies have done so out of a traditional dislike for Labor party politicians and antipathies toward Arabs, not out of support for Eretz Yisrael hashlema. Nor do they tend to identify, politically or emotionally, with the settlers across the Green Line, whose budgets were successfully portrayed in 1992 as coming at the expense of their communities. One important sentiment that does exist within the subcultures that comprise the *edot hamizrah* (the "Eastern communities"), and that suggests the transferability of their political allegiance in times of crisis, is a desire for "a strong leader" who makes his listeners feel he is telling them the truth, no matter what the consequences—an attraction from which right-wing politicians such as Begin, Shamir, Sharon, and Eitan have benefited.[97] Significantly, the image of "a strong leader" is precisely what a premier following the strategy outlined here would naturally project—as did de Gaulle in his dramatic radio and television appearances during the crises of 1960 and 1961 and as Churchill did in his Bradford speech (see Chapters 6 and 8).

The prognosis for successful exploitation of a regime crisis by an anti-annexationist government is also enhanced by the fact that in recent years Israeli Arabs, Russian immigrants, and ultraorthodox Jews have been the fastest growing segments of the Israeli population. Not surprisingly, Israeli Arabs strongly support establishment of a Palestinian state in the territories. In the 1992 elections, Russian immigrants voted heavily in favor of the Labor party and its secular-dovish allies. Indeed there is virtually no support among these immigrants for religious life-styles or parties and little interest in living in West Bank settlements. If large amounts of economic aid for Israel were seen to hang in the balance, if those leading the challenge were doing so in the name of religious or mystically nationalist ideological principles, and if the army's support for the political solution espoused by the government were clear, these new citizens would almost certainly rally to the side of an Israeli government facing a regime challenge.[98] Excluding the highly visible but politically unpredictable Lubavitch sect, most ultraorthodox Jews reject the Messianic claims of Gush Emunim, viewing Israel as a state like any other state (which happens to have a majority of Jews) whose laws must be obeyed so that the protection and benefits of an effective and generous government can continue to be enjoyed by the Torah-faithful. Even those ultraorthodox Jews living in thoroughly *haredi* West Bank settlements make it clear that if and when their rabbis tell them to leave the territories, they will do so without complaint or protest.[99]

Based on comparison of the British and French cases, however, it is also clear that Israeli scenarios cannot be carefully weighed without considering the character of the nationalist movement in the outlying territory(ies) and the dialectical relationship of that movement with the metropole. In the conclusion of Chapter 8 a number of factors were identified which helped explain the comparative readiness of the Irish nationalist movement to accept a fairly radical compromise of their objectives in 1921, including the spatial decomposition of the Irish problem versus the virtually unwavering insistence by the FLN on rapid and complete French withdrawal from all of Algeria (including the Sahara). The main point was that the failure of Irish Protestants to prevent the mobilization of Irish nationalist sentiment within the British political arena, the conservative influence of the Catholic church, and the British policies of land redistribution to Irish farmers produced an Irish nationalist movement whose "physical force" wing was ultimately subordinated by a bourgeois leadership well practiced in the arts of political compromise, accommodation, and administration—a leadership whose credibility remained intact even as it joined with the British to suppress the militant wing of the movement.[100] In the French case, by contrast, a more drastic denial of political space to middle-class, professional, and religious elites among Algerian Muslims, explained by the systematic success of the pieds noirs and their metropolitan allies in preventing any effective mobilization of Algerian nationalist sentiment within the French political system, contributed to a revolutionary movement dominated by individuals outside the country and by specialists in violence. The effectiveness of these nationalist leaders depended on strict adherence to the achievement of independence for all of Algeria. Indeed they could not hope to survive anything more than minor concessions or relatively insubstantial forms of cooperation with the French authorities.

The dialectical relationship between Israelis and Palestinians has led to a Palestinian national movement whose characteristics place it, on most dimensions, somewhere between the relatively accommodative representatives of Irish nationalism, who signed and enforced the Anglo-Irish treaty, and the uncompromising FLN leadership, whose narrow range of maneuver helps account for its refusal of virtually all concessions, even in the face of staggering losses and military defeat. In general, levels of Israeli repression are less destructive than those prevailing in Algeria from 1954 to 1962 but substantially more rigorous than British policies in Ireland. From 1967 to 1992, Israel forbade free political activity to Palestinians in the occupied territories (including expanded East Jerusalem). Since Palestinians in the territories are not Israeli citizens, or even, Israeli "nationals" (as the Algerians were French "nationals"), they have not been a factor within Israeli electoral or coalition politics. On the other hand, despite constraints and repression, Palestinian professional, educational, labor, and business organizations have been allowed to function (under varying degrees of harassment). Elections within those organizations, an independent though censored Palestinian press in East Jerusalem, participation in demonstrations and symposia within the Green Line, and alliances with Israeli Arabs and sympathetic Jews have provided enough political space for leaders to arise whose skills and credibility are linked to their ability to maneuver in a complex political arena.

Confronted, however, with a series of aggressively annexationist Israeli governments, this leadership has found itself under severe pressure. Large-scale land expropriation, harsh and humiliating treatment by Israeli soldiers and settlers, deportations, and extensive use of collective punishment have left thousands of Palestinians with a personal desire for revenge, providing Palestinian extremists with plenty of recruits for anti-Israeli or anti-Arab terrorism. Against this background, regional events such as the Iranian Revolution, the Lebanese Civil War, and the Gulf War have fueled an Islamic fundamentalist trend which rejects, in principle, the "separate-state" solution to the Palestinian problem espoused by the PLO and its supporters in the occupied territories, including (since 1987) the Unified National Command of the Uprising. With deep roots in the teeming refugee camps of Gaza and the West Bank, Muslim fundamentalists in 1992 carried out increasingly bloody and provocative attacks, on both Jews and politically mainstream Palestinians, designed to torpedo neogitations with Israel.

As in the past so in the future, popular sentiment among the Palestinians is likely to oscillate within a triangle of fury, hope, and despair. The fury of Palestinians inhibits internal or external leaders from making substantial concessions beyond agreeing to an independent state in the occupied territories as a final settlement of Palestinian political claims, and limits the maneuvering room of those willing to seek such an outcome over a long time period. Specifically, the substantial influence of Muslim fundamentalism constrains the subtlety and length of Israeli strategies of serial decomposition—a rescaling mechanism that requires "good behavior," unity, patience, and discipline from Palestinian partners as a method of camouflaging the end result of a series of interim arrangements. Israeli leaders committed to state contraction are indeed likely to be forced into a difficult choice. To prevent rejectionist extremism among Palestinian fundamentalists and others from disrupting the entire process, they will need to increase the credibility of their Palestinian interlocutors. This will require measures such as negotiations with the PLO, transfer of public land to an interim Palestinian authority, or commitments to share sovereignty in expanded Jerusalem which are themselves likely to prompt a more dangerous and less conveniently timed regime crisis than Israeli leaders would prefer to confront.

But the hope and despair of Palestinians, in contrast to their fury, suggest another kind of outcome, especially when considered in light of the development of the British-Irish relationship in the nineteenth century. The Great Famine of the 1840s cast the Irish into a pit of despair. After a generation, hopes revived as Irish nationalists, with help from British Liberals, fought for and eventually secured a place in British politics. Maneuvering between Unionists and Liberals, the Irish Home Rule party used what had become in political fact as well as in name a "binational" state (the United Kingdom of Great Britain and Ireland) as a first stage on the way to a separate Irish state (established in most of Ireland in 1922).

In the absence of a successful process of Israeli state contraction, a despairing Palestinian population in the West Bank and Gaza Strip might well enable Israel to maintain control over these territories on a nonhegemonic basis. Palestinian hopes would then focus on a process similar to that which occurred in nineteenth-century Britain—the transformation of Israel into a binational Jewish-Arab state within which Palestinian political power might eventually organize around a movement for "home rule" or even secession. Indeed it is conceivable that within a generation a similar dynamic will unfold—that Israeli Jewish secularists, doves, and progressives, out of their own political interests, will join with Arab voters inside of Israel and Palestinian leaders from the territories to demand equal citizenship rights for all inhabitants of the West Bank and Gaza Strip. If successful, such a campaign would set the stage for a new round of struggles over the shape of the state—either over the granting of political autonomy cum independence to heavily Arab areas or over a new definition of the country capable of attracting the loyalty of majorities in both the nations that inhabit it.[101]

Conclusion

The British and French cases show how difficult it has been, since the epoch of nationalism began, for "alien" states to institutionalize their rule on a hegemonic basis over large, nationally ambitious populations concentrated within historic homelands. In the contemporary period, during which the principle of national self-determination is even more strongly established as an international norm, the obstacles to successful Israeli state-building in the West Bank and Gaza Strip would seem even more daunting than those confronted earlier in this century by British Unionists in Ireland and partisans of Algérie française.[102]

I have argued that for Israel to relocate the problem of the territories across the ideological hegemony threshold would require either the conversion of most Israelis to the integralist and fundamentalist doctrines associated with Gush Emunim, the political and cultural integration of West Bank and Gaza Arabs into Israeli society, or the deportation of most Palestinian Arabs from these areas. Even its strongest advocates do not believe that Gush Emunim's redemptionist vision is capable of becoming the common sense of the mass of Israelis without the construction of international circumstances that would leave Israelis virtually no other choice. The ideological and cultural basis of Israel as a Jewish-Zionist state makes democratic integration even less plausible as a designed solution than it was in Britain for the Irish Catholics or in France for the Algerian Muslims. Finally, the wholesale deportation of Palestinians would represent an even greater insult, to even stronger international norms, by a state even more vulnerable to international pressure, than were the most repressive of British and French policies in Ireland and Algeria.

Accordingly, for all its difficulties, state contraction is the more likely route to the eventual stabilization of Israel's relationship to the West Bank and Gaza. As I have argued, this will require relocating the problem across the regime threshold. I have outlined a number of ways in which the rescaling mechanisms used by British and French leaders could be combined within the Israeli-Palestinian case to achieve such an outcome. Nothing in my analysis or my comparisons enables me to predict which of these combinations is most likely to be attempted, or whether and when any one of them will be successful. The point of the attention I have given to one particular scenario, combining realignment, serial decomposition, and utility-function change achieved within the context of a deliberately orchestrated internal crisis, is not to predict its occurrence but to highlight the conditions which suggest its relative plausibility in the Israeli-Palestinian case.

Combined with the judgment that Israel will not be able to institutionalize its control of the territories on a hegemonic basis, application of my two-threshold model predicts that Israel will not stabilize its relationship to the territories without disengaging from them, that it will not disengage from them without managing threats of regime disruption, and that the decisive stage in the process will not be the negotiation or implementation of an agreement with the Arabs, but an outcome in the struggle among Jews—the rescaling of the problem inside Israel from one that can threaten the regime to one that can threaten only incumbents.

There are two corollaries of this last point. First, diplomatic and political efforts to promote solutions based on disengagement are not important because they could lead directly to the implementation of a withdrawal-based agreement, but because they create opportunities for Israeli anti-annexationists to form winning coalitions and move decisively toward their goal. Second, the character of the process that leads to state contraction, by affecting the generosity of the arrangements for Palestinian self-determination, will determine whether or not future generations of Israelis will be left with a Northern Ireland—style problem of residual Palestinian national claims. Comparison of the British-Irish and French-Algerian relationships suggests that the higher the risks and the more decisive the Israeli moves toward state contraction in the short term, the more stable the Israeli-Palestinian relationship is likely to be in the long run.

In the meantime, both annexationists and anti-annexationists are learning more about the requirements of state-building and state contraction. With the problem of what to do with the territories located as close to the regime threshold as it has been for most of the last decade, annex-ationists are learning that there is no "point of no return," no single achievement, that will give them victory in their struggle with the anti-annexationist camp. Building settlements brought them part way toward their goal, but attaining their state-building objectives in the whole Land of Israel means constructing hegemony, not settlements—images and rou-tines, not roads and houses. One difficulty, however, is that the militant mobilization necessary to prevent state contraction at the regime threshold tends to interrupt the habits of thought and sentiment upon which a new hegemonic conception of the expanded state could be built. What anti-annexationists are learning is that Palestinians resisting the occupation must be seen as partners, not enemies, and that state contraction will mean not only winning control of the government, but managing and exploiting the more fundamental challenges that will accompany decisive steps to-ward state contraction.

CHAPTER ELEVEN

A Theory of States and Territories:
Extensions and Implications

The overall concern of this book has been to apply a theory of punctuated institutional transformation to the problem of change in the territorial composition of three states. Now it is time to show that the theory is generalizable, that it poses questions, suggests explanations, and "predicts facts" in a much wider variety of settings than the three cases I have examined. Its generalizability extends along two main axes: applications to more instances of state expansion and contraction; and applications to other processes of institutionalization.

In the late 1960s, Andrei Amalrik asked if the Soviet Union would last until 1984.[1] That year came and went, and Amalrik's question seemed no more relevant than it had when his book was published. The Soviet state's command over its vast territories seemed unshakeable. And then suddenly the Soviet state was gone. When the authors of the August 1991 coup tried to preserve the state in its old configuration and with its old regime, their attempt collapsed as quickly as some thought the movement toward democracy would once the old guard took out its heavy guns. In place of the Soviet Union, an array of successor states emerged within borders whose institutionalization was among their most vital and difficult tasks. What can account for the suddenness and scope of these transitions?

The Soviet state inherited most of its borders from the tsarist regime. Tsarist policies of military expansion and imperial rule created so vast and heterogeneous a domain that any subsequent regime would be hard pressed to mystify claims to authority on a purely national or ethnic basis. This was not a problem for the Bolsheviks, whose ultimate objective was to legitimize claims to authority primarily on the basis of class or party affiliation. To support this effort, images of a modern, Russian-speaking "Soviet" personality were advanced. More significant, however, were Stalin's appeals to "Mother Russia" sentiment while faced with the Nazi onslaught, and efforts by Lenin and Stalin's successors to bolster Communist party authority by acknowledging ethnic solidarities and co-opting nationalist elites within the smaller borders of the various republics.[2] In any event, since Soviet governments did not institutionalize a conception of the shape of the state independent of the socialist character of the regime, there were no strong cultural or psychological barriers to prevent questions about the shape of the state, or nationalist-based demands for "secession," from emerging once the Communist-dominated regime was in retreat.

The suddenness of the Soviet Union's contraction into Russia, the disappearance of the socialist regime, and the virtual elimination of the Communist party were due to an unsuccessful attempt by Mikhail Gorbachev to separate and preserve the territorial shape of the Soviet state, as a weakly institutionalized feature of its existence, from other features which he desired to deinstitutionalize, remove, and reinstitutionalize in substantially different form. In essence Gorbachev sought to overthrow hegemonic beliefs about the character of economic and political decision-making, strip regime-level commitments from these dimensions of the Soviet state, and then reinstitutionalize at least a semidemocratic polity and a quasi-market economy—all the while preserving the state's territorial composition and the dominant position of the Communist party.

Against a background of Soviet claims to superpower status and a U.S. military challenge that was increasingly difficult to match, of Soviet commitments to uphold norms covered under the Helsinki accords which clashed directly with the routine practices of the Soviet state, and gross discrepancies between the economic claims of Soviet socialism and its accomplishments, Gorbachev wielded slogans of *glasnost* and *perestroika* as weapons in a war of position to put basic economic and political questions on the country's agenda. But the forces for change that had accumulated beneath the decrepit hegemonic conceptions inherited from the Brezhnev era were overwhelming. Gorbachev's attempt to transform fundamental aspects of the Soviet hegemonic project into "ordinary" policy questions, that is, his attempt to cross backward through the regime threshold along these dimensions, precipitated a regime crisis which climaxed in the failed coup. In lieu of careful application of the rescaling mechanisms I have discussed, neither the regime itself, that is, the legal rules for governing competition within the *Soviet* state, nor the dominance of the CPSU (Communist Party of the Soviet Union) could survive the war of maneuver Gorbachev's policies precipitated.

Gorbachev's attempt, almost simultaneously, to relocate critical aspects of the Soviet state across both thresholds unleashed forces that were un-controllable (or at least, in the event, uncontrolled). What was to have been an exercise in state contraction, from designated economic and po-litical domains of state control, gave way instead to state collapse. Un-protected by hegemonic conceptions of its naturalness, the territorial shape of the state ruled by Moscow as including all fifteen republics was thrown open to question. Territorially based solidarities and irredentist sentiments thereby became ordinary usable resources for competing politicians strug-gling to install new regimes within the husk of the Soviet Union and take power within them. The result was a proliferation of independent republics out to rationalize their boundaries according to some principle (usually nationalist) that could serve the interests of elites positioned to benefit from them. In part because he lacked a new hegemonic conception for a post-Soviet "Russian" state for which he could stand as a credible ex-emplar, Gorbachev himself, along with his party, was rendered politically irrelevant, plunging Russia into a regime crisis and a protracted war of maneuver.

The Soviet/Russian experience points up certain key themes in my treat-ment of the British, French, and Israeli cases. It illustrates how intimately the territorial shape of a state, the character of the regime institutionalized within its borders, and the power position of incumbent elites are linked to one another. It highlights the importance of treating the embeddedness of the shape of the state as one among many dimensions of its institutional coherence. It supports a view of institutionalization as a process of ac-cumulating more fundamental kinds of expectations about limits on the possibility of change and of seeing deinstitutionalization as a process of losing those expectations. It illustrates how the discontinuities of institu-tional construction, labeled in my model as two "thresholds," help explain how long-term cumulative processes of change can be translated quickly, chaotically, but in recognizable patterns, into nonlinear transformations.[3] It also shows, as I have demonstrated in the British, French, and Israeli cases, how prevailing international norms and shifting balances of power influence outcomes in wars of position and maneuver by reinforcing or inhibiting the efforts of the protagonists.

Each of these propositions is illuminated just as clearly by consideration of ties between territories and states in contemporary Africa. As countless scholars have observed, the borders of African states in the postwar era were artifactual desiderata of European colonialism and its demise. As independent African states emerged, native elites came to power by iden-tifying themselves with established borders and the bureaucratic apparatus of the colonial states that operated within them. These political entrepre-neurs understood the danger of challenges to their authority which could be mounted if legitimacy were granted to claims for "national self-determination" advanced by ethnic or tribal groups within their borders—movements that would be led by opposing elites with better credentials to exploit such solidarities and lead the smaller states that would be built around them. Internationally, and in the Organization of African Unity, it was recognized that unless the "artificial" borders drawn in the colonial era were treated as sacrosanct, that is unless the idea of changing them was hegemonically excluded from political agendas, not only would the leadership position of those running the newly independent states be jeopardized, but the continent as a whole would be in danger of dissolving into fratricidal conflict. The failure of both the Katanga and Biafran secessionist movements was an early demonstration of the powerful consensus among African elites and the international community in support of the principle that the borders of colonial states would not be changed.[4]

After more than thirty years of independence, however, the hegemonic status of the belief that African borders are immutable, and thereby excluded from calculations about how Africans can respond to the exigencies of their existence, appears to be breaking down. In South Africa the collapse of apartheid as a hegemonic project and de Klerk's attempt to manage a regime-threshold transition from authoritarianism to multiracial democracy have pushed some conservative Afrikaners toward more drastic forms of partition than the black "homelands" project. Meanwhile prospects for stable majority rule are clouded by internecine struggles in which tribal identities are mobilized against the African National Congress's appeal to a South African "nation" incubated within the boundaries of the South African state. In the rest of the continent, the generation of elites who took over the colonial states has largely passed from the scene. Where they failed to build nations to correspond to the states they governed, and where regimes have not been institutionalized capable of containing competition for political power, it will be increasingly difficult to prevent new elites from mobilizing "irredentist" or "secessionist" sentiments as vehicles for their own ambition and self-preservation. Religious, tribal, regional, racial, and ethnic identities are all available avenues for such mobilization, each offering images of the proper shape of the political community which conflict with established national state boundaries.

Under such circumstances Africa faces, among its other woes, the possibility of cascading patterns of fragmentation and attachment. This is particularly the case because, with the end of the cold war, the Great Powers have less interest in preventing such processes. In the Persian Gulf the overwhelming importance of the region's oil resources induced the United States, Britain, and France forcefully to uphold the principle of the territorial integrity of established states against Iraq's attempted annexation of Kuwait. In that way, and in that area, the Great Powers at least postponed the time when carving up one's neighbors or one's own country will be perceived as ordinary options for pursuing political power. Even so, continuing U.S. pressure against the Saddam Hussein regime has been modulated by explicit concerns that Iraq not split into pieces.

Events in the Persian Gulf, of course, are of unusual interest to the Great Powers. In Africa and elsewhere the Great Powers lack interests important enough to warrant intervention. Where overriding geopolitical or economic interests do not obtain, belief in the permanence of borders may be exposed as but a tenuous construction, depriving weak regimes of the protection afforded by hegemonic beliefs which help keep territorial demands off of political agendas.

Morocco, for example, has had surprisingly little difficulty proceeding toward the incorporation of the western Sahara. Much of what was Liberia is now ruled by several of its neighbors. In the Horn of Africa there has been some Great Power action in support of famine relief, but careful avoidance of involvement in the political problems raised by the implosion of Somalia and the unraveling of Ethiopia. This seeming lack of interest may be compared to substantial U.S. and Soviet intervention during the 1970s and 1980s, when military and economic aid was poured into those weak but strategically useful states, helping to overcome great discrepancies between the claims of sovereign authority advanced by their governments and the actual abilities of those governments to elicit allegiance or even compliance within the territories they claimed as their states. In the absence of hegemonic barriers to change in the shape of African states or outside resources capable of substituting for them, what has happened in Somalia, Ethiopia, Morocco, and Liberia may well happen in Chad, Mozambique, Zaire, and Sudan.[5]

On other continents as well, elites positioned to benefit from territorial expansion or contraction will find little to restrain them from launching wars against their neighbors or regime-threatening challenges against their governments. Certainly this has been true of Serbia and of Serbian nationalists in Croatia and Bosnia. Iranian involvement in Afghanistan under the banner of Islam, and the competition of Turkey, Iran, and Pakistan for influence among the untested Muslim states of central Asia suggest the possible emergence of a vast area in which processes of territorial expansion and contraction, with enormous consequences for the stability of regimes in competing countries, would not be interrupted by the military intervention of the Great Powers. Meanwhile students of the subcontinent wonder whether Indian democracy is sufficiently institutionalized at the regime level to contract rather than collapse in response to Hindu exclusivism and Muslim separatism, or to destroy or deflect these movements so effectively that the image of a united India whether Hindu or secular nationalist, can itself become hegemonic. A somewhat similar question is posed by Turkey's rule of northern Cyprus. Only if and when constitutional democracy in Turkey is itself institutionalized hegemonically, or at least well beyond the regime threshold, will any Turkish government be likely to entertain options for a negotiated withdrawal of Turkey authority from Cyprus.

An even larger field for the application of this theory and its underlying framework is the comparative historical study of territorial expansion and contraction. Implicit in my abstract formulation of the theory as pertaining to the institutionalization of states is a claim that in principle it applies just as well to the expansion, contraction, and/or collapse of ancient empires, absolutist monarchies, early modern national states, nineteenth- and twentieth-century European empires, and "subnational" separatism, as it does to the specific instances of British, French, and Israeli expansion and contraction analyzed in detail in this volume.

For example, if we interpret the Augustan principate as a new regime for governing the Roman state, explanations for its establishment could be sought in the dramatic opportunities which territorial expansion can create for new myths, new classes, and new solidarities to become politically salient.[6] Yet the incompleteness of the Augustan transformation might also be tested as an explanation for subsequent failures of the empire. Thus continued commitment to republican myths (including the continued, formal, authority of the Roman Senate, and Caracalla's formal extension of "Roman" citizenship to all free males in the empire in 212 C.E.) may well have interfered with the development of an appropriately imperial/absolutist political formula. In the absence of the technologies and empathies capable of supporting development of a "Roman nation" throughout the entire area ruled by Rome, only such a formula, purged of republican ideas, could have been sufficiently hierarchical to have institutionalized Roman rule hegemonically. Its unavailability may help explain why Diocletian opted for a self-defeating but temporarily effective brand of coercive totalitarianism at the end of the third century, and why the Caesaro-papist Eastern Roman Empire, unburdened by the residue of republicanism, survived for so much longer than its Western counterpart.

My model posits state contraction as an undertheorized process which cannot be addressed as the simple reverse of expansion. Thus the "racheting" effect of the thresholds, making expansion through them in the state-building direction easier to accomplish than contraction, may help explain why increases in Roman power could lead to its expansion from a city-state in Latium to the dominant power in all of Italy, to a Mediterranean Empire, to the ruler of most of Europe and Asia Minor, while the progressive decrease in its power position beginning in the middle of the second century was not matched by similarly steady processes of strategic contraction. Similar analyses could be conducted of the failure of the nineteenth-century Ottoman reformists or progressive elements within the Austro-Hungarian Empire to consider imperial contraction as feasible options for saving these states. Which barriers, within the centers of these empires, were most salient in blocking such options: hegemonic conceptions which effectively excluded their contemplation, threats of regime collapse if disengagement were attempted, or only hesitation by incumbents to risk implementing unpopular policies?

Approached from the perspective of this theory, study of the transformation of feudal principalities into large absolutist states would focus not so much on power differentials between juxtaposed principalities but on the activities and pressures of elites positioned to benefit from an enlargement of the state as against more parochial elements able to calculate that enlargement of the domain would disadvantage them. Complex patterns of expansion or contraction of territorial dominion usually attributed by historians to marriage and inheritance among noble houses and dynasties would be a topic of particular interest. Were these acquisitions and detachments of land under the rubric of marriage and inheritance the actual mechanisms accomplishing these changes or were they indicators of changing power balances within and among states?[7] What hegemonic conceptions prevailed within each budding state, and throughout European Christendom, which allowed such an impressively fluid means of linking changing state capacities to changing territorial composition? How was change in those conceptions linked to regime-level institutionalization of the territorial shape of kingdoms—developments which the theory suggests would have led to a sharp decline in the transfer of territory via marriage and inheritance?

David Laitin and Thomas Callaghy have suggested that the crystallization of absolutist states in Europe evokes the challenges and opportunities confronting many state-builders in contemporary Africa. To measure the limits of this analogy requires identifying and evaluating the role of distinctive hegemonic conceptions in late medieval and early modern Europe.[8] Reflecting Roman imperial, Christian, and monarchical notions of authority, these conceptions appear to have provided a legitimizing framework for aggregating territories without simultaneously requiring a "nation-building" effort to unite their populations. Similar if less salient conceptions are present in African political mythologies. But instead of receiving support externally, African leaders who style themselves as kings or "emperors" stand in direct contradiction to internationally hegemonic norms of democracy and "national self-determination." The European-style absolutist path to national state formation may thus not be available in Africa.

One question of considerable historical and theoretical moment concerns the timing of European nationalisms. Did they emerge as a prelude to or as a consequence of the crystallization of large territorial states? Treatments of the subject could be invigorated by seeking instances of disputes within these states over whether to conquer, retain, or abandon particular territories—territories whose integration would affirm or contradict nationalist principles. The terms of these debates, and their outcomes, could shed light on what elites took for granted, or had to act as if they took for granted, about the norms governing the organization of political space. A war of position over the nature of the state would be discerned when arguments over territorial aggrandizement or contraction posed nationalist criteria (Is it good or necessary for the nation?) against monarchical or other criteria (Is it good or necessary for the king, dynasty, or empire?). A state would be judged to have become a "national state" when disputes about when or whether to engage in territorial aggrandizement were found to be grounded solely in nationalist terms. The failure of most European nationalists (or their opponents) to win these wars of position in the nineteenth century would be used to account for the prolonged admixture in most of them of national, monarchical, and/or imperial criteria. Failure to exclude nonnationalist principles of authority would then help explain the "imperial" expansion of these states into other continents, while the vitality of parochial, nationalist sentiments would help explain their systematic failure to create either more inclusive national formulas or genuinely imperial arrangements with which to institutionalize their rule of global empires beyond either the regime or hegemonic thresholds.

Scholarship on mid-twentieth-century decolonization has focused most often on the rise of nationalist movements in the colonized areas, on the "realization" by metropolitan leaders that the end of empire was at hand, on the efforts of colonial officials to devise beneficial arrangements for the transfer of power, and on the impact of variation in the pace and character of particular decolonizations on the nature of postcolonial states. These are factors whose importance is compatible with a view of European colonialism as predominantly an array of relatively lightly institutionalized state-building relationships. But the approach adopted here would also encourage alternatives to the standard image of decolonization as an inevitable retreat precipitated by global changes in the balance of power and the rise of powerful anticolonialist movements among indigenous populations.

In addition to understanding decolonization as a rational and timely response to changes that removed the profitability of particular colonial situations, the end of European domination in these areas could be explained as the result of the failure of European imperialists to institutionalize their rule of most colonial territories beyond the hegemonic or even regime thresholds, within the metropoles themselves. Where regime-level institutionalization did occur—not only in Britain and France with respect to Ireland and Algeria, but in the Netherlands regarding Indonesia and in Portugal vis-à-vis Angola, synchronous metropolitan responses to rising costs were not the decisive factors producing disengagement. Instead separation was delayed well beyond the point of "nonprofitability" and then implemented with great rapidity—a pattern associated with the decisiveness of the struggle to cross the regime threshold in the state-contracting direction and thus make the "irrationality" of continued rule politically determinative for metropolitan governments.

One significant advantage of thereby taking imperialism seriously as a state-expanding project is abandonment of teleological distinctions between "internal colonialism," within "states" whose institutional consolidation is deemed a fact of life, and "imperialism," conducted within empires deemed incapable of institutional consolidation. Regardless of the specific content of the political formula used to legitimize and mystify authority over wide territories—imperial, religious, national, and so forth—what distinguishes a dominance relationship over a region "inside" the state from a dominance relationship over a region "outside" the state is the presence of a well-institutionalized belief within the dominant core that the region under consideration is immutably bound to it.

Students of these relationships will decide for themselves whether to require institutionalization at the regime or the hegemonic level as sufficient for their purposes, or to proceed, as I have done in this study, by focusing on the political dynamics of change in the level of institutionalization. However, without a concept of the shape of the state as an institutionalized dimension of its existence, and without qualitative measures of institutionalization, analysts must rely on a priori or legalist demarcations of state boundaries. Even among the most careful practitioners, this lack leads to serious taxonomic problems. Michael Hechter, for example, classified Ireland as an internal colony while treating Irish independence as the result of "secession" rather than "decolonization."[9] Michael Doyle's definition of empire as "effective control . . . of a subordinated society by an imperial society" essentially denies the possibility of imperial authority experienced as legitimate and forces him to exclude the late Roman Empire from his category of "empire" at precisely the time he describes it as having reached "an imperial apotheosis." His distinction between metropolitan state-building (subordination within one society) and empire-building (subordination of one society by another) begs the question of how the shape and limits of a society are constituted, while forbidding questions to be asked about "imperial" routes to the construction of national states—routes followed by Wessex, England, the Île de France, Piedmont, Castile, and Prussia, which entailed changes in the boundaries of states and societies.[10]

From the point of view of separatist movements within well-institutionalized states (such as the Quebecois in Canada or the Basques in Spain), the problem as posed from the perspective of this theory is equivalent to that faced by the Irish nationalists in the 1830s. Many of the specific hypotheses advanced in this book about the requisites for crossing each of the two thresholds are directly applicable. The challenge first is to break apart hegemonic conceptions within the political class of the central state. Victory in this war of position is not signified by movement toward satisfaction of demands for autonomy or a greater share of resources, but by a shift in the ground of rejection of the separatist program. Once separatist demands are discussable among politically ambitious elites, then alliances can be formed with "metropolitan" sympathizers or at least those able to profit from a struggle to reduce the size of the state—a struggle that could lead eventually to a war of maneuver. A successful outcome at this stage would transform the question of separation of the territory into a policy question for successive governments rather than a problem portending a regime crisis for any government wishing to solve it by satisfying separatist demands. Whether through diachronic treatment of one separatist movement through several stages of struggle or via cross-cultural treatment of several movements at the same stage, one interesting focus for research would be variation in the character and consequence of separatist violence. Another would be examining links between the level of state institutionalization along nonterritorial dimensions and the prospects for state contraction, as opposed to collapse, disintegration, or civil war, in response to separatist challenges.

The relationship between a state's level of institutionalization along nonterritorial dimensions and its morphological flexibility was discussed in the conclusion to Chapter 5. Differences between the solidity of the constitutional monarchy in Britain and the precarious institutional status of the Fourth Republic in France were cited to help explain the different consequences of hegemonic failure regarding the territorial shape of those states. The same relationship is apparent today in the case of the European Community. The members of the EC are states with well-institutionalized regimes, moving toward amalgamation of many functions (currency, border controls, indirect taxation) previously associated with their separate sovereignties. While the territorial shape of the constituent states remains the same, other aspects of their existence as states are attenuated. The process of attenuation represents a deinstitutionalization of practices and expectations at the individual state level which are reinstitutionalized at the community level. Whatever the results of current efforts to implement provisions of the Maastricht Treaty, the capacity of the western European states to entertain such transformations without suffering regime-level disruptions is remarkable. It presents a striking contrast to Gorbachev's spectacular failure to preserve the territorial shape of the Soviet Union while instrumentalizing and reinstitutionalizing economic and political features. The comparison suggests fruitful lines of inquiry into the ability of some societies stably to instrumentalize spheres of activity that other societies require to be institutionalized at the regime or hegemonic level.

Viewed through the lens of this theory, the evolution of the EC raises other promising questions. If the concept of a United States of Europe has not achieved hegemonic status among Europeans, to what extent has the movement for European unification been a carrier of counterhegemonic formulas in various "national" settings? In which countries after World War II did the EC face intact hegemonic notions about the indivisibility of state sovereignty, and how and when were its victories achieved over them? What accounts for the delay in the movement toward European integration experienced in the 1970s? Can the dynamics identified by older federalist, diffusionist, and neofunctionalist theories of regional integration be reconsidered to identify the counterhegemonic and rescaling strategies that were more effective in some political, economic, and cultural contexts, and in some stages of the integration process, than in others?

One possibility is that western Europe will eventually experience some of the same strains that led to the disintegration of the USSR in the immediate aftermath of its reinstitutionalization debacle. The fortunes of cultural separatist movements in Britain and France ebbed in the 1980s because of the solidity of hegemonic conceptions of the shape of these states and because of the economic resources controlled by "national" centers. But as many traditional attributes of western European states are separated from their territorial shape, as institutions previously treated as hegemonic are instrumentalized, and as new images of a unified "Europe" gain support, expectations of territorial stability in what is left of these "national states" may weaken substantially. If so, cultural separatist demands for autonomy may gain renewed vigor. The result could be a raft of state-contraction battles whose progress could be traced and explicated by direct application of the categories and hypotheses presented in this study.

As my specific comments about the Roman, Soviet, and western European examples suggest, there is nothing about the theoretical apparatus I have presented that limits its application only to questions pertaining to the institutionalization of state borders. In principle, the theory should be applicable to institutionalization and deinstitutionalization processes along other salient dimensions, including the two dimensions that have attracted more scholarly attention than any others—the extent of state autonomy from society, and the democratic versus authoritarian character of regimes. Investigations of the relative autonomy of the state could, for example, be reformulated on the basis of measurements of the kinds of disruptions associated with state expansion into realms (industrial organization and policy, biological reproduction, education and the arts, the press, etc.) that previously may have been separated from the state merely by policy decisions of incumbents or by expectations and beliefs about the nature of state-society relations institutionalized at either the hegemonic or regime level.

Broadly applied, the theory presented here can link two important streams of scholarship focused on the explanation of democracy and its preservation or breakdown. One, exemplified by the work of both Barrington Moore, and Gabriel Almond and Sidney Verba,[11] begins by identifying either distributions of power among classes and strata standardly featured in the histories of large states or the accretion of deeply embedded expectations and beliefs about politics. These different configurations of power or culture are then classified as more or less conducive to the emergence of stable democratic regimes. Democracy or its absence is thereby explained by differences in historical conjunctures which for different states produced different social arrays and different cultural dispositions. In effect this kind of argument explains variation in the institutionalization of democracy as a function of the presence or absence of circumstantial endowments likely to support democracy's construction as a hegemonic feature of life in a particular state, likely, in other words, to be institutionalized beyond the ideological hegemony threshold. From this angle, stable democracy will emerge in states not predisposed to produce it only as a result of the radical consequences of defeat in interstate war or following an internal war of position whose long-term consequence would be to "reconstruct" the contextual realities of politics.

Representatives of the second approach are Juan Linz and his collaborators and Ruth and David Collier. Their work asks questions about transitions, breakdowns, and reequilibrations of democratic and authoritarian regimes, focusing on the problematic institutionalization of democracy beyond the regime threshold.[12] From this perspective the emergence and maintenance of democracy are seen as contingent upon the outcome of wars of maneuver surrounding the regime threshold. Accordingly, explanations for democracy and its demise hinge on specified characteristics of regimes and the talents and choices of competing elites directly aware of the payoffs associated with the construction, preservation, or breakdown of democracy and prepared to act illegally to prevail over their rivals.

The purpose of this book has primarily been to explain similarities and differences among three complex and intrinsically interesting histories. More generally, however, my analysis of institutional change as comprised of both linear and nonlinear processes was designed to capture the essential quality of any institution as a set of particular kinds of interruptions (discontinuities) in the seamless web of causality and in the fluidity with which pressures translate into changes corresponding to their weight and vector. More generally still, I advanced the notion of thresholds, and of wars of maneuver and position surrounding them, to help model in the political domain the same kind of "cusp catastrophes," "phase transitions," and "chaotic" patterns which natural scientists observe when continuous processes intersect with significant discontinuities in the physical world.

With this thrust toward general theory in mind, let me emphasize that in the cases of territorial metamorphosis I have discussed as well as in other cases or institutional spheres to which the theory could be applied, our objective should not be full accounts of the cases but better, more widely relevant answers to interesting questions. The stories I have told are intricate but necessarily incomplete. The explanations I have offered are potent but necessarily limited. My main concern has been to produce better explanations by joining different kinds of questions within the same analytic field. As institutions contain different kinds of impediments to the liberation or disruption of human affairs—some at the level of consciousness, some at the level of rules, and some at the level of partisanship—so questions posed about institutions must vary. If those questions can be situated in systematic relation to one another, as I have sought to do, more patterns can be discovered and those discovered portrayed more vividly. Since patterns from one perspective are explanations from another, the vividness of those patterns is a limit, but the only limit, to the quality of our explanations.

Abbreviations

AML	Amis du Manifeste et de la Liberté
CANAC	Veterans' Action Committee
CRS	Compagnies Républicaines de Securité
CRUA	Comité Révolutionnaire d'Unité d'Action
FAF	French Algerian Front
FLN	Front de Liberation Nationale; National Liberation Front
FNF	Front National Française
GPRA	Gouvernement Provisoire de la République Algérienne
IDF	Israel Defense Forces
IFOP	Institute Français d'opinion publique
IRA	Irish Republican Army
IRB	Irish Republican Brotherhood
MRP	Mouvement Républicaine Populaire
MTLD	Movement for the Triumph of Democratic Liberties
NRP	National Religious Party
OAS	Organisation Armée Secrète
OS	Special Organization
PCF	Parti Communist Français
PORI	Public Opinion Research Institute
PPA	Parti Progressiste Algérien
Ratz	Civil Rights Movement (Israel)
RAF	Rassemblement pour l'Algérie Française
RIC	Royal Irish Constabulary
SFIO	Parti Socialiste—Section Française de l'Internationale Ouvrière

UDMA	Democratic Union for the Algerian Manifesto
UDSR	Union démocratique et socialiste de la résistance
UNR	Union pour la Nouvelle République; unofficial Gaullist party
USRAF	Union for the Safeguarding and Renewal of French Algeria
UT	Territorial Units; Unités Territoriales
UUC	Ulster Unionist Council
UVF	Ulster Volunteer Forces

Appendix

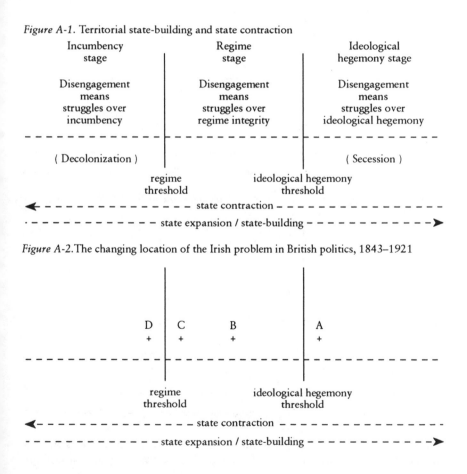

Figure A-1. Territorial state-building and state contraction

Incumbency stage	Regime stage	Ideological hegemony stage
Disengagement means struggles over incumbency	Disengagement means struggles over regime integrity	Disengagement means struggles over ideological hegemony
(Decolonization)		(Secession)

regime threshold   ideological hegemony threshold

◄ – – – – – – – – – – – – – – state contraction – – – – – – – – – – – – – –

· – – – – – – – – – – – state expansion / state-building – – – – – – – – – – –►

Figure A-2. The changing location of the Irish problem in British politics, 1843–1921

D | C   B   A
+   +   +   +

regime threshold   ideological hegemony threshold

◄– – – – – – – – – – – – – – state contraction – – – – – – – – – – – – – – –

– – – – – – – – – – – – state expansion / state-building – – – – – – – – – – –►

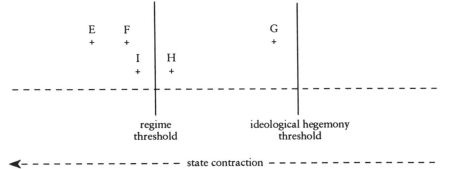

Figure A-3. The changing location of the Algerian problem in French politics, 1946–1962

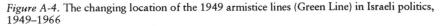

regime
threshold

ideological hegemony
threshold

◀- - - - - - - - - - - - - - state contraction - - - - - - - - - - - - - - - -

- - - - - - - - - - - - - state expansion / state-building - - - - - - - - - ▶

Figure A-4. The changing location of the 1949 armistice lines (Green Line) in Israeli politics, 1949–1966

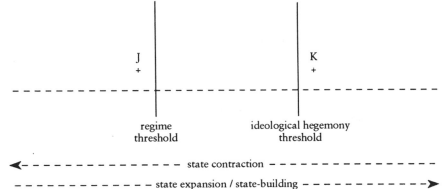

regime
threshold

ideological hegemony
threshold

◀- - - - - - - - - - - - - state contraction - - - - - - - - - - - - - - -

- - - - - - - - - - - - - state expansion / state-building - - - - - - - - - - ▶

Figure A-5. The changing location of the West Bank and Gaza Strip problem in Israeli politics, 1967–1992

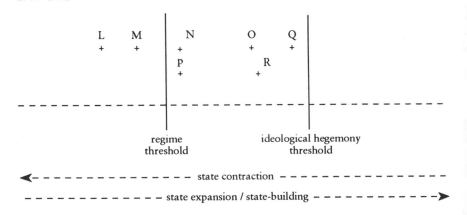

regime
threshold

ideological hegemony
threshold

◀- - - - - - - - - - - - - - state contraction - - - - - - - - - - - - - - -

- - - - - - - - - - - - - state expansion / state-building - - - - - - - - - - ▶

Note: In Figs. A-3 and A-5, the placement of points along the Y axis is for display purposes only and has no significance for the purposes of the model.

Notes

INTRODUCTION TO PART I

1 There is a significant scholarly tradition of interest in the causes and consequences of generic variation in the size and shape of states. Such studies normally link prevailing technologies of production, war, or revenue extraction to modal sizes of states in various regions or historical eras. A classic example is Karl Wittfogel, *Oriental Despotism* (New Haven: Yale University Press, 1964). Recent examples include David Friedman, "A Theory of the Size and Shape of Nations," *Journal of Political Economy* 85 (1977) 59–77; Margaret Levi, "The Predatory Theory of Rule," *Politics and Society* 10 (1981) 462–64; and Peter Katzenstein, "Small Nations in an Open International Economy: The Converging Balance of State and Society in Switzerland and Austria," in *Bringing the State Back In,* ed. Peter Evans, Dietrich Rueschemeyer, and Theda Skocpol (Cambridge: Cambridge University Press, 1985) 227–51. The questions posed by such studies are related to, but very different from, those explored here concerning variation in size of individual states with respect to the life of the polities whose borders they are usually taken to frame.

2 Max Weber, "Politics as a Vocation," in *From Max Weber: Essays in Sociology,* ed. H. H. Gerth and C. Wright Mills (New York: Oxford University Press, 1958) 78. There are other formulations to be found in Weber's work. This one is followed by a reminder: "Note that 'territory' is one of the characteristics of the state."

3 For examples of Weberian applications that emphasize or pass over without comment the "given" territorial shape of the state, see Joel S. Migdal, *Strong Societies and Weak States: State-Society Relations and State Capabilities in the Third World* (Princeton: Princeton University Press, 1988) 19; Charles Tilly, "Western State-Making and Theories of Political Transformation," in *The Formation of National States in Western Europe,* ed. Tilly (Princeton: Princeton Uni-

versity Press, 1975) 638; Thomas M. Callaghy, *The State-Society Struggle: Zaire in Comparative Perspective* (New York: Columbia University Press, 1984) x; Alfred Stepan, *The State and Society: Peru in Comparative Perspective* (Princeton: Princeton University Press, 1978) xi–xiv; Richard Rose, *Is the United Kingdom a State?* Studies in Public Policy no. 114 (Glasgow: Centre for the Study of Public Policy, University of Strathclyde, 1983) 2–5; idem, *Governing without Consensus* (Boston: Beacon, 1971) 26–27 and 512n; Guenther Roth, "Personal Rulership, Patrimonialism, and Empire-Building in the New States," *World Politics* 20 (January 1968) 194–206; Joshua B. Forrest, "The Quest for State 'Hardness' in Africa," *Comparative Politics* 20 (July 1988) 423; Edward S. Greenberg, "State Change: Approaches and Concepts," in *Changes in the State: Causes and Consequences,* ed. Edward S. Greenberg and Thomas F. Mayer (Newbury Park, Calif.: Sage, 1990) 12–13; Giacomo Luciani, "Introduction," in *The Arab State,* ed. Luciani (Berkeley: University of California Press, 1990) xviii; and Margaret Levi, *Of Rule and Revenue* (Berkeley: University of California Press, 1988) 1.

4 See in particular Norman J. G. Pounds and Sue Simons Ball, "Core-Areas and the Development of the European States System," *Annals of the Association of American Geographers* 54 (1964) 24–40; Charles Tilly, "Reflections on the History of European State-Making," in *The Formation of National States in Western Europe,* 7, 40–42, 76; and idem, "Western State-Making and Theories of Political Transformation," 601–38; Stein Rokkan, "Dimensions of State Formation and Nation-Building: A Possible Paradigm for Research on Variations within Europe," in *The Formation of National States in Europe,* 562–600. Otto Hintze, "The Formation of States and Constitutional Development: A Study in History and Politics," in *The Historical Essays of Otto Hintze* (New York: Oxford University Press, 1975) 161–65; Juan Linz, "Early State-Building and Late Peripheral Nationalism against the State: The Case of Spain," in *Building States and Nations: Analyses by Region,* ed. S. N. Eisenstadt and Stein Rokkan (Beverly Hills, Calif.: Sage, 1973) 2:33–106; and Samuel E. Finer, "State-Building, State Boundaries and Border Control," *Social Science Information* 13 (August–October 1974) 79–126. Analyses which advance or rely on strategic explanations for the determination of boundaries include Artistide Zolberg, "Strategic Interactions and the Formation of Modern States: France and England," *International Social Science Journal* 32 (1980) 687–716; Charles Tilly, *Coercion, Capital, and European States, A. D. 990–1990* (Cambridge, Mass.: Basil Blackwell, 1990) 130–43; Otto Hintze, "Military Organization and State Organization," in *The Historical Essays of Otto Hintze,* 180–215; Gianfranco Poggi, *The Development of the Modern State: A Sociological Introduction* (Stanford: Stanford University Press, 1978) 90–93. For an application of this approach in the American context see Thomas R. Hietala, *Manifest Design: Anxious Aggrandizement in Late Jacksonian America* (Ithaca, N. Y.: Cornell University Press, 1984).

5 J. P. Nettl, "The State as a Conceptual Variable," *World Politics* 20 (July 1968) 564–67. Rosenau labels "territory" one of four "static attributes [of a state] and not core phenomena subject to variation." James N. Rosenau, "The State in an Era of Cascading Politics," in *The Elusive State: International and Comparative Perspectives,* ed. James A. Caporaso (Newbury Park, Calif.: Sage, 1989) 18.

6   The literature pertaining to boundaries between state and society is too large and well known to be cited extensively here. For literature reviews that mirror its undertheorization of the territorial boundaries of states see Theda Skocpol, "Bringing the State Back In: Strategies of Analysis in Current Research," *Bringing the State Back In,* 3–37; Su-Hoon Lee, *State-Building in the Contemporary Third World* (Boulder, Colo.: Westview Press, 1988); and Karen Barkey and Sunita Parikh, "Comparative Perspectives on the State," *Annual Review of Sociology* 17 (1991) 523–49. For a critical analysis of the reification of boundaries between state and society that is acknowledged as applicable to the political construction of boundaries between states see Timothy Mitchell, "The Limits of the State: Beyond Statist Approaches and Their Critics," *American Political Science Review* 85 (March 1991) 77–96.

For a theoretically significant attempt to link African boundaries to political outcomes among competitors for power within postcolonial states see William J. Foltz, "Political Boundaries and Political Competition in Tropical Africa," in *Building States and Nations,* 1:357–83. For a politically sophisticated treatment of boundary formation at the "molecular" level see Peter Sahlins, *Boundaries: The Making of France and Spain in the Pyrenees* (Berkeley: University of California Press, 1989).

7   Concerning the externally reinforced constructedness of state boundaries in Africa see Robert H. Jackson, *Quasi-States: Sovereignty, International Relations and the Third World* (Cambridge: Cambridge University Press, 1990); and Jeffrey Herbst, "The Creation and Maintenance of National Boundaries in Africa," *International Organization* 43 (Autumn 1989) 673–92.

8   The Golan Heights and the Sinai peninsula were also captured by Israeli forces in the 1967 war, from Syria and Egypt respectively. Sinai was returned to Egypt under the terms of the Camp David Accords. Except for a small slice of the Golan Heights returned to Syria after the 1973 war, Israel has remained in occupation of this area. Approximately 12,000 Israeli settlers lived on the Golan Heights in 1992, among approximately 18,500 Syrian Druze. Ninety percent of the Golan's Syrian inhabitants fled or were expelled during the 1967 fighting. Many questions identical to those posed in this book about the West Bank and Gaza Strip can be raised about the continuation of Israeli rule of the Golan. For reasons of space, and because the Golan is generally not viewed by Israelis as part of the "Land of Israel," they are not addressed here.

1. ISRAEL AND THE WEST BANK AND GAZA STRIP

1   If one excludes expanded East Jerusalem, these figures would be 1.7 million Arabs and 110,000 Jews (1992).

2   Gloria H. Falk, "Israeli Public Opinion: Looking toward a Palestinian Solution," *Middle East Journal* 39 (Summer 1985) 254; and Russell A. Stone, *Social Change in Israel: Attitudes and Events, 1967–79* (New York: Praeger, 1982) 41.

3   This figure was given by the director general of the ministry. *Maariv,* January 12, 1983. According to Meron Benvenisti's figures, construction in the West Bank

accounted for 27 percent of Israel's public construction budget in 1984 and 30 percent in 1985. In 1984–85, 52.5 percent of Israel's total expenditures on roads was spent in the West Bank. Meron Benvenisti, *1986 Report: Demographic, Economic, Legal, Social and Political Developments in the West Bank* (Jerusalem: West Bank Data Project, 1986) 52–53.

4   For details of the scale and nature of Likud annexationist activities during this period see Tzvi Shuldiner, "The Real Cost of Settlements," *Haaretz,* July 25, 1980; Benvenisti, *1986 Report;* Ian Lustick, "Israel and the West Bank after Elon Moreh: The Mechanics of De Facto Annexation," *Middle East Journal* 35 (Autumn 1981) 557–77; Meron Benvenisti, *The West Bank Data Project: A Survey of Israel's Polices* (Washington, D. C.: American Enterprise Institute, 1984); Geoffrey Aronson, *Creating Facts: Israel, Palestinians and the West Bank* (Washington, D. C.: Institute for Palestine Studies, 1987) 59–156; and Ann Mosely Lesch and Mark Tessler, *Israel, Egypt, and the Palestinians: From Camp David to Intifada* (Bloomington: Indiana University Press, 1989) 194–222 and 238–54; Fawzi A. Gharaibeh, *The Economies of the West Bank and the Gaza Strip* (Boulder, Colo.: Westview Press, 1985); Meron Benvenisti and Shlomo Khayat, *The West Bank and Gaza Atlas* (Jerusalem: West Bank Data Project, 1988); *Jerusalem Post,* December 3, 1986; Yisrael Tomer, "The Mystery: How Much Was Invested in the Settlements?" *Yediot Acharonot,* November 9, 1983, translated by the Joint Publications Research Service, *Joint Publication Research Service Report: Near East and South Asia* (hereafter JPRS) 84781, November 18, 1983, pp. 42–45; and idem, *Two Decades of Settlement: Twenty Years since the Six Day War* (Hebrew) (Jerusalem: Ministry of Housing and Construction, 1987).

5   Meron Benvenisti, quoting himself, in an article published in *Davar,* October 9, 1988, the second in a series of three articles entitled "Nevertheless, Irreversible." See also, for a slightly amended version of these articles, Meron Benvenisti, *The Club and the Sling: Territories, Jews and Arabs* (Hebrew) (Jerusalem: Keter, 1988) 11–55. Unless otherwise indicated, all translations from Hebrew and French sources are my own.

6   "From Israel: Keeping Israel Jewish," interview with Abba Eban, *Moment Magazine* 7 (June 1982) 26, 29.

7   Interviews with Elias Freij, in *Haolam Hazeh,* March 16, 1983, translated in JPRS 83216, April 7, 1983, pp. 68, 71; and in *Al-Majallah* 186, September 3–9, 1983, translated in JPRS 84686, November 4, 1983, pp. 65–67; and King Hussein, April 30, 1983, transcribed in *Daily Report: Middle East and Africa,* Foreign Broadcast and Information Service (FBIS), May 2, 1983, p. F1. (The daily publication of the Foreign Broadcast and Information Service reporting on the Middle East has undergone several changes in its exact title. Hereafter FBIS designates the *Daily Report* pertaining to the Middle East on the date specified, regardless of its exact title.) For Mubarak's speech to the United Nations General Assembly, September 28, 1983, transcribed in FBIS, September 29, 1983, p. D3. For Shawa's opinion see Zvi Barel, "The List of the Agreed upon Six," *Haaretz,* January 20, 1983; and *Jerusalem Post International Edition,* week ending February 26, 1983. For use of Benvenisti's findings to exhort anti-annexationists to immediate action (before the elimination of withdrawal options) see also David Richardson, "Frus-

tration and Despair," *Jerusalem Post,* June 10, 1983; Yehuda Litani, "Quasi Faits Accomplis," *Haaretz,* January 14, 1983, translated in JPRS 82800, February 3, 1983, p. 62.

8   Benvenisti, *The West Bank Data Project,* 64. For the revised prediction of one hundred thousand West Bank settlers, see p. 60. This formulation was originally published on October 13, 1984, in the *New York Review of Books* in an article by Benvenisti titled "The Turning Point in Israel."

9   "For Tens of Thousands," *Nekuda,* 30, June 27, 1981, p. 2. *Nekuda* is a monthly journal published by the association of Jewish settlements in the West Bank and Gaza. It is virtually an official organ of Gush Emunim (Bloc of the Faithful), the umbrella organization of ideologically motivated settlers which has emerged as the single most powerful extraparliamentary political group in Israel's history. Founded in the mid–1970s to advance "the redemption process" and ensure fulfillment of the "destiny of the Jewish people" by restoring the whole, or "completed," Land of Israel to Jewish sovereignty, Gush has worked closely with Likud governments as a vanguard of and lobbyist for accelerated settlement of the territories. See Ian S. Lustick, *For the Land and the Lord: Jewish Fundamentalism in Israel* (New York: Council on Foreign Relations, 1988).

10   FBIS, January 28, 1983, p. 14; and January 26, 1983, transcribed from ITIM (News Service of Israel).

11   Aryeh Dayan, "The Last Option: Reactions," *Koteret Rashit,* 68, March 21, 1984, p. 18. For similarly delighted endorsements of Benvenisti's findings by Likud politicians, officials in charge of planning and implementing settlement programs, and sympathetic journalists, see remarks by Mikha'el Dekel, deputy minster of agriculture and head of settlement affairs in the second Begin government, and Mattitiyahu Drobles, director of the operational section of the World Zionist Organization/Jewish Agency Settlement Department, *Yoman Hashavua,* November 12, 1982, in FBIS, November 12, 1982, p. I16; Jerusalem Domestic Service broadcast, March 2, 1983, transcribed in FBIS, March 3, 1983, p. I6; and *Nekuda,* no. 61, July 18, 1983, p. 4. See also comments by Drobles's aide, Ze'ev Ben-Yosef, *Maariv,* January 11, 1983; Minister of Communication Mordechai Tzippori, announcement by the Communications Ministry spokesman, carried by ITIM, October 24, 1983, and translated in JPRS 84669, November 2, 1983; Ehud Olmert, *Harper's Magazine,* December 1984, p. 47; Ariel Sharon, Israel Defense Forces broadcast, December 21, 1982, transcribed by FBIS, December 22, 1982, p. I3; David Levy, *Yediot Acharonot,* November 25, 1983, in FBIS, November 28, 1983, p. I5; Meir Ben-Gur, "Benvenisti's Lesson," *Maariv,* April 30, 1984; and Yosef Harif, *Maariv,* December 7, 1984.

12   Editorial, "The End of an Era," *Nekuda,* no. 75, July 6, 1984, p. 6. For evidence of the excitement and optimism among settlers during this period see also editorial, "The Government Is Freezing Its Promises," *Nekuda,* no. 72, April 16, 1984, p. 6; Eliakim Haetzni, "Leave the Past Alone," *Nekuda,* no. 75, July 6, 1984, p. 9; editorial, "Best Wishes to the Absorption Campaign," *Nekuda,* no. 58, May 17, 1983, pp. 2–3; and *Nekuda,* no. 59, June 10, 1983, p. 11.

13   Dani Rubinstein, "The Pitfall of the Territories—To Its Climax," *Davar,* January 11, 1982. See also idem, "Deluxe Annexation," *New Outlook* 24 (June

1981) 16–20, 48. For similar if not always quite so categorical assessments offered during this period see *Al-Hamishmar,* April 1, 1983; Yehuda Litani in *Haaretz,* March 12, 1985; and idem, "On the Way to Shchem 'Illit'," *Koteret Rashit,* December 15, 1982, pp. 6–10, 20; Shmuel Toledano, "Those Who Prophesy Doom Are Right," *Haaretz,* April 6, 1982, translated in JPRS 80962, June 2, 1982, pp. 53–55; and a series of articles by Yosef Goell, "Settlement and Suburbia," January 7, 1983; "Promised Lands," January 14, 1983; "Roads to Roam," January 21, 1983; "Stumbling Blocks," January 28, 1983; all in the *Jerusalem Post.*

14   Litani, "Quasi Faits Accomplis," 62.

15   Amos Elon, "The View from Mount Gerizim," *Haaretz,* February 4, 1983.

16   Amos Elon, "Stepping up Annexation," *Haaretz,* February 26, 1982, translated in JPRS 80730, May 5, 1982, pp. 90–92. See also idem, "Towards an Apartheid State," *Haaretz,* December 10, 1982; and idem, "A Day in the Life of Shaul Friedlander," *Haaretz,* April 22, 1983. For other examples, during this period, of dovish portrayals of the imminent approach of the "point of no return," see Hirsch Goodman, "Questions of Democracy," *Jerusalem Post,* August 19, 1983; Lova Eliav, "Sever Israel's Twin," *New York Times,* October 13, 1983; and Shlomo Avineri, "West Bank Options," *Jerusalem Post International Edition,* week ending August 18, 1983.

17   Interview with Yuval Neeman, *Maariv,* February 24, 1984, translated in FBIS, February 28, 1984, p. I4.

18   Meron Benvenisti, "The Second Republic," *Jerusalem Post,* January 7, 1987. See also idem, *1986 Report,* 91.

19   Benvenisti, *The Sling and the Club,* 78.

20   See Benvenisti, *1986 Report,* 93–95; idem, *The Sling and the Club,* 87–88. For a similar view see Allan E. Shapiro, "The Rule of Law and the West Bank," *Jerusalem Post,* June 14, 1983.

21   See, for example, "Conversation with Shulamit Aloni: I Am Tired to Death," *Bamahane,* November 30, 1983. On the depressed withdrawal from public affairs by many dovish-liberal Israelis in this period, known as "internal emigration," see the remarks of Peace Now leader Avishai Margalit, interviewed by Joanna Yehiel in "What Next for Peace Now?," *Jerusalem Post International Edition,* week ending October 12, 1985, p. 13; and Yehoshafat Harkabi, *The Fateful Choices before Israel,* Essays on Strategy and Diplomacy, no. 7 (Claremont, Calif.: Keck Centre for International Strategic Studies, 1987) 22.

22   Jerusalem Domestic Service broadcast, April 27, 1984, transcribed in FBIS, May 1, 1984, p. I6.

23   All these Eban quotes are from an interview with the editors of *Moment Magazine,* June 1984, pp. 21–22. For similar condemnations of "defeatism" by anti-annexationists persuaded by Benvenisti's arguments, see David Twersky, "Annexation with a Human Face," *Jerusalem Post,* September 15, 1983; and comments by Mattitiyahu Peled and Shulamith Aloni in Aryeh Dayan, "The Last Option: Reactions," *Koteret Rashit,* March 21, 1983, pp. 18–19.

24   Abba Eban, "The Central Question," *Tikkun* 1 (1986) 22. For similar attacks on Benvenisti and his irreversibility thesis see Raanan Weitz, "Facts about the West Bank," *Haaretz,* April 24, 1985; Dayan, "The Last Option," 18–19; Avra-

ham Schweitzer, "The Illusion of Settlement," *Haaretz,* December 3, 1982; idem, "The Ash-Shuf Precedent Applies to the West Bank," *Haaretz,* April 29, 1984, translated in FBIS, May 1, 1984, p. 17; and Aryeh Ya'ari, "Benvenisti's Analysis or 'The Road to Hell Is Paved with Good Intentions' " (Hebrew) mimeo, International Center for Peace in the Middle East, Tel Aviv, March 1984.

25 Boaz Evron, "Too Late for the Settlers," *Yediot Acharonot,* May 2, 1986, translated in *Israel Press Briefs,* no. 45 (May–June 1986) 11.

26 Abba Eban, "Reflecting on Negotiations," *Jerusalem Post,* June 22, 1984. For similar dovish rejections of Benvenisti's argument see Aryeh Ya'ari, "The Israeli Tragedy," *Al Hamishmar,* October 11, 1985, translated in *Israel Press Briefs,* no. 39 (October 1985) 18. See also David Shaham, "Israel Can Undo Expansion," *New York Times,* June 8, 1984; Raanan Weitz, "Facts on Paper in the West Bank," *Haaretz,* April 24, 1985; and editorial, *Haaretz,* "Parasitical Lifestyle in the West Bank," November 26, 1985, translated in *Israel Press Briefs,* no. 40 (December 1985) 21. See also, regarding the impossibility of annexing the territories, Yehoshaphat Harkabi, *The Bar Kokhba Syndrome: Risk and Realism in International Politics* (Chappaqua, N.Y.: Rossel Books, 1983) 171–75, 180.

27 A mere 180 votes separated the totals of the "coalitionable" parties favoring complete absorption of the territories from those favoring territorial withdrawal in exchange for peace. Likud, Tehiya, the National Religious party, Morasha, and Ometz together received 875,001 votes. The Labor Party, Yahad, Shinui, and the Civil Rights Movement together received 874,821 votes. The result of this deadlock was the first "national unity government," in which the Labor and Likud parties were forced into a coalition together because neither could form a government with its own ideologically supportive allies.

28 Nor did this election permit either the Labor party or the Likud to form its own government. So another national unity government was established, but with the Likud as the dominant partner, and Yitzhak Shamir as prime minister, Labor leader Shimon Peres as foreign minister, and no rotation.

29 "To Stop the Reagan Plan," *Nekuda,* no. 80, November 23, 1984, p. 6.

30 See in particular two detailed and prominent articles by Hagai Segal, "What Happened to the 100,000 Plan?" *Nekuda,* no. 105, December 9, 1986, pp. 8–11, 38–39; and "The Great Land Robbery," *Nekuda,* no. 108, March 13, 1987, pp. 8–11, 40–41.

31 Editorial, "Peace in Exchange for Peace," *Nekuda,* no. 88, June 24, 1985, pp. 4–5.

32 Editorial, "The Crisis in the National Movement," *Nekuda,* no. 90, August 23, 1985, p. 6.

33 *Shared Rule: The Only Realistic Option for Peace* (Jerusalem: Jerusalem Centre for Public Affairs, 1983). See also Ze'ev Schiff, "The Spectre of Civil War in Israel," *Middle East Journal* 39 (Spring 1985) 233–36.

34 Larry L. Fabian, "Red Light, West Bank," *Foreign Policy* 50 (Spring 1983) 63, 69. For examples of American and European observers, mostly critical of the Likud government, who joined in the assessment at this time that withdrawal from the West Bank was no longer possible, see also Amos Perlmutter, "Peres Couldn't Return the Land," *New York Times,* September 4, 1984; Arthur Hertzbreg, "Israel

and the West Bank: The Implications over Permanent Control," *Foreign Affairs* 61 (Summer 1983) 1064, 1070; Michael Sterner, "Managing U.S.-Israeli Relations," *American-Arab Affairs* 6 (Fall 1983) 19; Conor Cruise O'Brien, "Why Israel Can't Take 'Bold Steps' for Peace," *Atlantic Monthly*, October 1985, pp. 45–55; Geoffrey Aronson, "Israel's Irreversible Expansion," *New York Times*, June 8, 1984; Ann M. Lesch, "Israeli Settlements on the West Bank: Mortgaging the Future," *Journal of South Asian and Middle Eastern Studies* 7 (Fall 1983) 23; and Peter Grose, *A Changing Israel* (New York: Vintage, 1985) 73, 88, 125–26.

35 *New York Times*, August 3, 1983. In response to questions about this statement the State Department repeated its view that calling for the "dismantling of the existing settlements" was "an impractical demand." *Washington Post*, August 4, 1983.

36 See Michal Sela's report of Nusseibeh's article on this topic and her conversation with him, *Koteret Rashit*, November 13, 1985, translated in *Israel Press Briefs*, no. 40 (December 1985) 11–12.

37 *Jerusalem Post*, February 25, 1987. For a more detailed examination of Nusseibeh's position in relation to Benvenisti's thesis see Salim Tamari's discussion of a paper presented by Nusseibeh to an East Jerusalem symposium convened in June 1987 to discuss the twentieth anniversary of the Israeli occupation. Salim Tamari, "The Palestinian Movement in Transition: Historical Reversals and the Uprising," *Journal of Palestine Studies* 20 (Winter 1991) 59–60.

38 *Jerusalem Post International Edition*, week ending June 13, 1987.

39 *Yediot Acharonot*, December 6, 1987, translated in FBIS, December 7, 1987, p. 43. On Nusseibeh's views as expressed to Amirav see also Ze'ev Schiff and Ehud Ya'ari, *Intifada: The Palestinian Uprising—Isreal's Third Front* (New York: Simon and Schuster, 1990) 275. See as well Elias Freij's announcement of his opinion that "the time has come for the inhabitants of the territories to become full-fledged [Israeli] citizens." *Yediot Acharonot*, January 13, 1988, translated in FBIS, January 14, 1988, p. 51. For an analysis of the impact of the image of an irreversible process of de facto annexation on PLO policies see Ian Lustick, "Points of No Return: Palestinians, the PLO, and De Facto Annexation," paper presented at the 1983 Middle Eastern Studies Association Convention, Chicago, Ill., November 4, 1983.

40 For his attack on the "fantasies" of the annexationists, and the exaggerations and simplistic thinking reflected in Benvenisti's analysis (compared with his own "realism"), see especially Yehoshafat Harkabi, *Fateful Decisions* (Hebrew) (Tel Aviv: Am Oved, 1986) 66, 82–83, 315–20. See also Abba Eban, "Return to Reason," *Jerusalem Post*, February 13, 1984. On the idea of territorial compromise as "an unrealistic illusion" or "vain dreams," see representative remarks by Minister of Construction of Housing David Levy and Deputy Prime Minister Yitzhak Shamir, reported in *Haaretz*, January 16, 1986, translated in FBIS, January 21, 1986, p. I6.

41 Chagai Segal, "Reports of the Death of the Settlements Are Exaggerated," *Hadashot*, May 2, 1989. Segal is himself a Gush Emunim activist.

42 Jonathan Frankel, "The State of Israel and the Liberal Crisis," *Jewish Quarterly* 32 (1985) 37.

43 Dani Rubinstein, "Back to the Green Line," *Davar*, July 8, 1988, translated in *Israel Press Briefs*, no. 60 (July–August 1988) 13.

44 Graham E. Fuller, *The West Bank of Israel: Point of No Return?* (Santa Monica, Calif.: Rand, 1989).

45 "Beginning to Get Used to It," *Politika*, no. 28 (September 1989) 1.

46 Quotation transcribed from a tape recording of the symposium, available at the Van Leer Institute, Jerusalem.

47 Two months later Benvenisti published an article describing his "irreversibility" thesis as meaning that Israeli rule of the West Bank and Gaza Strip would persist "as long as the unity of the Jewish political centre is maintained." Meron Benvenisti, "Parting from the West Bank, the Gaza Strip—and from Yossi Sarid," *Haaretz*, March 2, 1990.

48 Concerning Ben-Nun's leadership of the "consensus-building" wing of Gush Smunim see Lustick, *For the Land and the Lord*, 119.

49 Yoel Ben-Nun, "Topic: The Challenge of the General Staff to the Council of Torah Sages," *Nekuda*, no. 139, March–April 1990, pp. 26–28. For other signs of a reversal among settlers who before the intifada had judged de facto annexation an unstoppable process, see Nadav Shrgai, in *Haaretz*, December 22, 1989; Michael Capra, "Fear, Five Minutes from Kfar Saba," *Maariv*, March 11, 1988; Beni Katzover, "Eradicate the Intifada, Encourage Expansion of the Jewish Family, a Revolution in Settlement, Encourage Arab Emigration, Impose Sovereignty on All the Land of Israel," *Nekuda*, no. 130, June 2, 1989, pp. 14–16. See also Ezra Zohar, "The Momentum of Settlement Will End the Intifada," *Nekuda*, no. 127, October 2, 1989, pp. 31, 66; and Uri Elitzur, "Annexation of a Palestinian State: There Is No Third Solution," *Nekuda*, no. 141, June 1990, pp. 16–18; "It's beginning to be serious; lend a hand...," letter signed by Zvika Slonim, director, Eretz Yisrael Academy, dated February 14, 1989; and Reuven Pedatzur, in *Haaretz*, April 27, 1990, translated in JPRS 90036, July 7, 1990, pp. 37–38.

2. THRESHOLDS OF STATE-BUILDING AND STATE CONTRACTION

1 See, inter alia, Michael Bar-Zohar, *Facing a Cruel Mirror* (Hebrew) (Tel Aviv: Yediot Acharonot Books, 1990) 22–28; Tom Segev, *1949: The First Israelis* (New York: Free Press, 1986) 39–40; and Yoram Nimrod, "Ceasefire or Peace," *Davar*, April 14, 1989.

2 As one well-known Betar song goes, "The Jordan has two banks, one is ours and so is the other." Betar was the eastern European Jewish youth movement led by the founding father of Revisionist Zionism, Ze'ev Jabotinsky, in the 1920s and 1930s. It continues today in Israel as the youth organization of Herut. On Begin's own unswerving espousal of territorial maximalism after 1948, and his ability to keep Herut wedded to this concept, see Yonathan Shapiro, *Chosen to Command* (Hebrew) (TelAviv: Am Oved, 1989).

3 Milton Viorst, "Annexation Is Reversible," in *Is Annexation Reversible?* Discussion Paper 6 (Tel Aviv: International Center for Peace in the Middle East, 1985) 34.

4 Ibid., 31.

5 Abba Eban, "Democracy in Israel—1984," *Spectrum,* January–February 1984, p. 23.

6 Aryeh Dayan, "The Last Option," *Koteret Rashit,* March 14, 1984, p. 42.

7 For explicitly colonial descriptions of Israel's relationship to the territories by advocates of "decolonization" see Immanuel Sivan, "How to Extricate Ourselves from a Colonial Situation," *Davar,* August 22, 1986; and idem, "From Myth to History," in *Arab Political Myths* (Hebrew) (TelAviv: Am Oved, 1988) 173–209; Ze'ev Sternhell, in *Tikkun* 2 (1987) 61–62; Arieh Ya'ari, "Meron Benvenisti's 'Communal' Myth," *New Outlook* 33 (May/June 1990) 39. In 1989 Sivan began describing Israel as having entered a "crisis of decolonization," signaling the beginning of what he predicted would be a long and difficult process of disengagement. Immanuel Sivan, "A Crisis of Decolonization," *Politika,* no. 28 (September 1989) 6–8.

8 Meron Benvenisti, *The West Bank Data Project: A Survey of Israel's Policies* (Washington, D.C.: American Enterprise Institute, 1984) 65. See also idem, *1986 Report: Demographic, Economic, Legal, Social and Political Developments in the West Bank* (Jerusalem: West Bank Data Project, 1986) 50. For similar judgments about the practical political impact of a growing and organized constituency of settlers see, from one side of the political spectrum, Allan E. Shapiro, "The Federal Formula," *Jerusalem Post International Edition,* week ending January 8, 1983; and from the other, Mordechai Nisan, "The Yesha Council: Political Work," *Nekuda,* no. 24, February 20, 1981, pp. 4–5, 15.

9 Dayan, "The Last Option," 42. See also David Shaham, "Israel Can Undo Expansion," *New York Times,* June 8, 1984.

10 Yehoshafat Harkabi, *Israel's Fateful Hour* (New York: Harper and Row, 1988) 65–69, 124. This edition is an English translation, with some omissions and revisions, of *Fateful Decisions,* published in Hebrew in 1986. See also remarks made in a lecture Harkabi delivered on April 4, 1985, published under the title *The Arab-Israeli Conflict: Future Perspective* (Tel Aviv: International Center for Peace in the Middle East, 1985) 3.

11 Yoram Peri, *Between Battles and Ballots* (Cambridge: Cambridge University Press, 1982) 284–85; David Twersky, "Is Peace Really Possible?" *Jerusalem Post International Edition,* week ending December 14, 1985; and Dan Margalit, "Squaring the Circle," *Politika,* no. 28 (September 1989) 36–37. See especially Sammy Smooha's discussion of his "continuing occupation" model of Israeli rule of the territories in "Four Models and One More," *Politika,* nos. 14–15 (June 1987) 61–63.

12 See, for example, Dani Rubinstein's comments in *Al-Hamishmar,* April 1, 1983; Yoel Marcus, "Begin Is Alive, Truly Alive," *Haaretz,* April 15, 1983; Saul Cohen, *The Geopolitics of Israel's Border Question,* Jaffe Center for Strategic Studies, Tel Aviv University, Study No. 7 (Boulder, Colo.: Westview Press, 1986) 100; Haim Ganzu, "Another Right-Wing Revolution," *Haaretz,* May 14, 1990; Yaakov Sharett, *The State of Israel Is No More* (Hebrew) (Tel Aviv: Tesher, 1988); Giora Goldberg and Ephraim Ben-Zadok, "Gush Emunim in the West Bank," *Middle Eastern Studies* 22 (January 1986) 71–72. This article was originally published in Hebrew in 1983.

13   See also a document published in April 1981 by the Yesha Council of Jewish Settlements ("Yesha" is an acronym for "Judea, Samaria, and Gaza"), titled "Manifesto Regarding the Unity of the Land and the State," *Nekuda*, no. 26, April 3, 1981, p. 3.

14   Remarks of Deupty Labor and Social Affairs Minister Ben-Tzion Rubin, Jerusalem Domestic Service broadcast, April 12, 1983, transcribed by the Foreign Broadcast Information Service, *Daily Report: Near East and South Asia* (hereafter FBIS), April 13, 1983, p. I2.

15   Haim Tzaban was the official within the Land Settlement Department of the Jewish Agency responsible for producing the document (under the direction, as explained in Chap. 1, of both Mattitiyahu Drobles and Mikhael Dekel). Tzaban was chairman of the Steering Committee for Master Plans for the Regional Councils of Judea and Samaria. Haim Tzaban et al., *Master Plan for the Settlement of Samaria and Judea: Development Plan for the Area for the Years (1983–86)* (Hebrew) (Jerusalem: World Zionist Organization Settlement Department and State of Israel Ministry of Agriculture, 1983).

The title is misleading in that the document actually contains two plans, one a part of the other. The larger plan is a "master plan" describing the commitments and resources seen as necessary to transform the West Bank into an inseparable part of Israel by the year 2010. The subplan, set forth in considerably more detail, includes the specific objectives to be accomplished between 1983 and 1986 and identifies the resources required to achieve those objectives. Neither plan includes the Gaza Strip within its purview.

16   Ibid., 15.

17   With high levels of infrastructural investment slated for the initial years of the plan, the amount of money scheduled to be spent for *each* of the eighty thousand settlers to be transferred to the West Bank between 1983 and 1986 was $17,820. Computed from figures provided ibid., 62–64. For a detailed analysis of this and other aspects of the Tzaban plan see Ian S. Lustick, "The 'Irreversibility' of Israel's Annexation of the West Bank and Gaza Strip: A Critical Evaluation," study written under contract no. MDA908–85-M-1381 for the Department of Defense, October 1985, pp. 35–41.

18   Even under their most optimistic projections of Jewish and Arab population growth rates, they still projected that in the year 2010 Arabs would constitute a 65% majority of the West Bank population. Tzaban et al., *Master Plan for the Settlement of Samaria and Judea*, 18–19, 39–40.

19   Ibid., 19–34.

20   Ibid., 18, 20–22, 34–39, and 56–57.

21   Ibid., 39, 56–57, and 131.

22   The Yamit district in northeastern Sinai contained five thousand Jewish settlers when it was evacuated and returned to Egypt in April 1982, according to the terms of the Israel-Egypt peace treaty. In the preface to the Tzaban plan, a half dozen well-known Gush Emunim personalities—mayors of settlements, activists, and technical experts—were thanked for their contributions.

23   "Where to Now...," *Nekuda*, no. 43, May 21, 1982, pp. 16–17, 26.

24   Interview with Rabbi Yisrael Ariel, "Burn the Old Maps," *Nekuda*, no. 46, August 6, 1982, p. 20.

25 Pinchas Wallerstein, "Settlements Are Not Enough," *Nekuda,* no. 44, June 11, 1982, p. 5.

26 "A Foreign Flame," *Nekuda,* no. 68, January 13, 1984, p. 3 (emphasis added). In 1984 the World Zionist Organization, "in cooperation with Amana, the settlement movement of Gush Emunim, and the Council of Cities and Settlements in Judaea, Samaria, and Gaza," published an eighty-five-page booklet, *New Dimensions: Aliyah to Judaea, Samaria, and Gaza.* It began by contrasting the "images of tents and portable generators" associated with settlements in the territories in the mid–1970s with a growing presence that "day after day, month after month ...became...a new reality." "A majority of Israelis," it continued, "has come around to the early settlers' bedrock vision and conviction that Judea, Samaria, and Gaza are not some distant, foreign tracts, but rather an inseparable part of Israel." Immigration and Absorption Division, World Zionist Organization, *New Dimensions: Aliyah to Judaea, Samaria, and Gaza* (New York: World Zionist Organization, 1984) 1. Arab inhabitants of the areas were not mentioned. A map included with the booklet named each Jewish settlement and prominent Jewish cities and towns inside Israel proper, but bore no designation whatsoever of Arab cities, towns, or villages.

27 Yoel Ben-Nun, "State of Israel vs. Land of Israel," *Nekuda,* no. 74, April 16, 1984, p. 29.

28 Quoted in Eli Tabor, "Why Is Youth Moving Towards the Right?" *Yediot Acharonot* (supplement), August 10, 1984, pp. 1, 18. See also Milla Ohel, "The Process of Ideological Boundary Blurring and Its Consequences," *New Outlook* 26 (May 1983) 25.

29 Basheer Teri, "Dani, Age Eighteen," *Koteret Rashit,* no. 131, June 5, 1985, p. 16. For similar judgments that the Green Line had not been erased from the imagination of Israelis, but implying that its disappearance would, in fact, be decisive, see Herbert Kelman, "Not Too Late for a Palestinian-Israeli Solution," *New York Times,* January 21, 1988; Smooha, "Four Models and One More," 61–63; Itzhak Galnoor, in *Tikkun,* February 2, 1986, p. 62; and Misha Louvish, "The Spectre of the Green Line," *Jerusalem Post,* October 14, 1986.

30 This definition builds on Douglass C. North's conception of a state—an organization that "specifies property rights" and "whose boundaries are determined by its power to tax constituents." I omit his additional requirement that it possess "a comparative advantage in violence" as an unnecessary definitional exclusion of an important hypothesis. Douglass C. North, *Structure and Change in Economic History* (New York: Norton, 1981) 17 and 21.

31 Quoted and translated in Juan J. Linz in *The Breakdown of Democratic Regimes: Crisis Breakdown and Reequilibrium* (Baltimore: Johns Hopkins University Press, 1978) 100n.

32 Joseph R. Strayer, *On the Medieval Origins of the Modern State* (Princeton: Princeton University Press, 1970) 5.

33 On this general point see William Foltz, "Political Boundaries and Political Competition in Tropical Africa," in *Building States and Nations: Analyses by Region,* ed. vol. 2, S. N. Eisenstadt and Stein Rokkan (Beverly Hills, Calif.: Sage, 1973) 357–83.

34   Andrew J. R. Mack, "Why Big Nations Lose Small Wars: The Politics of Asymmetric Conflict," *World Politics* 27 (January 1975) 175–200. For a conceptually identical problem see Joseph S. Kraemer, "Revolutionary Guerrilla Warfare and the Decolonization Movement," *Polity* 4 (Winter 1971) 137–58.

35   Stephen D. Krasner, "Approaches to the State: Alternative Conceptions and Historical Dynamics," *Comparative Politics* 16 (January 1984) 233.

36   Theda Skocpol, "Bringing the State Back In: Strategies of Analysis in Current Research," in *Bringing the State Back In,* ed. Peter B. Evans, Dietrich Rueschemeyer, and Theda Skocpol (Cambridge: Cambridge University Press, 1985) 21. See also the comments of the editors of this volume, pp. 253–55 and 360–61.

37   Krasner, "Approaches to the State," 234.

38   Ibid.

39   Ibid., 234–35, 243–44.

40   The conditions under which this can be achieved among the population of a core state, when it is not accompanied by similar processes of institutionalized legitimation among disenfranchised or repressed populations of the integrated territory, is an important *empirical* question. My own studies of the system of control over Arab inhabitants of Israel (Green Line borders) and of British and French state-building failure in Ireland and Algeria suggest the complexity of the question, but also the possibility of finding systematic answers. Ian Lustick, *Arabs in the Jewish State: Israel's Control of a National Minority* (Austin: University of Texas Press, 1980); and idem, *State-Building Failure in British Ireland and French Algeria* (Berkeley: Institute of International Studies, University of California, 1985).

41   Technically this is not quite the case, as we shall see in regard to the status of French Algeria before World War II (Chap. 4), since in the absence of significant sources of strain, the particular borders of a state need not appear on its political agenda even if the conception of those borders has not been institutionalized on a hegemonic basis.

42   This argument is fully developed in Lustick, *State-Building Failure.*

43   After the overthrow of the Fourth Republic, Phillip Williams amended his previously published study to suggest that not until the Algerian problem had France ever had to face political strains as serious as those posed by the Irish question in Britain. Philip M. Williams, *Crisis and Compromise: Politics in the Fourth Republic* (Hamden, Conn.: Archon, 1964) v. Two books that touch on this comparison but whose primary focus is on the Northern Ireland issue in British politics since 1922 are Hugh Roberts, *Northern Ireland and the Algerian Analogy: A Suitable Case for Gaullism?* (Belfast: Athol, 1986); and Frank Wright, *Northern Ireland: A Comparative Analysis* (Totowa, N.J.: Barnes and Noble, 1987).

44   Concerning this type of "variation-finding comparison," see Charles Tilly, "Linkers, Diggers, and Glossers in Social History," mimeo, New School for Social Research, May 1987, pp. 12–15.

45   Excluded from this study are processes leading from the Irish Revolt of 1798 to the establishment of the Union between Great Britain and Ireland—a British

conception of the shape of their state which, as we shall see, enjoyed hegemonic status in the mid-nineteenth century.

INTRODUCTION TO PART II

1 Tom Segev, *1949: The First Israelis* (New York: Free Press, 1986) 6.

2 In fact my application of Gramscian analysis is not only consistent with Gramsci's most consistent formulation of his ideas but corresponds to his own development and use of the concept to address the question of the shape and size of the Italian state. See Antonio Gramsci, *The Modern Prince and Other Writings*, ed. Louis Marks (New York: International Publishers, 1957) 164; and, idem, "Notes on Italian History," *Selections from the Prison Notebooks of Antonio Gramsci*, ed. Quintin Hoare and Geoffrey Nowell-Smith (New York: International Publishers, 1971) 97–100 and 104–14. For additional citations and discussion see Ian S. Lustick, "Becoming Problematic: Breakdown of a Hegemonic Conception of Ireland in Nineteenth-Century Ireland," *Politics and Society* 18, no. 1 (1990) 42–44. For Gramsci's use of the notion of "common sense" to convey the meaning individuals attach to hegemonic beliefs see *The Modern Prince*, 60–67, 103–4, and 141. For examples of different interpretations see Gwyn A. Williams, "The Concept of '*Egemonia*' in the Thought of Antonio Gramsci: Some Notes on Interpretation," *Journal of the History of Ideas* 21 (October–December 1960) 586–99; and Joseph Femia, "The Gramsci Phenomenon: Some Reflections," *Political Studies* 27 (September 1979) 484–92. For an excellent attempt to operationalize the concept in an empirical domain see David Laitin, *Hegemony and Culture* (Chicago: University of Chicago Press, 1986).

3 Laclau and Mouffe provide a systematic argument for why and how Gramsci's concept of hegemony should be seen as applicable to discrete dimensions of political life rather than necessarily centered in a comprehensive, class-based formula for apprehending social reality. Ernesto Laclau and Chantal Mouffe, *Hegemony and Socialist Strategy: Towards a Radical Democratic Politics* (London: Verso, 1985) 69, 86–87, and 136–44.

4 Since no direct access to thought processes is possible, it may even be safest (though not necessary) to assume from the outset that all concepts available to the analyst are (or were) also available to the subject.

3. BECOMING PROBLEMATIC

1 See Figure A-2 in the Appendix for a depiction of this shift as plotted on the model described in Chapter 2. Point A in that diagram represents the location of the Irish problem in British politics in the 1830s and 1840s, when the concept of Ireland as an integral part of the United Kingdom enjoyed hegemonic status. Point B represents the relocation of the problem across the ideological hegemony threshold in the state-contracting direction as manifest in the 1886 debate over home rule that I analyze in this chapter.

2   Gustave de Beaumont, *Ireland: Social, Political, and Religious,* 2 vols., ed. W. C. Taylor (London: Richard Bentley, 1839) 2: 325–26.

3   Ibid., 324–25.

4   Ibid., 328.

5   Seymour Drescher, *Tocqueville and England* (Cambridge: Harvard University Press, 1964) 114.

6   Count Camille Benso Cavour, *Thoughts on Ireland: Its Present and Future,* trans. William B. Hodggson (London: Trübner, 1868) 106.

7   Ibid., 104–5.

8   Ibid., 106.

9   Lawrence J. McCaffrey, *Daniel O'Connell and the Repeal Year* (Lexington: University of Kentucky Press, 1966) 106–10.

10   *Illustrated London News* 2, June 24, 1843.

11   *Illustrated London News* 2, May 20, 1843.

12   *Illustrated London News* 2, June 24, 1843.

13   "The United Irishmen and the Repeal Agitation," *Westminster Review* 40 (August 1843) 38.

14   Ibid. As noted earlier, determination that a belief has hegemonic status does not mean that contrary scenarios are literally "unthinkable"—that they "cannot be imagined" or are "not imagined." I emphasize here that what distinguishes an ideologically hegemonic belief is the absence from defenses of it of serious if-then argumentation about outcomes based on change in the conditions it references.

15   Ibid., 37.

16   Ibid., 39.

17   P. S. O'Hegarty, *A History of Ireland under the Union* (London: Methuen, 1952) 62.

18   In 1834 O'Connell declared in Parliament that he would oppose "separation" as long as he lived. *Hansard Parliamentary Debates,* 3rd ser. (hereafter *Hansard*) vol. 22 (1834), col. 1156.

19   Patrick O'Farrell, *England and Ireland since 1800* (London: Oxford University Press, 1975) 37.

20   Oliver MacDonagh, *Ireland: The Union and Its Aftermath* (London: Allen and Unwin, 1979) 13.

21   *Hansard* 22 (1834), col. 1093.

22   Ibid., col. 1158.

23   *Hansard* 23 (1834), col. 291.

24   McCaffrey, *Daniel O'Connell and the Repeal Year,* 206.

25   *Hansard* 22 (1834), cols. 1172–73.

26   Ibid., col. 1191.

27   *Hansard* 23 (1834), col. 69. William Gladstone, then a young and reticent member of Parliament, heard Peel's address and in his diary called it a "splendid speech." *The Gladstone Diaries,* ed. M. R. D. Foot (Oxford: Clarendon Press, 1968) 2: 103, entry for April 25, 1934.

28   Before the 1870s the term "British Empire" referred not to British possessions overseas but to the United Kingdom itself. See below pp. 70, 74 and 148.

29   *Hansard* 23 (1834), col. 71.

30 Ibid., col. 95. For additional examples see Peel's characterization of Repeal as "insane," *Hansard* 70 (1843), col. 302; and as "utterly impossible," ibid., col. 297.

31 *Hansard* 23 (1834), col. 76.

32 Ibid., col. 92.

33 *Hansard* 71 (1843), col. 464.

34 *Hansard* 22 (1834), col. 296.

35 Ibid.

36 *Hansard* 69 (1843), cols. 9–10.

37 Ibid., col. 9.

38 *Hansard* 72 (1844), col. 685.

39 *Hansard* 22 (1834), col. 1289.

40 Ibid., col. 1324.

41 Ibid., col. 1289.

42 *Hansard* 69 (1843), cols. 1612–13. See also remarks by Sir Frederick Shaw, an Irish Protestant representing Dublin University and a former Irish privy councillor. Ibid., col. 1143.

43 Ibid., cols. 1040–41.

44 Ibid., col. 174.

45 Ibid., col. 1074.

46 *Hansard* 22 (1834), col. 298.

47 For an exhaustive discussion of the changing use of the term "empire" in nineteenth-century British politics, see Richard Koebner and Helmut Dan Schmidt, *Imperialism: The Story and Significance of a Political Word, 1840–1960* (Cambridge: Cambridge University Press, 1964) 27–134.

48 *Hansard* 22 (1834), col. 235. This is also what Peel meant in the passage quoted earlier (p. 66). See also the remarks of Lord Lyndhurst, *Hansard* 70 (1843), col. 1179; the earl of Roden, *Hansard* 69 (1843), col. 5; Lord Eliot, *Hansard* 70 (1843), col. 699; and Lord Brougham in the House of Lords, *Hansard* 69 (1843), col. 9.

49 For the extraordinarily contrived official, and thus instructive, argument that the *peaceable* nature of the Repeal meetings supported government charges of their *violent* intent and illegality, see Home Secretary James Graham's speech to the House of Commons justifying the banning of Repeal meetings in February 1844. *Hansard* 62 (1844), col. 772.

50 *Hansard* 304 (1886), col. 1239.

51 Donald Southgate, *The Passing of the Whigs: 1832–1886* (London: Macmillan. 1962) 413.

52 R. Barry O'Brien, *The Life of Charles Stewart Parnell* (New York: Harper and Brothers, 1898) 2:158.

53 *Hansard* 306 (1886), col. 681.

54 Ibid., col. 691.

55 Ibid., cols. 675–76.

56 Thomas John Dunne, "Ireland, England and Empire, 1868–1886: The Ideologies of British Political Leadership," Ph.D. diss., Cambridge University, 1975, p. 227.

57 *Hansard* 306 (1886), col. 698. Identical sentiments were voiced by other

Unionist leaders, including Sir Michael Hicks-Beach, *Hansard* 306 (1886), col. 1214.

58 Ibid., cols. 1214–15.

59 Indeed Chamberlain declared his willingness to vote, in principle, for home rule. Whether an actual bill could be devised to satisfy his insistence on the "real and effective" supremacy of the Imperial Parliament was a separate question. Ibid., cols. 677, 683.

60 Ibid., col. 1160.

61 Nicholas Mansergh, *The Irish Question, 1840–1921* (Toronto: University of Toronto Press, 1975) 160–61.

62 *Hansard* 304 (1886), col. 1242.

63 Ibid., col. 1263.

64 *Hansard* 305 (1886), col. 1764.

65 Ibid., col. 1761.

66 Ibid.

67 For example, the Ulster organization formed in 1886 to mobilize anti–home rule sentiment in Ireland and Britain called itself the Ulster Loyalist Anti-Repeal Union. D. C. Savage, "The Origins of the Ulster Unionist Party, 1885–86," *Irish Historical Studies* 7 (March 1961) 195. See also speeches by Hartington, *Hansard* 304 (1886), col. 1249; and Henry James, *Hansard* 305 (1886), col. 917. See also R. E. Quinault, "Lord Randolph Churchill and Home Rule," *Irish Historical Studies* 21 (September 1979) 377–403.

68 *Hansard* 306 (1886), cols. 684–85.

69 *Hansard* 304 (1886), col. 1257.

70 *Hansard* 306 (1886), col. 1158.

71 *Hansard* 304 (1886), cols. 1320–21.

72 For warnings of violent resistance to home rule and debate over that prospect see remarks by Protestant MPs from Ulster, including Edward MacNaghten, C. E. Lewis, and Colonel King-Harman, *Hansard* 305 (1886), cols. 677–78; and 306 (1886), cols. 536 and 1049–50. See also Savage, "Origins of the Ulster Unionist Party, 1885–86," 185–208. The final vote on the Home Rule Bill took place on June 8, 1886. On June 8, 9, and 10, Protestant rioting in Belfast left seven people dead and required army intervention before order could be restored. Savage, "Origins of the Ulster Unionist Party," 207.

73 See, for example, the remarks of Edward MacNaghten, representing the Protestant constituency of North Antrim in Ulster, in *Hansard* 306 (1886), cols. 553–54.

74 William Ewart Gladstone, *Special Aspects of the Irish Question* (London: John Murray, 1892) 12. See also p. 52.

75 *Times*, December 20, 1887.

76 Ibid.

4. WHERE AND WHAT IS FRANCE?

1 Preventing the French-Algerian relationship from becoming a subject of metropolitan political debate were: the security of France's hold over its overseas

possessions, Algeria's submergence within the French Empire as a whole in the consciousness of most French people, the domination of Algerian affairs by the colon population, and beliefs by French-educated Muslims that Algeria was rightfully a part of the French republic. On this last factor see Salah el-Din el-Zein el-Tayeb, "The Europeanized Algerians and the Emancipation of Algeria," *Middle Eastern Studies* 22 (April 1986) pp. 206–35.

2   As Miles Kahler has observed, "the empire in France was not constructed to bolster the position of a particular governing class or a political party; instead, it served to bolster a regime, the Third Republic." Miles Kahler, *Decolonization in Britain and France: The Domestic Consequences of International Politics* (Princeton: Princeton University Press, 1984) 81. See also Agnes Murphy, *The Ideology of French Imperialism, 1871–1881* (New York: Howard Fertig, 1968) 14–15 and 139–228; D. Bruce Marshall, *The French Colonial Myth and Constitution-Making in the Fourth Republic* (New Haven: Yale University Press, 1973) 12, 29, and chap. 2, "The Republican Consensus," 43–74; Paul Clay Sorum, *Intellectuals and Decolonization in France* (Chapel Hill: University of North Carolina Press, 1977) 205ff.; Jean-Claude Vatin, *L'Algérie politique histoire et société* (Paris: Presses de la Fondation Nationale des Sciences Politiques, 1983) 160.

3   Ernest Lavisse, *Histoire de France contemporaine* (Paris: Hachette, 1922) 9:539.

4   For the activities of the various colonial societies and the Parti Colonial, see Stuart Michael Persell, *The French Colonial Lobby, 1889–1938* (Stanford: Hoover Institution Press, 1983) 7–36; Carlton J. H. Hayes, *France: A Nation of Patriots* (New York: Columbia University Press, 1930) 216–25; and Christopher M. Andrew and A. S. Kanya-Forstner, *The Climax of French Imperial Expansion, 1914–1924* (Stanford: Stanford University Press, 1981) 9–32. Regarding the apathy and/ or hostility of public opinion toward the empire in the late nineteenth and early twentieth centuries see Herbert Ingram Priestly, *France Overseas: A Study of Modern Imperialism* (New York: Appleton-Century, 1938); and John Humphrey, "Nationalism and the Colonial Situation in Algeria under French Rule: 1830–1962," Ph.D. diss., Department of Politics, York University, 1976. For general discussion of the traditional lack of popular French enthusiasm for their empire see Ellen Hammer, "The French Empire Today," in *Modern France,* ed. Edward Mead (New York: Russell and Russell, 1964) 455; and Jean-Baptiste Duroselle's argument concerning "introversion" as the dominant characteristic of French political culture "Changes in French Foreign Policy since 1945," in *In Search of France,* ed. Stanley Hoffmann et al. (New York: Harper Torchbooks, 1963) 305–58.

5   Georges Spillmann, *De l'empire a l'hexagone* (Paris: Librairie Académique Perrin, 1981) 173.

6   Raoul Girardet, "L'apothéose de la 'plus grande France': L'idée coloniale devant l'opinion française (1930–1935)," *Revue Française de Science Politique* 28 (December 1968) 1086–87.

7   Patrick McCarthy, *Camus* (New York: Random House, 1982) 66–69; Dorthea Gallup, "The French Image of Algeria: Its Origin, Its Place in Colonial Ideology, Its Effect on Algerian Acculturation," Ph.D. diss., Department of History, Uni-

versity of California, Los Angeles, 1973, 312–29. See Girardet, "L'apothéose de la "plus grande france," 1091–92; Sheila Collingwood-Whittick, "The Colonial Situation in Algeria and Its Literary Reflection," Ph.D. diss., Birkbeck College, University of London, 1980, 17–36.

8 Manuela Semidei, "De l'empire a la décolonisation a travers les manuels scolaires," *Revue Française de Science Politique* 16 (February 1966) 56–71; Semidei's findings are supported by Ageron's analysis of intensive educational and propaganda efforts on behalf of French colonialism in the interwar period. See Charles Robert Ageron, *France coloniale ou parti colonial* (Paris: PUF, 1978) 250–59.

9 Girardet, "L'apothéose de la "plus grande france," 1085–86.

10 Ibid., 1089. Concerning France's imperial strategy of *mise en valeur* see Albert Sarraut, *Mise en valeur des colonies françaises* (Paris: Payot, 1923).

11 Girardet, "L'apothéose de la "plus grande France,' " 1095. See also Ageron, *France colonial ou parti colonial,* 259–60.

12 L. Gray Cowan, "The New Face of Algeria," *Political Science Quarterly* 66 (September 1951) 358. See also Girardet, "L'apothéose de la "plus grande France,' " 1098–99 and 1107–10; and Albert Sarraut, *Grandeur et servitude coloniales* (Paris: Editions Sagittaire, 1931).

13 Louis Milliot, *Le gouvernement de l'Algérie* (Paris: Comité National Metropolitain du Centenaire de l'Algérie; Cahiers du Centenaire de l'Algérie, 1930) 6–7 and 10; see also Jacques Berque, *French North Africa: The Maghrib between Two World Wars* (New York: Praeger, 1967) 222–24.

14 Georges Weill, "Les républicans français et l'Algérie," *Revue de l'Histoire des Colonies* 24 (1931) 292. The image, consistent with the Pirenne thesis, is of Europe displaced from the Mediterranean by the power of medieval Islam. See also Milliot, *Le gouvernement de l'Algérie,* 48 (conclusion). For spectacular characterizations of France's contribution to Algerian development and Algeria's role in demonstrating and revivifying France's Roman legacy, see Georges Rozet, *Algeria* (Paris: Algeria Centenary Publications, Horizons de France, 1929). The dedication of this beautifully composed volume of photographs and narrative description is a succinct but comprehensive statement of the French view of their imperial mission in North Africa. "To the Memory of those French soldiers who, one hundred years ago, freed Algeria from the yoke of Barbary, then restored it to its true destiny by inaugurating therein 'French Peace,' to the memory of those colonists who died at their task, to all those determined workers who, with the loyal collaboration of the natives, contribute to the work of human civilization and add to the national greatness. To all young Frenchmen for whom it is a duty to get to know new France and to hear its call, this book is dedicated, on the occasion of the Centenary of Algeria."

15 A. Demaison, *Exposition coloniale internationale: Guide officiel* (Paris, 1931) 17.

16 Girardet, "L'apothéose de la 'plus grande France,' " 1093.

17 *Keesing's Contemporary Archives* (1931) 1:99. The quotation is from Girardet, "L'apothéose de la 'plus grande France,' " 1092; see also 1112–13. For a similar judgment about the success of colonialist propaganda in changing French attitudes toward the empire in the early 1930s see Jacques Marseille, *Empire*

colonial et capitalisme français: Histoire d'un divorce (Paris: Albin Michel, 1984) 371. For amplifications of the intended message to the French themselves of both the Algerian Centenary and the Colonial Exhibition see Gabriel Hanotaux (G.H.), "Introduction a la vie coloniale: Colons," *Le Temps* (colonial supplement), October 7, 1930; Maurice Reclus, "The Imperial State," *Le Temps* (colonial supplement), October 14, 1930; Paul Strauss, "Jules Ferry et Léon Gambetta," *Le Temps,* May 26, 1931, p. 3.

18   Pierre Henry, "L'opinion publique française et le problème colonial," *Sondages,* 3 August 1939, quoted in Girardet, "L'apothéose de la 'plus grande France,' " 1112–13. Demographic analysis of the results suggest that respondents having the strongest attachment to overseas France were those under thirty and over sixty, that is, those whose education had included the new emphasis on greater France or those whose formative years included experience of World War I.

19   These included a project to establish Maison de la France d'Outre-Mer, for regular conferences of colonial officials, the organization in 1934 of an Interministerial Committee on Muslim Affairs, an attempt, also in 1934, to set up a prestigious Ministry of Overseas France, with an undersecretary for North Africa, and creation in 1935 of a High Mediterranean Committee, responsible directly to the president. Robert Montagne, "Comment organiser politiquement l'empire français," *Politique Etrangère* 33 (1938–39) 156–57, 160, and 181. Montagne later served as director of the Centre des Hautes Études d'Administration Musulmane. For a similar evocation of the imperatives which ought to have been governing French policy toward its empire in the late 1930s see Georges Hardy, *Histoire de la colonisation française* (Paris: Larose, 1938) 156.

20   Marshall, *The French Colonial Myth,* 74 and 14. See also Tony Smith, *The French Stake in Algeria: 1945–1962* (Ithaca, N. Y.: Cornell University Press, 1978).

21   Girardet "L'apothéose de la 'plus grande France,' " 1104–7.

22   Marshall, *The French Colonial Myth,* 70.

23   Xavier Yacono, *Les étapes de la décolonisation française* (Paris: Presses Universitaires de France, 1971) 48.

24   On the difference of perspective between Vichy and the Free French regarding the role of the empire see Marshall, *The French Colonial Myth,* 75–80. See also *The Complete War Memoirs of Charles de Gaulle* (New York: Simon and Schuster, 1972) 53–141. Concerning wartime planning for the empire by both the Free French and Vichy see, for the Free French, Jacques Chaban-Delmas, *Brazzaville: Conférence africaine française,* République Française (Paris: Ministere des Colonies, 1945); and for Vichy, René Maunier, *L'empire français: Propos et projects* (Paris: Librairie du Recueil Sirey, 1943); and Ageron, *France coloniale ou parti colonial?* 269–82.

25   Concerning the impact of June 1940 and its catastrophic aftermath on French attitudes toward the idea of decolonization see Duroselle, "Changes in French Foreign Policy since 1945," 341.

26   Concerning the extent of North African participation in the French war effort between 1939 and 1945 see Spillmann, *De l'empire a l'hexagone,* 192–206.

27   Hammer, "The French Empire Today," 467. Hammer's essay was written in 1950.

28 *Le Temps,* May 31, 1931, quoted in Girardet, "L'apothéose de la 'plus grande France,' " 1094.

29 De Gaulle radio broadcasts from London, January 18, 1942, and March 18, 1943, in Charles de Gaulle, *Discours et messages, 1940–1946* (Paris: Editions Berger-Levrault, 1946) 180 and 296. See also Georges Bidault, *Resistance: The Political Autobiography of Georges Bidault* (New York: Praeger, 1967) 283.

30 Sorum, *Intellectuals and Decolonization in France,* 30.

31 For an excellent discussion of this rivalry see Charles-Robert Ageron, *Histoire algérie contemporaine, 1830–1979* (Paris: Presses Universitaire de France, 1964) 89–90.

32 Quoted in Marshall, *The French Colonial Myth,* 93.

33 See, for example, ibid., 195; and Gordon Wright, *The Reshaping of French Democracy* (New York: Reynal and Hitchcock, 1948) 144.

34 Smith, *The French Stake in Algeria,* 53.

35 Quoted in Roger Quilliot, *La SFIO et l'exercice du pouvoir: 1944–1958* (Paris: Fayard, 1972) 148. Regarding demographic fears and the importance of the image of "France of 100 million," see also Wright, *The Reshaping of French Democracy,* 144.

36 Chaban-Delmas, *Brazzaville,* 77.

37 Ibid.

38 Wright, *The Reshaping of French Democracy,* 145.

39 *Brazzaville,* 75.

40 Sorum, *Intellectuals and Decolonization in France,* 16.

41 Quoted in Marshall, *The French Colonial Myth,* 205.

42 Quoted by Pascal Muselli from Tixier speech in Algiers, June 29, 1945. *Journal officiel, Assemblée Consultative Provisoire* (hereafter *JO, ACP*), July 10, 1945, p. 1355. For similar sentiments see R. Pierron, "Retour d'Algérie: The Situation Remains Serious—Part I," *Le Monde,* July 8, 1945; idem, "Retour d'Algérie: The Franco-Muslim Problem—Part II," *Le Monde,* July 10, 1945; Jacques Driand, "The North African Crisis: The French Malaise," *Le Monde,* May 18, 1945; idem, "The North African Crisis: Europeans and Natives," *Le Monde,* May 24, 1945. See also Manfred Halpern, "The Algerian Uprising of 1945," *Middle East Journal* 2 (April 1948) 191–202.

43 *JO, ACP,* July 10, 1945, pp. 1344–1417. Instructively the leading Algerian Muslim participant in this discussion—José Aboulker—condemned both Messali Hadj, leader of the most militant wing of the Algerian nationalist movement, and the colons as "separatist" in their contention that "Algiers is not Paris." See ibid. 1352.

44 In their gratitude for colonial loyalty during the war and their enthusiasm for making the empire a basis for France's leading role in the world, the founders of the Fourth Republic created a myth of the Brazzaville Conference which focused primarily on the expansive and generous elements in the conference's recommendations. What had been essentially a small conclave of French colonial officials anxious to protect their fiefdoms and committed above all to the "unbreakable political unity of the French world" was transformed into a visionary event, expressive of the genius of France in devising a totally new kind of "federalist" technique for resolving colonial relationships.

45   Robert Delavignette, "L'Union française," *Esprit*, July 1945, 229.

46   Ibid., 230, emphasis in original.

47   Ibid., 214.

48   Ibid., 223. The need for the French to make semantic changes conforming to new political and empathic "realities" is a common theme among French writers on the topic in this period. See E. De Curton, "The Colonies and the Constitution—Part I," *Le Monde*, July 11, 1945, and Jean de la Roche and Jean Gottmann, *La federation française* (Montreal: Editions de l'Arbre, 1945) 563–65.

49   De la Roche and Gottmann, *La federation française,* 233–34.

50   See Sorum, *Intellectuals and Decolonization in France,* 184–95. For a detailed exposition of this vision of France's vocation see de la Roche and Gottmann, *La federation française.* This volume includes an essay by Félix Eboué, a native of French Guiana who rallied early to the Gaullist cause during the war and served as governor-general of French Equatorial Africa. For examples of similar thinking from across the political spectrum see Edouard Depreux (Socialist), quoted in Marshall, *The French Colonial Myth,* 264; Marc Rucart (Communist), *JO, ACP,* July 1945, p. 1379; André Mercier (Communist) quoted in Marseille, *Empire colonial et capitalisme francais,* 371; Marcel Poimboeuf (MRP), *JO, ACP,* July 1945, p. 1417; General Jacques-Philippe Leclerc (Gaullist), quoted in "Preface" in Emile Dehon, *Une nouvelle politique colonial de France* (Paris: Flammarion, 1945); Auguste Rencurel (Algerian settler and Radical party member), *JO, ACP,* July 1945, pp. 1363–67; Joseph Costa, *JO, ACP,* July 1945, p. 1377; Pierre Cot (Radical-Indépendant), quoted in Sorum, *Intellectuals and Decolonization in France,* 30. Concerning French Communist commitments to the French Union and the PCF's opposition to colonial independence in Africa after World War II see David Caute, *Communism and the French Intellectuals: 1914–1960* (New York: Macmillan, 1964) 208–9; and Jean-Marie Domenach's comments, quoted in Sorum, *Intellectuals and Decolonization in France,* 23.

51   De Gaulle, *Discours et messages,* 454.

52   Ibid., 503. See also P. O. Lapie, "The New Colonial Policy of France," *Foreign Affairs* 23 (1944) 104–11.

53   De la Roche and Gottmann, *La federation française,* 563, 16ff., and 559.

54   Ibid., 19 and 22.

55   Ibid., 24.

56   See *Le Monde*'s response to the Allies, conference at Hot Springs, Va., in January 1945 which called for international supervision of previous colonies. *Le Monde,* January 21–22, 1945; and Sorum, *Intellectuals and Decolonization in France,* 31; de la Roche and Gottmann, *La federation francaise,* 575; and Spillmann, *De l'empire a l'hexagone,* 251 and 255–56. For accusations that Allied propaganda during and after the occupation of Algeria was responsible for the Sétif disturbances see remarks by Pascal Muselli, *JO, ACP,* July 10, 1945, pp. 1355–56, and Auguste Rencurel, ibid., p. 1365.

57   Marshall, *The French Colonial Myth,* 4, also 13.

58   Socialist leader Felix Gouin, prime minister of the provisional government from January to June 1946, quoted ibid., 114.

59   Of the sixty-four delegates elected to the first Constituent Assembly from overseas France, twenty-three were noncitizen natives.

60   De Curton, "The Colonies and the Constitution," pts. 1 and 2, *Le Monde,*
July 11, 1945, and July 14, 1945. Quotations are from part 1. Emphasis in original.
61   *Journal officiel, Assemblée Nationale Constituante élue le 21 octobre 1945*
(hereafter *JO, ANC-1*), March 23, 1946, p. 1033.
62   Wright, *The Reshaping of French Democracy,* 40, 142.
63   Sorum, *Intellectuals and Decolonization in France,* 45.
64   Quilliot, *La SFIO et l'exercice du pouvoir,* 146.
65   Ibid., 147.
66   Ibid.
67   The law, which remained in force even after the defeat of the draft constitution
in the April referendum, left open the question of how implementing legislation
in each overseas territory or department would "give effect" to the political equality
implicit in this new Lex Caracalla.
68   Wright, *The Reshaping of French Democracy,* 201. For details see Marshall,
The French Colonial Myth, 229; and Rudolf von Albertini, *Decolonization: The
Administration and Future of the Colonies* (New York: Africana Publishing, 1982)
387. Only eight of seventy-five meetings of the first Constituent Assembly dealt
with the French Union, compared to fully one-third of the second Constituent
Assembly meetings. Quilliot, *La SFIO et l'exercice du pouvoir,* 152.
69   Albertini, *Decolonization,* 389.
70   *Journal officiel, Assemblée Nationale Constituante élue le 2 juin 1946* (hereafter *JO, ANC-2*), August 27, 1946, p. 3334.
71   Wright, *The Reshaping of French Democracy,* 198 and 208.
72   Ibid., 208.
73   Marshall, *The French Colonial Myth,* 309, his translation.
74   Sorum, *Intellectuals and Decolonization in France,* 37; Marshall, *The French
Colonial Myth,* 310.
75   Marshall, *The French Colonial Myth,* 286.
76   René Maunier, *L'empire français: Propos et projects* (Paris: Librairie du Recueil Sirey, 1943) 24, 58–59, 69, and 138. For a list of similar books published
under the Vichy regime and relevant portions of the Vichy draft constitution see
Ageron, *France colonial ou parti colonial,* 272.
77   Yacono, *Les etapes de la décolonisation française,* 62–63.
78   *Brazzaville,* recommendations adopted by the Brazzaville conference, pt. 1,
sect. A.
79   Ibid., 75. Concerning the Roman, indeed "Constantinian," outlook of the
men of Brazzaville see Yacono, *Les etapes de la décolonisation française,* 57.
80   *Brazzaville,* 74.
81   Marshall, *The French Colonial Myth,* 295.
82   From official summaries of party positions on the October referendum as
printed on a pre-referendum poster.
83   For examples of such maps see *Atlas du Bottin* (Paris: Annuaire du Commerce,
1947); *Atlas du XXe siècle* (Paris: Fernand Nathan, c. 1948); and *Atlas historique
and géographique Vidal-Lablache* (Paris: Armand Colin, 1951). For discussion of
these mapmakers' failure to include Algeria within maps of "France," as opposed
to maps of the "French Union," see note 110.
84   Raoul Girardet, *L'idee coloniale en France: 1871–1962* (Paris: Table Ronde,

1972) 194–95 and 320n. See also Quilliot, *La SFIO et l'exercice du pouvoir,* 149–50.

85   Article 80 of the Fourth Republic Constitution.

86   François Borella, *L'évolution politique et juridique de l'Union française depuis 1946* (Paris: R. Pichon et R. Durand-Auzias, 1958) 159. This volume also lists the changes in Algeria's status incorporated within various pieces of legislation advanced between October 1946 and March 1947.

87   Such tolerance did not extend to explicit calls for Algerian independence. When at least one Muslim deputy implied the simple possibility of Algerian independence by mentioning separation from France as a conceivable occurrence— admitting that many Muslims would find such a rupture painful—he sparked an outraged response to the effect that under no circumstances could it be construed that the Assembly was considering the actual separation of Algeria from France. *Journal officiel, Débats parlementaires* (hereafter *JO*), August 10, 1947, p. 4196.

88   *JO,* August 10, 1947, p. 4202. Before final passage of the statute, Rabier resigned as rapporteur for the bill in protest against amendments made on the floor of the Assembly that reduced Muslim influence in the Algerian Assembly.

89   Ibid., 4196.

90   *JO,* August 19, 1947, pp. 4428–29.

91   Comment by Charles Serre, *JO,* August 10, 1947, p. 4223.

92   Communique issued August 18, 1947, quoted in de Gaulle, *Discours et messages,* 107.

93   *JO,* August 10, 1947, p. 4190.

94   Comments by Daniel Boisdon, *JO,* August 10, 1947, p. 4196. For a detailed lawyerly critique of the statute as contrary to the constitution, see the remarks of the MRP deputy Paul Viard, dean of the Faculty of Law at the University of Algiers, *JO,* August 19, 1947, pp. 4511–16.

95   *JO,* August 10, 1947, p. 4196.

96   Article 1, Organic Statue of Algeria, Law No. 47–1853, September 20, 1947.

97   See Quilliot, *La SFIO et l'exercice du pouvoir,* 266–68; Dorothy Pickles, *Algeria and France* (New York: Praeger, 1963) 30.

98   Manfred Halpern, "Recent Books on Moslem-French Relations in Algeria," *Middle East Journal* 3 (April 1949) 212–13; Vatin, *L'Algérie politique histoire et société,* 243–47.

99   See Michel Deveze, *La France d'outre-mer: De l'empire colonial a l'union française, 1938–1947* (Paris: Hachette, 1948) 318.

100   Quilliot, *La SFIO et l'exercice du pouvoir,* 441.

101   See, for example, contributions to a special issue of *Esprit,* edited by Jean-Marie Domenach, titled "Last Chances for the French Union," *Esprit,* July 1949; and Charles-André Julien, "From the French Empire to the French Union," *International Affairs* 26 (October 1950) 502.

102   Wright, *The Reshaping of French Democracy,* 148.

103   Borella, *L'évolution politique et juridique de l'Union française,* 447.

104   Concerning French expectations that the processes set in motion by the loi cadre would indeed lead to independence see Quilliot, *La SFIO et l'exercice du pouvoir,* 592–603; and Yves Person, "French West Africa and Decolonization,"

in *The Transfer of Power in Africa: Decolonization, 1940–1960,* ed. Prosser Gifford and Wm. Roger Louis (New Haven: Yale University Press, 1982), esp. 162.

105 Alfred Grosser, *Affaires extérierures: La politique de la France, 1944–1984* (Paris: Flammarion, 1984) 130.

106 See Foreign Minister Robert Schuman's address to the United Nations General Assembly (UNGA), 7th sess., November 10, 1952, A/PV. 392, pp. 193–200.

107 Remarks of M. Alphand, UN General Committee, 10th sess., September 22, 1955, A/Bur/SR.103, p. 7.

108 Concerning the difficulty of categorizing Algeria's historical relationship to France—labeling it "anomalous," "hybrid," or "unique"—see Priestly, *France Overseas,* 119–59; Duroselle, "Changes in French Foreign Policy since 1945," 340; Halpern, "Recent Books on Moslem France Relations in Algeria," 211; Marshall, *The French Colonial Myth* p. 70; and Robert Deemer Lee, "Regional Politics in a Unitary System: Colonial Algeria, 1920–1954," Ph.D. diss., Columbia University, 1972, p. 7.

109 See Ernest Lavisse, *Histoire de France* (Paris: Armand Colin, 1933) 318–22; idem, *Histoire de France: Course elementaire* (Boston: D. C. Heath, 1919) 181–84; and Albert Malet, *L'epoque contemporaine* (Paris: Hachette, 1920) 1 and 563–85; Raoul Blanchard and D. Faucher, *Cours de géographie: La France et ses colonies* (Paris: Gedalge, c. 1931) 49–51 and 59.

110 For examples of maps labeled "France" which omit Algeria (and it is difficult to find maps so labeled which include Algeria), see *Atlas departemental Larousse* (October 1914); Jean Moles, "Map of 'France' " Ministry of Public Works and Transport, Bureau of Tourism, Paris, 1947; M. Michel-Levy, "Geological Map of France," Ministry of Public Works, Paris, 1933; *Administrative Division of France, 1943* (Washington, D.C.: Office of Strategic Services, 1944); *Administrative Division of France, 1947* (Washington, D.C.: Department of State, Map Division, 1947); *Atlas du Bottin* (Paris: Annuaire du Commerce, 1947); and *Atlas historique and géographique Vidal-Lablache* (Paris: Armand Colin, 1951). Several of these atlases also contain maps of the French Union or of Africa which depict Algeria submerged within the category of the French Union, though sometimes its status as a collection of departments is noted. In this regard see especially P. Pollacchi, *Atlas colonial français: Colonies protectorates, et pays sous mandat* (1929); and idem, *Atlas du XXe siècle* (Paris: Fernand Nathan, c. 1948).

111 Louis François and Robert Mangin, *La France et son empire* (Paris: Hachette, 1942). See also pp. 6, 290, 311–13, and 472–73.

112 M. M. Knight, "French Colonial Policy: The Decline of 'Association,' " *Journal of Modern History* 5 (June 1933) 222

113 Delavignette, "L'Union française," 220n.

114 Marshall, *The French Colonial Myth,* 140.

115 See L. Gray Cowan, "The New Face of Algeria, Part II," *Political Science Quarterly* 66 (December 1951) 521–22 and 531. Article 6 of the NATO treaty, signed in 1949, stipulates that "an armed attack on one or more of the Parties is deemed to include an armed attack on the territory of any of the Parties in Europe or North America, [or] on the Algerian Departments of France."

116   Charles-Robert Ageron, "L'opinion française devant la guerre d'Algérie," *Revue Française d'Histoire d'Outre-Mer* 63 (1976) 259.

117   Such ideas were dismissed in short order as liable to turn control of "metropolitan affairs" over to "non-metropolitans" or were considered camouflage for creating a political base for separatist ambitions. See Robert Montagne, "Evolution in Algeria," *International Affairs* 22 (January 1947) 47.

118   *JO*, August 10, 1947, p. 4223. Among the phrases used by colon deputies to describe Algeria were "an integral part of France," "a French province of the same type as Burgundy, Flanders, Brittany, Comte..., or Savoy," "a prolongation of the fatherland," "our Mediterranean province," and "a prolongation of the metropole." These designations were supported by assertions of cultural, ecological, historical, and ethnic affinities that spanned the Mediterranean, explaining the inevitability and naturalness of Algeria's integration into France. See, for example, remarks by Auguste Rencurel, *JO, ANC-2*, August 22, 1946, p. 3229.

119   These were among the characterizations used by many members of the Provisional Consultative Assembly during discussions held in July 1945 of Algeria and the Sétif uprising. See comments in *JO, ACP* by Marc Rucart, July 11, 1945, pp. 1379–80; Auguste Rencurel, July 10, 1945, p. 1363; Adrien Tixier, July 18, 1945, p. 1409; and Jean-Pierre Bloch, July 10, 1945, p. 1346. Because of the prominence of West African soldiers and German mercenaries among the French forces in Indochina, fewer than 10 percent of the casualties on the French side during the Indochina war were metropolitan Frenchmen. See Alan C. Lamborn, "Domestic Politics, Risk, and French Colonialism," paper presented at the 1990 Annual Meeting of the American Political Science Association, San Francisco, p. 12.

120   Quoted in Quilliot, *La SFIO et l'exercice du pouvoir*, 612.

121   *Le Monde*, November 6, 1954, quoted in Albertini, *Decolonization*, 458; Quilliot, *La SFIO et l'exercice du pouvoir*, 606. In February 1955, Mitterrand, describing the essence of the Mendès-France government's stance toward Algeria, told the National Assembly that "l'Algérie, c'est la France!" had been the "very dogma of our policy." Catherine Nay, *The Black and the Red: François Mitterrand—the Story of an Ambition* (San Diego: Harcourt Brace Jovanovich, 1987) 188–89.

122   Translated in Alistair Horne, *Savage War of Peace: Algeria, 1954–1962* (New York: Penguin, 1979) 98. For judgments that the government's rhetoric in response to the outbreak of the rebellion mirrored widespread or near-universal attitudes in France at the time see ibid., 99; Wilifred Knapp, *A History of War and Peace: 1939–1965* (London: Oxford University Press, 1967) 451; and Quilliot, *La SFIO et l'exercice du pouvoir*, 612.

123   Jacques Soustelle, inaugural speech to the Algerian Assembly, February 23, 1955, reprinted as Appendix I in *Aimee et souffrante Algérie* (Paris: Plon, 1956) 264–65.

124   Alexander Werth, *The Strange History of Pierre Mendès-France and the Great Conflict over French North Africa* (London: Barrie Books, 1957) 279.

125   Soustelle, *Aimee et souffrante Algérie*, 207.

126   Prime Minister Edgar Faure, from a radio broadcast of September 25, 1955, quoted in Alfred Grosser, *Affairs extérieures: La politique de la France, 1944–1984* (Paris: Flammarion, 1984) 131. Between Soustelle and Faure's interior min-

ister—Bourgès-Maunoury—there were no disagreements whatsoever, "neither in basic conceptions, nor in the details of everyday activity." Soustelle, *Aimee et souffrante Algérie,* 10.

127 *JO,* March 9, 1956. Translated by Elizabeth Hobgood Murphrey, "Jacques Soustelle and the Passing of French Algeria," Ph.D. diss., Duke University, Department of History, 1976, p. 132.

128 UNGA, 11th sess. First Committee, February 4, 1957, A/C.1/SR.830, p. 99.

129 *New York Times,* February 5, 1957, as quoted in Edgar S. Furniss, Jr., *France: Troubled Ally* (New York: Council on Foreign Relations, 1960) 198.

130 UNGA, 11th sess. First Committee, February 4, 1957, A/C.1/SR.830, pp. 99–100; A/C.1/SR.831, p. 108; and February 6, 1957, A/C.1/SR.835, pp. 133–35.

131 Embassy of France, Press and Information Service, "France Overseas" New York, 1956. Instructively, the term "French Union" does not appear on the map. France's island possessions in the Carribean, also organized as overseas departments, are presented as black dots, but Algeria is pointedly listed separately as a category parallel to "overseas departments." This cartographic expression of a shift in hegemonic project from the French Union to French Algeria is apparent as early as 1953 in a similar map published in Hubert Deschamps *Les méthodes et les doctrines coloniales de la France* (Paris: Armand Colin, 1953) 201.

132 In 1955 the United Nations delegates of many states, including the United States, Britain, the Netherlands, Norway, New Zealand, and Belgium, expressed support for the French position that Algeria was a part of France. By 1957 the United States had retreated from official endorsement of the French view, though the United States opposed including of the Algerian question on the UN agenda and carefully avoided criticizing the French position.

133 Albertini, *Decolonization,* 465.

134 According to Tony Smith, "the central factor holding France in North Africa" and preventing the disposition of Algeria from being considered as "an end to be weighed against the means to secure it or against other ends" was a particular "image or perception the French political elite had of their nation and the place of Algeria in relation to its future." Smith, *The French State in Algeria,* 27, 172, and 176. Until 1956, according to Dorothy Pickles, "the only point on which virtually the whole of France was united was that Algerian independence was unthinkable and unmentionable." Pickles, *Algeria and France,* 9. "Algeria really is," argued a noted Swiss scholar in 1955, "a natural continuation of France beyond the Mediterranean, and really is a French creation. Even the name of 'Algeria' was first given to this sterile, nameless, and history-less country by the French." Herbert Luethy, *France against Herself* (New York: Praeger, 1955) 236. The French government was delighted with Luethy's analysis. See "Algeria Is a French Creation," *France Actuelle* 5, July 15, 1956, pp. 4–5. See also Edward Behr, "The Algerian Dilemma," *International Affairs* 34 (July 1958) 280.

135 Remarks by the rapporteur for the bill, Jacques Genton, *JO,* March 30, 1955, p. 2130.

136 *JO,* March 31, 1955, p. 2171. The amendment was defeated by a vote of 585 to 4.

137 In 1984 the Museum of the Army in Paris featured exhibits on every one

of France's "wars" (including Bugeaud's conquest of Algeria in the 1830s and the Indochina War) except the conflict in Algeria from 1954 to 1962.

138 Martin Harrison, "Government and Press in France during the Algerian War," *American Political Science Review* 58 (June 1964) 276.

139 Ibid., 274 and 277.

140 Quoted in William G. Andrews, *French Politics and Algeria* (New York: Appleton-Century-Crofts, 1962) 155 (emphasis added).

141 UNGA, 11th sess., First Committee, February 4, 1957, A/C.1/SR.830, p. 99; A/C.1/SR.831, pp. 105 and 107 (emphasis added).

142 UNGA, 11th sess., First Committee, February 6, 1957, A/C.1/SR.835, p. 134 (emphasis added). For similar syntactical patterns in Soustelle's presentations to French audiences see, for example, his discussion of Algeria's crucial economic importance "to France," the responsibilities of "the French of France" to Algeria, and the "contributions of the Metropole" to the betterment of native living conditions in Algeria. Jacques Soustelle, *Le drame algérien et la décadence française* (Paris: Plon, 1957) 30–34 and the text of an address on Radio Algiers, January 26, 1956, quoted in Soustelle, *Aimee et souffrante algérie*, 277.

143 See Embassy of France, Press and Information Service, "Basic Facts on Algeria," *French Affairs*, no. 24 (November 1955); and idem, "A New Agrarian Policy in Algeria: The Soustelle Plan," *French Affairs*, no. 26 (November 1955).

144 *Les Temps Modernes* 11 (October 1955) 577–78.

145 Raymond Aron, *La tragédie algérienne* (Paris: Plon, 1957) 4–5. Though published in this edition in 1957, the first half of the book from which this and subsequent quotations were taken first appeared in April 1956.

146 Ibid., 32.

147 Jacques Soustelle, *Le drame algérien et la décadence française: Response a Raymond Aron* (Paris: Plon, 1957) 22.

148 Ibid., 21.

149 Ibid., 28–33.

150 Ibid., 24.

151 For convenient summaries of the questions asked in these polls and responses to them see Andrews, *French Politics and Algeria*, 17–22; and Ageron, "L'opinion française devant la guerre d'Algérie," 256–85. These polls were originally published in various issues of *Sondages*. In September 1957 the pollsters changed the question of how long Algeria would remain French, rewording it to read "ten years" instead of "five years."

152 Ageron, "L'opinion française devant la guerre d'Algérie," 265.

153 Ageron observes that it took approximately eighteen months of war in Indochina before polls showed a majority of the French willing to negotiate with the Viet Minh, and two and a half years of war before 49 percent thought Indochina should be independent. Within twenty-one months of war in Algeria, a majority of French registered their willingness to negotiate with the FLN, but it took, Ageron stresses, almost five years before 55 percent of the French came to favor Algerian independence. Ageron concludes that French opinion on the war became increasingly divided in the mid–1950s, but taking into account the "guidance" which events in Indochina, Tunisia, and Morocco could be expected to have given to public opinion on Algeria, he is struck by the relative lag in French responses to

the Algerian War. Ageron explains this lag by the cognitive resistance of the French public toward treating Algeria according to Cartiérist principles of political or economic expediency. Ageron, "L'opinion française devant la guerre d'Algérie," 283–84. The author of Cartiérisme, Jacques Cartiér, editor of *Paris-Match,* was himself unwilling to apply his principles of economic expediency to Algeria.

154 See figure A–3 in the Appendix where points E (Union of free consent), F (Union of tutelary subordination), and G (Algérie française) represent the variable success of these hegemonic projects and the changing location of the Algerian problem in French politics during this period. Point H represents the location of the Algerian problem at the end of the Fourth Republic and the beginning of the Fifth Republic.

5. PATTERNS OF HEGEMONIC CHANGE

1 Gramsci used these military metaphors mainly to explain why the Russian Revolution, characterized by a short, sharp seizure of power, had not been and would not be repeated in the industrial states of Europe and America. In these countries authority structures were well institutionalized and elaborately legitimized by an ideologically and culturally integrated civil society. Before state power itself could be seized, the state would have to be successfully confronted on the ideological plane and deprived of its hegemonic resources. See Joseph V. Femia, *Gramsci's Political Thought: Hegemony, Consciousness, and the Revolutionary Process* (Oxford: Clarendon Press, 1987) 50–55 and 205–9.

I use Gramsci's metaphors and concepts but move from his predominant emphasis on a revolutionary process conceived as devoted to the transformation of an entire political system to a focus on struggles over one particular constituitive (and constituted) element of the state—its territorial shape. For a systematic argument for why and how Gramsci's concept of hegemony is applicable to discrete dimensions of political life, rather than necessarily centered in a comprehensive, class-based formula for apprehending social reality, see Ernesto Laclau and Chantal Mouffe, *Hegemony and Socialist Strategy: Towards a Radical Democratic Politics* (London: Verso, 1985) 69, 86–87, and 136–44.

2 Antonio Gramsci, "The Modern Prince," in *The Modern Prince and Other Writings,* ed. Louis Marks (New York: International Publishers, 1957) 169 and 184.

3 Ibid., 166 and 174ff.

4 Ibid., 154–55. For a fascinating attempt to establish the extent of "exploitation" which can, or cannot, be contained by hegemonic conceptions, see Adam Przeworski, "Material Bases of Consent: Economics and Politics in a Hegemonic System," in *Political Power and Social Theory: A Research Annual,* ed. Maurice Zeitlin (Greenwich, Conn.: JAI Press, 1980) 1:21–65.

5 For a similar characterization of Gramsci on this point, applied to the development of an Irish nationalist counterhegemonic project, see David Cairns and Shaun Richards, *Writing Ireland: Colonialism, Nationalism and Culture* (Manchester: Manchester University Press, 1988) esp. 13–21.

6 Gramsci, *The Modern Prince,* 147 and 183.

7 In this they show their understanding of Gramsci's primary dictum: "Whatever one does, one always plays somebody's game, the important thing is to seek in every way to play one's own game, i.e. to win completely." Ibid., 152.

8 The proportion of space alloted by the *Times* to Irish affairs is a useful measure of the attention given Ireland by the British political class because the newspaper was, by far, the most popular daily among British elites, and also because it tended to downplay news pertaining to Ireland. Proportions depicted equal the percentage of column inches devoted to Ireland and Irish affairs in *Palmer's Index to the Times Newspaper*.

9 John Stuart Mill, *John Stuart Mill on Ireland*, ed. Richard Ned Lebow (Philadelphia: Institute for the Study of Human Issues, 1979) 3 and 6. See also Lebow's introductory essay in this volume, "J. S. Mill and the Irish Land Question," 13. For other contemporary observers sympathetic to Ireland who characterized Fenian terrorism as crucial to the eventual realization of Irish rights see Anthony Trollope, *Phineas Finn* (London: Penguin, 1972; first published 1869) 703–4; and Karl Marx, as quoted in John Newsinger, " 'A great blow must be struck in Ireland': Karl Marx and the Fenians," *Race and Class* 24 (1982) 159. On the role of Fenian violence in obtaining "a hearing for moderation" in Britain see F. S. L. Lyons, *Ireland since the Famine* (London: Fontana, 1973) 141–42.

10 *London Quarterly Review* 124 (January–April 1868) American ed., pp. 134 and 137. David Thornley's judgment on the matter is in accord with most specialists on British-Irish history: "The eruption of the fenian conspiracy shattered the complacent illusions of both islands... [giving] striking demonstration... of the impermanence of the Irish settlement and of her unplacated grievances." David Thornley, *Isaac Butt and Home Rule* (London: Macgibbon and Kee, 1964) 14. See also D. G. Boyce, *The Irish Question and British Politics, 1868–1986* (London: Macmillan Education, 1988) 6; Thomas John Dunne, "Ireland, England and Empire, 1868–1886: The Ideologies of British Political Leadership," Ph.D. diss. Cambridge University, 1975, p. 48; Robert Blake, *The Conservative Party from Peel to Churchill* (London: Eyre and Spottiswoode, 1970) 10; and T. W. Moody, "The New Departure in Irish Politics, 1878–79," in *Essays in British and Irish History*, ed. H. A. Cronne et al. (London: Frederick Muller, 1949) 308.

11 Quoted in *London Quarterly Review* 124 (January–April 1868) American ed. p. 147.

12 *Hansard*, May 31, 1869, quoted in John Morley, *Life of Gladstone* (New York: Macmillan, 1905) 1:875–76 (emphasis added).

13 Using the land issue as "the engine that would pull the train of self-government to its destination" was just what James Fintan Lalor, thirty years earlier, had advanced as Ireland's best strategy for winning national rights. T. W. Moody, *Davitt and Irish Revolution: 1846–82* (Oxford: Clarendon Press, 1981) 332–33.

14 Ibid., 482; Robert Ensor, *England: 1870–1914* (Oxford: Clarendon Press, 1985; first published 1936) 78.

15 R. V. Comerford, *The Fenians in Context: Irish Politics and Society, 1848–82* (Dublin: Wolfhound Press, 1985) 223.

16 T. W. Moody called the Land War "the greatest mass-movement of modern Ireland." J. L. Garvin called it "nothing less than the strongest native revolt for

over two hundred years." Quoted in Conor Cruise O'Brien, *Parnell and His Party, 1880–1890* (Oxford: Clarendon Press, 1957) 5–6. In this same vein see George Dangerfield, *The Damnable Question: One Hundred and Twenty Years of Anglo-Irish Conflict* (Boston: Little, Brown, 1976) 18; T. W. Moody, "Fenianism, Home Rule, and the Land War," in *The Course of Irish History*, ed. T. W. Moody and F. X. Martin (Cork: the Mercier Press, 1987) 286; and L. P. Curtis, *Coercion and Conciliation in Ireland: 1880–1892* (Princeton: Princeton University Press, 1963) 9.

17 Ireland was the leading issue in the elections of 1886 and 1892. The parliamentary strength of Irish nationalists was determinative of governing coalitions as a result of elections in 1885, 1892, January 1910, and December 1910. The Irish settlement of 1921 was a key factor in the government's defeat in the 1922 election.

18 Concerning the role of "incurable contradictions" in producing the "organic crises" from which wars of position arise see Gramsci, *The Modern Prince*, 166.

19 The introduction of cloture brought an end to this tactic in February 1881.

20 For appraisals of Parnell's contribution to reopening the Irish question see Curtis, *Coercion and Conciliation in Ireland,* 12; Lyons, *Ireland since the Famine,* 200; Peter Marsh, *The Discipline of Popular Government: Lord Salisbury's Domestic Statecraft, 1881–1902* (Sussex: Harvester, 1978) 84; and especially O'Brien, *Parnell and His Party.*

21 See Eric R. Wolf, *Peasant Wars of the Twentieth Century* (New York: Harper and Row, 1968) 240–41.

22 Leaders of the revolt later estimated their strength at the outset as nine hundred to three thousand. William Quandt, *Revolution and Political Leadership: Algeria, 1954–1968* (Cambridge: MIT Press, 1969) 93.

23 Alistair Horne, *A Savage War of Peace: Algeria, 1954–1962* (New York: Penguin, 1977) 140.

24 *Sondages: Revue Française de l'Opinion Publique* 16, no. 4 (1954) 12.

25 Charles-Robert Ageron, "L'opinion française devant la guerre d'Algérie," *Review Française d'Histoire d'Outre-Mer* 63, no. 231 (1976) 259.

26 I. R. Campbell, "Political Attitudes in France to the Algerian Question, 1954–62, with Special Reference to the Centre National des Indépendants," Ph.D. Diss., Nuffield College, Oxford, 1972, p. 4.

27 Jean-Franois Sirinelli, "Guerre d'Algérie, guerre des petitions? Quelques jalons," *Revue Historique* 279 (1988) 79.

28 William G. Andrews, *French Politics and Algeria* (New York: Appleton-Century-Crofts, 1962) 28. Andrews found similarly large jumps from 1955 to 1956 in his study of *France-Soir,* a popular, large-circulation newspaper, and *L'Humanite,* the official newspaper of the French Communist party.

29 Sondages 20, no. 4 (1958) 5.

30 Faure speech to French National Assembly, *New York Times,* August 6, 1955.

31 Embassy of France, "Constructive Action of the French Government in Algeria," *French Affairs,* no. 40 (January 1957) 1.

32 Embassy of France, "Algeria," *French Affairs,* no. 24 (November 1955) 3; *New York Times,* May 26, 1957; and Edgar S. Furniss, Jr., *France: Troubled Ally* (New York: Council on Foreign Relations, 1960) 213.

33   *New York Times,* April 19, 1956.

34   *New York Times,* April 13, 1956.

35   Harold Callender, "France's Old Ailments Plague Her Once Again: Drain of Algeria, Lack of Hard Money Combine against Mollet," *New York Times,* May 26, 1957; Joseph Kraft, *The Struggle for Algeria* (Garden City, N.Y.: Doubleday, 1961) 162.

36   Harold Callender, "The Plight of France: An Appraisal of Her Need for Peace in Algeria to Ease Ills in Economy," *New York Times,* June 22, 1957.

37   J. J. Carré, P. Dubois, and E. Malinvaud, *French Economic Growth* (Stanford: Stanford University Press, 1975) 389.

38   Germaine Tillion, *Algeria: The Realities* (New York: Knopf, 1958) 106–7.

39   Ageron, "L'opinion française devant la guerre d'Algérie," 262.

40   Furniss, *France: Troubled Ally,* 213; *New York Times,* October 19, 1957.

41   Horne, *A Savage War of Peace,* 153.

42   Pierre Vidal-Naquet, *Torture: Cancer of Democracy* (Middlesex: Penguin, 1963) 27.

43   Martin Harrison, "Government and Press in France during the Algerian War," *American Political Science Review* 58 (June 1964) 276–79.

44   For an excellent discussion of the torture issue and its significance see Paul Clay Sorum, *Intellectuals and Decolonization in France* (Chapel Hill: University of North Carolina Press, 1977) 113–29.

45   From the *Principles of Political Economy,* quoted in Richard Ned Lebow, "J. S. Mill and the Irish Land Question," in *John Stuart Mill on Ireland,* 8–9; (emphasis added by IL). This paragraph's characterization of Mill's early thinking regarding Irish land issues is drawn from Lebow's essay.

46   John Stuart Mill, "England and Ireland" (1868), reprinted in *John Stuart Mill on Ireland,* 8.

47   Ibid., 9.

48   See Clive Dewey, "Celtic Agrarian Legislation and the Celtic Revival: Historicist Implications of Gladstone's Irish and Scottish Land Acts 1870–1886," *Past and Present* 64 (August 1974) 30–70; and Oliver MacDonagh, *Ireland: The Union and Its Aftermath* (London: George and Unwin, 1977) 47–48.

49   Henry Sumner Maine, *Lectures on the Early History of Institutions* (New York: Henry Holt, 1875) 360.

50   A. V. Dicey, *Lectures on the Relation between Law and Public Opinion in England during the Nineteenth Century* (London: Macmillan, 1926: first published 1905) 55–69, 399–400, and 456–61. This volume contains the text of lectures given at Harvard and Oxford universities between 1898 and 1905.

51   Seamus Deane, *Celtic Revivals* (London: Faber and Faber, 1985) 22.

52   Ibid., 25.

53   Ibid.

54   Matthew Arnold, *Irish Essays* (London: Spottiswoode, 1882) 76–78 and 88–89. See also Deane, *Celtic Revivals,* 21–23, which traces Arnold's attitude to the influence of Edmund Burke.

55   T. E. Kebbel, ed., *Selected Speeches of the Late Right Hon. the Earl of Beaconsfield* (London: Longmans, 1882) 2:527–28.

56 An 1878 speech by Disraeli quoted in Dunne, "Ireland, England and Empire, 1868–1886," 118.

57 Charles Dilke, *Greater Britain* (Philadelphia: J. B. Lippincott, 1869) 1:226.

58 J. R. Seeley, *The Expansion of England* (Boston: Little, Brown, 1905; first published 1883) 88–89.

59 Ibid., 201–2.

60 See Peter Marshall, "The Imperial Factor in the Liberal Decline, 1880–1885," in *Perspectives of Empire,* ed. John E. Flint and Glyndwr Williams (London: Longman Group, 1973) 144.

61 Dewey, "Celtic Agrarian Legislation and the Celtic Revival," 36 and 56–61. In 1869 Gladstone used the same historicist logic in his campaign to disestablish the (Anglican) Church of Ireland and in his escalating attack on the Protestant ascendancy as an alien, three-branched "upas tree" that had to be uprooted. See Morley, *Life of Gladstone,* 1:880–82, 920–21, and 2:42–44.

62 Dewey, "Celtic Agrarian Legislation and the Celtic Revival," 31, 59, and 63.

63 Orthodox political economy justified coercion in Ireland by defining Irish peasant defense of customary tenant rights as atavistic or criminal. See ibid., 34.

64 Ibid., 58–59.

65 William Ewart Gladstone, *Special Aspects of the Irish Question* (London: John Murray, 1892) 49.

66 Concerning the strength of the jingoist sentiment in the 1870s and 1880s see Marshall, "The Imperial Factor in the Liberal Decline, 1880–1885," 130–47.

67 Edward Dicey, "A Malcontent Liberal's Plea," *Fortnightly Review* 38 (October 1885) 469.

68 John Tyndall, quoted in Thomas Dunne, "*La trahison des clercs:* British Intellectuals and the First Home-Rule Crisis," *Irish Historical Studies* 23 (November 1982) 139. This article is an excellent source for tracing what might in late twentieth-century parlance be called a "neoconservative" backlash against the "bleeding heart" liberalism of Gladstone and the "Little England" movement in general. See also John Roach, "Liberalism and the Victorian Intelligentsia," *Cambridge Historical Journal* 13, no. 1 (1957) 58–81; and Marshall, "The Imperial Factor in the Liberal Decline, 1880–1885."

69 See Wolfgang J. Mommsen, "Power Politics, Imperialism, and National Emancipation, 1870–1914," in *Nationality and the Pursuit of National Independence* ed. T. W. Moody (Belfast: Appletree Press, 1978) 121–140.

70 Boyce, *The Irish Question and British Politics, 1868–1986,* 33. Concerning traditional British stereotypes of the Irish see Richard Ned Lebow, *White England, Black Ireland* (Philadelphia: Institute for the Study of Human Issues, 1976) 38–70. For the contribution of racialist thinking to Unionist policy toward Ireland see L. P. Curtis, *Anglo-Saxons and Celts: A Study in Anti-Irish Prejudice in Victorian England* (Bridgeport, Conn.: Conference on British Studies, 1968) 98–107.

71 Salisbury's remarks were made in his address to the National Union of Conservative Associations, May 15, 1886, just prior to the vote on Gladstone's first Home Rule Bill. Marsh, *The Discipline of Popular Government,* 92. See below for further discussion of the significance of this speech.

Many British intellectuals had, like Salisbury, begun their public life in the Indian civil service. In the intellectual climate described above, it became increasingly natural for them to use British authoritarianism in India, not parliamentary government in England, as a model for ruling Ireland and for assisting in the development of the "lower race" inhabiting that island. Marshall, "The Imperial Factor in the Liberal Decline, 1880–1885," 136–39.

72 See William Langer, *The Diplomacy of Imperialism: 1890–1902* (New York: Knopf, 1956) 71–82; and Max Beloff, *Britain's Liberal Empire, 1897–1921,* 2d ed. (London: Macmillan, 1987) 22–25.

73 With an extravagance "not untypical" of the hopes of British imperialists, Cecil Rhodes described his intention to establish "a Secret Society, the true aim and object whereof shall be the extension of British rule throughout the world... especially the occupation by British settlers of the entire Continent of Africa, the Holy Land, the Valley of the Euphrates, the Isles of Cyprus and Candia, the whole of South America, the Islands of the Pacific not heretofore possessed by Great Britain, the whole of the Malay Archipelago, the seaboard of China and Japan, the ultimate recovery of the United States of America as an integral part of the British Empire." This passage, taken from Rhodes's will, was written in 1877. On the representative tone and content of the sentiments expressed in this passage see Michael Howard, "Empire, Race and War in Pre–1914 Britain," in *History and Imagination,* ed. Hugh Lloyd-Jones et al. (New York: Holmes and Meier, 1982) 342ff.

74 See Marshall, "The Imperial Factor in the Liberal Decline, 1880–1885," 135–37. The argument has been most forcefully and systematically developed by Thomas Dunne. See Dunne, "Ireland, England and Empire, 1868–1886."

75 Ireland's demotion in this way is reflected in Peter Marshall's description of Sir Garnet Wolseley, not Gladstone, as the "hero of the age... defending the Empire against Irish, Egyptian, and Boer nationalism while despising the politicians whose orders deprived him of further glory." Marshall, "The Imperial Factor in the Liberal Decline, 1880–1885," 138. For a thorough discussion of the changing connotation of the terms "empire" and "imperialism" in British political discourse, which points out the gradual submergence of Ireland within wider applications of these words, see Richard Koebner and Helmut Dan Schmidt, *Imperialism: The Story and Significance of a Political Word* (Cambridge: Cambridge University Press, 1964) esp. 168.

76 Edward Dicey, "Mr. Gladstone and Our Empire," *Nineteenth Century* 2 (September 1877) 294–95.

77 Ibid., 294.

78 Ibid., 301.

79 Dicey, "A Malcontent Liberal's Plea," 469–70.

80 *Hansard* 306 (1886), col. 1223. Concerning the direct influence of the 1867 Canadian legislation on Gladstone's thinking on Ireland in 1885 see Dunne, "Ireland, England and Empire, 1868–1886," 240.

81 Concerning the extent to which Gladstonian liberals shared in the imperialist discourse most closely associated with the Unionists, see Dunne, "Ireland, England, and Empire, 1868–1886," 239–40 and 268; and Koebner and Schmidt, *Imperialism,* 168–72.

82 Gladstone, *Special Aspects of the Irish Question,* 47.

83 Quoted from Gladstone's letter to Hartington, December 17, 1885, in Morley, *Life of Gladstone,* 2:503.

84 Ibid., 532. See also Gladstone, *Special Aspects of the Irish Question,* 19.

85 Dunne, "Ireland, England and Empire, 1868–1886," 108.

86 Chamberlain, *Hansard* 304 (1886), cols. 1204–6; *Hansard* 306 (1886), col. 697; from Morley, *Life of Gladstone,* 2:556–57.

87 Beloff, *Britain's Liberal Empire, 1897–1921,* 28n. Concerning Rhodes's view of Parnellite home rule as part of an imperial federation see O'Brien, *Parnell and His Party,* 7.

88 In his Crystal Palace speech, cited above, which anticipated much British thought and political life of the last quarter of the nineteenth century, Disraeli argued for a consolidation of the British Empire that would include imperial tarrifs, self-government for "distant colonies," English rights there to "unappropriated lands," and "a representative council in the metropolis." Quoted in Kebbel, *Selected Speeches of the Late Right Honorable the Earl of Beaconsfield,* 2:530.

89 For a discussion of parallel and reinforcing trends in French art and literature during the late 1940s and early 1950s, especially a discussion of "polyculture," see Jean-Pierre Rioux, *The Fourth Republic* (Cambridge: Cambridge University Press, 1987) 430–35.

90 Concerning change in Catholic church thinking on colonialism and its impact on French Catholics in the 1950s see Raoul Girardet, *L'idée coloniale en France: 1871–1962* (Paris: Table Ronde, 1972) 266–76. Regarding general intellectual trends in post-war France and their relationship to decolonization see Sorum, *Intellectuals and Decolonization in France,* esp. 212–37.

91 See Sorum, *Intellectuals and Decolonization in France,* 211–12. This ethnocentrism was as true of most radical anticolonialists, such as Sartre, as it was of more mainstream thinkers such as André Siegfried, Maurice Duverger, and Charles Moraze.

92 Ibid., 211. In 1951, four years after the bloody suppression of unrest in Madagascar, Minister for Overseas France François Mitterrand declared that the future of that country would be "within the French Republic." Xavier Yacono, *Les étapes de la décolonisation française* (Paris: Presses Universitaires de France, 1982) 76.

93 Sorum, *Intellectuals and Decolonization in France,* 211.

94 On the "modernist" movement among French businessmen, and the impression caused by the enormous economic boost to Holland following Dutch disengagement from Indonesia, see Jacques Marseille, *Empire colonial et capitalisme français: Histoire d'un divorce* (Paris: Albin Michel, 1984) 11–15 and 350–65; and Sorum, *Intellectuals and Decolonization in France,* 244. For an enthusiastic portrayal of Mendès-France as the exemplar of this approach see Jean Hoffmann, "France's New Hope," *Foreign Affairs* 3 (Winter 1954–55) 225–38.

95 Regarding Cartiér's influence see Nathalie Ruz, "Le 'cartiérisme' et l'Algérie (1956–1961) a travers la presse parisienne," paper presented at the conference La guerre d'Algérie et les français, at Institut d'Histoire du Temps Present, Paris, December 15–17, 1988, p. 8.

96   Ibid.. For a systematic treatment of the "divorce" between economic rationality and political sentiment in explaining the difficulties of French decolonization, see Marseille, *Empire colonial et capitalisme français.*

97   Stanley Hoffmann, "Paradoxes of the French Political Community," in *In Search of France,* ed. Stanley Hoffmann et al. (New York: Harper Torchbooks, 1963) 75.

98   Girardet, *L'idée coloniale en France,* 248.

99   Ibid., 244–45.

100   Ibid., 248.

101   Ibid., 244.

102   Ibid., 249. Two additional works that attribute decisive importance to these psychological factors in explaining French reactions to decolonization, and that identify the dynamic leading to associations of disengagement from overseas territories with "decadence" and national humiliation, are Sorum, *Intellectuals and Decolonization in France,* and Tony Smith, *The French Stake in Algeria, 1945–1962* (Ithaca N. Y.: Cornell University Press, 1978).

103   Jean Dutourd, *The Taxis of the Marne* (New York: Simon and Schuster, 1957), 230.

104   See Chapter 7 for a discussion of the link between the French army's reaction to Dien Bien Phu, and other colonial defeats, and its commitment to Algérie française.

105   Hoffmann, "Paradoxes of the French Political Community," 92.

106   Laurence Wylie, "Social Change at the Grassroots," in *In Search of France,* 217.

107   Miles Kahler, *Decolonization in Britain and France* (Princeton: Princeton University Press, 1984) 331; Horne, *A Savage War of Peace,* 148–49. On the importance of Poujade's exploitation of the Algerian issue for his electoral success see Rioux, *The Fourth Republic,* 250.

108   See Dutourd, *The Taxis of the Marne,* 105; and Jacques Soustelle, *Le drame algérien et la décadence française: Reponse à Raymond Aron* (Paris: Plon, 1957) 3–8 and 14–20, and 64–70.

109   Smith, *The French Stake in Algeria,* 182.

110   Dutourd, *The Taxis of the Marne,* 113.

111   On this point see Odile Rudelle, "Le gaullisme devant la crise de l'identité républicaine," paper presented at the international colloquium of CNRS (Centre National des Républicains Sociaux), Institut d'Histoire du Temps Present, December 15–17, 1988, Paris, pp. 8–11. See also Stanley Hoffman and Inge Hoffmann, "De Gaulle as Political Artist: The Will to Grandeur," in *Decline or Renewal? France since the 1930s,* ed. Stanley Hoffman et al. (New York: Viking Press, 1974) 217.

112   For a thorough analysis of how de Gaulle's appeal to the French in these terms corresponded to a natural but carefully cultivated extension of both his private and public persona, see Hoffman and Hoffmann, "De Gaulle as Political Artist," 202–53.

113   Ibid., 503n.

114   Charles de Gaulle, *Discours et messages: Dans l'attente, February 1946–April 1958* (Paris: Plon, 1970) 633 and 642.

115   Herbert Luthy, "The French Intellectuals," in *The Intellectuals,* ed. George B. de Huszar (Glencoem Ill.: Free Press, 1960) 447. Reprinted from *Encounter,* August 1955, pp. 5–15.

116   Hoffman and Hoffmann, "De Gaulle as Political Artist," 234–35.

117   Ibid., 235–36.

118   Quoted by Gerald S. Graham, *A Concise History of the British Empire* (New York: Viking, 1970) 162.

119   See John Patrick Rossi, "Home Rule and the Liverpool By-election of 1880," *Irish Historical Studies* 19 (September 1974) 156–68.

120   Disraeli's letter to the duke of Marlborough, which served as his election manifesto, quoted in Richard B. Cook, *The Grand Old Man* (Publishers Union, 1898) 454. On Disraeli's early practice of "blending the Irish and Imperial issues" see Koebner and Schmidt, *Imperialism,* 168.

121   From the conclusion of Gladstone's last Midlothian address of 1880, quoted in John Morley, *Life of Gladstone,* 2:218.

122   This discussion of the differing strategies Churchill and Salisbury advanced in response to Gladstone's formula is based on Marsh, *The Discipline of Popular Government,* 47–119.

123   Quoted in Ensor, *England: 1870–1914,* 87.

124   Marsh, *The Discipline of Popular Government,* 34.

125   Ibid., 98–99.

126   Ibid., 92.

127   Ibid., 68. See also Alan O'Day, *The English Face of Irish Nationalism: Parnellite Involvement in British Politics, 1880–86* (Dublin: Gil and Macmillan, 1977) 178; and Curtis, *Coercion and Conciliation,* 34 and 95.

128   For a strong and detailed argument about the decisiveness of imperialist sentiments in the defeat of home rule, and the ascendancy of the Unionist Party under Salisbury's leadership after 1886, see Dunne, "Ireland, England, and Empire."

129   Marsh, *The Discipline of Popular Government,* 102. See also for details of Salisbury's use of his anti-Irish credentials to outmaneuver both Churchill and his other rival for supremacy within the Tory party—Sir Stafford Northcotte. Marsh also suggests that Salisbury's "blazing indiscretions" with respect to the Irish were carefully calculated to prevent the emergence of a Whig-led center party which would exclude both the right wing of the Conservative party that he represented and the Radical portion of the Liberal party. Ibid., 110.

130   In February 1886 Churchill confided to a political ally that he had "decided some time ago that if the GOM [i.e., the Grand Old Man—William Gladstone] went for Home Rule, the Orange card would be the one to play. Please God it may turn out the ace of trumps and not the two." Conor O'Clery, *Phrases Make History Here: Political Quotations on Ireland* (Dublin: O'Brien Press, 1986) 25.

131   Morley, *Life of Gladstone,* vol. 1; J. L. Hammond, *Gladstone and the Irish Nation* (London: Longman, 1938); Baron Eversley, (Shaw-Lefevre), *Gladstone and Ireland: The Irish Policy of Parliament from 1850–1894* (London: Methuen, 1912); Herbert Gladstone, *After Thirty Years* (London: Macmillan, 1928).

132   The quote, by Henry Broadhurst, is in C. C. Lubenow, *Parliamentary Politics*

and the Home Rule Crisis: The British House of Commons in 1886 (Oxford: Clarendon Press, 1988) 1.

133 Curtis, *Coercion and Conciliation in Ireland,* 69.

134 J. C. Beckett, *The Anglo-Irish Tradition* (Ithaca, N.Y.: Cornell University Press, 1976) 115.

135 Between 1861 and 1881, the percentage of the Irish population eligible to vote rose from 3.6 percent to only 4.4 percent. But in 1885 that percentage jumped to 14.3 percent. For a thorough analysis of changes in the British and Irish franchise see K. Theodore Hoppen, "The Franchise and Electoral Politics in England and Ireland, 1832–1885," *History* 70 (June 1985) 202–17. These percentages are calculated from data provided by Hoppen and Brian Mercer Walker, in "The Irish Electorate, 1865–1915," *Irish Historical Studies* 18 (March 1973) 359–406.

136 Quoted in Nicholas Mansergh, *The Irish Question, 1840–1921* (Toronto: University of Toronto Press, 1975) 140.

137 Quoted in Morley, *Life of Gladstone,* 1:383.

138 Ibid., 873.

139 Ibid., 877; Robert Blake, *The Conservative Party from Peel to Churchill* (London: Eyre and Spottiswoode, 1970) 110.

140 Mansergh, *The Irish Question, 1840–1921,* 141.

141 Concerning the "symbolic significance" of Gladstone's early Irish legislation see Lyons, *Ireland since the Famine,* 146.

142 T. A. Jenkins, *Gladstone, Whiggery and the Liberal Party* (Oxford: Clarendon Press, 1988); Robert Kee, *Ireland: A History* (London: Abacus, 1982); Dunne, "Ireland, England and Empire"; James Loughlin, *Gladstone, Home Rule, and the Ulster Question, 1882–1893* (Dublin: Gill and Macmillan, 1986). The phrase "eccentric historicism" comes from Dunne, "Responses to Gladstonian Home Rule and Land Reform," *Irish Historical Studies* 25 (November 1987) 435. Kee, *Ireland: A History,* 131; Marsh, *The Discipline of Popular Government,* 84; A. B. Cooke and John Vincent, *The Governing Passion: Cabinet Government and Party Politics in Britain, 1885–86* (New York: Harper and Row, 1974) 55–56; D. A. Hamer, "The Irish Question and Liberal Politics, 1886–1894," *Historical Journal* 12, no. 3 (1969) 511–32.

143 William Ewart Gladstone, "The Irish Question, 1886," in *Special Aspects of the Irish Question,* 6.

144 Ibid., 2.

145 Ibid., 4.

146 Ibid., 20.

147 Ibid., 12. According to Dunne, Gladstone's private correspondence during the period strengthens his claims to have been engaged, since the early 1870s, in a process of indirect political education on the question of political autonomy of Ireland. Dunne, "Ireland, England, and Empire," 59–60. Focusing solely on the content and not the terms of the discourse, Cooke and Vincent instructively describe this speech as Gladstone's most hostile attack on home rule. Cooke and Vincent, *The Governing Passion,* 49–50.

148 See John Vincent, "Gladstone and Ireland," Raleigh Lecture on History in *Proceedings of the British Academy* (1978) 209–11 and 219–20.

149   Morley, *Life of Gladstone,* 2:380–81.
150   For an example of the complex formulations which Gladstone developed in the 1870s to oppose home rule while shifting the terms of discourse about it in a way calculated to advance its prospects, see his article in the *Freeman's Journal* of January 26, 1874, quoted in Lawrence J. McCaffrey, "Home Rule and the General Election of 1874 in Ireland," *Irish Historical Studies* 9 (September 1954) 194.
151   Speech delivered in Cork in January 1885, quoted in Kee, *Ireland: A History,* 131.
152   Marsh, *The Discipline of Popular Government,* 85.
153   Dunne, "Ireland, England, and Empire," 164–65.
154   From a federal version of a home rule legislature, Chamberlain's idea narrowed to an administrative reform that would replace "the absurd and irritating anachronism known as Dublin Castle... [with a] Metropolitan Board of works on a larger and more important scale... [with] no power of initiating special taxation." Dunne, "Ireland, England, and Empire," 169; see also C. H. D. Howard, "Joseph Chamberlain, Parnell, and the Irish 'Central Board' Scheme, 1884–85," *Irish Historical Studies* 8 (September 1953) 324–61.
155   Dunne, "Ireland, England, and Empire," 222–24.
156   Ibid., 210–14.
157   Donald Southgate, *The Passing of the Whigs: 1832–1886* (London: Macmillan, 1962) 414–16.
158   Marsh, *The Discipline of Popular Government,* 84.
159   Gladstone, *Special Aspects of the Irish Question,* 52.
160   Ibid., 53–54. For the argument that the great importance of the crisis of 1886 was that the British regime, in particular the party system, found a way to integrate within the framework of more-or-less regular party rivalry the potentially revolutionary question of the disposition of Ireland, see Lubenow, *Parliamentary Politics and the Home Rule Crisis,* 323–24.
161   Churchill's career was cut short by syphilis. His mental acuity deteriorated rapidly, and he died in 1895 at the age of forty-six.
162   With the creation of the Irish Free State in 1922, the United Kingdom of Great Britain and Ireland became the United Kingdom of Great Britain and Northern Ireland.
163   As we shall see in Chapter 6, eventually the Irish question did threaten British stability. Once problematized, the struggle over Ireland's status became an important part of efforts to change the institutional structure of British politics by ending the House of Lords's veto. Some, such as Lord Milner, even hoped that violent agitation against home rule would set the stage for fairly radical transformations in the British political system.
164   The extent to which these fundamental differences in British and French political history, and the potentially different roles played by the presence or absence of a coherent ideological framework, may be attributed to cultural differences between the "pragmatic" English and the "Cartesian" French is an important question, both empirically and theoretically. The question, however, lies well beyond the scope of this study.

INTRODUCTION TO PART III

1 Remarks at the Israel-Diaspora Institute conference Israel as a Jewish Democratic Society, March 1988, Herzlyia, Israel.

6. THE IRISH QUESTION IN BRITISH POLITICS, 1886–1922

1 According to Lyons, "between 1903 and 1920 nearly nine million acres had changed hands and two million acres more were in the process of being sold." F. S. L. Lyons, *Ireland since the Famine* (London: Fontana, 1973) 219. On Balfour's policies, in addition to ibid., 202–23, see L. P. Curtis, *Coercion and Conciliation in Ireland, 1880–1892: A Study in Conservative Unionism* (Princeton: Princeton University Press, 1963).

2 The liaison began in 1880. By 1886 Parnell and Mrs. O'Shea were living together and had two children of their own. Hoping to share in a large inheritance due his wife, and able to extort political favors from Parnell by his acquiesence, Capt. William O'Shea kept silent. But in 1889 he sued his wife for divorce, pushing Parnell's adulterous relationship into public view.

3 H. W. McCready, "Home Rule and the Liberal Party, 1899–1906," *Irish Historical Studies* 12 (September 1963) 319–23.

4 Aware of the continued unpopularity of home rule with many British constituencies, the Liberals were reluctant to emphasize it as a part of their platform. Before the January 1910 election, Redmond extracted a public commitment from Asquith to "self-government" for Ireland only by threatening to deprive the Liberals of "every Irish vote in England." In the campaign prior to the December 1910 election the Liberals managed to avoid public and explicit endorsements of home rule, unless forced to answer direct questions. George Dangerfield, *The Damnable Question: One Hundred and Twenty Years of Anglo-Irish Conflict* (Boston: Little, Brown, 1976) 55; and A. T. Q. Stewart, *The Ulster Crisis* (London: Faber and Faber, 1967) 24.

5 For a thorough analysis of the tendency for English constituencies to vote Unionist during this period (based in substantial measure on anti-Irish, anti–home rule sentiment), compared to the anti-Unionist majorities consistently registered in Scotland, Wales, Cornwall, and Ireland, see Neal Blewett, *The Peers, the Parties and the People: The British General Elections of 1910* (Toronto: University of Toronto Press, 1972).

6 The penal laws were a discriminatory code that systematically deprived Catholics in Ireland of political rights and most rights to education, land ownership, religious expression, and entry into trades and professions. Imposed in the early 1700s by the Protestant Ascendancy in Ireland, the penal laws enforced the majority Catholic community's economic and political subordination for nearly one hundred years. See Maureen Wall, *Catholic Ireland in the Eighteenth Century* (Dublin: Geography Publications, 1989) 1–61.

7 Conor O'Clery, *Phrases Make History Here* (Dublin: O'Brien Press, 1986) 25.

8 D. C. Savage, "The Origins of the Ulster Unionist Party, 1885–86," *Irish Historical Studies* 12 (March 1961) 197.

9 O'Clery, *Phrases Make History Here*, 26 (emphasis added).

10 D. C. Savage, "The Origins of the Ulster Unionist Party, 1885–86," 196.

11 Ibid., 196–203. James Loughlin, *Gladstone, Home Rule, and the Ulster Question, 1882–1893* (Dublin: Gill and Macmillan, 1986) 168.

12 Loughlin, *Gladstone, Home Rule, and the Ulster Question, 1882–1893*, 169. This was the opinion of the *Pall Mall Gazette*'s Ulster reporter at the end of May 1886.

13 Ibid., 170.

14 Savage, "The Origins of the Ulster Unionist Party, 1885–86," 203.

15 A Belfast newspaper reported that the men drilling in Richhill, County Armagh, were " 'members of the Grand Orange Army,' and that their exercises were publicly delcared to be 'preparations for the civil war to be waged against the Queen's forces in resisting Home Rule.' " Charles Townshend, *Political Violence in Ireland: Government and Resistance since 1848* (Oxford: Clarendon Press, 1983) 191.

16 Lyons, *Ireland since the Famine*, 293.

17 Robert Kee, *Ireland: A History* (London: Abacus, 1982) 140. For details regarding this convention see Peter Gibbon, *The Origins of Ulster Unionism: The Formation of Popular Protestant Politics and Ideology in Nineteenth-Century Ireland* (Manchester: Manchester University Press, 1975) 130–38.

18 Townshend, *Political Violence in Ireland*, 191.

19 Kee, *Ireland: A History*, 140. For details concerning preparations for armed resistance at this time see Stewart, *The Ulster Crisis*, 32. See also Patrick Buckland, *Ulster Unionism and the Origins of Northern Ireland* (Dublin: Gill and Macmillan, 1973) 17.

20 Kee, *Ireland: A History*, 140. See also Saunderson's speech to his Ulster constituents, *Times*, December 20, 1892.

21 Loughlin, *Gladstone, Home Rule, and the Ulster Question*, 168–69.

22 Thomas MacKnight, *Ulster as It Is* (London: Macmillan, 1896) 2:238. MacKnight was the editor of the *Northern Whig*, a leading newspaper in Belfast.

23 Buckland, *Ulster Unionism and the Origins of Northern Ireland*, 15.

24 Ibid., 18.

25 Alvin Jackson, *The Ulster Party: Irish Unionists in the House of Commons, 1884–1911* (Oxford: Clarendon Press, 1989) 126–29.

26 Loughlin, *Gladstone, Home Rule, and the Ulster Question*, 235–36. Loughlin also discusses the extent to which Gladstone's personal views were tinged with a strong animus against Ulster Protestants.

27 Ibid., 292.

28 Stewart, *The Ulster Crisis*, 32–33. On the origins of the Ulster Unionist Council see F. S. L. Lyons, "The Irish Unionist Party and the Devolution Crisis of 1904–5," *Irish Historical Studies* 6 (March 1948) 1–22.

29 Jackson, *The Ulster Party*, 319–26. Jackson concludes his study of how Ulster's "holy war" against home rule developed with a discussion of E. J. Saunderson's death in 1906 and his replacement as leader of Ulster Unionism by Carson. Jackson identifies the change in leadership style between Saunderson and Carson as emblematic of the radical change in the political significance of Unionism's extra-constitutional dimension which took place in the years prior to World War I.

30 Patricia Jalland, *The Liberals and Ireland: The Ulster Question and British Politics to 1914* (New York: St. Martin's 1980) 59.

31 Jackson, *The Ulster Party*, 316.

32 A. T. Q. Stewart, *Edward Carson* (Dublin: Gill and Macmillan, 1981) 73.

33 Jackson, *The Ulster Party*, 315.

34 Ibid., 315–18. Weapons training and other military exercises were legalized (ironically) by a law permitting justices of the peace to authorize drilling and other military operations by civilians "to render citizens more efficient for the purpose of maintaining the constitution of the United Kingdom." Stewart, *The Ulster Crisis*, 69–71.

35 Passed first by the House of Commons on January 16, 1913, the third Home Rule for Ireland Bill was defeated by the House of Lords two weeks later, passed a second time by the Commons on July 7, 1913, defeated a second time by the Lords one week later, and passed for a third and, under the terms of the Parliament Act, final time by the House of Commons on May 25, 1914. The bill received the royal assent, and thereby went on the statute books, on September 18, but its implementation was suspended for the duration of World War I. Superseded by the Government of Ireland Act in 1920, it was never actually applied.

36 Charles Craig, *Hansard* 39 (1912), cols. 114–15.

37 D. J. Hickey and J. E. Doherty, *A Dictionary of Irish History, 1800–1980* (Dublin: Gill and Macmillan, 1980) 542–43.

38 J. J. Horgan, *The Complete Grammar of Anarchy* (Dublin: Maunsel, 1918) 13; Hickey and Doherty, *A Dictionary of Irish History, 1800–1980*, 542–43.

39 A number of the Covenanters, as they came to be called, signed their names in blood. For an evocative description of the solemnity of the event and the extraordinary feat of organization it entailed see Stewart, *The Ulster Crisis*, 63–66.

40 Ibid., 69–70.

41 George Dangerfield, *The Strange Death of Liberal England, 1910–1914* (New York: Perigree, 1935) 135.

42 Stewart, *The Ulster Crisis*, 73–84 and 122–23.

43 Stewart, *Edward Carson*, 81; and idem, *The Ulster Crisis*, 85–86.

44 Speech delivered on September 7, 1913. See O'Clery, *Phrases Make History Here*, 41.

45 Ibid., 40.

46 Dangerfield, *The Strange Death of Liberal England*, 135. For added information about British officers prepared to come "across the water" in the event of armed conflict see Stewart, *The Ulster Crisis*, 120–21; and Jalland, *The Liberals and Ireland*, 215.

47 Jalland, *The Liberals and Ireland*, 133.

48 Stewart, *The Ulster Crisis*, 119. According to the intelligence reports of Dublin Castle, the Ulster Volunteers had 41,000 men at their disposal in April 1913, 57,000 in September, and nearly 77,000 in November. But weapons were in much shorter supply. Dublin Castle counted 10,000 rifles as available to the UVF in October 1913, rising to 17,000 in December. Jalland, *The Liberals and Ireland*, 134.

49 Stewart, *The Ulster Crisis*, 120.

50 For the most detailed account available of the importation of arms into Ulster during this period see Stewart, *The Ulster Crisis*, especially 184–212 and 244–49.

Several weeks before the operation it was still unknown even to middle-level commanders within the UVF, who bitterly complained of their leaders' apparent unwillingness to acquire a substantial supply.

51 Townshend, *Political Violence in Ireland,* 253.

52 Stewart, *The Ulster Crisis,* 126–28.

53 Ibid., 77.

54 "The Irish Crisis," *Round Table* 4 (March 1914) 214.

55 Sheila Lawlor, *Britain and Ireland, 1914–23* (Totowa, N.J.: Barnes and Noble, 1983) 4.

56 Ibid., 3.

57 "The Amending Bill and the King's Conference," *Round Table* 4 (Fall 1914) 719–20.

58 Ibid., 720.

59 The classic study of the Conservative party's anticonstitutionalist radicalization during this period is Dangerfield, *The Strange Death of Liberal England.* For more recent scholarship which only supports Dangerfield's portrayal of the Tory leaders as viewing Liberal party rule as intrinsically illegitimate see Patrick Buckland, *Ulster Unionism and the Origins of Northern Ireland* (Dublin: Gill and Macmillan, 1973) 51–52; Robert Blake, *The Unknown Prime Minister: A Biography of Bonar Law* (London: Eyre and Spottiswoode, 1955) 128; Roy Jenkins, *Asquith* (London: Collins, 1964) 275–76; and Neal Blewett, *The Peers, the Parties and the People,* 412.

60 Quoted from *The Faber Book of Political Verse,* ed. Tom Paulin (London: Faber and Faber, 1986) 330.

61 Law served as chancellor of the exchequer in Lloyd George's coalition cabinet during World War I and as prime minister from 1922 to 1923.

62 Dangerfield, *The Strange Death of Liberal England,* 96 (emphasis in original).

63 Stewart, *The Ulster Crisis,* 54.

64 The city had been saved in part because a chain "boom" laid by the besiegers across the river approaching the city had been cut by the English rescuers. In 1912, as in 1689, Law told the Ulstermen: "You hold the pass, the pass for the Empire .... The Government by their Parliament Act have erected a boom against you, a boom to cut you off from the help of the British people. You will burst that boom. The help will come and when the crisis is over men will say of you in words not unlike those once used by Pitt, 'You have saved yourselves by your exertions, and you will save the Empire by your example.' " O'Clery, *Phrases Make History,* 37; and Blake, *The Unknown Prime Minister,* 128.

65 Horgan, *The Complete Grammar of Anarchy,* 9.

66 Remarks by Law at Blenheim Palace, July 24, 1912, as quoted in Blake, *The Unknown Prime Minister,* 130 (emphasis added).

67 Blake, *The Unknown Prime Minister,* 132.

68 Ibid., 152.

69 F. E. Smith, [Birkenhead] *Unionist Policy and Other Essays* (London: Williams and Norgate, 1913) 122–25. In September 1913, Smith earned the nickname "Galloper" for serving as the aide-de-camp to the UVF commander in chief, General George Richardson, during a review of seven thousand Volunteers in Balmoral.

70 Blake, *The Unknown Prime Minister,* 152.

71 *Times,* November 4, 1913.

72 Ibid.

73 Horgan, *The Complete Grammar of Anarchy,* 26. See also John D. Fair, "The Anglo-Irish Treaty of 1921: Unionist Aspects of the Peace," *Journal of British Studies* 12 (November 1972) 133.

74 Denis Gwynn, *The Life of John Redmond* (London: George G. Harrap, 1932) 239.

75 A. M. Gollin, *Proconsul in Politics: A Study of Lord Milner in Opposition and in Power* (New York: Macmillan, 1964) 183–84.

76 Stewart, *The Ulster Crisis,* 131.

77 Ibid., 132–34. See also Buckland, *Ulster Unionism and the Origins,* 52.

78 Gollin, *Proconsul in Politics,* 185.

79 Ibid., 212.

80 Ibid., 185–87.

81 Ibid., 185–88.

82 Ibid., 195–96.

83 Ibid., 182.

84 Milner's papers contain a long list of contributions, including £30,000 from Waldorf Astor, £10,000 from Lord Rothschild, and £10,000 from the duke of Bedford. Gollin, *Proconsul in Politics,* 187–88.

85 Dangerfield, *The Damnable Question,* 79–80. See also Blake, *The Unknown Prime Minister,* 173ff.

86 Gollin, *Proconsul in Politics,* 190.

87 In fact the Unionist leadership on this particular issue overestimated the enthusiasm of their followers for initiatives that so directly endangered the well-being of the army. Conservative backbenchers as well as many officers criticized the plan. Law himself appeared to hesitate. See Gollin, *Proconsul in Politics,* 204–7.

88 *Hansard* 59 (1914), cols. 2264–65.

89 Ibid., col. 2264.

90 Stewart, *The Ulster Crisis,* 150.

91 *Daily Telegraph,* March 25, 1914, quoted in O'Clery, *Phrases Make History,* 45.

92 Jalland, *The Liberals and Ireland,* 239–40. While some infantry units obeyed orders to enter Ulster, soldiers in two Belfast regiments threw down their arms and declared against home rule when ordered to muster for parade through Ulster. Stewart, *The Ulster Crisis,* 157; "Mutiny in Belfast," *Washington Post,* March 22, 1914.

93 Kee, *Ireland: A History,* 149–50.

94 *Washington Post,* March 21, 1914.

95 Stewart, *The Ulster Crisis,* 171.

96 Jalland, *The Liberals and Ireland,* 243. By May 1914, according to Jalland, the government "assumed it had lost the military power required either to enforce its original home rule policy or to impose a compromise settlement on its own terms on an unwilling Ulster." Ibid., 242.

97 Gollin, *Proconsul in Politics,* 201.

98 Ibid., 215.

99 Ibid., 215–18. Milner's preparations even included design of a currency to be used by the new government of Ulster.

100 Ibid., 218.

101 Blake, *The Unknown Prime Minister*, 203.

102 Dangerfield, *The Damnable Question*, 117.

103 Gollin, *Proconsul in Politics*, 219.

104 O'Clery, *Phrases Make History*, 46.

105 Blake, *The Unknown Prime Minister*, 205; Jalland, *The Liberals and Ireland*, 249.

106 After the Curragh mutiny, as the incident is popularly if somewhat inaccurately known, Law and most other Unionist leaders abandoned as unnecessary the idea of amending the annual Army Act. Milner alone continued to advocate amending the act as a way to bring about destruction of the government and open opportunities for redesigning the British Constitution. Gollin, *Proconsul in Politics*, 207–8.

107 Blake, *The Unknown Prime Minister*, 159.

108 For judgments that only the outbreak of war in Europe prevented the eruption of civil war or political collapse in the United Kingdom, see Blake, *The Unknown Prime Minister*, 121; Stewart, *The Ulster Crisis*, 231; *The Crisis of British Unionism; The Domestic Political Papers of the Second Earl of Selborne, 1885–1922*, ed. D. G. Boyce (London: Historians' Press, 1987) xiii; Lyons, *Ireland since the Famine*, 310; Jalland, *The Liberals and Ireland*, 260; Robin Wilson, "Imperialism in Crisis: The 'Irish Dimension,'" in *Crises in the British State, 1880–1930*, ed. Mary Langan and Bill Schwarz (London: Hutchinson, 1985) 164; Blewett, *The Peers, the Parties and the People* (Toronto: University of Toronto Press, 1972) 413; Edward David, *Inside Asquith's Cabinet* (New York: St. Martin's, 1977) 160; Dangerfield, *The Damnable Question*, 79; Gollin, *Proconsul in Politics*, 172; Townshend, *Political Violence in Ireland*, 261; J. E. Kendle, "The Round Table Movement and 'Home Rule All Round,'" *Historical Journal* 11, no. 2 (1968) 346; and Boyce, *The Irish Question and British Politics, 1868–1986* (London: Macmillan, 1988) 52. For comparable evaluations made by contemporary observers see "The Irish Question," *Round Table* 4 (December 1913) 47; and Frederick S. Oliver, *The Alternatives to Civil War* (London: John Murray, 1913) 56–60.

109 Roy Jenkins, *Asquith* (London: Collins, 1964) 335.

110 Jalland, *The Liberals and Ireland*, 76.

111 Ibid., 59.

112 Ibid., 92, 126, and 128.

113 *Hansard* 307 (1886), cols. 1719–20.

114 "The Home Rule Bill," *The Round Table: A Quarterly Review of the Politics of the British Empire* 3 (December 1912–September 1913) 120. Jalland, *The Liberals and Ireland*, 103.

115 "The Home Rule Bill," 124.

116 David, *Inside Asquith's Cabinet*, 126.

117 Tax revenue to be collected from relatively wealthy Ulster was a key ingre-

dient in the self-financing aspect of home rule. Jalland, *The Liberals and Ireland,* 108–15.

118   Ibid., 113.

119   Ibid., 162–64. While Asquith protested that use of the term "civil war" was inappropriate (at least in 1913), the king disagreed. "Will not," he asked Asquith, "the armed struggle between those sections of the people constitute Civil War, more especially if the forces of Ulster are reinforced from England, Scotland, and even the Colonies, which contingency I am assured is highly probable?" Townshend, *Political Violence in Ireland,* 267n; Jenkins, *Asquith,* 283–86.

120   Jenkins, *Asquith,* 282.

121   Jalland, *The Liberals and Ireland,* 213.

122   Ibid., 215.

123   Jackson, for example, has described the process of "Ulsterization," and the growing inclination to view extraconstitutional forces as decisive in the home rule crisis, as having relegated Westminster to "a secondary theatre of a phoney war, whose front line lay, appropriately, in Ulster itself." Jackson, *The Ulster Party,* 326.

124   Jalland, *The Liberals and Ireland,* 202.

125   *Hansard* 59 (1914), cols. 925, 934.

126   "The Ulster Situation," speech by Winston S. Churchill at Bradford, March 14, 1914, in *The Complete Speeches of Winston Churchill 1897–1963,* vol. 3, *1914–22* (London: Chelsea House, 1974) 2233.

127   *Hansard* 60 (1914), cols. 78–79. See also remarks by Walter Long, *Hansard* 60 (1914), col. 1050.

128   For these quotations, the text of the official resolution, and detailed descriptions of the demonstration, see the *Times,* April 4 and 6, 1914.

129   Jalland, *The Liberals and Ireland,* 239. On the cabinet's conviction, following the Curragh incident, that the army would likely split apart if ordered to enforce home rule, see Blake, *The Unknown Prime Minister,* 192 and 200.

130   Jalland, *The Liberals and Ireland,* 246.

131   Jenkins, *Asquith,* 316–17.

132   In a public statement issued on June 6, Redmond cited the unreliability of the regime governing the United Kingdom as the key factor leading to the change in his position. Denis Gwynn, *The Life of John Redmond* (London: George G. Harrap, 1932) 317.

133   Ibid., 325–26.

134   The meeting of the Ulster Provisional Government was presided over by Edward Carson and ostentatiously protected by an armed guard of the Ulster Volunteer Force. Volunteers were authorized by the provisional government to carry arms openly, with or without licenses, and plans were drawn up for the evacuation of women and children. Buckland, *Irish Unionism,* 64. For the Bonar Law quote see Jalland, *The Liberals and Ireland,* 260.

135   Townshend, *Political Violence in Ireland,* 261. The armies were the Ulster Volunteer Force, the Irish National Volunteers, James Larkin's small socialist/ nationalist Citizen Army in Dublin, the British army, and, if it is to be included, the Royal Irish Constabulary.

136   This shift is plotted in Figure A-2 in the appendix as a move from point C to the right of the regime threshold to point D to the left of it.

137   Despite lackadaisical recruiting efforts by Kitchener in Ireland, and an unwillingness to grant Irish Catholics special insignia or designated units, 94,000 Irish Catholics were serving in the British army in January 1917 (compared to 64,000 Irish Protestants). Gwynn, *The Life of John Redmond*, 536.

138   Trevor Wilson, *The Downfall of the Liberal Party, 1914–1935* (London: Collins, 1966) 61–69.

139   John M. McEwen, "The Liberal Party and the Irish Question during the First World War," *Journal of British Studies* 12 (November 1972) 116. In Asquith's view, it was not impossible that Lloyd George's undeniable gifts as a negotiator could result in an agreement including immediate establishment of a southern Irish government with Irish representatives remaining in Westminster. This would have the welcome effect of bolstering the strength of Redmond's party, whose eighty MPs were a vital part of Asquith's political base. Jenkins, *Asquith*, 398–99.

140   Gollin, *Proconsul in Politics*, 349.

141   D. G. Boyce, *Englishmen and Irish Troubles: British Public Opinion and the Making of Irish Policy, 1918–22* (Cambridge: MIT Press, 1972) 33–35; idem, "British Conservative Opinion, the Ulster Question, and the Partition of Ireland, 1912–21," *Irish Historical Studies* 17 (March 1970) 94.

142   In private Carson acknowledged that "I still detest Home Rule for any part of Ireland as much as I ever did, but I could not look forward to forcible resistance in Ulster after the war with any feelings except those of horror." Quoted from a July 3, 1916, letter from Carson to Liverpool Unionist party boss Archibald Salvidge, in Stanley Salvidge, *Salvidge of Liverpool* (London: Hodder and Stoughton, 1934) 154.

143   Jenkins, *Asquith*, 399–402. See also F. S. L. Lyons, *John Dillon: A Biography* (Chicago: University of Chicago Press, 1968) 398–99.

144   Lyons, *John Dillon*, 402. See Blake, *The Unknown Prime Minister*, 287–88, for a more flattering interpretation of Law's response to rank-and-file Unionist opposition to home rule. Like Lyons's analysis, however, Blake also emphasizes Law's partisan calculations as determinative. Blake identifies the impact of the episode on Law's leadership position within the Conservative party as of particular consequence.

145   Wilson, *The Downfall of the Liberal Party*, 70. See also *The Political Diaries of C. P. Scott 1911–1928*, ed. Trevor Wilson (Ithaca, N. Y.: Cornell University Press, 1970) 126.

146   Wilson, *The Downfall of the Liberal Party*, 70.

147   Trevor Wilson, *The Myriad Faces of War* (Cambridge: Basil Blackwell, 1986) 227–38.

148   David W. Savage, "The Parnell of Wales Has Become the Chamberlain of England: Lloyd George and the Irish Question," *Journal of British Studies* 12 (November 1972) 86–108.

149   The incumbent-level character of Lloyd George's concerns during this period, if not the particularities of his calculations, was well known to T. P. O'Connor and evident in the criterion O'Connor offered Lloyd George in private as the

rationale for action on the Irish question. A member of Parliament representing Irish immigrants in Liverpool, O'Connor was the Irish nationalist whose ties to the prime minister were longest and closest. In March 1917, O'Connor urged him to act generously and quickly, otherwise the government would be driven to coercion. "What does that mean," he asked Lloyd George, "to your future political career? Is it not the beginning of that necessary and inevitable dependence on the Tory forces which would paralyse your future work as a reformer?" Lyons, *John Dillon,* 412.

150　After a bitter debate throughout the winter of 1915–16, the government conscripted unmarried British males in January 1916 and married men in April.

151　On April 13, 1917, the British ambassador in Washington reported: "The Irish Party are of very great political importance at the present moment. The question is one which is at the root of most of our troubles with the United States. The fact that the Irish question is still unsettled is continually quoted against us as a proof that it is not wholly true that the fight is one for the sanctity of engagements or the independence of small nations." Quoted in Gwynn, *The Life of John Redmond,* 543. See pp. 543–44 for Wilson's personal message to Lloyd George on the need for an Irish settlement. Concerning the imperative to do something about Ireland which American entry into the war created see also Dangerfield, *The Damnable Question,* 254; Boyce, "British Conservative Opinion," 95; Gollin, *Proconsul in Politics,* 428–29; and Stephen Hartley, *The Irish Question as a Problem in British Foreign Policy, 1914–18* (New York: St. Martin's, 1987) 133–39 and 193–99.

152　On the sensitivity of relations between Carson and Lloyd George in this period, not only regarding Ireland but also naval policies toward the protection of convoys, see Gollin, *Proconsul in Politics,* 422–23; Ian Colvin, *The Life of Lord Carson* (New York: Macmillan, 1937) 3:240; Gwynn, *The Life of John Redmond,* 544; *The Political Diaries of C. P. Scott, 1911–1928,* 283; Lyons, *John Dillon,* 414; Dangerfield, *The Damnable Question,* 255.

153　Thomas Jones, *Whitehall Diary: Ireland, 1918–1925,* ed. Keith Middlemas (London: Oxford University Press, 1971) 8 and 10.

154　In only sixteen days, from March 21 to April 6, battle casualties on the western front were 7,000 officers and 105,000 enlisted men. Jones, *Whitehall Diary,* 2.

155　Redmond himself died in March 1918, but even before his death, and before the obvious failure of the Irish Convention, a series of by-election victories over Redmonite candidates by leaders of the Easter Rising (running with the endorsement of Sinn Fein) had signaled its demise.

156　See *The Crisis of British Unionism: The Domestic Political Papers of the Second Earl of Selborne,* 215–16; a manifesto issued by Edward Carson, published in the *Times,* May 8, 1918; Boyce, "British Conservative Opinion," 97.

157　Lawlor, *Britain and Ireland,* 14. Even without conscription, according to Winston Churchill's account, Britain was required to station 60,000 troops in Ireland during the war to maintain security, which was only just counterbalanced by the 60,000 Irish soldiers who enlisted in the British Army. Winston S. Churchill, *The World Crisis: The Aftermath* (London: Thornton Butterworth, 1929) 281.

158   *The Political Diaries of C. P. Scott, 1911–1928*, 338, 342, 345, and 348; Dangerfield, *The Damnable Question*, 292; and Jones, *Whitehall Diary*, 2. See also D. G. Boyce, "How to Settle the Irish Question: Lloyd George and Ireland, 1916–1921," in *Lloyd George: Twelve Essays*, ed. A. J. P. Taylor (New York: Atheneum, 1971) 142. Boyce comments gingerly on what he calls a "lack of direction in Lloyd George's Irish policy" during this period.

159   Charles Townshend, *The British Campaign in Ireland, 1919–1921: The Development of Political and Military Policies* (Oxford: Oxford University Press, 1978) 14. Long made his comment in a memo dated December 31, 1918.

160   Michael Collins, minister for home affairs and then finance in the Dail government established in 1919, was (secretly) a member of the Supreme Council of the IRB and eventually its president. He was also adjutant general of the Volunteers. Collins was primarily responsible for the military side of the struggle for Irish statehood from the end of World War I until his death during the Civil War, in August 1922. See Lyons, *Ireland since the Famine*, 387–88 and 410–11.

161   Ibid., 416.

162   Boyce, *Englishmen and Irish Troubles*, 51. For details concerning widespread arson, pillage, and indiscriminate killings by police, black and tans, and auxiliaries in retaliation for IRA killings, see Townshend, *The British Campaign in Ireland, 1919–1921*, 115 and 223; Hickey and Doherty, *A Dictionary of Irish History, 1800–1980*, 36; and Joseph M. Curran, *The Birth of the Irish Free State, 1921–1923* (Alabama: University of Alabama Press, 1980) 39. Between January 1919 and July 1921, government forces are estimated to have killed 752 IRA or Sinn Fein operatives and Irish civilians and wounded 866. Available figures show that in only the first six months of 1921, nearly 4,500 were interned. Lyons, *Ireland since the Famine*, 417. During the same period the government blamed Sinn Fein and the IRA for 381 civilian casualties, the death of 555 policemen and soldiers, and the wounding of more than 1,000 others. Townshend, *The British Campaign in Ireland, 1919–1921*, 214.

163   For details concerning the powers and responsibilities alloted to these legislatures and those retained by the British government see R. B. McDowell, *The Irish Convention, 1917–18* (London: Routledge and Kegan Paul, 1970) 197–98.

164   See Boyce, *Englishmen and Irish Troubles*, 81; Kenneth O. Morgan, *Consensus and Disunity: The Lloyd George Coalition Government, 1918–1922* (Oxford: Clarendon Press, 1979) 131; and C. L. Mowat, "The Irish Question in British Politics (1916–1922)," in *The Irish Struggle*, ed. Desmond Williams (Toronto: University of Toronto Press, 1966) 147–49. A *Manchester Guardian* editorial of June 10, 1921, for example, compared repression in Ireland to the "crimes of the Hessian troops at the time of the Rebellion."

165   Boyce, *Englishmen and Irish Troubles*, 75.

166   Dorothy Macardle, *The Irish Republic* (London: V. Gollancz, 1937) 319.

167   Ibid., 432.

168   This formula was composed by Lloyd George and accepted by De Valera, amid government threats to renew the war.

169   Curran, *The Birth of the Irish Free State*, 276.

170   The 1937 constitution made Ireland a republic in all but name. On Easter

Monday 1949 this too changed when the country's name became the Republic of Ireland.

171 Macardle, *The Irish Republic,* 460–61; G. A. Hayes-McCoy, "The Conduct of the Anglo-Irish War (January 1919 to the Truce in July 1921)," in *The Irish Struggle* 66. Lyons quotes the IRA commander Michael Collins as saying later that his forces could not have held out more than three more weeks had it not been for the cease-fire. See Lyons, *Ireland since the Famine,* 427.

172 Boyce, *Englishmen and Irish Troubles.* 180; see also Townshend, *The British Campaign in Ireland,* 186.

173 Boyce, *Englishmen and Irish Troubles,* 107.

174 Letter written by Lloyd George to Bonar Law, June 7, 1921, quoted in Blake, *The Unknown Prime Minister,* 428.

175 Jones, *Whitehall Diary,* 12. On the absence of a coherent policy toward Ireland during this period see Morgan, *Consensus and Disunity,* 126–27; and Lawlor, *Britain and Ireland,* 39–40.

176 Morgan, *Consensus and Disunity,* 180.

177 A. J. P. Taylor, *English History, 1914–1945* (London: Pelican, 1970) 179.

178 Morgan, *Consensus and Disunity,* 180.

179 This account of the rise and fall of the "fusionist" initiative in 1919 and early 1920 is primarily drawn from Morgan's fine analysis of the episode in *Consensus and Disunity,* 174–91. See also Wilson, *The Downfall of the Liberal Party,* 192–98.

180 Morgan, *Consensus and Disunity,* 186–87.

181 These contacts were established by Alfred Cope, one of Lloyd George's key men at the Munitions Ministry during the war. Cope was transferred to Ireland in 1920 as assistant undersecretary. See Morgan, *Consensus and Disunity,* 129. In early April 1921, Lloyd George told Lord Riddell that he had established contact through an intermediary with Michael Collins, but thought it necessary for a personal meeting. His reluctance to meet with Collins stemmed only from his fear of its political repercussions in Britain. *Lord Riddell's Intimate Diary of the Peace Conference and After, 1918–1923* (New York: Reynal and Hitchcock, 1934) 289.

182 "Dominion home rule" or "dominion self-government" were terms suggesting a Canadian or South African kind of independence within the British Empire, or, as it was increasingly referred to, the British Commonwealth.

183 Boyce, "How to Settle the Irish Question," 151–52.

184 Salvidge, *Salvidge of Liverpool,* 190.

185 Boyce, "How to Settle the Irish Question," 151–54; For Lloyd George's response to a bishops' protest against repression in Ireland, see the *Manchester Guardian,* April 22, 1921.

186 Churchill, *The World Crisis,* 290.

187 Jones, *Whitehall Diary,* 63–70.

188 *Manchester Guardian,* June 24, 1921. See also the *Times,* June 25, 1921. Middleton, a longtime leader of southern Unionists, was at this time personally engaged in arranging secret meetings between Sinn Fein representatives and a variety of southern Unionist notables. Patrick Buckland, *Irish Unionism: The Anglo-Irish and the New Ireland, 1885–1922* (Dublin: Gill and Macmillan, 1972) 235.

189   Townshend, *British Campaign in Ireland,* 181–83.

190   Ibid., 189–90.

191   J. A. Spender, *Great Britain: Empire and Commonwealth, 1886–1935* (London: Cassell, 1936) 610; Lyons, *Ireland since the Famine,* 426; and Townshend, *The British Campaign in Ireland,* 175.

192   The committee was chaired by Austen Chamberlain and included Sir Laming Worthington-Evans—the sternest hawk in the cabinet—Balfour, and Henry Wilson (at that time chief of the imperial general staff).

193   Macardle, *The Irish Republic,* 459.

194   Dangerfield, *The Damnable Question,* 328. For details see the *Manchester Guardian,* June 24, 1921. See also Lord Beaverbrook, *The Decline and Fall of Lloyd George* (New York: Duell, Sloan and Pearce, 1963) 66.

195   Concerning the calculations behind Lloyd George's dramatic change in policy toward Sinn Fein see Lawlor, *Britain and Ireland,* 86–87; Dangerfield, *The Damnable Question,* 327–29; Frank Pakenham, *Peace by Ordeal* (London: Sidgwick and Jackson, 1935) 64–70; and Boyce, *Englishmen and Irish Troubles,* 136–41.

196   Dangerfield, *The Damnable Question,* 328.

197   Selborne, for example, who considered "the Irish rebellion [as] only part of a worldwide Bolshevist conspiracy against England," sadly noted that "a very large majority in the country are quite determined that the government shall have an unfettered chance to work out their policy to the conclusion of some form of semi-Dominion government for the South of Ireland if they can." *The Crisis of British Unionism: The Domestic Political Papers of the Second Earl of Selborne,* 227 and 231.

198   John D. Fair, "The Anglo-Irish Treaty of 1921: Unionist Aspects of the Peace," *Journal of British Studies* 12 (November 1972) 138. See also Boyce, "How to Settle the Irish Question," 159.

199   Boyce, "How to Settle the Irish Question," 159.

200   "You can get a fresh deal for Ireland," Tim Healy told Arthur Griffith just prior to the Anglo-Irish negotiations, "but you can only get as much as the Conservative Party can be persuaded to give you. The Premier himself is in the chains to the Conservatives in this matter. Nonetheless, the great mass of sensible Conservative opinion will give you much if you handle the situation sensibly." Quoted in Beaverbrook, *The Decline and Fall of Lloyd George,* 97. Healy's contemporaneous judgment is supported by Fair, "The Anglo-Irish Treaty of 1921," 134–49. See also Dangerfield, *The Damnable Question,* 345.

201   Ian Colvin, *The Life of Lord Carson,* 3:410–15.

202   Pakenham, *Peace by Ordeal,* 260.

203   Mowat, "The Irish Question in British Politics (1916–1922)," 141. See also Lawlor, *Britain and Ireland,* 153. Winston Churchill, for one, thought that the treaty was "fatal" for Lloyd George. In this he likened Lloyd George to other great English statesmen—Essex, Strafford, Pitt, and Gladstone—whose careers had suffered from their attempts to resolve the great question. "But Lloyd George falls with this weighty difference, that whereas all these others, however great their efforts and sacrifices, left behind them only a problem, he has achieved—must we not hope?—a solution." Churchill, *The World Crisis,* 307.

204   Boyce, *The Irish Question and British Politics, 1868–1986,* 65.

7. THE ALGERIAN QUESTION IN FRENCH POLITICS, 1955–1962

1 Quoted in Melvin Richter, "Tocqueville on Algeria," *Review of Politics* 25 (July 1963) 369.

2 For a similar analysis see Raymond Aron, *France: Steadfast and Changing: The Fourth to the Fifth Republic* (Cambridge: Harvard University Press, 1960) 106–7.

3 The changing location of the Algerian problem in French political life in this period is summarized in the Appendix in Figure A-3. The zenith of the effort to establish Algérie française as hegemonic can be identified as point G (1955–56) to the left of the ideological hegemony threshold. By late 1957 and early 1958, however, the Algerian question's "location" had shifted to point H, close to the regime threshold. The regime threshold was crossed in the state-contracting direction in 1961, represented by the Algerian problem's subsequent location as point I.

4 For the most detailed discussion of this "game" available see Nathan Leites, *On the Game of Politics in France* (Stanford: Stanford University Press, 1959).

5 This excluded the Communists after 1947 and the Poujadists after 1956.

6 Interview with Mendès-France conducted in 1980, quoted in Jean Lacouture, *Pierre Mendès France* (New York: Holmes and Meier, 1984) 307.

7 *New York Times,* January 30, February 4 and 5, 1955.

8 This might not have been the case had the French Communist party been considered an eligible coalition partner. However, cold war criteria excluded the votes of nearly 100 Communist deputies, returned to the National Assembly as a result of the 1951 general elections, and the 140 Communist deputies elected in 1956. With Communist deputies excluded from the coalition considerations of every other party, strong anticolonialist sentiment in the one-quarter of the electorate represented by the PCF was deprived of effective expression in the composition of governments. For example, after Mendès-France was driven from office, Christian Pineau, a Socialist leader with decidedly dovish inclinations toward Algeria, was asked to form a government. Although supported by both Socialists and Radicals, Pineau was unwilling to consider forming a Popular Front with the Communists. He therefore lost his investiture vote, 312 to 268, with the Indépendants, Gaullists, and Peasants opposing him on the right and the Communists on the left. See in particular Alfred Grosser, *La IVe République et sa politique extérieure* (Paris: Armand Colin, 1972) 398.

9 Also known as the *modérés,* the Indépendant party was a loose array of conservative politicians and the largest right-wing political party in France.

10 Concerning the Moroccan crisis as a kind of prelude to the Algerian crisis of 1958, see Alexander Werth, *The Strange History of Pierre Mendès-France and the Great Conflict over French North Africa* (London: Barrie Books, 1957) 207–43.

11 Philip M. Williams, "The French Election of 1956: The Campaign," *Political Studies* 4, no. 2 (1956) 175; George Armstrong Kelly, *Lost Soldiers: The French Army and Empire in Crisis, 1947–1962* (Cambridge: MIT Press, 1965) 166. The elaborate voting rules governing Fourth Republic parliamentary elections, combined with the complexity of the political map, make it difficult to summarize

the results of the 1956 election. The Communists remained the largest party, receiving more than 25 percent of the vote and increasing their representation in the Assembly by more than 40 percent. The Socialists and the MRP both slipped somewhat. The Mendèsiste Radicals increased their share of the vote as well as their representation in the Assembly, while "Faurist" Radicals lost some support. The Indépendants increased their share of the popular vote, but the size of their representation in the Assembly hardly changed. The Gaullists lost most heavily, with much of their support going to the populist, proto-fascist Poujadist movement, which stunned observers by receiving 12.1 percent of the votes and fifty-two seats.

12   Official translation of Mollet's speech published in Charles S. Maier and Dan S. White eds., *The Thirteenth of May: The Advent of de Gaulle's Republic* (New York: Oxford University Press, 1968) 74–75.

13   For the former interpretation see Alistair Horne, *A Savage War of Peace: Algeria, 1954–1962* (New York: Penguin, 1977) 150; Werth, *The Strange History of Pierre Mendès-France,* 291–94; Jean-Pierre Rioux, *The Fourth Republic, 1944–1958* (Cambridge: Cambridge University Press, 1987) 265; and André Philip, quoted in Harvey G. Simmons, *French Socialists in Search of a Role, 1956–1967* (Ithaca, N.Y.: Cornell University Press, 1970) 25–26. For the latter, see Charles A. Micaud, *Communism and the French Left* (New York: Praeger, 1963) 212 and 226; and Philip M. Williams, *French Politicians and Elections, 1951–1969* (Cambridge: Cambridge University Press, 1970) 6–7. The continuity of policy toward Algeria, from the Mollet government through those of Bourgès-Maunoury (June 1957 to September 1957) and Gaillard (November 1957 to April 1958), is epitomized in Lacoste's position as minister in charge of Algeria in each of these cabinets.

14   The analysis that follows has benefited substantially from that of Kahler, who stresses "the demands of coalition formation" as the key factor in explaining Mollet's behavior and his "tenacious defense" of his Algerian policy. Miles Kahler, *Decolonization in Britain and France: The Domestic Consequences of International Politics* (Princeton: Princeton University Press, 1984) 196–201.

15   From "General Directive No. 1," issued by Robert Lacoste as resident-minister in Algeria to the French officers stationed in Algeria, May 19, 1956. Published in Maier and White, *The Thirteenth of May,* 94 (emphasis added).

16   The responses were as follows: Yes, have confidence in the present government to settle the Algerian problem—April 1956, 37 percent; July 1956, 38 percent; March 1957, 39 percent; No, do not have confidence in the present government to settle the Algerian problem—April 1956, 27 percent; July 1956, 30 percent; March 1957, 30 percent. The polls were conducted by IFOP, published in various issues of *Sondages,* and conveniently tabulated in Rioux, *The Fourth Republic, 1944–1958,* p. 298.

17   Charles-Robert Ageron, "L'opinion française devant la guerre d'Algérie," *Revue Française d'Histoire d'Outre-Mer* 63, no. 231 (1976) 264.

18   William G. Andrews, *French Politics and Algeria* (New York: Appleton-Century-Crofts, 1962) 21.

19   Ageron, "L'opinion française devant la guerre d'Algérie," 261.

20 Ibid., 262.

21 Andrews, *French Politics and Algeria*, 20.

22 Ibid.

23 Ageron, "L'opinion française devant la guerre d'Algérie," 262.

24 Ibid., 264–65. For a similar overall appraisal of available polling data regarding French views toward Algeria see John Talbott, "French Public Opinion and the Algerian War: A Research Note," *French Historical Studies* 9 (Fall 1975) 354–61.

25 Concerning Mollet's secret contacts with the FLN in early 1956 and their importance in maintaining student support for his government at that time see Michel de La Fourniere, "Les etudiants face au declenchment de la guerre d'Algérie, 1954–1957," paper presented at the conference La guerre d'Algérie et les français, at the Institut d'Histoire du Temps Present, Paris, December 15–17, 1988.

26 Simmons, *French Socialists in Search of a Role*, 73.

27 I. R. Campbell, "Political Attitudes in France to the Algerian Question, 1954–62 with Special Reference to the Centre National des Indépendants," Ph.D. diss., Nuffield College, Oxford University, 1972, p. 620. In sharp contrast to resolutions rejecting the slogan of "integration" and calling for new, fair elections in Algeria, passed by Socialist congresses in October 1955, a motion of support for Mollet's pacification and integrationist policy received overwhelming approval from the SFIO National Congress held in June and July 1956. The vote was 3,308 to 363. Simmons, *French Socialists in Search of a Role*, 73 and 293. See also *Le Monde*, October 14, 1955; Campbell, "Political Attitudes in France to the Algerian Question, 1954–62," 101–2 and 618; and Kahler, *Decolonization in Britain and France* 202.

28 On the relationship between PCF willingness to tone down its anticolonialist position in return for enhanced possibilities for joining a government, see David Caute, *Communism and the French Intellectuals, 1914–1960* (New York: Macmillan, 1964) esp. 210–11.

29 Horne, *A Savage War of Peace*, 157.

30 Alexander Werth, *The De Gaulle Revolution* (London: Robert Hale Ltd., 1960) 7.

31 Horne, *A Savage War of Peace*, 157 and 160.

32 *L'Année Politique* (1957) 2–3 and 11–12; Edgar S. Furniss, Jr., *France: Troubled Ally* (New York: Council on Foreign Relations, 1960) 209.

33 Duncan MacRae, Jr., *Parliament, Parties, and Society in France, 1946–1958* (New York: St. Martin's, 1967) 161; and Kahler, *Decolonization in Britain and France*, 202.

34 MacRae, *Parliament, Parties, and Society in France, 1946–1958*, 161.

35 See especially Andrews, *French Politics and Algeria*, 199.

36 *L'Année Politique* (1957) 59–61.

37 Andrews, *French Politics and Algeria*, 76–78 and *L'Année Politique* (1957) 244–45. The following description of the loi cadre legislation introduced by the Bourgès-Maunory and Gaillard governments is drawn from Andrews's account, which itself is based on the daily political reportage of *Le Monde*, and from *L'Année Politique* (1957) 84–87 and 244–47.

38 Andrews, *French Politics and Algeria,* 81, quoting *Le Monde,* quoting Mitterrand.

39 Ibid., 85–86, quoting *Le Monde.*

40 In June, 12 of 21 Social Republicans had voted for Bourgès-Maunoury's investiture, with 8 abstaining or not voting. In September, no Social Republicans voted to support the government, 17 voted no confidence, and 4 did not take part. In June, 67 of the 103 deputies representing the closely allied Indépendant and Indépendant Peasant parties had voted for Bourgès-Maunoury's investiture, with none voting against and 32 either abstaining or not voting. In September, of the 110 deputies representing what were now arranged as the Indépendant, Peasants for Social Action, and Peasant Parties, only 46 supported the government, while 51 voted no confidence, and 13 either abstained or did not vote. *L'Année Politique* (1957) 63 and 94.

41 Rioux, *The Fourth Republic, 1944–1958,* 295; Andrews, *French Politics and Algeria,* 88–90 and 160; *L'Année Politique* (1958) 250–51.

42 Werth, *The Strange History of Pierre Mendès-France,* 220–25; and Furniss, *France: Troubled Ally,* 118.

43 *New York Times,* January 15, 1956. For survey of French opinion in April 1956 linking the crisis in Algeria to fears of a regime collapse, see *New York Times,* April 30, 1956. On the readiness of "certain leaders from most of the major political parties...to subvert the Republic itself rather than lose Algeria to the rebels," see T. Alexander Smith, "Algeria and the French *Modérés:* The Politics of Immoderation?" *Western Political Quarterly* 18 (1965) 117.

44 Jean Rous, "Quelle solution en Algérie?" *Revue Socialiste,* no. 96 (April 1956) 344.

45 Werth, *The De Gaulle Revolution,* 2. The same motivation, according to Werth, was present in the cover-up of the torture murder of mathematics professor Maurice Audin in June 1957. See ibid., 16n.

46 *Le Monde,* June 30/July 1, 1957.

47 Henri Alleg, *The Question* (New York: George Braziller, 1958) 57–58.

48 Kahler, *Decolonization in Britain and France,* 193.

49 Ibid., 193, 200, and 357; see also Campbell, "Political Attitudes in France to the Algerian Question, 1954–62," 44.

50 The pattern here is closely analogous to the way threats to parliamentary authority materialized in connection with the first two Irish Home Rule bills before emerging as decisive in blocking implementation of the third.

51 "By the end of 1957," according to I. R. Campbell, "there were some forty conservative deputies willing to precipitate a crisis in the regime rather than agree to a policy of concessions in Algeria." Campbell, "Political Attitudes in France to the Algerian Question, 1954–62," xviii–xix.

52 *L'Année Politique* (1957) 538–39; excerpts from the official translation in Maier and White, *The Thirteenth of May,* 84–86.

53 Rioux, *The Fourth Republic, 1944–1958,* 285.

54 Simmons, *French Socialists in Search of a Role,* 67. See also Werth, *The De Gaulle Revolution,* 20.

55 Rioux, *The Fourth Republic, 1944–1958,* 493n.

56 *Le Monde,* March 15, 1958, quoted in Werth, *The De Gaulle Revolution,* 27; *New York Times,* March 14, 1958. Alexander Werth interprets the episode, "though unimportant on the face of it ... [as] nevertheless highly indicative of the Government's loss of authority ... a warning to everybody ... that *the police could not be depended on by the Fourth Republic.*" Werth, *The De Gaulle Revolution,* 28 (emphasis in original).

57 Rioux, *The Fourth Republic, 1944–1958,* 296–97.

58 Werth, *The De Gaulle Revolution,* 32n.

59 *L'Année Politique* (1958) 42–43.

60 Ibid., 41.

61 *New York Times,* March 2 and 20, 1958.

62 *New York Times,* April 27, 1958.

63 Joseph Kraft, *The Struggle for Algeria* (Garden City, N.Y.: Doubleday, 1961) 173–74.

64 Werth, *The De Gaulle Revolution,* 62. *New York Times,* May 11, 1958. The wrath of Algérie française partisans against Pflimlin was fueled by a widely discussed article he published on April 23, 1958, in *Nouvel Alsacien.* "We refuse," he had written, "to be forced into the dilemma: rigidity or abandonment. We believe that a third policy exists ... to engage in discussions with representatives of those who fight us to determine the modalities for a cease fire and for guaranteeing free elections." J. R. Tournoux, *Secrets d'état* (Paris: Plon, 1960) 246.

65 Merry Bromberger and Serge Bromberger, *Les 13 complots du 13 mai: Ou la deliverance de Gulliver* (Paris: Artheme Fayard, 1959) 133; Kraft, *The Struggle for Algeria,* 173.

66 Maier and White, *The Thirteenth of May,* 213.

67 Tournoux, *Secrets d'état,* 246–47.

68 Werth, *The De Gaulle Revolution,* 55.

69 In their well-known book on the subject, *Les 13 complots du 13 mai,* Merry and Serge Bromberger claim to have identified thirteen separate but overlapping plots.

70 Werth, *The De Gaulle Revolution,* 44–45; Kelly, *Lost Soldiers,* 216–18. After the revolt of May 1958, Colonel Trinquier offered a toast: "Neguib est au pouvoir; vive Nasser!" The same image was cultivated by the civilian ultras of Algiers. See Horne, *A Savage War of Peace,* 299.

71 Kelly, *Lost Soldiers,* 14–16; Raoul Girardet, "Civil and Military Power in the Fourth Republic," in *The Thirteenth of May,* 109.

72 Girardet, "Civil and Military Power in the Fourth Republic," 116.

73 On the psychological impact of isolation and reduced social and economic status on French officers during this period see ibid., 115–16; Orville D. Menard, *The Army and the Fifth Republic* (Lincoln: University of Nebraska Press, 1967) 50–75. See also Jean Larteguy's novels, *The Centurions* (New York: Dutton, 1962), and *The Praetorians* (New York: Dutton, 1963).

74 On the French army's doctrine of revolutionary war see Kelly, *Lost Soldiers,* 107–25.

75 Ibid., 8.

76 Menard, *The Army and the Fifth Republic,* 43–44 and 121–27.

77 "For the military," wrote Edgar Furniss, "the antics of the last Fourth Republic governments provided conclusive evidence that fundamental political change was overdue and must come soon, if the hierarchical authority of the armed forces were to escape utter destruction." Furniss, *France: Troubled Ally,* 177.

78 Prior to Chassin, the honorary president of the Indochina Veterans' Association, thousands of whose members rioted in Paris the day after the May 13 revolt in Algiers, was Raoul Salan.

79 Menard, *The Army and the Fifth Republic,* 103–4.

80 Bromberger and Bromberger, *Les 13 complots du 13 mai,* 69.

81 Kelly, *Lost Soldiers,* 224. For details of Operation Resurrection see Bromberger and Bromberger, *Les 13 complots du 13 mai,* 310; Werth, *The De Gaulle Revolution,* 48; Horne, *A Savage War of Peace,* 180–81; and Kelly, *Lost Soldiers,* 133.

82 Concentrated mainly in the area of Algiers, this force was comprised of reservists who served four days per month. Horne's comment on this militia is that "it resembled in more ways than one the Ulster Defence Force." Horne, *A Savage War of Peace,* 275–76.

83 Richard Brace and Joan Brace, *Ordeal in Algeria* (Princeton: Van Nostrand, 1960) 210.

84 Werth, *The De Gaulle Revolution,* 63–64.

85 Ibid., 43–44. Sérigny's *L'Echo d'Alger* editorials, May 11–12 and 15, 1958, can be found in Maier and White, *The Thirteenth of May,* 216–18 and 259–61. See also Furniss, *France: Troubled Ally,* 320.

86 Kelly, *Lost Soldiers,* 213–14. For examples of similar judgments about the decisive role of the Gaullists in provoking and "channeling" the events of May 13 into a movement for the return of de Gaulle and the fall of the Fourth Republic see Nicholas Wahl, *The Fifth Republic: France's New Political Agenda* (New York: Random House, 1959) 18; Roy C. Macridis and Bernard E. Brown, *The De Gaulle Republic: Quest for Unity* (Homewood, Ill.: Dorsey Press, 1960) 63; and Philip M. Williams, *Wars, Plots and Scandals in Post-War France* (Cambridge: Cambridge University Press, 1970) 133.

87 The derogatory phrase was coined by Michel Debré in his attack on the Fourth Republic published in 1957, *Ces princes qui nous gouvernent* (Paris: Plon, 1957), one of the staunchest "Algeria firsters" in de Gaulle's circle of confidants and one of the chief architects of the May revolt. Debré served as justice minister in de Gaulle's cabinet formed on June 1, and as prime minister under the Fifth Republic from January 1959 to April 1962.

88 Murphrey, "Jacques Soustelle and the Passing of French Algeria," Ph.D. Diss., Duke University, 1976, 164; Raoul Girardet, *L'idée coloniale en France, 1871–1962* (Paris: la Table Ronde, 1972) 263–64.

89 Suspected of having been involved in the Salan assassination and coup attempt of January 1957, Debré was under constant police surveillance. Horne, *A Savage War of Peace,* 274.

90 *Courrier de la Colère,* December 20, 1957, as quoted in Georges Bidault, *Resistance: The Political Autobiography of Georges Bidault* (New York: Praeger, 1967) 223.

91   *New York Times,* March 1, 1958.

92   Brace and Brace, *Ordeal in Algeria,* 198; Macridis and Brown, *The De Gaulle Republic,* 69–71; Tournoux, *Secrets d'état,* 180–83 and 257n.

93   Murphrey, "Jacques Soustelle and the Passing of French Algeria," 160.

94   Jacques Fauvet in *Le Monde,* March 4, 1958, and Alain de Sérigny, *L'Echo d'Alger,* April 17, 1958, in Maier and White, *The Thirteenth of May,* 174–75 and 189.

95   Quoted in Werth, *The De Gaulle Revolution,* 361.

96   Murphrey, "Jacques Soustelle and the Passing of French Algeria," 167.

97   Quoted in Macridis and Brown, *The De Gaulle Republic,* 70.

98   Ibid., 65.

99   According to a *L'Express* exposé, one-third of the USRAF membership was armed in 1957. Werth, *The De Gaulle Revolution,* 105–6.

100   Macridis and Brown, *The De Gaulle Republic,* 69. Delbecque later described himself as "the organizer of the Movement of the Thirteenth of May. I made it my business to be in the right place, at the right time, to exploit in General de Gaulle's favor the upheaval that was bound to take place." Concerning Delbecque's central role see also Tournoux, *Secrets d'état,* 219–20; and Bromberger and Brombergre, *Les 13 complots du 13 mai,* 105ff.

101   Horne, *A Savage War of Peace,* 276.

102   Williams, *Wars, Plots, and Scandals in Post-War France,* 135; Macridis and Brown, *The De Gaulle Republic,* 71.

103   Bromberger and Bromberger, *Les 13 complots du 13 mai,* 112.

104   Williams, *Wars, Plots, and Scandals in Post-War France,* 135n and 136.

105   Ibid., 137.

106   Macridis and Brown, *The De Gaulle Republic,* 76.

107   Murphrey, "Jacques Soustelle and the Passing of French Algeria," 170.

108   Three weeks after these events Trinquier proudly described his involvement in the "subversion" of May 13. He told a meeting of Algiers students on June 7 that "we committed subversion on May 13, by overthrowing the established power by illegal means." Leites, *On the Game of Politics in France,* 149.

109   For the text of communiqué, see Maier and White, *The Thirteenth of May,* 239–40.

110   See Aron, *France: Steadfast and Changing,* 116.

111   On the absence of top-ranking officers willing to accept the post of chief of staff or even to support the government against Algiers, and on the ineffectiveness of quick increases in military budgets to elicit this support, see Menard, *The Army and the Fifth Republic,* 118; John Steward Ambler, *The French Army in Politics, 1945–1962* (Columbus: Ohio State University Press, 1966) 247; and Furniss, *France: Troubled Ally,* 331–32.

112   *Le Monde,* December 6, 1958, quoted in Maier and White, *The Thirteenth of May,* 322; Menard, *The Army and the Fifth Republic,* 125.

113   Kraft, *The Struggle for Algeria,* 191.

114   Rioux, *The Fourth Republic, 1944–1958,* 305.

115   Maier and White, *The Thirteenth of May,* reprinted official translation, 287.

116   Werth, *The De Gaulle Revolution,* 127.

117   Tournoux, *Secrets d'etat,* 361.

118   Bromberger and Bromberger, *Les 13 complots du 13 may,* 359. Telegrams from de Gaulle, via Major Vitasse, signaling Algiers to move forward with Operation Resurrection and then stop it were presented at the April 1962 trial of General Jouhaud. See Menard, *The Army and the Fifth Republic,* 129–30.

119   Werth, *The De Gaulle Revolution,* 127; Brace and Brace, *Ordeal in Algeria,* 241.

120   Quoted in Macridis and Brown, *The De Gaulle Republic,* 92.

121   From *Le Monde,* May 31, 1958, quoted in Furniss, *France: Troubled Ally,* 344. American intelligence had actually informed the French government that an invasion of the mainland was about to take place. For judgments that the fear of civil war was genuine within the attentive public of France and decisive in its embrace of de Gaulle, see Werth, *The De Gaulle Revolution,* 2; Michel Dobry, *Sociologie des crises politiques* (Paris: Presses de la Fondation Nationale des Sciences Politiques, 1986) 233n; Brace and Brace, *Ordeal in Algeria,* 244–49; Rioux, *The Fourth Republic 1944–1958,* 310–11; and Dorothy Pickles, *The Government and Politics of France* (London: Methuen, 1973) 28. For a detailed analysis of the regime's vulnerability in May 1958 to violent threats against it, see Williams, *Wars, Plots, and Scandals in Post-War France,* 150–54. "Always avoid civil war," Williams quotes Jules Moch as commenting, "especially when you are sure to lose."

122   Bromberger and Bromberger, *Les 13 complots du 13 mai,* 406–8; Menard, *The Army and the Fifth Republic,* 128.

123   Horne, *A Savage War of Peace,* 297. The anxieties created by the Algiers coup in the minds of French "republicans" are easily understandable if one remembers, as they did, how General Francisco Franco had used his forces in Spanish Morocco to overthrow the Spanish republic in July 1936. Interior Minister Jules Moch actually sent telegrams to prefects throughout France ordering them, in the event of a military takeover, to form an underground resistance and organize mass strikes and other actions. Bromberger and Bromberger, *Les 13 complots du 13 may,* 382–83; Tournoux, *Secrets d'état,* 391–92. In these days André Malraux also portrayed the Fourth Republic as heading toward a Spanish-style civil war. It would last three years, he predicted, "there will be a million dead. There will be no more France as a great nation; it will be finished." Janet Flanner [Genet], *Paris Journal: 1944–65,* ed. William Shawn (New York: Harcourt Brace Jovanovich, 1965) 377.

124   "Message of M. René Coty, President of the French Republic to the French Parliament on May 29, 1958," translated and distributed by the Embassy of France, Press and Information Division, *French Affairs,* no. 58 (May 1958).

125   Furniss, *France: Troubled Ally,* 342.

126   "The army," as Nathan Leites put it, "threatened to make war on the political class." Leites, *On the Game of Politics in France,* 154.

127   See Coty's warning quoted in Chapter 4. Coty threatened to ask Mitterrand to form a Popular Front government and then resign if the Assembly refused his advice to accept de Gaulle.

128   On the irresistibility of the "Gaullist wave" for the majority of Socialist

parliamentarians see George A. Codding, Jr., and William Safran, *Ideology and Politics: The Socialist Party of France* (Boulder, Colo.: Westview Press, 1979) 148.

129   Sirius [Hubert Beuve-Méry], quoted in *Le Monde,* John Talbott, *The War without a Name: France and Algeria, 1954–1962* (New York: Knopf, 1980) 132–33.

130   De Gaulle's "full powers" authorized his government "to take any action it viewed as necessary in the fields of taxation, economy, production, military reorganization and Algerian and North African affairs." Robert A. Diamond, ed., *France under De Gaulle* (New York: Facts on File, 1970) 15.

131   Mendès-France remarks are reprinted from the *Journal officiel,* June 1, 1958, pp. 3377–79.

132   Thomas Hobbes, *Leviathan* (New York: Collier, 1962) 100.

133   Maier and White, *The Thirteenth of May,* 331 (emphasis added).

134   "In a short speech," de Gaulle later wrote, "I tossed them the words, seemingly spontaneous but in reality carefully calculated, which I hoped would fire their enthusiasm without committing me further than I was willing to go." De Gaulle, *Memoirs of Hope Renewal and Endeavor* (New York: Simon and Schuster, 1970) 47. De Gaulle's distrust of the military men and the Europeans in Algeria is reflected in his decision that security for his Algiers visit would be provided not by the paratroopers who had helped bring him to power, but by naval infantry units unconnected to the events of the past month. Werth, *The De Gaulle Revolution,* 183.

135   In Mostaganem, shortly before returning to France, de Gaulle did use, for the first (and what would be the last) time, the phrase "Algérie française."

136   Werth, *The De Gaulle Revolution,* 186–87.

137   Kelly, *Lost Soldiers,* 249. On de Gaulle's initially diffident treatment of the army see C. S. Sulzberger, "The Army's Guerrilla War against de Gaulle," *New York Times,* November 15, 1958; idem, "De Gaulle: The Role of the Giants," *New York Times,* June 4, 1958. For the overwhelming integrationist and Algérie française sentiment in the army that de Gaulle found himself facing in fall 1958, see Laurent Theis and Philippe Ratte, *La guerre d'Algérie ou le temps des meprises* (Tours: Mame, 1974) 215–16.

138   At the beginning of August 1958, Henry Ginger of the *New York Times* observed that French political thinking was still dominated by the same kind of "threats of a Right-wing military coup and of civil war" that preceded de Gaulle's takeover. André Siegfried, the doyen of French political scientists, remarked at the time that approval of de Gaulle's draft constitution in the upcoming referendum was "imperative if we do not wish to find ourselves again tomorrow on the verge of civil war." Henry Ginger, "Fears of a Coup Still Vex France," *New York Times,* August 3, 1958.

139   These transfers were accomplished mainly through promotions and honors. Menard, *The Army and the Fifth Republic,* 158.

140   For a description of how de Gaulle thwarted Soustelle's plans for an election system that might have produced a decisive parliamentary majority in favor of Algérie française, and for turning the UNR into a mass movement in favor of *intégration,* see Werth, *The De Gaulle Revolution,* 356–58 and 364–66.

141   Horne, *A Savage War of Peace,* 311.

142   C. L. Sulzberger, *The Test: De Gaulle and Algeria* (New York: Harcourt, Brace, and World, 1962) 121.

143   For an account of his conversations see Menard, *The Army and the Fifth Republic,* 147–48.

144   Horne, *A Savage War of Peace,* 347 and 354.

145   *L'Année Politique* (1959) 106–7.

146   Ibid., 109–10; Kelly, *Lost Soldiers,* 249.

147   This account of Operation Veronique is based on *L'Année Politique* (1959), and on Menard, *The Army and the Fifth Republic,* 150–54, which itself relies heavily on Merry Bromberger, Serge Bromberger, Georgette Elgey, and J.-F. Chauvel, *Barricades et colonels* (Paris: Artheme Fayard, 1960). See also Bernard E. Brown, "The Army and Politics in France," *Journal of Politics* 23 (May 1961) 268.

148   *L'Année Politique* (1959), 110.

149   Bromberger et al., *Barricades et colonels,* 59.

150   Sixty (European) Algerian deputies boycotted the meeting during which the vote was held. Most of the no votes were cast by Indépendants and Communists. There were twenty-eight abstentions. Soustelle, conveniently, was visiting French possessions in the South Pacific. See *L'Année Politique* (1959) 115–121.

151   *Economist,* January 30, 1960, 433.

152   Ibid., 374.

153   Concerning the details of this plot see Bromberger et al., *Barricades et colonels,* 67–85.

154   Kelly, *Lost Soldiers,* 261.

155   Ibid., 256–63; Horne, *A Savage War of Peace,* 349–52.

156   Talbott, *The War without a Name,* 153.

157   Massu's interview, translated from the German, was published in *Le Monde* on January 20, 1959. These excerpts are from Menard, *The Army and the Fifth Republic,* 160–61 and Horne, *A Savage War of Peace,* 357.

158   Bromberger et al., *Barricades et colonels,* 154; Horne, *A Savage War of Peace,* 358. See de Gaulle, *Memoirs of Hope,* 78.

159   Menard, *The Army and the Fifth Republic,* 168–69. Massu is reported, in this conversation, to have retracted his advice of the previous day against launching another May 13–style revolt.

160   Services in Algiers were paralyzed by the strike for eight straight days. Bromberger et al., *Barricades et colonels,* 169.

161   Menard, *The Army and the Fifth Republic,* 176.

162   Ibid., 174–75.

163   Bromberger et al., *Barricades et colonels,* 287.

164   Already confused by rivalries among their leaders—especially Ortiz and Lagaillarde—the disorientation of the pieds noirs was further aggravated by an unauthorized radio address by Delouvrier containing passionate expressions of sympathy for the courage of the men on the barricades, pleas to the army to avoid fratricidal conflict, promises of an Algeria that would be "freely and incontrovertibly French," and dire warnings of the consequences of defying de Gaulle.

165   Kelly, *Lost Soldiers,* 275.

166   These excerpts from de Gaulle's address of January 29, 1960, are quoted from the text as translated in Macridis and Brown, *The De Gaulle Republic,* 376–79.

167   Sulzberger, *The Test,* 127–28.

168   Williams, *Wars, Plots, and Scandals in Post-War France,* 177. The essay in which this quote appears was originally published in January 1961.

169   *New York Times,* February 1, 1960.

170   Brace and Brace, *Ordeal in Algeria,* 338.

171   Smith, "Algeria and the French *Modérés,*" 127–28.

172   The first sentence in the *New York Times's* front-page, headline article of January 27, 1960 (Henry Ginger, datelined Paris, January 26), was "French democracy hung in the balance tonight."

173   The real uncertainty felt by government ministers about the military's response and the vividness of their fears for the survival of the Fifth Republic are stressed in most accounts of the Barricades Rebellion. See, for example, Kelly, *Lost Soldiers,* 266, 273–74; Menard, *The Army and the Fifth Republic,* 172–78; Horne, *A Savage War of Peace,* 365–66; *France under De Gaulle,* 30; Kraft, *The Struggle for Algeria,* 236; Sulzberger, *The Test,* 124–25; and Bromberger et al., *Barricades et colonels,* 254–55, 270, 286–87, and 296–98.

174   Bromberger et al., *Barricades et colonels,* 297. Guillebon's conditions were not accepted. The post was finally filled by Pierre Messmer, a reserve officer recalled from active duty.

175   Debré and Guillaumat, the only ministers to visit Algeria during the crisis, were both severely shaken by what they had seen and heard from the colonels. Debré had been "paralyzed by the fear of provoking a military putsch by a false move." After returning to Paris, he worried that a junta had already formed and that civil war would erupt if he could not persuade de Gaulle to acquiesce in the demands of the Algiers colonels. Sobbing, Debré reportedly told his ministers that "he envied those whose faith did not prohibit them from committing suicide." Bromberger et al., *Barricades et colonels,* 287 and 292. Debré's Assembly speech is translated in Macridis and Brown, *The De Gaulle Republic,* 379.

176   Bernard Tricot, *Les sentiers de la paix: Algérie, 1958–1962* (Paris: Plon, 1972) 140–42. The quotation is from article 16 of the Constitution of the Fifth Republic.

177   Kelly, *Lost Soldiers,* 268. Kelly's is the outstanding study of French civil-military relations during this period. He observes that these guarantees were of great importance to the army: "It is possible that this act alone forestalled Army complicity in the insurrection." For the role played by General Ely, chief of the general staff, in communicating de Gaulle's reassuring promises to Challe and the rest of the Algerian high command see Brace and Brace, *Ordeal in Algeria,* 348–50.

178   Bromberger et al., *Barricades et colonels,* 300. "I have already said it," de Gaulle is reported to have told the colonels, "Now the Algerians must say it!"

179   *New York Times,* January 28, 1960.

180   Translation of de Gaulle's speech of January 29, 1960, reprinted in Macridis and Brown, *The De Gaulle Republic,* 377.

181   Aron, *France: Steadfast and Changing,* 189. The usually well-informed Israeli Embassy in Paris was also convinced, during this period, that de Gaulle would be overthrown. Uzi Benziman, "The Scheme of the Jesuit," *Haaretz,* September 29, 1989. For judgments by other observers that Algeria's disposition remained a regime-threatening problem after January 1960 see Brace and Brace, *Ordeal in Algeria,* 357, 365, and 378–79; Flanner, *Paris Journal,* 443 and 453; Campbell, "Political Attitudes in France to the Algerian Question," 525ff. Jean Planchais, "The Army, the Regime, and Algeria," *Le Monde,* March 11 and 12, 1960; Sulzberger, *The Test,* 120–48; and "The King and the Barons," *Economist,* February 6, 1960, 500–502.

182   Menard, *The Army and the Fifth Republic,* 185–87; Horne, *A Savage War of Peace,* 373–74 and 381; Ambler, *The French Army in Politics, 1945–1962,* 258.

183   Jean Lacouture, *De Gaulle* (London: Hutchinson, 1970) 176.

184   Quoted in Horne, *A Savage War of Peace,* 376.

185   Quoted ibid., 376 and 378; and Kelly, *Lost Soldiers,* 295.

186   *Le Monde,* March 6–7, 1960, quoted and translated in Menard, *The Army and the Fifth Republic,* 193.

187   Charles-Robert Ageron, *L'Algérie algérienne de Napoléon III à de Gaulle* (Paris: Sindbad, 1980) 249. Concerning the "concessions" de Gaulle appeared to the army to have made during this tour see Brown, "The Army and Politics in France," 273.

188   For the reaction among French supporters of Algerian self-determination to reports of de Gaulle's conversations with the officers during his Algeria visit see Horne, *A Savage War of Peace,* 377; *L'Année Politique* (1960) 27; and the *New York Times,* March 4 and 11, 1960.

189   The GPRA was established by the FLN in September 1958 as a "government in exile."

190   Concerning the problematic loyalty of the army to the Fifth Republic, and perceptions of its "veto" over Algerian policy in the year following the Barricades Rebellion, see Brown, "The Army and Politics in France," 266, 274, 276, and 278.

191   *L'Année Politique* (1960), 655–56.

192   Text of speech reprinted in *L'Année Politique* (1960) 660–61. Partially translated in De Gaulle, *Memoirs of Hope,* 90.

193   These quotations are from de Gaulle's radio and television address on December 20, 1960. *L'Année Politique* (1960) 663.

194   De Gaulle's December 31, 1960, broadcast, in *L'Année Politique* (1960) 664–65.

195   Horne, *A Savage War of Peace,* 428–29.

196   Eight Europeans and 112 Muslims were killed in these disturbances. Horne, *A Savage War of Peace,* 433.

197   Diamond, *France under De Gaulle,* 39.

198   *L'Année Politique* (1961) 645.

199   *L'Année Politique* (1960) 60–61.

200   Flanner, *Paris Journal*, 442.

201   *L'Année Politique* (1960) 61; Murphrey, "Jacques Soustelle and the Passing of French Algeria," 235 and 242–43.

202   *L'Année Politique* (1960) 115.

203   *New York Times*, April 19, 1961.

204   *L'Année Politique* (1960) 313n, 314, and 318–20; Roy C. Macridis and Bernard E. Brown, *Supplement to "The De Gaulle Republic: Quest for Unity"* (Homewood, Ill.: Dorsey Press, 1963) 19.

205   See Jean Planchais, "The Army, the Regime, and Algeria," pt. 2, *Le Monde*, March 12, 1960.

206   Ibid.

207   Horne, *A Savage War of Peace*, 418–19. Article 5 of the Fifth Republic Constitution names the president of the republic as "the guarantor of national independence [and] of the integrity of the territory."

208   Talbott, *The War without a Name*, 203.

209   The following week Challe discussed his plans with Soustelle and other members of the Vincennes Committee. See Paul Henissart, *Wolves in the City: The Death of French Algeria* (New York: Simon and Schuster, 1970) 74.

210   Menard, *The Army and the Fifth Republic*, 208; and Horne, *A Savage War of Peace*, 450.

211   While the colonels and Salan's Madrid group prepared for a violent takeover in Paris as well, Challe's real commitment to action in the metropole is less than clear. Challe appears to have hoped it would not be necessary. At his trial he claimed he had intended to achieve a quick and total military victory over the FLN. That victory, in his view, combined with the army's defiance of the Paris government, would bring an end to de Gaulle's political career and precipitate the political collapse of the Fifth Republic—without military action in the metropole. See Kelly, *Lost Soldiers*, 316–17.

212   Henissart, *Wolves in the City*, 53.

213   Kelly, *Lost Soldiers*, 320.

214   Among those apprehended was General Jacques Faure, who was to have led twenty-two hundred paratroopers who had taken up positions in the forests near Paris. Reinforced by sympathetic civilians and tanks from a military base in the vincinity, these troops were to have seized the Élysée Palace and other public buildings in Paris. With Faure's arrest, the paras stayed in hiding and eventually dispersed.

215   Reprinted from official translation, in Macridis and Brown, *Supplement to "The De Gaulle Republic,"* 106–7.

216   *L'Année Politique* (1960) 54–55.

217   Some months later two regular paratroop regiments were also dissolved. The divisions they belonged to were reorganized and transferred to metropolitan France. *New York Times*, November 5, 1961.

218   Horne, *A Savage War of Peace*, 531. According to Vitalis Cros, police chief of Algiers in 1962, there were four times as many OAS attacks in the city in the

six months from December 1961 to June 1962 as there were FLN attacks during the six and a half years of war. Cros made the statement during an interview conducted by Peter Batty for the film "The Suitcase or the Coffin," part 5 in a series titled *The Algerian Revolution,* by Batty Productions, London, 1987.

219 See Talbott, *The War without a Name,* 212–14; Kelly, *Lost Soldiers,* 327. Those who received the death sentence were Generals Salan, Jouhaud, and Gardy, and Colonels Argoud, Broizat, Gardes, Godard, and Lacheroy.

220 De Gaulle, *Memoirs of Hope,* 110.

221 *L'Année Politique* (1961) 153–54.

222 Ibid., 153–54. Accounts vary between two thousand and four thousand as to the exact number of officers summoned to Strasbourg. See Henissart, *Wolves in the City,* 237–38, for a description of the scene. Kelly sums up the mood in the army at the time of this meeting by quoting two unnamed officers: "Nobody has spoken of politics for the last six months." "We've been kicked in the gut." Kelly, *Lost Soldiers,* 329.

223 This was the judgment of Jacques Coup de Fréjac, director of information in Delegate-General Morin's office in Algiers: "The day after the putsch of April it was clear that from the point of view of the political preoccupations of the government the *pieds noirs* were, unfortunately for them, 'history.' " Quoted in Theis and Ratte, *La guerre d'Algérie ou le temps des meprises,* 280.

224 For the argument that OAS violence weakened the French bargaining position see Tricot, *Les sentiers de la paix,* 241; for the opposite view see Raymond Aron, "The General and the Tragedy," *Encounter* 19 (August 1962) 21.

225 Kelly, *Lost Soldiers,* 335.

226 Jean Lacouture, *Pierre Mendès France,* 391.

227 Simmons, *French Socialists in Search of a Role,* 112.

228 Ibid., 112–13; *L'Année Politique* (1961) 171; Martin Harrison, "The French Experience of Exceptional Powers: 1961," *Journal of Politics* 25 (February 1963) 146. As Martin Harrison argues in his analysis of the use of article 16 in response to the April putsch attempt, de Gaulle maintained its provisions in force for months after the legally necessary "circumstances" (such as "a grave and immediate threat" to the institutions of the republic) were absent. Harrison stresses de Gaulle's desire to accomplish incumbent-level objectives, including a long-desired overhaul of the civil service and the establishment of precedents for the use of article 16 which would help him shift the weight of political authority within the Fifth Republic even more profoundly toward the president and away from Parliament. Harrison notes that during summer 1961, de Gaulle and his ministers allowed Parliament to meet but did not acknowledge its right to pass legislation or consider motions of censure in connection with recurrent agitation by French farmers or in criticism of the government's use of the constitution. Harrison, "The French Experience of Exceptional Powers, 1961," 139–58. Similarly see Jacques Chastenet's analysis in *L'Année Politique* (1961) xi.

229 Harrison, "The French Experience of Exceptional Powers," 153.

230 On de Gaulle's successful use of this motif in connection with the Algerian War see Talbott, *The War without a Name,* 239. For classic examples see the texts of his October 3, and December 29, 1961, broadcasts. *L'Année Politique* (1961)

674 and 681. Right-wing critics of the government even went so far as to suggest that some if not all of the assassination attempts against de Gaulle in 1961 and 1962 were staged by the Élysée Palace itself, with the political payoff surrounding the anxiety they would produce foremost in mind. For evidence supporting the plausibility of this accusation see Kelly, *Lost Soldiers,* 342.

231   See Talbott, *The War without a Name,* 245; Williams, *Wars, Plots, and Scandals in Post-War France,* 218; Andrews, *French Politics and Algeria,* 197; Horne, *A Savage War of Peace,* 505 and 544.

232   See, for example, C. L. Mowat, "The Irish Question in British Politics (1916–1922)," in *The Irish Struggle,* ed. Desmond Williams (Toronto: University of Toronto Press, 1966) 141.

233   They were protesting de Gaulle's opposition to a united Europe.

8. Regimes at Risk

1   Perry Anderson brilliantly demonstrates the presence of these contradictory usages in Gramsci as well as the availability (within Gramsci's writings) of an approach to the relationship between wars of position and wars of movement which is also consistent with my deployment of the concepts. Anderson, "The Antinomies of Antonio Gramsci," *New Left Review* 100 (November 1976–January 1977) 55–75. See also Joseph V. Femia, *Gramsci's Political Thought: Hegemony, Consciousness, and the Revolutionary Process* (Oxford: Clarendon Press, 1987) 51–56 and 205–9.

2   See, for example, Gramsci's discussion of the importance of distinguishing "different stages and levels in the 'relations of forces,' " in order to avoid conflating incidental or occasional causes with organic factors and in order to appreciate dialectical relations obtaining among different kinds of political competition. Antonio Gramsci, "The Modern Prince," in *The Modern Prince and Other Writings,* ed. Louis Marks (New York: International Publishers, 1957) 164–73. On transitions between wars of maneuver and wars of position see also Gramsci, "State and Civil Society," in *Selections from the Prison Notebooks of Antonio Gramsci,* ed. Quintin Hoare and Geoffrey Nowell-Smith (New York: International Publishers, 1971) 238–39.

3   Gramsci, "State and Civil Society," 219–21.

4   Ibid., 220.

5   Juan J. Linz, *The Breakdown of Democratic Regimes: Crisis, Breakdown, and Reequilibration* (Baltimore: Johns Hopkins University Press, 1978); Samuel P. Huntington, *Political Order in Changing Societies* (New Haven: Yale University Press, 1968); Gabriel A. Almond, Scott C. Flanagan, and Robert J. Mundt, eds., *Crisis, Choice, and Change: Historical Studies of Political Development* (Boston: Little, Brown, 1973). For Albert O. Hirschman's original analysis of sequential solutions as an instance of reform-mongering, and the short shrift he gives to its applicability in cases of severe polarization, see Hirschman, *Journeys toward Progress* (New York: Twentieth Century Fund, 1963), esp. 276–97.

6   Huntington, *Political Order in Changing Societies,* 346–55.

7   According to Linz, regime breakdown occurs or is threatened when the parties supporting the regime cannot compromise on an important question and one of them attempts a solution with the suppport of forces that the opposition perceives as disloyal. This instigates polarization within the society, which creates distrust among those who in other circumstances would have supported the regime. It is only a slight exaggeration to label such problems unsolvable, for a solution acceptable to a majority among the regime-supporting parties cannot be found. Linz, *The Breakdown of Democratic Regimes,* 50.

8   Ibid., 40 and 88.

9   Ibid., 71 and 100n.

10   The others are social mobilization theory, system functionalism, and leadership.

11   Scott Flanagan, "Models and Methods of Analysis," in *Crisis, Choice, and Change,* 98.

12   Brian Barry, "Review Article: 'Crisis, Choice, and Change,' Part II," *British Journal of Political Science* 7 (1977) 219. Barry's exhaustive and trenchant critique of the Almond, Flanagan, and Mundt volume convincingly dismisses it as an enormous, and often inappropriate, checklist. The one portion of the work which Barry sees as making a real contribution is the attempt to apply game-theoretic concepts to the analysis of dynamic, regime-level, political situations. The review essay was published in two parts, part 1 in vol. 6 (1976) 99–113; and part 2 in vol. 7 (1977) 217–53.

13   Patricia Jalland, *The Liberals and Ireland: The Ulster Question and British Politics to 1914* (New York: St. Martin's, 1980) 167. See also, regarding Lloyd George's support for the tough Churchillian approach described below, John Grigg, *Lloyd George: From Peace to War, 1912–1916* (Berkeley: University of California Press, 1985) 119.

14   "The Ulster Situation," March 14, 1914, from *The Complete Speeches of Winston Churchill, 1897–1963,* ed. Robert Rhodes James, vol. 3 (1914–22) (London: Chelsea House, 1974) 2227–28.

15   Ibid., 2230.

16   Ibid.

17   The fleet was to be comprised of seven battleships ordered from an anchorage off the Spanish coast and specially loaded with field artillery; two light cruisers ordered from Bantry Bay in the southwest of Ireland to Belfast Lough; two training ships summoned to Dundalk, just south of the Ulster coast; and eight Home Fleet destroyers. The battleships and the destroyers were to assemble at Lamlash, a naval base on the Isle of Arran sixty miles from the coast of Ulster. These and other details concerning British government preparations for a crackdown on Ulster are drawn from A. T. Q. Stewart's discussion of the events in *The Ulster Crisis* (London: Faber and Faber, 1967) 141–50.

18   Michael Laffan, *The Partition of Ireland, 1911–1925* (Dublin: Dundalgan Press, 1983) 41–42; George Dangerfield, *The Damnable Question: One Hundred and Twenty Years of Anglo-Irish Conflict* (Boston: Little, Brown, 1976) 85–86; Roy F. Foster, *Modern Ireland: 1600–1972* (New York: Penguin, 1988) 469. Charles Townshend argues against the existence of a Churchillian/government

"plot," while endorsing the political wisdom of such an approach had it been adopted. Charles Townshend, *Political Violence in Ireland* (Oxford: Clarendon Press, 1987) 269–74. See also note 21 below.

19   In Jalland's account, Asquith's reluctance to rock the parliamentary boat by admitting the seriousness of the Ulster problem deprived him of timely opportunities in 1912 and 1913 to include compromises in the terms of the bill which could have neutralized UVF opposition without sacrificing the support of Redmond's party. Specifically, she argues that had a scheme for Ulster home rule, within a larger Irish home rule, been incorporated from the beginning within the third Home Rule Bill, the regime crisis of 1914 could have been avoided. In essence her argument is not with the decision to decompose the Irish problem as a means of crossing the regime threshold, but with the inefficient, risk-laden manner in which a more drastic decomposition than might have been required was implemented. Jalland, *The Liberals and Ireland*, 48–49 and 68–77.

20   On Asquith's leadership style see ibid., 35; and Robert Ensor, *England: 1870–1914* (Oxford: Clarendon Press, 1936) 407–8. In this sense, at least, Churchill had clearly been mistaken in his Bradford speech, when he said that "those who think that these events can be adjusted by the use of threats of violence against the Government do not know the British democracy; they do not know England; they do not know Yorkshire; and *they do not know Asquith*." Churchill, "The Ulster Situation," 2230.

21   Stewart provides substantial evidence that in addition to the unanimous belief of rank-and-file UVF members, Unionist leaders such as Bonar Law, Carson, and Long (who enjoyed direct access to classified information through Sir Henry Wilson, director of military operations) were convinced a government "plot," including the military occupation of Ulster and the arrest of Unionist leaders, had come very close to implementation. Stewart, *The Ulster Crisis*, 171–75 and 265n. Milner and Bonar Law were both convinced that the Churchill strategy for isolating their cause from the sympathy of British opinion was likely to work if carried forward vigorously. See A. M. Gollin, *Proconsul in Politics: A Study of Lord Milner in Opposition and in Power* (New York: Macmillan, 1964) 207 and 215; and Laffan, *The Partition of Ireland, 1911–1925*, 35 and 39.

For powerful presentations of the circumstantial evidence pointing toward government intentions to precipitate a showdown, see remarks in the House of Commons by Lord Charles Beresford, *Hansard* 60 (1914), cols. 378–79; Arthur Balfour, ibid., cols. 407–14; Bonar Law, ibid., cols. 423–34; and F. E. Smith, ibid., cols. 866–90. See also the *Times* of March 24, 1914, "The Plot That Failed," which concluded that there had indeed existed "a deliberate conspiracy to provoke and intimidate Ulster."

Of Churchill's tortured efforts to deny attempting to follow through on the tactical implications of his Bradford speech, Robert Rhodes James, the editor of Churchill's collected speeches, commented that his statement to the House of Commons on March 30, 1914, "can most charitably be described as disingenuous. More critical observers would employ harsher adjectives." *Complete Speeches of Winston S. Churchill, 1897–1963*, 3:2273.

22   See Didier Maus, "La guerre d'Algérie et les institutions de la république,"

paper presented at the conference "La guerre d'Algérie et les français, at the Institut d'Histoire du Temps Present, Paris, December 15–17, 1988, pp. 4–9.

23 William G. Andrews, *French Politics and Algeria* (New York: Appleton-Century-Crofts, 1962) 178.

24 For a convenient catalog of these and other changes associated with the new constitution, the emergence of the Fifth Republic as a quasi-monarchical, presidential regime, and the relationship of the new constitutional order to Algerian policy, see ibid., chap. 5–8, esp. pp. 133, 172–74, and 178.

25 Alexander Werth, *The De Gaulle Revolution* (London: Robert Hale Ltd., 1960) ix–x.

26 Ibid., x.

27 For a systematic examination of the "situationally defined" nature of charismatic authority, with direct reference to de Gaulle, see Michel Dobry, *Sociologie des crises politiques* (Paris: Presses de la Fondation Nationale des Sciences Politiques, 1986) 227–33.

28 Stanley Hoffmann, "Preface," in Alfred Grosser, *French Foreign Policy under De Gaulle* (Boston: Little, Brown, 1965) vii.

29 There is considerable debate over how sharp an image de Gaulle had in 1958 of his hopes for Algeria, of how fine an understanding he possessed of the difficulties that would confront a policy of disengagement, and of how great a role planning versus trial and error played in the unfolding drama. For portrayals of de Gaulle's Algerian policies as confused, contradictory, and fundamentally "empirical" see Grosser, *French Foreign Policy under De Gaulle*, 31–33; Laurent Theis and Philippe Ratte, *La guerre d'Algérie ou le temps des meprises* (Tours: Mame, 1974) 209–10; and Raoul Girardet, *L'idée coloniale en France: 1871–1962* (Paris: Table Ronde, 1972) 283. For interpretations that fault de Gaulle either for not realizing sooner that Algerian independence was inevitable or for overestimating the difficulties of reaching a negotiated settlement based on independence see Alistair Horne, *A Savage War of Peace; Algeria, 1954–1962* (New York: Penguin Books, 1977) 303, 308, 314–15; Edward Behr, *The Algerian Problem* (New York: Norton, 1961) 219–20 and 223; Roy C. Macridis and Bernard E. Brown, *The De Gaulle Republic: Quest for Unity* (Homewood, Ill.: Dorsey Press, 1960) 322; and Aron's account of his contemporaneous view of de Gaulle's Algerian policy in Raymond Aron, *Memoirs: Fifty Years of Political Reflection* (New York: Holmes and Meier, 1990) 261. The dominant and most convincing view, however, is the "Machiavellian" interpretation endorsed here. See Philip M. Williams, *Wars, Plots, and Scandals in Post-War France* (London: Cambridge University Press, 1970) 181–82, 201–2; Richard Brace and Joan Brace, *Ordeal in Algeria* (Princeton: Van Nostrand, 1960) 364–65; George Armstrong Kelly, *Lost Soldiers: The French Army and Empire in Crisis, 1947–1962* (Cambridge: MIT Press, 1965) 288–92; Dorothy Pickles, *Algeria and France: From Colonialism to Cooperation* (New York: Praeger, 1963) 126–29; Raymond Aron, "The General and the Tragedy," *Encounter* 19 (August 1962) 23; Horne, *A Savage War of Peace*, 377–81; and Bernard Tricot's analysis as presented to Theis and Ratte, in *La guerre d'Algérie ou le temps des meprises*, 223–26.

Macridis and Brown, whose study of de Gaulle published in 1960 portrayed his policy as disjointed and empirical, shifted their ground substantially in a supplement published three years later. In *Supplement to "The De Gaulle" Republic* (Homewood, Ill.: Dorsey Press, 1963) 13–15, they lean toward what is here described as a "Machiavellian" interpretation—qualifying their view only by saying that "one cannot rule out the possibility that de Gaulle's Algerian policy evolved pragmatically." For a similar but more rapid shift in Aron's assessment see Aron, *Memoirs*, 261–62.

Evidence for the role of calculated deceit in de Gaulle's Algerian strategy is also available from his own writings (prior to 1958) on the necessity for mystery and even deceit as characteristics of "heroic" leadership under crisis conditions. See Charles de Gaulle, *The Edge of the Sword* (New York: Criterion Books, 1960) 42–43 and 58–59. The book was originally published as *Le fil de l'épée* (Paris, 1935).

30   Charles de Gaulle, *Memoirs of Hope: Renewal and Endeavor* (New York: Simon and Schuster, 1970) 44–46.

31   For evidence that de Gaulle was convinced well before June 1958 that Algeria would eventually be independent from France see Charles-Robert Ageron, *L'Algérie algérienne de Napoléon III à de Gaulle* (Paris: Sindbad, 1980) 239–51; Jean Lacouture, *De Gaulle* (London: Hutchinson, 1970) 173–76; C. L. Sulzberger, "De Gaulle: III—The Oracle and Algeria," *New York Times*, June 9, 1958; Theis and Ratte, *La guerre d'Algérie ou le temps des meprises*, 208.

32   De Gaulle, *Memoirs of Hope*, 46–47 and 69. See Kelly, *Lost Soldiers*, 291, concerning "policies designed to placate the Army and hold it shy of the brink of rebellion." On the same point see Grosser, *French Foreign Policy under De Gaulle*, 40; and C. L. Sulzberger, *The Test: De Gaulle and Algeria* (New York: Harcourt, Brace, and World, 1962) 142–46.

33   Quoted in Kelly, *Lost Soldiers*, 352.

34   Jacques Soustelle, *L'esperance trahie*, quoted in Kelly, *Lost Soldiers*, 289. For similar interpretations of de Gaulle's behavior by his enemies see Georges Bidault, *Resistance: The Political Autobiography of Georges Bidault* (New York: Praeger, 1967); and Alfred Fabre-Luce, *The Trial of Charles de Gaulle* (New York: Praeger, 1963). Prime Minister Debré's presence at the head of de Gaulle's government and his anguished but ultimately total acceptance of de Gaulle's Algerian policies were tremendously significant. They helped de Gaulle camouflage his ultimate intentions and disadvantaged partisans of Algérie française by postponing the point at which they could agree that, even with Debré as prime minister, de Gaulle was leading France out of Algeria. See Theis and Ratte, *La guerre d'Algérie ou le temps des meprises*, 218.

35   This was of course a complete reversal of de Gaulle's strategy for bringing down the Fourth Republic—a strategy of insisting that all questions of policy and principle be combined within the single, clear imperative of recomposing the regime.

36   In their account of the Barricades Rebellion, Bromberger et al. depict the colonels as hesitant to fully support the ultras because de Gaulle's political salami tactics prevented the immediate issue from being framed as "exit from Algeria," the only question on which, they thought, the army would "be able to be aroused

to revolt." Merry Bromberger, Serge Bromberger, Georgette Elgey, and J.-F. Chauvel, *Barricades et colonels* (Paris: Artheme Fayard, 1960) 290.

37 On the relationship between the discipline of the UNR in support of de Gaulle and restriction of the bargaining power of both the Socialists, on the left, and the Indépendants, on the right, see I. R. Campbell, "Political Attitudes in France to the Algerian Question, 1954–62, with Special Reference to the Centre National des Indépendants," Ph.D. diss., Nuffield College, Oxford, 1972, pp. 82–90.

38 On the sharpening divisions within the Indépendant party over Algeria see T. Alexander Smith, "Algeria and the French *Modérés:* The Politics of Immoderation?" *Western Political Quarterly* 18 (1965) 116–34. See also Campbell, "Political Attitudes in France to the Algerian Question, 1954–62," 525–26; and Miles Kahler, *Decolonization in Britain and France: The Domestic Consequences of International Politics* (Princeton: Princeton University Press, 1984) 117–29 and 158–59.

39 Campbell, "Political Attitudes in France to the Algerian Question, 1954–62," 534ff.

40 For an analysis of the failure of French intellectuals to effect substantial change in mass attitudes see Paul Clay Sorum, *Intellectuals and Decolonization in France* (Chapel Hill: University of North Carolina Press, 1977) 232–41.

41 De Gaulle never wanted to depend on support for his policies from those whose opposition to the war could too easily be interpreted as "unpatriotic." Right up until 1962, government seizures of leftist newspapers whose editorial line supported the self-determination policy were more numerous than seizures of rightwing newspapers and journals which supported the antiregime activities of the Algérie française lobby. Martin Harrison, "Government and Press in France during the Algerian War," *American Political Science Review* 58 (June 1964) 277. In metropolitan France, police actions against anti-OAS demonstrators were harsh and bloody. In 1960 the government began to allow publication of books that were extremely critical of the war effort, and especially of the pieds noirs. Two of these books, written by pieds noirs—*La guerre d'Algérie* by Jules Roy and *Les français d'Algérie* by Pierre Nora—were especially influential. Roy's book, published in October 1960, became a best-seller. See John Talbott, *The War without a Name: France in Algeria, 1954–1962* (New York: Knopf, 1960) 176.

42 Girardet, *L'idée coloniale en France,* 282.

43 Nathalie Ruz, "Le 'cartiérisme' et l'Algérie (1956–1961) à travers la presse parisienne," paper presented at the conference La guerre d'Algérie et les français, at the Institut d'Histoire du Temps Present, Paris, December 15–17, 1988, pp. 8–9.

44 See, for example, the following front-page *Le Monde* articles signed by Sirius (an alias used by *Le Monde* editor Hubert Beuve-Méry): "Colonialism and Nationalism," April 26, 1958; "L'Algérie française," April 27–28, 1958; "Pourquoi," September 17, 1959; and "Criminelle folie," January 26, 1960. See also Ruz, "Le 'cartiérisme' et l'Algérie," 17.

45 Ruz, "Le 'cartiérisme' et l'Algérie," 11.

46 Concerning the application of Catholic anticolonialist sentiment to Algeria see William Bosworth, "The French Catholic Hierarchy and the Algerian Question"

Western Political Quarterly 15 (December 1962) 667–80. On this point see also Michael K. Clark, *Algeria in Turmoil: A History of the Rebellion* (New York: Praeger, 1959) 205–11.

47   For examples of de Gaulle's studied avoidance of public clarity regarding his plans for Algeria in 1957 and 1958 see the communiqué issued September 12, 1957, in Charles de Gaulle, *Discours et messages: 1946–1958* (Paris: Plon, 1970) 654; text of the press conference, reprinted in Charles S. Maier and Dan S. Whiter, eds., *The Thirteenth of May: The Advent of de Gaulle's Republic* (New York: Oxford University Press, 1968) 287–93; and de Gaulle's letter to President Auriol, May 26, 1958, quoted in Werth, *The De Gaulle Revolution,* p. 160. It is also far easier to explain his one and only public use of the phrase "Vive l'Algérie française!" on June 6, 1958, in Mostaganem, as a calculated deception than as an isolated expression of his real belief. For their treatment of this point see Pickles, *Algeria and France,* 133; and Grosser, *French Foreign Policy under De Gaulle,* 29–40.

48   Grosser, *French Foreign Policy under De Gaulle,* 38.

49   Horne, *A Savage War of Peace,* 62–64; Ruz, "Le 'cartiérisme' et l'Algérie," 4.

50   See Ruz, "Le 'cartiérisme' et l'Algérie," 15–22; Jacques Marseille, *Empire colonial et capitalisme français: Histoire d'un divorce* (Paris: Albin Michel, 1984) 367–73; and Kahler, *Decolonization in Britain and France,* 294–95.

51   R. Cartiér and H. Grandet, *L'Algérie sans mensonge,* quoted in Ruz, "Le 'cartiérisme' et l'Algérie," 19–20.

52   Ruz, "Le 'cartiérisme' et l'Algérie," 23–24.

53   From de Gaulle's April 11, 1961, press conference. See Marseille, *Empire colonial et capitalisme français,* 373. In 1955, Algerian living standards were estimated to be one-sixth of those in metropolitan France. See David S. McLellan, "The North African in France: A French Racial Problem," *Yale Review* 44 (March 1955) 422. During the course of the revolution this gap can only have increased.

54   Ruz, "Le 'cartiérisme' et l'Algérie," 15–22.

55   Stanley Hoffmann, "Paradoxes of the French Political Community," in *In Search of France,* ed. Hoffmann et al. (New York: Harper Torchbooks, 1963) 85.

56   Kelly, *Lost Soldiers,* 293.

57   Girardet, *L'idée coloniale en France,* 283.

58   See Gollin, *Proconsul in Politics,* 173, 179–80, 191–93 and 215; and Dangerfield, *The Damnable Question,* 87–88.

59   The operational goals of Irish nationalists also changed, emphasizing direct efforts to achieve an independent republic rather than focusing on home rule or some sort of federal arrangement. See Desmond Ryan, "Sinn Fein Policy and Practice (1916–1926)," in *The Irish Struggle,* ed. Desmond Williams (Toronto: University of Toronto Press, 1966) 31–40.

60   On the options open to Lloyd George and his ruthless exploitation of the inexperience, gullibility, and anxieties of the Irish negotiators in 1921, see Frank Pakenham [Lord Longford], *Peace by Ordeal: The Negotiation of the Anglo-Irish Treaty, 1921* (London: Sidgwick and Jackson, 1972) 250–59.

61   On British "war weariness" and its implications for public attitudes toward

Ireland see John D. Fair, "The Anglo-Irish Treaty of 1921: Unionist Aspects of the Peace," *Journal of British Studies* 12 (November 1972) 135; and D. G. Boyce, *Englishmen and Irish Troubles: British Public Opinion and the Making of Irish Policy, 1918–22* (Cambridge: MIT Press, 1972) 46.

62 Technically it is incorrect to speak of the twenty-six counties that comprised the Irish Free State as southern Ireland since one of them, Donegal, extends farther north than any other part of Ireland. After the implementation of the Anglo-Irish treaty the formal name of the British state was changed to reflect the contraction in its territory that had been effected—from the United Kingdom of Great Britain and Ireland, to the United Kingdom of Great Britain and Northern Ireland.

63 These figures are calculated from census figures listed in W. E. Vaughan and A. J. Fitzpatrick, eds., *Irish Historical Statistics* (Dublin: Royal Irish Academy, 1978) 66–68. The categories of religious denomination are Roman Catholic, Church of Ireland (Anglican), Presbyterian, Methodist, and other. It can be presumed that most of the "other" category is comprised of Jews.

64 Pierre Bourdieu, *The Algerians* (Boston: Beacon, 1962) 63.

65 Alain Peyrefitte, *Faut-il partager l'Algérie?* (Paris: Plon, 1961) 143–51.

66 While the Ulster Volunteer Force was formed and commanded by Irish Protestant politicians, the "territorial units" comprised of pieds noirs were extensions of the French army and directed by active duty army officers. On the latter point see Stuart H. Van Dyke, "French Settler Politics during the Algerian War, 1954–1958," Ph.D. diss., University of Chicago, 1980, 218ff.

67 Thomas C. Schelling, *The Strategy of Conflict* (Oxford: Oxford University Press, 1968) 53–80 and 111.

68 Germaine Tillion, *Algeria: The Realities,* trans. Ronald Matthews (New York: Knopf, 1958) 74–75.

69 Peyrefitte, *Faut-il partager l'Algérie?* 192–93.

70 During the summer of 1961 Peyrefitte's articles were expanded into the book just cited.

71 Peyrefitte, *Faut-il partager l'Algérie?* 3–4.

72 See Sulzberger, *The Test,* 154, 175–76; Campbell, "Political Attitudes in France to the Algerian Question, 1954–62," 332; John C. Cairns, "Algeria: The Last Ordeal," *International Journal* 17 (Spring 1962) 89–91. See also de Gaulle, *Memoirs of Hope,* 114–23.

73 See Ian Lustick, *State-Building Failure in British Ireland and French Algeria,* Research Monograph 63 (Berkeley: Institute of International Studies, University of California, 1985) 36–37.

74 Hereward Senior, *Orangeism in Ireland and Britain, 1795–1836* (London: Routledge and Kegan Paul, 1966) 216–64.

75 In 1936, for example, strikes and other forms of mass opposition by Europeans in Algeria, and intense lobbying by their representatives in Paris, blocked passage of the Blum-Violette package of political and economic reforms. The pieds noirs also played a key role in rigging Algerian elections in 1921, 1948, and 1951 and in turning virtually all the reforms contained in the 1947 Algerian Statute into a dead letter.

76 See F. S. L. Lyons, "The Passing of the Irish Parliamentary Party (1916–

1918)," in *The Irish Struggle*, 95; and especially David Fitzpatrick, *Politics and Irish Life: 1913–1921* (Dublin: Gill and Macmillan, 1977) 105–7 and 282–83.

77 See Patrick Lynch, "The Social Revolution That Never Was," in *The Irish Struggle*, 31–40.

78 Foster, *Modern Ireland*, 485 and 492. De Valera's image of Ireland was more reactionary than revolutionary. He envisioned an Arcadian, village-centered Ireland, celebrating its Gaelic identity through the revival of lost folkways. Despite his reputation for intransigence and his opposition to the Anglo-Irish treaty De Valera agreed with the provisional government's 1921 renunciation of the use of force against Ulster Unionists, and he considered restoration of the political unity of Ireland an objective to be pursued over the course of several generations. See John Bowman, *De Valera and the Ulster Question, 1917–1973* (Oxford: Clarendon Press, 1982) esp. 43–49 and 305–38. Regarding de Valera's bucolic vision of Ireland see Foster, *Modern Ireland*, 538.

79 See Tillion, *Algeria: The Realities*; and Horne, *A Savage War of Peace*, 62–65 and 155.

80 Lustick, *State-Building Failure*, 73–76.

81 Horne, *A Savage War of Peace*, 471.

82 For profiles of the origins of the "nine historics"—the founding chiefs of the Algerian revolt—and of their unwavering commitment to violent revolution, see Horne, *A Savage War of Peace*, 75–77. Concerning the predominance among the revolutionary elite of men skilled not in organization, but violence, see William B. Quandt, *Revolution and Political Leadership: Algeria, 1954–1968* (Cambridge: MIT Press, 1969) 66–96. The most important effort by an FLN leader to come to terms with the French was made by Si Salah, an internal army commander who succeeded in meeting personally with de Gaulle, but who was subsequently arrested by the FLN and killed (while an FLN prisoner) by the French. See Talbott, *War without a Name*, 191–96.

83 Michel Launay, *Paysans Algériens: La Terre, La Vigne et les Hommes*, quoted in Eric R. Wolf, *Peasant Wars of the Twentieth Century* (New York: Harper Torchbooks, 1969) 229–30.

84 On the central role, in radical Irish nationalism, played by middle-class elements in the towns and cities of Ireland, and the reluctance of peasant proprietors to become involved in violent resistance, see Patrick Lynch, "The Social Revolution That Never Was," in *The Irish Struggle*, 42; Lyons, *Ireland since the Famine*, 405; and Michael Hopkinson, *Green against Green: The Irish Civil War* (New York: St. Martin's, 1988) 10–11. On the "conservative nationalism" of Irish farmers, before and after the creation of the Irish Free State, see Foster, *Modern Ireland*, 513, 515, and 521. Concerning the primary role in the Algerian Revolution played by FLN recruitment of impoverished peasants see Jean-Claude Vatin, *L'Algérie politique: Histoire et société* (Paris: Presses de la Fondation Nationale des Sciences Politiques, 1983) 306; and Jacques Soustelle, *Aimée et souffrante Algérie* (Paris: Plon, 1956) 26. Franz Fanon offered the classic analysis of the psychological relationship between the absolute degradation of Algerian peasants by French colonialism and their embrace of violent forms of resistance. Franz Fanon, *The Wretched of the Earth* (New York: Grove Press, 1968). See also Wolf, *Peasant Wars of the Twentieth Century*, 244–46.

85   On the links between Islam and nationalism in the Algerian Revolution see Charles-Robert Ageron, "Le nationalisme algérien: De l'Islam à la révolution," *Revue Populaire* 99 (July 1956) 126–34; and Wolf, *Peasant Wars of the Twentieth Century*, 226–30 and 247.

86   John Stubbs, "The Impact of the Great War on the Conservative Party," in *The Politics of Reappraisal, 1918–1939*, ed. Gillian Peele and Chris Cook (New York: St. Martin's, 1975) 16–19; John D. Fair, "The Anglo-Irish Treaty of 1921: Unionist Aspects of the Peace," *Journal of British Studies* 12 (November 1972) 133. See also Chapter 6, above, "British Tories and Ulster Rebels: A Regime-Threatening Alliance."

87   On this point see Anne Sa'adah's illuminating discussion of French liberalism as afflicted by the "politics of exclusion" versus the "politics of inclusion" characteristic of British and French liberalism. Sa'adah, *The Shaping of Liberal Politics in Revolutionary France: A Comparative Perspective* (Princeton: Princeton University Press, 1990).

88   Didier Maus, "La guerre d'Algérie et les institutions de la république," 26–27.

89   For a detailed analysis of the divisions within the Algerian elite after independence see Quandt, *Revolution and Political Leadership*. But for an important qualification on the way he frames the problem, see Vatin, *L'Algérie politique*, 304–6. The tumultuous course of Algerian politics since 1988 highlights the importance of the course and outcome of the struggle with France as affording Algeria a twenty-five-year window of opportunity for state consolidation.

90   On Lloyd George's fear of this eventuality, and the role a too-generous Irish settlement might play in its occurrence, see Sheila Lawlor, *Britain and Ireland, 1914–23* (Totowa, N.J.: Barnes and Noble, 1983) 129–32.

91   Concerning the change in southern Irish Protestant (Unionist) opinion between 1918 and 1920, from steadfast devotion to the Union to support for a return to law and order which, it was believed, only an Irish government in Dublin could effect, see Patrick Buckland, *Irish Unionism: The Anglo-Irish and the New Ireland: 1885–1922* (Dublin: Gill and Macmillan, 1972) 195–271. As a result of emigration, and the withdrawal of largely Protestant police and military personnel, the Protestant population of the twenty-six counties decreased from 327,000 in 1911 to 221,000 in 1926 (7.4 percent of the Free State's total population). For figures on which this percentage was calculated and for a discussion of the solicitousness of Free State leaders toward Southern Irish Protestants see ibid., 285–301.

92   Historians rightly emphasize that in the rhetoric of the anti-treaty side of the civil war, it was not partition but the formal absence of "the Republic" which was most prominent. But this emphasis on the abstract notion of a republic, and the severe Anglophobia associated with it, was a direct result of the "blood sacrifice" of the 1916 rising—an event which dramatically changed the course of the Irish nationalist struggle. The rising would not have occurred or would not have had the same catalytic effect had the terms of the third Home Rule Bill been implemented in 1914. See Dangerfield, *The Damnable Question*, 136–220; and F. X. Martin, "The Origins of the Irish Rising of 1916," in *The Irish Struggle*, 14–17.

93   Robert Blake, for one, concludes his massive biography of Bonar Law with the verdict that had Bonar Law not helped direct as effective a regime challenge

as he had in the 1912–14 period, the partition of Ireland half a dozen years later would not have occurred. Robert Blake, *The Unknown Prime Minister: A Biography of Bonar Law* (London: Eyre and Spottiswoode, 1955) 531.

9. ISRAEL AND THE WEST BANK AND GAZA STRIP

1 Zeev Tsur, *From the Partition Dispute to the Allon Plan* (Hebrew) (Ramat Ephal: Tabenkin Institute, 1982) 9. For similar judgments see Yossi Beilin, *The Price of Unity: The Labor Party until the Yom Kippur War* (Hebrew) (Revivim: Leor Publishers, 1985) 25–28, 41, and 45; and Baruch Kimmerling, *A Conceptual Framework for the Analysis of Behavior in a Territorial Conflict: The Generalization of the Israeli Case*, Jerusalem Papers on Peace Problems, no. 25 (Jerusalem: Leonard Davis Institute for International Relations, 1979) 16–18 and 23–25.

2 Ofira Seliktar, *New Zionism and the Foreign Policy System of Israel* (Carbondale: Southern Illinois University Press, 1986) 92; and Rael Jean Isaac, *Israel Divided: Ideological Politics in the Jewish State* (Baltimore: Johns Hopkins University Press, 1976), 41.

3 Yitzhak Tabenkin, *Settlement: Idea and Praxis* (Hebrew) (Tel Aviv: Kibbutz Hameuchad, 1983) 35 and 55–66.

4 From the manifesto of the Whole Land of Israel Movement, August 1967, reproduced and translated in Isaac, *Israel Divided*, 165. Isaac provides a thorough depiction of the Land of Israel Movement, albeit one that construes it as considerably more devoted to religious values than the evidence warrants. For an excellent collection of essays and lectures reflecting the thinking of the movement see Aharon Ben-Ami, ed., *The Book of the Whole Land of Israel* (Hebrew) (Tel Aviv: Freedman, 1977).

5 Yisrael Harel, editor of the semi-official Gush Emunim settler journal *Nekuda*, was editor of the Whole Land of Israel Movement's newspaper, *Zot Haaretz*, from 1967 to 1969.

6 On the rise of Gush Emunim and its philosophy see Gideon Aran, "From Religious Zionism to Zionist Religion: The Roots of Gush Emunim," in *Studies in Contemporary Jewry*, ed. Peter Medding (Bloomington: Indiana University Press, 1986) 2:116–43; Uriel Tal, "Foundations of a Political Messianic Trend in Israel," *Jerusalem Quarterly*, no. 35 (Spring 1985) 36–45; and Tzvi Yehuda Hacohen Kook, *Lehalacha Tziboor* (Jerusalem: Bein Hachomot, 1987). The latter volume is a collection of the public statements and teachings of Tzvi Yehuda on political issues.

7 Both the Likud and Gush Emunim have considered themselves in the position of exploiting the other for the sake of different long-term objectives. They have been able to work together because on the decisive political question of the geographical shape of the state, Gush Emunim and the dominant Herut core of Likud have shared a fundamentally similar "state idea." On the ideology of Gush Emunim and its complex relationship between Gush Emunim and the Likud see Ian S. Lustick, *For the Land and the Lord: Jewish Fundamentalism in Israel* (New York: Council on Foreign Relations, 1988), esp. 37–52. For the notion of the Likud/ Gush Emunim hegemonic project as a "competing state idea" see Saul Cohen, *The*

Geopolitics of Israel's Border Question, Jaffe Center for Strategic Studies, Tel Aviv University, Study No. 7 (Boulder, Colo.: Westview Press, 1986) 46; Baruch Kimmerling, "Between the Primordial and the Civil Definitions of the Collective Identity: Eretz Israel or the State of Israel," in *Comparative Social Dynamics,* ed. Erik Cohen, Moshe Lissak, and Uri Almagor (Boulder, Colo.: Westview, 1983) 262–83.

8   Interview in *Yoman Hashavua,* November 17, 1983, translated in FBIS, November 21, 1983, p. 13.

9   In a 1963 letter to the Israeli author Haim Guri, David Ben-Gurion called Begin "a thoroughly Hitlerite type" who, if raised to power, would "put his thugs into the army and police headquarters and will rule just like Hitler ruled Germany." See the Hebrew edition of Michael Bar-Zohar's biography *Ben-Gurion* (Tel Aviv: Am Oved, 1975–77) 3:1547. See also Myron J. Aronoff, "Establishing Authority: The Memorialization of Jabotinsky and the Burial of the Bar-Kochba Bones in Israel under the Likud," in *The Frailty of Authority,* ed. Myron J. Aronoff, vol. 5 of *Political Anthropology* (New Brunswick, N. J.: Transaction Books, 1986) 105–30. On the general phenomenon of constructing a new "civil religion" or a "new Zionism" after 1967 see sources listed below in note 66.

10   On the objectives and mechanics of the Likud's annexationist progam see Ann Mosely Lesch and Mark Tessler, *Israel, Egypt, and the Palestinians: From Camp David to Intifada* (Bloomington: Indiana University Press, 1989) 194–222; Ian Lustick, "Israel and the West Bank after Elon Moreh: The Mechanics of De Facto Annexation," *Middle East Journal* 35 (Autumn 1981) 557–77; Meron Benvenisti, *The West Bank Data Project: A Survey of Israel's Policies* (Washington, D.C.: American Enterprise Institute, 1984) 19–63; Geoffrey Aronson, *Creating Facts: Israel, Palestinians and the West Bank* (Washington, D.C.: Institute for Palestine Studies, 1987) 59–116; Ilan Peleg, *Begin's Foreign Policy, 1977–1983: Israel's Move to the Right* (New York: Greenwood Press, 1987) 95–142; Bernard Avishai, *The Tragedy of Zionism: Revolution and Democracy in the Land of Israel* (New York: Farrar, Straus and Giroux, 1985) 311–13.

See below for an analysis of the incumbent-level political competition driving the policies implemented by Labor governments in the occupied territories from 1967 to 1977.

11   See Eliezer Schweid, *Homeland and Land of Destiny* (Hebrew) (Tel Aviv: Herzl Press, 1974), with an English edition titled *The Land of Israel: National Home or Land of Destiny,* trans. Deborah Greniman (Rutherford, N. J.: Herzl Press, 1985); and Eliezer Livneh, *Israel and the Crisis of Western Civilization* (Hebrew) (Tel Aviv: Schocken, 1972); and many of the contributions to Ben-Ami *The Book of the Whole Land of Israel,* especially Natan Alterman, "Five Portions," 11–18; Haim Hazan, "Real Things," 19–21; "Yonatan Aharoni, "Every Jew and Mt. Ephraim," 40–44; Dov Yosephi, "A Humane Solution to the Demographic Problem," 345–50. Schweid presents a revealing analysis of the difficulty of maintaining, without religious belief, an all-important "transcendental dimension" to beliefs about territorial expansion. For his discussion of how to use religion in order to achieve the politically necessary level of "inner certainty" see Schweid, *The Land of Israel,* 197–212.

12   Moshe Dayan, *A New Map—Different Relations* (Hebrew) (Tel Aviv: Safrit

Maariv, 1969) 173. See also Shabtai Teveth, *Moshe Dayan: The Soldier, the Man, the Legend* (Boston: Houghton Mifflin, 1973) 342. Teveth emphasizes that immediately following the Six Day War, Dayan tended to avoid advocating the clear delineation of enlarged borders, preferring to blur the question of actual annexation by stressing the establishment of secure Israeli presence within and rights to the whole Land of Israel. Teveth shows how dramatically different this stance was from Dayan's Ben-Gurionist propensity in the 1950s to insist on the "paramount" importance of clearly delineating the armistice lines as Israel's borders. Indeed by mid-1968, Dayan's approach shifted toward implementing policies that would bring an end to the military government as a "temporary institution" and replace it with the Israeli government as the accepted authority in the territories as in Israel itself. See Teveth, *Moshe Dayan*, 183 and 349.

13 Dayan, *A New Map*, 162–63. In a broadcast over Israeli army radio in August 1971, Dayan cited this book as providing the overall framework for his policy toward the West Bank and Gaza Strip. See *New Middle East*, no. 37 (October 1971) 33–34.

14 Dayan, *A New Map*, 164 and 179.

15 Ibid., 177.

16 Ibid., 178. (emphasis added). For Dayan at his most philosophical and most categorical about the impossibility of gaining peace from the Arabs on the basis of territorial or any other sort of concessions, see "A Soldier Reflects on Peace Hopes," Dayan's speech as defense minister to the Israel Army Staff and Command College, *Jerusalem Post*, September 27, 1968. For treatments of Dayan's thinking in this regard and of his influence on Israeli policy toward the territories in the early years of the occupation see Amos Perlmutter, *Israel: The Partitioned State* (New York: Scribner's, 1985) 216–21; and Aronson, *Creating Facts*, 19–31.

17 Jerusalem Domestic Service broadcast, December 6, 1982, transcribed in FBIS, December 6, 1982, p. I11.

18 Ann Mosely Lesch, *Israel's Occupation of the West Bank: The First Two Years* (Santa Monica, Calif.: Rand, 1970) 8.

19 Concerning the energetic efforts of Likud governments to promote the larger "map image" of the state in Israeli schools and atlases, see the editorial "David Levy's Geography Lesson," *Jerusalem Post*, August 20, 1986; David Arnow, "Maps Matter," *The Forum* 3, no. 1 (Autumn 1990) 17–18; *Davar*, May 31, 1988. For the concept of "map image" and its role in the construction of a hegemonic image of the shape of a state see John Bowman, *De Valera and the Ulster Question, 1917–1973* (Oxford: Clarendon Press, 1982) 11–25.

20 Baruch Kimmerling, *Zionism and Territory: The Socio-Territorial Dimensions of Zionist Politics*, Research Series No. 51 (Berkeley: Institute of International Studies, University of California, 1983) 174.

21 Editorial, "Witch Hunt," *Jerusalem Post*, April 5, 1982; and *Jerusalem Post*, April 20, 1982. Report by Agence France Presse, October 27, 1981, JPRS 79364, November 3, 1981, p. 37.

22 *Jerusalem Post*, January 18 and March 7, 1983.

23 Concerning this and related shifts in Israeli political discourse see Hanna Herzog, *Contest of Symbols: The Sociology of Election Campaigns through Israeli*

Ephemera (Cambridge: Harvard University Library, 1987) 84–85; and Baruch Kimmerling, "Between the Primordial and the Civil Definitions of the Collective Identity: *Eretz Yisrael* or the State of Israel," in *Comparative Solical Dynamics,* ed. Erik Cohen, Moshe Lissak, and Uri Almagor (Boulder, Colo.: Westview Press, 1983) 262–83.

24 Concerning the legal and administrative technicalities involved in creation of the "civilian administration" see Jonathan Kuttab and Raja Shehadeh, *Civilian Administration in the Occupied West Bank: Analysis of Israeli Military Government Order No. 947* (Geneva: Law in the Service of Man, 1982).

25 For example the West Bank was divided into five administrative districts (Shomron, Binyamin, Etzion, Jordan Valley, and Judea). These regulations are detailed in a thirty-five-page military order, no. 892. See Kuttab and Shehadeh, *Civilian Administration in the Occupied West Bank,* 58. See also David Newman, *Jewish Settlement in the West Bank: The Role of Gush Emunim,* Occasional Papers Series No. 16 (Durham, N. C.: University of Durham, Center for Middle Eastern and Islamic Studies, 1982) 57 and 62; and Jerusalem Domestic Service broadcast, December 16, 1980, transcribed in JPRS 77082, December 31, 1980, p. 57.

26 Regarding road building in the West Bank as a central feature of Israeli state-building under the Likud see Benvenisti, *The West Bank Data Project,* 23, 60, and 89; and Haim Tzaban et al., *Master Plan for the Settlement of Samaria and Judea: Development Plan for the Area for the Years 1983–86* (Hebrew) (Jerusalem: World Zionist Organization Settlement Department and State of Israel Ministry of Agriculture, 1983) 27–29. Concerning the inauguration of regular bus service to West Bank settlements and the extension of Israeli communications and electrical grids see *Maariv,* January 13 and April 13, 1983; *Davar,* September 28, 1983.

27 Concerning the "spillover" of Israeli legislation into the territories in connection with opportunities otherwise available to enterprising Israelis able to exploit the legal and administrative significance of the Green Line see Shlomo Maoz, "Judea and Samaria as a Tax Shelter," *Haaretz,* April 15, 1983; *Haaretz,* February 18, 1983; *Davar,* March 15, 1983; Benvenisti, *The West Bank Data Project,* 42–43; and idem, *1986 Report: Demographic, Economic, Legal, Social, and Political Developments in the West Bank* (Jerusalem: Jerusalem Post, 1986) 37–45.

28 See Mark Heller, "Politics and Social Change in the West Bank since 1967," in *Palestinian Society and Politics,* ed. Joel S. Migdal (Princeton: Princeton University Press, 1980) 200–201; Mark Allan Heller, "Foreign Occupation and Political Elites: A Study of the Palestinians," Ph.D. diss., Harvard University, 1976, pp. 228–30; Hillel Frisch, "From Armed Struggle over State Borders to Political Mobilization and Intifada within It: The Transformation of PLO Strategy in the Territories," *Plural Societies* 19, nos. 2–3 (1990) 99–100; and Simcha Flapan, "The Long Search for Peace: A Progressive Israeli View," in *Security in the Middle East: Regional Change and Great Power Strategies,* ed. Samuel F. Wells, Jr., and Mark A. Bruzonsky (Boulder, Colo.: Westview Press, 1987) 168.

29 Considerable evidence now exists that between 1948 and 1955, Syrian, Egyptian, and Jordanian governments made overtures to Israel designed to move quietly toward a regularization of relations and even peace. According to most accounts these efforts generally met with an unenthusiastic response from Israeli govern-

ments. Following the 1956 attack on Egypt by Israel, Britain, and France, these attempts ended and were replaced by extreme hostility expressed strongly in private as well as in public by most Arab leaders. See Tom Segev, *1949: The First Israelis* (Hebrew) (Jerusalem: Domino Press, 1984) 20–55; and Saadia Touval, *The Peace Brokers: Mediators in the Arab-Israeli Conflict, 1948–1979* (Princeton: Princeton University Press, 1982) 106–33.

30   Avi Shlaim and Avner Yaniv, "Domestic Politics and Foreign Policy in Israel," *International Affairs* 56 (1980) 244. There is an extensive literature identifying political factionalism as the source of Israel's immobile foreign policy between 1967 and 1977. See Mordechai Nisan, *Israel and the Territories: A Study in Control* (Ramat Gan: Turtle Dov Press, 1978) 22–29; Nadav Safran, "Israel's Internal Politics and Foreign Policy," in *Political Dynamics in the Middle East,* ed. Paul Y. Hammond and Sidney S. Alexander (New York: American Elsevier, 1972) 178–93; Ernest Stock, "Foreign Policy Issues," in *The Elections in Israel—1969,* ed. Alan Arian (Jerusalem: Jerusalem Academic Press, 1972) 43–47 and 57–60; Dan Margalit, *Broadcasting from the White House: The Rise and Fall of the National Unity Government* (Hebrew) (Tel Aviv: Otpaz, 1971) 147–49; Don Peretz, "Israel's 1969 Election Issues: The Visible and the Invisible," *Middle East Journal* 24 (Winter 1970) 32 and 39; Efraim Torgovnik, "Election Issues and Interfactional Conflict Resolution in Israel," *Political Studies* 20 (March 1972) 79–87; Samuel J. Roberts, *Party and Policy in Israel: The Battle between Hawks and Doves* (Boulder, Colo.: Westview Press, 1990) 31–41; and Yael Yishai, *Land or Peace: Whither Israel?* (Stanford: Hoover Institution Press, 1987) 62–99.

31   Concerning Israeli policies before 1973 designed to prevent a central Palestinian leadership from emerging in the West Bank as a candidate for negotiations see Moshe Ma'oz, *Palestinian Leadership on the West Bank: The Changing Role of the Arab Mayors under Jordan and Israel* (London: Frank Cass, 1984) 87–88.

32   Quoted in Shlaim and Yaniv, "Domestic Politics and Foreign Policy in Israel," 243. See also Nadav Safran, *Israel: Embattled Ally* (Cambridge: Harvard University Press, 1978) 175.

Golda Meir became prime minister in June 1969, thereby helping the Labor party avoid a sharp leadership struggle between Allon and Dayan. Before the Knesset Meir quoted from the official guidelines of Eshkol's government as a token of her government's continued adherence to a policy of warding off internal debates by avoiding definite decisions. She stated, "Israel will persist in its willingness to negotiate without pre-conditions with each of its neighboring states for signing a peace treaty. In the absence of peace treaties Israel would firmly retain the status determined by the cease-fire and would ameliorate its position with regard to the fundamental needs of its security and development." Quoted in Yishai, *Land or Peace?,* 5.

33   See Yishai, *Land or Peace?,* 6–8.

34   See Yisrael Galili's account of the strictly incumbent-level considerations surrounding Labor's decision to accept the 1970 U.S. peace initiative, in Galili, *Continuous Struggle* (Hebrew) (Tel Aviv: Kibbutz Hameuchad, 1987) 43–47. Galili was the only member of the cabinet who had participated in the top rank of the Zionist leadership before the creation of the state and was Meir's most trusted and influential minister.

Within Gahal itself, Begin's decision to leave the government on this issue was extremely controversial and intimately connected to his own career prospects. The vote in support of his move was 117 to 115. It appears he was motivated to leave the government at this time after calculating that only by insisting on the primacy of his party's ideological commitment to the whole Land of Israel could he protect his own preeminence against challenges from those within both Herut and the Liberal party whose appeals were based on patronage and satisfaction of social and economic demands. See Yonathan Shapiro, *Chosen to Command: The Road to Power of the Herut Party—A Socio-Political Interpretation* (Hebrew) (Tel Aviv: Am Oved, 1989) 171–73; Sasson Sofer, *Begin: An Anatomy of Leadership* (Oxford: Basil Blackwell, 1988) 90; and Michael Brecher, *Decisions in Israel's Foreign Policy* (London: Oxford University Press, 1974) 494–95.

35 The largely negative Israeli response to Sadat's 1971 proposals is covered by the sources listed above in note 30. Concerning the role of coalition-related considerations in prompting Golda Meir to reject Hussein's "Hashemite Kingdom" or "Federation" plan in 1972 see Tzvi El-Peleg, *Hussein's Federation Plan: Factors and Responses* (Hebrew) (Tel Aviv: Shiloach Research Center for the Middle East and Africa, 1977) 28.

36 See Matti Golan, *The Secret Conversations of Henry Kissinger: Step-by-Step Diplomacy in the Middle East* (New York: Quadrangle, 1976) 216–27; Safran, *Israel: Embattled Ally*, 536–38; Yitzhak Rabin, *The Rabin Memoirs* (Boston: Little, Brown, 1979) 240–41; and Yishai, *Land or Peace?*, 94.

37 Of course these efforts exploited the settlement and land acquisition policies and administrative precedents fostered by Dayan during previous Labor party–led governments.

38 David Halevy, "(Obstructed) Probe Spurs Resignation," *Washington Star*, August 7, 1980. See also Peleg, *Begin's Foreign Policy*, 121. In this same period the press was full of reports by Israeli journalists, such as that of the leftist gadfly Uri Avnery, of "an armed secret movement in the state . . . that is a threat to the authority of the law in Israel, a threat to democracy and the peace camp and its leaders, to the state's foreign relations, and very possibly to the government of Israel itself." Uri Avnery quoted in *Haolam Hazeh*, June 11, 1980. For details of publicly discussed suspicions of active Jewish undergrounds and government cover-ups in 1980 see also *New Outlook* 23, 4 (June–July 1980) 2–4; Amnon Kapeliouk, *Al-Hamishmar*, June 6, 1980; Nahum Barnea, *Davar*, June 6, 1980; and Amnon Denkner, in *Haaretz*, June 6, 1980. These excerpts were translated in *Journal of Palestine Studies* 10 (Autumn 1980) 142–49.

39 The text of the Karp Report was translated into English and published as *The Karp Report: An Israeli Government Inquiry into Settler Violence against Palestinians on the West Bank* (Washingdon, D.C.: Institute for Palestine Studies, 1984). The chief of staff at the time, Rafael Eitan, was an outspoken supporter of incorporating the West Bank and Gaza Strip into Israel. It was during this period that he initiated the practice of arming groups of settlers as reserve militia units responsible for patrolling local districts in the territories. After the Lebanon War and Eitan's departure from the army he founded Tzomet (Movement for Zionist Renewal) on a superhawkish platform of annexation, thorough settlement, and an "iron fist" against Arab dissidents. Tzomet allied itself briefly with Tehiya, but

ran independently in the 1988 and 1992 elections. In 1990, Tzomet joined the government and Eitan was named minister of agriculture.

40 Equally shocking to many Israelis were reports of how the wounded had been taunted by counterdemonstrators with references to "Ashke-Nazis" and shouts that "Hitler should have taken care of all of you." For an eyewitness account see Shulamit Hareven, "Eyewitness," *New Outlook* 26 (March–April 1983) 13–17. Only a few months prior to this event Gush Emunim evinced its own sense that polarization between the annexationist and anti-annexationist camps had reached dangerous levels. As a gesture of its willingness to engage in dialogue with its political opponents, Gush Emunim invited Amoz Oz, Israel's best-known novelist and a leading dove, to a lengthy discussion about the dangers of civil war. Amoz Oz, *In the Land of Israel* (New York: Harcourt Brace Jovanovich, 1983) 127–53. For a Hebrew transcript of his actual, somewhat more pungent, remarks, see *Nekuda,* no. 53, January 14, 1983, pp. 16–24.

41 For a listing of seventeen violent attacks by the Terror against Terror group which occurred between December 1983 and March 1984 see *Haaretz,* March 7, 1984. For a detailed account of the Gush Emunim underground's attacks on the Arab mayors and its preparations to destroy the Muslim shrines on the Haram el-Sharif see Haggai Segal, *Dear Brothers: The West Bank Jewish Underground* (Jerusalem: Beit-Shammai Publications, 1988). The author was convicted for his own participation in the group's activities. For elaborate coverage of the clashes between soldiers and settlers in the Sinai settlements see *Nekuda,* nos. 42, 43, and 44, April 7, May 21, and June 11, 1982.

42 A comparison of the changes in the proportion of the metropolitan population represented by Protestants in Ireland, Europeans in Algeria, and Israelis in the West Bank (including expanded East Jerusalem) and Gaza Strip shows that when the regime threshold was passed in the Israeli case (between 1982 and 1984), the Israeli proportion (of settlers to metropolitan population) rose to the level (between 2 percent and 3 percent) that prevailed during the regime crises of 1911–14 in Britain and 1958–61 in France.

For public manifestations of such thinking very early in Gush Emunim's career see 1975 interviews with Rabbis Hanan Porat, Yoel Ben-Nun, and Yochanan Fried, in Yair Kotler, "The Fanatics: Gush Emunim's Leaders," *Haaretz* (weekend supplement), September 5, 1975; Amnon Sella and Yael Yishai, *Israel the Peaceful Belligerent, 1967–79* (New York: St. Martin's, 1986) 209; and Rabbi Tzvi Yehuda Kook's characterization of the government in 1976 as having "no authority whatever in matters concerning renunciation, expropriation of land, or denial of our ownership in land [or] ... in matters concerning the right of the people of Israel and of all our brothers and sisters, wherever they are, to have this land." *Yediot Acharonot,* June 23, 1976.

43 Concerning the intentions of the Yamit demonstrators and the government's calculated participation in orchestrating the confrontation as a manageable but emotionally "traumatic" clash over Jewish attachment to the Land of Israel see Gabi Sheffer, "Was It Really a Trauma? Wider Political Implications of the Removal of Israeli Settlements from Sinai," *Journal of Applied Behavioral Science* 23 (February 1987) 117–29; *Hatzofe,* September 3, 1981; Dan Margalit, "Toward

Withdrawal," *Haaretz*, October 15, 1981; interview with the Tehiya member of Knesset Geula Kohen, *Yediot Acharonot*, October 19, 1981; David Oren, "Withdrawal and Persuasion," *Haaretz* (weekend supplement), October 23, 1981; Uzi Benziman, "Chosen Few in the Salient," *Haaretz*, October 26, 1981; Avraham Tal, "Operation Trauma 82," *Haaretz*, April 27, 1982; editorial, *Jerusalem Post*, May 2, 1982; "Liberated Territory," a paid advertisement in *Haaretz*, April 30, 1982; Amnon Kapeliouk, "The Staging of Yamit," *New Statesman*, May 7, 1982.

44 Poll conducted by Dahaf, reported in Charles S. Liebman, "The Religious Component in Israeli Ultra-Nationalism," *Jerusalem Quarterly*, no. 41 (Winter 1987) 128; Sammy Smooha, "Political Intolerance: Threatening Israel's Democracy," *New Outlook* 29 (July 1986) 29; poll conducted by the Van Leer Institute, reported in *Israleft Biweekly News Service*, no. 266, July 10, 1985, p. 6. Concerning Kach's substantially greater appeal to the Israeli public than to Israeli elites in 1984 and 1985 see Michal Shamir, "Kach and the Limits to Political Tolerance in Israel," *Jerusalem Letter/Viewpoints*, October 27, 1987.

45 Jacob Talmon, "The Homeland Is in Danger," *Haaretz*, March 31, 1980. For early predictions of violent clashes over the future of the territories, centering on threats of Gush Emunim challenges to the regime or "leftist" designs forcibly to eliminate Gush Emunim see Ehud Sprinzak, "Extreme Politics in Israel," *Jerusalem Quarterly*, no. 5 (Fall 1977) 33–47; Avi Ben-Zion, "On Fraternal Conflict in Israel" (Hebrew), *Bitzaron*, no. 328 (March 1977) 99–104. Aluph Hareven, "From the Seizure of Outposts to the Seizure of Authority?" *Haaretz*, October 19, 1979; Dani Rubinstein, *On the Lord's Side: Gush Emunim* (Hebrew) (Tel Aviv: Hakibbutz Hameuchad, 1982) 173–79; Tsvi Raanan, *Gush Emunim* (Hebrew) (Tel Aviv: Sifriat Poalim, 1980) 169–73; and Ehud Sprinzak, *Each Man Right in His Own Eyes: Illegalism in Israeli Society* (Hebrew) (Tel Aviv: Sifriat Poalim, 1986). For increasingly pointed analyses of the prospects for violent upheavals and regime breakdown that began appearing in front-rank Israeli academic work in 1982 see Mark A. Heller, *A Palestinian State: The Implications for Israel* (Cambridge: Harvard University Press, 1983) 115–16; and Yoram Peri, *Between Battles and Ballots* (Cambridge: Cambridge University Press, 1982) 284–87.

46 Meron Benvenisti, "The Turning Point in Israel," *New York Review of Books*, October 13, 1983, p. 12.

47 Benvenisti, *1986 Report*, 83. The text of this report, completed in January 1986, covers the period 1984–85.

48 Daniel J. Elazar, "Begin's Two-Year Government," in *Israel at the Polls, 1981*, ed. Howard R. Penniman and Daniel J. Elazar (Bloomington: Indiana University Press, 1986) 245 and 264; Giora Goldberg and Efraim Ben-Zadok, "Regionalism and an Emergent Territorial Cleavage: The Jewish Settlements in the Administered Territories," *Medina, Mimshal, ve-Yachasim Benleumiyim*, no. 21 (Spring 1983) 69–70; Aryeh Shalev, *Defense Line in Judea and Samaria* (Hebrew) (Tel Aviv: Kibbutz Hameuchad, 1982) 16; Sella and Yishai, *Israel the Peaceful Belligerent*, 1967–79, 77–126; Gershon Shafir, "Changing Nationalism and Israel's 'Open Frontier' on the West Bank," *Theory and Society* 13 (November 1984) 824; Uriel Tal, "Foundations of a Political Messianic Trend in Israel," *Jerusalem Quarterly*, no. 35 (Spring 1985) 38–45; and Baruch Kimmerling, "Exchanging Territories for

Peace: A Macrosocial Approach," *Journal of Applied Behavioral Science* 23 (February 1987) 13–33.

49   *Haaretz,* August 12, 1980; 23.9 percent answered yes.

50   Twenty-two percent agreed with this statement in 1983, with the number rising to 35 percent in August 1985 and 38 percent in September 1986. *Jerusalem Post International Edition,* week ending October 11, 1986. Late in 1989 the Smith Institute poll found that 52 percent of its respondents were "prepared to consider the deportation of Palestinians if a way is not found to make peace." *Haaretz,* November 10, 1989, from FBIS, November 14, 1989, p. 51.

51   *Koteret Rashit,* March 9, 1983. Twenty-seven percent of respondents said they thought Peace Now should be outlawed; 38 percent of Likud voters so responded. Twenty-two percent of respondents thought Gush Emunim should be outlawed; 16 percent of Labor party voters so responded. Sixty percent (including 71 percent of Likud voters) said the Committee for Solidarity with Beir Zeit (a Jewish group supporting students and faculty at a West Bank university) should be outlawed.

52   In this first survey on this question, 18.7 percent favored the idea. *Jerusalem Post,* January 13, 1984.

53   As reported by Christopher Hitchens, in *The Nation,* August 16–23, 1986, p. 103.

54   For reports of this research by various scholars and polling organizations see Donald S. Will, "Zionist Settlement Ideology and Its Ramifications for the Palestinian People," *Journal of Palestine Studies* 11 (Spring 1982) 53; Sammy Smooha, "Political Intolerance," 28; *Al-Hamishmar,* March 20, 1983; Ephraim Yuchtman-Yaar, "The Test of Israel's Arab Minority," *Israeli Democracy,* Spring 1988, pp. 42–46; *Haaretz,* June 8, 1988; Yochanan Peres and Ephraim Ya'ar, "Gender and Democracy," *Israeli Democracy,* Summer 1989, pp. 23–26 (regarding polls done in 1989); *Jerusalem Post,* January 24, 1990; Nurit Kahana, "According to Professor Sammy Smooha, the State of Israel Is Not a Real Democracy," *Haaretz,* June 5, 1990 (regarding polls done in 1988); and Kalman Benyamini, "Political and Civic Opinions of Israel's Jewish Youth," mimeo, Psychology Department, Hebrew University, June 1990 (regarding polls done in 1989 and 1990).

55   Gadi Wolfsfeld, *The Politics of Provocation: Participation and Protest in Israel* (Albany: SUNY Press, 1988) 2 and 164. Drawing on separate survey research data for the same and subsequent years, other Israeli researchers came to similar conclusions and offered similar warnings. See Michal Shamir and John Sullivan, "The Political Context of Tolerance: The United States and Israel," *American Political Science Review* 77 (December 1983) 911–28; Mina Tzemach and Ruth Tzin, "Attitudes of Adolescents toward Democratic Values," paper presented to the Van Leer Institute in Jerusalem, September 1984; Michal Shamir and John L. Sullivan, "Jews and Arabs in Israel: Everybody Hates Somebody, Sometime," *Journal of Conflict Resolution* 29 (June 1985) 283–305; and Michal Shamir, "Political Intolerance in a Polarized Society: Israel in the 1980s," paper presented at the annual meeting of the Association for Israel Studies, New York City, June 6–7, 1988; Yochanan Peres, "Most Israelis Are Commited to Democracy," *Israeli Democracy,* February 1987, pp. 16–19.

56   For examples of columns and editorials from this period which raised such warnings and concerns see Amos Elon, "Renaissance or Death Agony," *Haaretz,* October 12, 1979, translated in *Israleft: Biweekly News Service,* no. 157, November 1, 1979, p. 3; Ze'ev Schiff, *Haaretz,* June 6, 1980; "Destroying the Rule of Law in the Army," *Haaretz* August 24, 1980; Dan Margalit, "Leave Gadi in Prison," *Haaretz,* January 11, 1981; editorial, *Yediot Acharonot,* January 13, 1982; Hirsch Goodman, *Jerusalem Post,* March 12, 1982; A. Dunker, *Haaretz,* March 3, 1982; David Twersky, "Overflowing Sewer," *Jerusalem Post,* August 17, 1983; Charles Hoffman, "Israel Democracy's Fragile Base," *Jerusalem Post International Edition,* week ending March 5, 1983; Shlomo Ben-Ami, "Not in a Vacuum," *Hotam,* February 18, 1983; Moshe Auman, "Removing the Menace," *Jerusalem Post,* February 23, 1983; Ruth Bondi, "On the Road to '1984,' " *Davar* (weekly supplement), April 15, 1983; Ehud Ben-Ezer, "Were We Silent?" *Davar,* May 20, 1983; Shaul Friedlander, quoted in Amos Elon, *Haaretz,* April 22, 1983; editorial, "Jewish Terror," *Haaretz,* August 4, 1983; Yoel Marcus, "Alone in the End," *Haaretz,* April 3, 1984; Sadia Rahamim, "Sharon and 'The Original Sin,' " *Koteret Rashit,* no. 102, November 14, 1984; Dan Horowitz, "Israel: Ripe for Fascism," *Davar,* December 7, 1984; and Yoel Ben-Nun, "Why in *Koteret Rashit?*" *Koteret Rashit,* no. 114, February 6, 1985, pp. 36–37. For a literary treatment of the theme of Israel's transformation into a totalitarian society see Amos Kenan, *The Road to Ein Harod* (London: Al Saqi, 1986), first published in Hebrew by Am Oved in 1984.

57   In these years the editorial line of the *Jerusalem Post* reflected the thinking of moderate-to-dovish elements within the Labor party. I counted editorials as indicating the contemplation of regime threats if they contained references to the possibility of violent conflict between Jews as an accompaniment to efforts to withdraw from occupied territories or if they explicitly characterized political developments pertaining to the conflict over the disposition of the territories as threatening the foundations of Israeli democracy and the rule of law. A large number of editorials deploring the influence and popularity of Meir Kahane's Kach organization were not coded for inclusion in this category. I thank Marshall Billingslea for his help in conducting this analysis.

58   Quoted in Dan Horowitz, *Yediot Aharonot,* June 6, 1980. Translated in *Journal of Palestine Studies* 10 (Autumn 1980) 146–47.

59   FBIS, May 4, 1982, p. 115; FBIS, September 23, 1982, pp. 119–20.

60   See *Jerusalem Post International Edition,* week ending February 26, 1983.

61   From the Proceedings of the Knesset, December 27, 1983, quoted in "Oh What a Nice Kulturkampf," *Nekuda,* no. 70, March 2, 1984, p. 27.

62   Jerusalem Television Service broadcast, June 5, 1985, transcribed in FBIS, June 6, 1985, p. 16. For similar fears expressed by another Labor party leader, Gad Yaakobi, see "The Crucial Decision: What Kind of Israel Do We Want?" *Yediot Acharonot,* October 1985, translated in *American-Israel Civil Liberties Coalition Newsletter* 4 (Spring 1986).

63   For Yitzhak Navon's address to the nation on Independence Day, 1983, see transcription of a Jerusalem Domestic Service broadcast, April 17, 1983, FBIS, April 18, 1983, pp. 14–5. See also *Jerusalem Post,* September 7, 1983, concerning

President Herzog's New Year's message; and speeches delivered on Independence Day in 1984 and 1985 by Herzog, state of Israel, Office of the President, May 6, 1984, and April 25, 1985.

64   Several right-wing politicians, including Likud Knesset deputies Dov Shilansky and Michael Eitan, refused to sign, declaring their inability to endorse the division of the Land of Israel, which they considered at least implicit in the declaration's wording concerning the United Nations Partition Resolution.

65   Just after the election the secretary of the Board of Rabbis of Judea and Samaria contacted a senior Labor party leader to "reassure him" in the wake of reports that settlers were stockpiling weapons. Amos Levav, "We Have Encircled the Arab Population Centers in Judea and Samaria," *Yediot Acharonot* (supplement), July 24, 1992, translated in JPRS-NEA-92–108, p. 8. See also questions and answers during a news conference given by the prime minister-elect Rabin, June 26, 1992, Israel Radio broadcast, June 27, 1992, transcribed in FBIS, July 2, 1992, p. 26.

66   See, inter alia, Lilly Weissbrod, "From Labour Zionism to New Zionism: Ideological Change in Israel," *Theory and Society* 10 (November 1981) 777–803; idem, "Core Values and Revolutionary Change" *The Impact of Gush Emunim* ed. David Newman (London: Croom Helm, 1985) 70–72; Amnon Sella, "Custodians and Redeemers: Israeli Leaders' Perceptions of Peace, 1967–1979," *Middle Eastern Studies* 22 (April 1986) 248; David Newman, "Introduction: Gush Emunim in Society and Space," in *The Impact of Gush Emunim,* 1–2; Ofira Seliktar, "The New Zionism," *Foreign Policy,* no. 51 (Summer 1983) 118; idem, *New Zionism and the Foreign Policy System of Israel,* 74, 159, and 271; Amnon Rubinstein, *The Zionist Dream Revisited: From Herzl to Gush Emunim and Back* (New York: Schocken, 1984) 106–7; and Bernard Avishai, *The Tragedy of Zionism: Revolution and Democracy in the Land of Israel* (New York: Farrar, Straus and Giroux, 1985) 235–71. For a discussion of the transformation of Israel's "civil religion" which emphasizes change in parameters of political culture other than the territorial shape see Charles S. Liebman and Eliezer Don-Yehiya, *Civil Religion in Israel* (Berkeley: University of California Press, 1983).

67   See especially works by Myron J. Aronoff, "Establishing Authority: The Memorialization of Jabotinsky and the Burial of the Bar-Kochba Bones in Israel under the Likud," in *The Frailty of Authority,* 105–30; idem, *Israeli Visions and Divisions* (New Brunswick, N.J.: Transaction Books, 1989) 10–11; and idem, "Political Polarization: Contradictory Interpretations of Israeli Reality," in *Cross-Currents in Israeli Culture and Politics,* ed. Myron J. Aronoff, vol. 4 of *Political Anthropology* (New Brunswick, N.J.: Transaction Books, 1984) 14. For assessments judging the hegemonic projects of the Likud and/or of Gush Emunim as failures or as incompletely successful see Avram Schweitzer, *Israel: The Changing National Agenda* (London: Croom Helm, 1986) 90–91; Peleg, *Begin's Foreign Policy,* 89–90 and 117–20; Eliezer Don-Yehiya, "Jewish Messianism, Religious Zionism and Israeli Politics: The Impact and Origins of Gush Emunim," *Middle Eastern Studies* 23 (April 1987) 215–34; and Lustick, *For the Land and the Lord,* 12–14 and 177–80.

68   For typical claims about the supposed existence of an unbreakable national

consensus barring complete withdrawal from the territories, the establishment of a Palestinian state, and/or negotiations with the PLO see Shmuel Shnitzer "The Question and Answer Game," *Maariv,* February 27, 1981; Benjamin Akzin et al., *Shared Rule: The Only Realistic Option for Peace* (Jerusalem: Jerusalem Center for Public Affairs, 1983) 2–4 and 16; Haggai Eshed, "The Only Way Out," *Jerusalem Letter: Viewpoints,* no. 28, April 29, 1983; and Samuel J. Roberts, *Party and Policy in Israel: The Battle between Hawks and Doves* (Boulder, Colo.: Westview Press, 1990) 164–66.

69 See *Maariv,* March 18, 1977. Contrast this article with Harkabi's depiction of the PLO as firmly committed to Israel's destruction in his book, written in 1975, *Arab Strategies and Israel's Response* (New York: Free Press, 1977) 27–77. Harkabi's 1970 book, *Arab Attitudes toward Israel* (English edition) (Jerusalem: Keter, 1972) was based on a comprehensive review of books on Israel published in the Arab world and had an enormous impact on Israeli opinion, establishing a monolithic and extremely pessimistic Israeli view of Arab political attitudes. Harkabi coined the word "politicide" to summarize the Arab objective of "killing a state." His point-by-point analysis of the PLO's founding charter was widely circulated by Israel's Ministry of Information in the early 1970s. It was designed to prove, by textual analysis, that the PLO's slogan of a "democratic secular state" in Palestine was only a cover for the destruction of the Jewish state and the annihilation or expulsion of its Jewish citizens. For this and other early Harkabi analyses of the PLO see Yehoshaphat Harkabi, *Palestinians and Israel* (Jerusalem: Keter, 1974).

70 Had Arab citizens of Israel been included in these polls, the proportion of affirmative replies would likely have been 7 percent to 8 percent higher. Also during this period, when Israeli Jews were asked whether they positively favored establishment of a Palestinian state as opposed to whether they would be willing to accept such an outcome, the proportion of affirmative responses was regularly less than 10 percent. Sources for polling data regarding negotiations with the PLO are *Haaretz,* December 20, 1976, reporting a PORI poll; *Haaretz,* February 9, 1977, reporting a PORI poll; *Jerusalem Post,* September 28, 1979, reporting PORI polls; *Yediot Acharonot,* May 23, 1980, reporting polls by the Israel Institute for Applied Social Research; *Haaretz,* October 2, 1981, reporting a PORI poll; *Jerusalem Post,* October 2, 1986, reporting polls conducted by Hanoch Smith (June 1983; August 1985; February 1986; June 1986; September 1986); *Jerusalem Post,* January 30, 1986, reporting a poll by Dahaf; *Haaretz,* June 8, 1988, reporting a poll by Modi'in Ezrahi; poll by Hanoch Smith Research Foundation and Dahaf, reported in Mark Tessler, "The Intifada and Political Discourse in Israel," *Journal of Palestine Studies* 19 (Winter 1990) 56; *Yediot Acharonot,* September 23, 1987; *Yediot Acharonot* and *Haaretz,* September 1, 1988; *Jerusalem Post,* September 2, 1989; Asher Arian and Raphael Ventura, *Public Opinion in Israel and the Intifada: Changes in Security Attitudes, 1987–88,* JCSS Memorandum No. 28 (Tel Aviv: Tel Aviv University Jaffee Center for Strategic Studies, 1989) 33; *Yediot Acharonot,* December 23, 1988, reporting a Dahaf poll, in FBIS, December 28, 1988, p. 31; *Yediot Acharonot,* February 10, 1989, reporting a Dahaf poll transcribed in FBIS, February 13, 1989; *Maariv,* March 24, 1989, reporting a Dahaf poll by Mina

Tzemach in transcribed FBIS, March 27, 1989; Hanoch Smith polls reported in *New York Times*, April 2, 1989; *Hadashot*, March 27, 1991, reporting polls conducted by Ephraim Yaar for the Israel Institute for Democracy.

71 Giora Goldberg, Gad Barzilai, and Efraim Inbar, *The Impact of Intercommunal Conflict: The Intifada and Israeli Public Opinion*, Policy Studies No. 43 (Jerusalem: Leonard Davis Institute for International Relations, February 1991) 7 and 19. See also the analysis of Yosi Alpher, deputy director of the Center for Strategic Studies in Tel Aviv, who commented in March 1990 that "Today we have a situation that was considered absurd a year ago: What do they talk about within the Likud—whether we are already talking to the PLO and if that will lead to a Palestinian state? These issues, after all, were taboo!" *Davar*, March 16, 1990.

72 Jerusalem Television Service, February 26, 1985, transcribed by FBIS, February 27, 1985, pp. I4–5.

73 Meir Merhav, "A Consensus of Nonsense," *Jerusalem Post*, March 10, 1985. See also Asher Maniv, "The Cost of the PLO Taboo," *Jerusalem Post International Edition*, week ending March 7, 1987.

74 See remarks to this effect quoted from speeches by Arik Sharon, David Levy, and Yitzhak Shamir to a joint meeting of the central committees of parties supporting Jewish settlement of the West Bank and Gaza Strip. *Jerusalem Post*, April 8, 1985. For Shamir's public characterization of the emergence of a Palestinian state as a "risk one has to take," see *Jerusalem Post*, July 28, 1986. For a particularly vivid depiction of building anti-PLO hegemonic conceptions as a dangerously uncompleted task, see the analysis presented by Yossi Ben-Aharon, one of Shamir's closest advisers, in 1987. Quoted in Noam Chomsky, "Israel's Role in U.S. Foreign Policy," in *Intifada: The Palestinian Uprising against Israeli Occupation*, ed. Zachary Lockman and Joel Beinin (Boston: South End Press, 1989) 269–70.

75 See, for example, Orna Kadash, "Conversation with Shulamit Aloni: 'I Am Tired to Death," *Bamachane*, no. 15, November 30, 1983.

76 See Nahum Barnea's editorial in the liberal-dovish journal *Koteret Rashit*, " 'Yallah' Peace Now," on the "pathetic" condition of the Peace Now movement, no. 225, March 25, 1987, p. 3; his article on Amos Oz's withdrawal from the political scene, "Oz Searches for the Way Home," *Koteret Rashit*, no. 260, November 25, 1987, pp. 26–28; and Adi Ophir's argument that despite the "institutionalization" of Israeli rule of the territories, struggling over "the terms of Israeli political discourse" to prevent its "legitimization" was still a vital task for opponents of the state-building process. Ophir, "Occupation: A Perspective from the Israeli Left," *Tikkun* 2 (1987) 66–71. To mark the twentieth anniversary of the beginning of Israeli rule over the territories, and to help at least remind its readers of the West Bank problem, the editors of *Koteret Rashit* commissioned an Israeli novelist, David Grossman, to write a collection of articles based on an extended series of visits to the area. Many of these short pieces were published in a special issue of the journal, no. 230, April 29, 1987, and appeared later in a widely read English edition, *Yellow Wind* (New York: Farrar, Straus and Giroux, 1988). Grossman concluded his impressions with an essay reflecting his own pessimism and that of the "peace camp" as a whole, titled "The First Twenty Years." "I have a bad feeling," he wrote, "I'm afraid that the existing situation will continue exactly as it is for another ten or twenty years."

77 Lustick, *For the Land and the Lord,* 168–76. Concerning the shift within Gush Emunim during this period away from confrontationism toward political strategies appropriate for building ideological hegemony see Yoel Ben-Nun, "To Fill the Vacuum Left by Gush Emunim," *Nekuda,* no. 102, September 5, 1986, p. 10; Menachem Froumin, "I Am Splitting," *Nekuda,* no. 104, November 7, 1986, pp. 10–11, 31; Eliakim Haetzni, "No Need for Transfer," *Nekuda,* no. 113, August 28, 1987, pp. 10–11; Beni Katzover, "To the Schismatics Let There Be No Hope," *Nekuda,* no. 106, January 9, 1987, pp. 10–12; Beni Katzover, "Shaking Off the Feeling of Inferiority," *Nekuda,* no. 111, June 30, 1987, pp. 18–19 and 31; editorial, "TAKAM Joins in the Chorus of 'It's Coming to Me,' " *Nekuda,* no. 107, February 13, 1987, p. 7; Menachem Froumin, "Overcoming the Contemptuous Inclination," *Nekuda,* no. 108, March 13, 1987, pp. 22–23; Daniella Weiss, "I Never Said the Kibbutz Was a Failure," *Nekuda,* no. 108, March 13, 1987, pp. 26–27; Yossi Artziel, "A Movement instead of Gush," *Nekuda,* no. 109, April 14, 1987, pp. 26–27; editorial, "Twenty Years from the Liberation, Five Years from the Uprooting," *Nekuda,* no. 110, May 27, 1987, p. 6; Moshe Ben-Yoseph [Hagar], "Transfer and Gush Emunim," *Nekuda,* no. 113, August 28, 1987, p. 30; Amiel Unger, "Our Public Must Align Itself into One National Camp," *Nekuda,* no. 116, December 1987, pp. 16–19 and 38; Yoska Shapira, "The Media Connection," *Nekuda,* no. 116, December 1987, pp. 20–21 and 39.

78 See Tessler, "The Intifada and Political Discourse in Israel," 43–61.

79 Gideon Doron, "To Know the Price and to Change," *Haaretz,* May 5, 1990. For a much earlier analysis coming to a similar conclusion, but without the benefit of polling data, see Shlomo Gazit, "Our Common Denominator on the Palestinian Question," *Davar,* August 13, 1982. See also Perlmutter, *Israel: The Partitioned State,* 256. By 1989 at least one Likud spokesman was unwilling to claim any more for a "national consensus" than opposition to relinquishing strategic control over the occupied territories. See Zalman Shoval, "The Peace Initiative: Still the Best Bet," *Jerusalem Post,* July 11, 1989.

80 Transcribed from Jerusalem Domestic Service broadcast, May 3, 1988, by FBIS, May 3, 1988, p. 38; *Al-Hamishmar,* April 19, 1988. As early as August 1986 a report appeared in the Israeli media quoting Peres as having characterized Labor's position as unwilling to negotiate with the PLO "so long as it does not accept Resolutions 242 and 338 and does not abandon terror." *Jerusalem Post,* August 16, 1986.

81 *Al-Ahram,* September 11, 1988, translated in FBIS, September 13, 1988, p. 39. Rabin was at that time minister of defense. Peres was finance minister and deputy prime minister.

82 Jerusalem Domestic Service broadcast, August 7, 1988, transcribed by FBIS, August 9, 1988, p. 35.

83 *Jerusalem Post,* September 1, 1988. See also the remarks by Labor Minister Mordechai Gur, reported in *Yediot Acharonot,* December 18, 1988, characterizing the PLO as "an obvious and full partner in political talks to solve the Middle East conflict."

84 *Peace Now: Newsletter to Our Friends in North America* 5 (Winter–Spring 1989) 7.

85 For three years Israeli military intelligence had submitted analyses corrobor-

ating the PLO's acceptance of the principle of a "two-state solution" to be attained through political and diplomatic means. Early in 1989 the intelligence branch submitted an official report to Prime Minister Shamir identifying negotiations with the PLO as the only way to end the intifada. *Al-Hamishmar,* July 1, 1988. Concerning Shamir's efforts to purge the Israel Defense Forces of intelligence officers who would come to conclusions tending to "legitimize the PLO," see Robert Friedman, in a *Village Voice* article reported in *Hadoar,* February 17, 1989.

86 See Yitzhak Rabin's studied avoidance of repeated opportunities to make his traditional vow of refusal to ever negotiate with the PLO: Jerusalem Domestic Service broadcast, June 27, 1990, transcribed in FBIS, June 29, 1990, p. 28. For an example of Peres's intricate formulations indicating readiness to negotiate with the PLO but refusal to say so explicitly see the transcript of an extended interview by Dan Margalit, broadcast on March 23, 1989, transcribed in FBIS, March 24, 1989, pp. 24–27. For Gur's public announcement of his support for negotiations with the PLO see Jerusalem Domestic Service broadcast, January 4, 1989, transcribed in FBIS, January 5, 1989, p. 25; for a similar position articulated by Shahal see Jerusalem Domestic Service broadcast, February 12, 1989, transcribed in FBIS, February 13, 1989; p. 37; and Uzi Baram, in *Haaretz,* June 18, 1989. In one of his first moves as minister of police in the Rabin government established in July 1992, Shahal called for the decriminalization of meetings between Israelis and PLO members.

87 *Hadashot,* February 24, 1989.

88 Tessler, "The Intifada and Political Discourse in Israel," 57.

89 *Hadashot,* January 3, 1990, reporting a poll conducted under the supervision of Avraham Diskin, a Hebrew University political scientist.

90 Akiva Eldar, "Under Shamir's Sheep's Clothing," *Haaretz,* January 31, 1989. Translated in FBIS, February 2, 1989, p. 33.

91 Independence Day interview with Prime Minister Yitzhak Shamir, *Jerusalem Post,* May 9, 1989.

92 See PORI polls, reported by *Haaretz,* July 11, 1980, and November 8, 1985; polls of the Institute for Applied Social Research, reported by *Yediot Acharonot,* May 23, 1980; Arian and Ventura, *Public Opinion in Israel and the Intifada,* 34; and *Yediot Acharonot,* September 1, 1988. Some of these polls asked whether Israelis "should agree" to a Palestinian state, not whether they would be "willing to accept" such a state.

93 PORI poll, reported in *Haaretz,* February 23, 1981.

94 Israel Institute of Applied Social Research poll, reported by the institute's scientific director Eliahu Katz, in *Jerusalem Post International Edition,* week ending August 27, 1988.

95 *Jerusalem Post,* September 14, 1988. Shortly after the outbreak of the intifada, a minor cause celebre transpired when Moshe Amirav, a Likud central committee member, was forced to resign from the party after traveling to Romania in what appears to have been an unauthorized attempt to arrange indirect negotiations between Shamir and PLO leaders. For details on Amirav's activities see Pinchas Inbari, in *Al-Hamishmar,* September 28, 1987. For the ouster of another Herut politician, Aryeh Naor, on similar grounds, see editorial, *Maariv,* January 17, 1988.

96   See Ariel Sharon, in *Yediot Acharonot,* March 28, 1991, translated in JPRS-NEA-91–029, May 17, 1991, p. 13, According to Sharon's often-stated view, the Hashemite Kingdom of Jordan, east of the Jordan River, should be considered a Palestinian state. Similar comments by Eliyahu Ben-Elissar, a Herut veteran and then chair of the Knesset Foreign Affairs and Security Committee, broadcast on Israeli television, December 17, 1990, transcribed in FBIS, December 18, 1990, p. 38. In a striking illustration of the shift of the burden of proof in public discourse about negotiations with the PLO, Yitzhak Shamir quoted a recent poll showing that 80 percent of Israeli Jews opposed establishment of a "PLO state" in order to "discredit the views that there is a majority in Israel supporting the idea of a Palestinian state," and show that "the majority of Israelis were opposed to talks with the PLO." Jerusalem Domestic Service broadcast, February 7, 1989, transcribed in FBIS, February 7, 1989, p. 31.

97   Conducted by Teleseqer Research Institute, reported by *Yediot Acharonot,* March 14, 1990.

98   For longitudinal compilations and overall surveys of polling data, some stressing Israeli intransigence and some the potential for flexibility, but all reflecting the stability and evenness of the split in Israel on this basic question, see Abel Jacob, "Trends in Israeli Public Opinion on Issues Related to the Arab-Israeli Conflict," *Jewish Journal of Sociology* 16 (December 1974) 187–208; Russell A. Stone, *Social Change in Israel: Attitudes and Events, 1967–79* (New York: Praeger, 1982) 14–45; Gloria Falk, "Israeli Public Opinion: Looking toward a Palestinian Solution," *Middle East Journal* 39 (Summer 1985) 247–69; Yadin Kaufmann, "Israel's Flexible Voters," *Foreign Policy,* no. 61 (Winter 1985–86) 109–24; *Jerusalem Post,* April 2, 1988; *Maariv,* February 17, 1989.

99   Asher Arian, "A People Apart: Coping with National Security Problems in Israel," *Journal of Conflict Resolution* 33 (December 1989) 623 and 627.

100   Not until 1984, however, did official Israeli maps eliminate the section of the Green Line that divided the Israeli and (former) Jordanian municipalities and begin designating the line separating expanded East Jerusalem from the rest of the West Bank as an international boundary.

101   For examples of the use of this technique in connection with various diplomatic attempts to move the "peace process" forward see [Poles], "Camp David: The Second Half," *Haaretz,* May 7, 1982; public remarks by National Religious party member of Knesset Hayim Druckman, October 10, 1982, Israel Defense Forces broadcast, transcribed by FBIS, October 12, 1982, p. I9; Moshe Zaq, "A Magic Word Called Federation," *Maariv,* October 13, 1982; reports from *Maariv,* November 5, 1985, and Jerusalem Domestic Service broadcast, November 5, 1985, of objections by Ariel Sharon and Gush Emunim settlers against the contradiction between proposals to negotiate with Jordan and the terms of the 1980 Jerusalem Law, in FBIS, November 5, 1982, pp. I2–3; and remarks by Ariel Sharon to his political associates while celebrating the establishment of a personal residence in the Muslim Quarter of the Old City, *Haaretz,* May 25, 1989.

102   For an early 1980s discussion of the extent to which Israeli rule over expanded Jerusalem had (and had not) been established in such a manner as to "def[y] a rational cost-benefit calculus" see Heller, *A Palestinian State,* 116–26.

103   See, for example, remarks by Communications Minister Amnon Rubinstein,

Jerusalem Domestic Service broadcast, June 14, 1985, transcribed by FBIS, June 17, 1985, p. I4; and by Yossi Sarid, Jerusalem Domestic Service broadcast, October 7, 1986, transcribed by FBIS, October 8, 1986, p. I1.

104 Israel Defense Forces broadcast, July 3, 1988, transcribed by FBIS, July 8, 1988, p. 32.

105 Interview with the defense minister, Israel Defence Forces broadcast, April 14, 1987, transcribed by FBIS, April 15, 1987, p. I2.

106 Government of Israel, Central Bureau of Statistics, *Statistical Abstract of Israel,* annual, note to table 1, no. 1.

107 In 1981 one Gush Emunim activist neatly expressed the imperative of hegemonic construction when he described "the only way" to prevent the separation of Israel from expanded East Jerusalem. He stated, "There is only one way and that is to change the idea of dividing the city into something that is utterly ridiculous, as is the idea of returning the Arabs to Cordoba or Andalusia today—ridiculous." Beni Ricardo, "Yesha and Jerusalem," *Nekuda,* no. 26, April 3, 1981, p. 11. See Shamir's speech before the Likud Knesset faction indicating that the redivision of the city was only too conceivable, Israel Defense Forces broadcast, March 14, 1990, transcribed by FBIS, March 14, 1990, p. 16. See also, and especially, Sharon's speech before the Likud central committee, where he castigated his rivals in the Likud as well for their betrayal of the "united Jerusalem." "In fact, the capital, the heart of the Jewish people, has again been partitioned. The Israeli Government has reconciled itself to this situation." Israel Defense Forces broadcast, February 12, 1990, transcribed by FBIS, February 12, 1990, p. 14.

108 *Divrei HaKnesset* (Proceedings of the Knesset), March 15, 1990, from FBIS, March 15, 1990, p. 32 (emphasis added). The substantial change in the willingness of Labor party leaders to consider publicly adjustments in the status of expanded East Jerusalem and/or its residents is also apparent from the contrast between Labor's agreement to the participation of East Jerusalemites in the proposed negotiations and elections of 1990 and its opposition to comparable proposals during the autonomy negotiations in 1980–82. See Abba Eban, "Autonomy—The Hour of Truth," *Al-Hamishmar,* January 15, 1982.

109 Jerusalem Domestic Service broadcast, March 28, 1990, transcribed by FBIS, March 28, 1990, p. 18.

110 *Haaretz,* May 16, 1990; and *Maariv,* May 16, 1990.

10. HEGEMONIC FAILURE AND REGIME CRISIS IN ISRAEL

1 Space does not permit a full analysis here of Ben-Gurion's construction of the 1949 armistice lines as hegemonic or the opposition and defeat of those whose political interests were compromised by it. For sources relevant to such an analysis see, in addition to those listed in Chap. 9, note 1, Michael Keren, *The Pen and the Sword: Israeli Intellectuals and the Making of the Nation-State* (Boulder, Colo.: Westview Press, 1989) esp. 35–36; idem, *Ben Gurion and the Intellectuals: Power, Knowledge, and Charisma* (Dekalb: Northern Illinois University Press, 1983) esp. 122–28; Yitzhak Tabenkin, *Settlement: Idea and Praxis* (Hebrew) (Tel Aviv: Kibbutz Hameuchad, 1983) esp. 28–29, 35, 39–41, and 55–64; Mitchell Cohen, *Zion*

and State: Nation, Class and the Shaping of Modern Israel (Oxford: Basil Blackwell, 1987); Ezer Weizman, *On Eagles' Wings* (London: Weidenfeld and Nicolson, 1976) 253–54; David Ben-Gurion, *Rebirth and Destiny of Israel* (New York: Philosophical Library, 1954) 444–45, 452, 466, 489, and 501. On the link between Ben-Gurion's policy of retaliation raids, designed to reduce incursions by encouraging more thorough Jordanian and Egyptian domination of the West Bank and Gaza Strip, and Israeli acceptance of the armistice lines as "the factual and legal basis for the territorial limits of Israel," see Avraham Avi-hai, *Ben Gurion State-Builder: Principles and Pragmatism, 1948–1963* (New York: Wiley, 1974) 128; and Shlomo Aronson, *Conflict and Bargaining in the Middle East: An Israeli Perspective* (Baltimore: Johns Hopkins University Press, 1978) 10–11. Also relevant are pp. 6–9 and 379n.

2 Even a leading anti-annexationist such as Abba Eban, in a celebrated phrase uttered in the aftermath of the 1967 war, referred to the 1949 boundaries as "Auschwitz borders."

3 *Livnot ulehivanotba,* "to build and to be built by," was a prestate Labor Zionist slogan.

4 Editorial, "Long Is the Road to Redemption," *Nekuda,* no. 105, December 9, 1986, p. 6. For a dovish Israeli observer's analysis emphasizing the absence of Arab citizenship in the occupied territories as the decisive obstacle to the hegemonic aspirations of the annexationists see Sammy Smooha, "Four Models and One More," *Politika,* nos. 14–15 (June 1987) 61–63.

5 *Yediot Acharonot,* April 11, 1988; *Jerusalem Post,* June 7, 1989; Bank of Israel President Michael Bruno, quoted in Joel Bainerman, "Intifadah Alters Investment Trends," reprinted from *Jerusalem Post* (supplement), in JPRS-NEA-90–019, March 30, 1990, p. 48.

6 *Haaretz,* April 2, 1991. Btzelem also reported that during this period, 85 additional Arabs, including 30 babies, died shortly after exposure to tear gas.

7 *Davar,* October 31, 1989.

8 *Maariv,* November 17, 1989. See also descriptions by Israeli security services officers of the unprecedented breadth and scope of involvement by Palestinians in resistance activities. Jerusalem Domestic Service broadcast, December 6, 1989, transcribed in FBIS, December 15, 1989, p. 29.

9 *Maariv,* September 5, 1990.

10 See "The Human Costs of the Uprising," *Palestine Human Rights Campaign Newsletter* 11 (January 1991). Virtually all observers agree that the army's estimates of injuries inflicted are extremely low, partly because of Palestinian efforts to evade capture by the authorities. Levels of casualties, as well as destruction and seizure of property (mainly via home demolitions, fines, the uprooting of trees, extended curfews, disciplinary tax collection in kind, and violent and semiviolent searches), especially in proportion to the size of the Palestinian population, are much higher than those endured by Irish nationalists between 1918 and 1921, though not nearly as high as those endured by Algerian Muslims between 1954 and 1962. See also below, note 56.

11 See the cartoon by "Mushik" accompanying the article by Tedy Preus, "Creeping De-Annexation," *Davar,* May 27, 1989.

12 In personal interviews with Gush Emunim activists during spring 1988, this

was explicitly acknowledged as the motivation for exaggerating the participation of Israeli Arabs in violent aspects of the intifada. According to both the minister of police and a former deputy director of the security services, the intifada was virtually completely contained within the West Bank and Gaza Strip. *Maariv,* January 12 and *Maariv,* October 24, 1990. On the identity of Israeli Arabs, despite their strong sympathy for the intifada, as distinct from the Arabs of the territories, see Nadim Rouhana, "Palestinians in Israel: Responses to the Uprising," in *Echoes of the Intifada: Regional Repercussions of the Palestinian-Israeli Conflict,* ed. Rex Brynen (Boulder, Colo.: Westview Press, 1991) 97–118.

13   *Haaretz,* May 7, 1990; and *Maariv,* July 6, 1990.

14   *Jerusalem Post,* November 9, 1990. The Israeli sense of the territories as alien was especially pronounced in the Gaza Strip, where the intifada was triggered early in December 1987. See Jackson Diehl, "The Land Nobody Wants," *Washington Post National Weekly Edition,* week ending September 1, 1991, pp. 11–12. For the most comprehensive analysis of the intifada's contribution to the resurrection of the Green Line in Israeli consciousness see Mark Tessler, "The Impact of the *Intifada* on Israeli Political Thinking," in *Echoes of the Intifada,* 43–96.

15   A June 1992 poll of retired army generals and officers of equivalent rank in the security services showed 68 percent favored security arrangements based on withdrawal from the West Bank and Gaza Strip. Thirty-one percent favored annexation. *Jerusalem Post,* June 21, 1992.

16   I also note, at the end of Chapter 5, how the advocates of "Greater Britain," led by Joseph Chamberlain, Cecil Rhodes, and the Round Table group of tariff reformers, failed to establish their greatly enlarged conception of the shape of the British state in the face of enormous contradictions between the conflicting demands and identities of peoples in such a far-flung array of possessions and the real empathic capacities of those who inhabited the United Kingdom itself.

17   Giora Goldberg, Gad Barzilai, and Efraim Inbar, *The Impact of Intercommunal Conflict: The Intifada and Israeli Public Opinion,* Policy Studies No. 43 (Jerusalem: Leonard Davis Institute for International Relations, February 1991) 1.

18   The "end of the *status quo* as a tenable option" is one of the main conclusions reached by Goldberg, Barzilai, and Inbar, *The Impact of Intercommunal Conflict,* 12–13.

19   Thus does the Israeli government's glossy publication, distributed on the eve of the intifada, with its full-color photos of happy and prosperous Arabs cooperating with Israeli technicians, seem ridiculous rather than reassuring. See Office of the Coordinator of Government Operations in Judea, Samaria, and the Gaza District, *Judea, Samaria, and the Gaza District, 1967–1987* (Jerusalem: Carta, 1987).

20   Concerning the explicitly manipulative ways in which even those annexationist politicians ready to discuss eventual citizenship for Arabs in the territories think about the political meaning of that citizenship see Aryeh D. Cohen, "Neeman: Annex Territories and Give Arab Inhabitants Citizenship," press bulletin, Government Press Office, Jerusalem, April 3, 1984.

21   The only formulas that seem capable of overshadowing Palestinian nation-

alism among Arabs in the West Bank and Gaza Strip are Pan-Arab nationalism and Islamic fundamentalism, neither of which are more promising vehicles for facilitating the absorption of this population into a Jewish-Zionist-Israeli state than is Palestinian nationalism.

22   See Ian Lustick, "Is Annexation a Fact?" *New Outlook* 25 (April 1982) 14–17; Hagay Eshed, "Autonomy according to Sharon," *Davar*, November 13, 1981; and [Poles], "Camp David: The Second Half," *Haaretz*, May 7, 1982.

23   The best overall treatment of the Village Leagues phenomenon is Salim Tamari, "In League with Zion: Israel's Search for a Native Pillar," *Journal of Palestine Studies* 12 (Summer 1983) 41–56. See also a three-part article by Nura Sus in *Al-Fajr* (English), July 19–25, July 26–August 1, and August 2–8, 1981; and Tzvi Barel, "Autonomy of Area Village Leagues," *Haaretz*, September 2, 1982. For a different view, emphasizing the possibilities for success of the Village Leagues project, see Menachem Milson, "How to Make Peace with the Palestinians," *Commentary*, May 1981, pp. 25–35; and idem, *Israel, The Palestinians, and the Peace Process: A Conversation with Menachem Milson* (Hebrew) (Yad Tabenkin: Kibbutz Hameuchad Political Circle, February 1983). Milson resigned as head of the military government's civilian administration in fall 1982. See also Ahiya Yitzhaki, "Milson's Year on the West Bank," *Middle East Review* 18 (Winter 1986–87) 37–47.

24   Interview published in *Maariv*, June 26, 1992, reported in *Washington Post*, June 27, 1992.

25   Michael Inbar and Ephraim Yuchtman-Yaar, "The People's Image of Conflict Resolution: Israelis and Palestinians," *Journal of Conflict Resolution* 33 (March 1989) 42 and 46. See also *Monitin*, May 1986, whose annual survey of Israeli opinion showed that "only 46 percent of the population found the views of Kahane and his Kach Party 'totally unacceptable' ... 23 percent found the Kach program 'mistaken in general but partly right'; 17 percent found it correct in general but partly wrong; and 6 percent agreed with Kahane outright." Reported by Christopher Hitchens, "Minority Report," *The Nation*, August 16–23, 1986, p. 103.

26   *Haaretz*, November 10, 1989. Two-thirds of those willing to accept the idea of mass deportations identified themselves as supporters of the Likud or its political allies. In the June 1989 survey of the Israel Institute for Applied Social Research, a small majority of Jews favoring annexation of the territories also favored removing their Arab inhabitants (51 percent). Reported in *Jerusalem Post*, September 2, 1989. In May 1990, 51 percent of respondents in a Dahaf poll of Israeli Jewish youth answered affirmatively to the question "Are you for or against the expulsion of all Arabs from the areas of Judea and Samaria?" Yaron London, "Half Are in Favor," *Yediot Acharonot* (supplement), May 29, 1990. For other comparable polls during this period see *Maariv*, July 15, 1987, and *Haaretz*, June 8, 1988.

27   For unmediated statements of Kahane's positions toward Jews as well as Arabs see issues of his movement's journal published in the United States, *Kahane: The Magazine of the Authentic Jewish Idea*. See also Kahane's books, *They Must Go* (New York: Grosset and Dunlop, 1981); and *Uncomfortable Questions for Comfortable Jews* (Secaucus, N.J.: L. Stuart, 1987); and a representative op-ed piece, "For a Jewish State, Annex and Expel," *New York Times*, July 18, 1983.

28   Concerning Kahane's potential electoral strength among Likud-oriented con-

stituencies, see Gershon Shafir and Yoav Peled, "Thorns in Your Eyes: The So-cioeconomic Basis of the Kahane Vote," in *The Elections in Israel—1984*, ed. Asher Arian and Michal Shamir (Tel Aviv: Ramot, 1986) 189–206. For polls showing Kahane attracting enough support to be awarded eleven, four, and six to seven Knesset seats, see, respectively, *Haaretz*, August 27, September 22, 1985; *Hadashot*, August 22, 1988.

29 Mordechai Nisan, *The Jewish State and the Arab Problem* (Hebrew) (Tel Aviv: Hadar, 1986); Eliakim Haetzni, "Why I Went into a Coalition with Ka-hanists," *Nekuda*, no. 90, August 23, 1985, pp. 16–17; Moshe Ben-Yosef [Hagar], "For the Right of Transfer," *Nekuda*, no. 109, April 14, 1987, pp. 16–17 and 50.

Concerning the legitimizing effect of Kahanism on similar views prevailing within the annexationist camp see Gideon Rafael, *Jerusalem Post*, March 2, 1986; Amos Kenan, " 'Hello Dogs'—The Strategy of the Right," *Yediot Acharonot*, November 2, 1984; *New York Times*, August 5, 1985; editorial, "Arabs Out!" *Koteret Rashit*, no. 233, May 20, 1987, p. 3; editorial, "Transfer," *Koteret Rashit*, no. 240, July 8, 1987, p. 3; Aviezer Ravitzky, *The Roots of Kahanism: Consciousness and Political Reality* (Jerusalem: Shazar Library, Hebrew University of Jerusalem, 1986); Gerald Cromer, *The Debate about Kahanism in Israeli Society, 1984–1988*, Occasional Papers No. 3 (New York: Harry Frank Guggenheim Foundation, 1988) 30–32; and Avner Regev, in *Al-Hamishmar*, October 15, 1990.

30 *Maariv*, November 1, 1987. On Shapira's proposal as something to be dis-cussed as a reasonable option, and not rejected as morally horrifying, see editorial, "Hypocritical Reaction," *Nekuda*, no. 115, November 1987, p. 8.

31 Eyal Ehrlich, "The Man of the Future Is Arens," *Haaretz* (supplement), Feb-ruary 26, 1988. Concerning growing support for expulsion of Arabs within the central committees of the Likud and the National Religious party see Dan Margalit, "A Meeting, Half a Meeting," *Haaretz*, November 3, 1987, in FBIS, November 5, 1987, pp. 22–23.

32 Moledet received two seats in the 1988 elections and three in 1992. For a discussion of support for "transfer" ideas within the leadership of the annexationist camp that was crystallizing in the months just prior to the intifada see Avishai Ehrlich, "Is Transfer an Option?" *Israeli Democracy* 1 (Winter 1987–88) 36–38. For specifics see Hanan Porat, "Co-Existence Is Still Possible," *Nekuda*, no. 119, March 1988, pp. 44–45; *Jerusalem Post*, April 4, 1988; Tzvi Shiloah, in *Haaretz*, March 19, 1990; Ariel Sharon, interview, *Yediot Acharonot* (weekend supplement), January 19, 1990, translated in JPRS-NEA-90-017, March 21, 1990, p. 39; and Beni Katzover, "The Jews Are Coming, the Arabs Are Going," *Nekuda*, no. 145, November 1990, pp. 16–17 and 23.

33 See, for example, Yoel Ben-Nun, "Not to Be Nervous and Not to Be Made Nervous," *Nekuda*, no. 68, January 13, 1984, pp. 4–7.

34 *Davar*, November 22, 1985. Eliakim Haetzni, a firebrand lawyer living in Kiryat Arba, near Hebron, a leading Gush Emunim publicist, and subsequently a Tehiya party Knesset deputy, was the moving force behind the Yesha Council resolution. See Haetzni, *The Shock of Withdrawal in the Land of Israel* (Hebrew) (Jeruslem: Elisha, 1986) where he elaborates the rationale for treating the Peres government as equivalent to the Vichy regime in France. Concerning this episode

see also Yitzhak Taub, "The Era of Israeli Militias," *Al-Hamishmar*, June 18, 1985; Mark Gefen, "The Revolt in Judea and Samaria Is Coming Out of Hiding," *Al-Hamishmar*, November 8, 1985, in FBIS, November 15, 1985, p. 110; and Baruch Lior, "To Prepare the Generations for Prayer and War," *Nekuda*, no. 85, April 5, 1985, pp. 11–12.

35 Jerusalem Domestic Service broadcast, November 19, 1985, transcribed by FBIS, November 20, 1985, p. 14.

36 Jerusalem Domestic Service broadcast, November 11, 1985, transcribed in FBIS, November 12, 1985, p. 15.

37 *Haaretz*, December 11, 1986 (for the estimate of arms possessed by Gush Emunim settlers). On Zamir's advice to Rabin see Yoram Peri, "The IDF and the Settlers," typescript, 1987, pp. 90–91.

38 Based on the author's personal interviews with dozens of Israeli soldiers and family members during visits to Israel and the territories in spring 1988 and 1990. Concerning increased rates of suicide among soldiers and violent crime attributed to the influence of norms soldiers were constrained to adopt while serving in the territories see Ayala Malakh-Pines, "Violence Surges in Bad Times," *Haaretz*, October 23, 1989; *Yediot Acharonot*, September 5, 1989; *Al-Hamishmar*, July 6, 1990; and "The Intifada Influences the Crime Level," *Hadoar*, January 11, 1991; and Lilly Galili, "The Stones Didn't Touch Us," *Haaretz*, October 24, 1989 (reporting the results of surveys conducted by Asher Arian for the Jaffee Center for Strategic Studies at Tel Aviv University).

39 See Michael Capra, "Fear: Five Minutes from Kfar Saba," *Maariv* (supplement), March 11, 1988.

40 Incidents of soldiers hit by settlers firing at persons they thought were Arabs increased. Concerning verbal abuse and physical attacks by settlers on military personnel, anti-army riots by settlers, and organized incitement of soldiers to disobey orders restraining their use of firearms against Arabs, see Uriel Ben-Ami, "Israel of Two States," *Davar*, December 2, 1987; *Davar*, May 13, 1988; Ron Ben-Yishai, "The Zealots Want an Explosion," *Yediot Acharonot* (supplement), June 2, 1989; Ze'ev Schiff, "What Has Happened to the IDF during the Intifada?" *Haaretz*, June 16, 1989; *Yediot Acharonot*, September 3, 1989; interview with OC Central Command, General Yitzhak Mordechai, *Bamachane*, February 28, 1990, translated in JPRS-NEA-90-019, March 30, 1990, pp. 34–35; Michael Bar-Zohar, *Facing a Cruel Mirror: Israel's Moment of Truth* (Hebrew) (Tel Aviv: Sifrei Yediot Acharonot, 1990) 261. For settler complaints against the political bias of the IDF and the media see Shila Gal, "So How Would They Respond in the Jezereel Valley?" *Davar*, December 13, 1987; and Uri Urbach, "So Who Is Fit and Suitable to Serve in the Territories," *Hadashot*, November 6, 1989, translated in JPRS-NEA-90-001, January 4, 1990, pp. 18–19. For detailed background, including responses to settler complaints by commanding officers within the military government, see Yoram Peri, "The IDF and the Settlers," typescript, December 1987, pp. 52–63.

41 On the rationale for the Gush Emunim leaders hunger strike in early 1989 see "Hungry for Security," *Nekuda*, no. 126, January 6, 1989, pp. 10–11 and 45. For Shamir's promises to the hunger strikers that settlements would indeed be

increased and for their decision to end the strike see Jerusalem Domestic Service broadcast, January 3, 1989, transcribed in FBIS, January 5, 1989, p. 27; and on January 26, 1981, transcribed in FBIS, January 26, 1989, p. 36.

42   Concerning the emergence, objectives, and operations of these militias see *Maariv*, February 28, 1989; *Yediot Acharonot*, February 13, 1989; *Jerusalem Post*, February 13, 1989; Oron Meiri, "No Longer Underground," *Hadashot*, February 13, 1989; Ron Ben-Yishay, "Zealots Want Explosion," *Yediot Acharonot*, June 2, 1989; Ariela Ringel-Hoffman, "Touring and Shooting," *Yediot Acharonot*, June 2, 1989; and especially Yigal Sarna and Anat Tal-Shir, "Gil'ad's Private Army," *Yediot Acharonot*, April 6, 1990. For information on a manual circulating among West Bank settlers with detailed instructions for carrying out sabotage and assassination without being apprehended and resisting police interrogation techniques, see *Yediot Acharonot*, July 4, 1990. Policies implemented by the Likud-led government of June 1990 were designed to integrate most of these settler militias into the framework of army and police operations in the territories under the rubric of a "civil guard." See *Yediot Acharonot*, June 29, 1990.

43   Ariela Ringel-Hoffman, "The Crazy 5% Will Take Up Arms," *Yediot Acharonot*, January 20, 1989. For a lengthy article by a member of the Gush Emunim underground arrested in 1984 arguing that the army would not be able, as it had done in Yamit, to evacuate thousands of armed settlers from the West Bank, see Hagai Segal, "By Night They Train in the Fields," *Hadashot*, February 10, 1989.

44   *Haaretz*, November 10, 1988, reporting a survey done in August 1988 of four hundred heads of households from eleven settlements located in the northern bulge of the West Bank.

45   Shlomo Aviner, *Questions and Answers about the Intifada* (Hebrew) (Beit-El: Sifriat Beit-El in cooperation with the educational department of the Benjamin Regional Council, 1990) 57.

46   Baum is a veteran of Unit 101, the IDF's special operations battalion charged during the 1950s with conducting devastating raids into Jordanian territory. The unit was commanded by Ariel Sharon. Baum was also Sharon's right-hand man during his crackdown on resistance activity in the Gaza Strip in the early 1970s. On the "State of Judea" phenomenon see *Haaretz*, December 27, 1988; *Davar* December 30, 1988; Uriel Ben-Ami, "What He Does for the State," *Davar* (supplement), January 13, 1989; Nadav Shragi, "Dreams of a State of Judea on the Way," *Haaretz*, January 20, 1989; Rubik Rosenthal, "The State of Judea Exists," *Al-Hamishmar*, June 23, 1989; Yehoshua Meiri, "Hasamba or a New Irgun," *Haaretz* (supplement), January 19, 1990; *Hadashot*, January 19, 1990; and *Haaretz*, February 6, 1990.

47   In spring 1990 the police arrested Yoel Adler on suspicion of being a leader of the Sicarii. Adler was among the founders of the Tehiya party. Among those known to have received Sicarii death threats were Rabin, Peres, Aloni, Sarid, Zucker, Haim Oron, Avraham Burg, and other dovish politicians and peace activists. Assassination threats were also made on President Herzog and some ultraorthodox leaders suspected of readiness to help the Labor party form a government. Fires claimed to have been set by Sicarii arsonists burned the cars or residences of influential opinion leaders such as Mina Tzemach (the pollster), Dan

Margalit (a columnist), and Yair Tzaban (a Mapam member of Knesset). Publishers and writers such as Amos Schocken (publisher of *Haaretz*), Gershon Shaked, and Hayim Be'er were targets of phony explosives, as was the wife of Shimon Peres. In November 1989, bombs were placed near the homes of the rector of the Hebrew University and one other senior professor. On Sicarii-related incidents see *Yediot Acharonot*, April 6 and 18, 1990; and Jerusalem Domestic Service broadcast, November 24, 1989, p. 34; *Yediot Acharonot*, February 13, 1989; Yigal Sarna, "Sicarii: A New Jewish Underground?" *Yediot Acharonot* (supplement), March 24, 1989, pp. 13–15; editorial, "The Sicarii: A Danger to the Public," *Haaretz*, January 5, 1990; and *Al Hamishmar*, January 14, 1990. On the arrest of Adler see Jerusalem Domestic Service broadcast, June 26, 1990, transcribed by FBIS, June 28, 1990, p. 26.

48 Concerning the large majority of high-ranking officers whose political attitudes incline them toward territorial compromise see Ron Ben-Yishai in *Yediot Acharonot*, June 10, 1988; Israel Office of the American Jewish Committee, "High-Ranking Israeli Officers Enter the Debate," *Israeli Press Highlights*, June 10, 1988; and "Territorial Withdrawal in the West Bank and Gaza—On Condition," *Haaretz*, July 22, 1988. On the chief of staff's suppression of an article criticial of the army's policy toward the intifada by a major-general known for his pro-Likud views, see, *Hadashot*, April 21, 1989.

49 Speech by Dan Shomron, published in *Hadoar*, May 12, 1989, pp. 8–9; speech to the Tel Aviv Chamber of Commerce, reported by Jerusalem Television Service, September 22, 1989, in FBIS, September 25, 1989, p. 34; and an extended interview with Shomron broadcast on Jerusalem Domestic Service, June 16, 1989, transcribed in FBIS, June 16, 1989, pp. 25–26.

50 Editorial, *Jerusalem Post*, April 6, 1989.

51 *Hatzofe*, May 9, 1989, translated in FBIS, May 10, 1989, p. 25. Shomron made similar remarks in interviews broadcast over Jerusalem television on January 25, 1989 (transcribed in FBIS, January 27, 1989, pp. 29–34) and on May 20, 1990. On the political confrontation between the IDF's high command and right-wing ministers over policy toward the Palestinians in general and the intifada in particular see "The IDF and the *Intifada*," *Israel Press Highlights*, June 5, 1989; Yoram Peri, "Who Will Take the Territories Out of the IDF?" *Israeli Democracy*, Summer 1989, pp. 39–41; Ze'ev Schiff and Ehud Ya'ari, *Intifada: The Palestinian Uprising—Israel's Third Front* (New York: Simon and Schuster, 1987) 132–39.

52 Zeev Schiff, "The IDF Is Turning into a Police Force," *Haaretz*, December 11, 1990.

53 See Rabin's remarks before the Knesset, reported in editorial, *Jerusalem Post*, April 15, 1989. See also the attack by the National Religious party and Gush Emunim–affiliated politicians on Rabin and the IDF for not submitting options for crushing the uprising. *Al-Hamishmar*, May 4, 1989.

54 See an interview with Sharon during the lengthy maneuvering that resulted in establishment of the third Likud government in the spring of 1990, *Yediot Acharonot*, January 19, 1990, in JPRS-NEA-90-017, March 21, 1990, pp. 36–40. Sharon declared that he had a military solution to the intifada, and explicitly condemned Defense Minister Rabin for not issuing clear orders to the IDF to

"eradicate" Arab disturbances rather than "lower their level." In December 1988, Yitzhak Shamir said his remarks had been "distorted" in a report in which he had complained that a chief of staff from the Likud would be unacceptable to the army. *Hadashot,* December 21, 1988. Concerning the possibility of a "generals' revolt" against a right-wing government committed to the liquidation of the intifada, see an interview with Major General (Res.) Uri Or in *Hadashot,* March 7, 1990. See also *Yediot Acharonot,* June 13, 1990. Yossi Sarid warned that evacuation of villages from which intifada arsonists were suspected of operating, as advocated by Tehiya leader Geula Cohen, would be "the end of the army." Israel Defense Forces broadcast, June 25, 1990, transcribed in FBIS, June 25, 1990, p. 34.

55 Until mid-1991 the Israeli press was under strict orders to refrain from discussing these units. Their names—Shimshonim (Samsonites) and Duvduvenim (Cherries)—and activities were reported in the international media, however. See Dani Rubinstein, "Informers Shall Have No Hope," *Davar,* December 22, 1989; Pinchas Inbari, "Canny Exposure," *Al-Hamishmar,* June 24, 1991.

56 By the end of only eighteen months of the intifada, and leaving aside unreported infractions or those not pursued by the military police, the army prosecutor's office had opened files against more than fifteen hundred soldiers and officers for "improper or aberrant behavior." In the first two years of the intifada, forty-six soldiers and officers received jail sentences for abuses against Palestinians or their property. Btzelem reported that in nearly 50 percent of the fatal shootings of Palestinians, soldiers had fired illegally, and that of 102 instances in which children were killed by security forces, only one resulted in the jailing of a soldier. *Jerusalem Post,* November 27, 1989, and July 16, 1990. For the most fully documented study of child fatalities during the uprising see Anne Elizabeth Nixon, *The Status of Palestinian Children during the Uprising in the Occupied Territories,* vols. 1 and 2 (East Jerusalem: Swedish Save the Children, 1990). On the problem of cover-ups, vows of silence, falsified reporting within the IDF, and systematic failure to pursue investigations see *Davar,* September 6, 1988; *Haaretz,* June 26, 1990; Dani Rubinstein, "The Finish," *Davar,* May 19, 1989; Ze'ev Schiff, "What Has Happened to the IDF during the Intifada?" *Haaretz,* June 16, 1989; Avi Bineyahu, "Pardon as a Relief Valve for Investigations," *Al-Hamishmar,* September 19, 1989; Amnon Rubinstein in *Yediot Acharonot,* January 22, 1990; and *Jerusalem Post,* July 16, 1990. See especially a series of articles by Maya Rosenfeld concerning investigative procedures in cases of Palestinian fatalities: "The IDF Investigates Reasons for the Fatalities," *Etgar,* no. 3 (March 1990) 14–15, 23; "From Behind the Crack in the Wall: Justice Is in Another Place and Another Time," *Etgar,* no. 5 (June 1990) 18–19; and "It's All Buried in the Family," *Challenge* 1 (October 1990) 18–19, 34.

57 On "antidemocratic" tendencies triggered within the middle ranks of the IDF by the frustrations of coping with both the intifada and public criticism see Ze'ev Schiff, "Stones on the Media," *Haaretz,* September 4, 1989; and Avi Benayahu, "Not Only Relying on Bonuses," *Al Hamishmar,* March 18, 1990. By 1990 the army's concern with these tendencies was intensified by the fact that such a large proportion of new officers in the middle ranks (lieutenant, captain, and major)

who manifested these sentiments were of oriental Jewish extraction. Interviews with informants, April and May 1990. See *Jerusalem Post*, June 28, 1989. On the deterioration of standards within the IDF due to the intifada, including brutalization of soldiers, interruption of training, distortion of mission, and so forth, see Martin Van Krefeld, "Why Do I Say 'Shit'?" *Haaretz*, January 26, 1990; Ze'ev Schiff, "The IDF Is Turning into a Police Force," *Haaretz*, December 11, 1990; Ariela Ringel-Hoffmann, in *Yediot Acharonot* (supplement), December 8, 1989; Ron Ben-Yishai, "Excerpts from Givati Soldiers Verdict," May 28, 1989; Tami Lotem, in *Yediot Acharonot* (supplement), October 6, 1989; Yitzhak Tunik and Yosef Argaman, interview with Yitzhak Rabin, *Bamachane*, January 27, 1988, translated in JPRS-NEA-88–025, April 11, 1988, pp. 1–4; Amnon Rubinstein, in *Yediot Acharonot*, January 22, 1990; Yehiam Weitz, "Apocalypse Now," *Davar*, February 19, 1988; and Ron Ben-Yishai, in *Yediot Acharonot*, February 27, 1989.

58 Aryeh Stiu, "Even if You Pound the Leftist in a Mortar You Will Not Deprive Him of His Folly," *Nativ* 4 (January 1991) 66.

59 Zeev Schiff, "What Has Happened to the IDF during the Intifada?" *Haaretz*, June 16, 1989.

60 *Jerusalem Post*, April 10, 1988.

61 The overall slogan for the campaign leading up to the rally, which appeared all over the country on giant billboards, was *al taamod chasar Yesha*. The phrase is a triple pun in Hebrew, meaning (roughly) "don't stand there helplessly," "we cannot exist without Judea, Samaria, and Gaza," and "there is no basis for existence without salvation." Among those who addressed the huge crowd were David Levi, Rafael Eitan, and Chaim Druckman.

62 Interview with the author, Ariel, February 27, 1988.

63 Quoted by Uzi Benziman, "Poison Gas," *Haaretz*, July 24, 1989, translated in JPRS-NEA-89–067, October 19, 1989, p. 25.

64 *Jerusalem Post*, June 8, 1989.

65 Poll conducted by Dahaf, reported by *Yediot Acharonot*, June 8, 1989.

66 *Hadashot*, September 29, 1989. Interestingly, none of the top ten identified as "most hated" were Arabs; all were Jews. Concerning the accentuation of processes of polarization within Israeli public opinion as a result of the intifada see a longitudinal study of the same group of 416 respondents asked the same questions in December 1987 and 1988. Asher Arian and Raphael Ventura, *Public Opinion in Israel and the Intifada: Changes in Security Attitudes, 1987–88*, JCSS Memorandum No. 28 (Tel Aviv: Tel Aviv University, Jaffee Center for Strategic Studies, 1989) 5–8.

67 For details on efforts to establish extragovernmental dialogues between the two camps as a response to civil war fears see Shulamit Hareven, "Land or State?" *Yediot Acharonot*, June 30, 1989; *Haaretz*, June 4, 1989; Tzvi Gilat, "Ben-Nun Searches for Oz," *Yediot Acharonot*, June 8, 1989; interview with Yoel Ben-Nun, *Al-Hamishmar*, June 15, 1989, in JPRS-NEA-89–054, August 1989, pp. 49–52; *Davar*, June 8, 1989; Hagai Segal, "The Controversy Is Over the Limits of the Possible," *Hadashot*, March 3, 1989.

68 Interviews published in *Israeli Democracy*, Winter 1989, pp. 5–9. For examples of the intensity of public concern for Israel's political stability and antic-

ipations of internecine conflict see Elisheva Ayalon, "Then Let Everything Explode," *Hotam* (weekly supplement of *Al-Hamishmar*), May 19, 1989, translated in *From the Hebrew Press* 1 (September 1989) 2–7; Yehuda Ya'ari, "True Alarm— The Body's Place Means Nothing," *Davar*, September 22, 1989, translated in *From the Hebrew Press* 1 (January 1990) 16–23; editorial, *Al-Hamishmar*, June 4, 1989; Moshe Negbi, "The Slave Market Is Leading to Civil War," *Hadashot*, May 25, 1990; Gabi Nitzan, "Alibi," *Hadashot*, May 25, 1990; editorial, *Al-Hamishmar*, June 4, 1989; Natan Sharansky, quoted by Franz Schurman, Pacific News Service weekly collection, January 7–11, 1991, p. 1; Tzvi Gilat, "Our De Gaulle," *Hadashot* (supplement), July 14, 1989 (a detailed scenario of regime collapse in Israel surrounding the rise of Sharon *au pouvoir*).

69 Dvorah Getzler, "Licence for Violence," *Jerusalem Post*, July 14, 1989. For recent scholarly treatments of the threat of regime overthrow in connection with attempts to withdraw from the territories see Ira Sharkansky, *Ancient and Modern Israel: An Exploration of Political Parallels* (Albany: SUNY Press, 1991) 154–55; Yoram Peri, "From Political Nationalism to Ethno-Nationalism: The Case of Israel," in *The Arab-Israeli Conflict: Two Decades of Change*, ed. Abdalla M. Battah and Yehuda Lukacs (Boulder, Colo.: Westview Press, 1988) 41–53; and Ehud Sprinzak, *The Ascendance of Israel's Radical Right* (London: Oxford University Press, 1991).

70 *The West Bank and Gaza: Israel's Options for Peace*, Report of a Jaffee Center for Strategic Studies Study Group (Tel Aviv: Jerusalem Post Press, 1989) 106–9 and 147. For similar judgments by other Israeli scholars and commentators see Gad Barzilai, "National Security Crises and Voting Behavior: The Intifada and the 1988 Elections," in *The Elections in Israel—1988*, ed. Asher Arian and Michal Shamir (Boulder, Colo.: Westview Press, 1990) 74; Yaakov Sharret, *The State of Israel Is No More* (Hebrew) (Tel Aviv: Tesher, 1988); Hanna Ish-Hurwitz, "Forgivingness as Catastrophe," *Al-Hamishmar*, June 23, 1989; Amnon Rubinstein, "Signals of Weimar," *Haaretz*, May 21, 1990; and Giora Goldberg, "Israeli Politics—Styleless and Vapid," *Nativ* 14, no. 3 (May 1990) 23; and Michael Porter, ed., *The Internal Israeli Polarization Over the Territories as a Political Dilemma*, Israel-Diaspora Institute, Report No. 4, April 1988.

71 *Jerusalem Post*, March 27, 1990.

72 In response to a ruling by Israel's chief rabbis that, under the circumstances prevailing at the time, it was "forbidden" to make territorial concessions, Rabbi Shach told his students that "territories, as a value in themselves, meant nothing, especially when the government which held those territories did not live by the Torah and descrated the Sabbath." *Jerusalem Post*, August 14, 1989. Rabbi Ovadia Yosef, chief spiritual leader of Sephardic Jews in Israel, is also on record as favoring territorial compromise to achieve peace.

73 Jerusalem Television Service broadcast, March 22, 1990, transcribed in FBIS, March 23, 1990, p. 24. For the text of Shach's address on March 26 see *Haaretz*, March 28, 1990. Shach also wished to preserve the stability of an institutional framework within which, as he put it, his people could "steal apples" (i.e., benefit privately from public funds) as readily and with just as much profit as other Israeli interest groups.

74   The sequence to which I refer here is incumbent-level competition bringing a state-building annexationist government to power (1977); movement past the regime threshold in the state-building direction (1983); failure to establish the larger shape of the state as a hegemonic belief (1983–1987); and appearance of regime-level concerns as decisive in the calculations of both opponents and proponents of state contraction (1990).

75   See his lengthy and detailed address to the Labor party's central committee, broadcast live on Israeli television, transcribed in FBIS, April 11, 1990, pp. 33–38. On Peres's strategy in this regard see *Jerusalem Post*, December 2, 1989; and a television interview with Peres on Israel's Arabic language service, March 16, 1990, transcribed by FBIS, March 19, 1990, pp. 20–21. On the logic of an eventual alliance between anti-annexationists and the religious parties as a crucial ingredient in disengaging from the territories see Saul Cohen, *The Geopolitics of Israel's Border Question*, Jaffe Center for Strategic Studies, Tel Aviv University, Study No. 7 (Boulder, Colo.: Westview Press, 1986) 51; Haim Ganz, "Another Rightist Revolution," *Haaretz*, May 14, 1990; Aryeh Naor, "What Peres Can Do," *Haaretz*, March 22, 1990; and Boaz Shapira, "Peres' One Accomplishment," *Haaretz*, April 27, 1990.

76   On March 30, intense efforts by both Likud and Labor to court the ultraorthodox resulted in sudden new legislation authorizing more than $100 million for institutions linked to the religious parties. In accordance with a Supreme Court order, the terms of secret agreements reached between the Labor party, Agudat Yisrael, Likud renegades, and both Jewish and Arab members of the Communist party front Hadash were published. See Bina Barzel, "The Ball Is in the Hands of the Small Players," *Yediot Acharonot*, June 5, 1990; *Financial Times*, March 31, 1990; *Jerusalem Post*, April 4, 1990.

77   For Agudat Yisrael's position on this issue see Israel Defense Forces broadcast, April 11, 1990, transcribed by FBIS, April 11, 1990, pp. 31–32; and *Maariv*, March 25, 1990. See also remarks by Yitzhak Rabin reported in a Jerusalem Domestic Service broadcast, March 25, 1990, in FBIS, March 26, 1990, p. 13.

78   Address by Mordechai Gur to Labor party branch, Yahud, June 3, 1990. Gur is a former chief of staff and a prominent Labor party politician named to the post of deputy defense minister in July 1992.

79   Interviews with MKs and Labor party central committee members, Tel Aviv, Jerusalem, Beit-Berl, May and June 1990. For a public version of the position of the more "risk-averse" members of the Labor party, see Simcha Dinitz, in *Davar*, September 10, 1989. Dinitz associated himself with the Merkaz or "centrist" faction within the Labor party, as opposed to the more militantly dovish and less risk-averse faction known at that time as Force Seventeen, under the leadership of MKs close to Peres such as Haim Ramon and Yossi Beilin.

80   For example, Yehoshafat Harkabi, *The Fateful Choices before Israel*, Essays on Strategy and Diplomacy No. 7 (Claremont, Calif.: Keck Center for International Strategic Studies, 1987) 21; and Samuel J. Roberts, *Party and Policy in Israel: The Battle between Hawks and Doves* (Boulder Colo.: Westview Press, 1990) 138–39 and 165ff.

81   In 1989 a simulation analysis of the six most plausible schemes for electoral

reform showed that had any of them been implemented before the 1988 elections, none would have produced a substantively different coalitional outcome. Yoram Peri, ed., *Electoral Reform in Israel,* Report No. 5 (Ramat Aviv: Israel Diaspora Institute, 1989) 1–2 and 54–59. However, outcomes of Israeli elections are less predictable than in the past by virtue of the introduction of three hundred thousand Russian and Ethiopian immigrant voters before the 1992 elections. Disproportionate support from these groups for the Labor party accounted for much of the increase in its vote.

82   This is a lacuna in Immanuel Sivan's cogent analysis of the intifada as having provoked a "crisis of decolonization" in Israel and raised the threat of civil war. Because of this threat, Sivan argues, Israeli separation from the territories can occur only when the kind of realignment described here as "Caesarist" or "fusionist" is established, under the leadership of a de Gaulle–like leader, and based on what he calls a "genuine consensus" between Likud pragmatists and the anti-annexationist bloc. Immanuel Sivan, "The Crisis of Decolonization," *Politika,* no. 28 (September 1989) 6–9; and idem, "On the Eve of the Third Year of the *Intifada*," *Haaretz,* December 8, 1989. For other characterizations of such a political bloc as necessary for disengagement and as capable of emerging as a result of calculations by pragmatists in the Likud, encouragement from the army, and/or slow change in the attitudes of both Likud and Labor politicians see Dan Margalit, "Squaring the Circle," *Politika,* no. 28 (September 1989) 36–37; For an argument that only a massive external shock could produce forces great enough to achieve the wholesale recomposition of the Israeli regime see Giora Goldberg, "Israeli Politics—Styleless and Vapid," 22–23.

83   For anti-annexationist pleas for U.S. arm-twisting on this issue see Haim Zadok, "Who's Afraid of a U.S. Initiative?" *Jerusalem Post,* June 16, 1989; Gideon Samet, "Welcome American Pressure," *Haaretz,* February 18, 1988; comments by Yossi Beilin, *Jerusalem Post,* October 8, 1989; Akiva Eldar, "Man Does Not Live by Aid Alone," *Haaretz,* November 30, 1989; Letter to the editor, signed by twenty Israeli writers, *New York Times,* February 21, 1988; and interviews with Asa Kasher and Peace Now spokesman Amiram Goldblum, published, respectively, in *Challenge,* no. 2 (January–March 1991) 2–3; and no. 3 (May–June 1991) 4–5. According to a Hanoch Smith Institute poll of Israelis conducted in May 1991, a majority of respondents did not believe peace negotiations could be initiated in the absence of U.S. pressure. Reported in *Davar,* June 2, 1991.

84   Circumstances leading to an "imposed solution" came closest to realization in the final stages of the 1973 war. See especially Henry A. Kissinger, *Years of Upheaval* (Boston: Little, Brown, 1982) 538–91.

85   British disengagement from the twenty-six counties of southern Ireland was also eased by the massive losses of World War I, which reduced the amount of additional bloodshed (even Irish bloodshed) the British public was willing to tolerate. Similarly, whether at the regime threshold or after its passage, the specter of a future Arab-Israeli war fought with unconventional weapons may act as the functional equivalent of external pressure as a means of generating political support to overcome die-hard annexationist opposition to territorial compromise.

86   For Abba Eban's rejection of the Allon Plan as no longer relevant see Ilan

Shehori, in *Haaretz*, August 1, 1988. Ironically almost the only Israelis who continued to talk about the Allon Plan were Ariel Sharon, Israel Eldad, and other annexationists, who began advancing expansive versions of it as the basis for a new "national consensus." For Sharon and Eldad the virtue of the Allon Plan was precisely that thoroughgoing application of its terms, including settlement and enforcement of Israeli law throughout the areas targeted within it for absorption by Israel, would eliminate any real prospect for a political agreement entailing Israeli withdrawal from *any* territories. See Israel Eldad, "The Allon Plan, Conditionally," *Nekuda*, no. 62, August 13, 1983, pp. 18–19; idem, "I Have Not Fallen from 'The Ladder,' " *Nekuda*, no. 65, November 4, 1984, pp. 10–11 and 30; and news reports regarding Sharon's proposals to the cabinet to enforce Israeli law within the borders of the Allon Plan, Jerusalem Domestic Service broadcast, August 3, 1988, transcribed in FBIS, August 3, 1988, p. 22; and Israel Defense Forces broadcast, November 26, 1989, transcribed in FBIS, November 27, 1989, p. 26.

87 Toledano is a veteran of the security services, was in charge of the Israeli Arab minority from 1966 to 1967, and represented the Labor party in the Knesset.

88 Positive responses were also forthcoming from Palestinian sources. Polls conducted by Dahaf in December 1989 and January 1990, reported in Shmuel Toledano, "The 'Peace in Stages' Plan," *New Outlook* 33, 8 (August 1990) 23. For details on the Toledano plan see also Avital Inba, in *Davar* (supplement), March 16, 1990, JPRS-NEA-90–027, May 16, 1990, pp. 22–27.

89 Joseph Alpher and Shai Feldman, eds., *Israel, the West Bank and Gaza: Toward a Solution,* report of a Jaffee Center for Strategic Studies study group (Tel Aviv: Jerusalem Post Press, 1989) 7.

90 Ibid., 22. For a similar analysis reflecting the thinking of the Jaffee Center group see Yochanan Peres, interviewed in *New Outlook* 33, 8 (August 1990) 24–25.

91 Alpher and Feldman, *Israel, the West Bank and Gaza,* 17–22. For evidence that in 1992, Rabin's strategic conception of progress toward a permanent settlement was based on commitment to a fundamentally deceptive strategy of serial decomposition similar to that advanced by the Jaffee Center Report see detailed interviews he granted during the 1992 election campaign to *Der Spiegel* and *Davar* in April 1992, translated in FBIS, April 22, 1992, pp. 29–32.

92 In the Israeli context this scenario recalls a dramatic confrontation in 1948 when Ben-Gurion depicted the arrival of an Irgun arms ship, the *Altalena,* as a direct challenge to the integrity of the new state. In a bloody battle the ship was ordered sunk, in full view of Tel Aviv. The incident helped Ben-Gurion achieve the political ostracism of the Revisionists.

93 My specific argument is supported by Maoz who contends, building on Riker's work, that heresthetical techniques for framing and reframing major public issues are facilitated during "crisis conditions" perceived as "an extreme threat to basic values. . . . Framing is feasible to the extent that the group does not have the time to deal with multiple interpretations of the decision problem. The salami tactic is feasible because the problems of the moment preoccupy the decision-making process and prohibit analysis of the broad, long-term picture." Zeev Maoz, "Framing

the National Interest: The Manipulation of Foreign Policy Decisions in Group Settings," *World Politics* 43 (October 1990) 93. See also William Riker, *The Art of Political Manipulation* (New Haven: Yale University Press, 1986).

94 In any event these proportions are very close—2.9 percent in the Britain-Ireland case (1911), 2.3 percent in the France-Algeria case (1959), and 2.8 percent in the Israel–West Bank/Gaza Strip case (1992). The demographic weight of the settler population as a proportion of Israel's Jewish population depends greatly on whether Jews in expanded East Jerusalem are counted. If they are included, the proportion of settlers to the Israeli Jewish population rises to 6.4 percent. However, taking into account arrangements that would create Jewish and Arab boroughs in greater East Jerusalem, forming a united municipality with divided sovereignty, and in light of the substantial proportion of Jewish Jerusalemites who actually favor disengagement from the occupied territories, it seems highly unlikely that East Jerusalem would serve as a demographic anchor for settler resistance akin to Belfast and the European neighborhoods of Algiers and Oran.

95 Concerning the emergence of second-echelon Likud leaders, including some from Herut itself, whose pragmatism and potentially dovish inclinations suggest the potential for a split in the party if subjected to appropriately focused political pressures of the right intensity, see Uri Avneri's interview with Herzliya mayor Eli Landau, in *Haolam Hazeh*, February 14, 1990; Margalit, "Squaring the Circle," 36–37; Tzvi Gilat, "Likud Personalities, Factions Examined," *Yediot Acharonot* (supplement), October 13, 1989, title supplied and translated in JPRS-NEA-89-081, December 28, 1989, pp. 28–31.

96 These observations are based in part on discussions with informants, and with soldiers and officers on active duty in the Israeli army during 1990. The dovish inclinations of the Israeli officer corps were vividly displayed by a quasi-mutiny of one hundred of the highest-ranking officers in the army, who confronted Defense Minister Sharon after the massacre of Palestinians in the Sabra and Shatila camps to demand his resignation. The most vivid accounts of this confrontation appeared in *Sunday Times,* October 2, 1982. See also Jerusalem Domestic Service broadcast, October 3, 1982, transcribed in FBIS, October 4, 1982, pp. I4–5; Ariel Sharon, " 'The Red Line' in Officers' Criticism," *Maariv,* October 6, 1982, in FBIS, October 6, 1982, pp. I5–6; Yaacov Erez, "The Ground in the Defense Establishment Is Shaking under Sharon's Feet," *Maariv,* October 5, 1982, in FBIS, October 6, 1982, pp. I8–9; and Matti Golan, "On the Way to a Political Army," *Haaretz,* October 13, 1982, in FBIS, October 15, 1982, pp. I13–14.

97 See Sammy Smooha, "Internal Divisions in Israel at Forty," *Middle East Review,* Summer 1988, p. 34.

98 Concerning the political leanings of Soviet immigrants see *Davar,* May 3, 1991.

99 See, for example, an interview with Shmuel Zaiveld, mayor of the largest ultraorthodox settlement in the West Bank, Imanuel. *Hadashot,* April 23, 1991. The *halachic* (Jewish law) principles of *mipnei darchei hashalom* and *lo l'hitgaroot bagoyim* ("for the sake of peace" and "avoiding unnecessary aggravation of gentiles") provide an important doctrinal basis for protecting the safety and prosperity of their communities by accommodating political pressures.

100 Indeed the Irish Free State crushed the anti-treaty forces using British artillery and ammunition, inflicting more Irish casualties in the brief civil war than had been suffered during three years of Anglo-Irish struggle.

101 For some preliminary thinking about the dynamics of defacto binationalism in Israel see Ilan Peleg and Ofira Seliktar, eds., *The Emergence of a Binational Israel: The Second Republic in the Making* (Boulder, Colo.: Westview Press, 1989).

102 It is also worth remembering the effects of immoderate campaigns to promote "Greater Britain" and two global versions of the French Union. The one undermined a previously hegemonic belief in the United Kingdom regarding Ireland's inclusion within the state. The other reduced the chances for hegemonic establishment of Algérie française. This pattern suggests that Israeli attempts to stretch the size of the state far beyond what can be established hegemonically may ultimately jeopardize Israel's ability to advance or defend the hegemonic status of its pre-1967 borders, both at home and abroad.

11. A Theory of States and Territories

1 Andrei Amalrik, *Will the Soviet Union Survive until 1984?* (New York: Harper and Row, 1970).

2 Philip G. Roeder, "Soviet Federalism and Ethnic Mobilization," *World Politics* 43, no. 2 (January 1991) 196–232.

3 In his analysis of the suddenness of the eastern European revolutions of 1989, Timur Kuran applies a threshold model to the separate decisions of individuals to challenge established authority. Drawing on Václav Havel's notion of "living the lie," Kuran notes the vulnerability of nondemocratic systems where political discourse is built on what I term here "decrepit" hegemonic conceptions. Kuran approaches the same problem of linking nonlinear effects to linear causes posed in my analysis, but focuses on the specific mechanisms that accomplish this translation rather than, as I do, on the changing circumstances within which those mechanisms are put in motion. Kuran, "Now out of Never: The Element of Surprise in the East European Revolution of 1989," *World Politics* 44, no. 1 (October 1991) 7–48.

4 See Crawford Young, "Comparative Claims to Political Sovereignty: Biafra, Katanga, Eritrea," in *State versus Ethnic Claims: African Policy Dilemmas,* ed. Donald Rothchild and Victor A. Olorunsolu (Boulder, Colo.: Westview Press, 1983) 199–223.

5 For a survey of active and potential territorial and irredentist problems in Africa see Benyamin Neuberger, "Irredentism and Politics in Africa," in *Irredentism and International Politics,* ed. Naomi Chazan (Boulder, Colo.: Lynne Rienner Publishers, 1990) 97–110.

6 See Michael W. Doyle's insightful treatment of the "Augustan threshold" as marking a discontinuous change in the character of the Roman regime—a change that accompanied expansion of Rome's territorial domain and helps account for its long-term stability. Doyle, *Empires* (Ithaca, N.Y.: Cornell University Press, 1986) 92–98.

7   For an excellent example of research on marriage as a political mechanism in late medieval Europe see John F. Padgett and Christopher K. Ansell, "Elite Consolidation and Party Formation in Renaissance Florence: The Rise of the Medici, 1400–1434," paper presented at the annual conference of the American Political Science Association, San Francisco, September 1990.

8   This argument is adumbrated in David D. Laitin, *Language Repertoires and State Construction in Africa* (Cambridge: Cambridge University Press, 1992) ix; and Thomas M. Callaghy, *The State-Society Struggle: Zaire in Comparative Perspective* (New York: Columbia University Press, 1984).

9   Hechter tries to escape from the theoretical problem expressed by this taxonomic difficulty in two somewhat inconsistent ways. Early in his book he classifies territories whose inhabitants eventually accept the legitimacy of central authority as having been incorporated by processes of "national expansion." Territories whose inhabitants do not ascribe legitimacy to central authority he labels as having been subjected to "imperial expansion." But this post hoc solution means his model cannot be applied to contemporary cases. More serious still, it ignores the fact and future possibility of empires deemed legitimate by their inhabitants. At the end of the book Hechter admits "there is no hard and fast line" with which to distinguish "internal colonies" from either "peripheral regions" or "colonies," suggesting that the best approach might be a more impressionistic summation of political, administrative, legal, geographical, cultural, and historical measures of "integration." The main difficulty with this formulation is that it removes any analytic rationale for treating "internal colonialism" as qualitatively different from "overseas" imperialism. Michael Hechter, *Internal Colonialism: The Celtic Fringe in British National Development, 1536–1966* (Berkeley: University of California Press, 1975) 60–64 and 348–51.

10   Doyle, *Empires*, 30, 45, 92–103, and 353–69.

11   Barrington Moore, *Social Origins of Dictatorship and Democracy: Lord and Peasant in the Making of the Modern World* (Boston: Beacon, 1966); Gabriel A. Almond and Sidney Verba, *The Civic Culture: Political Attitudes and Democracy in Five Nations* (Princeton: Princeton University Press, 1963).

12   See David Collier and Deborah L. Norden, "Strategic Choice Models of Political Change in Latin America," *Comparative Politics* 24, no. 2 (January 1992) 229–44, for a convenient discussion of much of this literature. See also Juan J. Linz, *The Breakdown of Democratic Regimes: Crisis, Breakdown, and Reequilibration* (Baltimore: Johns Hopkins University Press, 1978); Juan J. Linz and Alfred Stepan, *The Breakdown of Democratic Regimes: Europe* (Baltimore: Johns Hopkins University Press, 1978); and Ruth Berins Collier and David Collier, *Shaping the Political Arena: Critical Junctures, the Labor Movement, and Regime Dynamics in Latin America* (Princeton: Princeton University Press, 1991).

Index

Abbas, Ferhat, 101, 131, 133, 135, 338–39
Africa, 1–2, 106, 133, 441–43
African National Congress (ANC), 442
Ageron, Charles-Robert, 118–19
Albertini, Rudolph von, 114
Algeria, 81, 90; centenary celebration in, 84; comparable episodes of state-building/contraction and, 46–50; Constantine plan for economic development of, 137, 274, 323; de Gaulle during World War II and, 87–88; Generals' Revolt in, 287–95; land reform in, 340; Moqrani Rebellion in (1870–71), 130; nationalism in, 130–32, 339–41, 434; Organic Statue of 1947 for, 102–3, 105, 242; Phillippe-ville Massacre in, 134–35; Sétif attack in, 89–90, 109, 131, 338; torture used by French army in, 138–39, 254, 320; viniculture in, 108–9; World War II and status of, 82. See also Algérie française
Algerian Revolution, 110–11, 240; aftermath of, 295–301; antiregime plots against Fourth Republic and, 258–65; army-settler-Gaullist takeover and, 257–58, 265–70; Barricades Rebellion and, 277–86; de Gaulle's rise to power and, 270–75; Fourth Republic collapse and, 252–58, 407; Generals' Revolt in Algeria and, 287–95; self-determination for Algeria and, 275–77; special powers

given to deal with, 114–16; wars of position and, 130–39
Algérie française, 134–35, 176; Algerian Revolution's aftermath and, 295–301; antiregime plots against Fourth Republic and, 258–65; army-settler-Gaullist takeover and, 257–58, 265–70; Barricades Rebellion and, 277–86; decomposition/realignment and pedagogy to change, 315–25; de Gaulle's rise to power and, 270–75; failure of, 149–60; Fourth Republic collapse and, 252–58; Generals' Revolt in Algeria and, 287–95; incumbent-level factors in debate over, 241–52; Mollet's adherence to, 407; resources not given to, 179; self-determination policy of de Gaulle and, 275–77
Allon Plan, 423–24
Almond, Gabriel, 304, 450
Aloni, Shulamit, 413–14
Anglo-Irish agreement of 1985, 1
Anglo-Irish War (1919–21), 226–37, 329–30
Arab negotiation overtures, 362–63, 366
Argoud, Antoine, 278, 280, 292
Army of France, 135, 344; antiregime plots from, 259–63; army-settler-Gaullist takeover and, 257–58, 265–70; Barricades Rebellion and, 277–86; de Gaulle's attention focused on, 274–76, 324, 431; Generals' Revolt in Algeria and, 287–95; Pflimlin government and, 258; reservists and draftees in, 137–38